The Handbook of Aging and Cognition

The Handbook of Aging and Cognition

Edited by

Fergus I. M. Craik
University of Toronto

Timothy A. Salthouse
Georgia Institute of Technology

LEA LAWRENCE ERLBAUM ASSOCIATES, PUBLISHERS
1992 Hillsdale, New Jersey   Hove and London

Copyright © 1992, by Lawrence Erlbaum Associates, Inc.
All rights reserved. No part of the book may be reproduced in
any form, by photostat, microform, retrieval system, or any other
means, without the prior written permission of the publisher.

Lawrence Erlbaum Associates, Inc., Publishers
365 Broadway
Hillsdale, New Jersey 07642

Library of Congress Cataloging-in-Publication Data

The handbook of aging and cognition / edited by Fergus I.M. Craik,
Timothy A. Salthouse.
      p.   cm.
Includes bibliographical references and index.
ISBN 0-8058-0713-6
1. Cognition in old age. 2. Cognition—Age factors.
I. Salthouse, Timothy A.
BF724.85.C64H36   1992
155.67—dc20   91-40681
                                                         CIP

Printed in the United States of America
10 9 8 7 6 5 4 3 2 1

Contents

PART II
NEUROPSYCHOLOGY AND NEUROSCIENCE

PART III
APPLICATIONS

Preface

This handbook had its origins when Larry Erlbaum raised the possibility to one of us of editing a state-of-the-art handbook dealing with the topic of aging and cognition. The two of us discussed this idea in the context of a broad-ranging discussion about the field of cognitive aging—its tremendous growth and its possible future directions—and this led to a discussion of the difficulties associated with keeping up with current research in the area. We had both written chapters for the excellent series of Handbooks of Aging edited by James Birren and Warner Schaie and liked the in-depth treatment that the earlier volumes of that series offered. Owing to the tremendous expansion of research on aging, later volumes in the Birren and Schaie series have opted for more limited reviews of a wide area—we thought that the time might be ripe for a return to fuller treatments of research topics, but necessarily within the more restricted area of cognitive changes associated with aging.

It seemed like a good idea at the time, and now that we have assembled our set of chapters it seems like an even better idea! The basic goal of the handbook was to present reviews of the core topics of cognitive psychology—attention, memory, knowledge representation, reasoning and spatial abilities, and language. Apart from our own contributions, we were extremely fortunate to attract some of the best people in the field to write these chapters—Alan Hartley, Leah Light, and Susan Kemper. But we also wished to set these reviews in a context of research from adjacent areas. For example, we were impressed by the volume and excellence of recent research in neuropsychology, and so invited Morris Moscovitch and Gordon Winocur to write a review of recent work in that area that would illuminate the processes of normal aging; we also invited Robert Nebes to write a more specific review of recent work on cognitive dysfunction in Alzheimer's disease. The area of cognitive neuroscience is another "context" area that we thought would provide some useful background and possible research leads to students of cognitive aging; accordingly we invited Gwen Ivy and her colleagues at the Scarborough Campus of the University of Toronto to review the neurobiology of aging, but also to make links, or point to potential links, between changes in brain structure and function on the one hand, and age-related changes in cognitive functioning on the other. We are particularly pleased with the success of this section on neuropsychology and neuroscience—it really does seem that these areas are now making good contact with work in cognitive psychology.

The third section is on applications of laboratory studies to real-life domains. Here we have two complementary chapters—one on human factors, and one on applied cognitive aging. The difference in emphasis is that whereas Neil Charness and Elizabeth Bosman talk primarily about human engineering methods and results in their Human Factors chapter, Denise Park takes results from the cognitive psychology laboratory and explores their application to some real-life problems of older people. In this sense then the handbook is really one of "Aging and Cognition Plus. . . ." We hope that readers share our enthusiasm for the useful perspectives that these context chapters give to the theories and findings in mainstream cognition.

We asked contributors to provide reviews and critical commentaries on the research within their assigned topic, rather than merely to give accounts of their own research programs. We feel that this makes for livelier reading, although it does mean that the reader may encounter different points of view on certain topics from time to time! The chapters are written primarily for other researchers in the fields of gerontology and cognitive psychology, but we believe that they are accessible both to students of these topics (at the graduate and advanced undergraduate levels) and to researchers in neighboring fields.

We are grateful to a number of people for their help and encouragement. In Toronto we thank Jennie Sawula, Marion Brand, and Ken Seergobin for their work on manuscript and index preparation. We also thank Judi Amsel and Christopher Pecci at Lawrence Erlbaum Associates for encouragement, support, and excellent help throughout the preparation and production phases. We are most grateful to the Natural Sciences and Engineering Research Council of Canada, the Canadian Networks of Centres of Excellence program, and the National Institute of Aging in the United

States for grant support that greatly facilitated our job as editors. Above all, we wish to thank the contributors to the volume for producing an excellent set of chapters, and for responding to our incessant nagging and niggling demands with tolerance and forebearance!

—Fergus Craik
—Timothy Salthouse

PART ONE

COGNITIVE PROCESSES

CHAPTER ONE

Attention

Alan A. Hartley
Scripps College

What is attention? William James (1890) provided a clear and eloquent definition that still is cited as appropriate and current despite the intervening century:

> Everyone knows what attention is. It is the taking possession by the mind, in clear and vivid form, of one out of what seem several simultaneously possible objects or trains of thought. Focalization, concentration, of consciousness are of its essence. It implies withdrawal from some things in order to deal effectively with others. (Vol. 1, pp. 403–404)

The definition is so straightforward and so consistent with common sense, however, that it may cause us to overlook the rich variety of phenomena that attention comprises.

Consider this scenario: An individual is driving along a busy and unfamiliar urban street. What has had possession of her mind for most of the drive is the talk she will be giving at her destination to a meeting of an organization. Because she is unfamiliar with the area, she must scan each corner for the street sign, often hidden in a confusing forest of utility poles, bus stops, and other signs. At the same time, she must monitor traffic in front and behind as well as stoplights, adjusting her speed and direction as necessary with the wheel, the transmission, the brake, and the clutch. When she detects a street sign, she must focus on it to read it and, then, if it is the street she has been seeking, make her way in a relatively short time and distance into the leftmost lane so that she can turn. Yet, throughout this episode, our driver would probably say, if asked, that she had been running over her speech in her mind.

What aspects of that very complicated but very common scenario involve attention? Would we agree with a narrow reading of James (1890) that it is only the taking possession of her mind by the speech she is to give that involves attention? Is not attention involved in scanning the street corner for a sign, detecting what is probably a sign, orienting the eyes toward it, and ignoring surrounding objects to extract the desired information—the street name—from the sign? Then, too, there is the continuing sequence of operations in which the surrounding traffic and the vehicle are checked, decisions are made, and adjustments are effected. These seem to us to happen almost automatically, except that errors occur—we shift from first gear to fourth when we meant to shift to second—and show that there had been some executive management of the sequence. Is that executive management a kind of attention? Was attention involved in managing simultaneous, or at least interleaved, tasks, like looking for the sign and watching traffic?

In a relatively short span, a variety of things took possession of our driver's mind. Some were very broad, such as considering her speech; some were very narrow, such as picking out the letters in the street name or downshifting from third to second gear. Some were part of a hierarchy of goals and subgoals concerned with getting to the destination. Lower level goals such as slowing the car could be satisfied without the higher level goals such as identifying the street name ever really losing possession of the mind. At the same time, the mind, even though possessed by this hierarchy, does not filter out extraneous external information that may require attention and action, such as a pedestrian unexpectedly stepping off a curb. Yet, in most cases, the mind is repossessed by its original content as soon as the exigency is handled.

James's (1890) definition emphasized the filtering aspect of attention. Other authors have echoed this (e.g., Eriksen & St. James, 1986; LaBerge, 1990a; LaBerge & Brown, 1989; Madden, 1990a; Shiffrin, 1988; Treisman & Gelade, 1980; Treisman & Gormican, 1988). Selection of certain information for priority processing explains how our driver attends to the street sign or to the pedestrian, but not how she manages both at the same time. For reasons such as this many authors also have incorporated a coordinative, executive function into the concept of attention (e.g., Gopher & Donchin, 1986; Hoyer & Plude, 1982; Madden, 1990a; Navon, 1984, 1985; Plude & Hoyer, 1985; Shiffrin, 1988; Wickens, 1984). There is considerable debate about what is managed and how it is managed (see, e.g., Navon, 1984, 1985), but there is agreement that simultaneous tasks often require special management that is not necessary when they are performed alone.

A refined definition of attention, then, is that it is responsible for selectively preparing for, maintaining the preparation for, and processing certain aspects of experience. Attention is also responsible for the coordination of multiple simultaneous tasks. The definition is still quite broad. It will be of heuristic value in reviewing research in attention, but it still may miss important distinctions in our example scenario.

Why Is Attention Important in Aging and Cognition?

For one answer to this question, all we need do is make the driver in our example 75 years old. It is clear that lapses of attention while driving can be dangerous or even fatal. Imagine that the demands of locating the street sign caused the driver to fail to notice the pedestrian stepping off the curb. Although it may be unfair to stereotype older drivers as slow, erratic, and inattentive, it is the case that they have more accidents per mile driven than middle-age adults and that they are convicted more often of sign, right-of-way, and turning violations but less often of speed and other major violations (Sterns, Barrett, & Alexander, 1985). McFarland, Tune, and Welford (1964) and Planek and Fowler (1971) also found that accidents due to neglect of or inattentiveness to relevant information were more common in the elderly. Kosnik, Winslow, Kline, Rasinski, and Sekuler (1988) found increases across the adult life span in self-reported difficulty with reading signs, locating a sign amidst other signs, reading a sign while moving, reading credits on TV, and other visual tasks. These difficulties may reflect problems in visual search and focused attention as well as purely visual function. If problems due to inattention in everyday life increase with age, then there are important practical reasons to better understand the aging of attention.

A second reason is theoretical. Age-related differences in cognitive functioning are ubiquitous. This makes it very attractive to look for a single, broad explanatory mechanism, or, at most, a very few mechanisms. Such mechanisms would have to be involved in most aspects of cognitive processing. Changes in such mechanisms could provide a parsimonious account for the widespread differences that are observed. Because attention is so broadly implicated in cognitive processing, it is an attractive candidate for one such mechanism.

AGING AND ATTENTION:
THEORIES AND THEORETICAL CONSIDERATIONS

The broadest theoretical explanation for age-related differences in attentional functioning is a reduction in the energy that fuels cognitive processing (Salthouse, 1985, 1988a, 1988b, 1988c, 1988d). If attention is viewed as the resource that enables processing and if the reduced energy is inferred only from the age-related differences in performance, then the explanation is perfectly circular, and not an explanation at all. If attention is viewed more restrictively as involved in selective filtering and in coordination of simultaneous tasks, reduced capacity might appear to serve as an explanation for many age-related differences in performance. There are difficulties. There may not be a fixed capacity because it may be possible to increase the amount of processing "fuel" available by increasing effort or arousal (Kahneman, 1973). Or, there may be fixed or variable capacities in several different pools (Wickens, 1984). Agreement on techniques for measuring attentional capacity independent of the performance to be explained would come only after there was agreement on the nature of the capacity or capacities. In addition, there may be an unfortunate coincidence of terms. Without agreeing on the precise meaning, it is possible that the selective attention that is disengaged, shifted, and engaged in response to cues or during visual search may be fundamentally different from the attentional energy that is said to be divided among simultaneous tasks. It would then be incorrect to use performance in any one class of attention-related tasks as a measure of attentional energy. The difficulties in selecting appropriate measures of attentional capacity also have been pointed out by Guttentag (1989) and Salthouse (1988a). At present, the hypothesis of reduced attentional energy in older adults is too ill-defined to make strong, testable predictions.

Hasher and Zacks (1988) recently proposed a more focused resource hypothesis. They posited that inhibitory functioning is reduced in older adults, and, specifically, that "older adults have attentional deficiencies in the mechanisms that control access to activation" (p. 168). Examples of reduced inhibition are more frequent intrusions of personal reminiscences into recall of text by older adults (Hasher & Zacks, 1988) and greater verbosity, that is, shifts of speech into a series of loosely associated recollections that stray far from the context that prompted the speech (Gold, Andres, Arbuckle, & Schwartzman, 1988). In this formulation, inhibition can be viewed as a resource; it is a basic operation that is a vital component of higher level information processing. Hasher and Zacks do not assert that there is some inhibitory capacity, some fixed pool of inhibition energy. Their formulation is different from space or energy notions of resource but not from speed notions (see Salthouse, 1985, 1988a, 1988c, 1988d). Reduced inhibition is an attractive explanatory construct because it could affect so many aspects of behavior, including those thought to reflect attention. If selection of one stimulus involves inhibition of competing stimuli, then we would expect older adults to be less effective in attentional filtering. Similarly, if managing more than one task involves temporarily inhibiting other tasks so that one may be executed, age differences should be observed in those situations also.

Plude and Hoyer (1985) proposed a theory more specifically concerned with attention. They postulated that spatial localization ability is impaired in old age. Spatial localization is not conceptualized as a resource whose capacity might be reduced; rather, it is a specific process that is a component of much of visual information processing. Not only does the postulate help organize findings, but also it makes strong predictions. There should be age differences in sequential search and the discrepancy should grow as the target/distractor similarity increases because older adults should find it more difficult to suppress processing of distractors. If age differences in search are due to impaired spatial localization, then there should be differences in visual search performance but not memory search performance, or, at the least, the two should be uncorrelated. Another prediction is that older adults should show greater benefits than younger adults for advance cues about the spatial location of a target. The greater benefits may be more apparent in tasks that require identification of targets than in those that require only detection because identification is dependent on the correct localization of features belonging to the target. By contrast, the impaired spatial localization hypothesis makes no direct predictions about age differences in dual-task performance.

There are two theories that are not, in fact, theories of attention at all. Each argues that what appear to be age differences in attention are artifacts of more fundamental age differences. The first theoretical position argues that age-related effects in attention are simply expressions of a general slowing of cognitive operations in old age (Cerella, 1985b; Hale, Myerson, & Wagstaff, 1987; Salthouse, 1985). There is good, direct evidence for behavioral slowing with age (e.g., Cerella, 1985b; Cerella, Poon, & Williams, 1980; Salthouse, 1985), and the slowing is certainly broad enough to explain age-related differences in a wide variety of high-level cognitive tasks.

There are two, subtly different versions of this position. These can be labeled the *strong* and *weak* theories of cognitive slowing. A strong theory specifies a mechanism that is responsible for the slowing, such as uniform slowing of synaptic transmission (cf. Birren, 1974) or information loss at each transmission (Myerson, Hale, Wagstaff, Poon, & Smith, 1990). Such a theory predicts the form of the functional relationship between reaction times for younger and older adults across tasks. The observed reaction times, in principle, can be adjusted for the predicted slowing to determine whether unexplained residuals remain. By contrast, a weak theory of slowing does not specify a mechanism, but rather, simply attempts to identify a function that provides a good fit to the relationship between younger and older adult performance. If the function fits well, it constitutes the theory. It provides only a description, not an explanation.

In principle, it is always possible to find a function that provides a good fit to a set of data. In practice, both strong and weak theories may be hard to falsify. Deviations can be discounted as experimental error (cf. Cerella, 1991). Weak theories may be particularly hard to falsify because functions of increasing complexity can be used to accommodate the data without any requirement that they be justified by basic assumptions about the origins of slowing.

Many researchers give slowing a special status. When reaction time is used as a dependent measure analyses often will be reported that ask whether the results could be accounted for by slowing alone. More precisely, the analyses ask whether the results could be accounted for by a strong theory of slowing that predicts a linear function relating older adult to younger adult reaction times. For example, Madden (1986, 1987) collected reaction times to an auditory probe secondary task. He used the proportional increase over a probe-alone baseline condition as the dependent measure. Hence, for an age effect to be significant it would have to show disproportionate slowing in older adults. Another approach that has been used is to regress the means across different conditions for the older adults on those for younger adults (e.g., Madden, 1984, 1985, 1989; McDowd & Craik, 1988; Plude & Doussard-Roosevelt, 1989). If increased complexity affects older adults disproportionately, then the best fitting function will be quadratic and a linear function will fit poorly.

The use of proportional measures has shown effects beyond those that can be accounted for by slowing (e.g., Madden, 1986, 1987). Of course, there are strong theories for which a proportional transformation would not remove all the effects of slowing (e.g., Myerson et al., 1990) but, in practice, most of the variance attributed to slowing would be removed. Plots of older–younger mean pairs have not. Cerella (1991) argued that the latter results should be given precedence; he has concluded that, once cognitive slowing has been accounted for in such a manner, there may be no age-related effects left to explain. The validity of his conclusion is examined after recent research in attention is reviewed. Where possible in the findings that are reviewed in this chapter the effects of proportional (or other similar transformations) are mentioned.

A second argument that age-related effects in attention are artifactual asserts that a reduction with age in the size of the functional visual field may have been mistaken for age changes in attention (Cerella, 1985a). It is clear that older adults have greater difficulty than younger adults in processing peripheral targets (Ball, Beard, Roenker, Miller, & Griggs, 1988; Cerella, 1985a; Cerella, Plude, & Milberg, 1987; Scialfa & Kline, 1988; Scialfa, Kline, & Lyman, 1987; Sekuler & Ball, 1986). As an example of how a reduced functional field of view could produce an appearance of impaired attentional functioning, consider a task requiring search for a target among distractors. If we suppose the items are scanned sequentially, then one item must be examined and, if it is not the target, it must be rejected and another must be selected from the periphery to be examined next. If younger adults were better able to localize and extract features from potential targets in the periphery, they would make better choices of items to examine next so their performance would be faster and probably more accurate and their advantage would increase with the size of the display.

This interpretation provides a simple, structural explanation for some attentional phenomena without any appeal to underlying cognitive processes or to resources that energize them. But this interpretation is too simple. It is not the case that visual acuity declines more rapidly with distance from the fovea for older than for younger adults, as some authors have asserted (e.g., Plude & Doussard-Roosevelt, 1989). Older adults exhibit more refractive error, but the age differences do not increase with distance from the fovea (Scialfa, Leibowitz, & Gish, 1989). Moreover, when a target is alone in the field, age differences in performance are unaffected by how far into the periphery it appears (Ball et al., 1988; Cerella, 1985a; Scialfa et al., 1987). The phenomenon of differentially greater difficulty with peripheral targets for older adults only occurs when the target is embedded in noise. Moreover, the effect may be exacerbated by increasing the difficulty of the processing required at the fovea (Ball et al., 1988). Thus, it is not purely a sensory or visual problem. The age difference cannot be compensated for by simply correcting refractive error or even by selecting the sizes of the letters to compensate for reduced acuity. The phenomenon must be more complex and at a higher level. In short, it appears to be a phenomenon that needs to be explained rather than an explanation for other phenomena. Whether it is an attentional phenomenon or not remains an open question.

In summary, there are several theoretical explanations for age-related differences in attention. They range from the very broad to the very specific, and they differ in whether they consider age-related changes in attention as real phenomena to be explained or as artifacts to be explained away. Each has advantages, but they all have clear limitations.

In addition to specific psychological theories of aging and attention, there is an important body of evidence from outside experimental psychology that may provide both important clues to understanding the aging of attention and constraints on the development of psychological theories. Neuropsychology, neurobiology, and neurochemistry all have expanded their understanding of attention substantially in recent years. Space does not allow more than a brief mention of the conclusions here. The interested reader should see Anderson (1987), Heilman, Watson, Valenstein, and Goldberg (1987), Posner and Petersen (1990), and Posner,

Petersen, Fox, and Raichle (1988) for integrative reviews, and chapters 6, 7, and 8 in this volume for both more general and more detailed discussions of developments in neuroscience relevant to aging. The present discussion briefly highlights conclusions directly relevant to attention.

A number of implications can be drawn from the neuroscientific evidence concerning the aging of attention. The evidence strongly supports the claim of a modular organization. There are a variety of different structures and systems, mediated by different neurotransmitters, carrying out attentional functions. It is clear that determining where a stimulus is and what it is are carried out by separate, semiindependent systems. This means that evidence for early selection of spatial locations could be consistent with a range of possibilities for encoding; it also means that unattended stimuli could affect responding (Allport, 1989). The effects of age in the two systems could well be different. It is also likely, even though attention may appear to involve early filtering of input, that filtering is the result of relatively late processing feeding back to control functioning at earlier levels.

Given these conclusions it seems unlikely there is some general attentional resource and that it changes uniformly with age. Aging is accompanied by neuronal loss in certain areas (such as the locus coeruleus), by increases in glial cells, by fewer dendrites and dendritic spines, by reductions in levels of some neurotransmitters and otherwise disturbed synaptic transmission, and by accumulation in neurons of inactive substances such as lipofuscin, melanin, and amyloid (Timiras, 1988). Given a wide variety of changes at many different levels, it is unlikely that age changes in the modules that together constitute attention will be uniform in their magnitude, time course, or qualitative effects. When we examine very complex tasks that require contributions from many processing modules, we may see a gradual, general decline that appears consistent with a loss of some undifferentiated resource. We easily could miss differential change by depending on behavioral measures that provide relatively rough-grained indicators of the interactive functioning of many modular components.

REVIEW OF EMPIRICAL FINDINGS

For convenience, research on aging and attention is divided into four categories: (a) studies of externally initiated shifts of attention such as priming and cuing, (b) studies of internally initiated shifts of attention such as search tasks, (c) dual-task studies that are presumed to involved division or sharing of attention, and (d) studies of sustained attention and vigilance.

Externally Initiated Shifts of Attention

Shifts of attention can be initiated by primes and cues, but also by expectancies and prompts. Because previous usages of these terms have been inconsistent, we should distinguish among the concepts.

An example of *priming* is that a subject can say whether *chair* is a word or not more rapidly if the preceding stimulus is *table* than if it is *olive* or XXXXX (e.g., Howard, 1983). Apparently, the relatedness of the two stimuli facilitates the processing of the second, perhaps because of residual excitation from the activation of the semantic information concerning the first stimulus (Collins & Loftus, 1975). The relationship need not be semantic: The stimuli can be identical or simply physically similar; they can be conceptually or categorically related; or they may only be assigned to the same response (Flowers & Reed, 1985). The important point for the present discussion is that the prime does not reduce uncertainty about the stimulus that will appear. In the example, *chair* is as likely to follow XXXXX as it is to follow *table*. Thus, priming as used here is presumed not to be the result of controlled, conscious preparation for an upcoming stimulus, but rather to reflect nonconscious, automatic processing. In addition to word meanings, other aspects of a target can be primed including its spatial location.

As an example of *cuing,* Nissen and Corkin (1985) presented an arrow pointing to either the left or right side of the display to indicate where the target was likely to appear. Unlike a prime, there is no necessary relation between a cue and the target it precedes, although there can be. Thus, had the cue been a box that appeared at the location where the target would be that would have been not only a cue but also it would have primed that location. Unlike a prime, a cue is informative about what will come next or where it will appear, so it allows for conscious, controlled preparation for a target. As with a prime, the task could be completed successfully even if the cue were completely ignored.

An experiment by Hoyer and Familant (1987) provides an example of an *expectancy.* Targets could appear in one of four locations. In one block, however, they occurred in one of the locations 80% of the time and the subjects were told that would happen. They could improve their performance by directing attention to that location. An expectancy, then, is like a cue except that the information about the target holds across a block of trials rather than for a single trial.

Schaie (1955) conducted a study in which a *prompt* was used. The subject saw a series of words written in either upper case or lower case. If the word was lower case, the task was to give a synonym; if it was upper case, the task was to give an antonym. The case in which the word was written was a prompt for the proper processing. In this example, the prompt accompanied the stimulus, but it also could have preceded or followed it. A prompt is unrelated to the stimulus to be processed and it conveys no information about what the stimulus will be or its location. Unlike a prime and a cue, a prompt cannot be ignored; it is essential to responding appropriately to the stimulus. Thus prompting should result in conscious, controlled preparation for specific processing of a stimulus.

Two general questions are asked in reviewing studies in each area. First, is there a reliable age difference in the effect and, if so, is the effect larger or smaller for older adults? Second, is there a difference in the time course of the effect? The approach is to present one or two representative studies in some detail, describing the methods and discussing interpretations. Using this as a context, related findings are summarized.

Priming

Burke, White, and Diaz (1987), following earlier work by Neely (1977), carried out an experiment that combined priming and cuing in a lexical decision task. There were four conditions. One pair of conditions involved standard priming procedures. The category name, *tree,* for example, was followed by a related word such as *elm* on 80% of the trials and by an unrelated word such as *fog* on 20% of the trials. When the instance is semantically related to the category, priming should occur. In addition, the category name is likely to be followed by an instance of that category. Because the category name is informative, it also should serve as a cue that an instance of that category is likely to follow. In the other two conditions, a category name such as *vegetable* was followed by a vegetable name only 20% of the time. It was followed by an animal name, such as *dog*, 80% of the time. Here the category name would serve as a cue for an animal name but it would prime vegetable names. Burke et al. (1987) reasoned that semantic relatedness should produce priming, which is relatively automatic, and should speed responses to a related target whether that target was expected—that is, cued—or not. Cuing should speed expected targets but slow unexpected ones whether the target was naturally related to the category name or not. The effects of priming were expected to occur more rapidly than those of cuing. To test this, they used two delays between the category name and the stimulus that was to be categorized as a word or nonword, 410 ms and 1,550 ms.

Priming effects were defined as the difference in reaction time between related and unrelated targets; cuing effects, as the difference between expected and unexpected targets. Many studies of priming include both semantically related primes and others presumed to be semantically neutral (e.g., XXXXX). Because of questions about whether such primes are, in fact, neutral (e.g., DeGroot, 1983; Jonides & Mack, 1984), those were not used.

Consistent with the predictions, priming effects decreased from the short to the long delay (from 7.6% of mean unrelated response time to 2.4%) whereas cuing effects increased (from 8.8% of mean unexpected response time to 14.1%). The most important finding was that there were no age differences in the size of the effects. Moreover, there was no evidence for differences in the time course of attentional engagement. The effect of a cue, allowing the subject to expect an instance of a particular category, was 63% as great at 410 ms for younger adults as it was at 1,550 ms; it was 62% as great for older adults. Of course, with only two time intervals, the coarse grain could conceal age differences in the time course.

This pattern of results, in which priming effects are equivalent in younger and older adults, has been found in a number of studies. Myerson, Ferraro, Hale, and Lima (1991) conducted a meta-analysis of 12 studies comprising 25 experimental conditions that used a lexical decision priming procedure and that found significant priming effects in younger adults. Significant age differences had been reported in only six of those conditions. Nonetheless, Myerson et al. calculated an average priming effect size of 65 ms for younger adults and 94 ms for older adults. The mean ratio of older to younger effect size was 1.90; the median was 1.50. A test calculated from the ratios they reported showed the average ratio was significantly greater than 1.00, $t(24) = 4.90, p < .05$. Myerson et al. argued that this result is just what would be expected if semantic activation, along with other central processing, were slowed in older adults (also see Howard, 1988). If every step in processing is slowed proportionally in older adults and if priming reduces the number of processing steps, then the absolute benefit of priming should be greater in older adults. The result is contrary to the assertion that automatic processes, such as priming, should be spared from age-related declines (Hasher & Zacks, 1979). In another study, Laver and Burke (1990) used formal meta-analytic techniques to summarize evidence from studies comparing lexical priming in younger and older adults. They, too, concluded that the age difference was reliably larger than zero.

In addition to the overall effect size, the time course of priming also can be examined. If early activation is automatic and later activation is controlled, and if automatic processes were spared the effects of aging, then the ratio of older to younger effect sizes should be close to 1.00 for short delays but should increase with longer delays. Myerson et al. (1991) reasoned that, if central processes are slowed in older adults, the ratio should remain constant as the delay increases. A more plausible interpretation is that central slowing should cause priming to run its course more slowly in older adults. From the findings of Myerson et al. we can predict that the peak effect should be at a delay 1.5 to 1.9 times longer in older adults than in younger adults. There should be an early period when younger adults show the effect and older adults do not, resulting in a ratio below 1.00. There should be a later period when older adults show the effect but when it is disappearing in younger adults, resulting in a sharply rising ratio. Myerson et al. found no relation between the effect ratio and the delay. The simple correlation was .17. Higher order polynomial functions fit to the data reported by Myerson et al. provide no substantial improvement. The predicted effects of slowing on the time course of priming are not seen when studies are aggregated.

Three studies have directly manipulated the delay (stimulus-onset asynchrony, SOA) between the prime and the target. Howard, Shaw, and Heisey (1986) found that the effect ratio rose from .27 at 150 ms SOA to .96 at 450 ms to 1.68 at 1,000 ms, although this change was not significant. Calculations from results reported by Balota and Duchek (1988, Figure 1) yield effect ratios of 2.50 for 200 ms SOA, 1.53 for 350 ms, 1.67 for 500 ms, 1.47 for 650 ms, and 1.29 for 800 ms. Although they used a pronunciation task rather than a lexical decision task, it is reasonable to expect similar time courses for the different priming tasks. Madden (1989) also varied the delay from the prime to the target. Because the primes were four- to seven-word sentences presented one word at a time, however, it is not possible to determine the effective stimulus onset asynchrony with any confidence. As with the aggregated studies, studies that directly manipulate SOA show no consistent relationship between SOA and the effect ratio.

The interpretation that is most consistent with the data is that the relative size of priming effects in older and younger adults does not change systematically with SOA. This is not consistent with the prediction that the time course of priming should be affected by slowing of central processes. This means that the interpretation offered for the overall larger priming effects in older adults cannot be extended to explain SOA effects. It would be tempting to explain away the failure to find a consistent lengthening of the time course of priming in older adults but, as can be seen, similar findings appear again in other, different paradigms.

In addition to the facilitatory priming seen in lexical decision tasks, there are also procedures that produce inhibitory or *negative priming*. For example, Tipper and Cranston (1985) presented pairs of letters, one in red, one in green. The participant's task was to identify letters in one of the colors, for example, green. In the critical condition, a letter written in red, that was to be ignored, could appear in green as the target on the next trial. Reaction times on those trials were reliably longer than those on which the target had not previously been a distractor. Presumably the active inhibition of the distracting item carried over to the next trial, slowing processing when it had become a target.

Following Hasher and Zacks's (1988) suggestion that inhibitory processes are impaired in old age, Tipper (1991) used a similar procedure on older adults and compared the results to those obtained on the task previously with younger adults (Tipper, Bourgue, Anderson, & Brehaut, 1989). Subjects saw two pictures; they were to identify the one at fixation. In an ignored repetition condition, the distractor picture from one trial could be the target on the next. Younger adults showed significant negative priming, with the ignored repetition trials 15 ms slower than control trials. Older adults showed a positive priming effect with distractors repeated as targets 26 ms faster. In two experiments using the same procedure as Tipper and Cranston (1985), Hasher, Stoltzfus, Zacks, and Rypma (1991) found significant negative priming effects of 9 ms and 8 ms in younger adults and nonsignificant effects of 2 ms and − 2 ms (a positive priming effect) in older adults.

In summary, despite the small effects it is reasonable to hypothesize that negative priming procedures may produce qualitatively different effects in younger and older adults.

The Stroop task is another procedure in which irrelevant information apparently is activated automatically and must be suppressed. The name of a color is printed in color; the task is to identify the color in which the word is printed. If the color is congruent with the word (e.g., *red* printed in red), the meaning of the word facilitates the response and need not be inhibited. If, however, the color is incongruent (e.g., *red* printed in green), processing of the word would interfere with the correct response and must be inhibited. The result is similar to priming because the word does not reduce uncertainty about the color and need not be consciously processed but does affect the response. There is evidence that times to name colors with incongruent words increase more rapidly with age than do times to name the color of colored bars (Cohn, Dustman, & Bradford, 1984; Comalli, Wapner, & Werner, 1962). If, however, the effect is expressed as the ratio of the time to name colored words to the time to name colored bars, compensating for the generally slower performance of older adults, the age effects disappear in the Cohn et al. study and are reduced substantially in the Comalli et al. study. Panek, Rush, and Slade (1984), however, found that the interaction of Stroop interference and age remained significant after a logarithmic transformation that should have removed effects of general slowing.

Rogers and Fisk (1991) studied Stroop-like interference effects using arithmetic equations. For example, the judgment that $3 \times 4 = 7$ is false is slower and more difficult than $3 \times 4 = 9$, presumably because the equation $3 + 4 = 7$ would be correct. They concluded that interference effects were greater in older adults than in younger adults; although if the reaction-time effects are expressed as a proportion of the reaction time to noninterfering equations, older adults actually show less interference (.17) than younger adults (.19). Rogers and Fisk also examined the change in interference over three 450-trial sessions. They found that younger adults differentially improved performance on the interfering equations whereas older adults did not; they concluded that older adults were impaired in their ability to learn to inhibit the activation of competing information. Examination of their results, however, shows (a) that the greatest improvement in accuracy was for older adults in the interfering equation condition, (b) that the proportional improvement in reaction time was very similar for all conditions for both older and younger adults (averaging .13 for each), and (c) that, in the final session, the interference effects were still very similar for older adults (.18) and younger adults (.17). As a consequence, Rogers and Fisk's claims about specific impairments in older adults should be viewed with caution.

The Stroop task has not been investigated systematically with older adults, for example, to explore the effects of separating the distracting word from the color block (Kahneman & Henik, 1981), or the effects of diluting the effect with the presence of neutral words (Kahneman & Chajczyk, 1983), or the effects of temporally separating the word and the color block (Dyer & Severance, 1973). Such investigations would provide more complete information on which to base conclusions about aging and inhibitory functioning.

Cuing

The effects of cuing can be measured in the benefits of a correct or valid cue and the costs of an incorrect or invalid cue. The usual measure of the benefits is the difference in reaction times between uncued and validly cued trials; costs are the difference between invalidly cued and uncued trials. As noted in the discussion of priming, there are reasons to doubt that uncued trials are truly neutral (Jonides & Mack, 1984), so some authors use costs plus benefits (the difference between invalidly and validly cued trials) as the measure of the effect of cues. Two types of cues have been used, cues to the location of the target and cues to its identity.

Location Cuing. Nissen and Corkin (1985) used a procedure in which the target was preceded by an arrow pointing to the visual hemifield in which it was likely to occur. The cue was valid on 80% of the cued trials and invalid on 20%. On noncued trials, a plus appeared.

The task was to detect the onset of a target, which appeared on every trial; there were no catch trials. Costs plus benefits were greater for older adults (50 ms) than for younger adults (28 ms). This was still true when the effects were expressed as a percentage of the overall average reaction time (18% for older adults, 12% for younger adults). Using a similar procedure, Hartley, Kieley, and Slabach (1990) also found that cuing effects were larger for older adults than for younger adults even when expressed as a proportion of valid cue reaction time.

Using a different procedure, Madden (1983) cued two of four possible target locations with a two-headed arrow pointing to the two locations. He gave only valid cues; thus there were only benefits, no costs. The benefits were larger for older adults than for younger adults with both absolute and relative measures. In contrast, when two of four possible locations were cued by asterisks appearing at the positions, the benefits were slightly smaller for older adults in absolute reaction times and noticeably smaller when expressed as proportions (Madden, 1986). The asterisks would have served as primes in addition to serving as cues because they appeared at the same location as the target.

Hartley et al. (1990, Experiment 3) also used a bar-marker cue that appeared at the likely location of the target. In that condition, they found that costs plus benefits did not differ for older and younger adults. When the results were expressed as a proportion of valid cue reaction times, costs plus benefits were slightly lower for older adults. Although the evidence is again limited, it appears possible that the effects of cues are larger for older adults than younger adults unless the cue also serves as a prime, in which case the effects are the same or smaller.

In Madden's (1986) experiment, a secondary tone reaction-time task was carried out concurrently. Performance on the tone task was expressed as a proportion of reaction time in a baseline tone-alone condition, to compensate for general slowing. Nonetheless, proportional tone reaction times were higher for older than for younger adults. For both groups, however, the reaction times were elevated for 100 ms and 200 ms after the cue appeared, but then dropped to asymptotic levels after 300 ms. Thus, the time course of processing the cue—presumably indexed by slowing in the secondary tone task—was the same for older and younger adults. Hartley et al. (1990) also looked at the time course of cue utilization by varying the SOA between the cue and the target. They found that costs and benefits emerged at least as early for older adults as for younger adults. In contrast, Hoyer and Familant (1987) found that benefits of a cue were significant for younger adults at a 250 ms SOA but did not reach significance for older adults until 750 ms. Cue benefits expressed as a proportion of neutral reaction time were substantially higher for younger adults: Younger adults increased from .16 at 350 ms SOA to .44 at 1,250 ms; older adults reached .12 for SOAs of 1,000 and 1,250 ms. It is difficult to interpret their results, however, because the task was simply to detect the appearance of a target and the cue was always correct. Thus the cue provided all the information needed to respond. Subjects may have determined the correct response and had to withhold it until the target actually appeared. Age differences in reaction times may have been due to differences in cue processing or differences in strategies for delaying a response or both.

Madden (1990b) also provided a cue that provided perfect information about where the target would appear but not what the target would be; the task was to determine whether the target was a *C* or an *X*. There were also no noncued trials, so that neither costs nor benefits could be measured. When distractors were absent younger adults showed reduced reaction times at the longest SOA, 183 ms; older adults showed no reduction. When distractors were present, younger adults improved monotonically from 50 ms to 183 ms SOA whereas older adults showed no significant reduction in reaction times until 183 ms. This effect remained significant even after a logarithmic transformation that would have removed age interactions due to general slowing. In the absence of comparison conditions, it is not possible to separate age differences in the informational effects of a cue from general effects on tonic arousal. Although the results of Hoyer and Familant (1987) and Madden (1990b) might be discounted on procedural grounds, a conservative conclusion is probably in order in that the presence or absence of age differences in the time course of cue utilization is still an open question.

Identity Cuing. Madden (1984) tested an assertion by Rabbitt (1979) that older adults are deficient in memory-driven but not in data-driven selective attention. He designated two letters as targets. Four-letter displays were presented and the task was to say whether one of the target items was present. In the data-driven cue condition, a letter presented as an advance cue meant that letter was likely to be the target. In the memory-driven cue condition, a letter presented as a cue meant the other letter in the target set was likely to be the cue. Notice that, in the data-driven cue condition, the letter serves as a cue, but it also should prime the target because it is physically identical. In the memory-driven cue condition, the letter is only a cue. The results showed no significant age differences in cue effects in either condition for absolute reaction times. If the costs plus benefits are expressed as a proportion of uncued reaction time, the proportions are larger for younger adults, particularly in the memory-driven cue condition (.31 for younger adults; .17 for older adults). A later experiment using only the memory-driven cue condition showed slightly higher cue benefits in older than in younger adults;

neither group showed any costs (Madden, 1985). When expressed as a proportion of noncued reaction times, benefits were slightly higher for younger adults (.23) than for older adults (.19). Hartley et al. (1990) presented the letters, *A* and *B,* and the digits, 1 and 2, as targets. An advance cue indicated whether the target was likely to be a letter or a number. Costs plus benefits were larger for older adults both in absolute terms and as a proportion of valid cue reaction time.

Both Madden (1985) and Hartley et al. (1990) examined the time course of identity cuing and found significant cuing effects at each SOA examined. Madden found no age difference in the benefits of 200 ms and 400 ms SOAs but found they were higher for older adults at 800 ms and 1,000 ms. When expressed as a proportion of uncued reaction time, benefits were higher for younger adults at SOAs of 200 ms and 400 ms (.23 and .25 for younger adults; .13 and .18 for older adults); they were similar at SOAs of 800 ms and 1,200 ms (.20 and .19 for younger adults; .21 and .22 for older adults). Hartley et al. found no change in costs plus benefits from 200 ms to 600 ms for either younger or older adults with the benefits remaining higher for older adults for both absolute and proportional measures. The evidence is limited and inconsistent. Madden found that younger adults realize the benefits of a cue more rapidly; Hartley et al. found no difference in the time course.

Expectancies

A cue creates an anticipation that the target on that trial will appear in a particular location or will have a particular characteristic. An expectancy is an anticipation that extends over a number of trials. Hoyer and Familant (1987) had subjects respond to the onset of a target in one of four locations by pressing one of four corresponding keys. They contrasted a condition in which the target appeared in one of the locations on 85% of the trials with another in which all four locations were equally likely. To strengthen the expectation, the distributions were explained to the subjects in the instructions. The difference between reaction times to the expected and unexpected locations was more than twice as large for older adults (291 ms) as for younger adults (119 ms). The difference is also larger for older adults (.46) than for younger adults (.30) when expressed as a proportion of reaction time in the equal frequency condition. Waugh, Fozard, Talland, and Erwin (1973) and Fozard, Thomas, and Waugh (1976) compared two-choice reaction times for trials on which the target on the preceding trial was repeated to those on which the target was alternated. Reaction times were generally faster for the alternated targets even though a repeated target would have been primed, as though the participants had an expectation for alternation. The advantage for the expected target was greater for older adults both in absolute reaction times and when expressed as a proportion of the reaction time to repeated targets. The studies reviewed here are consistent with the previous conclusion that the effects of cues are larger in older adults than younger adults.

Summary

The effects of externally initiated shifts of attention are generally larger for older adults than for younger adults when measured by absolute reaction times. There are two exceptions: (a) When a location is cued by a peripheral stimulus appearing at the location the effects are equivalent; (b) when a distractor on the preceding trial becomes the target on the next trial, younger adults show negative priming whereas older adults show no effect or positive priming (although the evidence on this point is preliminary at present). When the possibility of general slowing is taken into account by some form of proportional transformation, the results are much less clear. Age effects in semantic priming seem to disappear. Effects in Stroop interference may or may not. Effects of expectancies and of central location cues remain larger in older adults than in younger adults; effects of peripheral cues are smaller. Results with cuing of identity are mixed. Time course effects are still less clear. Either the results are mixed (semantic priming, location cuing, identity cuing) or the relevant studies have not been carried out (negative priming, Stroop effect).

Internally Initiated Shifts of Attention

The predominant view seems to be that search involves internally initiated shifts of attention in order to serially scan the possible targets. The search can be through a visual display of items or through items held in memory. Some stimuli can summon attention automatically. If the target is not found in this way, then the items must be selected and examined until it is. The reaction time increases monotonically with the load (display or memory set size), presumably because the number of items that need to be checked before a target is found increases with load. The process need not be serial, however. The search could be carried out in parallel. So long as the capacity were fixed, reaction time would be expected to rise with load because the limited capacity would have to be spread over more items.

Visual Search

Plude and Doussard-Roosevelt (1989) studied search for a target among distractors in a visual display. They contrasted a *feature* condition in which the target differed from the distractors on one feature (e.g., a green target among red distractors) with a *conjunction* condition in which the target differed on a combination of features (e.g., a green *X* among red *X*s and red and green *O*s). The theoretical model of Treisman and Gelade (1980) predicts that a target defined by a single feature can be selected preattentively; no attention-requiring search of the display is necessary. The target is said to "pop out"; reaction time is independent of display size. By contrast, reaction times in the conjunction condition increase linearly with display size, as though attention must be directed successively to each item. (As Duncan & Humphreys, 1989, noted, pop-out is not exclusive to feature search, nor is a display size effect exclusive to conjunction search.) The slopes of the functions relating reaction time to display size—presumed to give the time per comparison—often are found to be twice as high when there is no target in the display as when the target is present. The interpretation is that search must be exhaustive when the target is absent, but can be terminated as soon as the target is found when one is present and that will occur, on average, after half of the items have been scanned.

Plude and Doussard-Roosevelt (1989) found pop-out in the feature condition in both younger and older adults. The slopes of the display size functions did not differ from zero for either group ($-.35$ ms/item for younger adults, .55 ms/item for older adults). The conjunction conditions showed clear display size effects. Both groups had target-absent slopes that were approximately twice those for target-present (25.5 ms/item and 13.9 ms/item for younger adults; 49.6 ms/item and 25.4 ms/item for older adults). This indicates that the processing was qualitatively the same in both groups: exhaustive search in target-absent and self-terminating in target-present. Nonetheless, slopes were about twice as high in older adults as though they required twice as long to consider each display item.

In the standard conjunction condition, if the target were a red *X,* half of the distractors would share the color (red *O*s) and half would share the shape (green *X*s). Plude and Doussard-Roosevelt (1989) also included a condition in which two distractors shared the color and the remaining 2, 12, or 22 distractors shared the shape (e.g., two red *O*s and 2, 12, or 22 green *X*s). In such a case, younger adults appear to filter out the green items and concentrate their search on the smaller set of red items (Egeth, Virzi, & Garbart, 1984). If younger adults can take advantage of this perceptual grouping but older adults cannot, reaction time would be independent of display size in younger but not older adults. The age groups did not differ. Although the slopes were slightly above zero for both groups, even the largest was within the range considered to reflect pop-out by Treisman (Treisman & Gelade, 1980; Treisman & Gormican, 1988). Thus, both younger and older adults appear able to take advantage of the asymmetry to improve the efficiency of their search. Overall, the results of Plude and Doussard-Roosevelt's experiment indicate that the processes of visual search are similar, if slower, in older adults and in younger adults.

Gilmore, Tobias, and Royer (1985) also examined the effects of perceptual grouping on search. The target was embedded in zero, five, or nine distractors. In one condition the distractors were identical dot matrices, the same height and width as a letter. In other conditions, the distractors were different letters chosen to be either similar to each other (e.g., *A, H, W*) or dissimilar (e.g., *I, U, X*). The distractors were placed close together to promote perceptual grouping because of proximity. The different letters may not have been similar enough to result in perceptual grouping, but the matrices certainly should have been. When a target was present, the estimated time per comparison for younger adults was 9 ms/item for matrices and 21 ms/item for letters. The estimates for older adults were 35 ms/item for matrices and 25 ms/item for letters. When the target was absent, the pattern was quite different. For target absent, the estimates for younger adults were 2.5 ms/item for matrices and 52 ms/item for letters; for older adults, 1.2 ms/item and 35 ms/item. Gilmore et al. (1985) and Madden (1990a) concluded from these results that older adults may not be able to take advantage of perceptual grouping, contrary to the findings of Plude and Doussard-Roosevelt (1989). However, performance in the two age groups is qualitatively similar for all but the target-present conditions in which matrices were distractors. There is no satisfactory explanation for why pop-out should occur on target-absent but not target-present trials.

Memory Search

It is also possible to vary the number of items held in memory rather than the size of the display (e.g., Sternberg, 1966). A probe is presented and the subject must indicate whether it is an element of the memory set (present) or not (absent). Reaction times increase with memory set size as though the probe were successively compared to each memory set item. The results are similar to those from experiments varying display size in visual search, except that the slopes are often similar for both probe-present and probe-absent conditions. This is taken as evidence that exhaustive search is carried out in both conditions.

Strayer, Wickens, and Braune (1987) examined memory search in subjects aged 20–65 years. They used memory set sizes of two, three, or four. In addition to conditions with letters as the memory set, they also had spatial conditions in which the items were connected line segments. Overall, they found that the slope of the function relating response time to set size increased from 41 ms/item in the youngest group (20–26 years) to 57 ms/item in the oldest group (53–65 years). These age effects did not interact with whether the probe was present or absent in the memory set or whether the stimuli were letters or line segments. These results are consistent with those obtained by other investigators (Anders & Fozard, 1973; Anders, Fozard, & Lillyquist, 1972; Eriksen, Hamlin, & Daye, 1973; Ford, Roth, Mohs, Hopkins, & Kopell, 1979; Madden & Nebes, 1980; Marsh, 1975; Salthouse & Somberg, 1982). It appears that the rate of memory search slows with age.

Strayer et al. (1987) examined the process of memory search much more closely and reached a somewhat different conclusion. They also collected cortical event-related potentials and located the P300. P300 is a positive peak occurring about 300 ms after stimulus onset. Its exact temporal location is sensitive to changes in perceptual and cognitive processing but it is thought to be uninfluenced by response related processes (for a review, see Bashore, 1990). Strayer et al. found that P300 latency increased with set size and was longer when the probe was absent from the memory set than when it was present. P300 latencies showed a monotonic increase from the youngest to the oldest groups, but the difference fell short of significance. P300 latencies did not increase more rapidly with the increase in set size for older adults than younger adults as reaction times did. This is consistent with the conclusions of a meta-analysis of P300 studies by Bashore, Osman, and Heffley (1989).

If P300 reflects the effects of processing load independent of response-related processes, then the results of Strayer et al. (1987) indicate that the demands of memory search are no greater for older adults than for younger adults. The age differences that have been found in reaction time would appear to be the result of response-related processes. Their results are consistent with the interpretation that all subjects set progressively more conservative response criteria as set size increases and that this is more pronounced for older adults. Because there are questions about the mechanisms underlying P300, however, it would be well to reserve judgment on this conclusion until converging evidence is available.

If we considered only visual search, it would be attractive to explain age differences as due to impaired spatial localization in older adults (perhaps related to increased difficulty in handling information from the visual periphery in a crowded field). If the scan of items is serial, then, as the processing of one item is being completed, the next item to be selected must be located and a process executed to shift attention to that location. If older adults are less accurate at localizing the next item, it would take longer to finally settle attention on it, filter out the surround, and begin processing. However, the findings are quite similar for both visual and memory search: The search is qualitatively similar but slower in older than in younger adults. The findings of Strayer et al. (1987) raise the distinct possibility that the age differences in search are in processes related to setting the response criterion rather than in attentional selection.

Madden (1986) presented evidence consistent with this interpretation. He used a dual-task procedure in which reaction times to an auditory probe were used to infer the attentional demands of search. The dependent variable was the reaction time to the probe expressed as a proportion of reaction time in probe-only baseline trials. This served to compensate for general slowing in older adults. The proportional tone reaction times were higher with a set size of four items than with a set size of two items and they stayed elevated longer after the onset of the probe consistent with the interpretation that the processing of the larger set was more difficult and took longer. The proportional reaction times were higher throughout for older adults but the increase from a set size of two to a set size of four was not differentially greater for older adults and the time course of reaction time elevation was the same in both groups. In a second experiment, Madden compared the proportional tone reaction times for trials on which a response was required to others on which no response was required. Older adults showed significantly elevated reaction times when a response was required; younger adults showed no difference between response and no-response trials. Again, however, the time course of elevation was the same for younger and older adults. Madden's results are consistent with the interpretation that age differences as a function of load in search tasks may be a function of response-related processes.

Development of Automatic Search

In search tasks the same items may serve as targets on some trials and as distractors on others. This is called *varied mapping* (Shiffrin & Schneider, 1977). Alternatively, the sets of targets and distractors may be kept distinct. This is called *consistent mapping* (Shiffrin & Schneider, 1977). With sufficient training in a consistent mapping task, the time to recognize a target becomes independent of load, resembling the pop-out that occurs in feature search conditions. The processing is said to be automatic. In contrast, performance in varied mapping never becomes independent of load; search apparently remains controlled despite extended practice.

Typically consistent mapping conditions reduce age differences relative to varied mapping in both visual and memory search, although the slopes remain larger for older adults (Madden, 1982, 1983; Madden & Nebes, 1980; Plude & Hoyer, 1986; Plude et al., 1983). Madden (1982) and

Madden and Nebes (1980) found similar improvement with extended practice for both older and younger adults as though both were headed eventually toward asymptotic performance with reaction time independent of load. Fisk, McGee, and Giambra (1988) extended practice to 4,200 trials in both consistent mapping and varied mapping tasks (compared to 1,968 trials in Madden, 1986). Varied mapping slopes did not change with practice for any age group. Consistent mapping slopes, however, decreased 99% for younger adults and 82% for middle-aged adults, but only 65% for older adults.

Fisk and Rogers (1991) extended consistent mapping practice to 5,184 trials. In two experiments they found different results for memory and visual search in the last block of trials: Memory set size had a small effect on reaction time and the effect was the same for younger and older adults; visual display size, however, had a stronger effect that was significantly larger for older than for younger adults. They obtained the opposite result when they examined the last block from a total of 2,592 varied mapping trials: The effect of visual display size was the same in younger and older adults; memory set size had a significantly larger effect in older than in younger adults. Fisk and Rogers argued that, with extended practice in consistent mapping, the memory set can become categorized or unitized, removing the necessity for serial search. They concluded that both younger and older adults can do this. Visual targets, however, gain in attention-summoning strength relative to distractors only for younger adults, not for older adults. By contrast, in varied mapping neither of these processes is possible. Memory search performance remains dependent on the ability to maintain the memory set for that trial and to conduct a serial search of each item, so older adults are at a disadvantage. Because targets and distractors are interchangeable from trial to trial, no differential strengthening of targets is possible, so there is no advantage in visual search for younger adults.

Yet again, the evidence is limited, but the apparent conclusion is that there are age differences in search even after very extensive training.

Summary

Search appears to be carried out more slowly by older adults than by younger adults, although the difference in speed is not beyond what would be expected from generalized slowing. The pattern of results is similar suggesting that the processes of search do not change with age although the speed does. These conclusions appear not to hold after extended practice, when older adults are differentially slower for visual search in consistent mapping situations and for memory search in varied mapping situations.

Dual-Task Studies

Dual-task studies usually are thought of as requiring the division of attention between the two simultaneous tasks. An alternative is to think of them as requiring time sharing in which attention is shifted between the tasks. The available results do not allow us to distinguish between these possibilities. They also do not allow strong inferences about reduced cognitive resources in old age (e.g., Guttentag, 1989; Salthouse, 1988c). Nonetheless, such studies can address the question: Are older adults particularly disadvantaged when they must do two things at once? Two approaches are taken. The first is to aggregate studies and look for consistent age differences. This approach acknowledges that specific studies may have methodological shortcomings but presumes that any reliable effect should appear across studies. The second approach is to select those few studies that have avoided most of the problems in drawing inferences, and so, that should provide the best evidence.

Meta-Analysis of Divided-Attention Studies

In an unpublished study Kieley (1991) has analyzed the effect size in a large number of experiments. (In a formal meta-analysis, the effect size, d, is the standardized difference between the means for the two groups, here older and younger adults.) The studies are listed in Table 1.1. The studies fell in two general categories: dichotic listening-type tasks and dual-task procedures in which subjects simultaneously carried out two tasks of qualitatively different types. Tasks that primarily involved division of effort between two different kinds of processing on a single task were excluded (e.g., handling carries while doing mental addition).

Dichotic listening tasks typically involve hearing a short series of digit pairs. In each pair, one digit is channeled to the left ear; the other, to the right ear. The subject often is instructed to report all the digits heard in one ear, then all those heard in the other ear. These studies were motivated by Broadbent's (1958) filter model. The attentional filter was presumed to be set to the channel (the ear) to be reported first. Only after those items had been recalled could the selector be set to the other channel. In the interim, those items would have undergone decay, and performance would be worse than for the first-reported items.

There have been many variants on this basic procedure. In addition to digits (e.g., Caird, 1966; Craik, 1965), stimuli have included letters (e.g., Panek, Barrett, Sterns, & Alexander, 1978) and words (e.g., Schonfield, Trueman, & Kline, 1982). Subjects have been prompted before or after presentation about which channel to recall first (e.g., Clark & Knowles, 1973; Inglis & Ankus, 1965; Panek & Rush, 1981), or they may

TABLE 1.1
Studies Included in Meta-Analysis of Simultaneous Task Performance
by Kieley, Including Sample Sizes and Effect Size (*d*)

| Study | Sample Size | | *d* |
	Older	Younger	
Dichotic Listening			
Broadbent & Heron (1982)	8	6	2.15
Caird (1966)	20	20	.53
Craik (1965)	20	20	.86
	20	20	1.24
Inglis & Ankus (1965)	20	20	.71
	20	20	.99
	20	20	.80
Inglis & Caird (1965)	20	20	1.43
Inglis & Tansey (1967)	20	20	1.66
Mackay & Inglis (1963)	20	20	.53
Panek, Barrett, Sterns, & Alexander (1978)	25	25	.90
Parkinson, Lindholm, & Urell (1980)	8	8	2.36
	6	5	.94
Schonfield, Trueman, & Kline (1982)	10	10	.43
Dual-Task			
Baddeley, Logie, Bressi, Della Sala, & Spinnler (1986)	28	20	.31
Craik & McDowd (1987)	15	15	.82
Craik, Morris, & Gick (1988)	16	16	.37
	16	16	.37
Duchek (1984)	32	32	.26
Gick, Morris, & Craik (1988)	18	18	.34
Guttentag & Madden (1987)	14	14	.96
Kirchner (1958)	12	9	3.88
Kolbet (1985)	6	6	.63
	6	6	2.86
	6	6	1.99
Light & Anderson (1985)	25	25	.67
	20	20	.46
Lorsbach & Simpson (1988)	18	18	.87
Macht & Buschke (1983)	48	48	1.34
Madden (1986)	20	20	1.27
	18	18	2.41
	20	20	1.14
	16	16	1.55
Madden (1987)	24	24	1.36
McDowd (1986)	6	6	1.28
McDowd & Craik (1988)	16	16	1.28
	18	18	1.01
Morris, Gick, & Craik (1988)	24	24	.30
Park, Smith, Dudley, & La Fornza (1988)	60	59	.37

(Continued)

TABLE 1.1
(Continued)

| Study | Sample Size | | |
	Older	Younger	*d*
Dual-Task (Continued)			
Penner (1982)	24	24	.45
	24	24	.71
	24	24	.53
Salthouse & Somberg (1982)	16	16	.53
	16	16	4.08
Salthouse, Rogan, & Prill (1984)	24	24	.78
	16	16	.59
	16	16	.93
Somberg & Salthouse (1982)	16	16	.25
	16	16	.50
Talland (1966)	35	36	.88
	35	36	1.10
Teece (1982)	38	23	.62
Wickens, Braune, & Stokes (1987)	10	10	.37
Wright (1981)	12	12	.81

have been allowed simply to choose which to recall first (e.g., Caird, 1966; Inglis & Ankus, 1965).

The results are not without ambiguity. Some investigators have reported significant age-related decrements only for the channel reported second (e.g., Inglis & Caird, 1963; Mackay & Inglis, 1963) whereas others have found similar decrements in recall from both channels (e.g., Clark & Knowles, 1973; Craik, 1965; Inglis & Tansey, 1967; Schonfield et al., 1982). Parkinson, Lindholm, and Urell (1980) argued that age effects were the result of comparing groups with preexisting differences in digit span, whereas Inglis and Caird (1963) found differences despite matching for digit span. Dichotic listening performance could be interpreted as reflecting age differences in resources or in the costs of managing simultaneous tasks particularly when recall is prompted after presentation. It also could be interpreted as reflecting age differences in working memory, and so, may be less relevant than dual-task performance to age-related differences in attention.

The number of dual-task studies has increased steadily, with about three times as many appearing in the period 1983–1988 as in the preceding 5 years. This is probably due to the popularity of the resource metaphor and the attractiveness of dual-task methods as a test of reduced resources in older adults. Once again, a wide range of primary and secondary tasks has been used. The primary tasks have included visual search and other perceptual tasks (e.g., Broadbent & Heron, 1962; Guttentag & Madden, 1987; Kirchner, 1958; Lorsbach & Simpson, 1988; Madden, 1986, 1987; Salthouse & Somberg, 1982; Somberg & Salthouse, 1982), memory tasks (e.g., Craik, 1973; Craik & McDowd, 1987; Craik, Morris, & Gick, 1988; Gick, Craik, & Morris, 1988; Light & Anderson, 1985; Macht & Buschke, 1983; Morris, Gick, & Craik, 1988; Park, Smith, Dudley, & LaFornza, 1988; Rabinowitz, Craik, & Ackerman, 1982; Teece, Cattanach, Yrchik, Meinbresse, & Dessonville, 1982; Wright, 1981), motor skill tasks (e.g., Baddeley, Logie, Bressi, Della Sala, & Spinnler, 1986; McDowd, 1986; Somberg & Salthouse, 1982; Talland, 1962; Wickens, Braune, & Stokes, 1987), semantic processing (e.g., Duchek, 1984; McDowd & Craik, 1988; Penner, 1982), and problem solving (e.g., Duchek, 1984; Wright, 1981). Secondary tasks have included visual search (e.g., Craik & McDowd, 1987; McDowd & Craik, 1988), auditory detection (e.g., Duchek, 1984; Madden, 1986, 1987; McDowd, 1986; Park et al., 1988), visual detection (e.g., Macht & Buschke, 1983), semantic processing (e.g., Craik et al., 1988; Wright, 1981), and memory (e.g., Broadbent & Heron, 1962; Kirchner, 1958; Wickens et al., 1987). The tasks have covered a wide range of difficulties.

Formal meta-analytic procedures (Hedges, 1984) were applied to the sizes of the age effects in these studies. There was a powerful average effect (d = .99), and the 95% confidence interval for the true population effect size (δ) did not include zero (.88 < δ < 1.11), indicating that the age differences were reliable across studies. However, the effects were not homogeneous, indicating there were different factors producing the effects in different studies. Dichotic listening and related studies were separated from the remaining, dual-task studies. When this was done, there was a strong and internally homogeneous age effect for the dichotic-type tasks. Analysis of the dual-task studies yielded a powerful but heterogeneous effect. This means that the age effects in dual-task studies were not produced by the same factors as those in dichotic listening studies; the division or sharing of attention in the two types of tasks was not the same. This is consistent with the results of factor analyses by Wickens et al. (1987) who found that dichotic listening measures loaded on a different factor from other dual-task measures.

Kieley (1991) attempted to identify factors that contributed to the dual-task age effects. This was done by testing rationally derived subgroups of the studies to determine whether they had internally homogeneous age effects. He grouped the studies by the differences in age between the younger and older adults, by the education level of the subjects, by whether or not methodological problems such as nonequivalent baselines had been handled, by the type or modality or difficulty of the primary task, and by the dependent variables that were used. Although the number of studies in some of the groupings was small, the clearest evidence for homogeneous age effects within a grouping was for difficult primary tasks (although the effect size was smaller than for less difficult primary tasks rather than larger, as might have been expected) and for memory and motor primary tasks.

The results of the meta-analysis allow the qualified conclusion that there are real age differences in the ability to carry out two tasks simultaneously but that those differences can be produced by multiple underlying causes. The analyses did not identify what those causes might be.

Well-Controlled Divided-Attention Studies

The model for such studies is one conducted by Somberg and Salthouse (1982). In their experiments, subjects saw two overlapping four-item rectangular matrices. There were different item types in the two matrices. The target in each matrix was a small addition to one of the elements. The subject responded separately to the presence or absence of a target in each of the two matrices. To avoid age differences in performance on either of the tasks alone, Somberg and Salthouse equated performance across all subjects by adjusting the exposure duration for each matrix alone to achieve an 80%–90% accuracy criterion. In addition to the baseline conditions in which the subjects were to devote 100% of their attention to one task or the other, they also included three different joint emphasis conditions, 30%/70%, 50%/50%, and 70%/30%. This avoided the possibility of confounding caused by age differences in attention allocation policy because they could map out the entire performance operating characteristic (POC; see Fig. 1.1). Divided-attention costs were measured from the POC as shown in Fig. 1.1, by comparing the actual POC to the rectangular POC that would result if performance on both tasks remained at maximum when they were combined. The divided-attention costs were no different for younger adults than for older adults. In addition, the POCs were similarly shaped, indicating that both younger and older adults shift attentional emphasis similarly.

Salthouse, Rogan, and Prill (1984) used a similar approach but rather different tasks. They presented two lists, one of digits, one of letters. They adjusted the list lengths for each subject to be 75% of the subject's span for each type individually (so the two together were 150% of span). Again, they used different emphasis conditions and divided-attention costs were obtained in the same way. The divided-attention costs were reliably higher for older adults. This result held up across additional experiments conducted to rule out explanations based on response interference. Salthouse et al. argued that there are real age differences in information-processing

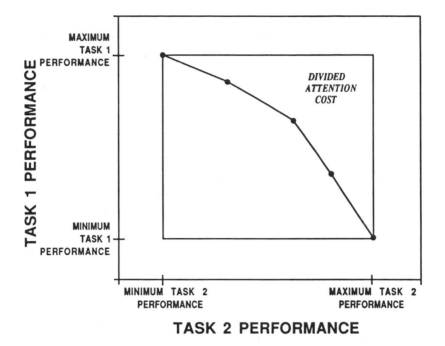

FIG. 1.1. Performance operating characteristic. Minimum and maximum performances are obtained when the subject is instructed to attend only to the other or only to that task. (Adapted from Somberg & Salthouse, 1982.)

operations such as "the initial allocation, subsequent redistribution, coordination, and monitoring of capacity-demanding encoding operations across the two concurrent tasks" (p. 619). They speculated that the difference between these results and those of Somberg and Salthouse (1982) was that the tasks in the later study were more complex—they required more component operations—so age differences would be expected to be larger. In addition, the tasks used by Somberg and Salthouse were more perceptual. Ponds, Brouwer, and van Wolffelaar (1988) used a design very similar to that of Salthouse et al. to study age differences when subjects had to keep an automobile on track in a driving simulator while simultaneously monitoring the status of a visual display. They obtained similar results: Divided-attention costs were higher in older adults than in middle-age or younger adults.

Korteling (1991) used a procedure in which perturbations in a left–right and an up–down tracking task were individually calibrated so that all individuals had the same average tracking error when each task was performed alone. When the tasks then were done simultaneously, older adults were less able to capitalize on synchronization of the two targets to improve dual-task performance.

The approach used in these studies is not intended to address the question of why age differences in the single tasks might occur (i.e., differences in digit or letter span when no other task was superimposed). It can ask, given that the demands of each task alone have been equated across age groups, whether there are age differences in concurrence costs. Salthouse et al. (1984) argued that there are. They attributed them to dynamic attentional capacity rather than any structural limitation or response competition. They went on to argue that age differences in divided-attention costs would be expected to rise with the complexity of tasks because the age differences in executing each step would compound as the number of steps increased. The problem is that the argument about complexity is based on the component tasks themselves. The assumption is that, if the component tasks are more complex, then the executive costs of managing them together will be greater.

This argument has prompted a number of researchers to use a different approach to examining age differences in concurrence costs. The alternative approach does not require any a priori assumptions about the relation of the concurrence costs to the composite tasks. An example is a study by McDowd and Craik (1988) in which they gave easy and difficult versions of both auditory and visual tasks. Each task was given alone and in combination with others, resulting in a total of 12 measures (the four tasks alone plus performance measures for visual and auditory in each of the four combined tasks). They plotted the older adults' mean reaction times as a function of the young adults' means. They argued that, if the requirements of managing simultaneous tasks act simply to increase complexity, then all points should lie along the same line. The implicit assumption is that divided attention may have costs, but, if the costs are proportionately the same in the two age groups, the points for conditions high in divided-attention costs should lie along the same line as that for other conditions. For the two experiments they reported, the r^2s were .81 and .88, providing strong evidence in support of their conjecture that older adults were not differentially affected by having to manage two tasks concurrently. A similar approach was used by Madden (1988) and Plude and Doussard-Roosevelt (1989) who reached similar conclusions.

Once again, any simple summary is likely to be wrong. Accepting that caveat, the most plausible interpretation of the findings from dual-task studies is that younger and older adults do not differ in the ability to allocate attention across conditions. There are age differences in absolute concurrence costs but not relative or proportional concurrence costs. The processes involved in doing two things concurrently are probably qualitatively quite similar in younger and older adults. The differences are caused by the fact that each of the component processes is affected by aging.

Sustained Attention: Vigilance

In sustained-attention tasks subjects must monitor an information source for occasional target events. Both controlled attending and general alertness and arousal are implicated in performance. The target events can be sensory—for example detecting double jumps in a clock hand that moves once per second (the Mackworth Clock Task; Giambra & Quilter, 1988; Surwillo & Quilter, 1964)—or cognitive—for example, monitoring a digit stream for occurrences of three odd, nonrepeated digits in sequence. The events can be relatively frequent—for example, one per 4 s on average (Parasuraman, Nestor, & Greenwood, 1989)—or relatively infrequent—for example, one every 162 s on average (Giambra & Quilter, 1988). Typical results show a decline in the likelihood of correctly detecting a target as the time on task increases; this is called the vigilance decrement. The results often are discussed in terms of the signal detection concepts of sensitivity (d') and response criterion (β).

In many tasks the decrement in hit rate is due to changes in β with d' remaining stable. The response criterion becomes more stringent over time. If the event rate is high and the targets impose a cognitive load or are perceptually degraded, the vigilance decrement is mediated by a change in d' (Nuechterlein, Parasuraman, & Jiang, 1983; Parasuraman, 1979; Parasuraman et al., 1989).

Surwillo and Quilter (1964) used the Mackworth Clock task in a 62-min session. There were no significant age differences in hits in the first 15 min, but older adults were clearly worse in the last 15 min. That is, the vigilance decrement was greater in older adults. Giambra and Quilter (1988) reviewed the analyses performed by Surwillo and Quilter, and concluded that the apparent age difference may have been a statistical artifact of splitting the sample at age 60 years for comparisons. Giambra and Quilter replicated the earlier study, testing a large number of individuals including 53 who had been tested 18 years before as a part of Surwillo and Quilter's study. They found no age differences in target detections. The likelihood of detection decreased with time but did so equivalently for all age groups. The number of detections was correlated significantly with both reaction time and measures of physiological arousal; those dependent variables declined along with hits. An absence of age differences also was reported by Gridley, Mack, and Gilmore (1986) and by Thompson, Opton, and Cohen (1963).

In contrast to Giambra and Quilter (1988), Parasuraman et al. (1989) used a cognitive task—detecting zeros in a stream of digits. The event rate was high—one per 4 s instead of one per 162 s—and the perceptual degradation of the stimuli was manipulated across conditions, resulting in conditions that might be expected to produce a vigilance decrement due to changes in d'. Correct detections declined over blocks, and did so more rapidly with degraded stimuli and for older adults. Sensitivity (d') was lower for older adults. It declined over blocks, but only in the most degraded condition. Most important, the change in d' was unaffected by age. The differentially larger decrement in hits in older adults than in younger adults combined with the equivalent changes in d' suggested that there may have been different changes in response criteria for younger and older adults. The change in β was somewhat greater in the older than in the younger adults (i.e., the criterion became more stringent), but the effect fell short of significance.

It is difficult to base strong conclusions on two studies. Nonetheless, both were carefully designed, used very different methods, and tested moderately large to very large samples. It is most likely the case, as Parasuraman et al. (1989) concluded, that "the process of sustained allocation of attentional capacity, as reflected in temporal changes in sensitivity, operates similarly in older as in younger adults" (p. 344).

CONCLUSIONS

The findings that have been reviewed in this chapter are summarized in Table 1.2. For each procedure, a generalization is offered about age-related effects and the evidence in support of that generalization is assessed. The evidence is characterized as *strong* if it is the result of a formal meta-analysis or if a number of studies have consistently produced the same result. It is characterized as *moderate* or *limited* if the results have been consistent, but there have been fewer studies. When different studies have produced qualitatively different results, the evidence is characterized as *mixed*. These are the data that must be explained by an adequate theory or theories of age-related differences in attention.

What is immediately clear from Table 1.2 is that there is relatively little evidence. For many of the procedures we cannot say with confidence what the result is that a theory should explain. There are relatively few studies and the results from those studies are, in some cases, inconsistent. The danger in drawing conclusions is pointed up by the evidence from semantic priming and dual-task procedures. If the results were simply listed, the evidence for age differences would have to be characterized as mixed. Yet, because there were enough similar studies to allow formal meta-analysis, it was discovered that there are reliable age differences. Because of the uncertainties about the evidence, the evaluation of theories of attention at best can be only tentative.

The theory that should be considered first is the version of the reduced resources hypothesis that explains age differences in attentional per-

TABLE 1.2
Summary of Age-Related Effects in Attention[a]

Phenomenon	Age-Related Effect	Evidence
Semantic Priming	Reaction-time benefit is approximately 1.5 times larger in older adults.	Strong
	No consistent age difference in time course.	Limited
Negative Priming	Reaction-time cost for targets that had been distractors in younger adults; not for older adults.	Limited
	Time course has not been investigated.	None
Stroop-Type Effects	Irrelevant stimuli produce larger reaction-time costs (incongruent) and benefits (congruent) for older adults.	Strong
	Time course has not been investigated.	None
Location Cuing	Reaction-time costs and benefits larger in older adults.	Moderate
	When the cue also primes the location, costs and benefits are similar for younger and older adults.	Moderate
	Some studies show no difference in time course; others consistent with longer time course in older adults.	Mixed
Identity Cuing	Reaction-time costs and benefits are the same or larger in older adults.	Limited
	One study found longer time course for older adults; another found no difference.	Mixed
Expectancy	Reaction-time benefits of expected targets are larger for older adults.	Moderate
Visual Search	Both younger and older adults show "pop-out" in single-feature search.	Moderate
	Conjunction search rates are qualitatively similar, but about twice as large in older adults.	Strong
	After extended practice with consistent mapping, display size effects are significantly larger for older adults; for varied mapping display size effects were the same.	Limited
Memory Search	Memory set size effects are greater for older adults for reaction time; they are similar for the P300 component of the event-related potential.	Strong
	After extended practice with consistent mapping, memory set size effects are small and are similar for younger and older adults; for varied mapping memory set size has a significantly larger effect for older adults.	Limited
Dichotic Listening	Younger adults perform better.	Strong
Dual-Task	Younger adults perform better.	Strong
Vigilance	For perceptual tasks and infrequent targets, sensitivity and the decline in sensitivity over time do not differ.	Moderate
	For cognitive tasks and frequent targets, sensitivity is lower for older adults, but the decline over time is similar.	Moderate

[a]Not shown in the table is that overall reaction times are longer for older adults in each task type.

35

formance, insofar as they are indexed by reaction time, as artifacts of general slowing (Birren, 1974; Birren, Woods, & Williams, 1980; Cerella, 1985b; Salthouse, 1985). Longer response latencies for older adults have been reported throughout this review. Cerella (1991) argued that generalized slowing may be sufficient to explain all age effects, that anomalous results can be attributed to sampling error, and that there may be no findings that require process-specific explanations. To review, the evidence in support of this claim is that, when the average performance for older adults in an experimental condition is plotted as a function of the average performance of younger adults in that condition without regard for the information-processing context of the experiment, the resulting plot is substantially linear with a slope greater than one. This is what would be expected if processing in any task were the same for younger and older adults, but the older adults were slowed by a constant amount at every step. (Various nonlinear functions have been suggested to provide slightly better fits—e.g., Cerella, 1985b, 1991; Myerson et al., 1990—but they do not change the general argument.)

An example of such an old–young plot is shown in Fig. 1.2. Each point

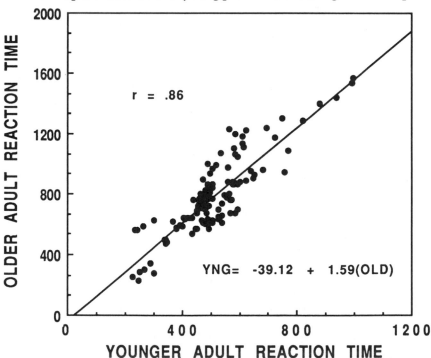

FIG. 1.2.   Mean older adult reaction time as a function of mean younger adult reaction time for 136 conditions from experiments showing disproportionate slowing with age.

represents 1 of 136 conditions from experiments reviewed in this chapter (Hartley et al., 1990; Hoyer & Familant, 1987; Madden, 1986, 1987, 1990b; Nissen & Corkin, 1985). Despite the heterogeneity of the experimental methods, there is a strongly linear reaction, $r = .86$. Each of the experiments was chosen, however, because it reported disproportionate age effects, that is, interactions of experimental factors with age that remained even when transformations were applied that should have removed effects of generalized slowing. The moral is clear. Slowing with age accounts for so much of the variance that it is easy to miss effects it cannot explain, particularly when aggregative techniques such as old–young plots are used.

What are the anomalies that cannot be accounted for by generalized slowing? The most important such evidence is the failure to find that the time course of priming, cuing, and activation during search were different in younger and older adults. Other evidence suggests that processing takes about 1.5 to 2.0 times longer in older adults. The time course of priming and cuing should be extended by a similar proportion; this effect should be as unmistakable as the slowing of overall reaction time. Yet there is no clear, consistent evidence of a lengthened time course in older adults. A second piece of evidence inconsistent with slowing is the finding of disproportionately larger effects of cues and expectancies in older adults. A third piece of evidence is that memory search resulted in age-related slowing in reaction time but not in the latency of the P300 component of the cortical evoked potential (Bashore et al., 1989; Strayer et al., 1987), although this is qualified by questions about what P300 measures. A fourth piece of evidence is that secondary-task measures show much larger effects on older adults than on younger adults when a response is required on the primary task than when it is not (Madden, 1986). These anomalies all converge on the explanation that the behavioral slowing that is observed may be largely the result of response processes. The processing of a cue or prime does not lead to a response. Rather, it affects the processing of the target, and it is that processing that leads to a response. Similarly, the P300 component is thought to reflect processes unrelated to responding. Plausible working hypotheses, then, are that age-related slowing may occur only in the decision and response stages of processing or that the slowing may be different in response stages from that in earlier stages. Procedures that allow separation of decision and response components from other components of processing will be valuable in evaluating these hypotheses.

There are other pieces of evidence that are inconsistent with simple slowing. One is the finding that reaction times in an auditory detection secondary task were higher for older adults than for younger adults, even when expressed as a proportion of reaction times on baseline trials

(Guttentag & Madden, 1987; Madden, 1986, 1987). Use of the proportional measure should have removed effects of general slowing. Another is the qualitatively different pattern of results obtained by Tipper (1991) and Hasher et al. (1991) in which young adults showed negative priming when a target had previously been a distractor whereas older adults showed no priming or positive priming. A third is the difference between younger and older adults in the pattern of memory set size and display size effects in consistent and varied mapping even after extensive practice (Fisk & Rogers, 1991).

This list of anomalies makes it clear that, even if a strong theory of generalized slowing is given theoretical priority, there are age-related attentional phenomena to be explained. A weak theory of slowing, of course, simply could incorporate these data, noting that they, too, obeyed a lawful relationship. Do the other theories of aging and attention that were described explain the anomalies?

The most specific theory of attention was the hypothesis that spatial localization is impaired in older adults (Plude & Hoyer, 1985). That hypothesis predicted that visual search performance should be worse in older adults than in younger adults, and this was found. The hypothesis makes no prediction about memory search, although we would at least expect visual and memory search to be uncorrelated in older adults. I know of no test of that correlation. The hypothesis also predicts that location cues would be more effective, which is the case. Again, it makes no prediction about identity cues, except perhaps that their effects would be uncorrelated with those of location cues. The hypothesis makes no prediction about priming, other than location priming, which should have a larger effect in older adults. It does not. The hypothesis also makes no prediction about performance in dual-task procedures or in procedures that involve facilitation or interference such as the Stroop task. The hypothesis of impaired spatial localization is limited in its predictions; it fails to explain most of the findings unexplained by slowing. The predictions it does make appear to have been supported except for the prediction that location priming would be more effective in older adults.

The hypothesis of reduced inhibitory functioning in old age (Hasher & Zacks, 1988) specifically predicts that interference and facilitation in the Stroop task should be greater in older than in younger adults. In contrast, negative priming should be greater in younger adults because they more successfully inhibit the distractors that later become targets. Both of these were found. The hypothesis makes no prediction about priming. Although the hypothesis does not make other predictions without additional assumptions, some predictions can be drawn. To the extent performing two tasks concurrently requires sharing, such that one task is inhibited while processing on the other is carried out, older adults would be expected to do less well than younger adults, and they do. If cuing of one location or aspect involves inhibiting processing of other locations or aspects and if older adults do this less effectively, then the costs of invalid cues should be less for older adults than for younger adults. This has not been found. Similarly, if search involves successively focusing on one item and temporarily inhibiting processing of nearby distractors and if older adults do this less well, then search should be worse for older than for younger adults. This should be true both for visual and memory search, and that is what has been found. We might well expect performance at the two to be correlated, but, again, this has not been tested. So, the reduced inhibition theory also fares well, but not all the predictions are confirmed. And, again, it fails to explain many of the findings left unexplained by slowing.

Toward a Cognitive Neuroscience of Aging and Attention

It is clear that aging and attention is by no means a mature field. The data are few and the theories are loosely specified (with the exception of some theories of slowing). What approaches can be taken so that, when a chapter such as this is written 5 or 10 years hence, there will be significant progress to report? One model is the emerging field of *cognitive neuroscience* (e.g., LeDoux & Hirst, 1986). Cognitive neuroscience can be defined loosely as the intersection of cognitive psychology, behavioral neuroscience, and artificial intelligence (or, more correctly, computational modeling of behavior).

Ideally, knowledge in each field would provide strong constraints to guide research in the others. For example, a formal specification of what is necessary to select some visual object for priority processing should place limits on the ways selection might be accomplished in human attention. Similarly, knowledge of the functional architecture of brain systems concerned with attention could provide strong constraints on theories of human attention. In practice, the ideal is not met. Often, too little is known in one field to provide clear guidance in another. Even when there are well-understood areas in two fields, they may not make contact. Most important, the constraints may never be strong enough to be of real value. Even if the phenomena of human selective attention could be specified unambiguously, there are a hopelessly large number of ways that could be instantiated in the biological substrates.

What has developed instead is an active process of cross-fertilization. Computational modelers have looked to cognitive psychology and cognitive psychologists have looked to neuroscience for hypotheses about how a function might be realized (e.g., LaBerge & Brown, 1989). Neuroscientists have looked to cognitive psychology for hypotheses about the brain's functions and how they should be conceived (Hirst & LeDoux, 1986). Cognitive psychologists and neuroscientists have borrowed techniques from each other (e.g., Bashore, 1990; Peterson, Fox, Snyder, & Raichle, 1990) and both have tested their theories by formalizing them as computational models (e.g., Granger, Ambros-Ingerson, & Lynch, 1988; LaBerge, 1990b). A similar cross-fertilization could be of substantial benefit to the cognitive psychology of aging and attention.

At the computational level a more precise characterization of the functions relating reaction times for younger and older adults in the same tasks would be desirable. Putative mechanisms that could explain behavioral slowing—strong theories of slowing—should be formalized and tested against the available evidence. Techniques of connectionist modeling may allow formalization of theories that are not mathematically tractable (McClelland & Rumelhart, 1986; Rumelhart & McClelland, 1986). One such mechanism is increased variability in old age in the arrival of axonal inputs at the dendritic tree of a neuron. If processing proceeded as in youth but the postsynaptic neuron simply had to wait for the last-arriving input, then generalized slowing would result. This model easily is expressed mathematically. If, instead, the delayed arrival of some inputs changed the information provided by the neuron to others with which it was linked, there could be qualitative changes in performance as well as generalized slowing. This mechanism would be explored more easily if realized as a connectionist neural network. Another theory that would profit from formalization as a computational model is that of impaired inhibitory functioning.

A more precisely specified weak theory of slowing also would be desirable. Linear, quadratic, or higher order functions suggest different underlying mechanisms. If different kinds of studies are fit by different specific functions from the same family, examination of the subsets could provide additional constraints. If the function is discontinuous (cf. Cerella, 1985b), then the search for common elements in each segment of the function is called for.

At the functional level of cognitive psychology, it probably will be fruitful to explore different ways to parse the phenomena of attention. The goal always has been to find subgroupings of studies that show internally homogeneous but externally heterogeneous patterns of age effects. Researchers in aging and attention have tended to adopt procedures used by cognitive psychologists studying attention in general. As a result, the phenomena are organized most naturally around those procedures (as has been done in this chapter). This may not be the ideal way to group them. As just described, old–young functions may provide a different way to parse the phenomena. Other parsings may come from neuroscience, which often organizes findings around brain structures.

As an example of such an organization at the neurochemical level, consider the central nervous system norepinephrine system (NE; e.g., Foote, Berridge, Adams, & Pineda, in press; Foote & Morrison, 1987). The NE system arises in the locus coeruleus and projects widely through the brain, in particular to the prefrontal cortex. It appears to be a critical component of cortically mediated attentional processes, serving to sharpen the difference between signal and noise. There is evidence for impairment in the NE system in older organisms (Arnsten & Goldman-Rakic, 1985). Such an impairment can be hypothesized to cause slowing and other changes, but it should do so particularly for tasks involving brain areas such as prefrontal cortex with projections from the locus coeruleus.

As an example at the neuroanatomical level, different networks of brain centers have been hypothesized to be involved in different aspects of attention (Posner, 1988; Posner & Petersen, 1990). Attention to different locations in space appears to be mediated by a posterior system involving parietal cortex, thalamus, and superior colliculus; attention to different cognitive operations appears to be mediated by the anterior cingulate cortex. Studies that tapped these different aspects of attention could be examined for differences in age-related effects.

The most important contributions from the neurosciences, however, may be methodological rather than theoretical. Cognitive psychologists studying aging already have adopted measures such as electroencephalogram (EEG) event-related potentials (see Bashore, 1990, for a review), skin conductance orienting responses (McDowd & Filion, in press), and cardiovascular responses (e.g., Jennings, Nebes, & Yovetich, 1990). Such measures can be very useful additions to an armamentarium that often is limited to reaction times and errors. Positron emission tomography (PET) techniques could be a useful adjunct to the study of aging and cognitive processes (e.g. LaBerge, 1990b; Peterson et al., 1990), but may be unavailable to many researchers.

In summary, cognitive neuroscience is an appealing model for the field of aging and attention to follow. Whether we do or not, the points remain that we need more data, we need innovative techniques to measure performance and innovative perspectives on the organization of the results, and we need more rigorous (and, consequently, more falsifiable) theoretical accounts of our findings. We have a long way to go to understand the driver in the scenario that opened the chapter. We have even farther to go to be able to use that understanding to make driving safer for her as she ages and for those who share the road with her.

REFERENCES

Allport, A. (1989). Visual attention. In M. I. Posner (Ed.), *The foundations of cognitive science* (pp. 631–682). Cambridge, MA: MIT Press.

Anders, T. R., & Fozard, J. L. (1973). Effects of age upon retrieval from primary and secondary memory. *Developmental Psychology, 9,* 411–415.

Anders, T. R., Fozard, J. L., & Lillyquist, T. D. (1972). Effects of age upon retrieval from short-term memory. *Developmental Psychology, 6,* 214–217.

Anderson, R. A. (1987). Inferior parietal lobule function in spatial perception and visuomotor integration. In V. B. Mountcastle, F. Plum, & S. R. Geiger (Eds.), *Handbook of physiology: Sec. 1, The nervous system: Vol. 5, Higher functions of the brain, Part 2* (pp. 483–518). Bethesda, MD: American Physiological Society.

Arnsten, A. F. T., & Goldman-Rakic, P. S. (1985). Alpha$_2$-adrenergic mechanisms in prefrontal cortex associated with cognitive decline in aged nonhuman primates. *Science, 230,* 1273–1276.

Baddeley, A., Logie, R., Bressi, S., Della Sala, S., & Spinnler, H. (1986). Dementia and working memory. *Quarterly Journal of Experimental Psychology, 38A,* 603–618.

Ball, K. K., Beard, B. L., Roenker, D. L., Miller, R. L., & Griggs, D. S. (1988). Age and visual search: Expanding the useful field of view. *Journal of the Optical Society of America (A), 5,* 2210–2219.

Balota, D. A., & Duchek, J. M. (1988). Age-related differences in lexical access, spreading activation, and simple pronunciation. *Psychology and Aging, 3,* 84–93.

Bashore, T. R. (1990). Age-related changes in mental processing revealed by analyses of event-related brain potentials. In J. W. Rohrbaugh, R. Parasuraman, & R. Johnson (Eds.), *Event-related brain potentials* (pp. 242–275). New York: Oxford University Press.

Bashore, T. R., Osman, A., & Heffley, E. F. III. (1989). Mental slowing in elderly persons: A cognitive psychophysiological analysis. *Psychology and Aging, 4,* 235–244.

Birren, J. E. (1974). Translations in gerontology—From lab to life: Psychophysiology and speed of response. *American Psychologist, 29,* 808–815.

Birren, J. E., Woods, A. M., & Williams, M. V. (1980). Behavioral slowing with age: Causes, organization, and consequences. In L. W. Poon (Ed.), *Aging in the 1980s: Psychological issues* (pp. 293–308). Washington, DC: American Psychological Association.

Broadbent, D. E. (1958). *Perception and communication.* London: Pergamon.

Broadbent, D. E. (1971). *Decision and stress.* London: Academic.

Broadbent, D. E., & Heron, A. (1962). Effects of a subsidiary task upon performance involving immediate memory by younger and older subjects. *British Journal of Psychology, 29,* 182–189.

Burke, D. M., White, H., & Diaz, D. L. (1987). Semantic priming in young and older adults: Evidence for age constancy in automatic and attentional processes. *Journal of Experimental Psychology: Human Perception and Performance, 13,* 79–88.

Caird, W. K. (1966). Aging and short-term memory. *Journal of Gerontology, 21,* 295–299.

Cerella, J. (1985a). Age-related decline in extrafoveal letter perception. *Journal of Gerontology, 40,* 727–736.

Cerella, J. (1985b). Information processing rates in the elderly. *Psychological Bulletin, 98,* 67–83.

Cerella, J. (1991). Age effects may be global, not local: Comments on Fisk and Rogers (1991). *Journal of Experimental Psychology: General, 120,* 215–223.

Cerella, J., Plude, D. J., & Milberg, W. (1987). Radial localization in the aged. *Psychology and Aging, 2,* 52–55.

Cerella, J., Poon, L. W., & Williams, D. M. (1980). Age and the complexity hypothesis. In L. W. Poon (Ed.), *Aging in the 1980s: Psychological issues.* Washington, DC: American Psychological Association.

Clark, I. F., & Knowles, J. B. (1973). Age differences in dichotic listening performance. *Journal of Gerontology, 28,* 173–178.

Cohn, N. B., Dustman, R. E., & Bradford, D. C. (1984). Age-related decrements in Stroop color test performance. *Journal of Clinical Psychology, 40,* 1244–1250.

Collins, A. M., & Loftus, E. F. (1975). A spreading-activation theory of semantic processing. *Psychological Review, 82,* 407–428.

Comalli, P. E., Jr., Wapner, S., & Werner, H. (1962). Interference effects of Stroop color-word test in childhood, adulthood, and aging. *Journal of Genetic Psychology, 100,* 47–53.

Craik, F. I. M. (1965). The nature of the age decrement in performance on dichotic listening tasks. *Quarterly Journal of Experimental Psychology, 17,* 227–240.

Craik, F. I. M. (1973, April). *Signal detection analysis of age differences in divided attention.* Paper presented at the American Psychological Association meetings, Montreal.

Craik, F. I. M., & McDowd, J. M. (1987). Age differences in recall and recognition. *Journal of Experimental Psychology: Learning, Memory, and Cognition, 13,* 474–479.

Craik, F. I. M., Morris, R. G., & Gick, M. L. (1990). Adult age differences in working memory. In G. Vallar & T. Shallice (Eds.), *Neuropsychological impairments of short-term memory* (pp. 247–267). Cambridge, England: Cambridge University Press.

DeGroot, A. M. B. (1983). The range of automatic spreading activation in word priming. *Journal of Verbal Learning and Verbal Behavior, 22,* 417–436.

Duchek, J. M. (1984). Encoding and retrieval differences between young and old: The impact of attentional capacity usage. *Developmental Psychology, 20,* 1173–1180.

Duncan, J., & Humphreys, G. W. (1989). Visual search and stimulus similarity. *Psychological Review, 96,* 433–458.

Dyer, F. N., & Severance, L. J. (1973). Stroop interference with successive presentations of separate incongruent words and colors. *Journal of Experimental Psychology, 98,* 438–439.

Egeth, H. E., Virzi, R. A., & Garbart, H. (1984). Searching for conjunctively defined targets. *Journal of Experimental Psychology: Human Perception and Performance, 10,* 32–39.

Eriksen, C. W., Hamlin, R. M., & Daye, C. (1973). Aging adults and rate of memory scan. *Bulletin of the Psychonomic Society, 1,* 259–260.

Eriksen, C. W., & St. James, J. D. (1986). Visual attention within and around the field of focal attention: A zoom lens model. *Perception & Psychophysics, 40,* 225–240.

Fisk, A. D., McGee, N. D., & Giambra, L. M. (1988). The influence of age on consistent and varied semantic-category search performance. *Psychology and Aging, 3,* 323–333.

Fisk, A. D., & Rogers, W. A. (1991). Toward an understanding of age-related memory and visual search effects. *Journal of Experimental Psychology: General, 120,* 131–149.

Flowers, J. H., & Reed, D. (1985, November). *Characteristics of visual context effects in visual classification tasks.* Paper presented at the meeting of the Psychonomic Society, Boston.

Foote, S. L., Berridge, C. W., Adams, L. M., & Pineda, J. A. (in press). Electrophysiological evidence for the involvement of the locus coeruleus in alerting, orienting, and attending. *Progress in Brain Research.*

Foote, S. L., & Morrison, J. H. (1987). Extrathalamic modulation of neocortical function. *Annual Review of Neuroscience, 10,* 67–95.

Ford, J. M., Roth, W. T., Mohs, R. C., Hopkins, W. F., & Kopell, B. S. (1979). Event-related potentials recorded from young and old adults during a memory retrieval task. *Electroencephalography & Clinical Neurophysiology, 47,* 450–459.

Fozard, J. L., Thomas, J. C., & Waugh, N. C. (1976). Effects of age and frequency of stimulus repetitions on two-choice reaction time. *Journal of Gerontology, 31,* 556–563.

Giambra, L. M., & Quilter, R. E. (1988). Sustained attention in adulthood: A unique, large-sample, longitudinal and multi-cohort analysis using the Mackworth Clock-test. *Psychology and Aging, 3,* 75–83.

Gick, M. L., Craik, F. I. M., & Morris, R. G. (1988). Task complexity and age differences in working memory. *Memory & Cognition, 16,* 353–361.

Gilmore, G. C., Tobias, T. R., & Royer, F. L. (1985). Aging and similarity grouping in visual search. *Journal of Gerontology, 40,* 586–592.

Gold, D., Andres, D., Arbuckle, T., & Schwartzman, A. (1988). Measurement and correlates of verbosity in elderly people. *Journals of Gerontology: Psychological Sciences, 43,* P27–P34.

Gopher, D., & Donchin, E. (1986). Workload—An examination of the concept. In K. R. Boff, L. Kaufman, & J. P. Thomas (Eds.), *Handbook of perception and human performance: Vol. 2. Cognitive processes and performance* (pp. 41/1–41/49). New York: Wiley.

Granger, R., Ambros-Ingerson, J., & Lynch, G. (1988). Derivation of encoding characteristics of layer II cerebral cortex. *Journal of Cognitive Neuroscience, 1,* 61–87.

Gridley, M. C., Mack, J. L., & Gilmore, G. C. (1986). Age effects on a nonverbal auditory sustained attention task. *Perceptual and Motor Skills, 62,* 911–917.

Guttentag, R. E. (1989). Age differences in dual-task performance: Procedures, assumptions, and results. *Developmental Review, 9,* 146–170.

Guttentag, R. E., & Madden, D. J. (1987). Adult age differences in the attentional capacity demands of letter matching. *Experimental Aging Research, 13,* 93–99.

Hale, S., Myerson, J., & Wagstaff, D. (1987). General slowing of nonverbal information processing: Evidence for a power law. *Journal of Gerontology, 42,* 131–136.

Hartley, A. A., Kieley, J. M., & Slabach, E. H. (1990). Age differences and similarities in the effects of cues and prompts. *Journal of Experimental Psychology: Human Perception and Performance, 16,* 523–538.

Hasher, L., Stoltzfus, E. R., Zacks, R. T., & Rypma, B. (1991). Age and inhibition. *Journal of Experimental Psychology: Learning, Memory, and Cognition, 17,* 163–169.

Hasher, L., & Zacks, R. T. (1979). Automatic and effortful processes in memory. *Journal of Experimental Psychology: General, 108,* 356–388.

Hasher, L., & Zacks, R. T. (1988). Working memory, comprehension, and aging: A review and a new view. In G. H. Bower (Ed.), *The psychology of learning and motivation* (Vol. 22, pp. 193–225). San Diego: Academic.

Hedges, L. V. (1984). Advances in statistical methods for meta-analysis. In W. H. Yeaton & P. M. Wortman (Eds.), *Issues in data synthesis: New directions for program evaluation* (pp. 25–42). San Francisco: Jossey-Bass.

Heilman, K. M., Watson, R. T., Valenstein, E., & Goldberg, M. E. (1987). Attention: Behavior and neural mechanisms. In V. B. Mountcastle, F. Plum, & S. R. Geiger (Eds.), *Handbook of physiology: Sec. 1, The nervous system: Vol. 5, Higher functions of the brain, Part 2* (pp. 461–481). Bethesda, MD: American Physiological Society.

Hirst, W., & LeDoux, J. E. (1986). Cognitive neuroscience: Final considerations. In J. E. LeDoux & W. Hirst (Eds.), *Mind and brain* (pp. 368–378). Cambridge, England: Cambridge University Press.

Howard, D. V. (1983). The effect of aging and degree of association on the semantic priming of lexical decisions. *Experimental Aging Research, 9,* 145–151.

Howard, D. V. (1988). Aging and memory activation: The priming of semantic and episodic memories. In L. L. Light & D. M. Burke (Eds.), *Language, memory, and aging* (pp. 77–99). New York: Cambridge University Press.

Howard, D. V., Shaw, R. S., & Heisey, J. G. (1986). Aging and the time course of semantic activation. *Journal of Gerontology, 41,* 195–203.

Hoyer, W. J., & Familant, M. E. (1987). Adult age differences in the rate of processing expectancy information. *Cognitive Development, 2,* 59–70.

Hoyer, W. J., & Plude, D. J. (1982). Aging and the allocation of attentional resources in visual information-processing. In R. Sekuler, D. Kline, & K. Dismukes (Eds.), *Aging and human visual function* (pp. 245–263). New York: Liss.

Inglis, J., & Ankus, M. N. (1965). Effects of age on short-term storage and serial rote learning. *British Journal of Psychology, 56,* 183–195.

Inglis, J., & Caird, W. K. (1963). Age differences in successive responses to simultaneous stimulation. *Canadian Journal of Psychology, 17,* 98–105.

Inglis, J., & Tansey, C. L. (1967). Age differences and scoring differences in dichotic listening performance. *Journal of Psychology, 66,* 325–332.

James, W. (1890). *The principles of psychology* (Vols. 1 & 2). New York: Holt, Rinehart & Winston.

Jennings, J. R., Nebes, R. D., & Yovetich, N. A. (1990). Aging increases the energetic demands of episodic memory: A cardiovascular analysis. *Journal of Experimental Psychology: General, 119,* 77–91.

Jonides, J., & Mack, R. (1984). On the cost and benefit of cost and benefit. *Psychological Bulletin, 96,* 29–44.

Kahneman, D. (1973). *Attention and effort.* Englewood Cliffs, NJ: Prentice-Hall.

Kahneman, D., & Chajczyk, D. (1983). Tests of the automaticity of reading: Dilution of Stroop effects by color-irrelevant stimuli. *Journal of Experimental Psychology: Human Perception and Performance, 9,* 497–509.

Kahneman, D., & Henik, A. (1981). Perceptual organization and attention. In M. Kubovy & J. R. Pomerantz (Eds.), *Perceptual organization* (pp. 181–211). Hillsdale, NJ: Lawrence Erlbaum Associates.

Kieley, J. (1990). *A meta-analysis and review of aging and divided attention.* Unpublished manuscript, Claremont Graduate School, Department of Psychology, Claremont, CA.

Kirchner, W. K. (1958). Age differences in short-term retention of rapidly changing information. *Journal of Experimental Psychology, 55,* 352–358.

Kolbet, L. L. (1985). Aging and the allocation of attentional resources: The influence of stimulus structure, preattentive organization and automaticity. *Dissertation Abstracts International, 46/*07B, 2475. (University Microfilms International No. AAC 8519858.)

Korteling, J. E. (1991). Effects of skill integration and perceptual competition on age-related differences in dual-task performance. *Human Factors, 33,* 35–44.

Kosnik, W., Winslow, L., Kline, D., Rasinski, K., & Sekuler, R. (1988). Visual changes in daily life throughout adulthood. *Journals of Gerontology: Psychological Sciences, 43,* P63–P70.

LaBerge, D. L. (1990a). Attention. *Psychological Science, 1,* 1–7.

LaBerge, D. (1990b). Thalamic and cortical mechanisms of attention suggested by recent positron emission tomography experiments. *Journal of Cognitive Neuroscience, 2,* 358–372.

LaBerge, D., & Brown, V. (1989). Theory and measurement of attentional operations in shape identification. *Psychological Review, 96,* 101–124.

Laver, G. D., & Burke, D. M. (1990, April). *Meta-analysis of differential priming effects in younger and older adults.* Paper presented at the Cognitive Aging Conference, Atlanta.

LeDoux, J. E., & Hirst, W. (1986). *Mind and brain.* Cambridge, England: Cambridge University Press.

Light, L. L., & Anderson, P. A. (1985). Working-memory capacity, age, and memory for discourse. *Journal of Gerontology, 40,* 737–747.

Lorsbach, T. C., & Simpson, G. B. (1988). Dual-task performance as a function of adult age and task complexity. *Psychology and Aging, 3,* 210–212.

Macht, M. L., & Buschke, H. (1983). Age differences in cognitive effort in recall. *Journal of Gerontology, 38,* 695–700.

Mackay, H. A., & Inglis, J. (1963). The effects of age on short-term auditory storage processes. *Gerontologia, 15,* 193–200.

Madden, D. J. (1982). Age differences and similarities in the improvement of controlled search. *Experimental Aging Research, 8,* 91–98.

Madden, D. J. (1983). Aging and distraction by highly familiar stimuli during visual search. *Developmental Psychology, 19,* 499–507.

Madden, D. J. (1984). Data-driven and memory driven selective attention in visual search. *Journal of Gerontology, 39,* 72–78.

Madden, D. J. (1985). Adult age differences in memory-driven selective attention. *Developmental Psychology, 21,* 655–665.

Madden, D. J. (1986). Adult age differences in the attentional capacity demands of visual search. *Cognitive Development, 1,* 335–363.

Madden, D. J. (1987). Aging, attention, and the use of meaning during visual search. *Cognitive Development, 2,* 201–216.

Madden, D. J. (1988). Adult age differences in the effects of sentence context and stimulus degradation during visual word recognition. *Psychology and Aging, 3,* 167–172.

Madden, D. J. (1989). Visual word identification and age-related slowing. *Cognitive Development, 4,* 1–29.

Madden, D. J. (1990a). Adult age differences in attentional selectivity and capacity. *European Journal of Cognitive Psychology, 2,* 229–252.

Madden, D. J. (1990b). Adult age differences in the time course of visual attention. *Journals of Gerontology: Psychological Sciences, 45,* P9–P16.

Madden, D. J., & Nebes, R. D. (1980). Aging and the development of automaticity in visual search. *Developmental Psychology, 16,* 377–384.

Marsh, G. A. (1975). Age differences in evoked potential correlates of a memory-scanning process. *Experimental Aging Research, 1,* 3–16.

McClelland, J. L., & Rumelhart, D. E. (1986). *Parallel distributed processing: Vol. 2. Psychological and biological models.* Cambridge, MA: MIT Press.

McDowd, J. M. (1986). The effects of age and extended practice on divided attention performance. *Journal of Gerontology, 41,* 764–769.

McDowd, J. M., & Craik, F. I. M. (1988). Effects of aging and task difficulty on divided attention performance. *Journal of Experimental Psychology: Human Perception and Performance, 14,* 267–280.

McDowd, J. M., & Filion, D. L. (in press). Aging, selective attention, and inhibitory processes: A psychophysiological approach. *Psychology and Aging.*

McFarland, R. A., Tune, C. S., & Welford, A. T. (1964). On the driving of automobiles by older people. *Journal of Gerontology, 19,* 190–197.

Morris, R. G., Gick, M. L., & Craik, F. I. M. (1988). Processing resources and age differences in working memory. *Memory & Cognition, 16,* 362–366.

Myerson, J., Ferraro, F. R., Hale, S., & Lima, S. D. (1991). *The role of global slowing in semantic priming and word recognition.* Manuscript submitted for publication.

Myerson, J., Hale, S., Wagstaff, D., Poon, L. W., & Smith, G. A. (1990). The information-loss model: A mathematical theory of age-related cognitive slowing. *Psychological Review, 97,* 475–487.

Navon, D. (1984). Resources—A theoretical soup stone? *Psychological Review, 91,* 216–234.

Navon, D. (1985). Attention division or attention sharing? In M. I. Posner & O. S. M. Marin (Eds.), *Attention and performance XI* (pp. 133–146). Hillsdale, NJ: Lawrence Erlbaum Associates.

Neely, J. H. (1977). Semantic priming and retrieval from lexical memory: Roles of inhibitionless spreading activation and limited capacity attention. *Journal of Experimental Psychology: General, 106,* 226–254.

Nissen, M. J., & Corkin, S. (1985). Effectiveness of attentional cueing in older and younger adults. *Journal of Gerontology, 40,* 185–191.

Nuechterlein, K., Parasuraman, R., & Jiang, Q. (1983). Visual sustained attention: Image degradation produces rapid sensitivity decrement over time. *Science, 220,* 327–329.

Panek, P. E., Barrett, G. E., Sterns, H. L., & Alexander, R. A. (1978). Age differences in perceptual style, selective attention, and perceptual-motor reaction time. *Experimental Aging Research, 4,* 377–387.

Panek, P. E., & Rush, M. C. (1981). Simultaneous examination of age related differences in the ability to maintain and reorient auditory selective attention. *Experimental Aging Research, 7,* 405–416.

Panek, P. E., Rush, M. C., & Slade, L. A. (1984). Locus of the age-Stroop interference relationship. *Journal of Genetic Psychology, 145,* 209–216.

Parasuraman, R. (1979). Memory load and event rate control sensitivity decrements in sustained attention. *Science, 205,* 924–927.

Parasuraman, R., Nestor, P., & Greenwood, P. (1989). Sustained-attention capacity in young and older adults. *Psychology and Aging, 4,* 339–345.

Park, D. C., Smith, A. D., Dudley, W., & LaFornza, V. (1988, April). *Memory performance as a function of age and competing contextual demands.* Paper presented at the Second Cognitive Aging Conference, Atlanta.

Parkinson, S. R., Lindholm, J. M., & Urell, T. (1980). Aging, dichotic memory and digit span. *Journal of Gerontology, 35,* 87–95.

Penner, S. (1982). *An investigation of age differences in divided attention and intrahemispheric competition.* Unpublished doctoral dissertation, University of Victoria, British Columbia.

Peterson, S. E., Fox, P. T., Snyder, A. Z., & Raichle, M. E. (1990). Activation of extrastriate and frontal cortical areas by visual words and word-like stimuli. *Science, 249,* 1041–1044.

Planek, T. W., & Fowler, R. C. (1971). Traffic accident problems and exposure characteristics of the aging driver. *Journal of Gerontology, 26,* 224–230.

Plude, D. J., & Doussard-Roosevelt, J. A. (1989). Aging, selective attention, and feature integration. *Psychology and Aging, 4,* 98–105.

Plude, D. J., & Hoyer, W. J. (1985). Attention and performance: Identifying and localizing age deficits. In N. Charness (Ed.), *Aging and human performance* (pp. 47–99). New York: Wiley.

Plude, D. J., & Hoyer, W. J. (1986). Age and the selectivity of visual information processing. *Psychology and Aging, 1,* 4–10.

Plude, D. J., Kaye, D. B., Hoyer, W. J., Post, T. A., Saynisch, M. J., & Hahn, M. V. (1983). Aging and visual search under consistent and varied mapping. *Developmental Psychology, 19,* 508–512.

Ponds, R. W. H. M., Brouwer, W. H., & van Wolffelaar, P. C. (1988). Age differences in divided attention in a simulated driving task. *Journals of Gerontology: Psychological Sciences, 43,* P151–P156.

Posner, M. I. (1988). Structures and functions of selective attention. In T. Boll & B. K. Bryant (Eds.), *Clinical neuropsychology and brain function: Research, measurement, and practice* (pp. 171–202). Washington, DC: American Psychological Association.

Posner, M. I., & Petersen, S. E. (1990). The attention system of the human brain. *Annual Review of Neuroscience, 13,* 25–42.

Posner, M. I., Petersen, S. E., Fox, P. T., & Raichle, M. E. (1988). Localization of cognitive operations in the human brain. *Science, 240,* 1627–1631.

Rabbitt, P. (1979). Some experiments and a model for changes in attentional selectivity with old age. In F. Hoffmeister & C. Muller (Eds.), *Brain function in old age: Evaluation of changes and disorders* (pp. 82–94). New York: Springer-Verlag.

Rabinowitz, J. C., Craik, F. I. M., & Ackerman, B. P. (1982). A processing resources account of age differences in recall. *Canadian Journal of Psychology, 36,* 325–344.

Rogers, W. A., & Fisk, A. D. (1991). Age-related differences in the maintenance and modification of automatic processes: Arithmetic Stroop interference. *Human Factors, 33,* 45–56.

Rumelhart, D. E., & McClelland, J. L. (1986). *Parallel distributed processing: Vol. 1. Foundations.* Cambridge, MA: MIT Press.

Salthouse, T. A. (1985). Speed of behavior and its implications for cognition. In J. E. Birren & K. W. Schaie (Eds.), *Handbook of the psychology of aging* (2nd ed., pp. 400–426). New York: Van Nostrand Reinhold.

Salthouse, T. A. (1988a). Effects of aging on verbal abilities: Examination of the psychometric literature. In L. L. Light & D. M. Burke (Eds.), *Language and memory in old age* (pp. 17–35). New York: Cambridge University Press.

Salthouse, T. A. (1988b). Initiating the formalization of theories of cognitive aging. *Psychology and Aging, 3,* 3–16.

Salthouse, T. A. (1988c). Resource-reduction interpretations of cognitive aging. *Developmental Review, 8,* 238–272.

Salthouse, T. A. (1988d). The role of processing resources in cognitive aging. In M. L. Howe & C. J. Brainerd (Eds.), *Cognitive development in adulthood* (pp. 185–239). New York: Springer-Verlag.

Salthouse, T. A., Rogan, J. D., & Prill, K. A. (1984). Division of attention: Age differences on a visually presented memory task. *Memory and Cognition, 12,* 613–620.

Salthouse, T. A., & Somberg, B. L. (1982). Skilled performance: Effects of adult age and experience on elementary processes. *Journal of Experimental Psychology: General, 111,* 176–207.

Schaie, K. W. (1955). A test of behavioral rigidity. *Journal of Abnormal and Social Psychology, 51,* 604–610.

Schonfield, D., Trueman, V., & Kline, D. (1982). Recognition tests of dichotic listening and the age variable. *Journal of Gerontology, 27,* 487–493.

Scialfa, C. T., & Kline, D. W. (1988). Effects of noise type and retinal eccentricity on age differences in identification and localization. *Journals of Gerontology: Psychological Sciences, 43,* P91–P99.

Scialfa, C. T., Kline, D. W., & Lyman, B. J. (1987). Age differences in target identification as a function of retinal location and noise level: Examination of the useful field of view. *Psychology and Aging, 2,* 14–19.

Scialfa, C. T., Leibowitz, H. W., & Gish, K. W. (1989). Age differences in peripheral refractive error. *Psychology and Aging, 4,* 372–375.

Sekuler, R., & Ball, K. (1986). Visual localization: Age and practice. *Journal of the Optical Society of America (A), 3,* 864–867.

Shiffrin, R. M. (1988). Attention. In R. C. Atkinson, R. J. Herrnstein, G. Lindsey, & R. D. Luce (Eds.), *Steven's Handbook of Experimental Psychology* (pp. 739–811). New York: Wiley.

Shiffrin, R. M., & Schneider, W. (1977). Controlled and automatic human information processing: 2. Perceptual learning, automatic attending, and a general theory. *Psychological Review, 84,* 127–190.

Somberg, B. L., & Salthouse, T. A. (1982). Divided attention abilities in young and old adults. *Journal of Experimental Psychology: Human Perception and Performance, 8,* 651–663.

Spence, A. P. (1989). *Biology of human aging.* Englewood Cliffs, NJ: Prentice-Hall.

Sternberg, S. (1966). High-speed scanning in human memory. *Science, 153,* 652–654.

Sterns, H. L., Barrett, G. V., & Alexander, R. A. (1985). Accidents and the aging individual. In J. E. Birren & K. W. Schaie (Eds.), *Handbook of the psychology of aging* (2nd ed., pp. 703–724). New York: Van Nostrand Reinhold.

Strayer, D. L., Wickens, C. D., & Braune, R. (1987). Adult age differences in the speed and capacity of information processing: 2. An electrophysiological approach. *Psychology and Aging, 2,* 99–110.

Surwillo, W. W., & Quilter, R. E. (1964). Vigilance, age, and response time. *American Journal of Psychology, 77,* 614–620.

Talland, G. A. (1962). The effect of age on speed of simple manual skill. *Journal of Genetic Psychology, 100,* 69–76.

Talland, G. A. (1966). Visual signal detection, as a function of age, input rate, and signal frequency. *The Journal of Psychology, 63,* 105–115.

Teece, J. J., Cattanach, L., Yrchik, D. A., Meinbresse, D., & Dessonville, C. L. (1982). CNV rebound and aging. *Electroencephalography and Clinical Neurophysiology, 54,* 175–186.

Thompson, L. W., Opton, E., Jr., & Cohen, L. D. (1963). Effects of age, presentation speed, and sensory modality on performance of a "vigilance" task. *Journal of Gerontology, 18,* 366–369.

Timiras, P. S. (1988). *Physiological basis of geriatrics.* New York: Macmillan.

Tipper, S. P. (1991). Less attentional selectivity as a result of declining inhibition in older adults. *Bulletin of the Psychonomic Society, 29,* 45–47.

Tipper, S. P., Bourgue, T., Anderson, S., & Brehaut, J. (1989). Mechanisms of attention: A developmental study. *Journal of Experimental Child Psychology, 46,* 353–376.

Tipper, S. P., & Cranston, M. (1985). Selective attention and priming: Inhibitory and facilitory effects of ignored primes. *Quarterly Journal of Experimental Psychology, 37A,* 591–611.

Treisman, A., & Gelade, G. (1980). A feature integration theory of attention. *Cognitive Psychology, 12,* 97–136.

Treisman, A., & Gormican, S. (1988). Feature analysis in early vision: Evidence from search asymmetries. *Psychological Review, 95,* 15–48.

Waugh, N. C., Fozard, J. L., Talland, G. A., & Erwin, D. E. (1973). Age, stimulus repetition, and reaction time. *Journal of Gerontology, 28,* 466–470.

Wickens, C. D. (1984). Processing resources in attention. In R. Parasuraman & D. R. Davies (Eds.), *Varieties of attention* (pp. 63–102). Orlando, FL: Academic.

Wickens, C. D., Braune, R., & Stokes, A. (1987). Age differences in the speed and capacity of information processing: 1. A dual-task approach. *Psychology and Aging, 2,* 70–78.

Wright, L. L. (1981). Aging, divided attention, and processing capacity. *Journal of Gerontology, 36,* 605–614.

CHAPTER TWO

Human Memory

Fergus I. M. Craik
University of Toronto

Janine M. Jennings
McMaster University

APPROACHES TO THE STUDY OF MEMORY

Research on adult age differences in human memory has been conducted very largely within the framework of current theoretical views of memory. Because the present review is organized in terms of the topics and concepts suggested by these approaches, it may be useful to provide an outline of the ways in which cognitive psychologists think about memory—its nature, components, and organization. This introduction may help the reader to absorb and integrate the many empirical results described, and to understand more clearly the theoretical motivation for the experimental questions asked by researchers. At the end of the review we attempt to evaluate the usefulness of some of the main theoretical ideas in light of the present empirical evidence.

All of the approaches described fall under the general heading of cognitive, information-processing points of view, because this has been the dominant perspective during the past decade. Within this tradition, a number of highly influential theoretical positions are not described—simply because they have not been used extensively to study age changes in memory (Anderson, 1983; Gillund & Shiffrin, 1984; McClelland & Rumelhart, 1986; Murdock, 1982; Paivio, 1971). A further limitation is that we concentrate largely on memory for specific events. Age differences in the acquisition and utilization of knowledge (semantic memory) are dealt with in chapter 3 by Leah Light. We focus on three broad theoretical orientations: memory stores, processing models, and memory systems.

Memory Stores

The notion that human memory is composed of different stores, containing information at successive stages of processing, was the dominant viewpoint in the 1960s and 1970s; it is still an influential and useful way to analyze the phenomena. According to the "modal model" (Murdock, 1967) incoming information is first held briefly in modality-specific sensory registers; if the information is selected by attentional processes it is then passed on to a limited-capacity short-term memory where it is integrated with previously learned information and enters conscious awareness. Finally, if further rehearsal and learning operations are carried out on the information, it is transferred to a more permanent long-term memory store. The general questions engendered by this approach concern the capacity of each store, the types of encoded representations held at the various stages, and the characteristics of forgetting. The stress is on encoding and storage of information; retrieval mechanisms are poorly specified.

Age differences in memory can be understood within this framework in terms of either biological changes to the structural components—for example, smaller capacity, faster decay, greater vulnerability to interference—or changes to the processing aspects, especially perhaps to the "transfer" of information from short-term to long-term storage. However, as pointed out by Craik and Lockhart (1972), once theoretical attention is fixed on transfer and other processes, it seems that more and more memory phenomena can be described in terms of these encoding and retrieval operations themselves, and that the structural notions of store and storage become less useful. A further criticism is that many characteristics of the stores do not appear to be constant, but instead vary from one experimental paradigm to another.

One current set of ideas that stemmed originally from the work on memory stores is Baddeley's (1986) model of *working memory*. This model combines structural components (e.g., the phonological store) and dynamic processes (e.g., the articulatory loop). The further inclusion of a superordinate system for managing the information flow among the various components (the "central executive") gives WM a key role in memory, learning, reasoning, and other cognitive processes. It has an obvious part to play in describing and understanding age differences.

Processing Models

As a reaction to some of the limitations of stores and structures, researchers suggested ways in which human memory could be described in terms of processing operations—mental activities rather than mental structures. Thus acquisition was discussed in terms of qualitatively different levels (or types) of processing (Craik & Lockhart, 1972) with context determining the specific way in which an event was encoded (Tulving & Thomson, 1973). Different types of rehearsal operations determine the final encoding achieved, and thus the event's potential memorability (Jacoby & Bartz, 1972; Woodward, Bjork, & Jongeward, 1973). Retrieval was viewed as the repetition or recapitulation of encoding operations (Kolers, 1973), with the effectiveness of retrieval cues depending on their involvement in the original encoding process (Tulving & Thomson, 1973). The phenomena ascribed to short-term or primary memory in the stores model were redescribed in terms of those mental representations that are currently active (e.g., Craik & Lockhart, 1972; Shiffrin, 1976), rather than as events held in a special storage mechanism. Some theorists suggested that sensory memory also could be described in terms of continued processing (e.g., Di Lollo, Arnett, & Kruk, 1982). One advantage of a processing approach is that it is possible to describe the mental activities of learning and remembering in the same terms as perceiving, attending, knowing, and acting. These other cognitive activities may even share some of the same processing operations (e.g., Craik, 1983; Shepard, 1984).

In these terms, age differences would be sought in such things as the types of processing operations carried out on events to be remembered, in the number of representations that can be maintained in an active state, in the ability to manage maintenance processing while simultaneously attending to new events, in the extent to which context influences the specificity of encoding, and in the ability to recapitulate original processing operations (with and without the help of cues) at the time of retrieval. One major disadvantage of current processing ideas is that they are usually rather vague and general, leading to the formulation of principles of operation rather than to the precise specification of mechanisms or procedures. By the same token they are difficult to confirm or disconfirm by crucial experiments. For these reasons, perhaps, a number of researchers have classified memory phenomena in terms of memory systems; such views represent a partial return to the idea of mental structures as opposed to processes. The language and concepts of memory systems theorists (e.g., Tulving, 1983) are also very congenial to neuropsychologists and neuroscientists who can identify systems and subsystems with specific brain structures and processes.

Memory Systems

Tulving (1972) drew the distinction between *episodic memory* for specific events and *semantic memory* for general knowledge; these two classes of memory were described as separate but interacting systems. Later experimental work (e.g., Jacoby & Witherspoon, 1982; Tulving, Schacter, & Stark, 1982) strongly suggested the existence of a further cognitive system that registered information that affected later performance, although the information did not give rise to conscious recollection of the time and place of its acquisition. This third system has been termed *procedural memory* and it is held to underlie performance on various motor and cognitive skills. One very striking finding that is relevant in the present context is that procedural memory appears to be unaffected in patients who are deeply amnesic for autobiographical events (e.g., Warrington & Weiskrantz, 1974). Tulving (1985b) suggested that procedural memory may be the most primitive memory system, with semantic memory, and finally episodic memory emerging as later evolutionary refinements. This phylogenetic progression may be echoed in development also, with episodic memory being the last to mature (Tulving, 1983). In this connection an obvious question is whether it is also the first to show losses as a function of aging.

Tulving and Schacter (1990) recently described a fourth system that they called the *perceptual representational system,* which is assumed to be presemantic and can function independently of the episodic and semantic memory systems. This system partly underlies the phenomenon of *priming,* in which subjects reveal memory from recently presented stimuli through their enhanced performance on various tasks, although they may not be aware that they have recently encountered the stimuli. Because the system contains a number of distributed traces of any object, rather than one abstract encoding, representation and access are considered to be "hyper-specific." Access to PRS does not involve conscious awareness, and the system is thought to develop early in life and to last into old age.

The systems view is not without its critics. Experimental dissociations between two abilities and/or tasks have provided some of the main evidence in favor of separate memory systems. However, several writers (e.g., Jacoby, 1983; Roediger, Weldon, & Challis, 1989) have pointed out that such dissociations may be explained more parsimoniously by the suggestion that different memory tasks require different types of information at encoding and retrieval for their optimal performance. So, for example, Jacoby's (1983) demonstration that perceptual identification improved with greater degrees of prior visual processing, whereas recognition memory performance was enhanced by greater amounts of conceptual processing, may be explained in terms of different task requirements rather than in terms of two distinct memory systems.

With respect to age differences, the obvious question is whether aging has a more detrimental effect on some systems than on others. The usefulness of the systems view, and of the other classifications described, are examined after reviewing the empirical evidence. The literature on memory and aging is now so extensive that the review must be selective— we focus on topics of current debate and largely on research reported in the last 10 years.

EMPIRICAL EVIDENCE

Sensory and Perceptual Memory

The earlier notion that sensory memory buffers hold automatically processed sensory information until it is "read out" by the processes of attention is gradually giving way to the idea that sensory processing proceeds in stages of increasing complexity, and that the phenomena of sensory memory reflect the continuing activity of ongoing analysis. That is, sensory information is not held passively in rapidly decaying stores, but the information is available to affect performance for as long as analysis continues (Di Lollo, 1980). If older people require more time to analyze a stimulus, this account makes the interesting prediction that sensory memory should apparently be longer lasting for older than for younger subjects under some conditions. Some evidence in line with this prediction was reported by Di Lollo et al. (1982). In their paradigm two 5 × 5 dot matrices were plotted simultaneously, side by side, on a computer screen. One matrix had all 25 dots present but the other had only 24 dots—the task was to decide which matrix had 24 dots. The dots were plotted serially, so visual persistence is required to integrate the patterns and see all 25 dots together. If the dots are plotted too slowly, the first dots will have faded from sensory memory before the last dots are presented, and the task will be impossible; typically 40 ms to 90 ms is required for efficient integration. Di Lollo et al. argued that efficient visual processing is associated with short visual persistence; they found that older subjects (aged 58–70 years) could accomplish the task at a slower plotting rate than was possible for younger people. Thus visual persistence (or time required for visual analysis) appears to be longer in older subjects— but in this case greater visual persistence is an indication of less efficient processing.

In contrast to the large number of studies of the effects of aging on other types of memory, relatively little work has been carried out on age differences in either visual (*iconic*) or auditory (*echoic*) sensory memory functions, although clearly there is interesting work to be done in the investigation of such differences in the early stages of visual and auditory processing. Some researchers (e.g., Hasher & Zacks, 1979; Mitchell, 1989; but, see also Light, 1991) have suggested that automatic processing and procedural memory functions are essentially unimpaired in the elderly; if this is a valid conclusion, it suggests that early processing stages (which are presumably common to implicit procedural and explicit episodic memory tasks) are also unimpaired by aging, and that the reasons for age-related deficits in explicit memory functions must be sought at later stages of processing. However, the opposite conclusion—that slight age-related deficits in early processing stages are amplified throughout subsequent stages—cannot be ruled out given our present knowledge.

Short-Term and Working Memory

The psychological literature on short-term memory is shot through with a variety of different terms and concepts that make it very confusing to many readers (Craik & Levy, 1976). We use the terms *primary memory* (PM) and *secondary memory* (SM) as suggested by Waugh and Norman (1965) to refer respectively to the holding of material in conscious awareness (PM), and the retrieval of information that has been dropped from conscious awareness (SM). In these terms even the immediate recall of a list of 20 words will contain PM and SM components (Waugh & Norman, 1965).

The concept of working memory (WM) refers to the processes and structures involved in simultaneously holding information in mind and using that information (often in combination with further incoming information) to solve a problem, make a decision, or learn some new concept. This active area of research has been stimulated and guided by the model of WM proposed by Baddeley (1986) and his colleagues, although others (e.g., Daneman & Tardif, 1987; Monsell, 1984) have suggested that WM is not so much one constant set of structures and processes (Baddeley's view) as an umbrella term for many similar short-term holding and computational processes associated with a wide range of cognitive skills and knowledge domains. Following this second viewpoint, Craik and Rabinowitz (1984) proposed that PM and WM should not be thought of as separate systems, but that specific short-term memory tasks could be regarded as having some mixture of PM and WM characteristics. To the extent that a task involves the passive holding and reproduction of a small amount of information it may be said to tap PM; if the task involves more complex manipulation and integration of information, or the simultaneous holding of information and processing further incoming information, it may be termed a WM task. In this sense, tasks lie on a continuum from relatively pure PM situations such as the reproduction of recency items in a free-recall list, to the complex holding and processing tasks devised by Baddeley and Hitch (1974), Daneman and Carpenter (1980), and others.

The notion of a continuum of short-term tasks is important in the cognitive aging context in that Craik and Rabinowitz (1984) suggested that age differences were slight or nonexistent in pure PM tasks, but that substantial age-related decrements existed in WM tasks.

Age Differences in Primary Memory. In the past decade Parkinson and his colleagues have reported a series of studies showing (contrary to the proposal by Craik & Rabinowitz, 1984) that older subjects do in fact show deficits in a variety of short-term memory tasks (e.g., Parkinson, 1982; Parkinson, Lindholm, & Inman, 1982). However, recent work has helped to clarify a number of the apparent discrepancies.

The recency effect in the free recall of word lists has been taken to reflect PM capacity. Parkinson et al. (1982) found that age-related decrements were as great in recency as in earlier portions of the serial position curve, and therefore concluded that age differences exist in both PM and SM. The same absence of an age by serial-position interaction in free recall was reported by Foos, Sabol, Corral, and Mobley (1987) and by Rissenberg and Glanzer (1987). However, Waugh and Norman (1965) pointed out some time ago that recall from recency positions draws to some extent on both PM and SM; in order to obtain pure PM estimates, recall from recency positions must be "corrected" for the probability that the items were recalled from SM. A second factor that affects recency is the subject's recall strategy; early in practice subjects attempt to recall words from the beginning of the list, but they later switch to the more efficient strategy of first recalling the last-presented words. This second strategy yields higher levels of recency, and a recency effect that more accurately reflects PM recall. In order to make valid age comparisons of PM, it is therefore necessary to equate subjects' strategies by asking subjects to recall the last-presented words first of all, and also to employ some procedure to isolate the PM component.

One recent study that incorporated both of these procedures was reported by Delbecq-Derouesné and Beauvois (1989). They examined free recall in 75 subjects ranging in age from 20 years to 86 years; 12 lists of 15 words were presented, and subjects were instructed to recall the final words in each list first of all. A word was counted as retrieved from PM provided that no more than seven words (presentations or recalls) intervened between its presentation and its retrieval; the remaining words were considered SM words (Tulving & Colotla, 1970). Table 2.1 shows that although total recall declined with age, this decline was almost entirely attributable to lower SM performance; for example, the ratio of recall levels between the oldest and the youngest groups is .93 for PM and .36 for SM. We therefore wish to maintain the position argued by Craik and Rabinowitz (1984) that, when the experiment allows a valid

TABLE 2.1
Immediate Free Recall: Mean Numbers of Words Recalled from
15-Word Lists as a Function of Age

	Age Range (in Years)				
	20–25	26–40	41–55	56–65	65–86
Total Recall	8.20	7.18	7.22	6.24	5.22
Primary Memory	3.97	3.75	3.98	3.80	3.69
Secondary Memory	4.23	3.43	3.24	2.44	1.53

Note. From Delbecq-Derouesné and Beauvois, 1989. The primary memory and second-ary memory components were calculated by the method of Tulving and Colotla, 1970.

measure of pure PM to be calculated, age-related differences are slight or nonexistent. However, such differences would be expected in other short-term memory tasks to the extent that the particular task involves an SM component.

Age Differences in Span.   Parkinson (1982) reported small but reliable age-related decrements in digit span in two studies (the mean spans for young and old were 6.4 and 5.8 respectively in one study, and 6.8 and 5.8 respectively in the second study). In the same vein, Johansson and Berg (1989) found small but reliable decrements over 5–10 years in a longitudinal study involving elderly participants aged 70–79 years. These investigators also found that participants who died during the course of the study showed greater declines in digit span in the years preceding death than did comparable participants who survived; it would be interesting to repeat this type of study with other memory measures. Salthouse and Babcock (1991) also reported two large-scale studies (N = 227 and N = 233 respectively) exploring the effects of age on various span measures. The correlations of digit span with age were – .34 and – .18 in Studies 1 and 2 respectively, and the corresponding correlations for word span were – .42 and – .32 respectively; all four correlations are highly reliable.

It thus seems clear that span measures do decline reliably with age, although the absolute differences in performance may not be great. The Salthouse and Babcock (1991) studies suggest that word span declines more with age than does digit span, and this possibility is in line with results reported by Wingfield, Stine, Lahar, and Aberdeen (1988). Salthouse and Babcock also reported larger negative correlations between age and WM span than between age and simple memory span for both digits and words; this result is discussed further in a later section. An interim conclusion might be that whereas simple span declines somewhat with increasing age, this decline is exacerbated if the task requires some manipulation of the items held or some computation performed upon them. Following this notion, Gick and Craik (reported by Craik, 1986) compared age differences on a standard digit-span task with performance on an alpha-span task. In this latter task, subjects were given a short list of words, and were required to repeat them back in correct alphabetical order. No age differences were found in digit span, but the same subjects showed a substantial age-related decrement in alpha span. The conclusion that the age-related decrement in span performance is larger when the task requires complex processing is supported also by the results of a small-scale meta-analysis reported by Babcock and Salthouse (1990, Table 2). In 19 out of 20 studies utilizing simple and complex span procedures, the ratio of young to older performance was greater in the complex than in the simple version of the task.

The most reasonable conclusion given the present evidence is that memory-span tasks do show a small but reliable drop with age. The relationships between span measures on the one hand and PM and SM on the other have not yet been fully worked out, but there is some evidence that span contains both PM and SM components (Parkinson et al., 1982). If this is so, the age-related drop in span performance may be attributable to the SM component of span. It is also tempting to attribute the larger correlations between age and word span (as opposed to digit span) to a larger SM component in word span—due possibly to the greater individuality and semantic content of words compared to digits—but this is quite speculative at present. As a final comment on span, digit-span and word-span tests are still used rather routinely as clinical tests of memory. Given the relative insensitivity of PM and span tasks to aging and even to amnesia (Baddeley & Warrington, 1970), it would be useful to develop clinical tests of short-term memory functioning that tap WM abilities.

Brown–Peterson Task. In the Brown–Peterson paradigm, a short series of letters or words is presented and studied briefly by the subject, whose attention is then fully diverted to an interpolated task (e.g., counting backwards in threes from a given number), which is continued for an interval usually ranging between 0 and 20 s; the subject then attempts to recall the original letters or words in their presented order. There is good agreement that normal aging has essentially no effect on the rate of forgetting observed in this task. This conclusion was reached by Craik (1977) on the basis of the experimental evidence then available. However, Inman and Parkinson (1983) pointed out that retrieval after 10 s or 15 s of rehearsal-preventing activity is probably from SM and that age differences therefore might be expected. These authors also commented on possible age differences in memory span and in the efficiency of rehearsal-preventing activities in previous studies, and suggested that different results might be obtained with better control of these factors. Their own study revealed lower recall levels and slightly faster forgetting rates in older subjects relative to a young control group, but they also found that these group differences were entirely attributable to lower span scores in the older group; when span was equated statistically no age differences remained.

In another well-controlled study, Puckett and Stockburger (1988) first determined word span for each subject and then used the subject's own span length to determine the number of words presented in the Brown–Peterson task. They also utilized demanding, self-paced interpolated tasks, and separated subjects who reported some covert rehearsal of the words during the retention interval from subjects who did not rehearse. The researchers found no age differences in either the level of recall or in the forgetting rate.

There is thus rather general agreement that short-term forgetting rates are not sensitive to normal aging when age differences in span and covert rehearsal are minimized. Three final comments may be made on this paradigm: First, it is surprising that no age differences are found, given the probability that at least item information is retrieved from SM after 15–20 s (Inman & Parkinson, 1983). Apparently, once the to-be-remembered information is encoded, forgetting rates are insensitive to the effects of aging. Second, in contrast to this conclusion, patients with Alzheimer's disease do show faster forgetting rates in the Brown–Peterson task (Dannenbaum, Parkinson, & Inman, 1989; Morris, 1986). Finally, although the task involves both storage and processing, we do not consider the Brown–Peterson paradigm to be a WM task. The crucial difference is that in WM tasks the subject is consciously attempting to maintain some information in mind while concurrently carrying out further operations, either on that information itself or on information relevant to the stored material. In the Brown–Peterson task, once the stored material is encoded it is dropped entirely from conscious awareness and the subject's processing resources are directed completely to an irrelevant task; the original material is then retrieved with some rapidly declining probability from SM. There is thus no conflict between the absence of age differences in the Brown–Peterson task and the finding of large age-related decrements in WM.

Age Differences in Retrieval Speed.   In line with the pervasive finding that older people are slower at performing many cognitive tasks (e.g., Salthouse, 1985), age-related decrements have been found by many investigators in the Sternberg memory-scanning paradigm (Sternberg, 1969). Some recent studies have added to our understanding of this situation, which presumably also reflects the ability to make rapid decisions and the retrieval of information from memory in general. Madden (1982) reported that older subjects, as well as their younger counterparts, were able to increase their rate of scanning when targets and distractors were made physically or conceptually distinct. This result was found also by Puglisi (1986) using three-dimensional objects as the targets. Both studies showed that set size effects could be reduced to zero in both young and old subjects when targets and distractors were distinctively different.

In related paradigms, other investigators have explored age differences in short-term memory search involving both PM and SM components. For example, Lorsbach and Simpson (1984) presented lists of 10 words followed by a probe word that could be identical to a list word, or a homonym or synonym of a list word. No age differences were found in the ability to identify target words, but older participants were slower, especially when the task required retrieval of semantic information from SM. Coyne, Allen, and Wickens (1986) also found that age differences in retrieval speed were greater when the information had to be retrieved from SM.

The literature thus seems consistent in the view that older subjects are slower on tasks of memory matching and retrieval, especially when information must be brought back to mind before a decision can be made. The studies also show that subjects of various ages respond in the same manner to variables that affect performance in search paradigms. Finally, the conclusion that age-related differences in primary memory are slight or nonexistent clearly must be qualified by the statement that age-related increases in response latency typically are found in PM, although even these age differences are often slight relative to the comparable age differences in retrieval latency found in SM tasks (Craik & Rabinowitz, 1984).

Age Differences in Working Memory

In general, there is now good agreement that older people do less well on WM tasks, and that such age differences underlie a variety of age-related deficits in cognitive performance. This view thus endorses the conclusions reached by Welford (1958) some 35 years ago. Whereas researchers agree on the overall effects of aging on WM tasks, there is less agreement on the nature of WM, its structural and processing components, its relation to the notion of processing resources, and the specific aspects of the concept that are most vulnerable to aging. For example, does aging affect storage or processing, does it affect both components, or does the answer obtained depend on the task in question?

Several researchers have reported results in line with the Craik and Rabinowitz (1984) suggestion that age differences increase as tasks vary from PM to WM. Wingfield et al. (1988) contrasted performance on digit span, word span, and a version of the Daneman and Carpenter (1980) WM span task. They found no age differences in digit span, a slight age-related decrement in word span, and a larger decrement in WM span. Similar results were reported by Dobbs and Rule (1989); they found slight age differences in digit span and in the Brown–Peterson task, but large age-related decrements in a WM task. Finally, in another recent study on different types of memory span, Wiegersma and Meertse (1990) found no age differences in span when the task required simple reproduction (e.g., digit span), but they did find substantial age-related differences in favor of younger subjects when the task required active production (e.g., production of the digits 1–9 in a random order). Interestingly, age differences on this latter task resemble results found previously by the authors on patients with frontal lobe lesions (Wiegersma, Van der Scheer, & Hijman, 1990).

There is some debate on the related issue of how task complexity affects the relation between age and performance. The conclusion reached by Welford (1958) on the basis of several perceptual-motor experiments was that increasing complexity was proportionately more detrimental to the performance of older subjects. Corresponding interactions between age and complexity were found in a series of studies on age differences in various WM tasks summarized by Craik, Morris, and Gick (1990), although not all increases in task complexity were more detrimental to the older participants. Specifically, age did interact with syntactic complexity of the sentences processed in two different WM paradigms, but age did not interact with the number of preloaded words in the Baddeley and Hitch (1974) paradigm, or with the number of sentences processed in the Daneman and Carpenter (1980) paradigm. Craik et al. tentatively concluded that aging has a greater detrimental effect on the active, decision-making aspects of processing than on the relatively passive or automatic storage aspects. The conclusion that older adults are relatively more impaired than their younger counterparts when task complexity is varied in cognitive tasks by increasing WM demands was reached also by Salthouse, Mitchell, Skovronek, and Babcock (1989). Their tasks tapped verbal reasoning, computational, and spatial abilities; it is important to note that performance levels were correlated among the tasks, and the effects of complexity were similar between verbal reasoning and spatial ability.

Further findings on the relations between age and task complexity in WM have been reported in an important series of studies by Salthouse and his colleagues (Babcock & Salthouse, 1990; Salthouse & Babcock,

1991; Salthouse, Babcock, & Shaw, 1991). These researchers have attempted to separate the contributions of structural (storage) aspects of WM from its operational (processing) aspects, and determine which aspect is particularly sensitive to aging. They illustrate this difference by analogy to a restaurant that can vary both in terms of its seating capacity (structural or passive storage) and in terms of the kitchen's ability to feed a given number of diners in a given time (operational or processing capacity). In one experiment (Babcock & Salthouse, 1990, Study 3) subjects performed five number-span tasks that differed systematically in their processing requirements. In the most difficult version, a series of arithmetic problems was presented (e.g., $4 + 1 = ?$; $5 - 2 = ?$; $8 + 4 = ?$); the subjects' task was to answer each problem as it appeared and then recall the series of second-presented digits in each problem (e.g., 1, 2, 4 in the preceding example) after all problems had been presented. In the second task, no arithmetic was required, simply a serially presented set of numbers to be recalled; the third task was identical, except that the numbers were presented simultaneously. The fourth and fifth tasks involved recognition memory for the numbers presented either serially (Task 4) or simultaneously (Task 5). The results are shown in Fig. 2.1. No interaction between age and task difficulty was found (contrary to

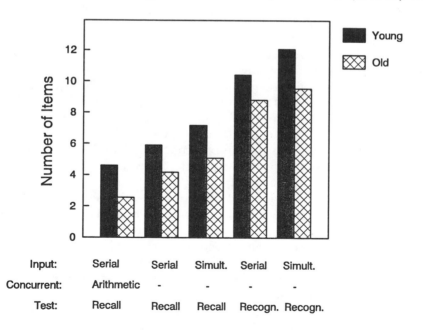

FIG. 2.1.   Mean performance levels on five number-span tasks (Babcock & Salthouse, 1990); solid bars represent young subjects and crosshatched bars represent older subjects.

the position of Craik & Rabinowitz, 1984) and the authors concluded that age-related differences in both storage and processing appear to contribute to the observed age differences in WM performance.

Salthouse et al. (1991) also varied both structural and operational aspects of WM tasks. As one example involving arithmetic operations, a visual display consisted of four quadrants and each quadrant could either be blank or contain a digit (presented serially). Successive displays then required the subject to add or subtract a given digit from the number originally presented in that quadrant; thus subjects had to keep a mental running total for the current value of one to four quadrants. Both the structural aspects (number of quadrants occupied) and processing aspects (number of subsequent arithmetic operations) could thus be varied. Although older subjects performed less well in general, age did not interact with either the number of items involved or the number of operations required. The authors suggested that once information is well encoded by older people, it is preserved equally well across successive processing operations. Alternatively, they suggested that age differences in operational capacity may exist only when processing requires a transformation resulting in a product that is more complex or more abstract.

In a large-scale study involving over 400 adults, Salthouse and Babcock (1991) examined age-related differences in computation span (with arithmetic operations) and listening span (with sentences). Significant age-related decrements were found in both measures; an attempt was then made to locate the source of the difficulty in factors relating primarily to storage capacity, processing efficiency, or in the effectiveness of coordinating simultaneous storage and processing. The results suggested that "processing efficiency is the most important determinant of age-related differences in working memory" (p. 770) but that these age-related effects are indirect—they are mediated by age-related reductions in simple speed of processing. This conclusion echoes Salthouse's (1982) previous suggestions that some apparent age differences in memory may reflect differences in processing speed.

Clearly, further empirical and conceptual work is required to resolve the apparent discrepancies and to sharpen the related concepts of WM, processing resources, and computational speed. One possibility is that age differences in short-term storage are relatively slight when the subjects' resources can be fully committed to storage, but that age-related differences appear when there is a conflict between storage and processing. In this vein, Zacks and Hasher (1988) suggested that older individuals give high priority to ongoing processing at the expense of other encoding processes, and that "storage capacity" is thereby apparently reduced. In a related comment, Salthouse (1990) suggested that age differences in WM may be attributable to reductions with age in the ability to monitor and coordinate concurrent demands on storage and processing, and not to storage differences as such. A meaningful separation between storage and processing may not even be possible, especially if WM storage is regarded as equivalent to holding information in mind. That is, both storage and on-line processing may entail processing activities that are fundamentally similar; both may draw on some limited pool of resources (which may be reduced in older people), or they may both compete for limited "capacity" in some other sense (e.g., Neumann, 1987). Different tasks, or different strategic goals, may influence the subject to emphasize one or another aspect of ongoing processing.

Meanwhile, the construct of WM, and its reduced efficiency in older people, is proving useful in related cognitive domains such as language. For example, Cohen (1988), following earlier work by Spilich (1983) and others, concluded that age differences in text comprehension and memory are caused by an age-related reduction in processing capacity. Zacks and Hasher (1988) implicated an age-related reduction in the efficiency of WM in subtly reduced abilities in comprehension and inference. Hartley (1988) did not find age differences in a WM task, although individual differences on the task did predict performance on text recall. Kemper (1988) also made use of the concept of WM, suggesting that age-related reductions in the complexity of spoken and written language may be attributable to reductions in WM capacity. Finally, Stine and Wingfield (1990) found that age differences in recall of discourse were accounted for in terms of differences in WM span—although this was true for simpler texts only; other factors come into play with more difficult texts. Against this general trend, Light and Anderson (1985) did not find relationships between WM span measures and text recall, although they did find that performance on all measures dropped with age.

As a final comment on this area of research, the concept of inhibition in cognitive processes has been rather neglected in recent years. However, in an interesting article, Hasher and Zacks (1988) proposed that inefficient inhibition in older individuals' WM processing allows entrance to WM of off-task information, resulting in an increased liability to daydream and to think of personal concerns, and an increased vulnerability to distraction. Such inefficient WM processing would be experienced as a difficulty in concentration, which is certainly a common complaint in the elderly. A further implication is that functional storage capacity will be reduced because WM becomes cluttered with irrelevant material. This seems to be a promising lead, although (in common with other concepts in the area) the ideas need to be sharpened and refined.

AGE DIFFERENCES IN ENCODING

There is general agreement that memory for specific events declines with age (e.g., Craik, 1977; Kausler, 1982; Salthouse, 1982); the experimental work reported in the last decade has therefore focused on finer grain descriptions of the deficit, and on possible underlying causes. Traditionally, psychological studies of memory have assumed three loci that might exhibit reduced efficiency—encoding or acquisition, storage, and retrieval. However, with the shift to process-oriented views, the notion of storage has become difficult to define in cognitive terms, although clearly it has a reality in biological terms. As a result, modern work on the psychology of memory has concentrated largely on the nature of encoding and retrieval processes, and on their interrelations. One possibility is that retrieval processes essentially recapitulate encoding processes (Craik & Jacoby, 1979; Kolers, 1973), in which case it might be expected that any factor associated with a reduction in processing efficiency (e.g., aging) necessarily would have parallel effects on both sets of processes (in some sense they are the same processes, although driven or initiated by different factors). However, in the present review we discuss encoding and retrieval separately, while bearing in mind that they are at least strongly interdependent.

Qualitative Differences in Encoding

We know from 50 years of research in verbal learning that the best way to encode information in memory is to form a representation that relates well to our existing organized knowledge structures, yet is also distinctive against the background of that knowledge. Do older people encode events in ways that are less rich, meaningful, and distinctive? An affirmative answer to this question implies that older people would show a parallel inefficiency in the depth and richness of comprehension (taking the viewpoint of Craik & Lockhart, 1972, and others, that encoding for memory involves nothing more than perception and comprehension of the event to be remembered). There is some evidence to this effect, although the case is not an overwhelming one (see Burke & Light, 1981). For example, Zacks and her colleagues (Zacks & Hasher, 1988; Zacks, Hasher, Doren, Hamm, & Attig, 1987) have shown that older people have greater difficulty recalling information that must be inferred, as opposed to explicitly stated, from text passages. This conclusion agrees with the earlier work of Gillian Cohen (Cohen, 1979), who suggested that age differences in text comprehension and memory are caused by an age-related reduction in processing capacity (Cohen, 1988).

The notion that processing capacity (or the related concepts of attentional resources and processing resources) declines with age is used extensively to account for age-related deficits in cognitive functioning (e.g., Craik & Byrd, 1982; Salthouse, 1982). In one variant of this approach, Craik (1983, 1986) argued that cognitive processing reflects an interaction between processes that are driven by external stimulation and those that are initiated from within the organism. These latter "self-initiated" processes are heavily dependent on available processing resources, and so may decline in effectiveness as the person ages. However, performance decrements may be reduced by minimizing the demands on diminished resources and maximizing the contributions of external stimulation or environmental support. As an example, recognition memory involves substantial environmental support because the target item is re-presented, in contrast to free recall which necessarily involves more self-initiated activity; in line with the preceding argument, age-related decrements are typically larger in recall than in recognition (Craik, 1986).

This logic may be extended to include well-learned schematic information as a further source of internal environmental support. That is, rich, meaningful, and distinctive encodings may be achieved either by presentation of a richly detailed stimulus (e.g., a picture) or by utilizing the subject's existing knowledge to enrich the stimulus (e.g., "remember the word *thatcher*"). This second method of enriching the encoded representation is presumably the one tapped in levels of processing studies (Craik & Tulving, 1975). "Deep" encodings are not achieved by virtue of expending more attentional resources, but by greater reliance on preexisting schematic knowledge.

These arguments suggest that age-related decrements in memory performance can be reduced either by the provision of greater environmental support at both encoding and retrieval, or by encouraging greater use of preexisting knowledge to enrich encoding and to recapitulate the same cognitive processes at the time of retrieval. Unfortunately, the experimental evidence does not permit such a tidy conclusion. Some studies indeed do show that more supportive encoding conditions are differentially beneficial to older adults; however, other experiments provide clear examples of equal benefits to older and younger subjects, whereas still others show disproportionate benefits to younger participants. Clearly, other factors are involved; some speculations are offered after a consideration of the evidence.

Greater Effects in Older Adults. In a study involving 64 younger (20–39 years) and 64 older adults (60–79 years), West and Boatwright (1983) presented words with semantic or acoustic orienting tasks, and subsequently tested retention in recognition and cued-recall tests using the original semantic or acoustic descriptions as cues. There were no age differences in recognition, and the age-related decrement in cued recall was least (82% vs. 73%) in the condition that paired a semantic orienting task with semantic cues at recall. In contrast, when an acoustic orienting task was paired with acoustic cues the corresponding recall values were 41% and 18% respectively. The authors concluded that older people have difficulty using effective semantic information spontaneously at encoding and retrieval, but can use it, thereby reducing age-related losses, when the tasks supply sufficient constraint and guidance. Rankin and Firnhaber (1986) had younger and older subjects generate common or distinctive adjectives to nouns, and followed this with free then cued recall, using the generated adjectives as cues. In line with West and Boatwright's results, age differences were least (90% vs. 82%) with cued recall using distinctive adjectives.

Rankin and Collins (1986) reported a similar study using 50 young and 50 elderly adults. Sentences containing an adjective were presented, and subjects either generated or were provided with further verbal material that elaborated the meaning of the sentence in a precise or imprecise way; later the original sentence frame was given as a cue for recall of the adjective. Hashtroudi, Parker, Luis, and Reisen (1989) used the same paradigm; both sets of results are shown in Table 2.2. The table shows that precise elaborators were more effective than imprecise elaborators in all cases, and that younger subjects recalled more target words when they themselves generated the elaborators. However, in the Rankin and Collins study, the older subjects performed best when the precise elaborator was provided (also, age differences were least in this condition), whereas in the Hashtroudi et al. study, older subjects performed best (and age differences were minimized) when the precise elaborators were generated. Differences between the experiments include the employment of a slightly older sample in the Rankin and Collins study (mean age was 73.4 years as opposed to 65.8 years in the Hashtroudi et al. study), and the use of incidental learning instructions by Rankin and Collins as opposed to intentional learning by Hashtroudi et al. There is evidence from other studies (e.g., Mitchell, Hunt, & Schmitt, 1986) that remedial manipulations that are effective with normal older adults are less effective with Alzheimer's patients; it therefore seems possible that in the course of normal aging subjects are progressively less able to benefit from the effects of encoding and retrieval manipulations that are effective at younger ages, especially under less than optimal experimental conditions.

The notion that compensatory benefits can accrue to older people was illustrated in a slightly different way by Bäckman (1986). He presented lists of short sentences for immediate free recall at either a fast or a slow

TABLE 2.2
Proportions of Target Words Recalled with
Generated and Provided Elaborators

	Base Sentence	Elaborator Provided		Elaborator Generated	
		Imprecise	*Precise*	*Imprecise*	*Precise*
Rankin & Collins (1986)					
Young	.63	.41	.65	.68	.84
Old	.34	.21	.52	.28	.41
Hashtroudi et al. (1989)					
Young	.51	.28	.72	.69	.76
Old	.27	.18	.35	.53	.66

rate; additionally, the sentences were presented visually, auditorily, or in both modalities simultaneously. Age differences were least when the lists were presented at a slow rate and in both modalities. Bäckman concluded that elderly subjects' encoding deficiencies may be offset by supportive task conditions.

A similar conclusion was reached by Park, Smith, Morrell, Puglisi, and Dudley (1990) in an experiment using line drawings of concrete objects. Each slide contained a target and a context object; the two objects were either related conceptually (e.g., a spider and an ant), related perceptually (a spider eating a cherry), or unrelated. At test the context object was given as a cue for the target. Age differences were greatest in the unrelated case, and older subjects' performance improved particularly in the conceptually related case. The authors argued in favor of the value of environmental support for the elderly, and also argued that this support is particularly effective when the context and target information are well integrated. The previous studies cited in this section have shown also that the case for compensation is strongest when conditions are supportive at both encoding and retrieval.

Equal Effects. A large number of studies show that some beneficial encoding manipulations have equal effects on younger and older subjects. Rankin and Collins (1985) found that older people benefited as much as their younger counterparts from the provision of precise elaborators for words in a sentence, although the young subjects showed a somewhat larger benefit when they generated their own elaborators. In a similar result using pictorial materials, Park, Puglisi, and Smith (1986) found that older and younger participants benefited equally from the provision of more elaborate pictorial embellishment; in this case memory was tested by recognition.

Two paradigms that have attracted a lot of interest in the past decade are the generation effect (Jacoby, 1978; Slamecka & Graf, 1978) and the beneficial recall and recognition associated with the performance of brief motor activities (Cohen, 1981; Saltz & Donnenwerth-Nolan, 1981). In the first paradigm, the finding is that even trivial amounts of cognitive effort expended on completing an incomplete word, often presented with a guiding context—for example, *quick* = *F__ST,* are associated with superior later recall and recognition of the completed word relative to the case when the whole word was presented (*quick* = *FAST*). Similar results are obtained when subjects must supply a missing word in a sentence frame. Several recent studies agree that the generation effect is of equivalent magnitude in younger and older adults (Johnson, Schmitt, & Pietrukowicz, 1989; McDaniel, Ryan, & Cunningham, 1989; Mitchell et al., 1986; Rabinowitz, 1989a) and there is also agreement that, despite this equivalence, younger subjects are better at identifying whether a word had been generated or read originally (Mitchell et al., 1986; Rabinowitz, 1989a).

In the second paradigm, subjects are presented with brief verbal commands such as "pick up the knife," "scratch your ear," and "knock on the table," which they either learn as a verbally presented list or act out. The finding is that the latter *subject-performed tasks* (SPTs) are recalled and recognized better than their verbal equivalents. Initial work examining age differences in this paradigm found that older people showed greater benefits than their younger counterparts (Bäckman, 1985; Bäckman & Nilsson, 1984, 1985), but subsequent work has tended to find equivalent effects in younger and older subjects (Cohen, Sandler, & Schroeder, 1987; Guttentag & Hunt, 1988; Kausler & Phillips, 1988; Nilsson & Craik, 1990). Reasons for the different results are still unclear. The crucial difference does not seem to be presentation rate, because both Cohen et al. and Nilsson and Craik used the 5-s presentation rate employed by Bäckman and his collaborators. Neither does list length appear to be the differentiating variable, because both Cohen et al. and Nilsson and Craik found equal effects of SPTs on young and older subjects in long and short lists. Obviously, further work is required to resolve the discrepancy.

A further situation in which young and older adults profit equally is one in which verbal material is retrieved shortly after presentation; this initial retrieval has a beneficial effect on later retrieval, probably both because the first test acts as "retrieval practice" and because it acts as a second encoding opportunity. Rabinowitz and Craik (1986) reported one such experiment in which two sets of three words each were presented; within each set the words were drawn from a single semantic category, and were preceded by the category name. Following 17 s of interfering activity one category was cued for recall. After 13 such trials, subjects were unexpectedly given tests of final free recall, cued recall, and recognition for all words; prior retrieval was associated with benefits in all three tests, and to an equal degree in young and old subjects. This result was confirmed using a slightly different manipulation by Kausler and Wiley (1991).

Greater Effects in Younger Adults. To round out the complex picture of age-related encoding effects, some studies have found that younger subjects profit more than do their older counterparts from some beneficial encoding situations. That is, the age difference is amplified, not reduced, as conditions improve. Some examples of this pattern are provided in experiments by Treat and Reese (1976), Erber, Herman, and Botwinick (1980), Craik and Rabinowitz (1985), Puglisi and Park (1987), and Rabinowitz (1989b). In the Erber et al. study, recall increased more for younger than older subjects when intentional learning instructions were added to the orienting task of checking whether specified letters were present in studied words. As encoding conditions were made more favorable, however (e.g., by providing a semantic orienting task), further recall gains were more or less equivalent in the two age groups. Craik and Rabinowitz found that younger subjects' word recall profited more than that of an older group as presentation rate was slowed from 1.5 s to 6 s per word. However, retention levels increased equally for the two age groups with recognition testing and with recall when a semantic orienting task was provided at encoding. Finally, Puglisi and Park found that both young and old participants showed benefits in picture recall when some picture completion was required at study, but that the younger subjects profited to a greater extent; similarly, Rabinowitz found that both age groups benefited from "optimal study conditions" for a long list of words (self-paced study, note taking, etc.) but that the younger group showed greater gains in recall under such conditions.

Conflicting Conclusions on Encoding. Some comments are made later on the apparently conflicting evidence provided by these various studies. One possibility is that a change in encoding conditions that leads to improved performance in a young group may be less supportive and thus less helpful for older subjects. For example, if a change of materials affords a better encoding, but only with the expenditure of extra effort, it may be that younger subjects will be more able to take advantage of the change. That is, not all changes that offer more support to younger subjects' encoding processes may be truly more supportive to the elderly.

Effects of Organization and Knowledge. Episodic memory clearly depends on the person's existing knowledge base (semantic memory or schemata) both to enrich encoding of the event in question and to facilitate its later retrieval. Is aging associated with any loss in the utilization of such schematic information? Studies in this area are somewhat difficult to interpret because memory for events is typically good when the new information is compatible with current knowledge, but sometimes can be superior when the new information is inconsistent with that knowledge. In the latter case the argument is that the person must carry out more extensive processing in order to resolve the inconsistency. With respect to age differences, several studies have shown that older subjects show the same pattern of recall and recognition performance as do young subjects as a function of the relations between new events and existing schemata and scripts (Arbuckle, Vanderleck, Harsany, & Lapidus, 1990; Bäckman, 1991; Hess, Donley, & Vandermaas, 1989; Hess, Vandermaas, Donley, & Snyder, 1987). The conclusion is therefore that older people continue to use schematic information to support encoding and retrieval in the same way as their younger counterparts. However, both Bäckman and Hess et al. suggested that elderly subjects are somewhat less effective at encoding information in relation to scripts and schematic prior knowledge—especially information that has little association with the script or schema and is therefore dependent on further processing for integration in memory. Thus, older people may benefit from schematic support in the same way as they benefit (under certain circumstances at least) from external environmental support.

Encoding Specificity. Memory researchers are in good agreement that the optimal retrieval cue for an encoded event is one that reflects the highly specific manner in which the event was originally encoded. This general idea, variously termed *the encoding specificity principle, transfer-appropriate processing,* and *repetition of operations*, is surely undeniable at this point. Presumably it applies to older learners just as much as to their younger counterparts. One hypothesis that relates to this point is that older people encode events in a more automatic, general fashion; that is, they do not elaborate events so fully, or modify them to the same extent to reflect the specific context in which they occur (Craik & Simon, 1980; Hasher & Zacks, 1979; Rabinowitz & Ackerman, 1982; Simon, 1979). We still find this idea attractive although it has not received overwhelming empirical support to date.

It should be stressed that even if older people do encode information in a more general manner, the encoding specificity principle (ESP) still applies to them in exactly the same way as it applies to younger adults; the difference would simply be that now general *retrieval cues* would be relatively more effective. These ideas were explored using word pairs by Rabinowitz, Craik, and Ackerman (1982). In the acquisition phase, target words were paired either with strong or weak associates, and these

TABLE 2.3
Proportions of Cued Recall as a Function of Age, Encoding-Cue
Combination, Materials, and Degree of Attention

	Encoding-Cue Combination						
	1 s-s	2 w-w	3 w-s	4 s-w	1–2	2–3	Encoding Type
Rabinowitz et al.							
Young - 5 s	92	85	68	07	07	17	Specific
Old - 10 s	92	62	67	00	30	– 05	General
Young - DA	83	56	59	01	27	– 03	General
Puglisi et al.							
Full Attention							
Young - Words	78	85	26	15	– 07	59	Specific
Old - Words	71	71	21	01	00	50	Specific
Divided Attention							
Young - Words	72	65	33	10	07	32	Specific
Old - Words	46	29	24	07	17	05	General
Old - Pictures	79	67	32	11	12	35	Specific

Note. From Puglisi et al., 1988, and Rabinowitz et al., 1982.

associates were used as cues at retrieval. In addition, the encoding and retrieval manipulations were crossed to yield four encoding-retrieval conditions: Strong-Strong, Weak-Weak, Weak-Strong, and Strong-Weak. That is, in the first two conditions the retrieval cues remained the same as at encoding, whereas in the other two conditions the cues were switched. The results are shown in Table 2.3. If subjects encode target items specifically with respect to the accompanying weak cues, then these same weak cues will be effective at retrieval; this is the pattern shown by younger subjects. If target words are not modified by weak contextual cues, however, such cues will be relatively ineffective at retrieval, although strong associates will be quite effective still, even if they were not present during acquisition. This pattern is demonstrated by the older group (with word pairs presented at a slower rate to equate the general level of performance), and also by a further young group who learned the word pairs under conditions of divided attention. Rabinowitz et al. concluded that when processing resources are diminished—in divided attention and arguably in older subjects—target items are encoded in a way that is less modified by specific contextual detail (e.g., weak associates) and therefore are given the more habitual "default" encoding in a more automatic fashion.

This line of research was extended by Park, Puglisi, Smith, and Dudley (1987) and by Puglisi, Park, Smith, and Dudley (1988). In the first study, these investigators found no evidence for general encoding in older adults, using pictures as stimuli and recognition as the test. In the second study, Puglisi et al. did find evidence for general encoding, but only when older subjects were tested with words (as opposed to pictures) and learned the words under divided attention conditions. When the older subjects were given pictures as stimuli, or learned under conditions of full attention, evidence for specific encoding was found (see Table 2.3). Thus the same patterns of results was found by Rabinowitz et al. (1982) and by Puglisi et al., but in the latter experiment conditions had to be made more difficult before the general pattern emerged. Plausibly, pictures "drive" a rich elaborate encoding somewhat automatically, whereas there is greater "optionality" associated with the encoding of isolated words; this suggestion is in line also with the stronger levels of processing effects associated with words than with faces (Patterson & Baddeley, 1977).

More generally, the suggestion is that older adults show a tendency to encode events in a less elaborated, more general way, and that this tendency can be exacerbated by reducing resources further (divided attention), but compensated for by utilizing rich materials (e.g., pictures), favorable encoding conditions, and bright subjects. That is, the same pattern of results holds throughout a series of studies; where a specific experiment falls on the pattern will depend on interactions among subjects, materials, encoding, and retrieval conditions (Jenkins, 1979). Clearly this is not the solution to the problem, but it provides a framework for understanding apparently diverse current results, and for planning further studies.

Three recent studies provide some further evidence that is at least in line with the notion of more general encoding in older adults under certain conditions. Hess et al. (1989) concluded that older subjects relied on relatively automatic encoding processes for events in a scripted context. Also, Hashtroudi, Johnson, and Chrosniak (1990) found that when younger and older adults were asked to recall perceived and imagined scenes, the older adults showed poorer recall of perceptual and spatial detail, although they showed good recall of thoughts and feelings. The authors concluded that their results were consistent with the idea that older adults encode only general and global features of presented information. More direct evidence comes from a study by Mäntylä and Bäckman (1990) in which subjects generated three descriptors to each of 40 nouns; the subjects returned after 3 weeks and were asked unexpectedly to again generate three descriptors. Older subjects showed less commonality of their responses from the first to the second occasion, but showed greater intersubject commonality, relative to younger adults.

That is, older people were both less consistent in their reactions to the target words from one occasion to the next and also gave more stereo-typed, less distinctive responses. In a second experiment, intrasubject consistency was found to be positively related to recall of the words given their self-generated descriptors as cues. The authors concluded that age-related differences in consistency of encoding may contribute to age-related deficits in episodic remembering.

Conclusions on Encoding Differences.   What are we to make of the situation in which there are good data to support the conclusions that (a) older people benefit more than do their younger counter-parts from more supportive encoding conditions, (b) older and younger subjects profit to the same extent, and (c) younger subjects profit to a greater extent. As suggested previously, the answer must lie in the complex interactions among acquisition variables, test variables, materials, and subjects (Bäckman, Mäntylä, & Herlitz, 1990; Craik, 1983; Jenkins, 1979). This state of affairs suggests that the experiments we perform should not examine a static slice through some combination of tasks, materials, and subjects, because in this case any pattern of results is "explainable" post hoc. Rather, meaningful patterns of data should be sought such that if the explanation under one combination is correct, then some change in the materials or task conditions should affect the results in a predictable way. That is, several "slices" through the data space should be explored. One implication of this suggestion is that future research should include much larger scale projects, involving several combinations of subjects, materials, and conditions.

Two recurring patterns of data are suggested by the preceding evidence. One is the notion that as encoding and retrieval conditions improve, subjects benefit to the extent that they are cognitively competent. That is, young subjects benefit to the greatest extent, middle-age and older subjects to a lesser extent, and Alzheimer's patients perhaps not at all (see Fig. 2.2, a). A more complex pattern is one in which younger subjects improve their performance to a greater extent initially but then asymp-tote at a functional ceiling depending on the materials, the subjects' skill, and so forth (Bäckman et al., 1990). Older subjects are less responsive initially, then start to improve, and finally achieve virtually the same level as that shown by the young (see Fig. 2.2, b). This second pattern has the advantage in that it allows for all three types of relationships (greater benefits to young subjects, equal effects, and compensation) illustrated in the preceding sections. As evidence that Fig. 2.2, b is not entirely fan-ciful, very much this pattern of results has been reported both by Treat and Reese (1976) and by Bäckman (1986).

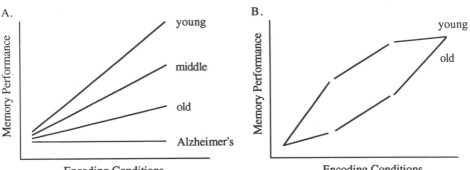

FIG. 2.2.   Theoretical functions relating memory performance to encoding conditions.

Effects of Context

A number of recent workers have suggested that one major reason for the poorer memory performance typically found in older people is an age-related failure to encode as much rich perceptual and conceptual detail associated with experienced events (Burke & Light, 1981; Craik & Simon, 1980; Rabinowitz et al., 1982; Simon, 1979). The effects of this comparative failure to encode contextual information are likely to include the formation of a less distinctive record of the event, possibly a more general and stereotyped encoding as discussed in the previous section, and a lessened effectiveness of environmental information to act as a retrieval cue at the time of remembering. A corollary of this position is that if the context is arranged to be particularly compatible with the target event, the resulting facilitation of integrating the event with its context should be especially beneficial to older people. The evidence on some of these points is convincing; on óthers it is less so.

Encoding Attributes.   There is good agreement that older subjects show a reduced ability to remember the specific manner in which verbal material was presented. For example, Kausler and Puckett (1980, 1981) demonstrated age-related decrements in memory for the case in which visually presented words were written, and for the voice in which auditorily presented words were spoken. These effects hold even when attribute recall is conditionalized on successful word recognition (Kausler & Puckett, 1981). Similar results, showing an age-related decrement in modality identification (whether words were presented auditorily or visually), were reported by Lehman and Mellinger (1984, 1986).

Age Differences in Reality Monitoring. A further topic of interest to memory researchers during the past decade has been the ability of subjects to distinguish experienced events from those that were merely imagined. This ability has been termed *reality monitoring* by Marcia Johnson and her co-workers (e.g., Johnson & Raye, 1981). If older people encode events less richly—especially with respect to environmental detail—an age-related decrement would be expected in this area; such findings have been reported recently by several investigators. Mitchell et al. (1986) had younger and older subjects either generate or read words in sentence contexts; the subjects were tested later for their ability to remember whether a word had been read or generated. Older people were significantly poorer at this task. The Mitchell et al. study sometimes is cited as evidence for no age deficit in reality monitoring, but it should be noted that the age difference was nonsignificant only when 3 of the 12 older subjects were dropped from the analysis. However, the data certainly do show the great variability in older subjects' ability to recollect the initial encoding context and that many older people perform at the level of their younger counterparts. Rabinowitz (1989a) also reported an age-related decrement in the ability to say whether a word had been generated or read by the subject.

Guttentag and Hunt (1988) had subjects either perform or imagine themselves perform a series of actions, and later asked the subjects to remember this aspect of the initial event. It has been suggested that age-related recall deficits may result from a failure of older adults to integrate events with their contexts at the time of encoding (McIntyre & Craik, 1987). The idea is that a failure to integrate items in this way will lead to a less elaborate encoding and will be associated, therefore, with poorer recall. On the other hand, good integration of events and their contexts will be associated with good recall of both the event itself and of the context given the event as a cue; that is, item recall and context recall should be correlated. Guttentag and Hunt found that older people were poorer at recalling both the actions and whether the activity was performed or imagined; however (contrary to the suggestion of McIntyre & Craik) such source judgments were no better for recalled than for nonrecalled items, and source judgments did not correlate reliably with recall levels in either age group. Arguably, item recall may correlate with context recall only in cases where item recall is accomplished or assisted by re-creating the context; when item recall is accomplished via other cues, then no correlation would be expected.

In similar studies, Hashtroudi et al. (1990) and Cohen and Faulkner (1989) also reported age-related deficits in source remembering. In the Hashtroudi et al. study, subjects either perceived or imagined real-life events such as packing a picnic basket; 3 weeks later, the older subjects were less able than the young group to recollect which events had been perceived and which imagined. In one experiment, Cohen and Faulkner had subjects perform, watch, or imagine short action sequences; an age decrement in source remembering was observed. In a second experiment with interesting practical implications, subjects watched a short film and then read an account of the sequence of events that did or did not contain misleading information. Cohen and Faulkner argued that if older people are less able to remember the source of information then they should be more likely to wrongly assert that misleading information in the story had actually occurred in the film, and this is the result that they found. Rather alarmingly, of the errors of this type made by older subjects, 37.5% of the responses were made with a confidence rating of "very sure," whereas only 9.4% of younger subjects' errors were given with this degree of confidence. Clearly, such results have major implications for the reliability of eyewitness testimony given by elderly respondents (the mean age of the older subjects was 70.4 years).

Hashtroudi, Johnson, and Chrosniak (1989) had subjects discriminate between words that had been spoken originally by one of two experimenters and words either spoken or simply thought by the subject. Older participants showed no significant decrement relative to the young group in distinguishing internal from external sources (e.g., words spoken by themselves from words spoken by an experimenter) but they were reliably poorer at discriminating between two self-generated events (words thought vs. words spoken by themselves) and between two externally generated events (words spoken by one or other of the experimenters). It seems that whereas older people show a decreased ability in general to recall details of the initial context, this age-related decrement can be ameliorated or enhanced by varying the similarity between the sources in question.

Two other interesting studies in this area were reported by Dywan and Jacoby (1990) and by Koriat, Ben-Zur, and Sheffer (1988). In the Dywan and Jacoby experiment subjects first learned a list of fictitious names; later they were given a fame judgment task in which the fictitious names were mixed up with the names of real, famous people. Older subjects showed a greater liability to judge a previously learned fictitious name as "famous," presumably because the feeling of familiarity associated with the name was misattributed to real-world fame rather than to the prior learning episode. The Koriat et al. study demonstrated poorer output monitoring in older people; in a free-recall task they were more likely to repeat words they had already recalled, and less likely to recognize that they had recalled specific words. In a follow-up experiment, subjects learned a word list and then were given a recognition list consisting of old (list words) and new (distractor) items, each of which was presented twice during the course of the recognition list; the subjects' task was to classify each recognition list word as old/new and first/second presentation. Older subjects were good at discriminating old from new items on their first presentation, but misclassified many second presentations. Probabilities of saying "new" when an item was old were .19 and .30 for young and old subjects respectively, but the probabilities of erroneously saying "first" to second presentations were .14 and .48 respectively. That is, older people are particularly weak at output monitoring; they are more likely to forget actions they already have performed, such as taking medication or telling an anecdote.

Source Amnesia and Source Forgetting. *Source amnesia* is the term used in neuropsychology to refer to the case in which a person remembers some information but cannot remember where or when the information was originally learned. Whereas this phenomenon may reach pathological levels in amnesic patients, it is clearly a commonly occurring aspect of everyday forgetting—for example, knowing a person but forgetting where you have seen him or her before. Schacter, Harbluk, and McLachlan (1984) demonstrated the effect in patients by teaching them made-up "facts" and then testing for the facts and their source after a few minutes had elapsed. Reasoning that if older people encode contextual information less fully, they should show more source amnesia than their younger counterparts, McIntyre and Craik (1987) reported that older subjects did exhibit substantial forgetting of where made-up facts had been learned; in this case the retention interval was 1 week. In a follow-up study, Craik, Morris, Morris, and Loewen (1990) showed that the degree of source amnesia within a group of older subjects was extremely variable (see also, Guttentag & Hunt, 1988; Mitchell et al., 1986), and that a measure of source amnesia was related to lower scores on some neuropsychological tests of frontal-lobe functioning. The suggestion here (following Schacter et al.) is that the great variability in source judgments shown by older groups may be attributable to individual differences in some aspects of frontal lobe performance. Specifically, it has been suggested (Schacter, 1987b; Shimamura & Squire, 1987) that the frontal lobes are responsible for integrating perceived events with their temporal and spatial contexts (but, see also Lewis, 1989, for an alternative view).

Source forgetting was the term used by Schacter et al. (1984) to denote the inability to remember the specific source of information (a particular speaker, say) within a general situation. Although Schacter et al. argued that source amnesia and source forgetting were qualitatively different phenomena, that claim is still debatable. An alternative position is presumably that all types of contextual information are vulnerable to the effects of aging, to frontal-lobe damage, and so forth, and that information that is less central to a perceiver's purposes when the event is initially processed will be most vulnerable. An even more general position is that all information in the event is vulnerable, but that contextual information is more liable to be lost than is the central, relatively salient gist of the event (see also, McIntyre & Craik, 1987). A corollary of the second position is that fact (or event) memory should be correlated with source memory. Fact and source were not correlated reliably in the sample of 24 older adults tested by Craik, Morris, Morris, and Loewen (1990), but the correlation was statistically significant in a group of 16 adults tested for fact and source recall after 6–8 weeks (Shimamura & Squire, in press). To add further complexity to the story, Schacter, Kaszniak, Kihlstrom, and Valdiserri (in press) recently reported a study in which older subjects showed more source forgetting for novel facts after 2 hr (which of two speakers initially presented the fact?), but only under certain experimental conditions. An age-related decrement in source recall was found when the two speakers presented the facts either in a blocked fashion or in a randomized fashion, but no age decrement in source recall was found when the facts were presented twice as often to the older group in order to eliminate age differences in fact recall. Clearly, more work is required to clarify both the role of aging in fact recall and its relations to source recall of various types, as well as the possible mediating effects of frontal-lobe dysfunction on recollection of source. The problems are likely to attract a lot of attention during the next decade, given the crucial importance of context and source to episodic remembering.

Environmental Support. Craik (1983, 1986) argued that the activity of remembering should be seen as an interaction between external information (from stimuli and their contexts) and internal mental processes (well-learned schematic information plus self-initiated processing). If older people carry out self-initiated processing less effectively, they should be at a disadvantage when such processing dominates a task (e.g., free recall), and perform relatively well in situations where the environment affords support at encoding and retrieval. Self-initiated processing may be particularly demanding of limited processing resources; if so, increased environmental support would be one way to achieve good performance when processing resources are reduced.

Several recent studies have provided evidence in line with this idea, although other investigators have challenged the findings. Waddell and Rogoff (1981) tested the ability of middle-age and elderly women to remember the spatial location of toy objects placed either in featureless cubicles or on a model landscape. A large age-related deficit was found in the first case, but none was found in the second. However, Park, Cherry, Smith, and Lafronza (1990) pointed out that the elderly women spent comparatively longer studying the landscape condition and that this may have affected the results. Sharps and Gollin (1987, 1988) published two interesting articles showing again that age-related decrements in the recall of spatial location of objects are greatly reduced when the objects are placed in a meaningful, structured context—for example, on a colored map or in a room, as opposed to on a plain background.

However, these experiments showing that the poorer performance of older subjects can be compensated for by the provision of rich, meaningful contexts must be evaluated in the light of other studies showing that younger and older people benefit equally from enriched contexts (Light, 1991). Zelinski and Light (1988) presented such an experiment. In their study, younger and older subjects showed equal improvements in memory for object locations on a map when fuller details were added to the map. Similarly, Park et al. (1990) found equal improvements in spatial memory for young and older participants as a function of increased richness of both the items to be remembered and their context. Enriched context had no effect on free recall of objects in this study. Sharps (1991) recently tried to resolve the discrepancy in results between the Park et al. study and those reported by Sharps and Gollin (1987). He pointed out that Park et al. used 40 objects that could be categorized into 10 categories; using Park's objects, Sharps replicated the Park et al. group's results—that is, an equal benefit to young and old with enriched context—whereas using the Sharps and Gollin objects, Sharps replicated his original finding— that is, an interaction between age and context. As in the work discussed previously, it appears that the results obtained in this paradigm depend on interactions among subjects, materials, study, and test conditions. Unsatisfactory though this state of affairs may be, cognitive aging researchers may simply have to accept this fact of nature and undertake experiments with multiple samples, materials, and tasks to obtain the full picture (see also, Hultsch & Pentz, 1980; Jenkins, 1979, for a discussion of this "contextualist" position).

AGE DIFFERENCES IN RETRIEVAL

Burke and Light (1981) argued persuasively that an age-related difficulty in retrieval was one major reason for poorer memory performance in the elderly. There seems little reason to doubt this assertion; work during the last decade has attempted to refine the analysis further. One suggestion, discussed earlier, is that age decrements should be alleviated to the extent that the task (or more generally, the environment) supports retrieval processes (Craik, 1983, 1986). Thus, recognition tasks should present less of a problem to the older person than recall tasks, because in the former situation useful information is re-presented that helps to induce appropriate mental operations. In the case of recall, the operations must be "self-initiated" by the subject, rather than be driven or induced by aspects of the external environment.

Schonfield and Robertson (1966) originally reported that age-related decrements were more severe in recall than in recognition, and this pattern has been replicated by other researchers. One exception is a study by White and Cunningham (1982) who found an interaction between age and recall/recognition, but they also found that the interaction disappeared when recognition was corrected for guessing. However, studies by Rabinowitz (1984, 1986) and by Craik and McDowd (1987) all found that age-related decrements were less in recognition than in recall. In answer to White and Cunningham's criticism that recognition is often not measured appropriately (i.e., differential guessing rates or false alarm rates are not taken into account), Craik and McDowd suggested carrying out an analysis of covariance on recall data, using d' recognition scores as the covariate. The point here is that d' scores yield a measure of recognition that is independent of guessing bias. After equating recognition performance between the age groups statistically in this fashion, Craik and McDowd found that substantial age-related decrements in recall still remained. In the same vein, Ceci and Tabor (1981) and Craik, Byrd, and Swanson (1987) showed that age differences were greater in free recall than in cued recall—again (arguably) the greater environmental support at retrieval is associated with reduced age-related decrements in performance. The Ceci and Tabor study also explored the dimension of cognitive flexibility in recall, by presenting drawings that were related to a series of themes (e.g., "associated with the North Pole") or were members of semantic categories (e.g., dwellings). Younger subjects showed more flexibility in moving from one type of organizer to the other during recall; also, greater flexibility was related to higher levels of recall.

One line of evidence suggests that recall is more effortful than recognition, and that this difference in required effort may be especially detrimental to the older person. Macht and Buschke (1983) gave participants a reaction-time (RT) task to perform while they were recalling a list of words; RT was increased above a resting baseline level by concurrent recall to a greater extent in the case of the elderly subjects. This finding was replicated by Craik and McDowd (1987), who also demonstrated that a recall task was more detrimental to concurrent RT than was a recognition task.

Researchers have started to dissect the tasks of recall and recognition to uncover the component processes involved in carrying them out. One widely accepted view is that recognition memory involves a fast-acting, relatively automatic "familiarity" component, followed by a slower, more effortful process concerned with the recollection of original contextual information. This second type of information is usually necessary because the question asked is "Did this item occur in the experimental list?" not "Have you *ever* seen this item before?" Evidence is accumulating to the effect that age differences in the familiarity component are small or nonexistent, although age differences in the context recall component of recognition do exist (Rabinowitz, 1984). The results of the Dywan and Jacoby (1990) experiment on famous names also could be interpreted as showing that the familiarity component of recognition is intact in older people, although the feeling of familiarity may be misattributed to prior general knowledge rather than to recent exposure. A related technique introduced by Tulving (1985a) has subjects state for each recognized item whether they consciously recollected its prior occurrence on the study list ("remember" items) or whether they recognized the item on some other basis ("know" items); one possible basis for "knowing" as opposed to "remembering" is presumably general familiarity. Parkin and Walter (1992) recently demonstrated that the proportion of know items increases, if anything, with age, whereas the proportion of remember items declines in older subjects. The dissociation between familiarity and recollective experience clearly is related to notions of implicit and explicit memory tasks, and to the distinction between procedural and episodic memory systems; these suggested classifications are discussed briefly at the end of the chapter.

Two interesting studies have explored the interactions between prior knowledge and recent experience in retrieval tasks. Reder, Wible, and Martin (1986) presented stories to younger and older participants and then asked them either to discriminate between plausible facts that were or were not present in the stories, or to judge the plausibility of statements regardless of whether they had been presented in the story. Older subjects were poorer than their younger counterparts on the first task, but not on the second. The authors commented that there is an age-related loss in the ability to make exact memory matches and careful inspection of retrieved propositions, but not in the ability to make judgments on the basis of plausible inferences. Bäckman (1991) carried out a face recognition experiment in which he found that subjects of all ages were better at recognizing famous faces from their own age cohort; further, young subjects and young-old adults (mean age = 66 years) showed the same superior recognition performance for same-cohort unfamiliar faces, whereas two elderly groups (mean ages = 76 and 85 years) showed no effect of age of face. Bäckman concluded that crystallized semantic knowledge is used to perform episodic memory tasks at all ages, although in the elderly there is a gradual loss in the ability to utilize subtler aspects of prior knowledge.

AGE DIFFERENCES IN NONVERBAL MEMORY

Critics have complained rightly that memory researchers have tended to concentrate almost exclusively on studying memory for verbal materials—digits, letters, words, sentences, and stories—whereas memory in everyday life is much more often concerned with remembering factual information, faces, object locations, and appointments. In response to such criticisms, and in the context of the broader theorizing encouraged by the cognitive approach, researchers have turned increasingly to the study of nonverbal materials over the past 10–15 years; this trend has been apparent also in the aging literature. The broader perspective is certainly welcome, but it should be noted that the general principles of human memory induced from experiments on verbal learning and memory appear to be equally applicable to the results obtained with pictures, faces, and other materials. The general pattern of age-related declines in ability also hold, but again these losses can be offset by using stimuli that are familiar and are compatible with prior knowledge, by using learning situations that encourage rich and elaborate encoding, and by using retrieval tasks that readily reinstate the initial encoding operations.

Memory for Pictures.   Park, Puglisi, and their colleagues have carried out an impressive series of studies on age changes in memory for pictures. One major conclusion is that age differences in recognition of scenes or drawings are typically slight (Park et al., 1986; Rybarczyk, Hart, & Harkins, 1987; Till, Bartlett, & Doyle, 1982). This conclusion holds for retention intervals up to 48 hr, but at longer retention intervals young people appear to have the advantage (Park et al., 1986; Park, Royal, Dudley, & Morrell, 1988). Exceptions to the finding of only slight age-related decrements in picture recognition have been reported also (Park, Puglisi, & Sovacool, 1983; Trahan, Larrabee, & Levin, 1986), although in both these studies the poorer performance of older subjects is largely attributable to age-related increases in false alarm rates; hit rates were virtually unchanged across age groups. Further exceptions occur when the recognition decision is made particularly difficult by using very similar distractor items. Thus, Till et al. (1982) found that young subjects were better than older adults at distinguishing presented scenes from very similar scenes, and Bartlett, Till, Gernsbacher, and Gorman (1983) found the same results using distractors that were reversed versions of target pictures.

In contrast to the small age-related effects in recognition memory, age deficits are found typically in experiments using free or cued recall as the measure of performance. For example, Puglisi and Park (1987) reported a superiority of young over older participants in recalling a series of line drawings, though both age groups profited from an encoding condition in which the drawings were incomplete (cf. the generation effect in verbal memory). Again, age differences were reported in a cued-recall study of line drawings (Park, Smith et al., 1990), although the age-related deficit was greatest when the target and its context (later used as the retrieval cue) were poorly integrated and least when target and context were well integrated. Further, older adults profited more from the well-integrated context, in line with some of the results described in the section on verbal memory.

Memory for Faces. Recent work on age differences in face recognition corroborates the findings from studies of drawings and scenes; that is, age differences are slight unless the encoding conditions were unfavorable or fine discriminations were required at the time of test. Thus, Bartlett and Leslie (1986) found that young adults were superior to older adults in face recognition when the stimuli were photographs showing only one view of the face and when the distractors were the same face seen with a different expression or in a different pose. No age differences were reported when subjects studied four different views or poses of the face at input or when a target face had to be distinguished from an entirely new face. In a second study, Bartlett, Leslie, Tubbs, and Fulton (1989) did find an age-related decrement in the ability to distinguish photos of previously presented faces from photos of entirely new faces. However, only one viewing had been permitted in the encoding phase, and the result depended entirely on an age-related increase in false alarms—there were no age differences in hit rates. This last result thus replicates the findings using scenes as materials (Park et al., 1983; Trahan et al., 1986). A further result reported by Bartlett et al. (1989) was that when older subjects recognized a previously presented face presented at test with a different expression or pose, they were less able than younger people to say exactly what had been changed; they detected a difference, but could not say how the photo had changed.

Finally, a study by Bäckman and Herlitz (1990) found that both healthy older subjects and elderly demented patients found photographs of famous personalities from the 1940s more familiar than photographs of personalities from the 1980s. However, only the healthy older people were able to profit from this knowledge in an episodic recognition test; that is, they recognized "dated" photographs better than "contemporary" photographs, whereas the patients showed no difference between the two classes of materials. The authors concluded that older people can utilize prior knowledge to enrich stimulus encoding, but that Alzheimer's patients cannot (see also, Nebes, chapter 8 of this volume). Further work by Bäckman (1991) has shown that even normal aging is associated with some loss in the ability to utilize subtler aspects of prior knowledge.

Memory for Spatial Information.   Hasher and Zacks (1979) suggested that certain aspects of experienced events were encoded relatively automatically and thus should be immune to the detrimental effects of aging; they included temporal and spatial attributes in this category. Although the studies reviewed in this section make it clear that this position cannot be maintained, the theoretical statement served a useful purpose in stimulating research in the area. Interestingly, more recent findings in the neuropsychological literature have yielded exactly the opposite prediction—that spatial and temporal attributes may be especially vulnerable to the effects of aging! This latter position follows from research on patients with frontal-lobe lesions; the patients show marked deficits in remembering where or when events occurred (Janowsky, Shimamura, & Squire, 1989; Schacter et al., 1984). If normal aging is accompanied by some inefficiency of frontal-lobe functioning (Craik, Morris, Morris, & Loewen, 1990; Schacter, 1987b), then some losses in memory for spatiotemporal information would be expected (see the section Memory for Source).

Three studies published in 1983 (Light & Zelinski, 1983; Park et al., 1983; Pezdek, 1983) present good converging evidence that memory for spatial information declines with advancing age in the adult years. In general, subsequent studies have confirmed this finding, with some caveats. Because research on spatial memory does not carry the burden of a crystallized classical methodology, the experiments tend to be innovative and use a variety of techniques tapping both laboratory and real-life skills. This diversity makes the converging conclusions all the more convincing.

The most commonly used paradigm is one in which subjects are shown verbal material or pictures or objects in a spatial matrix and later have to replace the items in their original positions. Using this technique, several researchers have found substantial age-related differences in both recall and recognition of spatial location (Naveh-Benjamin, 1987, 1988; Salthouse, Kausler, & Saults, 1988). Similarly, in a large-scale study, Moore, Richards, and Hood (1984) found a progressive decline in the ability to recall the location of a series of wooden shapes in subjects age 19–76 years. The same general finding was reported by Cherry and Park (1989) using a 3-D Plexiglas display. In this study, memory for location was better when meaningful objects were used, but the benefit associated with meaningfulness was no greater for the older adults.

Some investigators have used model towns or streetscapes to test for spatial memory. For example, Bruce and Herman (1986) found an age-related deficit in the ability to replace model buildings accurately on a map; the authors interpreted their results as supporting Pezdek's (1983) suggestion of an encoding difficulty in the elderly. The finding of an age-related deficit in recognition of spatial information (Naveh-Benjamin, 1988) is also in line with the encoding deficit view. In an earlier study, Bruce and Herman (1983) showed subjects photographs of street scenes and later presented photographs of the same locations for recognition; the test photographs were taken either from the same angle (0° shift) or from a perspective shifted 90° or 180° from the original. Recognition in all subjects declined from 0° through 180° to 90°, and the age-related deficit was greatest for the 90° condition. In another realistic experiment, Evans, Brennan, Skorpovich, and Held (1984) asked subjects to recall the buildings from a familiar part of their city, and also to locate the buildings on a grid. Despite the fact that the older adults in the study had lived in the area longer, they were substantially poorer than younger adults at both tasks. One comment here is that older adults may have excellent knowledge of real-life spatial information when they are using it, but have more difficulty expressing it under the somewhat abstract and artificial circumstances of a laboratory experiment. The push to assess abilities under real-life conditions should be encouraged!

One interesting debate in this area concerns the role of contextual information in compensating for age-related deficits in spatial memory. As described in a previous section, studies by Waddell and Rogoff (1981) and Sharps and Gollin (1987, 1988) suggest that a rich, meaningful context differentially enhances the performance of older adults. Evidence for such compensatory effects has not been found by other workers, however, either in the case where the items were made more meaningful (Cherry & Park, 1989; Park et al., 1983) or in the case where the spatial environment was made more supportive (Park, Cherry, Smith, & Lafronza, 1990; Zelinski & Light, 1988). This may be another case of the fuller picture emerging only after subject × materials × encoding × retrieval interactions are thoroughly explored (e.g., older adults profit differentially only from highly meaningful objects located in realistic surroundings), but for the moment the evidence is poised between compensation and equal effects for young and old.

Frequency and Temporal Effects. Several studies have explored adult age differences in the ability to judge how many times an event has occurred. Hasher and Zacks (1979) suggested that such frequency information is encoded automatically, and thus is not sensitive to strategies or the effects of aging. The consensus emerging from recent studies is that there may be some age-related decline in the accuracy of frequency judgments, but the effects are small and are perhaps restricted to situations in which some strategic processing can in fact occur.

Initially, the studies reported tended to confirm Hasher and Zacks's (1979) prediction of no age-related effects in frequency judgments (e.g., Attig & Hasher, 1980; Kausler & Puckett, 1980). Further studies revealed small but significant effects in favor of younger adults (e.g., Kausler, Lichty, & Hakami, 1984; Kausler, Salthouse, & Saults, 1987). Sanders, Wise, Liddle, and Murphy (1990) recently suggested that when processing is truly incidental, and thus relatively "shallow," age differences disappear; they presented evidence in support of this contention. They further suggested that in intentional learning situations, more elaborate strategic processes are switched in, and that such processing is differentially helpful to frequency judgments of younger subjects. This viewpoint is in line with previous findings of Kausler and Hakami (1982) that age differences in frequency judgments were found with "relevant" (attended) words, but no age difference was found with relatively unattended words.

The temporal order of events ("recency judgments") has been another object of theoretical interest, and a few studies have examined age differences in this ability. One recent example is by Naveh-Benjamin (1990). He presented a list of 20 words serially and later asked subjects to reconstruct the original order of presentation. An age-related decline in performance was found, although the difference was not large—mean correlations between judged and actual orders were $+.51$ for younger subjects and $+.36$ for the older group. The topics of temporal and frequency-of-occurrence memory are potentially interesting ones—but the studies could stand an infusion of more creative and realistic paradigms.

AGE DIFFERENCES IN MEMORY OF THE PAST
AND FOR THE FUTURE

Remote Memory. Although older people often report anecdotally that their memories of youthful experiences are much clearer than memories of recent events, the scientific literature has not supported this contention. In general, when memory for factual historical events has been assessed, it appears that performance declines from the present to the past (see Erber, 1981, for a review). Recent experiments mostly support this conclusion, although it should be noted that the studies tap memory for public events or for personalities in the news, as opposed to personal (and probably more emotional) autobiographical experiences; it remains possible that such personal memories behave somewhat differently.

This is difficult research to do because such factors as the degree of initial learning (reflecting interest in and attention paid to the events in question), amount of subsequent rehearsal or retrieval of the material, and exposure to further intervening material of a similar nature are largely uncontrolled. Nonetheless, some recent experiments have provided important leads. For example, Rubin (1982) carried out an extensive diary study on college-age subjects and was able to plot a retention function for autobiographical memories dating from 1 hr to 18 years previously. The forgetting function for these real-life events was essentially identical to that obtained previously by Wickelgren (1974) for verbal materials learned in the laboratory; the data were well fitted by a single trace retention function that was an exponential multiplied by a power function. Similar results were reported by Squire (1989). He devised a questionnaire for TV shows that had been shown for one season only; the shows had been aired from 1 year to 15 years previously. Multiple-choice recognition scores were adjusted for the number of weeks a particular show had run, and it was found that the adjusted scores declined monotonically over the 15 years. Again, the data were well fitted by either an exponential or a power function. Squire divided his participants into three age groups of 77 subjects (mean ages = 30.3, 39.8, and 54.1 years respectively) to examine age-related changes in forgetting functions. Age differences between the groups were slight (although it should be noted that the age range was also small), with the younger group showing a slightly steeper forgetting function than the old. Performance at the longest retention interval (11–15 years) was equivalent (50% compared to the chance level of 25%) for all three age groups.

Bahrick (1979, 1984) reported some extremely elegant work examining memory for real-life knowledge over periods of up to 50 years. In one case (Bahrick, 1979) the information concerned the spatial layout of a city that the respondents once had lived in, and in another (Bahrick, 1984) the information was a second language that respondents had learned in school. In both cases, the general finding was that memory for these types of well-learned knowledge declined exponentially for 3–6 years, but then showed very little further change over the period 6–25 years. Further declines were evident after 25 years. Bahrick referred to the stable middle period as a "permastore" for learned materials. Age is necessarily confounded with retention interval in these studies, but the data provide a wealth of information for students of real-life learning across the adult years.

Another careful study examining memory for public events was reported by Howes and Katz (1988). They devised a questionnaire for public events dating from 1920 to 1981, and covering a wide range of content areas. Their basic findings were that, using both recall and recognition as measures, memory for public events increases over the teenage years, and remains relatively constant thereafter. Thus, unlike the studies described earlier, there was essentially no forgetting of remote events and no recency effect for events that had happened in the last few years. The reason for the discrepancy is unclear; the salience of the events assessed is one possible source of difference—that is, very salient public events are likely to form part of the subjects' permastore of historical knowledge.

A technique to evoke personal autobiographical memories has been used with increasing frequency in recent years. Subjects are presented with a single word and asked to describe a personal memory that the word evokes; they then attempt to date the memory as precisely as possible. Using this technique, Fitzgerald and Lawrence (1984) presented participants ranging from junior high school students to elderly adults with either nouns or emotional words as memory prompts. As shown in Table 2.4, the remoteness of the memory evoked increased as a function of the subject's age (understandably), and emotional words evoked memories that were considerably more recent than the memories evoked by nouns. This latter result may occur because people have stored some particularly striking event involving a place or person (e.g., policeman, airport, dancer) in something like a personal semantic memory that is relatively crystallized, whereas being asked about an emotional event (e.g., tender, disgusted) necessitates an active search for an occasion on which that emotion was felt. The second case may bias the search toward more recent memories. Fitzgerald and Lawrence also reported the interesting finding that certain emotional words evoke memories that are either recent or from the more distant past differentially for various age groups. For example, "fearful" evokes relatively old memories in college students, but recent memories in older adults. Clearly, some qualitative analysis of words and their evoked memories is also possible with this technique.

Finally, Rubin, Wetzler, and Nebes (1986) described a quantitative model based on several studies using the memory evocation method. They presented convincing evidence that memory for personal events declines from the present back into the past in a similar fashion for younger and

TABLE 2.4
Remoteness of Memories Evoked by Emotional Words or Common Nouns

| Age Group | Event Age (Months) | |
	Emotional Word	Noun
Junior High	3.3	6.2
College	14.3	31.4
Middle Age	49.5	98.2
Older Adults	83.2	211.7

Note. From Fitzgerald and Lawrence, 1984.

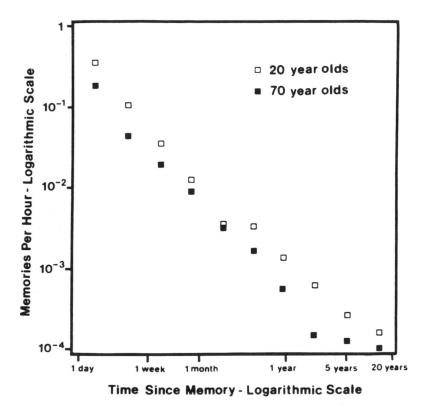

FIG. 2.3.   Mean number of memories per hr reported from subjects' lives
as a function of the age of those memories (Rubin et al., 1986).

older subjects, and that this retention curve is well described by a power
function (see Fig. 2.3). Two further components are required to fit the
data over the entire life span: first, a childhood amnesia component to
account for the underrepresentation of memories from the first few years
of life, and second, a reminiscence component in participants older than
40 years to account for the overrepresentation of memories from the years
10–30. This last factor does not appear to reflect better encoding of events
in these years, however, but differential sampling from that period, which
for most people is rich in salient life events.

Prospective Memory.   Craik (1986) proposed that age-related
decrements in memory performance were observed to the extent that
the task in question necessitated much self-initiated processing on the
part of the subject. He further suggested that remembering to carry out
some future action (prospective memory) should be particularly
vulnerable to the effects of aging, because typically the subject must

"remember to remember" at some future time. Some studies have reported results in line with Craik's view. For example, Dobbs and Rule (1987) asked subjects to remember to ask for a red pen at a given point in the experiment, and to date a questionnaire they would later fill out at home; subjects over 70 years were much more likely to forget these instructions than were younger participants. Similarly, Cockburn and Smith (1988, 1991) gave a battery of memory tests to subjects of various ages; older people were more likely to forget to ask for the return of a hidden belonging, to arrange a future appointment, and to deliver a message as requested.

These results are in line with the common complaint of older people that they are becoming more forgetful and absentminded about daily events. However, a number of recent reports have cast doubt on the blanket assertion that prospective memory inevitably declines with age. First, Moscovitch (1982) reported a study in which subjects were asked to phone the lab on various future dates and times. If anything, older people were better at remembering to do this task—to some extent because they took more care to set up reminders for themselves (e.g., by placing a note near the telephone). The same result was reported by Maylor (1990) in a large-scale study involving over 300 female subjects. She found that remembering to perform future actions correlated positively with age in those subjects who made active use of external cues, but negatively in a smaller subset of subjects who attempted to remember "by themselves." It thus seems possible that prospective memory ability declines with age unless the older person takes active steps to compensate for his or her growing difficulties by relying progressively more on external mnemonic aids. There is evidence to support the notion that younger adults rely more on mental strategies like rehearsal, whereas older adults rely on external aids (Loewen, Shaw, & Craik, 1990).

In an interesting recent study, Einstein and McDaniel (1990) found no age differences in a prospective memory experiment in which subjects had to press a key whenever an infrequently occurring target word was presented as part of an ongoing experiment. Performance by both age groups was better if the target word was unfamiliar (e.g., *monad* as opposed to *method*), and the authors commented that the effectiveness of an external prompt is likely to depend on its salience. They also pointed out that there is no need to argue (as Craik, 1986, did) that all prospective memory situations require self-initiated activity; if a person takes care to set up a future reminder (a note by the telephone, a letter by the front door) prospective memory will be strongly supported by the environment, and no age differences would be expected. By this view age differences in prospective memory will depend on (a) the level of forward strategic planning shown by the individual, (b) the salience of the reminding event, and (c) the ability of the individual to carry out self-initiated mnemonic activities. In line with these conclusions, Einstein, McDaniel, Cunfer, and Guynn (1991) found age differences on a task in which subjects were asked to perform an action every 10 min (a time-based task presumed to be high in self-initiated retrieval), but no age differences on a task in which subjects performed an action whenever a particular word was presented (an event-based task presumed to be relatively low in self-initiated retrieval).

In summary, it appears that prospective memory abilities do decline with age, especially in situations where the environment offers few cues as reminders. However, older people often take active steps to overcome this inefficiency by ensuring that their environment does provide salient events to trigger future actions.

AGING AND MEMORY SYSTEMS

The notion that human memory comprises several distinct systems has been enormously influential in recent years. Tulving (1972, 1983) distinguished *episodic memory*—the ability to recollect specific events from one's personal past—from *semantic memory*—general knowledge about the world, acquired through learning. In his later writings, Tulving (1985b) suggested that *procedural memory*—the influence of earlier experiences on present performance—be thought of as a third system, and that the three systems are arranged in a monohierarchical fashion, with procedural memory supporting semantic memory which in turn supports episodic memory. Tulving further suggested that this organization may reflect both evolutionary and developmental trends; that is, procedural memory is the most primitive system and the one to develop first in infants, whereas episodic memory develops late and is found in higher mammals only. A second implication of this reasoning is that episodic memory should be the system most vulnerable to brain injury or inefficiency (and thus to the effects of aging), and that procedural memory should be least affected. The results described later are in good agreement with this principle, although they also may be accounted for in other terms.

Procedural memory has been used to describe a wide variety of abilities ranging from motor skills to the effect of prior exposure of a word on its subsequent identification. Because a very wide range of cognitive (and physiological) procedures must be involved in these tasks, we describe some relevant experiments under the more neutral terminology of *implicit memory,* contrasting age differences in tasks that do not require recollection of the original event with age differences on *explicit memory*

tasks, such as recall and recognition, that do require conscious recollection of the preceding episode.

Age Differences in Implicit Memory.   The general area of implicit
memory (or memory without awareness) has been well reviewed by
Jacoby and Witherspoon (1982), Schacter (1987b), and Richardson-
Klavehn and Bjork (1988). Good reviews of adult age differences on such
indirect tests of memory are provided by Light and Burke (1988), Chiarello
and Hoyer (1988), and Graf (1990). One of the most striking results found
with implicit tests of memory is that amnesic patients, despite their profound deficiency on explicit memory tests, demonstrate a level of performance that is comparable to that found with a normal population
(Richardson-Klavehn & Bjork, 1988; Schacter, 1987a). This suggests that
amnesics have retained some memorial abilities that can support unconscious remembering. Moreover, their performance has served as a
useful analog for research with the elderly (Light & Burke, 1988), implying that older adults may show little if any impairment on indirect
memory tasks relative to young individuals.

One task that has been used in this context is lexical decision, in which
subjects are required to decide rapidly whether a presented string of letters forms a real word. Age differences are minimal in this task (though
see later), suggesting that the structures concerned with language remain
intact in the course of normal aging (Bowles & Poon, 1981, 1985). The
task can be extended to examine the effects of presenting either the identical word or a related word at some time prior to the lexical decision;
the amount and duration of priming can be studied in this way. Several
studies have reported no reliable differences between young and old subjects in this respect (Howard, 1983; Madden, 1986; Moscovitch, 1982),
although all three studies did find an age-related decrement in explicit
memory tasks for the presented words. A similar study by Mitchell (1989)
explored the effect of repetition of line drawings at various lags on naming latency for the pictured object; he too found no significant differences
between young and old. A further extension of the priming technique
has been to study implicit memory for new associations. These studies
involve presenting subjects either with sentences or unrelated word pairs.
Following presentation, subjects are asked to make a word recognition
judgment, and the latency of their response is recorded. Faster recognition judgments are made when a target is preceded by a word that was
presented with it during study, suggesting that a new association was
formed and remembered without awareness. Again, age differences are
minimal in this task (Howard, Heisey, & Shaw, 1986; Rabinowitz, 1986).
One caveat in connection with priming tasks involving decision latency
is that older adults' responses are almost always slower; the baseline

latencies therefore differ between young and old groups, and older subjects, consequently, have more room for improvement.

However, other experimental techniques have also yielded negligible age-related differences. For example, Howard (1988) adopted the homophone spelling bias task introduced by Jacoby and Witherspoon (1982). She presented written homophones that were biased toward their more infrequent spelling (e.g., *reed* as opposed to *read*). Her subjects later showed memory without awareness when they produced these infrequent spellings as responses to auditorily presented words on a spelling test. Moreover, these spelling bias scores were not significantly different for young (30%) and old (34%) participants. Perceptual identification tasks in which subjects are presented with visually degraded stimuli, or intact stimuli under very fast viewing conditions, also demonstrate the influence of unaware remembering. Subjects are better able to identify old items (that have already been shown prior to the task) than new items, and this effect holds equally for the elderly (Light & Singh, 1987).

The most common indirect tests used in current memory research involve either stem or word fragment completion. Typically, subjects are presented with a list of words, followed by a task in which they are given either the first few letters of a word (stem completion) or some of the word's letters interspersed with blanks (word fragment completion), and asked to complete the word. Although many of the completions come from the earlier list, subjects are asked merely to complete the item with the first word that comes to mind; they are not asked to think back to the earlier list. Memory, however, is revealed because the subjects tend to complete the items with the words they have just seen, and elderly subjects are not significantly different from young subjects in this regard (Light & Singh, 1987; Light, Singh, & Capps, 1986). A particularly striking illustration of the dissociation between implicit and explicit memory is provided by Light and Singh who compared performance on word stem completion and cued recall using the same stems as cues. They altered only the instructions for the two tests; subjects were told to use the word stems either to deliberately recall words from the study list (cued recall) or to complete the stems with whatever word came to mind (word-stem completion). Again, no age difference was found on the indirect memory test, but a large age-related decrement was found in cued recall.

The literature thus provides strong converging evidence for an absence of age-related effects in tests of implicit memory. There are some exceptions to this general statement. For example, Rose, Yesavage, Hill, and Bower (1986) found age differences on the spelling bias test; Howard, Shaw, and Heisey (1986) found an age-related decrement in priming in lexical decision; Chiarello and Hoyer (1988) found age differences in both stem completion and cued recall. However, the important conclusion again follows from the general pattern of results—that age differences are substantially larger in tests of explicit remembering involving conscious recollection than they are in tests of implicit memory.

Episodic and Semantic Memory.   The literature on age differences in knowledge representation and utilization is reviewed elsewhere in this volume (see chapters 3 and 5), so this brief section focuses on the contrast between retrieval of information from the semantic and episodic memory systems. Again, the general finding is that age differences in semantic memory functioning are minimal, whereas age-related decrements in episodic remembering are the rule. For example, Light and Anderson (1983) found no age differences in the ability to use generic knowledge to generate scripts relating to everyday activities, although young subjects were superior at recognition and recall of such scripted activities. Similarly, Albert, Heller, and Milberg (1988) and Mitchell (1989) reported studies showing no age decrement (until the 70s at least) in naming objects from line drawings, yet substantial age-related decrements in explicit tests of recall and recognition.

An interesting exception to this general pattern is provided by Bowles and Poon (Bowles, 1989; Bowles & Poon, 1985). They found large age-related decrements in a task in which word definitions were provided, and subjects had to retrieve the specified word. The authors suggested that retrieval deficits in semantic memory processing are found when subjects are provided with stimulus information that is conceptual rather than orthographic. A similar point was made by Albert et al. (1988). There is an interesting parallel here to the greater problems experienced by older people when dealing with inferential as opposed to verbatim information (Cohen, 1979; Zacks & Hasher, 1988).

Some Comments on Aging and Memory Systems.   The literature thus provides a very consistent picture—age differences are minimal in procedural (or implicit) memory tasks, slight or nonexistent in semantic memory tasks unless the retrieval cues require conceptual or inferential processing, yet are large in episodic memory tasks. In addition, some workers (e.g., Mitchell, 1989; Mitchell, Brown, & Murphy, 1990) have provided convincing evidence for the independence of performance levels between episodic and procedural, and between episodic and semantic memory tasks. But are these findings best described in terms of memory systems, or are there alternative ways of accounting for the same data?

One point that calls into question the usefulness of experimental dissociations as a method for distinguishing independent systems is that dissociations are found between tasks that are supposedly representative of a single system (Witherspoon & Moscovitch, 1989). An alternative account (Jacoby, 1983; Roediger et al., 1989) suggests that different tasks simply require different types of information for their optimal performance, so that certain encoding manipulations will have large effects on some tasks but little effect on others. Similarly, if older people retain intact certain types of processing but are deficient in others, then no age differences will be found on tasks requiring the intact processing but age-related deficits will be found on tasks requiring the deficient processes.

Whereas age differences are typically slight on many semantic memory tasks, the finding of substantial age differences when words must be retrieved in response to definitions (Bowles & Poon, 1985) suggests strongly that it is not the system that declines in efficiency as a function of age, but rather the type of processing operation that must be performed to accomplish the task. One of the most common complaints of elderly people is their difficulty in remembering names—a semantic memory task. In the same way, age-related decrements in episodic memory may be either large or slight depending again on the process required and the level of support provided by the task. Thus (as detailed in previous sections) age differences are large in unsupported free recall, yet relatively slight in cued recall and recognition when the initial context is reinstated.

Two other comments may be made on points raised by workers in this area. Several researchers (e.g., Burke, White, & Diaz, 1987; Madden, 1986) have commented that because age differences are minimal in priming tasks involving semantic activation of the lexicon, this implies that semantic processing is intact in general; therefore age-related deficits in episodic memory cannot be attributable to a deficit in semantic encoding. In our opinion, this view of semantic processing is too monolithic; it is altogether unlikely that semantic processing is one thing, either present or absent. Further, the type of semantic processing required to support good episodic retention may differ considerably from the type of processing required to facilitate lexical access.

A second comment concerns the notion of environmental support. Light and Singh (1987) pointed out that they found no age differences on the stem completion task (where the first three letters of a target word were re-presented) yet did find reliable age differences, favoring the young subjects in recognition (where the whole word was re-presented). Reasonably enough, they claimed that this result contradicts the proposal by Craik (1983, 1986) that age differences should decline with greater levels of environmental support—in this case, re-presentation of the whole word. However, it should be borne in mind that although subjects write down or check off the target word in both tasks, the mental processes involved are substantially different; in stem completion the subject produces the first word that comes to mind, whereas in recognition the task is to decide whether a given word was present on a former occasion. That is, recognition memory necessarily involves recollection of the original encoding context—arguably an effortful procedure—whereas stem completion does not; it merely demands that the subject complete the stem with the first word that comes to mind. It is again clear, however, that more direct evidence for differences in effort or self-initiated processing must be obtained.

CONCLUSIONS AND FUTURE DIRECTIONS

Light (1991) recently provided an excellent systematic review of memory and aging. Her conclusions are somewhat pessimistic in tone, because the evidence does not provide clear support for any one of the four hypotheses that she considers; these are that age-related differences in memory are attributable to a failure of metamemory, to semantic deficits, to an impairment of deliberate recollection, or to a reduction in processing resources. Although we agree with Light that the current evidence does not permit unequivocal acceptance of any one of these positions, and strongly endorse her view that theoretical positions should be abandoned if they fail to generate confirming data, we are inclined to take a more optimistic position. If, as we have suggested in the present review, understandable patterns of data will emerge only after the interactions among subjects, materials, and encoding and retrieval variables are taken into account, the search for order and consistency must move to a level higher than the individual experiment. That is, it may be insufficient to accept the negative evidence from one experiment (however well designed and carried out) as a basis for rejecting a hypothesis, if there is also good evidence in favor of the hypothesis. Rather, some higher level principle must be sought that predicts one pattern of results in one set of conditions, yet a different pattern in another set.

A case in point is the differential benefits observed for younger and older subjects as encoding conditions are made more favorable. As detailed earlier, there is now good evidence for three different conclusions: that older subjects benefit differentially, that younger subjects benefit differentially, and that the two groups show equivalent benefits. The next phase of research must be to provide experimental bridges among these sets of results—to elucidate the factors that modulate the basic patterns. A simple yet elegant demonstration of such an experimental bridge was provided some years ago by Epstein, Phillips, and Johnson (1975). In a cued-recall task involving noun pairs, is it more beneficial to encode the pairs initially by generating a semantic similarity or a difference between the words? Epstein et al. showed that if the words are related (*boot, shoe*) generating a difference is more beneficial, whereas if the words are unrelated (*fence, helicopter*) generating a similarity leads to superior performance in the later cued-recall test. The higher level principle thus seems to be that a good encoding should involve both semantic organization and distinctive information to differentiate the event from the organized background (Einstein & Hunt, 1980; McDaniel, Einstein, Dunay, & Cobb, 1986). In our view it is unlikely that any one of the hypotheses evaluated by Light (1991) or the various theoretical frameworks described in the present chapter will emerge as *the* valid way in which to describe age-related changes in memory. Rather, these viewpoints, frameworks, and hypotheses will continue to be useful to the extent that they generate striking, unexpected, and robust empirical phenomena. The hope is that once the field is better stocked with benchmark paradigms and results, we will have a much clearer idea of what we mean by such currently vague concepts as environmental support, working-memory capacity, and processing resources.

Future Directions. A number of perspectives, issues, and techniques seem likely to generate useful data over the next 5–10 years of research. One is the growing commonality of interests between "traditional" cognitive aging researchers and neuropsychologists (see chapters 7 and 8 of this volume). In particular, the similarities between the phenomena of normal aging and those exhibited by patients with frontal-lobe lesions (e.g., difficulties of "central executive" integration, failures of forward planning, overdependence on the current context) may lead to profitable interactions between the areas. The rapidly growing field of cognitive neuroscience (see chapter 6 of this volume) also may provide new pointers and paradigms within the next decade.

Another potentially useful bridge may be built between cognitive aging researchers and cognitive scientists. Connectionist and other computer modelers are generating extremely sophisticated and powerful sets of ideas, and these ideas are being applied to neuropsychological problems (e.g., Hinton & Shallice, 1991).

Within the domain of cognitive psychology, the further specification of working-memory functions and their roles in encoding, retrieval, and future planning is likely to remain an important task. A related question is whether the vague yet compelling notion of processing resources can be defined and specified more clearly. The role of inhibition—and age-related failures to inhibit irrelevant processing (Hasher & Zacks, 1988)—remains to be clarified. Studies of prospective memory, spatial memory, implicit memory, and the role of context in encoding and retrieval, are all likely to form exciting research foci. New methods such as Jacoby's (1991) technique for dissociating automatic and intentional aspects of recollection and Tulving's (1985a) separation of know and remember are likely to stimulate new lines of research. Finally, the current emphasis of governments and funding agencies on practical implications of research should lead to an acceleration of activity in the areas of memory rehabilitation and training, and in practical problems such as the reliability of the older witness.

ACKNOWLEDGMENTS

Preparation of this chapter was supported by grants from the Natural Sciences and Engineering Research Council of Canada, and from the Network of Centres of Excellence Program to the Canadian Aging Research Network (CARNET). We thank Tim Salthouse and Sheila Kerr for helpful comments on an earlier draft.

REFERENCES

Albert, M. S., Heller, H. S., & Milberg, W. (1988). Changes in naming ability with age. *Psychology and Aging, 3,* 173–178.

Anderson, J. R. (1983). *The architecture of cognition.* Cambridge, MA: Harvard University Press.

Arbuckle, T. Y., Vanderleck, V. F., Harsany, M., & Lapidus, S. (1990). Adult age differences in memory in relation to availability and accessibility of knowledge-based schemas. *Journal of Experimental Psychology: Learning, Memory, and Cognition, 16,* 305–315.

Attig, M., & Hasher, L. (1980). The processing of frequency occurrence information by adults. *Journal of Gerontology, 35,* 66–69.

Babcock, R. L., & Salthouse, T. A. (1990). Effects of increased processing demands on age differences in working memory. *Psychology and Aging, 5,* 421–428.

Bäckman, L. (1985). Further evidence for the lack of adult age differences on free recall of subject-performed tasks: The importance of motor action. *Human Learning, 4,* 79–87.

Bäckman, L. (1986). Adult age differences in cross-modal recoding and mental tempo, and older adults' utilization of compensatory task conditions. *Experimental Aging Research, 12,* 135–140.

Bäckman, L. (1991). Recognition memory across the adult life span: The role of prior knowledge. *Memory & Cognition, 19,* 63–71.

Bäckman, L., & Herlitz, A. (1990). The relationship between prior knowledge and face recognition memory in normal aging and Alzheimer's disease. *Journals of Gerontology: Psychological Sciences, 45,* P94–P100.

Bäckman, L., Mäntylä, T., & Herlitz, A. (1990). The optimization of episodic remembering in old age. In P. B. Baltes & M. M. Baltes (Eds.), *Successful aging: Perspectives from the behavioral sciences* (pp. 118–163). New York: Cambridge University Press.

Bäckman, L., & Nilsson, L. G. (1984). Aging effects in free recall: An exception to the rule. *Human Learning, 3,* 53–69.

Bäckman, L., & Nilsson, L. G. (1985). Prerequisites for lack of age differences in memory performance. *Experimental Aging Research, 11,* 67–73.

Baddeley, A. D. (1986). *Working memory.* London: Oxford University Press.

Baddeley, A. D., & Hitch, G. J. (1974). Working memory. In G. H. Bower (Ed.), *The psy-chology of learning and motivation* (Vol. 8, pp. 47–90). New York. Academic.

Baddeley, A. D., & Warrington, E. K. (1970). Amnesia and the distinction between long- and short-term memory. *Journal of Verbal Learning and Verbal Behavior, 9,* 176–189.

Bahrick, H. P. (1979). Maintenance of knowledge: Questions about memory we forgot to ask. *Journal of Experimental Psychology: General, 108,* 296–308.

Bahrick, H. P. (1984). Semantic memory content in permastore: Fifty years of memory for Spanish learned in school. *Journal of Experimental Psychology: General, 113,* 1–26.

Bartlett, J. C., & Leslie, J. E. (1986). Aging and memory for faces versus single views of faces. *Memory & Cognition, 14,* 371–381.

Bartlett, J. C., Leslie, J. E., Tubbs, A., & Fulton, A. (1989). Aging and memory for pictures of faces. *Psychology and Aging, 4,* 276–283.

Bartlett, J. C., Till, R. E., Gernsbacher, M., & Gorman, W. (1983). Age-related differences in memory for lateral orientation of pictures. *Journal of Gerontology, 38,* 439–446.

Bowles, N. L. (1989). Age and semantic inhibition in word retrieval. *Journal of Gerontology, 44,* 88–90.

Bowles, N. L., & Poon, L. W. (1981). An analysis of the effect of aging on recognition memory. *Journal of Gerontology, 37,* 212–219.

Bowles, N. L., & Poon, L. W. (1985). Aging and retrieval of words in semantic memory. *Journal of Gerontology, 40,* 71–77.

Bruce, P. R., & Herman, J. F. (1983). Spatial knowledge of young and elderly adults: Scene recognition from familiar and novel perspectives. *Experimental Aging Research, 9,* 169–173.

Bruce, P. R., & Herman, J. F. (1986). Adult age differences in spatial memory: Effects of distinctiveness and repeated experience. *Journal of Gerontology, 41,* 774–777.

Burke, D. M., & Light, L. L. (1981). Memory and aging: The role of retrieval processes. *Psychological Bulletin, 90,* 513–546.

Burke, D. M., White, H., & Diaz, D. L. (1987). Semantic priming in young and older adults: Evidence for age constancy in automatic and attentional processes. *Journal of Experimental Psychology: Human Perception and Performance, 13,* 79–88.

Ceci, S. J., & Tabor, L. (1981). Flexibility and memory: Are the elderly really less flexible? *Experimental Aging Research, 7,* 147–158.

Cherry, K. E., & Park, D. C. (1989). Age-related differences in three-dimensional spatial memory. *Journals of Gerontology: Psychological Sciences, 44,* P16–P22.

Chiarello, C., & Hoyer, W. J. (1988). Adult age differences in implicit and explicit memory: Time course and encoding effects. *Psychology and Aging, 3,* 358–366.

Cockburn, J., & Smith, P. T. (1988). Effects of age and intelligence on everyday memory tasks. In M. M. Gruneberg, P. E. Morris, & R. N. Sykes (Eds.), *Practical aspects of memory: Current research and issues* (Vol. 2, pp. 132–136). Chichester, England: Wiley.

Cockburn, J., & Smith, P. T. (1991). The relative influence of intelligence and age on everyday memory. *Journals of Gerontology: Psychological Sciences, 46,* P31–P36.

Cohen, G. (1979). Language comprehension in old age. *Cognitive Psychology, 11,* 412–429.

Cohen, G. (1988). Age differences in memory for text: Production deficiency or processing limitations? In L. L. Light & D. M. Burke (Eds.), *Language, memory, and aging* (pp. 171–190). New York: Cambridge University Press.

Cohen, G., & Faulkner, D. (1989). Age differences in source forgetting: Effects on reality monitoring and on eyewitness testimony. *Psychology and Aging, 4,* 10–17.

Cohen, R. L. (1981). On the generality of some memory laws. *Scandinavian Journal of Psychology, 22,* 267–281.

Cohen, R. L., Sandler, S. P., & Schroeder, K. (1987). Aging and memory for words and action events: Effects of item repetition and list length. *Psychology and Aging, 2,* 280–285.

Coyne, A. C., Allen, P. A., & Wickens, D. D. (1986). Influence of adult age on primary and secondary memory search. *Psychology and Aging, 1,* 187–194.

Craik, F. I. M. (1977). Age differences in human memory. In J. E. Birren & K. W. Schaie (Eds.), *Handbook of the psychology of aging* (pp. 384–420). New York: Van Nostrand Reinhold.

Craik, F. I. M. (1983). On the transfer of information from temporary to permanent memory. *Philosophical Transactions of the Royal Society of London, Series B, 302,* 341–359.

Craik, F. I. M. (1986). A functional account of age differences in memory. In F. Klix & H. Hagendorf (Eds.), *Human memory and cognitive capabilities, mechanisms and performances* (pp. 409–422). North Holland: Elsevier.

Craik, F. I. M., & Byrd, M. (1982). Aging and cognitive deficits: The role of attentional resources. In F. I. M. Craik & S. Trehub (Eds.), *Aging and cognitive processes* (pp. 191–211). New York: Plenum.

Craik, F. I. M., Byrd, M., & Swanson, J. M. (1987). Patterns of memory loss in three elderly samples. *Psychology and Aging, 2,* 79–86.

Craik, F. I. M., & Jacoby, L. L. (1979). Elaboration and distinctiveness in episodic memory. In L. G. Nilsson (Ed.), *Perspectives in memory research* (pp. 145–166). Hillsdale, NJ: Lawrence Erlbaum Associates.

Craik, F. I. M., & Levy, B. A. (1976). The concept of primary memory. In W. K. Estes (Ed.), *Handbook of learning and cognitive processes: Attention and memory* (Vol. 4, pp. 133–175). Hillsdale, NJ: Lawrence Erlbaum Associates.

Craik, F. I. M., & Lockhart, R. S. (1972). Levels of processing: A framework for memory research. *Journal of Verbal Learning and Verbal Behavior, 11,* 671–684.

Craik, F. I. M., & McDowd, J. M. (1987). Age differences in recall and recognition. *Journal of Experimental Psychology: Learning, Memory, and Cognition, 13,* 474–479.

Craik, F. I. M., Morris, R. G., & Gick, M. L. (1990). Adult age differences in working memory. In G. Vallar & T. Shallice (Eds.), *Neuropsychological impairments of short-term memory* (pp. 247–267). Cambridge, England: Cambridge University Press.

Craik, F. I. M., Morris, L. W., Morris, R. G., & Loewen, E. R. (1990). Aging, source amnesia, and frontal lobe functioning. *Psychology and Aging, 5,* 148–151.

Craik, F. I. M., & Rabinowitz, J. C. (1984). Age differences in the acquisition and use of verbal information. In H. Bouma & D. G. Bouwhuis (Eds.), *Attention and performance X* (pp. 471–499). Hillsdale, NJ: Lawrence Erlbaum Associates.

Craik, F. I. M., & Rabinowitz, J. C. (1985). The effects of presentation rate and encoding task on age-related memory deficits. *Journal of Gerontology, 40,* 309–315.

Craik, F. I. M., & Simon, E. (1980). Age differences in memory: The roles of attention and depth of processing. In L. W. Poon, J. L. Fozard, L. Cermak, D. Arenberg, & L. W. Thompson (Eds.), *New directions in memory and aging: Proceedings of the George Talland memorial conference* (pp. 95–112). Hillsdale, NJ: Lawrence Erlbaum Associates.

Craik, F. I. M., & Tulving, E. (1975). Depth of processing and the retention of words in episodic memory. *Journal of Experimental Psychology: General, 104,* 268–294.

Daneman, M., & Carpenter, P. A. (1980). Individual differences in working memory and reading. *Journal of Verbal Learning and Verbal Behavior, 19,* 450–466.

Daneman, M., & Tardif, T. (1987). Working memory and reading skill re-examined. In M. Coltheart (Ed.), *Attention and performance XII* (pp. 491–508). Hillsdale, NJ: Lawrence Erlbaum Associates.

Dannenbaum, S. E., Parkinson, S. R., & Inman, V. W. (1989). Short-term forgetting: Comparisons between patients with dementia of the Alzheimer type, depressed, and normal elderly. *Cognitive Neuropsychology, 5,* 213–233.

Delbecq-Derouesné, J., & Beauvois, M. F. (1989). Memory processes and aging: A defect of automatic rather than controlled processes? *Archives of Gerontology and Geriatrics, Suppl. 1,* 121–150.

Di Lollo, V. (1980). Temporal interaction in visual memory. *Journal of Experimental Psychology: General, 109,* 75–97.

Di Lollo, V., Arnett, J. L., & Kruk, R. V. (1982). Age-related changes in the rate of visual information processing. *Journal of Experimental Psychology: Human Perception and Performance, 8,* 225–237.

Dobbs, A. R., & Rule, B. G. (1987). Prospective memory and self-reports of memory abilities in older adults. *Canadian Journal of Psychology, 41,* 209–222.

Dobbs, A. R., & Rule, B. G. (1989). Adult age differences in working memory. *Psychology and Aging, 4,* 500–503.

Dywan, J., & Jacoby, L. L. (1990). Effects of aging on source monitoring: Differences in susceptibility to false fame. *Psychology and Aging, 5,* 379–387.

Einstein, G. O., & Hunt, R. R. (1980). Levels of processing and organization: Additive effects of individual item and relational processing. *Journal of Experimental Psychology: Human Learning and Memory, 6,* 588–598.

Einstein, G. O., & McDaniel, M. A. (1990). Normal aging and prospective memory. *Journal of Experimental Psychology: Learning, Memory, and Cognition, 16,* 717–726.

Einstein, G. O., McDaniel, M. A., Cunfer, A. R., & Guynn, M. J. (1991). *Aging and prospective memory: Examining the influences of self-initiated retrieval processes and mind wandering.* Manuscript submitted for publication.

Epstein, M. L., Phillips, W. D., & Johnson, S. J. (1975). Recall of related and unrelated word pairs as a function of processing level. *Journal of Experimental Psychology: Human Learning and Memory, 104,* 149–152.

Erber, J. T. (1981). Remote memory and age—A review. *Experimental Aging Research, 7,* 189–199.

Erber, J. T., Herman, T. G., & Botwinick, J. (1980). Age differences in memory as a function of depth of processing. *Experimental Aging Research, 6,* 341–348.

Evans, G. W., Brennan, P. L., Skorpovich, M. A., & Held, D. (1984). Cognitive mapping and elderly adults: Verbal and location memory for urban landmarks. *Journal of Gerontology, 39,* 452–457.

Fitzgerald, J. M., & Lawrence, R. (1984). Autobiographical memory across the life-span. *Journal of Gerontology, 39,* 692–698.

Foos, P. W., Sabol, M. A., Corral, G., & Mobley, L. (1987). Age differences in primary and secondary memory. *Bulletin of the Psychonomic Society, 25,* 159–160.

Gillund, G., & Shiffrin, R. M. (1984). A retrieval model for both recognition and recall. *Psychological Review, 91,* 1–67.

Graf, P. (1990). Life-span changes in implicit and explicit memory. *Bulletin of the Psychonomic Society, 28,* 353–358.

Guttentag, R. E., & Hunt, R. R. (1988). Adult age differences in memory for imagined and performed actions. *Journals of Gerontology: Psychological Sciences, 43,* P107–P108.

Hartley, J. T. (1988). Aging and individual differences in memory for written discourse. In L. L. Light & D. M. Burke (Eds.), *Language, memory, and aging* (pp. 36–57). New York: Cambridge University Press.

Hasher, L., & Zacks, R. T. (1979). Automatic and effortful processes in memory. *Journal of Experimental Psychology: General, 108,* 356–388.

Hasher, L. & Zacks, R. T. (1988). Working memory, comprehension, and aging: A review and a new view. In G. H. Bower (Ed.), *The psychology of learning and motivation* (Vol. 22, pp. 193–225). New York: Academic.

Hashtroudi, S., Johnson, M. K., & Chrosniak, L. D. (1989). Aging and source monitoring. *Psychology and Aging, 4,* 106–112.

Hashtroudi, S., Johnson, M. K., & Chrosniak, L. D. (1990). Aging and qualitative characteristics of memories for perceived and imagined complex events. *Psychology and Aging, 5,* 119–126.

Hashtroudi, S., Parker, E. S., Luis, J. D., & Reisen, C. A. (1989). Generation and elaboration in older adults. *Experimental Aging Research, 15,* 73–78.

Hess, T. M., Donley, J., & Vandermaas, M. O. (1989). Aging-related changes in the processing and retention of script information. *Experimental Aging Research, 15,* 89–96.

Hess, T. M., Vandermaas, M. O., Donley, J., & Snyder, S. S. (1987). Memory for sex-role consistent and inconsistent actions in young and old adults. *Journal of Gerontology, 42,* 505–511.

Hinton, G. E., & Shallice, T. (1991). Lesioning an attractor network: Investigations of acquired dyslexia. *Psychological Review, 98,* 74–95.

Howard, D. V. (1983). The effects of aging and degree of association on the semantic priming of lexical decisions. *Experimental Aging Research, 9,* 145–151.

Howard, D. V. (1988). Aging and semantic activation: The priming of semantic and episodic memories. In L. L. Light & D. M. Burke (Eds.), *Language, memory, and aging* (pp. 77–100). New York: Cambridge University Press.

Howard, D. V., Heisey, J., & Shaw, R. J. (1986). Aging and the priming of newly learned associations. *Developmental Psychology, 22,* 78–85.

Howard, D. V., Shaw, R. J., & Heisey, J. (1986). Aging and the time course of semantic activation. *Journal of Gerontology, 41,* 195–203.

Howes, J. L., & Katz, A. N. (1988). Assessing remote memory with an improved public events questionnaire. *Psychology and Aging, 3,* 142–150.

Hultsch, D. F., & Pentz, C. A. (1980). Encoding, storage, and retrieval in adult memory: The role of model assumptions. In L. W. Poon, J. L. Fozard, L. S. Cermak, D. Arenberg, & L. W. Thompson (Eds.), *New directions in memory and aging: Proceedings of the George A. Talland memorial conference.* Hillsdale, NJ: Lawrence Erlbaum Associates.

Inman, V. W., & Parkinson, S. R. (1983). Differences in Brown–Peterson recall as a function of age and retention interval. *Journal of Gerontology, 38,* 58–64.

Jacoby, L. L. (1978). On interpreting the effects of repetition: Solving a problem versus remembering a solution. *Journal of Verbal Learning and Verbal Behavior, 17,* 649–667.

Jacoby, L. L. (1983). Remembering the data: Analyzing interactive processes in reading. *Journal of Verbal Learning and Verbal Behavior, 22,* 485–508.

Jacoby, L. L. (1991). A process dissociation framework: Separating automatic from intentional uses of memory. *Journal of Memory and Language, 30,* 513–541.

Jacoby, L. L., & Bartz, W. H. (1972). Rehearsal and transfer to LTM. *Journal of Verbal Learning and Verbal Behavior, 11,* 561–565.

Jacoby, L. L., & Witherspoon, D. (1982). Remembering without awareness. *Canadian Journal of Psychology, 36,* 300–324.

Janowsky, J. S., Shimamura, A. P., & Squire, L. R. (1989). Source memory impairment in patients with frontal lobe lesions. *Neuropsychologia, 27,* 1043–1056.

Jenkins, J. J. (1979). Four points to remember: A tetrahedral model of memory experiments. In L. S. Cermak & F. I. M. Craik (Eds.), *Levels of processing in human memory* (pp. 429–446). Hillsdale, NJ: Lawrence Erlbaum Associates.

Johansson, B., & Berg, S. (1989). The robustness of the terminal decline phenomenon: Longitudinal data from the digit-span memory test. *Journals of Gerontology: Psychological Sciences, 44,* P184–P186.

Johnson, M. K., & Raye, C. L. (1981). Reality monitoring. *Psychological Review, 88,* 67–85.

Johnson, M. M., Schmitt, F. A., & Pietrukowicz, M. (1989). The memory advantages of the generation effect: Age and process differences. *Journals of Gerontology: Psychological Science, 44,* P91–P94.

Kausler, D. H. (1982). *Experimental psychology and human aging.* New York: Wiley.

Kausler, D. H., & Hakami, M. K. (1982). Frequency judgments by young and elderly adults for relevant stimuli with simultaneously presented irrelevant stimuli. *Journal of Gerontology, 37,* 438–442.

Kausler, D. H., Lichty, W., & Hakami, M. K. (1984). Frequency judgments for distractor items in a short-term memory task: Instructional variation and adult age differences. *Journal of Verbal Learning and Verbal Behavior, 23,* 660–668.

Kausler, D. H., & Phillips, P. L. (1988). Instructional variation and adult age differences in activity memory. *Experimental Aging Research, 14,* 195–199.

Kausler, D. H., & Puckett, J. M. (1980). Adult age differences in recognition memory for a non-semantic attribute. *Experimental Aging Research, 6,* 349–355.

Kausler, D. H., & Puckett, J. M. (1981). Adult age differences in memory for modality attributes. *Experimental Aging Research, 7,* 117–125.

Kausler, D. H., Salthouse, T. A., & Saults, J. S. (1987). Frequency-of-occurrence memory over the adult lifespan. *Experimental Aging Research, 13,* 159–161.

Kausler, D. H., & Wiley, J. G. (1991). Effects of short-term retrieval on adult age differences in long-term recall of actions. *Psychology and Aging, 6,* 661–665.

Kemper, S. (1988). Geriatric psycholinguistics. In L. L. Light & D. M. Burke (Eds.), *Language, memory, and aging* (pp. 58–76). New York: Cambridge University Press.

Kolers, P. A. (1973). Remembering operations. *Memory & Cognition, 1,* 347–355.

Koriat, A., Ben-Zur, H., & Sheffer, D. (1988). Telling the same story twice: Output monitoring and age. *Journal of Memory and Language, 27,* 23–39.

Lehman, E. B., & Mellinger, J. C. (1984). Effects of aging on memory for presentation modality. *Developmental Psychology, 20,* 1210–1217.

Lehman, E. B., & Mellinger, J. C. (1986). Forgetting rates in modality memory for young, mid-life, and older women. *Psychology and Aging, 1,* 178–179.

Lewis, R. S. (1989). Remembering and the pre-frontal cortex. *Psychobiology, 17,* 102–107.

Light, L. L. (1991). Memory and aging: Four hypotheses in search of data. *Annual Review of Psychology, 43,* 333–376.

Light, L. L., & Anderson, P. A. (1983). Memory for scripts in young and older adults. *Memory & Cognition, 11,* 435–444.

Light, L. L., & Anderson, P. A. (1985). Working-memory capacity, age, and memory for discourse. *Journal of Gerontology, 40,* 737–747.

Light, L. L., & Burke, D. M. (1988). Patterns of language and memory in old age. In L. L. Light & D. M. Burke (Eds.), *Language, memory, and aging* (pp. 244–271). New York: Cambridge University Press.

Light, L. L., & Singh, A. (1987). Implicit and explicit memory in young and older adults. *Journal of Experimental Psychology: Learning, Memory, and Cognition, 13,* 531–541.

Light, L. L., Singh, A., & Capps, J. L. (1986). Dissociation of memory and awareness in young and older adults. *Journal of Clinical and Experimental Neuropsychology, 8,* 62–74.

Light, L. L., & Zelinski, E. M. (1983). Memory for spatial information in young and old adults. *Developmental Psychology, 19,* 901–906.

Loewen, E. R., Shaw, R. J., & Craik, F. I. M. (1990). Age differences in components of metamemory. *Experimental Aging Research, 16,* 43–48.

Lorsbach, T. C., & Simpson, G. B. (1984). Age differences in the rate of processing in short-term memory. *Journal of Gerontology, 39,* 315–321.

Macht, M. L., & Buschke, H. (1983). Age differences in cognitive effort in recall. *Journal of Gerontology, 38,* 695–700.

Madden, D. J. (1982). Age differences and similarities in the improvement of controlled search. *Experimental Aging Research, 8,* 91–98.

Madden, D. J. (1986). Adult age differences in visual word recognition: Semantic encoding and episodic retention. *Experimental Aging Research, 12,* 71–78.

Mäntylä, T., & Bäckman, L. (1990). Encoding variability and age-related retrieval failures. *Psychology and Aging, 5,* 545–550.

Maylor, E. A. (1990). Age and prospective memory. *Quarterly Journal of Experimental Psychology: Human Experimental Psychology, 42,* 471–493.

McClelland, J. L., & Rumelhart, D. E. (1986). *Parallel distributed processing: Explorations in the microstructure of cognition: Vol. 2. Psychological and biological models.* Cambridge, MA: MIT Press.

McDaniel, M. A., Einstein, G. O., Dunay, P. K., & Cobb, R. E. (1986). Encoding difficulty and memory: Toward a unifying theory. *Journal of Memory and Language, 25,* 645–656.

McDaniel, M. A., Ryan, E. B., & Cunningham, C. J. (1989). Encoding difficulty and memory enhancement for young and older readers. *Psychology and Aging, 4,* 333–338.

McIntyre, J. S., & Craik, F. I. M. (1987). Age differences in memory for item and source information. *Canadian Journal of Psychology, 41,* 175–192.

Mitchell, D. B. (1989). How many memory systems? Evidence from aging. *Journal of Experimental Psychology: Learning, Memory, and Cognition, 15,* 31–49.

Mitchell, D. B., Brown, A. S., & Murphy, D. R. (1990). Dissociation between procedural and episodic memory: Effects of time and aging. *Psychology and Aging, 5,* 264–276.

Mitchell, D. B., Hunt, R. R., & Schmitt, F. A. (1986). The generation effect and reality monitoring: Evidence from dementia and normal aging. *Journal of Gerontology, 41,* 79–84.

Monsell, S. (1984). Components of working memory underlying verbal skills: A "distributed capacities" view. In H. Bouma & D. G. Bouwhuis (Eds.), *Attention and performance X* (pp. 327–350). Hillsdale, NJ: Lawrence Erlbaum Associates.

Moore, T. E., Richards, B., & Hood, J. (1984). Aging and the coding of spatial information. *Journal of Gerontology, 39,* 210–212.

Morris, R. G. (1986). Short-term forgetting in senile dementia of the Alzheimer's type. *Cognitive Neuropsychology, 3,* 77–79.

Moscovitch, M. (1982). A neuropsychological approach to perception and memory in normal and pathological aging. In F. I. M. Craik & S. Trehub (Eds.), *Aging and cognitive processes* (pp. 55–79). New York: Plenum.

Murdock, B. B., Jr. (1967). Recent developments in short-term memory. *British Journal of Psychology, 58,* 421–433.

Murdock, B. B., Jr. (1982). A theory of the storage and retrieval of item and associative information. *Psychological Review, 89,* 609–626.

Naveh-Benjamin, M. (1987). Coding of spatial location information: An automatic process? *Journal of Experimental Psychology: Learning, Memory, and Cognition, 13,* 595–605.

Naveh-Benjamin, M. (1988). Recognition memory of spatial location information: Another failure of automaticity. *Memory & Cognition, 16,* 437–445.

Naveh-Benjamin, M. (1990). Coding of temporal order information: An automatic process? *Journal of Experimental Psychology: Learning, Memory, and Cognition, 16,* 117–126.

Neumann, O. (1987). Beyond capacity: A functional view of attention. In H. Heuer & A. F. Sanders (Eds.), *Perspectives on perception and action* (pp. 361–394). Hillsdale, NJ: Lawrence Erlbaum Associates.

Nilsson, L. G., & Craik, F. I. M. (1990). Additive and interactive effects in memory for subject-performed tasks. *European Journal of Cognitive Psychology, 2,* 305–324.

Paivio, A. (1971). *Imagery and verbal processes.* New York: Holt, Rinehart & Winston.

Park, D. C., Cherry, K. E. Smith, A. D., & Lafronza, V. N. (1990). Effects of distinctive context on memory for objects and their locations in young and elderly adults. *Psychology and Aging, 5,* 250–255.

Park, D. C., Puglisi, J. T., & Smith, A. D. (1986). Memory for pictures: Does an age-related decline exist? *Psychology and Aging, 1,* 11–17.

Park, D. C., Puglisi, J. T., Smith, A. D., & Dudley, W. N. (1987). Cue utilization and encoding specificity in picture recognition by older adults. *Journal of Gerontology, 42,* 423–425.

Park, D. C., Puglisi, J. T., & Sovacool, M. (1983). Memory for pictures, words, and spatial location in older adults: Evidence for pictorial superiority. *Journal of Gerontology, 38,* 582–588.

Park, D. C., Royal, D., Dudley, W., & Morrell, R. (1988). Forgetting of pictures over a long retention interval in young and older adults. *Psychology and Aging, 3,* 94–95.

Park, D. C., Smith, A. D., Morrell, R. W., Puglisi, J. T., & Dudley, W. N. (1990). Effects of contextual integration on recall of pictures by older adults. *Journals of Gerontology: Psychological Sciences, 45,* P52–P57.

Parkin, A. J., & Walter, B. M. (in press). Recollective experience, normal aging, and frontal dysfunction. *Psychology and Aging, 7.*

Parkinson, S. R. (1982). Performance deficits in short-term memory tasks: A comparison of amnesic Korsakoff patients and the aged. In L. S. Cermak (Ed.), *Human memory and amnesia* (pp. 77–96). Hillsdale, NJ: Lawrence Erlbaum Associates.

Parkinson, S. R., Lindholm, J. M., & Inman, V. W. (1982). An analysis of age differences in immediate recall. *Journal of Gerontology, 37,* 425–431.

Patterson, K. E., & Baddeley, A. D. (1977). When face recognition fails. *Journal of Experimental Psychology: Human Learning and Memory, 3,* 406–417.

Pezdek, K. (1983). Memory for items and their spatial locations by young and elderly adults. *Developmental Psychology, 19,* 895–900.

Puckett, J. M., & Stockburger, D. W. (1988). Absence of age-related proneness to short-term retroactive interference in the absence of rehearsal. *Psychology and Aging, 3,* 342–347.

Puglisi, J. T. (1986). Age-related slowing in memory search for three-dimensional objects. *Journal of Gerontology, 41,* 72–78.

Puglisi, J. T., & Park, D. C. (1987). Perceptual elaboration and memory in older adults. *Journal of Gerontology, 42,* 160–162.

Puglisi, J. T., Park, D. C., Smith, A. D., & Dudley, W. N. (1988). Age differences in encoding specificity. *Journals of Gerontology: Psychological Sciences, 43,* P145–P150.

Rabinowitz, J. C. (1984). Aging and recognition failure. *Journal of Gerontology, 39,* 65–71.

Rabinowitz, J. C. (1986). Priming in episodic memory. *Journal of Gerontology, 41,* 204–213.

Rabinowitz, J. C. (1989a). Judgments of origin and generation effects: Comparisons between young and elderly adults. *Psychology and Aging, 4,* 259–268.

Rabinowitz, J. C. (1989b). Age deficits in recall under optimal study conditions. *Psychology and Aging, 4,* 378–380.

Rabinowitz, J. C., & Ackerman, B. P. (1982). General encoding of episodic events by elderly adults. In F. I. M. Craik & S. Trehub (Eds.), *Aging and cognitive processes* (pp. 145–154). New York: Plenum.

Rabinowitz, J. C., & Craik, F. I. M. (1986). Prior retrieval effects in young and old adults. *Journal of Gerontology, 41,* 368–375.

Rabinowitz, J. C., Craik, F. I. M., & Ackerman, B. P. (1982). A processing resource account of age differences in recall. *Canadian Journal of Psychology, 36,* 325–344.

Rankin, J. L., & Collins, M. (1985). Adult age differences in memory elaboration. *Journal of Gerontology, 40,* 451–458.

Rankin, J. L., & Collins, M. (1986). The effects of memory elaboration on adult age differences in incidental recall. *Experimental Aging Research, 12,* 231–234.

Rankin, J. L., & Firnhaber, S. (1986). Adult age differences in memory: Effects of distinctive and common encodings. *Experimental Aging Research, 12,* 141–146.

Reder, L. M., Wible, C., & Martin, J. (1986). Differential memory changes with age: Exact retrieval versus plausible inference. *Journal of Experimental Psychology: Learning, Memory, and Cognition, 12,* 72–81.

Richardson-Klavehn, A., & Bjork, R. A. (1988). Measures of memory. *Annual Review of Psychology, 39,* 475–543.

Rissenberg, M., & Glanzer, M. (1987). Free-recall and word finding ability in normal aging and senile dementia of the Alzheimer's type—The effect of item concreteness. *Journal of Gerontology, 42,* 318–322.

Roediger, H. L., Weldon, M. S., & Challis, B. H. (1989). Explaining dissociations between implicit and explicit measures of retention: A processing account. In H. L. Roediger & F. I. M. Craik (Eds.), *Varieties of memory and consciousness: Essays in honour of Endel Tulving* (pp. 3–41). Hillsdale, NJ: Lawrence Erlbaum Associates.

Rose, T. L., Yesavage, J. A., Hill, R. D., & Bower, G. H. (1986). Priming effects and recognition memory in young and elderly adults. *Experimental Aging Research, 12,* 31–37.

Rubin, D. C. (1982). On the retention function for autobiographical memory. *Journal of Verbal Learning and Verbal Behavior, 21,* 21–38.

Rubin, D. C., Wetzler, S. E., & Nebes, R. D. (1986). Autobiographical memory across the lifespan. In D. C. Rubin (Ed.), *Autobiographical memory* (pp. 202–221). Cambridge, England: Cambridge University Press.

Rybarczyk, B. D., Hart, R. P., & Harkins, S. W. (1987). Age and forgetting rate with pictorial stimuli. *Psychology and Aging, 2,* 404–406.

Salthouse, T. A. (1982). *Adult cognition: An experimental psychology of human aging.* New York: Springer-Verlag.

Salthouse, T. A. (1985). *A theory of cognitive aging.* Amsterdam: North Holland.

Salthouse, T. (1990). Working memory as a processing resource in cognitive aging. Special issue: Limited resource models of cognitive development. *Developmental Review, 10,* 101–124.

Salthouse, T. A., & Babcock, R. L. (1991). Decomposing adult age differences in working memory. *Developmental Psychology, 27,* 763–776.

Salthouse, T. A., Babcock, R. L., & Shaw, R. J. (1991). Effects of adult age on structural and operational capacities in working memory. *Psychology and Aging, 6,* 118–127.

Salthouse, T. A., Kausler, D. H., & Saults, J. S. (1988). Investigation of student status, background variables, and feasibility of standard tasks in cognitive aging research. *Psychology and Aging, 3,* 29–37.

Salthouse, T. A., Mitchell, D. R., Skovronek, E., & Babcock, R. L. (1989). Effects of adult age and working memory on reasoning and spatial abilities. *Journal of Experimental Psychology: Learning, Memory, and Cognition, 15,* 507–516.

Saltz, E., & Donnenwerth-Nolan, S. (1981). Does motoric imagery facilitate memory for sentences? A selective interference test. *Journal of Verbal Learning and Verbal Behavior, 20,* 322–332.

Sanders, R. E., Wise, J. L., Liddle, C. L., & Murphy, M. D. (1990). Adult age comparisons in the processing of event frequency information. *Psychology and Aging, 5,* 172–177.

Schacter, D. L. (1987a). Implicit memory: History and current status. *Journal of Experimental Psychology: Learning, Memory, and Cognition, 13,* 368–379.

Schacter, D. L. (1987b). Memory, amnesia, and frontal lobe dysfunction. *Psychobiology, 15,* 21–36.

Schacter, D. L., Harbluk, J. L., & McLachlan, D. (1984). Retrieval without recollection: An experimental analysis of source amnesia. *Journal of Verbal Learning and Verbal Behavior, 23,* 593–611.

Schacter, D. L., Kaszniak, A. W., Kihlstrom, J. F., & Valdiserri, M. (1991). The relation between source memory and aging. *Psychology and Aging, 6,* 559–568.

Schonfield, D., & Robertson, B. A. (1966). Memory storage and aging. *Canadian Journal of Psychology, 20,* 228–236.

Sharps, M. J. (1991). Spatial memory in young and elderly adults: The category structure of stimulus sets. *Psychology and Aging, 6,* 309–312.

Sharps, M. J., & Gollin, E. S. (1987). Memory for object locations in young and elderly adults. *Journal of Gerontology, 42,* 336–341.

Sharps, M. J., & Gollin, E. S. (1988). Aging and free recall for objects located in space. *Journals of Gerontology: Psychological Sciences, 43,* P8–P11.

Shepard, R. N. (1984). Ecological constraints on internal representation: Resonant kinematics of perceiving, imagining, thinking and dreaming. *Psychological Review, 91,* 417–447.

Shiffrin, R. M. (1976). Capacity limitations in information processing, attention, and memory. In W. K. Estes (Ed.), *Handbook of learning and cognitive processes* (Vol. 4, pp. 177–236). Hillsdale, NJ: Lawrence Erlbaum Associates.

Shimamura, A. P., & Squire, L. R. (1987). A neuropsychological study of fact memory and source amnesia. *Journal of Experimental Psychology: Learning, Memory, and Cognition, 13,* 464–473.

Shimamura, A. P., & Squire, L. R. (in press). The relationship between fact and source memory: Findings from amnesic patients and normal subjects. *Psychobiology.*

Simon, E. (1979). Depth and elaboration of processing in relation to age. *Journal of Experimental Psychology: Human Learning and Memory, 5,* 115–124.

Slamecka, N. J., & Graf, P. (1978). The generation effect: Delineation of a phenomenon. *Journal of Experimental Psychology: Human Learning and Memory, 4,* 592–604.

Spilich, G. J. (1983). Life-span components of text processing: Structural and procedural differences. *Journal of Verbal Learning and Verbal Behavior, 22,* 231–244.

Squire, L. R. (1989). On the course of forgetting in very long-term memory. *Journal of Experimental Psychology: Learning, Memory, and Cognition, 15,* 241–245.

Sternberg, S. (1969). On the discovery of processing stages: Some extensions of Donders' method. *Acta Psychologica, 30,* 276–315.

Stine, E. A. L., & Wingfield, A. (1990). The assessment of qualitative age differences in discourse processing. In T. M. Hess (Ed.), *Aging and cognition: Knowledge organization and utilization* (pp. 33–92). Amsterdam: North Holland.

Till, R. E., Bartlett, J. C., & Doyle, A. H. (1982). Age differences in picture memory with resemblance and discrimination tasks. *Experimental Aging Research, 8,* 179–184.

Trahan, D. E., Larrabee, G. J., & Levin, H. S. (1986). Age-related differences in recognition memory for pictures. *Experimental Aging Research, 12,* 147–150.

Treat, N. J., & Reese, H. W. (1976). Age, pacing, and imagery in paired-associate learning. *Developmental Psychology, 12,* 119–124.

Tulving, E. (1972). Episodic and semantic memory. In E. Tulving & W. Donaldson (Eds.), *Organization of memory* (pp. 382–404). New York: Academic.

Tulving, E. (1983). *Elements of episodic memory.* New York: Oxford University Press.

Tulving, E. (1985a). Memory and consciousness. *Canadian Psychology, 26,* 1–12.

Tulving, E. (1985b). How many memory systems are there? *American Psychologist, 40,* 385–398.

Tulving, E., & Colotla, V. A. (1970). Free recall of trilingual lists. *Cognitive Psychology, 1,* 86–98.

Tulving, E., & Schacter, D. L. (1990). Priming and human memory systems. *Science, 247,* 301–306.

Tulving, E., Schacter, D. L., & Stark, H. A. (1982). Priming effects in word-fragment completion are independent of recognition memory. *Journal of Experimental Psychology: Learning, Memory, and Cognition, 8,* 336–342.

Tulving, E., & Thomson, D. M. (1973). Encoding specificity and retrieval processes in episodic memory. *Psychological Review, 80,* 352–373.

Waddell, K. J., & Rogoff, B. (1981). Effect of contextual organization on spatial memory of middle-aged and older women. *Developmental Psychology, 17,* 878–885.

Warrington, E. K., & Weiskrantz, L. (1974). The effect of prior learning on subsequent retention in amnesic patients. *Neuropsychologia, 12,* 419–428.

Waugh, N. C., & Norman, D. A. (1965). Primary memory. *Psychological Review, 72,* 89–104.

Welford, A. T. (1958). *Ageing and human skill.* London: Oxford University Press.

West, R. L., & Boatwright, L. K. (1983). Age differences in cued recall and recognition under varying encoding and retrieval conditions. *Experimental Aging Research, 9,* 185–189.

White, N., & Cunningham, W. R. (1982). What is the evidence for retrieval problems in the elderly? *Experimental Aging Research, 8,* 169–171.

Wickelgren, W. A. (1974). Single-trace fragility theory of memory dynamics. *Memory & Cognition, 2,* 775–780.

Wiegersma, S., & Meertse, K. (1990). Subjective ordering, working memory, and aging. *Experimental Aging Research, 16,* 73–77.

Wiegersma, S., Van der Scheer, E., & Hijman, R. (1990). Subjective ordering, short-term memory and the frontal lobes. *Neuropsychologia, 28,* 95–98.

Wingfield, A., Stine, A. L., Lahar, C. J., & Aberdeen, J. S. (1988). Does the capacity of working memory change with age? *Experimental Aging Research, 14,* 103–107.

Witherspoon, D., & Moscovitch, M. (1989). Stochastic independence between two implicit memory tasks. *Journal of Experimental Psychology: Learning, Memory, and Cognition, 15,* 22–30.

Woodward, A. E., Bjork, R. A., & Jongeward, R. H., Jr. (1973). Recall and recognition as a function of primary rehearsal. *Journal of Verbal Learning and Verbal Behavior, 12,* 608–617.

Zacks, R. T., & Hasher, L. (1988). Capacity theory and the processing of inferences. In L. L. Light & D. M. Burke (Eds.), *Language, memory, and aging* (pp. 154–170). New York: Cambridge University Press.

Zacks, R. T., Hasher, L., Doren, B., Hamm, V., & Attig, M. S. (1987). Encoding and memory of explicit and implicit information. *Journal of Gerontology, 42,* 418–422.

Zelinski, E. M., & Light, L. L. (1988). Young and older adults' use of context in spatial memory. *Psychology and Aging, 3,* 99–101.

CHAPTER THREE

The Organization of Memory in Old Age

Leah L. Light
Pitzer College

Memory for written or spoken discourse is most likely to be a natural by-product of language comprehension (Bransford & Johnson, 1972; Craik, 1983). Comprehension requires both that the memory structures which represent our knowledge about language and about the world at large be intact and that the processes which operate on these knowledge structures be effective. Hence, any changes in memory structures or in processes that impact on natural language understanding would be expected to have negative consequences for memory in old age. Indeed, one frequently cited account of age-related memory impairments is that older adults have a specific impairment in language comprehension which results in impoverished semantic encoding of new information (e.g., Cohen, 1979, 1988; Craik & Byrd, 1982; Craik & Rabinowitz, 1984). In this chapter, the focus is on a circumscribed set of issues that relate to the representation of knowledge in memory and to the role that general world knowledge has in comprehension and memory for new information in young and older adults. The chapter is divided into two sections. The first discusses the representation of conceptual information in young and older adults. The second considers the representation of general world knowledge in comprehension and memory.

THE REPRESENTATION
OF CONCEPTUAL INFORMATION

The possibility that comprehension failures are responsible for memory impairment in old age has been tested within the framework of network models of memory (e.g., Anderson, 1983; Collins & Loftus,. 1975). According to Anderson, all factual knowledge, both semantic and episodic, is organized in networks consisting of nodes, which stand for concepts or propositions, and these nodes are connected by associative pathways. When a concept is encountered, its node is activated, and activation also spreads along associative pathways to related nodes, making them more available for additional cognitive processing. Spreading activation is viewed as the mechanism underlying retrieval of both semantic and episodic information. Both rapid, automatic processes and slower, expectation-driven, attentional, or effortful, processes are involved in spreading activation (Neely, 1977; Posner & Snyder, 1975). These activation processes, both automatic and attentional, play an important part in natural language understanding. They have been implicated in perception of words in spoken or written form (McClelland & Rumelhart, 1981), in determining the syntactic structure of sentences (Tanenhaus, Dell, & Carlson, 1987), and in deriving the meaning of single sentences and entire discourses (Kintsch, 1988). Activation of pragmatic or general world knowledge embodied in schemata is necessary for making inferences, for establishing the topic of a discourse, and for determining the antecedents of pronouns. Hence, differences across age either in the way knowledge is represented in memory or in the way that activation proceeds could result in comprehension differences and these, in turn, could produce age decrements in memory. A similar line of reasoning has been used to account for memory deficits in Alzheimer's disease. Weingartner, Grafman, Boutelle, Kaye, and Martin (1983) have suggested that deficits in retrieval of semantic memory underlie problems in remembering recent events in this dementia. Bayles and Kaszniak (1987) have also made a case for the centrality of a semantic deficit to memory impairment in Alzheimer's disease, but, unlike Weingartner et al., they implicated deterioration in both semantic structures and access to them. To the extent, then, that there are commonalities between normal aging and Alzheimer's disease, we might expect to find differences in the representation or retrieval of concepts in young and older adults.

In this section, we examine research bearing on possible age differences in conceptual organization, drawing upon studies of the representation of individual word meanings, schematic information, and everyday problem solving. One point that should be clear from the discussion of network models is that conclusions about age differences in mental representation require assumptions about age constancy in the processes that act on mental structures. Different tasks impose different processing constraints and the outcomes from experiments using these tasks therefore may be discrepant. For instance, it has been observed that Alzheimer's disease patients have difficulty in generating specific properties of objects but that their response times for deciding that the object and its properties are related show the same profile as that of normal adults (e.g., Nebes & Brady, 1988). Focusing on the latency data leads to the conclusion that conceptual structure is intact, whereas focusing on the generation data would lead to the opposite conclusion. In short, when considering the outcome of particular studies, it is also necessary to evaluate the constraints of the paradigms involved.

The Representation of Word Meanings

Evidence about possible age differences in the representation of word meanings comes from a variety of sources, including word-finding difficulties, responses to word association tasks, semantic priming in lexical decision and word naming, and judgments of similarity or relatedness of concepts.

Word-Finding Difficulties. Word-finding problems are characteristic of Alzheimer's disease. These problems are manifested in spontaneous speech, where they are indexed by increasing use of circumlocutions rather than specific terms, and by empty phrases, indefinite terms, and pronouns without antecedents (see Nebes, 1989, for a review). They also show up in verbal fluency tasks in which people are given a fixed amount of time to generate as many words as they can that meet specific criteria, such as beginning with a particular letter or being members of particular categories. For instance, Ober, Dronkers, Koss, Delis, and Friedland (1986) asked subjects to name items found in a supermarket. Demented patients not only produced fewer items overall, but also produced fewer items within a semantic subcategory than normal elderly and were more likely to just name a subcategory (e.g., vegetables) without producing category members. Finally, both confrontation naming (e.g., Huff, Corkin, & Growdon, 1986) and naming to definition (Rissenberg & Glanzer, 1987) are severely impaired in Alzheimer's disease. These changes are no doubt subject to multiple causation. For instance, using pronouns without antecedents may reflect a deficit in pragmatic aspects of language leading to a reduction in consideration for the needs of listeners. Reductions in verbal fluency may represent changes in attentional aspects of memory search in Alzheimer's disease. Increasing frequency of circumlocutions and problems in both object naming and naming to definition may reflect specific deficits in retrieval of lexical information from semantic memory. However, any or all of these also may indicate changes in either the completeness or the organization of conceptual knowledge. That is, if semantic representations in Alzheimer's disease contain fewer features or if the associations between concepts and their attributes have a different distribution of strengths than they do in normal individuals, then changes such as those just described would not be unexpected.

Normal aging also is accompanied by increased word-finding difficulties. For instance, in retelling stories, pronouns may be used without antecedents (e.g., Cohen, 1979; Obler, 1980; Pratt, Boyes, Robins, & Manchester, 1989; Ulatowska, Cannito, Hayashi, & Fleming, 1985). One possibility is that memory for character names is impaired and that the use of pronouns is a strategy for coping with this memory problem. Alternatively, problems in retrieving specific words may be the underlying cause. In spontaneous speech, there is also some evidence for increased frequency of pauses, which may signal word-finding problems, but the findings are not consistent across studies (e.g., Cooper, 1990; Kynette & Kemper, 1986).

Declines in verbal fluency often are reported in studies of normal aging (e.g., Brown & Mitchell, in press; Howard, 1980; McCrae, Arenberg, & Costa, 1987; Obler & Albert, 1985; Schaie & Parham, 1977), although they are not always found (e.g., Craik, Byrd, & Swanson, 1987). Surprisingly, fine-grained analyses comparing the protocols of young and older adults similar to those conducted by Ober et al. (1986) have not been undertaken for fluency tasks, so that we have no way of knowing exactly why older adults produce fewer words. One possibility is that older adults are simply slower (in either writing or speaking or in carrying out other cognitive operations) and therefore are penalized by the short time (usually less than 90 s) allocated for word generation. However, providing longer time periods for responding does not result in similar asymptotes for young and old (Brown & Mitchell, in press).

Decreased verbal fluency, however, should not be interpreted as evidence for loss of word meanings in old age. There is little evidence for a decline in vocabulary size as people grow older (e.g., Salthouse, 1982, 1988). Nor is there any reason to believe that older adults are prone to loss of meanings for individual words or domains as has been reported in both Alzheimer's disease (e.g., Chertkow, Bub, & Seidenberg, 1989) and aphasia (e.g., Warrington & Shallice, 1984). Older adults nevertheless do have more word-finding difficulties than young adults. For instance, they have more tip-of-the-tongue experiences in which words are temporarily unretrievable, but these words ultimately do become available (Burke, MacKay, Worthley, & Wade, 1991; Cohen & Faulkner, 1986).

(Although Maylor, 1990a, did not find an increase in tip-of-the-tongue experiences in a naming-to-definition task, her stimuli were names of objects, nonobject nouns, adjectives, and verbs—categories of items for which Burke et al. found little age difference in number of tip-of-the-tongue experiences.) For both young and older adults, persistent alternates that come to mind during tip-of-the-tongue states are virtually always from the same grammatical class as the target, suggesting that the organization of these grammatical classes is intact in old age (Burke et al., 1991). Older adults do produce fewer semantic features of the targets than young adults when in a tip-of-the-tongue state (Maylor, 1990b). This could be interpreted as a loss of semantic associations in old age. However, phonological features also are produced less often (Burke et al., 1991; Maylor, 1990a). These results are consistent with a transmission deficit in old age which reduces the availability of both semantic and phonological information (cf. Burke et al., 1991). Thus, in tip-of-the-tongue experiences, it is probably access to the phonological realizations of words from semantic information that is problematic, not the structure of the semantic concepts themselves.

Picture-naming errors also increase in old age, though perhaps not until the eighth decade of life (e.g., Albert, Heller, & Milberg, 1988; Borod, Goodglass, & Kaplan, 1980; Van Gorp, Satz, Kiersch, & Henry, 1986; but see Mitchell, 1989, for a finding of no age difference). The most frequent type of naming error for all age groups is a semantically related word. An increase with age in the proportion of semantically related errors could be indicative of word-finding problems, if the errors are circumlocutions (e.g., "cutting the wood" for "sawing"), or could signal a breakdown in organization or activation of information within specific semantic domains if the errors are near synonyms or responses in the same category as the correct word. On an action-naming task, Bowles, Ober, and Albert (1987) found that the frequency of semantically related errors increased more with age than did the frequencies of near synonyms and circumlocutions. When their frequencies are converted to proportions, however, this effect disappears, with about two thirds of all errors being semantically related words for both old and young. Neither Albert et al. nor Nicholas, Obler, Albert, and Goodglass (1985) differentiated between near synonyms and semantically related errors. In neither case, however, do the data suggest that the relative frequency of semantic associations increases with age; both show drops in the proportion of semantically related errors and increases in the proportion of circumlocutions. These results seem more in keeping with lexical retrieval failures than with semantic deficits. An additional reason for believing that confrontation naming errors in old age arise from difficulties in accessing lexical entries from semantic information is that phonemic cues are equally helpful as hints to young and older adults and semantic cues are not very helpful to either age group (Nicholas et al., 1985).

Finally, evidence with respect to older adults' ability to produce words when given their definitions is mixed. Rissenberg and Glanzer (1987) found no age differences for either concrete or abstract common words, but others report age differences on this task. Maylor (1990a) found that the number of correct responses to definitions of rare words dropped from the 50s to the 70s. Older adults produce fewer words in naming-to-definition tasks when neutral or unrelated primes are given, but not when the correct response or a word beginning with the same initial letters is used as the prime (Bowles & Poon, 1985), again suggesting a problem in lexical access rather than in availability of semantic information. In the Bowles and Poon study, however, older adults were slowed more than young adults when semantically related primes were given and were more likely to err by giving the prime as the target word in this condition. One interpretation of this result is that older adults have difficulty in rejecting the semantically related primes as the targets; this would suggest loss of semantic information needed to distinguish between concepts. However, in this study, the correct word also was used as a prime on some trials, possibly engendering the use of a strategy whereby the prime is first examined to determine if it is the target. When the correct word was not used as a prime, young and older adults did not differ in responses to semantically related targets, suggesting that the age difference in the earlier study was due to strategy differences rather than to breakdown of semantic fields (Bowles, 1989). This interpretation is bolstered by Maylor's (1990a) finding that both age and semantic relatedness of a potential blocking word presented after the definition affected correct responses, but that these factors did not interact; in her study no targets were presented as potential blockers.

In sum, older adults exhibit some of the same types of word-finding difficulties that Alzheimer's patients do, although the severity of the problem is considerably less in normal aging. The evidence, however, is generally consistent with the hypothesis that word-finding problems in old age arise from a deficit in the transmission of activation from semantic to phonological concepts and provide scant evidence for age-related changes in semantic organization as such.

Word Associations.   In free-association tasks, the instructions are to give the first word that comes to mind when a stimulus word is presented. According to semantic network models, presentation of the stimulus word activates the node standing for this concept. Activation also spreads automatically from this node to all concepts having attributes in common with it and hence sharing pathways with it. The first word to come to mind should be the one whose concept has the most shared properties or whose semantic distance is the smallest. In controlled-association tasks, further restrictions are placed on the response to be given. For instance, the task may be to produce a superordinate of the word or a physical characteristic of an object or an action that can be performed with the object. Here, network models would assume that there is a compound stimulus consisting of the word and the type of response to be produced. Activation from this compound stimulus may converge automatically on an appropriate response. Alternatively, all properties of the stimulus concept may be activated and the concept associated with the pathway labeled with the appropriate relation may be selected as the response. Both types of word association task provide data relevant to determining whether semantic organization varies with age.

There are indications that the characteristics of word associations remain the same across age. First, in free-association tasks, young adults typically produce paradigmatic rather than syntagmatic responses in free-association tasks. That is, they are more likely to give as responses words that are in the same grammatical class as the stimulus and that share features of meaning with it. Syntagmatic responses, words that differ in grammatical class from the stimulus and that may occur sequentially in the same sentence with the stimulus, are less common. Syntagmatic responding decreases in frequency, at least for some form classes, as children grow older (Nelson, 1977). Moreover, paradigmatic responding decreases in Alzheimer's disease (Santo Pietro & Goldfarb, 1985). A decline in paradigmatic responding in old age would suggest changes in the relative strengths of certain kinds of associations or loss of particular types of associations. Although Riegel and Riegel (1964) reported a drop in the percentage of paradigmatic responses in their German-speaking sample, this result has not been replicated in other investigations that were careful to take into account the verbal abilities of the subjects (Burke & Peters, 1986; Lovelace & Cooley, 1982; Scialfa & Margolis, 1986).

Second, Burke and Peters (1986) found that neither young nor older adults produced responses that were phonemically similar to stimulus words. Sensory characteristics of objects also were given infrequently as associates by members of either age group. There have been suggestions that older adults encode verbal materials more shallowly, that is, in terms of phonological properties or more surface characteristics of objects (e.g., Craik, 1977; Eysenck, 1974; see Light, 1991, for a review). This would be especially likely to occur if the pattern of existing associations were different in old age so that phonological connections were spared whereas associations based on meaning were differentially lost. Burke and Peters's finding argues against such loss of features.

Third, there is evidence that young and older adults show the same extent of specificity in the associations that they produce. Lovelace and Cooley (1982) asked young and older adults to free associate to groups of three words. The word triads were of three types: (a) three members of the same category (e.g., *onion, carrot, spinach*), (b) three words sharing a sensory property (e.g., *snow, teeth, pearl*), or (c) three words sharing both category membership and having a common property (e.g., *cherry, apple, cranberry*). Responses were categorized as superordinates (category name), coordinates (members of the same category), adjectival (a shared sensory characteristic), function (a verb that described a shared function or a noun related to that function), or miscellaneous. Category triads evoked mostly superordinates and property triads evoked mostly adjectivals. Triads that shared both category membership and sensory properties evoked superordinates slightly less often than category triads did; they also evoked adjectivals much less frequently than did property triads, though more often than category triads. Function terms were produced about 10%–15% of the time for both category and category + property triads. However, the distribution of responses across types was very similar for young and older adults, suggesting that the relative strengths of different types of associations do not vary across age.

The triad task used by Lovelace and Cooley (1982), though billed as a free-association task, is similar to controlled-association tasks in that subjects were requested to provide a response evoked by the triad as a whole. This instruction would appear to require some analysis as to the nature of the commonality among triad members and might be interpreted as a controlled-association task. Indeed, results of controlled-association tasks support conclusions drawn from the triad task. For instance, Nebes and Brady (1988) asked young and older adults to produce three types of responses to words naming objects—a characteristic action, a distinctive physical feature, and a general associate. The percentage of acceptable responses did not differ reliably across age, although older adults made somewhat fewer correct responses for features and associates. Similarly, Stine (1986) asked people to produce up to seven properties for each of 12 nouns in a category. The breakdown of attributes into those referring to physical features, functional features, specifiers (elaborations on functions that specify their objects), category names, and exemplars was very similar for young and old. The one exception was that older adults were more likely than young adults to enumerate alternative features for an object or to name a dimension without choosing a particular value (e.g., "can be white or green or purple"). The import of this is not clear, but it may mean simply that older adults are being more careful to be precise; they also are more likely to give elaborations when naming objects, saying "propeller on an airplane" rather than just "propeller" (Nicholas et al., 1985).

Howard (1980) asked young, middle-aged, and older adults to generate members of 21 taxonomic categories. She then computed the correlations, for each category, between the frequencies with which members of all pairs of age groups produced particular items. Across all 21 categories, the mean values were .85 for the young–old correlation and .90 for both the young–middle and middle–old correlations. Similar results also have been obtained by Brown and Mitchell (in press). In another study, Howard (1979) collected normative data on property associations and observed similar patterns of production frequencies across age. On the assumption that frequency of response reflects associative strength between stimulus words and responses, the results of these studies strongly suggest that the strengths of particular types of associations do not vary across age.

There has been some debate as to whether older adults' associative responses are more variable than those of younger adults. Variability has been defined in a number of different ways, including the number of different responses given to a word, the number of unique responses generated, and the proportion of subjects producing the most common response to a word. As noted by Burke and Peters (1986), response variability would be expected to increase if older adults have atypical associations or if features important to meaning were absent. And indeed, the word associations of patients with Alzheimer's disease do become more idiosyncratic (Santo Pietro & Goldfarb, 1985). Although some studies have reported that normal older adults produce a greater number of different associates or more unique associates (Riegel & Riegel, 1964; Tresselt & Mayzner, 1964), such differences generally are not observed when young and older adults are carefully equated on education or on verbal ability as assessed by vocabulary tests (Bowles, Williams, & Poon, 1983; Burke & Peters, 1986; Howard, 1979, 1980; Lovelace & Cooley, 1982; Scialfa & Margolis, 1986). Moreover, there is little evidence for age-related differences in proportion of people producing the most common responses in their own age group or in proportion of people producing the most common response in previously published norms (Bowles et al., 1983; Burke & Peters, 1986; Howard, 1979, 1980; Perlmutter, 1979; Riegel & Riegel, 1964; Scialfa & Margolis, 1986; but see Tresselt & Mayzner, 1964, for contradictory evidence, and Lovelace & Cooley, 1982, for mixed results).

Before leaving the topic of word associations, there is one final point to be made. Although patterns of word associations remain remarkably stable across age, the specific items produced are not always identical. In Lovelace and Cooley's (1982) study, the most commonly produced response was the same for young and older adults for 45 of the 56 stimulus words. For all but two of the other stimulus words, the most common response of the old was one of the three most frequent responses of the young. On the other hand, agreement was lower in Burke and Peters's (1986) study; agreement in the top three responses was only 61.5% in their samples of young and old. The meaning of such findings is not easy to assess. Because test–retest reliability is not available, it is impossible to tell whether differences across age represent variations in mental contents that exceed what would be expected if individuals within an age group were tested on two occasions. Overall, our review of this literature shows considerable stability in the types of responses that older adults make and in the production frequencies for particular associates.

Lexical Decision and Word-Naming Tasks.   It takes less time to decide whether a string of letters is a word or to simply name a target when it is preceded by a semantically related prime word or by an appropriate sentence context than when it is preceded by an unrelated prime (Meyer & Schvaneveldt, 1971; Stanovich & West, 1983). Such semantic priming effects generally are interpreted as evidence for spreading activation in a network and, therefore, similar patterns of semantic priming in young and older adults would constitute evidence for the intactness of the semantic system.[1] That is, differences across age in the sensitivity of priming to variations in the associative strength of primes and targets, or to different prime-target semantic relationships, or to sentence contexts would suggest a semantic deficit. As we note later, however, the available evidence from semantic priming studies points to the absence of such a deficit.

Howard (1983a) varied category dominance of prime-target pairs in a lexical decision task. High-dominance pairs included targets that were common responses to the category name in a controlled-association task (*bird-robin*) whereas low-dominance pairs had less frequently produced targets (*bird-duck*). Young and older adults had equivalent amounts of priming regardless of category dominance. Unfortunately, however, high-dominance pairs failed to produce larger priming effects, a surprising result, so it is not easy to interpret her results. Less ambiguous results were obtained by Balota and Duchek (1988) who varied associative strength between prime and target in a word-naming task. Half of their prime-target pairs consisted of category-exemplar pairs, divided between high- and low-category dominance pairs, and the remainder consisted of free associates, again divided between pairs of high and low associative strength. There was a small, but reliable, tendency for the effect of associative strength on magnitude of priming to be larger for the old than

---

[1]A cautionary note is in order here. In our discussion we assume the existence of lexical entries in a network representation. This assumption has been called into question (Seidenberg & McClelland, 1989).

for the young, perhaps because older adults are slower in lexical access, giving an opportunity for greater spread of activation prior to response.

With respect to type of association, comparable priming effects have been obtained in young and old with a variety of prime-target relationships. For instance, Howard, McAndrews, and Lasaga (1981) asked subjects to respond "yes" when two letter strings were both words and "no" if either was a nonword. Positive responses to word pairs were speeded to the same extent in young and old when both were members of the same category (*rain snow*) and when one word was a descriptive property of the other (*rain wet*). Burke and Yee (1984) presented sentences containing verbs that implied instruments (e.g., *The cook cut the meat*) and then tested lexical decision for these instruments (e.g., *knife*) or for unrelated words (e.g., *key*); the magnitude of the priming effect (the difference in latency between related and unrelated words) did not vary with age.

Finding that facilitation effects remain about the same with age across a range of associative strengths and associative relationships provides support for the proposition that the structure of word meanings is unaffected by aging. Because neither lexical decision nor naming of single words requires an explicit statement of the relationships between primes and targets, however, it constitutes relatively weak support for this proposition. That is, priming effects would be expected to stay the same if associations between concepts were intact even if the nature of the relationship (its label) were no longer available. Priming sometimes is observed in patients who perform poorly on overt semantic judgment tasks (Milberg & Blumstein, 1981). In the case of sentence-priming tasks, however, facilitation would not be expected unless subjects were able to integrate the meanings of individual words to produce a semantic reading of the sentence as a whole. Thus, the fact that older adults show at least as much facilitation in lexical decision and naming tasks as young adults when sentence primes are used provides stronger evidence that word meanings are intact in old age. For instance, in Madden's (1986) study, lexical decision for the word *books* was faster when it was preceded by the congruous prime *The accountant balanced the* than when it was preceded by the neutral prime *They said it was the,* and the extent of this facilitation was similar across age. Similar results have been obtained in other studies (Burke & Harrold, 1988; Burke & Yee, 1984; Cohen & Faulkner, 1983; Madden, 1988, 1989; Nebes, Boller, & Holland, 1986).

Thus far, we have been concerned primarily with the similarity of *patterns* of priming across age. The sheer *magnitude* of priming effects also might be informative about conceptual organization. Chiarello (1990) noted that "if semantic representations were degraded, lost, or no longer 'hooked up' with related meanings, or if lexical representations were no longer indexed semantically, then all semantic priming would be preclud-ed'' (p. 6). One implication of this is that even moderate amounts of dis-ruption of the semantic system could have repercussions for activation processes. Hence, finding reduced semantic priming in old age might sug-gest damage to the conceptual system. However, other interpretations of such findings also would be possible. To the extent that semantic prim-ing involves attentional processing and older adults are deficient in at-tention, reductions in priming would be expected in old age. Also, obtaining priming effects presumably depends on the prime having been processed semantically (Smith, Theodor, & Franklin, 1983). As noted earli-er, older adults are sometimes said to process semantic information less thoroughly than younger adults (but see Light, 1991). If this were true, reduced priming effects in old age would be unsurprising.

Finding enhanced priming in old age also might be consistent with im-paired semantic memory (cf. similar arguments about priming after brain injury by Chiarello, 1990). In some network models, activation from a node is divided among pathways leading from that node so that the amount of activation for a particular pathway would depend on the num-ber of other pathways leading from its node of origin (Anderson, 1983). If old age were accompanied by a reduction in the number of associa-tions per concept, the remaining associations might show enhanced prim-ing. Chertkow et al. (1989) tested this hypothesis for patients with Alzheimer's disease by first identifying for each one concepts that were degraded. These were concepts for which patients could not answer ques-tions probing semantic knowledge and that often were not named when presented as pictures. On Anderson's hypothesis, more priming should be expected for intact concepts than for degraded concepts, but the op-posite was found. There was markedly greater priming for degraded con-cepts, possibly because the background level of activation for these was very low in patients. Comparable studies of normal aging are probably not feasible because older adults show next to no evidence for impaired lexical concepts (but see later).

Even if larger semantic priming effects were obtained for normal older adults than for young adults, interpretation of such findings would be subject to accounts other than semantic impairment. Young adults show larger priming effects for words that are difficult to access because they have been visually degraded (e.g., Stanovich & West, 1983). Children who are less skilled readers and, hence, are slower to access words, show greater priming than children who are better readers (West & Stanovich, 1978). When lexical access is slowed, there is more time for activation to spread from prime to target, enhancing the beneficial effects of prime-target relatedness. If older adults were generally slower in accessing lex-ical information, larger semantic priming effects in old age would be anticipated even on the assumption of an intact conceptual system. Indeed, there is evidence for both larger priming effects and for slower lexical access in old age. A recent meta-analysis (Laver & Burke, 1990) found generally larger semantic priming effects in the old than in the young. Moreover, when lexical access is slowed by stimulus degradation, the increase in the magnitude of semantic facilitation in lexical decision is greater for the old than for the young (Madden, 1988; but see Cerella & Fozard, 1984, for a different result in a word-naming task). Madden suggested that older adults are slower in early stages of the word recognition process such as feature extraction and that this slowing is exacerbated by visually degrading stimuli. Older adults are slower to name words than are young adults (e.g., Nebes et al., 1986; Thomas, Fozard, & Waugh, 1977). They also derive a greater benefit from short delays (on the order of 300 to 450 ms) in a word-naming task in which overt pronunciation is withheld until a signal is given, a finding compatible with the hypothesis that they are slower to access information in the mental lexicon (Balota & Duchek, 1988). Although Cerella and Fozard failed to find an age difference in the benefit accruing from a delay in a pronunciation task, they used only a 1,000 ms delay, a point in time at which Balota and Duchek found no age difference in benefit; Cerella and Fozard also computed benefit by taking the difference between delayed pronunciation time and pronunciation time in a normal semantic priming study, a procedure that compares latencies under quite different conditions. We might note at this juncture that the time it takes to pronounce a word is also much greater in Alzheimer's disease than in normal aging (e.g., Nebes et al., 1986) so that slowed lexical access may play a role in producing enhanced semantic priming in patients, though other factors also may be important (Chertkow et al., 1989).

To summarize, finding similar effects of associative strength and type of association on the magnitude of semantic priming in young and older adults provides crude support for the hypothesis that meaning is represented similarly across age. Examination of the absolute size of the age difference in facilitation, however, does not yield readily interpretable evidence but is again consistent with an intact semantic system accompanied by slowing of lexical access in old age.

Judgments of Similarity. Another approach taken in explorations of possible age differences in structure of conceptual knowledge involves the use of tasks that require judgments about similarity between pairs of objects. Three rather different methods have been used. In the first, young and older adults have been asked to decide whether two words are related in some way and response latency and accuracy are measured. For instance, people may be asked to judge whether two words mean approximately the same thing (Hertzog, Raskind, & Cannon, 1986; Madden, 1985), to decide whether a word names a category member or whether two words belong to the same category (Eysenck, 1975; Hertzog et al., 1986; Mueller, Kausler, & Faherty, 1980; Petros, Zehr, & Chabot, 1983), or just to decide whether two words are related, without the precise nature of the relation being specified (Byrd, 1984; Nebes & Brady, 1988). Although older adults are slower than young adults to make semantic judgments, their error rates are no higher, suggesting the availability of information about relationships queried or, when the judgment is about simple relatedness, the availability of information that an association exists. In some studies (Byrd, 1984; Hertzog et al., 1986; Mueller et al., 1980; Petros et al., 1983), the category instances varied in production frequency (response dominance). More frequently produced category members are rated as being more typical or central to a category and generally are responded to more quickly in semantic judgment tasks. In all studies that varied typicality, the extent to which typicality affected response latency was the same across age, suggesting that category structure is similar across age (but see later).

Despite these findings, there are some investigations that make this conclusion a bit less unequivocal. For instance, performance on the Wechsler Adult Intelligence Scale (WAIS) Similarities subtest, which requires the statement of a way in which two things are related, declines with age (see Salthouse, 1982, for a review), though cohort differences in education may be a factor here (Birren & Morrison, 1961). Older adults also perform more poorly on tests in which particular relationships are explicitly queried. For instance, Riegel (1959) found that young and older adults equated on ability to select synonyms on a multiple-choice test had problems in choosing antonyms, in selecting salient properties (A GRANARY always has: grain, elevator, cellar, mice, *entrance*), in choosing two coordinates for a target when a superordinate is not actually stated (GRANARY belongs with: field, *stable,* farm, *barn,* plough), and in solving verbal analogies tests that require computation of similarity relationships (GRANARY is related to CORN as STABLE is related to: field, *cows,* grain, cottage, farmer). These tasks are more specific in the knowledge they tap than tasks that involve production of properties or judgments of similarity or category membership; they require the abstraction and, in some cases, the verbalization of relationships between two objects. Judgments of relatedness do not require that a basis for similarity be explicitly retrieved and judgments of the category membership or synonymity of two words do not require the production of these words. It may be that older adults are impaired in these areas, but that semantic structure is indeed intact. A similar issue has emerged in studies of the semantic deficit in Alzheimer's disease—that is, the possibility that semantic structure may be preserved in the face of difficulties in accessing semantic information by directed search (see Nebes, 1989, for a review). The contrast between studies of semantic priming, which indirectly tap semantic structure, where an age-related impairment of priming has not been demonstrated, and studies requiring overt retrieval of semantic information, where there may be age-related differences in performance, is reminiscent of the pattern of intact and impaired episodic memory in old age. Here, too, older adults show preserved performance on indirect tests of memory but not on direct tests (see Light, 1991, and chapter 2 of this volume for reviews).

A second way of using similarity judgments to examine conceptual structure involves more direct ratings of the similarity of objects. Three studies have used this technique. Stine (1986) asked young and older adults to list up to seven properties for 12 fruits or 12 vehicles and also to rate the similarity of pairs of objects within their assigned domain. She then computed a measure of similarity for each pair of objects which incorporated both common and distinctive features listed for the two objects. This measure was used to predict the similarity ratings. Although young adults appeared to use both common and distinctive features in assigning ratings, older adults relied more heavily on distinctive features. Also, relative use of perceptual and function-related features differed for young and old. For the young, both common and distinctive perceptual features predicted similarity ratings, but for the old only distinctive features were predictive. Specifiers, a type of functional elaborator, contributed to rating predictions for the old, but not for the young. These results argue for a difference in the way in which young and older adults make similarity judgments, but do not tell us whether people of different ages actually differ in how similar they judge two objects to be.

Howard (1983b) used multidimensional scaling to get at this question. Adults in each decade of age from the 20s through the 70s rated the similarity of all pairs of 16 animals and also rated the animals on six scales (small–large, domestic–wild, nonpredatory–predatory, bad–good, weak–strong, passive–active). Two-dimensional scaling solutions produced the best fits to the data for all ages, with the two dimensions appearing to be predacity and size. However, adults in their 60s and 70s weighted predacity somewhat less heavily in doing their ratings. It is unclear whether such a difference reflects a difference in semantic structure or whether it reflects a different strategy for rating objects.

Anooshian and Samuelson (1985–1986) examined the extent to which young and older adults relied on a semantic dimension (their own past experience with an object) or a more superficial dimension (alphabetic order of object names) to rate similarity of animals or diseases. The extent to which past experience emerged as a dimension in multidimensional scaling declined with age whereas the presence of an alphabetic dimension did not. From this, the authors argued that older adults encode less deeply. This would seem to be faulty reasoning, however, inasmuch as no effort was made to identify the nature of dimensions actually used by older adults. The number of dimensions needed to fit the data did not vary with age, leading to the conclusion that encoding elaborativeness did not vary with age. With some stretching, we might argue that similarity in number of dimensions for young and old solutions supports the existence of age constancy in number of associations activated during similarity judgments, though it does not speak to issues of the number of associations actually available in a network.

The third way in which perception of similarity has been studied involves the use of sorting tasks. The issue here is whether young and older adults use the same bases for sorting pictures of objects into groups. Different sorting strategies might reflect differential strength of particular types of associations in different age groups. Indeed, age differences in classification have been reported, with older adults being less likely to sort pictures on the basis of taxonomic similarity and more likely to make relational-thematic groupings by putting together things that are used in the same activity (Annett, 1959; Cicirelli, 1976; Kogan, 1973; Pearce & Denney, 1984). This outcome is difficult to interpret, however, because of age differences in education in these studies; no age differences in type of sort were found by Laurence and Arrowood (1982) who tested highly educated groups. Moreover, there are no age differences in ability to select items that belong to a particular taxonomic category when people are told the basis for selecting items (Flicker, Ferris, Crook, & Bartus, 1986) or in ability to explain the basis for either taxonomic or thematic sorts when these are done spontaneously (Smiley & Brown, 1979). There is an assumption in sorting studies that taxonomic sorts are more "advanced," possibly because the prevalence of a taxonomic basis for sorting increases with age in childhood. However, there are many natural categories that are not based on the simple sharing of attributes (Lakoff, 1987), including categories based on such goals as saving things from a fire or escaping from the Mafia (Barsalou, 1983). Hence, this assumption seems ill-founded.

On balance, then, tasks involving judgments of similarity give us our first glimpse of possible age differences in semantic structure. There is some evidence that older adults are less able to articulate the basis for similarity between concepts or to select words that bear particular relationships to target words on multiple-choice tests. There is also some evidence that older adults may base their similarity judgments on different dimensions than young adults or weight these dimensions differently. The available evidence, however, does not permit us to decide between explanations based on strategy differences in assigning similarity ratings and explanations based on age-related variation in semantic structure. Finally, age differences in the way in which adults group items in a sorting task are not always informative about the underlying nature of mental representations.

Schemata

As should be clear from the preceding discussion, information is not stored randomly. Rather, our memories of our experiences in the world are organized in a meaningful way. There have been many ways of conceptualizing the knowledge structures that accomplish this, including fairly general ideas of schemata (Bartlett, 1932) as well as more concrete and restricted proposals about the representation of ordered series of actions embodied in scripts (Schank & Abelson, 1977) or Memory Organization Packets (Schank, 1982). More recently, Sharkey (1990) discussed connectionist approaches to knowledge structures. Despite the diversity of ways of thinking about the organization of general world knowledge, there has been agreement that schemata play a central role in language comprehension and memory (but see Alba & Hasher, 1983, for a critique of this view). Schemata are believed to guide expectations about what will be said next, to facilitate perception of individual words, to aid in integration of old and new information, and to serve as guides to retrieval (e.g., Anderson & Pichert, 1978; Bransford & Johnson, 1972; Sanford & Garrod, 1981; Sharkey, 1986). Comprehension and communication in old age could be severely impaired either if young and older adults did not have similar knowledge structures or if there were differences in the efficiency of accessing or modifying these structures. There is evidence for deterioration of knowledge about routine activities in Alzheimer's disease (Weingartner et al., 1983). Here we explore the extent to which knowledge structures are similar in young and normal old people. The issue of access to schematic information during discourse comprehension and memory is taken up later.

The available evidence speaks to the similarity of conceptual organization across age in some (though not necessarily all) domains. There is a close correspondence in the ways in which young and older adults view many activities of daily life. Schank and Abelson (1977) suggested that we represent our knowledge of these stereotypic action sequences as "scripts." These scripts specify conventional roles, props, action sequences, reasons for engaging in an activity (goals), and expected outcomes. College students share beliefs about the structure of such scripts and can rate reliably such properties of actions as their centrality, distinctiveness, and standardness (Bower, Black, & Turner, 1979; Galambos,

1986). When young and older adults are asked to generate a sequence of actions that are typically performed by most people in carrying out an activity (e.g., writing a letter to a friend or getting up in the morning), the production frequencies of particular actions are very similar across age (Hess, 1985; Light & Anderson, 1983). Moreover, correlations between age groups are very high when people are asked to rate how typical or necessary an act is for completing an activity (Hess, 1985; Light & Anderson, 1983), to rate its importance in understanding an event sequence (Hess, Donley, & Vandermaas, 1989), or to rate the importance of particular ideas in a passage describing a house to homebuyers or burglars (Hess & Flannagan, in press). These shared views can be quite detailed and veridical. For instance, young and older adults hold similar beliefs about the particular objects that are subject to shoplifting, about the actions likely to be performed in the course of stealing them, and about the characteristics of the shoplifters who take them; these beliefs also correspond quite closely to actual thefts in a major metropolitan department store (List, 1986). There are indications, however, that not all knowledge structures are identical in young and older adults. When asked to generate personal rather than culturally generic scripts, there are differences in the prominence of certain actions (Hess, 1992; Ross & Berg, 1992). For example, young adults, as the parents of adolescents know well, spend a lot more time on personal appearance than do older adults. The import of this finding is not clear inasmuch as it is possible to simultaneously hold shared cultural beliefs and recognize individual exceptions to them. Moreover, it is not known whether age/cohort differences in personal scripts are for optional actions or for actions that are central to the performance of an activity.

In addition to having shared beliefs about typical scripted activities, young and older adults share social stereotypes and have similar implicit theories of personality and cognition. There may be age differences in degree of traditional sex-role orientation, though Hess, Vandermaas, Donley, and Snyder (1987) found inconsistent results across two experiments; nevertheless, young and old do agree on the kinds of activities that are likely to be performed by men and women on a typical weekend. Young and older adults agree on the consistency of behaviors with personality traits (Hess & Tate, 1991). There is also considerable agreement across groups of young, middle-age, and older adults asked to generate attributes descriptive of people who are "wise, intelligent, perceptive, shrewd, and spiritual" or to rate how characteristic particular attributes are of wise people (Holliday & Chandler, 1986). However, there may be some age-related differences in intuitive notions about intelligence. Older people appear to believe that nontraditional intellectual abilities (such as everyday competence, knowledge and responsibility, and cognitive investment) are more central to the concept of intelligence (Berg, 1990).

Young and older adults also have similar ideas about the nature of psychopathology. Hochman, Storandt, and Rosenberg (1986) found that young and older women were equally adept in identifying descriptions of people as indicative of normal mental health, depression, senile dementia, paranoia, or hypochondriasis. There were no age differences in ratings of mental health or in the criteria used for making judgments about mental health. There were some differences in attributions about young and old women described as having various symptoms. Age of target person was viewed as a more important determinant of mental health for depressed and demented old women than for young women with the same symptoms. Also, physical complaints were more important determinants of ratings of older demented and paranoid women than of young women. However, there were no interactions with age of raters, indicating considerable mutuality in the perceptions of laypeople of different ages about mental health at different points in the life course.

There are both age-related similarities and age-related differences, however, in subjective beliefs about the course of adult development. Heckhausen, Dixon, and Baltes (1989) asked young, middle-aged, and older adults to rate adjectives describing a wide range of personality, social, and intellectual characteristics (e.g., skeptical, friendly, intellectual, wise, forgetful) on how likely they were to show increases across the life span, to rate how desirable they were, and to indicate decade of onset and closing age for each. Correlations between age groups for these variables were very high, indicating good agreement across age. For instance, the correlation between expected age of onset and desirability of trait was strongly negative, with the exceptions of *dignified* and *wise*. Nevertheless, there were some age differences. Older subjects rated more adjectives as showing developmental changes, suggesting an increase in the complexity of beliefs about old age. Middle-aged and older adults also made more use of intermediate values for age of onset of attributes whereas young adults tended to use the extremes of the scale. This suggests that with age comes a more attribute-specific and differentiated set of expectations about aging. A similar conclusion was reached by Brewer and Lui (1984) who found that older adults sorted pictures of old people into more groups than did young adults. In this domain, then, older adults may have more richly endowed conceptual structures than young adults.

There is also some evidence from the work of Kite, Deaux, and Miele (1991) for age differences in the contents of stereotypes about aging held by young and older adults. When asked to rate targets varying in age (35 or 65 years old) and sex (man or woman) on masculine and feminine traits, role behaviors, and physical characteristics, interactions between subject age and target age were observed for masculine traits and masculine role behaviors. There were no age differences in rating 35-year-old targets, but younger adults rated 65-year-old targets as less masculine than 35-year-old targets on these dimensions. When attributes specifically related to aging were rated, the factor structures that emerged were very similar for subjects in the two age groups. However, young adults viewed older targets as less physically attractive, less sociable, and more talkative than did older adults. Younger adults were thus less positive than older adults in their assessment of older targets on some dimensions.

Young and older adults share the view that memory problems increase in old age (Ryan, 1990). Erber (1989) reported that young adults, but not older adults, used a double standard, judging the memory failures of old people described in short vignettes as more severe than identical problems attributed to young people. This result, however, may have been due to older adults having forgotten the ages of the target figures. Under conditions when memory for the age of the target figures is more likely, both old and young show more concern for memory failures of older adults (Erber & Rothberg, 1991; Erber, Szuchman, & Rothberg, 1990); memory failures in the old, particularly those involving familiar, overlearned materials such as the name of a close friend, are more likely to be judged as indicating mental difficulty and warranting psychological or medical evaluation. Some age differences in ratings did emerge in these studies. Young adults were somewhat more likely than older adults to believe that memory problems were a sign of mental difficulty and required fewer occurrences of a problem before recommending evaluation; these results suggest that older adults are less bothered by memory problems than are young adults.

On the whole, then, studies of knowledge structures find considerable commonality across age. There are some differences in the specific content of personal scripts for everyday activities. Young and older adults weight some aspects of intelligence slightly differently. Young adults hold less positive views of the elderly than the elderly do of themselves. Young and old also make slightly different attributions about memory lapses in young and older adults. Such differences in the specific content of schemata presumably arise because of changes in daily routines with increased age, changing intellectual demands, changing experience with the aging process itself, and changing concerns about cognitive competence in old age. The existence of such differences serves as a warning that materials used in research on cognition in old age should be normed on appropriate samples (see Gillund & Perlmutter, 1988, and Hess, 1990, for reviews) and raises the possibility of differences of opinion on a variety of topics in adults of different ages, but causes no concern that the mechanisms operating on cognitive structures are different in young and older adults. Indeed, as shown by the studies to which we turn later, there is every reason to believe that young and older adults are affected similarly by experimental manipulations of schematic knowledge.

Everyday Problem Solving

Studies of everyday problem solving afford another window into the nature of the representation of knowledge in young and older adults. In a well-known series of experiments, Denney and Palmer (1981) examined the solutions offered by people of different ages to real-life problems in a variety of domains, such as coping with malfunctioning appliances, flooded basements, young children who are late getting home, witnessing a crime, and receiving threatening phone calls. Responses were scored by assigning points to each problem depending on the number of solutions offered as well as on the degree of reliance on self rather than others. A curvilinear relation between age and scores was obtained, with 40- and 50-year-olds outperforming both younger and older groups. This pattern of results is not eliminated by using problems thought to be more familiar to particular age/cohort groups (Denney, Pearce, & Palmer, 1982). The nature of the scoring system employed in these studies is rather arbitrary because it places greater weight on solutions that rely only on independent action. Such a system may be biased against older adults who either for physical reasons or because of cohort differences are more prone to rely on others. Also, in these studies, the problems were designed by the experimenters and there was no way of knowing whether they were equally familiar to all age groups or to the group to which they were targeted. Older adults are known to experience everyday "hassles" somewhat different from those of younger adults (Folman, Lazarus, Pimley, & Novacek, 1987). However, simply scoring the number of safe and effective solutions and using problems contributed by older adults does not change the outcome (Denney & Pearce, 1989).

From Denney's work we might conclude that, despite the similarity in scripts generated by young and older people, older adults have less extensive representations of knowledge about the kinds of problems that crop up in everyday life. Two facts militate against accepting this conclusion. First, scoring the number of solutions produced to a problem converts the task into a special kind of fluency task, and, indeed, fluency tasks that involve generating remote consequences for unusual situations do show age-related declines (McCrae et al., 1987). Second, other evidence suggests considerable overlap in the ways in which young and older adults think about everyday problems. Cornelius and Caspi (1987) constructed an Everyday Problem-Solving Inventory that samples situations in six domains: in experiences as a consumer, in dealing with complicated information, in managing a home, in dealing with interpersonal conflicts at home, in dealing with conflicts with friends, and in coping with conflicts at work. Rather than having people generate solutions, Cornelius and Caspi obtained ratings on the efficacy of four solutions to each problem. The alternatives for each problem were designed such that one referred to self-initiated, overt behaviors that deal directly with a problem, one referred to efforts to deal with the problem cognitively by solving the problem through logical analysis or changing one's appraisal of the problem, one included attempts to avoid or withdraw from a situation or to depend on others to solve it, and one illustrated avoidant thinking and denial. The problems first were normed by having a set of young, middle-aged, and older adults rate the effectiveness of each solution. The mean of their ratings was used as a standard of comparison for the ratings of a larger group of adults ranging in age from 20 to 78 years. Correlations of individual ratings with the combined judges' ratings showed increases over the life span in each of the six domains. Because ratings of problem familiarity increased with age for some domains and decreased for others, the larger correlation of older adults' ratings with those of the norming sample in this task cannot be due to greater problem familiarity. In research using a similar technique, Cornelius (1990) also showed that there is considerable agreement across age in judgments of the effectiveness of different strategies for coping with stressful situations involving losses, threats, and challenges (e.g., failing the vision test for a driver's license). In these studies, then, which do not involve generating solutions to practical problems, young and older adults are found to have similar views about problem solving in everyday situations.

It has been suggested that older adults may have a greater fund of practical wisdom in the domain of interpersonal relations which is demonstrated by their consideration of alternative perspectives in problem solving and the taking of a relativistic rather than an absolute stance on issues (e.g., Labouvie-Vief, 1985; Rybash, Hoyer, & Roodin, 1986). If true, this would suggest either a more complex structure for social domains or a difference in reasoning strategy, with older adults adopting more postformal reasoning. The evidence on this point is somewhat mixed. Blanchard-Fields (1986) found that middle-aged adults were more likely than younger adults to exhibit relativism in reasoning about social dilemmas in which contradictory perspectives were presented, but no older adults were included in her study. Sebby and Papini (1989), however, did include an older sample; they reported that middle-aged and older adults were more likely to be aware of subjective elements in interpreting problem premises and to recognize that "logic must, at times, be integrated with experience, lest logical solutions to real problems be confused with sensible solutions" (p. 65).

Smith and Baltes (1990) found somewhat different results. Their subjects participated in a life-planning task. They produced thinking-aloud protocols as they formulated plans for the protagonists in each of four problems. These problems varied in the age of the principal character (30 or 60 years) and in whether the decision to be made was normative or nonnormative with respect to age grading (e.g., a 28-year-old mechanic about to be laid off from his job must decide whether to move his family to another city to find employment or take on child-care and household responsibilities while his wife works). Judges scored each protocol on one of five dimensions related to Baltes and Smith's (1990) theory about the characteristics of the knowledge system underlying wise judgment or else evaluated the protocols against their own definition of wisdom. Only 11 of the 240 protocols were judged to reflect wise reasoning, but these were distributed evenly across the three age groups. However, there were marginally reliable differences favoring the young on other rating scales. Moreover, there was an interaction between subject age and target age, with older adults showing less wise ratings than the young on all but the old/nonnormative problem, for which there were no age differences. Compared with young and middle-aged adults, older adults showed less relativism, a lower level of factual knowledge about the type of problem encountered, and less insight about the young character problems. These results are noteworthy in that they suggest that relativistic thinking may depend on both age of subject and familiarity with the particular life situations involved. In this respect, they differ from those of both Denney and her colleagues (Denney & Pearce, 1989; Denney et al., 1982) and Cornelius and Caspi (1987).

Summary

In this section we have surveyed a considerable variety of methods used to assess the structure and content of conceptual knowledge in young and older adults. Little evidence for age-related changes in semantic knowledge has emerged. Although older adults have word-finding difficulties, the simplest explanation for these is that lexical access is impaired. There is great consistency in the type of word associations produced by young and older adults and little indication that word associations are more variable or idiosyncratic in the old. Semantic priming is preserved in old age and, in fact, there is evidence that older adults may show greater priming than young adults. Older adults are as accurate as young adults in deciding whether two concepts are related or whether they share particular aspects of meaning. Although the old do show declines on tasks that require the explicit statement or selection of the way in which words are related, it is not clear whether this result should be taken as signaling an alteration in semantic structures. The same result may be indicative of problems in accessing particular knowledge or even of shifts in the criteria for similarity without implicating a semantic deficit. There is surprising agreement across age in the contents of schemata involving activities, personality characteristics, and solutions for everyday problems. Where age differences do appear, such as in personal scripts or in ideas about aging or cognition, they seem to be related to particulars of the daily routines of young and older people or to life experiences that are not encountered until middle or late life. All in all, then, there is little reason to believe that normal aging is accompanied by changes in semantic structure or content. If such changes do not exist, they cannot be responsible for any age-related changes in comprehension or memory that do occur.

THE REPRESENTATION OF INFORMATION IN LANGUAGE COMPREHENSION AND MEMORY FOR DISCOURSE

With the exception of studies of semantic priming in sentence contexts, the experimental tasks discussed in the previous section primarily involved processing of single words or pairs of words. These paradigms have in common an underlying assumption about the nature of meaning, that is, that meanings are fixed and can be studied in isolation. Interpretations given to words in sentences and larger discourses, however, depend heavily on the contexts in which they are embedded and hence are derived from people's implicit theories about the way in which the world works (e.g., Johnson-Laird, 1983; Medin, 1989). Moreover, understanding a discourse involves constructing a mental model in which the entities referred to and their actions can be placed in a temporal, spatial, causal, and intentional framework (e.g., Bower & Morrow, 1990; Johnson-Laird, 1983; Sanford & Garrod, 1981). There are two questions here with respect to aging: (a) Do young and older adults share the same fund of general world knowledge to use as the basis for constructing such mental models? and (b) Are there age differences in the utilization of this knowledge, that is, in drawing inferences from sentences or in producing coherent mental representations of discourse? We already have received a positive answer to the first question. We turn now to the second question and consider studies comparing young and older adults with respect to inferences based on particularization of word meanings within sentences and short discourses, the role of schemata in memory for discourse, establishing coreference, and limitations on the use of general world knowledge in drawing inferences.

Particularization of Word Meanings in Sentences

The results of controlled-association studies and judgments of similarity or relatedness suggest that young and older adults share beliefs about the properties and functions of objects as well as the actions that may be performed with them. Properties of a word's meaning are not, however, equally salient across all situations. Although some core or central properties may always be activated regardless of context (Barsalou, 1982; Greenspan, 1986), particular linguistic contexts emphasize or highlight different aspects of meaning. Moreover, unemphasized properties may be inhibited (become less available) when other properties are activated (e.g., Tabossi & Johnson-Laird, 1980).

Two types of paradigms account for most studies of the specification of word meanings in context, cued recall and more on-line measures such as property verification. In a well-known study by Barclay, Bransford, Franks, McCarrell, and Nitsch (1974), the phrase "something heavy" was found to be a better retrieval cue than the phrase "something with a nice sound" for the sentence *The man lifted the piano,* but the reverse was true for the sentence *The man tuned the piano.* The heaviness of a piano is important for the operation of lifting but its tunefulness is not, whereas the sound of a piano is crucial in tuning but its weight is not. Retrieval cues are differentially effective because they match the encoded representation of the sentence to a greater or lesser degree (Tulving, 1983). The use of cued recall as a way of investigating the contents of memory representations has been criticized because it confounds processes occurring during comprehension, which are of principal interest here, with additional retrieval operations occurring at the time of recall (Keenan, Potts, Golding, & Jennings, 1990; McKoon & Ratcliff, 1990). For this reason, on-line measures that tap into the memory representation as comprehension occurs or shortly thereafter are preferable. A study by Tabossi and Johnson-Laird (1980) illustrates this methodology. Young adults read a sentence such as *The goldsmith cut the glass with the diamond* which biases the property of hardness, a neutral sentence such as *The film showed the person with the diamond,* or a sentence such as *The mirror dispersed the light from the diamond* which highlights a different property. They then judged whether a sentence such as *A diamond is hard* was true or false. Target sentences that biased appropriate properties produced faster responses than neutral sentences which, in turn, were faster than sentences biasing contextually inappropriate properties. From this, it may be concluded that relevant aspects of the meaning of *diamond* were activated during sentence comprehension whereas contextually inappropriate properties were inhibited, or alternatively, that the target sentence was easier to integrate with the relevant context sentence.

Conclusions about possible age differences in the specification of meaning in context may depend critically on the methodology used to investigate this question. For instance, Till and Walsh (1980) presented young and old adults with sentences such as *The chauffeur drove on the left side.* Memory was tested by free recall or by recall cued with nouns (here *England*) that referred to information not stated explicitly in the sentence but pragmatically implied by it. Young adults benefited more from the retrieval cues than older adults, except when subjects provided continuations for the sentences during presentation. We might conclude from this that pragmatic information is normally inferred by young but not by older adults. This conclusion, however, would be premature. In a follow-up study, Till (1985) presented young and old adults with a list of sentences such as *The hostess raised her glass* or *The hostess raised her glass as a toast* and later assessed memory by asking questions such as *Who proposed a toast?* Younger adults outperformed older adults when the sentences only invited inferences. Till interpreted this result as further evidence of age differences in processing inferential material. However, younger adults also recalled more than older adults when the answers to the questions were explicitly stated, rather than merely being implied by the original sentences. This suggests that memory for the sentences was simply poorer for older adults, not that older adults have a specific impairment in encoding or retrieving inferences.

Several studies have looked more closely at the role of context in particularizing specific aspects of word meaning across age with on-line procedures. Burke and Harrold (1988) used Tabossi and Johnson-Laird's (1980) property verification task to study selection of relevant properties of objects. Young and older adults both demonstrated inhibition of contextually inappropriate properties (e.g., the roundness of oranges for the sentence *The oranges satisfied the thirst of the hot children*), though only older adults showed activation of appropriate properties (here the juiciness of oranges). Burke and Harrold believe that this outcome occurred because older adults were slower to access target-property information during the verification task, so that there was more time for activation to spread. Burke and Harrold also found that young and older adults were equally likely to produce the appropriate properties when given the sentences and instructed to produce the first property that came to mind.

As discussed earlier, Burke and Yee (1984) found no age differences in the extent to which sentence context encouraged the inference that particular actions (e.g., cut) were performed with particular instruments (e.g., knife). In this instance, activation of the implied instrument was inferred from facilitation in a lexical decision task. Evidence for the presence of implied instruments in memory representations of both young and older adults also was obtained by Hess and Arnould (1986) in a recognition memory task. After reading sentences such as *She had swept the garage floor that morning,* young and older adults were equally likely to falsely recognize instruments such as *broom,* suggesting similar long-term encodings of implied information.

In another series of studies, Light, Valencia-Laver, and Zavis (1991) showed that young and older adults are equally likely to instantiate general terms in sentences, that is, to infer that particular category members are implied by sentence context. That such effects require the activation of general world knowledge should be clear from contrasting *The insect in the clover stung the professor* and *The insect in the woodwork concerned the professor.* General world knowledge leads us to draw the inference that the insect referred to in the first of these is a bee whereas the insect referred to in the second is a termite. In two experiments, young and older adults read sentences such as the aforementioned and then were tested for instantiation of general terms using a relatedness judgment task modeled after the property verification task of Tabossi and Johnson-Laird (1980) and Burke and Harrold (1988). A noun-property pair (e.g., *bee-insect*) was presented and the task was to decide whether the two words were related. The noun was either the category instance suggested by the sentence context or the noun suggested by an alternative sentence containing the same general term and the property was the category name. To the extent that sentence comprehension involves instantiation of general terms, we would expect that response times should be faster when the target exemplar is a category member that instantiates the category well in a given context than when there is a mismatch between biasing context and target exemplar. In one experiment, each sentence was followed by a relatedness judgment, so that comprehension was measured immediately after sentence reading. In the other, which involved delayed testing, a series of relatedness judgments followed each block of eight sentences. Matching effects were obtained in both experiments and these were of equal magnitude for young and old. A similar result was found in a third study that involved cued recall. Here, appropriate instances were found to be better retrieval cues for the sentences that biased their instantiations than for other sentences containing the same general terms. Although young adults recalled more sentences than older adults, the pattern of effects in cued recall was not sensitive to age.

These three studies of instantiation of general terms also bear on another issue. For each general term, one of the sentences biased a typical category member (e.g., *bee*) and the other biased an atypical category member (e.g., *termite*). As discussed earlier, category verification for words tested in isolation is faster for typical category members than for atypical category members and typical category members have higher production frequencies in exemplar generation tasks. These results suggest that typical instances are somehow more central to the meaning of categorical terms. It has been suggested that older adults not only make fewer inferences than young adults, but also that they encode more generally, that is, that their interpretations of word meanings are less affected by sentence context (e.g., Craik & Byrd, 1982; Rabinowitz, Craik, & Ackerman, 1982). If this were true and older adults encoded general terms in the same old way each time they encountered them, we would expect to find that older adults respond more rapidly to typical targets in the relatedness judgment task regardless of the sentence bias. However, this did not occur. We also might expect that general terms always would make better retrieval cues for older adults regardless of the category members biased by sentences, but this result was not obtained either.

The research described thus far offers strong support for the view that sentence comprehension is guided by general world knowledge to the same extent in young and older adults and, by inference, that the nature of this general world knowledge is the same across age. In the studies discussed, the inferences depended on knowledge of single word meanings in situations where the literal meaning of sentences was involved. It is possible, however, that access to general world knowledge in understanding more figurative language might be impaired in older adults. Verbrugge and McCarrell (1977) argued that comprehension of novel metaphors such as *Billboards are warts on the landscape* or *Billboards are the yellow pages of a highway* requires an inference about abstract systems of resemblance (the ground) linking the domain of a topic (billboards) and the domain of a vehicle (warts, yellow pages). The ground for the warts metaphor is something like *are ugly protrusions on a surface* whereas the ground of the yellow pages metaphor is *tell you where to find businesses in the area.* For pairs such as these, Verbrugge and McCarrell found that cuing recall with the appropriate, though unstated, ground was much more effective than cuing with the inappropriate ground. Using Tulving's (1983) logic, we could argue that this means that the relevant grounds were inferred during metaphor comprehension and became part of the memory representation for the sentence. Inferring the relationship between billboards and warts requires that we deduce the similarity between them. As noted earlier, detection of similarities is impaired in old age. Hence, it might be predicted that older adults should be less likely to infer the relevant relationships between topic and vehicle in novel metaphors and their memory for metaphorical sentences should be less improved by relevant cues.

Light, Albertson Owens, Mahoney, and La Voie (in press) tested this prediction. Young and older adults heard a list of metaphoric sentences twice and then were tested for cued recall with both relevant and irrelevant grounds. They then were given a second test with the sentence subjects as cues. Both young and older adults remembered more metaphorical sentences when the cues were appropriate grounds than when they were inappropriate grounds. Moreover, the appropriateness effect was greater for young adults. Because cued recall was very low when inappropriate grounds were used, it is possible that the interaction was due to a floor effect in sentence memory. However, analysis of just those sentences that were recalled correctly to sentence subject cues gave the same interaction. Thus, for sentences that could be recalled when the topic of the metaphor was given, so that their availability in memory was assured, the appropriateness effect was smaller for older adults, suggesting that they were less likely to make or store inferences about the grounds of the metaphors.

A second experiment, using a more on-line measure of metaphor comprehension, suggests that the age difference in the appropriateness effect in cued recall was due to differences in retrieval strategies across age groups rather than to age-related differences in initial metaphor comprehension. Young and older adults read a sentence on the screen of a monitor and then responded true or false to a property sentence. The critical sentences were metaphors with the property sentence being the ground of the appropriate metaphor half the time and of the alternative metaphor for the topic half the time. If the grounds of the metaphor are inferred during sentence comprehension, a ground sentence should be verified faster when preceded (primed) by a relevant metaphor than by a metaphor biasing the alternative ground. This was found to be true for both young and older adults, and there was no age difference in the magnitude of the appropriateness effect.

In a third experiment, subjects read a series of metaphoric sentences. After each one, they were given the sentence topic, which was also the topic of the metaphor, and were asked to state a property of the topic (e.g., *billboards*) that the sentence made them think of. On this task, adults over 70 years of age (though not those in their 60s) produced fewer metaphor-relevant properties than young adults did. This finding suggests that older adults may show a deficit in metaphor comprehension, but only when the task requires that an explicit interpretation be given; the priming task, which did not require an explicit statement of the meaning of the metaphor, showed no age difference.

To summarize, when on-line techniques are used to assess particularization of word meanings in sentences, age-related differences in comprehension are almost never found. Use of cued recall has given mixed results, with some studies finding age differences favoring the young and others reporting age constancy. The one study using false alarms in recognition as a marker for inferences based on single word meanings found no age differences (Hess & Arnould, 1986). Hess (1990) hypothesized that older adults have problems in retrieving inferences, so that direct measures of memory, such as cued recall, which require deliberate recollection, will show age effects, whereas indirect measures, which permit memory for inferences to be demonstrated without deliberate recollection, will show age invariance. On this view, recognition measures of memory for inferences, which rely more heavily on perceptual familiarity than on retrieval, should be insensitive to age. The available evidence is not altogether consistent with this position, because cued recall does not always produce age differences.

The Role of Schemata in Memory for Discourse

One large class of studies has examined the consequences of varying the availability of particular schematic information to young and old adults. The research strategy here is to develop sets of materials that are more comprehensible when people are given relevant background information about the perspective of the protagonist, the identity of the individuals being described, or the topic of the discourse. These studies uniformly find similar patterns of performance in young and older adults. For instance, both young and older adults draw inferences based on general world knowledge when that general world knowledge is activated during comprehension. Regardless of age, people told that a character suspects she is pregnant make inferences that are appropriate to this theme, as shown by false alarms on a recognition test (Zelinski & Miura, 1988), suggesting that they interpret the actions performed by the character in the light of her possible pregnancy. Both young and old people told that a passage containing few specific referents is about washing clothes later will believe that they have read about "dirty clothes" though these were previously only called "the stuff that needs treatment" in the passage itself (Arbuckle, Vanderleck, Harsany, & Lapidus, 1990). This result suggests that both young and older adults develop a mental model of the washing clothes passage that involves inferring the identities of relevant objects. A similar finding by Radvansky, Gerard, Zacks, and Hasher (1990) is consonant with this interpretation. These authors found that on a recognition test, young and older adults were more likely to confuse sentences such as *The judge got his contact lenses in the optician's* and *The judge got his contact lenses from the optician* than to confuse pairs such as *The judge answered a telephone call in the optician's* and *The judge answered a telephone call from the optician*; the two members of the first pair invoke the same mental model of a sale of contact lenses in an optician's shop whereas the second two sentences do not both refer to events occurring in the same location. Also, regardless of age, recall of obscure facts about well-known people is improved by providing information about the identity of those people (Arbuckle et al., 1990).

Activation of prior knowledge improves acquisition of relevant new information, and appears to do so equally for young and older adults. Regardless of age, people who are expert musicians remember more about passages dealing with music than with passages dealing with a domain (dogs) in which they lack expertise (Arbuckle et al., 1990). When asked to read a passage from the perspective of a homebuyer or from the perspective of a burglar, there are no age differences in the extent to which people remember more perspective-relevant information (Hess & Flannagan, in press). After forming an impression of a person, young and old give similar ratings of the consistency of traits with the person's behavior (Hess et al., 1987; Hess & Tate, 1991). The knowledge activated need not be directly relevant to the contents of what is to be learned to be beneficial. People have implicit theories, sometimes called story grammars, about the structure of narratives (e.g., Mandler & Johnson, 1977; Thorndyke, 1977; see Johnson-Laird, 1983, for a critique). When these assumptions are violated, for instance by scrambling the sentences within a story, both young and old recall less than when the same stories are presented in their canonical order (Mandel & Johnson, 1984; Smith, Rebok, Smith, Hall, & Alvin, 1983). They also tend to recall the stories in an order more closely resembling the standard form, suggesting that models of narrative structure affect the way in which information retrieval proceeds.

In these studies, what has been of interest is the presence or absence of particular schematic information, and the effects of this manipulation seem to be insensitive to age. Investigations of memory for scripted information, however, allow a more fine-grained look at the effects of schema relevance across age and have produced somewhat mixed results. In an experiment by Light and Anderson (1983), young and older adults read a narrative about a character named Jack who engaged in a number of activities as he went about his life. The actions in each activity varied in how typical or necessary they were to the activity. Consistent with findings by others (e.g., Bower et al., 1979; Graesser, Woll, Kowalski, & Smith, 1980), atypical activities were recalled and recognized better than typical activities on a test carried out within a few minutes of study. Moreover, the patterns of intrusions in free recall and false alarms in recognition were similar across age, with both being more frequent for unstated but typical actions. These results generally are interpreted as evidence that mental scripts have been activated and lead to inferences about commonly performed actions not mentioned in the text.

Hess and his colleagues (Hess, 1985; Hess et al., 1989) have replicated some aspects of these results, namely that patterns of intrusions in recall and recognition are constant across age. However, they also have found an interaction between age and typicality, such that age differences in retention are larger for atypical actions. Hess et al. (1989) attributed this to difficulties that older adults have in forming new connections when atypical actions, especially irrelevant atypical actions, are mentioned. Because the result occurs for both recall and recognition, Hess argued that the interaction does not arise from age differences in retrieval processes involving scripts, but rather stems from problems in establishing contextual links to atypical actions. Although this interpretation is supported by Hess's findings in two studies, he did not obtain parallel results elsewhere. For instance, age and relevance of information to reader perspective did not interact in two experiments conducted by Hess and Flannagan (1990). Nor did age interact with consistency of trait information to a sex-role stereotype in a memory task (Hess et al., 1987), though Hess and Tate (1991) did find an interaction between trait consistency and age. Finally, List (1986), in a study of memory for shoplifting episodes, observed no differential age effect as a function of the probability that different objects or actions would be involved in thefts. It is not clear that action typicality, trait inconsistency, and object probability are equivalent in the role they play in establishing mental models, so the importance of the discrepancies in results cannot be assessed with any certainty. It is clear, however, that with relatively few exceptions, the effects of schema availability are very similar across age.

Establishing Coreference

Comprehension of anaphoric devices, including pronouns and noun phrases that refer back to concepts previously introduced in a discourse, is crucial for establishing coherence, that is, for determining the links between what has been said before and what is being said now (Lesgold, 1972). Should older adults experience difficulty in determining coreference, their comprehension would be expected to suffer, with later forgetting a natural outcome of problems in initial integration of discourse. It is not surprising, then, that the use of general world knowledge by young and older adults in understanding noun-phrase anaphors and in determining the antecedents of referentially ambiguous pronouns has received considerable experimental attention.

Light and Albertson (1988) used a paradigm developed by Dell, McKoon, and Ratcliff (1983) to compare the performance of young and older adults in an on-line task that taps comprehension of noun-phrase anaphors during the reading of sentences in short paragraphs such as this one:

A burglar surveyed the garage set back from the street.
Several milk bottles were piled at the curb.
The banker and her husband were on vacation.
The criminal slipped away from the street lamp. (Anaphor)
A cat slipped away from the street lamp. (Unrelated)

In the Unrelated version of the paragraph (the first three lines and the last line), a new entity is introduced that does not corefer with any of the previously mentioned concepts. In the Anaphor version of the paragraph (the first four lines), the last sentence contains a referring expression, *the criminal,* which is a superordinate of the subject of the first sentence. Use of the definite article *the* signals that the concept *criminal* has been introduced earlier in the discourse and encourages the inference that the burglar mentioned in the first sentence and the criminal mentioned in the last sentence refer to the same individual. An inference is required here because there is no logical necessity that this be so. The presence of the definite article and the superordinate, together with our assumption that discourses are coherent, leads us to make the inference because doing so results in a comprehensible paragraph (Hobbs, 1979).

Young and older adults read paragraphs that were presented on a computer monitor in a word-by-word fashion, with all the words in a sentence remaining on the screen until the last word was presented. At two points in the presentation of the final sentence of the paragraph, after the anaphor or at the end of the sentence, a probe such as *burglar* was presented. The subject's task was to respond positively if the probe word had appeared in the paragraph and negatively if it had not. Response time for young and older adults was faster at both probe positions when there was an anaphor in the last sentence than when the last sentence was unrelated, indicating that the initial sentence becomes available in working memory more rapidly when the last sentence can be interpreted as referring to previously mentioned entities. Thus, the use of general world knowledge in making pragmatic inferences to establish noun-phrase coreference is similar in adults of different ages.

A series of experiments conducted by Zelinski and her colleagues (Zelinski, 1988) corroborates the findings of Light and Albertson (1988). In her experiments, Zelinski used sentence-reading time as an index of comprehension. One experiment compared young and older adults in two conditions illustrated by the following examples:

1. We donated a refrigerator to our church.
   The refrigerator will be much appreciated there.

  2. We donated an appliance to our church.
     The refrigerator will be much appreciated there.

In Example 1, the term *refrigerator* is repeated across sentences and there
is no question as to coreference, but in Example 2, an inference must
be drawn that the refrigerator is the appliance in question. Haviland and
Clark (1974) had shown that reading time for the second sentence is faster
when there are identical terms than when an inference based on context
must be made. Zelinski found that this increase in reading time was comparable for old and young adults, suggesting that drawing the inference
is no more difficult for old than for young people.
    A second experiment examined the effects of varying the generality
of the term in the first sentence of the pair. For instance, in Example 3
a general term is mentioned in the first sentence and instantiated in the
second sentence; in Example 4 a specific instance is given in the first sentence and a general term is used in the second:

  3. Some money lay in the middle of the sidewalk.
     The dollar was picked up by the elderly man.
  4. A dollar lay in the middle of the sidewalk.
     The money was picked up by the elderly man.

Garrod and Sanford (1977) found that it is easier to establish coreference
when a specific instance is mentioned first, possibly because mentioning
a general term first does not restrict the domain of possible exemplars
very much. Zelinski's (1988) results indicate that the effects of this variable are similar across age. Finally, in a third study, the effects of amount
of material intervening between mention of an exemplar and its coreferential general term were assessed. Across different antecedent-anaphor sentence pairs, the number of intervening sentences was zero, two, or four.
The intervening sentences referred to the exemplar, so the antecedent
of the anaphor was maintained in an activated state, or foregrounded.
Anaphor sentence-reading times increased with number of intervening
sentences, but this variable did not interact with age. The results of these
experiments point to the similarity in noun-phrase anaphor resolution
mechanisms in young and older adults.
    Assignment of pronouns to their antecedents is quite straightforward
when there is agreement as to gender and number. However, when there
is more than one candidate for an antecedent, as when two men or two
women are mentioned and the antecedent of *he* or *she* must be determined, the task is trickier. Under these circumstances, people rely on a
variety of heuristic devices (van Dijk & Kintsch, 1983). When the ambiguity lies within a sentence or a clause, the strategy of assigning the

pronoun to the first-mentioned individual, who is also likely to be the topic of the sentence, is a powerful heuristic. Hobbs (1979) reported that it works about 90% of the time in written texts and about 75% of the time in dialogues he examined. Thus, unless there are good reasons to do otherwise, people interpret a pronoun in the second clause of a complex sentence as being coreferential with the noun phrase that is signaled as topic by being in the subject position. Such good reasons include general world knowledge about what is involved in certain activities, the semantics of verbs used in the first clause of a sentence, and the use of linguistic devices that indicate a shift in topic. Age-related differences in any of these areas could result in differences in the ways in which young and older adults assign coreference and, therefore, in differences in the way in which a discourse is understood. The results of several studies conducted by Light and her colleagues indicate no basis for concern here and thus point to similarities across age in both general world knowledge and in discourse comprehension strategies.

In one study, Light and Capps (1986) examined the assignment of pronouns based on general world knowledge. Young and older adults heard pairs of sentences such as these, adapted from Hirst and Brill (1980):

5. Henry spoke at a meeting while John drove to the beach.
   He brought along a surfboard.
6. Henry spoke at a meeting while John drove to the beach.
   He lectured on the administration.

A decision as to the antecedent of the pronoun *he* in these examples cannot be made on the basis of number or gender because both *John* and *Henry* are male and singular. Rather, an inference based on general world knowledge is needed. Because surfboards are more likely to be found at the beach than at a meeting and because lecturing is more likely at a meeting than at the beach (though many of us continue to hope for conferences in Acapulco where this happy circumstance might occur), *John* is more likely to be selected as antecedent in Example 5 and *Henry* in Example 6. Light and Capps found that this was equally true for young and older adults when no sentences intervened between the initial, context-setting sentence and the sentence containing the pronoun. This result suggests that pragmatic constraints play the same role in assignment of antecedents to pronouns by young and older adults when memory load is low.

Pronoun assignment also can depend on very subtle nuances of verb meaning. Consider these two sentence fragments:

7. John apologized to Bill because he . . .

8. John blamed Bill because he . . .

These fragments contain verbs that have a property that Garvey and Caramazza (1974), following Chafe (1972), called "implicit causality." Although the pronoun *he* is referentially ambiguous here, our knowledge of situations involving apology and blame lead us to expect continuations that, in the case of *apologize,* assign the pronoun to John—that is, to the first-mentioned noun—and to Bill—the second noun—in the case of *blame*:

9. John apologized to Bill because he stepped on his foot.
10. John blamed Bill because he forgot to put the cat out.

As noted by Ehrlich (1980), the sentence frame *John blamed Bill because he* . . . is likely to be interpreted as: "At some time, Bill does something which is probably bad. This action is a reason for John to say something to someone about Bill's action, at some later time" (p. 248). Nonetheless, continuations that violate such expectations and assign the pronoun differently are possible in each case and are perfectly comprehensible:

11. John apologized to Bill because he was so upset at the criticism.
12. John blamed Bill because he was afraid he'd be accused himself.

Grober, Beardsley, and Caramazza (1978) found asking people to complete sentence fragments such as Examples 7 and 8 with a motive or reason appropriate to the action in the first part of the sentence, led to continuations that were usually consistent with the implicit causality of the verb. When the connective *but* was used, however, the implicit causality of the verb no longer governed pronoun assignment. Rather, the pronoun was assigned to the subject noun in the stem regardless of whether the verb biased the first- or second-mentioned individual. According to Grober et al., the connective *because* encourages continuations that explain the action referred to by the verb, whereas *but* invokes "a statement of what has happened which usually is the opposite of what might be expected on the basis of the behavior described in the clause" (p. 124). If older adults are insensitive to presuppositions about human interaction underlying the meanings of verbs in sentence fragments or if they do not respond to the meanings of various connectives, they should choose the sentence topic when assigning pronouns to complete sentence fragments. However, in an unpublished replication of the Grober et al. experiment, Light and Capps found that the sentence continuations of young and older adults were equally responsive to both the implicit causality of verbs and the presence of the connectives *because* and *but*.

These results, then, not only attest to the similarity of the mental representations of these classes of words across age, but also point to the similarity of the processes that operate on these representations during comprehension.

Neither pronouns nor other anaphoric devices can be used (or at least they should not be used) unless the writer or speaker has reason to believe that the reader or listener will be able to pick out the intended referent with ease. Givón (1983) marshalled an impressive array of evidence that natural languages contain a hierarchy of syntactic devices for coding the degree of topic continuity in sentences, with constructions at one end of the continuum used to indicate that the current topic is the same as the previous one and constructions at the other end used to signal topic change. The dimension underlying this hierarchy is markedness or explicitness of reference, with more explicit forms used when the degree of discontinuity is greatest. The four examples below (from Fletcher, 1984) are ordered with respect to explicitness:

13. *Zero anaphor.* Pete had intended to go bowling with Sam last night but broke his leg.
14. *Unstressed pronoun.* Pete had intended to go bowling with Sam last night but he broke his leg.
15. *Stressed pronoun.* Pete had intended to go bowling with Sam last night but *he* broke his leg.
16. *Noun phrase.* Pete had intended to go bowling with Sam last night but the guy broke his leg.

In these examples, the second clauses contain syntactic constructions that differ in markedness but that are all ambiguous in that there is no algorithm for computing whether they refer to the first- or second-mentioned person. In all four examples, the topic established in the first clause is Pete, the subject of the main clause. In Example 13, the subject of the subordinate clause is omitted and we infer that we are still talking about Pete, that is, that the topic has not changed. Similarly in Example 14, the use of the pronoun suggests a high degree of topic continuity. However in Example 15, the use of the stressed pronoun renders the situation less certain and we now may be inclined to interpret the second clause as referring to Sam. Finally, the noun phrase in Example 16 gives no clue as to who needs orthopedic care.

To investigate the degree to which young and old consider the markedness of syntactic forms when determining coreference, Light and Albertson Owens (unpublished data) used a technique developed by Fletcher (1984). Young and older adults were asked to read sentences of the four types shown, and to answer for each one a question that tapped interpretation of the second clause (e.g., *Who broke his leg?*). They tabulated the probability that the second clause was interpreted as consistent with the original topic. Consistent with the results obtained by Fletcher, the probability of maintaining the topic varied as a function of type of anaphor, with continuity maintained virtually all of the time for the zero anaphor (proportions of 1.00 for young and .98 for old), most of the time for unstressed pronouns (.92 for young and .87 for old), less frequently for stressed pronouns (.67 for young and .68 for old), and considerably less reliably for the noun phrases (.48 and .36). The pattern of responses is very similar across age and testifies to a shared understanding of how various syntactic constructions code topic continuity.

Thus far, we have considered topic selection when only one or two sentences are involved. Understanding a discourse requires the construction of a mental model of what the discourse is about based on the particular linguistic inputs a reader or listener is exposed to as well as relevant bits of general world knowledge. Narratives tend to have a single protagonist or main character who is often the topic of the narrative as a whole as well as of many of the individual sentences (Morrow, 1985). Other characters and events in the narrative are described from the point of view of the protagonist. The reader typically identifies the main protagonist and develops a model of the discourse in which this character is central. For this reason, the protagonist should be prominent in working memory and ambiguous pronouns should be interpreted as referring to the protagonist rather than to other characters, unless it is made clear by preceding portions of the story that attention has been shifted from the protagonist to some other person in order to advance the plot. These notions may be clarified by examining the four versions of the narrative below (taken from Morrow):

> Tom thought his friend Harry looked worried about something. He asked him what was wrong, but Harry acted very evasive. Tom thought his friend needed some distraction, so he took him to a fair. Tom wandered through the fairgrounds with his friend for a while and then they stopped by an exhibition hall. He asked Harry what he wanted to do, but the poor guy just shrugged his shoulders. Tom was beginning to feel a little irritated so he said he wanted to do something fun. They decided to split up for a while.
> (a) After Harry had gone into the hall, Tom walked toward the ferris wheel.
> (b) Tom walked toward the ferris wheel after Harry had gone into the hall.
> (c) After Tom had gone into the hall, Harry walked toward the ferris wheel.
> (d) Harry walked toward the ferris wheel after Tom had gone into the hall.
> He saw a friend and said hello. (pp. 310, 312)

In this narrative, Tom is the protagonist and the story is related from his point of view. In Versions (a) and (b), the critical sentence has Tom mentioned in the main clause and Harry in the subordinate clause. Use of the conjunction *after* signals that Tom's action followed Harry's action and suggests that the story line will continue with more information about Tom. In Versions (c) and (d), Harry is mentioned in the main clause and this signals a shift in topic, suggesting that Harry is prominent at this point in the narrative and that we next will learn something more about his activities. Morrow asked college students to read narratives such as this one and to identify the referent of the ambiguous pronoun in the last sentence of each narrative. Morrow's subjects were quite confident in choosing the character brought into prominence by the preceding sentence even when this required awareness of a topic shift. Moreover, the ordering of the main and subordinate clauses in the critical sentence played no role in the choices people made.

To determine whether young and older adults are equally likely to rely on character prominence in a narrative when assigning pronouns, thereby indicating that they are equally likely to detect topic shift, Light and Albertson Owens (unpublished data) asked young and older groups to read four passages like these and, after reading each one, to answer a question about the referent of the pronoun in the last sentence. Their subjects, both young and old, behaved very much like Morrow's. They most often chose as the referent of the pronoun in the target sentence the character named in the main clause of the critical preceding sentence, and they did so regardless of whether the main clause appeared first or second. It is clear that there are no age differences in sensitivity to topic shift when subjects read narratives such as this one.

Limitations of the Use of General World Knowledge in Drawing Inferences

There seems to be considerable evidence, then, that older adults draw pragmatic inferences based on general world knowledge. Nonetheless, there is reason to believe that, under certain circumstances, older adults are less likely to do so than young adults. These circumstances arise when inferences based on general world knowledge depend not on thematic information or on meanings of single words, but when information must be integrated across sentences in a discourse. For instance, Cohen (1981) asked young and older adults to read short texts in which either information was stated explicitly or a bridging inference based on prior world knowledge was called for. Examples of these texts, taken from Keenan and Kintsch (1974), are given next:

17. *Explicit text.* A carelessly discarded burning cigarette started a fire. The fire destroyed many acres of virgin forest.

18. *Implicit text.* A burning cigarette was carelessly discarded. The fire destroyed many acres of virgin forest.

After reading three texts of each type, subjects answered questions based on both explicit and implicit information. Although both young and older adults took longer to read the implicit texts, suggesting that the need for integrative activity was recognized equally by both groups, older adults responded correctly to fewer questions based on implicit texts; there was no age difference on questions based on explicit information.

In another study, Cohen (1979) found that older adults were not as good as younger adults in detecting anomalies based on factual knowledge. Detecting the anomalies required putting together pieces of information presented in different sentences, such as that a man is blind and that he was seen to be reading a newspaper. However, Light and Albertson (1988) found age differences in anomaly detection only in conditions in which integration of information across sentences was made difficult. Consider the differences between these two passages:

19. Next door to us there's an old man who's completely blind. He lives quite alone and nobody ever goes to visit him, but he seems to manage quite well. He has a guide dog and goes out with the dog every day to do his shopping. We often see him sitting on his porch reading his newspaper.

20. Next door to us there's an old man who's completely blind. He lives with his unmarried sister who works as housekeeper for a banker. She works long hours and rarely seems to get any time off to be with her brother. We often see him sitting on his porch reading his newspaper.

In both versions, the blindness of the old man is mentioned in the first sentence and the anomalous fact that he reads the newspaper is reported in the last sentence. Detecting the anomaly requires us to note that the old man is blind and that he was seen reading the newspaper, and to relate these facts to our knowledge that (barring Braille newspapers) reading requires vision. In neither version is blindness explicitly mentioned after the first sentence, but in Example 19 blindness continues to be salient in the discourse. In Example 20, the intervening material deals with the man's sister. The old man and his physical disability are no longer the focus of the discourse; they are in the background. Light and Albertson found that anomaly detection differed across age only for the backgrounded versions of the stories. However, memory for factual information needed to detect the anomaly was also less accurate in the old. When anomaly detection was conditionalized on memory for factual material, the age difference disappeared. These data suggest that difficulties in drawing pragmatic inferences arise because of problems in remembering relevant information rather than from problems in utilizing general world knowledge.

A similar conclusion was drawn by Light and Capps (1986). As discussed earlier, these investigators found that young and older adults were able to use general world knowledge to determine the antecedent of a referentially ambiguous pronoun when the sentence containing the pronoun followed immediately after a context-setting sentence. In another condition, two intervening sentences were inserted between the context-setting sentence and the sentence containing a pronoun, as in the following paragraph:

> John stood watching while Henry jumped across a ravine.
> The ground was so rocky and uneven that only goats used this path.
> There were no flowers but a few weeds grew here and there.
> He fell in the river.

The intervening sentences here were designed to avoid biasing pronoun assignment to either John or Henry, and in general could be said to background the information in the first sentence of a set so that it might no longer be available in consciousness or working memory. Under these circumstances, older adults were less accurate than young ones in deciding on the antecedent of the pronoun, though their performance was still quite good. The reason for this appears to be that older adults are more prone to forget the contents of the context-setting sentence than young adults and hence are unable to constrain their choices of antecedents based on pragmatic considerations. To demonstrate this, Light and Capps asked young and old to recall in writing the first sentence of the paragraph after making a pronoun assignment. Memory for the context-setting sentences was reduced in old age. When pronoun assignment was examined for just those paragraphs for which the context-setting sentences were correctly recalled, the probability of selecting the pragmatically biased antecedent was close to 1.00 for both age groups. The important point here is that when contextual information is available, older adults use it as much as young adults. Their models of discourse, however, will be inaccurate when information necessary to draw an inference is lost or inaccessible.

This conclusion is reinforced by a series of studies conducted by Hasher and Zacks (1988). In their studies, young and older adults read a series of passages in which information was presented explicitly, was readily inferred (Expected condition), or required a shift in interpretation (Unexpected condition). Examples of these passages follow:

> *Explicit and Expected versions.* The artist was busily painting one day when he received the phone call he had been expecting from his doctor's office.

He was concerned about the results of a series of lab tests he had taken. The artist was told that he had three more months (to live). He was shocked to hear this kind of news from his doctor. Although he had not been feeling well, he still had not expected to hear such bad news. His doctor expressed sympathy and hung up. Suddenly the painting was no longer important. The artist mixed himself a strong drink.

Unexpected version. The artist was concerned about having his painting ready for the exhibit deadline. While he was busily painting one day, he received a phone call. The artist was told he had three more months. He was shocked to hear this kind of news from his doctor. Although he had not been feeling well, he still had not expected to hear such bad news. His doctor expressed sympathy and hung up. Suddenly the painting was no longer important. The artist mixed himself a strong drink. (p. 199)

In each case, the target question asked what the artist had 3 more months to do. This fact is stated explicitly in one version of the passage and easily inferred from the schema evoked by the passage in the Expected version. However, in the Unexpected version, the first inference is likely to be that the artist has 3 months to complete his painting. Only later, as it becomes clear that the call is from his doctor and that he has been ailing, is it apparent that the 3 months is the artist's life expectancy. Older adults were as accurate as young adults when the target information was stated explicitly. Their ability to respond correctly to inference questions depended on presentation condition. When subjects listened to passages presented at a rate under the control of the experimenter, age differences were found for both Expected and Unexpected versions. When subjects could read the passages at their own pace but could see each sentence only once, age differences were found only for the Unexpected version. And when the entire passage could be viewed during reading, age differences disappeared entirely. These results are accommodated by the hypothesis that age differences in drawing inferences stem from difficulties in retrieving facts stated in the discourse that are relevant to the integration of old and new information, not to difficulties in accessing or using previously acquired general world knowledge.

Summary

In this section, we have reviewed research showing that older adults use general world knowledge in much the same way as do younger adults. Young and older adults are equally sensitive to the nuances of word meanings highlighted by particular sentence contexts, and this is true for sentences requiring metaphoric interpretation as well as for sentences not involving figurative language. Young and older adults are both responsive to the availability of thematic information relevant to a passage; memory is improved and pragmatic inferences are drawn when such information is present. Both young and older adults use a variety of strategies dependent on general world knowledge in understanding anaphoric devices. Older adults, however, are more impaired than young adults in use of general world knowledge when memory load is high.

CONCLUSIONS

Before closing, I would like to make several points about comprehension and memory in old age. The literature surveyed here indicates that young and normal older adults are remarkably similar in conceptual knowledge. There is little evidence for the kind of breakdown in semantic structure in normal aging that has been hypothesized in Alzheimer's disease. Young and older adults also seem to access general world knowledge during comprehension and retrieval in much the same way. Yet, there are age-related differences in the amount remembered by young and older adults, and this age deficit in memory has sometimes been laid at the door of a semantic deficit. For example, Craik and Byrd (1982) hypothesized that "older subjects' encodings will contain less associative and inferential information; their encodings go less beyond the information given" and that "an encoded event is less modified by the specific context in which it occurs for the older person" (p. 208). Rabinowitz et al. (1982) also suggested that older adults do not form distinctive, contextually specific, encodings of new information, but rather encode events "in the same old way" from one occasion to the next. Couched in the language of network models, the idea is that when older adults encounter an instance of a concept or schema, the pattern of activation depends on the strength of preexisting associations and not on the specifics of the current situation.

There are a number of reasons for caution in accepting this view (Light, 1991):

1. Our review turned up little evidence to suggest an age-related impairment in semantic organization or in semantic activation processes. Moreover, there does not seem to be much relationship between measures of conceptual knowledge and measures of memory for new information. Such relationships would be predicted by the semantic deficit hypothesis, because the mechanism underlying retrieval of both semantic and episodic information is spreading activation (Anderson, 1983). However, picture-naming accuracy is not a good predictor of performance on a delayed memory test (Albert et al., 1988; Mitchell, 1989). Nor is there a strong

correlation between magnitude of semantic priming and subsequent memory for the words in the priming task (see Light, 1991, for a review). One knowledge variable that does predict memory for new information is vocabulary test score. For instance, Hartley (1988) found that a factor including vocabulary was a significant predictor of text memory for both young and older adults. However, vocabulary scores tend to increase with age whereas text memory scores decrease with age. Hence, it is unlikely that loss of word meanings contributes to memory difficulties in old age. There seems, then, to be little basis for concluding that changes in semantic organization underlie memory deficits in old age. It is interesting to note, in this context, that anterograde amnesics may show severely impaired memory in the absence of a semantic deficit (Ellis & Young, 1988; Weingartner et al., 1983).

2. Evidence offered as support for increased generality and/or decreased encoding specificity in old age is subject to alternative interpretations. As discussed earlier, Hess (1985) suggested that older adults depend more on schematic information than young adults in remembering. His argument was based on the outcomes of his studies of script memory in which larger age differences were obtained in memory for atypical actions than in memory for typical actions. Because typical actions are more likely to be necessary or central to a script and hence are more likely to be performed each time a script is enacted, such results could be taken as evidence that older adults encode more generally. However, we believe that the reason older adults remember less atypical information is not that older adults have less elaborated knowledge structures or faulty access to these structures. The pattern of their intrusion errors in recall and false alarms in recognition shows that they are quite similar to young adults in the nature of inferences drawn about unstated but likely actions. Rather, what is going on seems to be a failure on the part of older adults to establish new connections in memory. That is, this seems to be just an example of a larger age difference in the formation of associations between weakly related events than between strongly related events (Light & Burke, 1988) and, in fact, Hess (1990; Hess et al., 1989) made just this point.

A similar interpretation also may be placed on studies of encoding specificity in young and older adults. Rabinowitz et al. (1982) suggested that in paired-associates tasks older adults, because of insufficient attentional resources, encode events in a stereotyped way from situation to situation, including only general or core semantic information, rather than the novel semantic information needed to integrate the pairs. In one of their experiments, young and older adults studied a list of word pairs, half of which were strong associates and half of which were weak associates. At test, the retrieval cues were the stimulus members of the studied pairs for half of the items and new extralist cues that were either strong or weak associates of the targets for the other half of the items. An encoding specificity effect is demonstrated when list cues produce better recall than new cues. When strongly associated pairs were studied, both young and old showed strong encoding specificity effects—that is, strong associates produced better recall than weakly associated new cues. When weakly associated pairs were studied, only the young showed better recall when the original weak cues were presented than when new strongly associated cues were given. This pattern of results was interpreted as support for the hypothesis that young and old both encode general aspects of target words but that only the young record novel, contextual information. A similar set of outcomes, comparable context effects for related but not unrelated word pairs, was obtained by Hess (1984). There are two points to be made about these results. First, they are not invariably obtained (see, e.g., Light et al., 1991, and Puglisi, Park, Smith, & Dudley, 1988), so their robustness is questionable. Second, even if reliable, they do not necessarily attest to differences in the specificity of semantic encoding. What they seem to suggest is, again, that older adults have difficulty in forming or retrieving associations between unrelated words. Interpreting such results as evidence of a semantic encoding deficit would mean that any age deficit in memory for new information is prima facie evidence for a semantic encoding deficit. This line of reasoning quickly can become circular unless it is established both that there is an age deficit in semantic encoding and that this semantic deficit is responsible for age differences in remembering new material. As noted earlier, there is very little evidence for either of these links in the argument (see also Burke & Light, 1981, and Light, 1991, for related points).[2]

3. The literature indicates that comprehension is no less influenced by specific linguistic context in the old than in the young. Particularization of word meanings in sentences, comprehension of anaphoric devices, and drawing pragmatic inferences are unimpaired in old age except when integration of information from earlier parts of a discourse is required.

---

[2]There is a sense in which it may be correct to say that older adults are "more schematic" in their memory. Older adults may make recognition memory judgments on the basis of fit to a schema rather than on the basis of memory for specific contextual information (Hess, 1990; Reder, Wible, & Martin, 1986). Their recall also may depend more on guesses based on plausible scenarios than the recall of young adults. Whether this is due to failure to encode the particulars of a situation or to age/cohort differences in the social construction of memory tasks is not clear at this time. There is some evidence, for instance, that older adults may be less likely than young adults to spontaneously engage in literal, text-based recall and more likely to prefer a knowledge-based integrative recall style which includes mention of pragmatic and psychological inferences invited by the text (Adams, Labouvie-Vief, Hobart, & Dorosz, 1990).

Moreover, studies of word recognition and naming (e.g., Cohen & Faulkner, 1983; Nebes et al., 1986) and studies of immediate memory for sentences (Wingfield, Poon, Lombardi, & Lowe, 1985) show that older adults are at least as sensitive as younger ones to semantic and syntactic constraints. Such findings are best understood as reflecting intact conceptual structures and intact activation of general world knowledge in old age whenever relevant information is available in working memory.

We do agree with Craik and Byrd (1982) that there is a sense in which "an encoded event is less modified by the specific context in which it occurs for the older person" (p. 208). It is important, however, to be precise in specifying the nature of this contextual information. Everything discussed in the second half of this chapter suggests that older adults are just as sensitive to linguistic or semantic context as young adults. What they seem to have a problem with is memory for "nonlinguistic" context. Older adults are less adept at monitoring the sources of information they have received. For example, they are not as good as young adults in recalling information about input modality (e.g., McIntyre & Craik, 1987), the case in which a word was printed (Kausler & Puckett, 1980), the sex of a speaker (Kausler & Puckett, 1981), or the color in which a word was printed (Park & Puglisi, 1985). Nor do older adults remember as much as young adults about the temporal and spatial contexts in which information was acquired (see Light, 1991, for a review). In this sense, then, it is quite accurate to say that the young establish more elaborate, more precise, more contextually specific memories than do the old. Maintaining the distinction between semantic and nonsemantic context should help in delineating the nature of the memory impairment found in old age. It may be that older adults' impairment in recall of nonlinguistic context is a reflection of their more general difficulty in formation of new associations.

ACKNOWLEDGMENT

Preparation of this chapter was supported by Grant R37 AG02452 from the National Institute on Aging.

REFERENCES

Adams, C., Labouvie-Vief, G., Hobart, C. J., & Dorosz, M. (1990). Adult age group differences in story recall style. *Journal of Gerontology: Psychological Sciences, 45,* P17–P27.
Alba, J. W., & Hasher, L. (1983). Is memory schematic? *Psychological Bulletin, 93,* 203–231.
Albert, M. S., Heller, H. S., & Milberg, W. (1988). Changes in naming ability with age. *Psychology and Aging, 3,* 173–178.

Anderson, J. A. (1983). A spreading activation theory of memory. *Journal of Verbal Learning and Verbal Behavior, 22,* 261–295.

Anderson, R. C., & Pichert, J. W. (1978). Recall of previously unrecallable information following a shift in perspective. *Journal of Verbal Learning and Verbal Behavior, 17,* 1–12.

Annett, M. (1959). The classification of instances of four common class concepts by children and adults. *British Journal of Educational Psychology, 29,* 223–236.

Anooshian, L. J., & Samuelson, J. A. (1985–1986). Age differences in processing: Assessments of depth, elaboration and encoding-retrieval compatibility with multidimensional scaling. *International Journal of Aging and Human Development, 22,* 271–289.

Arbuckle, T. Y., Vanderleck, V. F., Harsany, M., & Lapidus, S. (1990). Adult age differences in memory in relation to availability and accessibility of knowledge-based schemas. *Journal of Experimental Psychology: Learning, Memory, and Cognition, 16,* 305–315.

Balota, D. A., & Duchek, J. M. (1988). Age-related differences in lexical access, spreading activation, and simple pronunciation. *Psychology and Aging, 3,* 84–93.

Baltes, P. B., & Smith, J. (1990). Toward a psychology of wisdom and its ontogenesis. In R. J. Sternberg (Ed.), *Wisdom: Its nature, origins, and development* (pp. 87–120). New York: Cambridge University Press.

Barclay, J. R., Bransford, J. D., Franks, J. J., McCarrell, N. S., & Nitsch, K. (1974). Comprehension and semantic flexibility. *Journal of Verbal Learning and Verbal Behavior, 13,* 471–481.

Barsalou, L. W. (1982). Context-independent and context-dependent information in concepts. *Memory & Cognition, 10,* 82–93.

Barsalou, L. W. (1983). Ad hoc categories. *Memory & Cognition, 11,* 211–227.

Bartlett, F. C. (1932). *Remembering.* Cambridge, England: Cambridge University Press.

Bayles, K. A., & Kaszniak, A. W. (1987). *Communication and cognition in normal aging and dementia.* Boston: College-Hill.

Berg, C. A. (1990). What is intellectual efficacy over the life course? Using adults' conceptions to address the question. In J. A. Rodin, C. Schooler, & K. W. Schaie (Eds.), *Self-directedness: Causes and effects throughout the life course* (pp. 155–181). Hillsdale, NJ: Lawrence Erlbaum Associates.

Birren, J. E., & Morrison, D. F. (1961). Analysis of the WAIS subtests in relation to age and education. *Journal of Gerontology, 16,* 363–369.

Blanchard-Fields, F. (1986). Reasoning on social dilemmas varying in emotional saliency: An adult developmental perspective. *Psychology and Aging, 1,* 325–333.

Borod, J. C., Goodglass, H., & Kaplan, E. (1980). Normative data on the Boston Diagnostic Aphasia Examination, Parietal Lobe Battery, and the Boston Naming Test. *Journal of Clinical Neuropsychology, 2,* 209–215.

Bower, G. H., Black, J. B., & Turner, T. J. (1979). Scripts in memory for text. *Cognitive Psychology, 11,* 177–220.

Bower, G. H., & Morrow, D. G. (1990). Mental models in narrative comprehension. *Science, 247,* 44–48.

Bowles, N. L. (1989). Age and semantic inhibition in word retrieval. *Journal of Gerontology: Psychological Sciences, 44,* P88–P90.

Bowles, N. L., Obler, L. K., & Albert, M. L. (1987). Naming errors in healthy aging and dementia of the Alzheimer type. *Cortex, 23,* 519–524.

Bowles, N. L., & Poon, L. W. (1985). Aging and retrieval of words in semantic memory. *Journal of Gerontology, 40,* 71–77.

Bowles, N. L., Williams, D., & Poon, L. W. (1983). On the use of word association norms in aging research. *Experimental Aging Research, 9,* 175–177.

Bransford, J. D., & Johnson, M. K. (1972). Contextual prerequisites for understanding: Some investigations of comprehension and recall. *Journal of Verbal Learning and Verbal Behavior, 11,* 717–726.

Brewer, M. B., & Lui, L. (1984). Categorization of the elderly by the elderly: Effects of perceiver's category membership. *Personality and Social Psychology Bulletin, 10,* 585–595.

Brown, A. S., & Mitchell, D. B. (in press). Age differences in retrieval consistency and response dominance. *Journal of Gerontology: Psychological Sciences.*

Burke, D. M., & Harrold, R. M. (1988). Automatic and effortful semantic processes in old age: Experimental and naturalistic approaches. In L. L. Light & D. M. Burke (Eds.), *Language, memory, and aging* (pp. 100–116). New York: Cambridge University Press.

Burke, D. M., & Light, L. L. (1981). Memory and aging: The role of retrieval processes. *Psychological Bulletin, 90,* 513–546.

Burke, D. M., MacKay, D. G., Worthley, J. S., & Wade, E. (1991). On the tip of the tongue: What causes word finding failures in young and older adults? *Journal of Memory and Language, 30,* 542–579.

Burke, D. M., & Peters, L. (1986). Word associations in old age: Evidence for consistency in semantic encoding during adulthood. *Psychology and Aging, 1,* 283–292.

Burke, D. M., & Yee, P. L. (1984). Semantic priming during sentence processing by young and older adults. *Developmental Psychology, 20,* 903–910.

Byrd, M. (1984). Age differences in the retrieval of information from semantic memory. *Experimental Aging Research, 10,* 29–33.

Cerella, J., & Fozard, J. L. (1984). Lexical access and age. *Developmental Psychology, 20,* 235–243.

Chafe, W. L. (1972). Discourse structure and human knowledge. In J. Carroll & R. Freedle (Eds.), *Language comprehension and the acquisition of knowledge* (pp. 41–69). Washington, DC: Winston.

Chertkow, H., Bub, D., & Seidenberg, M. (1989). Priming and semantic memory loss in Alzheimer's disease. *Brain and Language, 36,* 420–446.

Chiarello, C. (1990). *The neurofractionation of semantic priming: Injured brains, half brains, and models of lexical-semantic memory.* Unpublished manuscript, Syracuse University, Department of Psychology, Syracuse, NY.

Cicirelli, V. G. (1976). Categorization behavior in aging subjects. *Journal of Gerontology, 31,* 676–680.

Cohen, G. (1979). Language comprehension in old age. *Cognitive Psychology, 11,* 412–429.

Cohen, G. (1981). Inferential reasoning in old age. *Cognition, 9,* 59–72.

Cohen, G. (1988). Age differences in memory for text: Production deficiency or processing limitations? In L. L. Light & D. M. Burke (Eds.), *Language, memory, and aging* (pp. 171–190). New York: Cambridge University Press.

Cohen, G., & Faulkner, D. (1983). Word recognition: Age differences in contextual facilitation effects. *British Journal of Psychology, 74,* 239–251.

Cohen, G., & Faulkner, D. (1986). Memory for proper names: Age differences in retrieval. *British Journal of Developmental Psychology, 4,* 187–197.

Collins, A. M., & Loftus, E. F. (1975). A spreading-activation theory of semantic processing. *Psychological Review, 82,* 407–428.

Cooper, P. V. (1990). Discourse production and normal aging: Performance on oral picture description tasks. *Journal of Gerontology: Psychological Sciences, 45,* P210–P214.

Cornelius, S. W. (1990). Aging and everyday cognitive abilities. In T. M. Hess (Ed.), *Aging and cognition: Knowledge organization and utilization* (pp. 411–459). Amsterdam: Elsevier.

Cornelius, S. W., & Caspi, A. (1987). Everyday problem solving in adulthood and old age. *Psychology and Aging, 2,* 144–153.

Craik, F. I. M. (1977). Age differences in human memory. In J. E. Birren & K. W. Schaie (Eds.), *Handbook of the psychology of aging* (pp. 384–420). New York: Van Nostrand Reinhold.

Craik, F. I. M. (1983). On the transfer of information from temporary to permanent storage. *Philosophical Transactions of the Royal Society of London, Series B, 302,* 341–359.

Craik, F. I. M., & Byrd, M. (1982). Aging and cognitive deficits: The role of attentional resources. In F. I. M. Craik & S. Trehub (Eds.), *Aging and cognitive processes* (pp. 191–211). New York: Plenum.

Craik, F. I. M., Byrd, M., & Swanson, J. M. (1987). Patterns of memory loss in three elderly samples. *Psychology and Aging, 2,* 79–86.

Craik, F. I. M., & Rabinowitz, J. C. (1984). Age differences in the acquisition and use of verbal information: A tutorial review. In H. Bouma & D. G. Bouwhuis (Eds.), *Attention and performance: X. Control of language processes* (pp. 471–499). Hillsdale, NJ: Lawrence Erlbaum Associates.

Dell, G. S., McKoon, G., & Ratcliff, R. (1983). The activation of antecedent information during the processing of anaphoric reference in reading. *Journal of Verbal Learning and Verbal Behavior, 22,* 121–132.

Denney, N. W., & Palmer, A. M. (1981). Adult age differences on traditional and practical problem-solving measures. *Journal of Gerontology, 36,* 323–328.

Denney, N. W., & Pearce, K. A. (1989). A developmental study of practical problem solving in adults. *Psychology and Aging, 4,* 438–442.

Denney, N. W., Pearce, K. A., & Palmer, A. M. (1982). A developmental study of adults' performance on traditional and practical problem-solving tasks. *Experimental Aging Research, 8,* 115–118.

Ehrlich, K. (1980). Comprehension of pronouns. *Quarterly Journal of Experimental Psychology, 32,* 247–255.

Ellis, A. W., & Young, A. W. (1988). *Human cognitive neuropsychology.* Hillsdale, NJ: Lawrence Erlbaum Associates.

Erber, J. T. (1989). Young and older adults' appraisal of memory failures in young and older adult target persons. *Journal of Gerontology: Psychological Sciences, 44,* P170–P175.

Erber, J. T., & Rothberg, S. T. (1991). Here's looking at you: The relative effect of age and attractiveness on judgments about memory failure. *Journal of Gerontology: Psychological Sciences, 46,* P116–P123.

Erber, J. T., Szuchman, L. T., & Rothberg, S. T. (1990). Everyday memory failure: Age differences in appraisal and attribution. *Psychology and Aging, 5,* 236–241.

Eysenck, M. W. (1974). Age differences in incidental learning. *Developmental Psychology, 10,* 936–941.

Eysenck, M. W. (1975). Retrieval from semantic memory as a function of age. *Journal of Gerontology, 30,* 174–180.

Fletcher, C. R. (1984). Markedness and topic continuity in discourse processing. *Journal of Verbal Learning and Verbal Behavior, 23,* 487–493.

Flicker, C., Ferris, S. H., Crook, T., & Bartus, R. T. (1986). The effects of aging and dementia on concept formation as measured on an object-sorting task. *Developmental Neuropsychology, 2,* 65–72.

Folman, S., Lazarus, R. S., Pimley, S., & Novacek, J. (1987). Age differences in stress and coping processes. *Psychology and Aging, 2,* 171–184.

Galambos, J. A. (1986). Knowledge structures for common activities. In J. A. Galambos, R. P. Abelson, & J. B. Black (Eds.), *Knowledge structures* (pp. 21–47). Hillsdale, NJ: Lawrence Erlbaum Associates.

Garrod, S., & Sanford, A. (1977). Interpreting anaphoric relations: The integration of semantic information while reading. *Journal of Verbal Learning and Verbal Behavior, 16,* 77–90.

Garvey, C., & Caramazza, A. (1974). Implicit causality in verbs. *Linguistic Inquiry, 5,* 459–464.

Gillund, G., & Perlmutter, M. (1988). Episodic memory and knowledge interactions across adulthood. In L. L. Light & D. M. Burke (Eds.), *Language, memory, and aging* (pp. 191–208). New York: Cambridge University Press.

Givón, T. (Ed.) (1983). *Topic continuity in discourse: A quantitative cross-language study.* Amsterdam: J. Benjamin's.

Graesser, A. C., Woll, S. B., Kowalski, D. J., & Smith, D. A. (1980). Memory for typical and atypical actions in scripted activities. *Journal of Experimental Psychology: Human Learning and Memory, 6,* 503–515.

Greenspan, S. L. (1986). Semantic flexibility and referential specificity of concrete nouns. *Journal of Memory and Language, 25,* 539–557.

Grober, E. H., Beardsley, W., & Caramazza, A. (1978). Parallel function strategy in pronoun assignment. *Cognition, 6,* 117–133.

Hartley, J. T. (1988). Aging and individual differences in memory for written discourse. In L. L. Light & D. M. Burke (Eds.), *Language, memory, and aging* (pp. 36–57). New York: Cambridge University Press.

Hasher, L., & Zacks, R. T. (1988). Working memory, comprehension, and aging: A review and a new view. In G. H. Bower (Ed.), *The psychology of learning and motivation* (Vol. 22, pp. 193–225). New York: Academic.

Haviland, S. E., & Clark, H. H. (1974). What's new? Acquiring new information as a process in comprehension. *Journal of Verbal Learning and Verbal Behavior, 13,* 512–521.

Heckhausen, J., Dixon, R. A., & Baltes, P. B. (1989). Gains and losses in development throughout adulthood as perceived by different age groups. *Developmental Psychology, 25,* 109–121.

Hertzog, C., Raskind, C. L., & Cannon, C. J. (1986). Age-related slowing in semantic information processing speed: An individual differences analysis. *Journal of Gerontology, 41,* 500–502.

Hess, T. M. (1984). Effects of semantically related and unrelated contexts on recognition memory of different-aged adults. *Journal of Gerontology, 39,* 444–451.

Hess, T. M. (1985). Aging and context influences on recognition memory for typical and atypical script actions. *Developmental Psychology, 21,* 1139–1151.

Hess, T. M. (1990). Aging and schematic influences on memory. In T. M. Hess (Ed.), *Aging and cognition: Knowledge organization and utilization* (pp. 93–160). Amsterdam: North Holland.

Hess, T. M. (1992). Adult age differences in script content and structure. In R. L. West & J. D. Sinnott (Eds.), *Everyday memory and aging: Current research and methodology* (pp. 87–100). New York: Springer-Verlag.

Hess, T. M., & Arnould, D. (1986). Adult age differences in memory for explicit and implicit sentence information. *Journal of Gerontology, 2,* 191–194.

Hess, T. M., Donley, J., & Vandermaas, M. O. (1989). Aging-related changes in the processing and retention of script information. *Experimental Aging Research, 15,* 89–96.

Hess, T. M., & Flannagan, D. A. (in press). Schema-based retrieval processes in young and older adults. *Journal of Gerontology: Psychological Sciences.*

Hess, T. M., & Tate, C. S. (1991). Adult age differences in explanations and memory for behavioral information. *Psychology and Aging, 6,* 86–92.

Hess, T. M., Vandermaas, M. O., Donley, J., & Snyder, M. (1987). Memory for sex-role consistent and inconsistent actions in young and old adults. *Journal of Gerontology, 42,* 505–511.

Hirst, W., & Brill, G. A. (1980). Contextual aspects of pronoun assignment. *Journal of Verbal Learning and Verbal Behavior, 19,* 168–175.

Hobbs, J. R. (1979). Coherence and coreference. *Cognitive Science, 3,* 67–90.

Hochman, L. O., Storandt, M., & Rosenberg, A. M. (1986). Age and its effect on perceptions of psychopathology. *Psychology and Aging, 1,* 337–338.

Holliday, S. G., & Chandler, M. J. (1986). *Wisdom: Explorations in adult competence.* Basel, Switzerland: Karger.

Howard, D. V. (1979). *Restricted word association norms for adults between the ages of 20 and 80* (Tech. Rep. No. NIA-79-2). Washington, DC: Georgetown University Press.

Howard, D. V. (1980). Category norms: A comparison of the Battig and Montague (1969) norms with the responses of adults between the ages of 20 and 80. *Journal of Gerontology, 35,* 225–231.

Howard, D. V. (1983a). The effects of aging and degree of association on the semantic priming of lexical decisions. *Experimental Aging Research, 9,* 145–151.

Howard, D. V. (1983b). A multidimensional scaling analysis of aging and the semantic structure of animal names. *Experimental Aging Research, 9,* 27–30.

Howard, D. V., McAndrews, M. P., & Lasaga, M. I. (1981). Semantic priming of lexical decisions in young and old adults. *Journal of Gerontology, 36,* 707–714.

Huff, F. J., Corkin, S., & Growdon, J. H. (1986). Semantic impairment and anomia in Alzheimer's disease. *Brain and Language, 28,* 235–249.

Johnson-Laird, P. N. (1983). *Mental models.* Cambridge, MA: Harvard University Press.

Kausler, D. H., & Puckett, J. M. (1980). Adult age differences in recognition memory for a nonsemantic attribute. *Experimental Aging Research, 6,* 349–355.

Kausler, D. H., & Puckett, J. M. (1981). Adult age differences in memory for sex of voice. *Journal of Gerontology, 36,* 44–50.

Keenan, J. M., & Kintsch, W. (1974). The identification of explicitly and implicitly presented information. In W. Kintsch, *The representation of meaning in memory* (pp. 153–166). Hillsdale, NJ: Lawrence Erlbaum Associates.

Keenan, J. M., Potts, G. R., Golding, J. M., & Jennings, T. M. (1990). Which elaborative inferences are drawn during reading? A question of methodologies. In D. A. Balota, G. B. Flores d'Arcais, & K. Rayner (Eds.), *Comprehension processes in reading* (pp. 377–402). Hillsdale, NJ: Lawrence Erlbaum Associates.

Kintsch, W. (1988). The role of knowledge in discourse comprehension: A construction-integration model. *Psychological Review, 95,* 163–182.

Kite, M. E., Deaux, K., & Miele, M. (1991). Stereotypes of young and old: Does age outweigh gender? *Psychology and Aging, 6,* 19–27.

Kogan, N. (1973). Creativity and cognitive style: A life-span perspective. In P. B. Baltes & K. W. Schaie (Eds.), *Life-span developmental psychology: Personality and socialization* (pp. 145–178). New York: Academic.

Kynette, D., & Kemper, S. (1986). Aging and the loss of grammatical forms: A cross-sectional study of language performance. *Language & Communication, 6,* 65–72.

Labouvie-Vief, G. (1985). Intelligence and cognition. In J. E. Birren & K. W. Schaie, *Handbook of the psychology of aging* (2nd ed., pp. 500–530). New York: Van Nostrand Reinhold.

Lakoff, G. (1987). *Women, fire, and dangerous things.* Chicago: University of Chicago Press.

Laurence, M. W., & Arrowood, A. J. (1982). Classification style differences in the elderly. In F. I. M. Craik & S. Trehub (Eds.), *Aging and cognitive processes* (pp. 213–220). New York: Plenum.

Laver, G. D., & Burke, D. M. (1990). *Are semantic priming effects equivalent in young and older adults?* Unpublished manuscript, Claremont Graduate School, Department of Psychology, Claremont, CA.

Lesgold, A. M. (1972). Pronominalization: A device for unifying sentences in memory. *Journal of Verbal Learning and Verbal Behavior, 11,* 316–323.

Light, L. L. (1991). Memory and aging: Four hypotheses in search of data. *Annual Review of Psychology, 42,* 333–376.

Light, L. L., & Albertson, S. (1988). Comprehension of pragmatic implications in young and older adults. In L. L. Light & D. M. Burke (Eds.), *Language, memory, and aging* (pp. 133–153). New York: Cambridge University Press.

Light, L. L., & Anderson, P. A. (1983). Memory for scripts in young and older adults. *Memory & Cognition, 11,* 435–444.

Light, L. L., & Burke, D. M. (1988). Patterns of language and memory in old age. In L. L. Light & D. M. Burke (Eds.), *Language, memory, and aging* (pp. 244–271). New York: Cambridge University Press.

Light, L. L., & Capps, J. L. (1986). Comprehension of pronouns in young and older adults. *Developmental Psychology, 22,* 580–585.

Light, L. L., Albertson Owens, S., Mahoney, P. G., & La Voie, D. (in press). Comprehension of metaphors by young and older adults. In J. Cerella, W. Hoyer, J. Rybash, & M. L. Commons (Eds.), *Adult information processing: Limits on loss.* San Diego: Academic.

Light, L. L., Valencia-Laver, D., & Zavis, D. (1991). Instantiation of general terms in young and older adults. *Psychology and Aging, 6,* 337–351.

List, J. A. (1986). Age and schematic differences in the reliability of eyewitness testimony. *Developmental Psychology, 22,* 50–57.

Lovelace, E. A., & Cooley, S. (1982). Free associations of older adults to single words and conceptually related word triads. *Journal of Gerontology, 37,* 432–437.

Madden, D. J. (1985). Age-related slowing in the retrieval of information from long-term memory. *Journal of Gerontology, 40,* 208–210.

Madden, D. J. (1986). Adult age differences in visual word recognition: Semantic encoding and episodic retention. *Experimental Aging Research, 12,* 71–77.

Madden, D. J. (1988). Adult age differences in the effects of sentence context and stimulus degradation during visual word recognition. *Psychology and Aging, 3,* 167–172.

Madden, D. J. (1989). Visual word identification and age-related slowing. *Cognitive Development, 4,* 1–29.

Mandel, R. G., & Johnson, N. S. (1984). A developmental analysis of story recall and comprehension in adulthood. *Journal of Verbal Learning and Verbal Behavior, 23,* 643–659.

Mandler, J. M., & Johnson, N. S. (1977). Remembrance of things parsed: Story structure and recall. *Journal of Verbal Learning and Verbal Behavior, 23,* 111–151.

Maylor, E. A. (1990a). Age, blocking and the tip of the tongue state. *British Journal of Psychology, 81,* 123–134.

Maylor, E. A. (1990b). Recognizing and naming faces: Aging, memory retrieval, and the tip of the tongue state. *Journal of Gerontology: Psychological Sciences, 45,* P215–P226.

McClelland, J. L., & Rumelhart, D. E. (1981). An interactive activation model of context effects in letter perception: Part 1. An account of basic findings. *Psychological Review, 88,* 375–407.

McCrae, R. R., Arenberg, D., & Costa, P. T. (1987). Declines in divergent thinking with age: Cross-sectional, longitudinal, and cross-sequential analyses. *Psychology and Aging, 2,* 130–137.

McIntyre, J. S., & Craik, F. I. M. (1987). Age differences in memory for item and source information. *Canadian Journal of Psychology, 41,* 175–192.

McKoon, G., & Ratcliff, R. (1990). Textual inferences: Models and measures. In D. A. Balota, G. B. Flores d'Arcais, & K. Rayner (Eds.), *Comprehension processes in reading* (pp. 403–421). Hillsdale, NJ: Lawrence Erlbaum Associates.

Medin, D. L. (1989). Concepts and conceptual structure. *American Psychologist, 44,* 1469–1481.

Meyer, D. E., & Schvaneveldt, R. W. (1971). Facilitation in recognizing pairs of words: Evidence of a dependence between retrieval operations. *Journal of Experimental Psychology, 90,* 227–234.

Milberg, W., & Blumstein, S. E. (1981). Lexical decision and aphasia: Evidence for semantic processing. *Brain and Language, 14,* 371–385.

Mitchell, D. B. (1989). How many memory systems? Evidence from aging. *Journal of Experimental Psychology: Learning, Memory, and Cognition, 15,* 31–49.

Morrow, D. G. (1985). Prominent characters and events organize narrative understanding. *Journal of Memory and Language, 24,* 304–319.

Mueller, J. H., Kausler, D. H., & Faherty, A. (1980). Age and access time for different memory codes. *Experimental Aging Research, 6,* 445–449.

Nebes, R. D. (1989). Semantic memory in Alzheimer's disease. *Psychological Bulletin, 106,* 377–394.

Nebes, R. D., Boller, F., & Holland, A. (1986). Use of semantic context by patients with Alzheimer's disease. *Psychology and Aging, 1,* 261–269.

Nebes, R. D., & Brady, C. B. (1988). Integrity of semantic fields in Alzheimer's disease. *Cortex, 24,* 291–299.

Neely, J. H. (1977). Semantic priming and retrieval from lexical memory: Roles of inhibitionless spreading activation and limited-capacity attention. *Journal of Experimental Psychology: General, 106,* 226–254.

Nelson, K. (1977). The syntagmatic-paradigmatic shift revisited: A review of research and theory. *Psychological Bulletin, 84,* 93–116.

Nicholas, M., Obler, L., Albert, M., & Goodglass, H. (1985). Lexical retrieval in healthy aging. *Cortex, 21,* 595–606.

Ober, B. A., Dronkers, N. F., Koss, E., Delis, D. C., & Friedland, R. P. (1986). Retrieval from semantic memory in Alzheimer-type dementia. *Journal of Clinical and Experimental Neuropsychology, 8,* 75–92.

Obler, L. K. (1980). Narrative discourse style in the elderly. In L. K. Obler & M. L. Albert (Eds.), *Language and communication in the elderly* (pp. 75–90). Lexington, MA: Heath.

Obler, L. K., & Albert, M. L. (1985). Language skills across adulthood. In J. E. Birren & K. W. Schaie (Eds.), *Handbook of the psychology of aging* (2nd ed., pp. 463–473). New York: Van Nostrand Reinhold.

Park, D. C., & Puglisi, J. T. (1985). Older adults' memory for the color of pictures and words. *Journal of Gerontology, 40,* 198–204.

Pearce, K. A., & Denney, N. W. (1984). A life-span study of classification preference. *Journal of Gerontology, 39,* 458–464.

Perlmutter, M. (1979). Age differences in the consistency of adults' associative responses. *Experimental Aging Research, 5,* 549–553.

Petros, T. V., Zehr, H. D., & Chabot, R. J. (1983). Adult age differences in accessing and retrieving information from long-term memory. *Journal of Gerontology, 38,* 589–592.

Posner, M. I., & Snyder, C. R. R. (1975). Attention and cognitive control. In A. Solso (Ed.), *Information processing and cognition* (pp. 55–85). Hillsdale, NJ: Lawrence Erlbaum Associates.

Pratt, M. W., Boyes, C., Robins, S., & Manchester, J. (1989). Telling tales: Aging, working memory, and the narrative cohesion of story retellings. *Developmental Psychology, 25,* 628–635.

Puglisi, J. T., Park, D. C., Smith, A. D., & Dudley, W. N. (1988). Age differences in encoding specificity. *Journal of Gerontology: Psychological Sciences, 43,* P145–P150.

Rabinowitz, J. C., Craik, F. I. M., & Ackerman, B. P. (1982). A processing resource account of age differences in recall. *Canadian Journal of Psychology, 36,* 325–344.

Radvansky, G. A., Gerard, L. D., Zacks, R. T., & Hasher, L. (1990). Younger and older adults' use of mental models as representations for text materials. *Psychology and Aging, 5,* 209–214.

Reder, L. M., Wible, C., & Martin, J. (1986). Differential memory changes with age: Exact retrieval versus plausible inference. *Journal of Experimental Psychology: Learning, Memory, and Cognition, 12,* 72–81.

Riegel, K. F. (1959). A study of verbal achievements of older persons. *Journal of Gerontology, 14,* 453–456.

Riegel, K. F., & Riegel, R. M. (1964). Changes in associative behavior during later years of life: A cross-sectional analysis. *Vita Humana, 7,* 1–32.

Rissenberg, M., & Glanzer, M. (1987). Free recall and word finding ability in normal aging and senile dementia of the Alzheimer's type: The effect of item concreteness. *Journal of Gerontology, 42,* 318–322.

Ross, B. L., & Berg, C. A. (1992). Examining idiosyncracies in script reports across the life span: Distortions or derivations of experience? In R. L. West & J. D. Sinnott (Eds.), *Everyday memory and aging: Current research and methodology* (pp. 39–53). New York: Springer-Verlag.

Ryan, E. B. (1990). *Beliefs about memory changes across the lifespan.* Unpublished manuscript, McMaster University, Department of Psychiatry and Office of Gerontological Studies, Hamilton, Ontario, Canada.

Rybash, J. M., Hoyer, W. J., & Roodin, P. A. (1986). *Adult cognition and aging.* New York: Pergamon.

Salthouse, T. A. (1982). *Adult cognition: An experimental psychology of human aging.* New York: Springer-Verlag.

Salthouse, T. A. (1988). Effects of aging on verbal abilities: Examination of the psychometric literature. In L. L. Light & D. M. Burke (Eds.), *Language, memory, and aging* (pp. 17–35). New York: Cambridge University Press.

Sanford, A. J., & Garrod, S. C. (1981). *Understanding written language: Explorations of comprehension beyond the sentence.* Chichester, England: Wiley.

Santo Pietro, M. J., & Goldfarb, R. (1985). Characteristic patterns of word association responses in institutionalized elderly with and without senile dementia. *Brain and Language, 26,* 230–243.

Schaie, K. W., & Parham, I. A. (1977). Cohort-sequential analyses of adult intellectual development. *Developmental Psychology, 13,* 649–653.

Schank, R. C. (1982). *Dynamic memory.* Cambridge, England: Cambridge University Press.

Schank, R. C., & Abelson, R. P. (1977). *Scripts, plans, goals, and understanding.* Hillsdale, NJ: Lawrence Erlbaum Associates.

Scialfa, C. T., & Margolis, R. B. (1986). Age differences in the commonality of free associations. *Experimental Aging Research, 12,* 95–98.

Sebby, R. A., & Papini, D. R. (1989). Problems in everyday problem solving research: A framework for conceptualizing solutions to everyday problems. In J. D. Sinnott (Ed.), *Everyday problem solving: Theory and applications* (pp. 55–72). New York: Praeger.

Seidenberg, M. S., & McClelland, J. L. (1989). A distributed, developmental model of word recognition and naming. *Psychological Review, 96,* 523–568.

Sharkey, N. E. (1986). A model of knowledge-based expectations in text comprehension. In J. A. Galambos, R. P. Abelson, & J. B. Black (Eds.), *Knowledge structures* (pp. 49–70). Hillsdale, NJ: Lawrence Erlbaum Associates.

Sharkey, N. E. (1990). A connectionist model of text comprehension. In D. A. Balota, G. B. Flores d'Arcais, & K. Rayner (Eds.), *Comprehension processes in reading* (pp. 487–514). Hillsdale, NJ: Lawrence Erlbaum Associates.

Smiley, S. S., & Brown, A. L. (1979). Conceptual preferences for thematic or taxonomic relations: A nonmonotonic age trend from preschool to old age. *Journal of Experimental Child Psychology, 28,* 249–257.

Smith, J., & Baltes, P. B. (1990). Wisdom-related knowledge: Age/cohort differences in response to life-planning problems. *Developmental Psychology, 26,* 494–505.

Smith, S. W., Rebok, G. W., Smith, W. R., Hall, S. E., & Alvin, M. (1983). Adult age differences in the use of story structure in delayed free recall. *Experimental Aging Research, 9,* 191–195.

Smith, M. C., Theodor, L., & Franklin, P. E. (1983). The relationship between contextual facilitation and depth of processing. *Journal of Experimental Psychology: Learning, Memory, and Cognition, 9,* 697–712.

Stanovich, K. E., & West, R. F. (1983). On priming by a sentence context. *Journal of Experimental Psychology: General, 112,* 1–36.

Stine, E. L. (1986). Attribute-based similarity perception in younger and older adults. *Experimental Aging Research, 12,* 89–94.

Tabossi, P., & Johnson-Laird, P. N. (1980). Linguistic context and the priming of semantic information. *Quarterly Journal of Experimental Psychology, 32,* 595–603.

Tanenhaus, M. K., Dell, G. S., & Carlson, G. (1987). Context effects and lexical processing: A connectionist approach to modularity. In J. L. Garfield (Ed.), *Modularity in knowledge representation and natural-language understanding* (pp. 83–110). Cambridge, MA: MIT Press.

Thomas, J. C., Fozard, J. L., & Waugh, N. C. (1977). Age-related differences in naming latency. *American Journal of Psychology, 90,* 499–509.

Thorndyke, P. (1977). Cognitive structures in comprehension and memory of narrative discourse. *Journal of Verbal Learning and Verbal Behavior, 9,* 77–110.

Till, R. E. (1985). Verbatim and inferential memory in young and elderly adults. *Journal of Gerontology, 40,* 316–323.

Till, R. E., & Walsh, D. A. (1980). Encoding and retrieval factors in adult memory for implicational sentences. *Journal of Verbal Learning and Verbal Behavior, 19,* 1–16.

Tresselt, M. E., & Mayzner, M. S. (1964). The Kent–Rosanoff word associations: Word association norms as a function of age. *Psychonomic Science, 1,* 65–66.

Tulving, E. (1983). *Elements of episodic memory.* Oxford, England: Clarendon.

Ulatowska, H. K., Cannito, M. P., Hayashi, M. M., & Fleming, S. G. (1985). Language abilities in the elderly. In H. K. Ulatowska (Ed.), *The aging brain: Communication in the elderly* (pp. 125–139). San Diego: College-Hill.

van Dijk, T. A., & Kintsch, W. (1983). *Strategies of discourse comprehension.* New York: Academic.

Van Gorp, W., Satz, P., Kiersch, M. E., & Henry, R. (1986). Normative data on the Boston Naming Test for a group of normal older adults. *Journal of Clinical and Experimental Neuropsychology, 8,* 702–705.

Verbrugge, R. R., & McCarrell, N. S. (1977). Metaphoric comprehension: Studies in reminding and resembling. *Cognitive Psychology, 9,* 494–533.

Warrington, E. K., & Shallice, T. (1984). Category specific semantic impairments. *Brain, 107,* 829–854.

Weingartner, H., Grafman, J., Boutelle, W., Kaye, W., & Martin, P. R. (1983). Forms of memory failure. *Science, 221,* 380–382.

West, R. F., & Stanovich, K. E. (1978). Automatic contextual facilitation in readers of three ages. *Child Development, 49,* 717–727.

Wingfield, A., Poon, L. W., Lombardi, L., & Lowe, D. (1985). Speed of processing in normal aging: Effects of speech rate, linguistic structure, and processing time. *Journal of Gerontology, 40,* 579–585.

Zelinski, E. M. (1988). Integrating information from discourse: Do older adults show deficits?. In L. L. Light & D. M. Burke (Eds.), *Language, memory, and aging* (pp. 117–132). New York: Cambridge University Press.

Zelinski, E. M., & Miura, S. A. (1988). Effects of thematic information on script memory in young and old adults. *Psychology and Aging, 3,* 292–299.

CHAPTER FOUR

Reasoning and Spatial Abilities

Timothy A. Salthouse
Georgia Institute of Technology

Although reasoning abilities and spatial abilities usually are considered to be distinct, they are treated together in this chapter because (a) measures of performance on reasoning and spatial tests are often highly correlated; (b) both abilities appear to represent a common, and meaningful, level of analysis intermediate between memory and complex thinking or decision making; and (c) there is only a limited amount of empirical literature concerned with the relations between age and each ability. The first and third points are self-explanatory, but the second point warrants some elaboration. Reasoning and spatial abilities typically are measured with tests or tasks that require not only the maintenance or preservation of information, but also that a sequence of operations or transformations be performed on the relevant information. However, unlike more complex and naturalistic problems requiring thinking or decision making, the quality of the answers or decisions is usually not dependent on either the amount or the type of knowledge one possesses. Reasoning and spatial abilities therefore can be considered somewhat more complex than memory ability, but simpler than many thinking or problem-solving abilities. Moreover, because tests of reasoning and spatial abilities often are included in cognitive assessment batteries used to predict performance outside the laboratory, they provide an important linkage between the level of elementary cognitive processes and real-world functioning.

Assessments of reasoning and spatial abilities obviously can vary in the extent to which prior knowledge is required for successful performance.

The current coverage nevertheless is restricted to tests or tasks presumed to require minimal amounts of special knowledge and generally involving such familiar stimulus materials as letters, numbers, or geometric figures. There are two reasons for this emphasis on novel or abstract tasks. The first is a desire to concentrate on the assessment of the efficiency of current processing and not on the appraisal of the products of prior processing. That is, the purpose of most tests of reasoning and spatial abilities is to determine the individual's level of functioning at the current time and not to inventory what he or she was able to accomplish at various times in the past. The influence of current processing efficiency generally is assumed to be greater when the stimulus materials are either highly overlearned, or equally novel, for most examinees, such that the primary determinant of individual differences in performance can be postulated to be the ability to execute the required operations.

The second reason for emphasizing novel or abstract tasks is to avoid possible confoundings between the age of the individual and the amount of experience he or she has received. Because not everyone will have had the same amount of experience with more natural activities, and because as people acquire expertise they often develop special methods of dealing with the information or materials in their specific domains, use of tasks involving natural or realistic materials or operations may lead to problems of distinguishing the pure or basic capabilities of the individual from the declarative and procedural knowledge he or she has acquired through experience.

Of course, objections can be raised against the use of novel or abstract tasks. Perhaps the major criticism is that the level, and perhaps even the method, of performance might vary according to the context in which the task is performed because processes may be adapted and modified to function in different contexts. The research literature on expertise has established that the availability of knowledge increases effectiveness in many ways, and hence conclusions based on tasks presumed to involve minimal knowledge may severely underestimate a given individual's true capabilities in situations in which he or she has extensive experience.

As alluded to earlier, cognitive tasks can be viewed as falling along an approximate hierarchy, with the preservation of information (some forms of memory) near the lower end of the hierarchy, preservation and transformation of information (reasoning and spatial abilities) near the middle of the hierarchy, and preservation, transformation, and integration of information with preexisting knowledge (decision making and judgment) near the top of the hierarchy. All levels of this hierarchy ultimately must be understood, including the highest level in which the knowledge acquired through experience is incorporated into the cognitive functioning of the individual. However, the primary assumption motivating the current review is that it is useful to attempt to understand age relations first with tasks and materials that probably do not vary much with respect to naturally varying experiential influences. Only after moderate understanding is achieved at that level would it then be meaningful to try to assess how variations in knowledge and experience might alter the patterns of age-related differences.

Furthermore, although it is possible that cognition in context, or enriched by experience, is substantially different than the type of cognition assessed by novel or abstract tasks, it seems unlikely that even if the various aspects of cognition are distinct, they would be completely independent. Indeed, a basic premise of most psychometric researchers has been that certain cognitive abilities or mental traits are transsituational or context-independent. One consequence of this assumption is that nearly all the empirical research concerned with relations between aging and higher order cognitive abilities, which has been heavily influenced by the psychometric tradition, has involved assessments assumed to minimize the influence of experiential variations. It is for this reason as much as any other, therefore, that the present review is restricted to tests and tasks sometimes assumed to be culture-fair, or context-independent.

Another restriction on the coverage in the current review is that many types of complex problem solving are excluded from consideration. Specifically, there is no discussion of problems with ambiguous or open-ended solutions, or of everyday problems in which the responses might reflect personality or cognitive style as much as, or possibly even more than, the level of a relevant cognitive ability.

Both reasoning and spatial abilities frequently are subdivided into narrower classifications such as inductive and deductive reasoning, or spatial orientation and spatial visualization. These classifications are largely ignored in this review. The principal reason for neglecting these presumably more precise categorizations is that there is still little consensus with respect to the precise number, or identity, of taxonomic classifications within each ability domain. Taxonomies derived from correlation-based procedures such as factor analysis are highly dependent on the specific tests or tasks included in the assessment battery, the form (e.g., speed or power, manipulative or paper-and-pencil, etc.) of assessment, and the analytical methods used to identify the factors. Psychometric tests and experimental tasks also can be classified according to the theoretical processes hypothesized to be required, but few of the existing process-based models have independent evidence of the validity of the analytical speculations. Finally, more precise classifications are primarily useful for understanding age-related effects when the magnitude of the age relations varies across different taxonomic categories or when the organization or classification of the abilities varies as a function of age. Little evidence for either of these patterns is available in the existing research literature, however, and hence finer distinctions among types of reasoning or spatial abilities appear neither necessary nor desirable at this time in discussing the relation between increased age and performance on tests of reasoning and spatial abilities.

The remainder of the chapter is organized into four major sections. An initial section is devoted to reviewing evidence establishing the existence, and approximate magnitude, of age-related effects on reasoning and spatial abilities. The second and third sections are concerned with distal, in the sense of temporally remote, and proximal, or concurrent, determinants of age differences in measures of reasoning and spatial abilities. The final section consists of a brief discussion of the strengths and weaknesses of alternative research strategies to investigate the relations between age and cognitive functioning.

DOCUMENTING THE AGE RELATIONS

It is desirable, before considering the research aimed at explaining the relations between age and reasoning and spatial abilities, to document the existence of those relations. The purpose of this first section is therefore to indicate the magnitude of the relations between age and performance of assorted psychometric tests or experimental tasks designed to assess reasoning and spatial abilities.

Sample items from two typical tests of reasoning ability and two typical tests of spatial ability are illustrated in Fig. 4.1. These particular tests were selected for illustration because each was administered to a sample of 383 adults between about 18 and 80 years of age in a recent project reported by Salthouse and Mitchell (1990). Number correct scores on each test were converted into z scores based on the distribution of scores of young adults (ages 18–29 years), and the frequency distributions plotted for the 45–85 adults in each decade. The data for the two reasoning tests are illustrated in Fig. 4.2, and the data for the two spatial tests are illustrated in Fig. 4.3. Notice that there is a clear tendency for the entire distribution of scores to shift to lower levels with increased age. Correlations between age and the measures illustrated in Figs. 4.2 and 4.3 were − .33 for both reasoning measures and − .42 for both spatial measures.

Similar patterns of age differences are evident in the performance of other tests. For example, Fig. 4.4 portrays results from three series completion tests, and Fig. 4.5 portrays results from three paper-folding tests. The data in each figure were derived from independent samples and somewhat different versions of each type of test. Despite these variations, the results reveal that the average 60-year-old in these samples performs

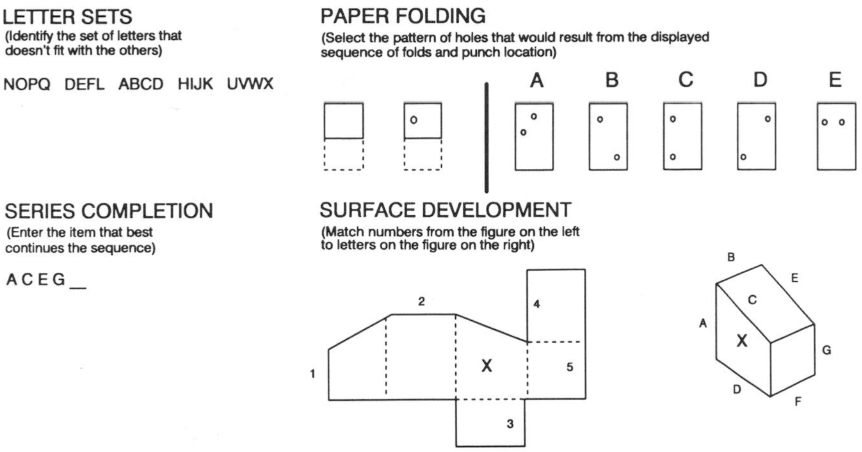

LETTER SETS
(Identify the set of letters that doesn't fit with the others)
NOPQ DEFL ABCD HIJK UVWX
PAPER FOLDING
(Select the pattern of holes that would result from the displayed sequence of folds and punch location)
A B C D E
SERIES COMPLETION
(Enter the item that best continues the sequence)
A C E G __
SURFACE DEVELOPMENT
(Match numbers from the figure on the left to letters on the figure on the right)
1 2 3 4 5 X
A B C D E F G X

FIG. 4.1. Illustration of sample problems in two typical tests of reasoning abilities, Letter Sets and Series Completion, and two typical tests of spatial abilities, Paper Folding and Surface Development.

Shipley Abstraction
Young Adult Standard Deviations
-4 -3.5 -3 -2.5 -2 -1.5 -1 -.5 0 .5 1 1.5 2 2.5 3 3.5 4
20s 30s 40s 50s 60s 70s
Letter Sets
Young Adult Standard Deviations
-4 -3.5 -3 -2.5 -2 -1.5 -1 -.5 0 .5 1 1.5 2 2.5 3 3.5 4
20s 30s 40s 50s 60s 70s
Age Decade

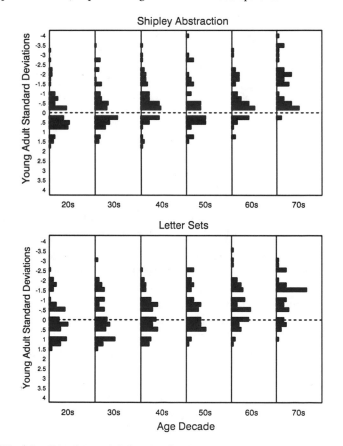

FIG. 4.2. Distribution by decade of average performance, in young adult standard deviation units, on the Shipley Abstraction (series completion) and Letter Sets tests (data from Salthouse & Mitchell, 1990).

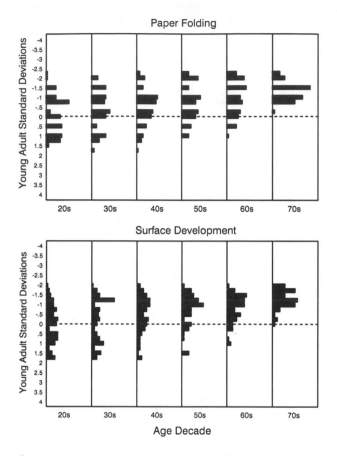

FIG. 4.3.   Distribution by decade of average performance, in young adult standard deviation units, on the Paper-Folding and Surface Development tests (data from Salthouse & Mitchell, 1990).

about .5 to 1.5 standard deviations (*SD*s) below the average 20-year-old.

Results from other projects in which adults of different ages were compared on measures of reasoning or spatial abilities are summarized in Tables 4.1 through 4.4. Tables 4.1 and 4.3 contain age-performance correlations, and Tables 4.2 and 4.4 indicate performance of older adults (generally with a mean age in either the 60s or the 70s) expressed in units of standard deviations of young adults (generally with a mean age in the early 20s). Data from measures of reasoning abilities are summarized in Tables 4.1 and 4.2, and data from measures assessing spatial abilities are summarized in Tables 4.3 and 4.4.

It is apparent in Figs. 4.2 through 4.5 and in Tables 4.1 through 4.4 that moderate to large relations exist between chronological age and performance on various tests of reasoning and spatial ability. The median

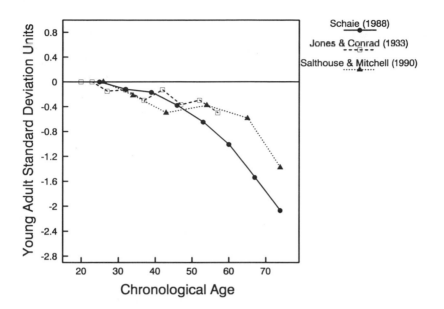

FIG. 4.4. Mean levels of series completion performance, in young adult standard deviation units, as a function of age in three independent projects.

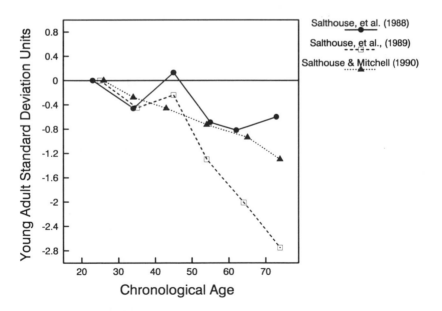

FIG. 4.5. Mean levels of paper-folding performance, in young adult standard deviation units, as a function of age in three independent projects.

age correlation is −.44 in Table 4.1 and −.38 in Table 4.3, and the median young-adult standard deviation score for older adults is −1.54 in Table 4.2 and −1.16 in Table 4.4. There is clearly overlap in the distributions at each age, and most of the variance in measured performance is unrelated to chronological age. Nevertheless, the age relations are substantial enough to warrant explanation, and hence the focus in the remaining sections of this chapter is on the examination of alternative explanations of this phenomenon.

TABLE 4.1
Correlations Between Age and Measures of Reasoning Ability

Measure	Correlation	Sample Size	Age Range (in Years)	Source
Raven's Matrices	−.46	183	21–83	Babcock (1991)
Raven's Matrices	−.50	90	19–71	Barr & Giambra (1990)
Raven's Matrices	−.27	567	26–64	Burke (1972)
Raven's Matrices	−.62	96	20–79	Davies & Leytham (1964)
Raven's Matrices	−.55	80	22–76	Edwards & Wine (1963)
Raven's Matrices	−.64	300	20–79	Heron & Chown (1967)
Raven's Matrices	−.51	240	20–79	Heron & Chown (1967)
Raven's Matrices	−.61	180	17–80	Hooper et al. (1984)
Raven's Matrices	−.49	67	21–92	Koss et al. (1991)
Raven's Matrices	−.57	221	20–80	Salthouse (1991a)
Raven's Matrices	−.62	96	20–79	Wilson (1963)
PMA Reasoning	−.49	102	20–70	Clark (1960)
PMA Reasoning	−.42	100	18–89	Cornelius (1984)
PMA Reasoning	−.53	611	25–81	Schaie (1989)
PMA Reasoning	−.60	628	25–81	Schaie (1989)
Shipley Abstraction	−.39	183	21–83	Babcock (1991)
Shipley Abstraction	−.33	200	16–65	Kraus et al. (1967)
Shipley Abstraction	−.29	198	25–75	Mason & Ganzler (1964)
Shipley Abstraction	−.47	221	20–80	Salthouse (1991a)
Shipley Abstraction	−.33	383	20–83	Salthouse & Mitchell (1990)
Series Completion	−.26	180	17–80	Hooper et al. (1984)
Series Completion	−.28	233	20–79	Salthouse et al. (1988)
Series Completion	−.39	708	17–101	McCrae et al. (1987)
Category Test	−.42	100	16–70	Aftanas & Royce (1969)
Category Test	−.40	289	18–72	Pierce et al. (1989)
Category Test	−.42	35	16–61	Prigatano & Parsons (1976)
Category Test	−.43	558	20–80	Schludermann et al. (1983)
Category Test	−.63	50	M = 40.8	Vega & Parsons (1967)

(Continued)

TABLE 4.1
(Continued)

Measure	Correlation	Sample Size	Age Range (in Years)	Source
Concept Identification	− .45	828 +	20s–80s	Arenberg (1988)
Concept Identification	− .44	60	18–85	Hoyer et al. (1979)
Letter Sets	− .32	183	21–83	Babcock (1991)
Letter Sets	− .39	100	18–89	Cornelius (1984)
Letter Sets	− .33	383	20–83	Salthouse & Mitchell (1990)
Figural Relations	− .27	100	18–89	Cornelius (1984)
20 Questions	− .52	45	21–71	Charness (1987)
Integrative Reasoning	− .41	228	20–82	Salthouse (1991a)
Integrative Reasoning	− .43	223	20–84	Salthouse (1991a)
Integrative Reasoning	− .53	120	20–79	Salthouse, Mitchell, Skovronek, & Babcock (1989)
Geometric Analogies	− .44	228	20–82	Salthouse (1991a)
Geometric Analogies	− .48	223	20–84	Salthouse (1991a)
Geometric Analogies	− .43	233	20–78	Salthouse et al. (1988)

TABLE 4.2

Performance of Older Adults (Mean Age in 60s or 70s) on Reasoning Ability Measures in Standard Deviations of Young Adults (Mean Age in 20s)

Measure	Old in Young SDs	Young N/Age	Old N/Age	Source
Raven's Matrices	− 2.84	20/18–20	20/60–69	Clayton & Overton (1976)
Raven's Matrices	− 3.10	35/M = 19	40/60–79	Cunningham et al. (1975)
Raven's Matrices	− 3.31	50/20–44	50/65–86	Panek & Stoner (1980)
Raven's Matrices	− 0.48	26/M = 36	30/M = 60	Riege et al. (1984)
Raven's Matrices	− 2.06	100/18–23	100/60–70	Schultz et al. (1980)
PMA Reasoning	− 5.19	37/18–22	48/64–91	Lachman & Jelalian (1984)
PMA Reasoning	− 2.18	40/18–28	40/60–84	Prohaska et al. (1984)
PMA Reasoning	− 1.62	24/19–29	24/56–73	Salthouse & Prill (1987)
Shipley Abstraction	− 0.59	20/20–30	20/60–70	Garfield & Blek (1952)
Category Test	− 2.01	15/15–35	14/51–75	Bigler et al. (1981)
Category Test	− 1.54	40/20–37	41/60–80	Mack & Carlson (1978)
Series Completion	− 1.69	24/19–29	24/56–73	Salthouse & Prill (1987)
Series Completion	− 1.25	45/21–42	45/60–79	Sward (1945)

(Continued)

TABLE 4.2
(Continued)

Measure	Old in Young SDs	Young N/Age	Old N/Age	Source
Figural Relations	−0.93	16/18–26	16/60–83	Kausler & Pukett (1980)
Figural Relations	−1.60	48/17–27	33/55–86	Kausler et al. (1981)
Figural Relations	−1.50	48/18–27	42/56–84	Kausler et al. (1982)
Concept Identification	−1.29	21/17–22	21/60–77	Arenberg (1968)
Concept Identification	−1.28	54/17–22	54/59–76	Hayslip & Sterns (1979)
Concept Identification	−2.03	54/17–22	54/59–76	Hayslip & Sterns (1979)
20 Questions	−1.50	14/20–29	14/60–69	Denney & Palmer (1981)
20 Questions	−1.51	16/20–29	16/60–69	Denney et al. (1982)
20 Questions	−1.58	32/14–35	32/60–83	Hartley & Anderson (1983a)
Syllogistic Reasoning	−0.66	39/20–29	24/60–69	Nehrke (1972)
Syllogistic Reasoning	−0.90	59/20–29	34/60–69	Nahrke (1972)
Picture Classification	−1.06	12,806/20–29	571/50+	Trembly & O'Connor (1966)

TABLE 4.3
Correlations Between Age and Measures of Spatial Ability

Measure	Correlation	Sample Size	Age Range (in Years)	Source
Block Design	−.32	933	25–64	Birren & Morrison (1961)
Block Design	−17	105	18–64	Goldfarb (1941)
Block Design	−.25	60	18–64	Goldfarb (1941)
Block Design	−.41	1480	20–74	Kaufman et al. (1989)
Block Design	−.57	67	21–92	Koss et al. (1991)
Block Design	−.51	120	20–84	Riege & Inman (1981)
Object Assembly	−.28	933	25–64	Birren & Morrison (1961)
Object Assembly	−.16	108	18–64	Goldfarb (1941)
Object Assembly	−.08	60	18–64	Goldfarb (1941)
Object Assembly	−.41	1480	20–74	Kaufman et al. (1989)
Object Assembly	−.59	67	21–92	Koss et al. (1991)
Picture Completion	−.28	933	25–64	Birren & Morrison (1961)
Picture Completion	−.23	108	18–64	Goldfarb (1941)
Picture Completion	−.31	60	18–64	Goldfarb (1941)
Picture Completion	−.38	1480	20–74	Kaufman et al. (1989)
Picture Completion	−.28	67	21–92	Koss et al. (1991)
Hooper VOT	−.36	100	16–70	Aftanas & Royce (1969)
Hooper VOT	−.59	120	20–80	Botwinick & Storandt (1974)

(Continued)

TABLE 4.3
(Continued)

Measure	Correlation	Sample Size	Age Range (in Years)	Source
Hooper VOT	−.45	193	25–75	Mason & Ganzler (1964)
Hooper VOT	−.38	231	25–75	Mason & Ganzler (1964)
Hooper VOT	−.42	75	20–72	Sterne (1973)
Hooper VOT	−.50	211	20–79	Tamkin & Jacobsen (1984)
Hooper VOT	−.37	60	41–85	Wentworth-Rohr et al. (1974)
Hooper VOT	−.69	21	39–60	Wentworth-Rohr et al. (1974)
PMA Space	−.42	102	20–70	Clark (1960)
PMA Space	−.41	611	25–81	Schaie (1989)
PMA Space	−.47	628	25–81	Schaie (1989)
Paper Folding	−.28	129	20–79	Salthouse et al (1988)
Paper Folding	−.53	120	20–79	Salthouse, Mitchell, Skovronek, & Babcock (1989)
Paper Folding	−.40	50	24–67	Salthouse, Babcock, Mitchell, Skovronek, & Palmon (1990)
Paper Folding	−.19	228	20–82	Salthouse (1991a)
Paper Folding	−.36	223	20–84	Salthouse (1991a)
Paper Folding	−.42	383	20–83	Salthouse & Mitchell (1990)
Embedded Figures	−.52	71	27–59	Arthur et al. (1990)
Embedded Figures	−.28	??	25–64	Barrett et al. (1977)
Embedded Figures	−.40	120	20–80	Botwinick & Storandt (1974)
Embedded Figures	−.37	200	20–82	Chown (1961)
Embedded Figures	−.20	160	23–77	Crosson (1984)
Embedded Figures	−.43	72	20–79	Lee & Pollack (1978)
Surface Development	−.34	88	22–49	Cobb et al. (1971)
Surface Development	−.37	50	24–67	Salthouse, Babcock, Mitchell, Skovronek, & Palmon (1990)
Surface Development	−.42	383	20–83	Salthouse & Mitchell (1990)
Perceptual Closure	−.49	320	30–69	Dirken (1972)
Perceptual Closure	−.33	544	20–50	Glanzer & Glaser (1959)
Perceptual Closure	−.20	129	20–79	Salthouse et al. (1988)
Perceptual Closure	−.58	80	20–68	Wasserstein et al. (1987)
Form Boards	−.22	50	24–67	Salthouse, Babcock, Mitchell, Skovronek, & Palmon (1990)
Form Boards	−.38	40	20–59	Weisenburg et al. (1936)
Cube Assembly	−.14	228	20–82	Salthouse (1991a)
Cube Assembly	−.31	223	20–84	Salthouse (1991a)
Cube Comparisons	−.54	50	24–67	Salthouse, Babcock, Mitchell, Skovronek, & Palmon (1990)

TABLE 4.4
Performance of Older Adults (Mean Age in 60s or 70s) on Spatial Ability
Measures in Standard Deviations of Young Adults (Mean Age in 20s)

Measure	Old in Young SDs	Young N/Age	Old N/Age	Source
Block Design	−1.56	24/20–24	278/60–64	Berkowitz (1953)
Block Design	−1.02	35/18–26	48/55–74	Hines (1979)
Block Design	−1.07	26/M = 36	30/M = 60	Riege et al. (1984)
Block Design	−1.53	20/18–35	20/63–77	Salthouse (1987b)
Block Design	−0.93	10/20–23	10/61–77	Salthouse (1987b)
Block Design	−1.06	27/18–24	20/55–68	Salthouse (1987b)
Embedded Figures	−1.68	46/17–27	45/60–89	Panek (1985)
Embedded Figures	−1.59	25/17–24	25/65–72	Panek et al. (1978)
Hidden Figures	−1.25	40/18–28	40/60–84	Prohaska et al. (1984)
Hidden Figures	−0.65	100/18–23	100/60–70	Schultz et al.(1980)
Knox Cubes	−1.16	174/20–29	174/60–69	Gilbert (1941)
Paper Folding	−1.74	40/18–28	40/60–84	Prohaska et al. (1984)
Object Rotation	−0.96	50/25–39	50/65–79	Pierce & Storandt (1987)
PMA Space	−0.83	50/20–25	50/61–65	Schaie (1958)
DAT Spatial Relations	−1.35	12/M = 19	12/M = 72	Adamowicz & Hudson (1978)
Form Boards	−1.90	20/21–33	20/62–86	Kirasic (1991)
Card Rotations	−1.53	18/19–29	19/65–80	Kliegl et al. (1990)
Cube Comparison	−1.29	20/21–33	20/62–86	Kirasic (1991)
Cube Comparison	−0.86	24/18–23	24/55–70	Salthouse & Skovronek (in press)
Cube Comparison	−0.77	26/17–27	25/60–79	Salthouse & Skovronek (in press)
Cube Comparison	−1.14	60/17–30	20/60–78	Salthouse & Skovronek (in press)

INVESTIGATING THE CAUSES OF AGE DIFFERENCES IN REASONING AND SPATIAL ABILITIES

Two general approaches have been employed to investigate possible explanations of adult age differences in reasoning and spatial abilities. Although they frequently are identified as corresponding to the psychometric and experimental traditions, a more meaningful basis for classification may be according to whether the causal determinants of the age-related phenomena are primarily distal or proximal in nature.

Research emphasizing distal determinants generally relies on the psychometric tradition of treating the total score on a test as the unit of analysis. That is, the score typically is not interpreted as the outcome of a series of conceptually distinct processes, but rather as an indication of the individual's relative standing in the population of potential examinees. Furthermore, researchers with a distal focus tend to be interested primarily in explanations based on factors originating at earlier periods in one's life and not on the specific nature of the processes responsible for producing the current level of performance.

Relatively little research has been reported linking performance on psychometric tests of reasoning and spatial abilities to intrinsic, or endogenous, changes such as hormonal shifts or maturationally determined cell loss. However, somewhat more research has been reported examining the influence of extrinsic or exogenous factors such as the type or amount of experience the individual has received. The two major sources of experiential influence that have been investigated in age-comparative research on cognition are cultural variation, as reflected in changes in the environment presumed to affect most people (e.g., mass communication, education, nutrition, etc.) and intraindividual variation corresponding to changes in the nature or frequency of the activities in which a particular individual engages at different periods in his or her life. Research relevant to both of these categories of experiential influences is reviewed in the following section.

Most of the research with a proximal focus has been conducted within the information-processing tradition of attempting to determine the processes responsible for performance on specific cognitive tasks. Because the measures of greatest interest are not the total scores on the tests or tasks but rather measures of presumably more fundamental components, this approach is analytical or decompositional in nature. The research focus is proximal because the explanatory mechanisms are concurrent, in the sense that the critical component is identified at the same period in one's life at which the performance impairments are reported. Process-oriented research designed to isolate or localize the proximal source of age differences in reasoning and spatial tasks is reviewed in the third section of the chapter.

DISTAL DETERMINANTS OF AGE DIFFERENCES

One frequently discussed class of experiential influences on adult age differences in cognitive functioning is that associated with changes in the external environment. It often is speculated that improvements in educational practices, or simply increases in overall cultural stimulation, have contributed to successively higher scores on measures of reasoning and spatial ability among more recently born individuals. The strongest evidence for this kind of generational improvement derives from time-lag comparisons in which scores are contrasted for people of the same age, but tested at different points in time. If changes in the environment have led to progressively more favorable conditions for the development of reasoning and spatial abilities, then one would expect people of later, or more recent, generations to perform at higher levels than people of earlier, or older, generations.

Rather dramatic evidence of time-lag improvements was reported by Flynn (1987) in analyses of scores of the Raven's Progressive Matrices Test administered to large percentages of the draft-age men in The Netherlands, Belgium, France, and Norway. Estimates of the gains in Raven's score computed by Salthouse (1991b) averaged about .05 *SD*s per year, or about 2.0 *SD* units over 40 years. A striking feature of these estimates is that they are nearly identical to the average annual difference derived from the young–old differences on the Raven's test summarized in Table 4.2. For example, the difference of − 2.06 *SD* units reported by Schultz, Kaye, and Hoyer (1980) between adults with average ages of 65 and 21 years is equivalent to an annual difference of − 2.06/44 = − .047. Moreover, the average of the five Raven's contrasts in Table 4.2 is − .054 young *SD* units per year. At least with these two sets of data from the Raven's test, therefore, it appears that unspecified changes in the external environment may have been responsible for increases in performance of nearly the same magnitude as the average decrease per year observed in cross-sectional studies of age differences.

What may be the only research project with data from relatively large samples of adults in both time-lag and cross-sectional comparisons is Schaie's (1988) Seattle Longitudinal Study. Figure 4.6 illustrates the mean (*M*) performance at each age grouping for the Reasoning (top panel) and Space (bottom panel) subtests from the Primary Mental Abilities Test Battery across five successive measurement occasions. These data are based on the values reported in Schaie (Table 8.1) for independent samples of

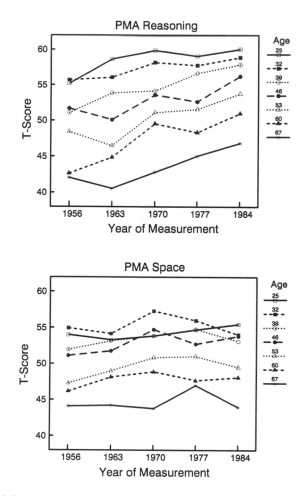

FIG. 4.6.   Mean level of Primary Mental Abilities Reasoning performance (top panel) and Space performance (bottom panel), in total sample T-score units, as a function of age and year of measurement (data from Schaie, 1988).

participants, and are expressed in T scores ($M = 50$ and $SD = 10$) computed from the distribution of scores of 3,442 individuals at the first assessment across the five test occasions.

The results in Fig. 4.6 indicate that slight to moderate time-lag improvements are present with each test, but that substantial cross-sectional age differences are also evident at each test occasion. Linear regression equations based on the mean values reported in Schaie's (1988) Table 8.1 reveal that the average slopes for the cross-sectional results were $-.36$ T-score units per year of age for the Reasoning measure, and $-.24$ T-score units per year of age for the Space measure. Similar analyses based on the time-lag results indicate that the average slopes were .20 T-score units per year of historical time for the Reasoning measure and .06 T-score units per year of historical time for the Space measure. When considered in combination, therefore, these results suggest that changes in the external environment may be associated with improvements in performance between 25% and 56% as great as those observed in cross-sectional comparisons.

Although results such as those just described are convincing in suggesting that the average level of performance on standardized tests of reasoning and spatial abilities has been improving over the last 25–50 years, the implications of these generational improvements for the interpretation of cross-sectional age differences are not yet obvious. Some authors have assumed that a discovery that successive generations perform at progressively higher levels on various cognitive tests necessarily makes cross-sectional comparisons based on those tests biased against older adults. This is not inevitably the case, however, because if the effects of the favorable environmental changes continue to accumulate throughout one's life, then the overall benefits attributable to improvements in the external environment actually might be greater for older adults than for young adults. Alternatively, time-lag effects may be irrelevant to the relations between age and cognitive performance if the consequences are uniform across the adult years, in a manner similar to how inflation results in increases in average income but does not necessarily alter the relation between age and income at any given period.

As discussed in Salthouse (1991b), estimates of the contribution of endogenous determinants of development may be too high, too low, or unbiased, when the average level of performance is increasing across successive generations because of favorable environmental changes. Before concluding that age comparisons from cross-sectional comparisons are confounded, it first must be determined whether the time-lag effects vary as a function of age and whether there is a maximum accumulation of time-lag benefits. Because reliable information on these issues is not yet available, it appears impossible at the current time to reach strong conclusions about the effects of environmental changes on age differences in reasoning and spatial abilities.

Experiential influences on cognitive functioning also can originate because of changes in the pattern of experiences occurring within a given individual. For example, one of the most popular interpretations of cognitive aging phenomena is the disuse hypothesis, which asserts that at least some age-related declines occur because as people grow older they no longer have as much experience with activities requiring abilities assessed in cognitive tests. Although versions of the disuse hypothesis frequently are discussed in both the popular and the scientific literature, this interpretation has been difficult to subject to rigorous investigation because of problems associated with establishing the actual frequencies of different experiences across an individual's lifetime. Nevertheless, there are a few studies in which the research participants might reasonably be expected to have high amounts of experience with spatial abilities.

Several of the relevant studies have involved aircraft pilots or air traffic controllers. Spatial abilities presumably are required in these occupations because spatial ability tests often are used to aid in the selection of candidates to receive training in these fields. Contrary to the expectation that continuous experience might preserve abilities, however, most of the reports have indicated that pilots and air traffic controllers exhibit patterns of age-related declines in the performance of assorted spatial tests similar to those evident in unselected samples of adults (e.g., Birren & Spieth, 1962; Cobb, Lay, & Bourdet, 1971; Glanzer & Glaser, 1959; Spieth, 1965; Trites & Cobb, 1964).

Three recent studies by Salthouse and his colleagues (Salthouse, 1991c; Salthouse, Babcock, Mitchell, Skovronek, & Palmon, 1990; Salthouse & Mitchell, 1990) are also relevant to the experiential interpretation of age differences in spatial abilities. Practicing architects were recruited to perform a battery of psychometric tests and experimental tasks assessing spatial ability in the Salthouse et al. project. In the Salthouse and Mitchell project, research participants were asked to perform several spatial ability tests, and in addition to rate the amount of experience they had with various activities presumed to require spatial visualization abilities. The self-report information then was used to classify the individuals as high, medium, or low in terms of experience involving spatial abilities. Special efforts were made to recruit mechanical engineers to participate in the Salthouse project because the experimental tasks were designed to be relevant to the interpretation of technical drawings of three-dimensional objects.

One of the major findings from these projects was that although the overall level of performance varied with amount of experience, similar relations between age and performance on the spatial tests were evident at each level of experience. This pattern is illustrated in Fig. 4.7, which portrays the number of items answered correctly in the Surface Development Test (see Fig. 4.1 for an illustration of a sample item on this test). Notice that although the architects and people reporting extensive experience with activities presumed to require spatial abilities perform at higher levels than people reporting lower amounts of experience, pronounced age trends are apparent in each group. These results seem to suggest that one's level of ability in young adulthood may influence the choice of an occupation or the type of activities in which one engages,

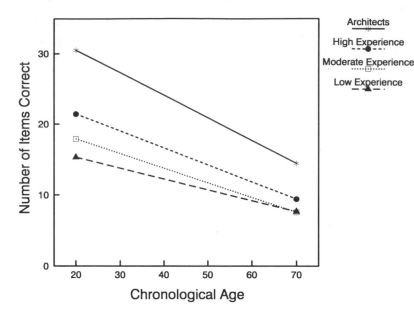

FIG. 4.7.   Regression lines indicating age relations in the Surface Development test (data of architects from Salthouse, Babcock, Mitchell, Skovronek, & Palmon, 1990, and data from the three experience groups from Salthouse & Mitchell, 1990).

but that experience does not alter the pattern of age-related declines in at least some tests of those abilities.

A recent research project conducted from a sociological perspective is also relevant to the issue of distal determinants of age differences in reasoning and spatial abilities. Lee (1991) analyzed data from a survey administered to a representative sample of 615 adults ranging between 18 and 88 years of age. The primary dependent variable in this study was an index of abstraction ability derived from responses to five questions asking whether two concepts had anything in common or asking for a rating of agreement with a statement about the classification of people or objects. This measure is clearly not optimal from the standpoint of psychological measurement because there was little evidence of convergent (e.g., high correlations with other measures of abstraction ability) or discriminant (e.g., low correlations with measures of cognitive style) validity and the reported reliability was rather low (i.e., coefficient alpha of .53). The study is nevertheless interesting because it represents a promising approach to the investigation of distal determinants of age differences in cognitive functioning.

The simple correlation between age and the abstraction index in the Lee (1991) study was − .30, a value within the range of those reported for more traditional measures of reasoning (see Table 4.1). However, the availability of measures of the respondent's educational attainment, the complexity of his or her occupation and current labor status, as well as the parents' educational attainment which served as a proxy for intellectual stimulation in childhood, allowed the influence of these variables to be examined in addition to age. The relation between age and abstraction after all these variables were considered was still statistically significant, but it was much reduced (i.e., to $-.12$). Lee therefore concluded that "a considerable proportion of the age-related deficit . . . is because older people were raised in less complex environments and have less formal educational experience . . . (and) . . . these factors are associated with employment in less complex jobs, and . . . older people are more likely to be retired" (p. 70).

Of particular interest in Lee's (1991) study was the finding that, distinct from other influences, occupational complexity was positively associated with the abstraction index. This result, together with a similar finding by Kohn and Schooler (1983) involving different measures of cognitive functioning, suggests that experience in one's job may influence the level of cognitive performance independent of any influences associated with increased age. What is not yet clear from this type of research is whether there are interactive effects of age and experience such that the age relations are moderated by type and amount of occupational experience.

Another area of research relevant to experiential influences on age differences in reasoning and spatial abilities is that involving attempts to manipulate the type or amount of experience an individual receives through the provision of practice or training. Although a number of studies have been reported in which various training or practice manipulations have been examined, inferences from most of them are limited either because the studies did not include age-related comparisons, or because the posttreatment assessment was very narrow, often consisting of the same test or task that was practiced or trained. These characteristics severely restrict the inferences that can be made about the effects of experience on age differences in reasoning or spatial abilities. Some kind of developmental comparisons seem essential to reach conclusions about age-related processes, and inclusion of other measures of the target ability are desirable to support statements about effects at the level of construct abilities rather than specific variables.

One project that did involve developmentally relevant comparisons and assessments at the level of theoretical constructs was reported by Willis and Schaie (1986). These investigators devised training programs intended to increase either spatial or reasoning abilities, and then administered the programs to individuals classified as having remained stable or having declined in one of those abilities across an interval of

14 years. The primary expectation from the disuse hypothesis was that the training-related gains would be selective, and greater for those individuals classified as having declined in that ability than for those classified as having remained stable.

Four separate tests of both reasoning and spatial abilities were administered before and after the training program. Although the tests involved distinct types of materials (e.g., geometric figures, objects, or letters for the spatial tests, and letters, words, and numbers for the reasoning tests), they were similar in that each of the reasoning tests involved series completion operations, and each of the spatial tests involved spatial rotation operations. Measures of performance in the four tests of each ability were combined to create a single score for either the reasoning construct or for the spatial ability construct for every research participant.

The training manipulations were found to be effective at improving performance across most of the measures of each target ability. However, the results failed to support the disuse interpretation of age-related cognitive decline because the improvements were not differential. That is, the amount of improvement in the construct scores was not significantly greater for individuals classified as having declined in the ability than for those classified as having remained stable. It therefore cannot be concluded from the Willis and Schaie (1986) results that the experiential manipulation remediated an experiential deficit because the training gains were nearly equivalent in magnitude for individuals reported to have declined in the ability from a previous assessment, and who might be postulated to have suffered from an experiential deficit, as for those who had not declined, and thus apparently had no experiential deficit that could have been eliminated with training. An alternative, and seemingly more plausible, interpretation of the results of the Willis and Schaie project is that the training did not modify processes responsible for the age-related differences in performance, but instead improved performance by affecting other mechanisms, such as the learning of new skills or strategies.

The currently available evidence concerning distal determinants of age differences in reasoning and spatial abilities is rather mixed. It does seem to be the case that the average level of performance has increased substantially across historical time, and experiential factors related to educational practices or general cultural stimulation may be responsible for most of these increases. However, it is not yet clear exactly what the existence of positive time-lag effects implies with respect to the pattern of age differences in cross-sectional contrasts, and other evidence relevant to experiential influences (e.g., comparisons of individuals with different amounts of experience and the lack of differential improvement in training studies) appears inconsistent with the expectations from the experiential-deprivation or disuse hypothesis.

PROXIMAL DETERMINANTS OF AGE DIFFERENCES

Research attempting to identify the concurrent or proximal processes that might be responsible for age-related impairments in reasoning and spatial abilities generally has relied upon within-task comparisons of measures presumed to represent different processing components. However, not all analytical research is necessarily decompositional because total scores also can be informative when the tasks are so simple that they can be inferred to involve a very limited number of processes. Examination of the pattern of age differences in simple tasks therefore may indicate whether the one or two processes presumably required by those tasks are sensitive to age-related influences.

One task that might be useful in this respect is the fluency task in which the examinee is requested to generate as many different items, or combinations of items, as possible within a limited time. Because fluency tasks require little manipulation or transformation of information, performance seems to reflect the individual's ability to rapidly generate alternatives satisfying specified constraints. Although not higher order cognition itself, this aspect of processing could be of considerable importance in more complex reasoning and spatial tasks.

Age-related differences have been reported in a variety of fluency tasks, ranging from the generation of words beginning with a particular letter (e.g., Birren, 1955; Mittenberg, Seidenberg, O'Leary, & DiGiulio, 1989; Schaie, 1958, 1988), to those requiring ideational responses such as devising new uses for common objects or specifying plot titles for short stories (e.g., Alpaugh & Birren, 1977; Alpaugh, Parham, Cole, & Birren, 1982; McCrae, Arenberg, & Costa, 1987), to those requiring figural responses by connecting lines to produce unique designs (e.g., Mittenberg et al., 1989; Ruff, Light, & Evans, 1987), to those requiring novel physical arrangements of blocks or other objects (e.g., Bromley, 1956, 1967), and finally to those requiring the generation of unique combinations of items (e.g., Muhs, Hooper, & Papalia-Finlay, 1979–1980; Sinnott, 1975). The consistency with which age differences have been reported across such a diverse set of stimulus materials provides convincing evidence that increased age is associated with reductions in the rapid generation of alternative formulations or conceptualizations.

A slightly more complex task, in that it can be hypothesized to involve several processing operations, is the 20-questions task. Participants in this task are instructed to determine the identity of a target element within a designated set by asking the fewest number of questions. Optimum performance, assuming that the targets are randomly selected, requires asking questions that eliminate one half of the possible alternatives with each answer. Poor performance therefore could originate because of a failure to appreciate the importance of this principle, because of an inability to formulate appropriate constraining questions, or because of difficulty in remembering the outcomes of prior questions.

One or more of these processes apparently is impaired with increased age because older adults frequently are reported to perform at lower levels than young adults on assorted versions of this task (e.g., Charness, 1987; Denney, 1980; Denney & Denney, 1982; Denney & Palmer, 1981; Denney, Pearce, & Palmer, 1982; Hartley & Anderson, 1983a, 1983b, 1986; Hybertson, Perdue, & Hybertson, 1982; Kesler, Denney, & Whitely, 1976; Rimoldi & Vander Woude, 1969). Although questioning efficiency has been found to vary with the nature of the stimuli (e.g., Denney, 1980; Kesler, Denney, & Whitely, 1976), the physical arrangement of the stimuli (e.g., Charness, 1987), the number of alternatives in the target set (e.g., Denney, 1980; Hartley & Anderson, 1983a, 1983b), and the number of problems to be solved simultaneously (e.g., Hartley & Anderson, 1983a), none of these manipulations has resulted in either the elimination or the substantial attenuation of the age differences.

Hartley and Anderson (1986) suggested that older adults were deficient relative to young adults in recognizing the effectiveness of the strategy of eliminating the greatest possible number of alternatives. Although this factor may contribute to the age differences, it does not appear to be the entire explanation because Hybertson et al. (1982) found that age differences in questioning efficiency persisted even after the efficient focusing strategy was demonstrated to the research participants and its use explicitly encouraged. An additional finding by Hybertson et al. was that older adults asked more irrelevant questions, more questions yielding no new information, and more repetitions of earlier questions. These results suggest that the poorer performance of older adults may have been attributable, at least in part, to some kind of memory limitations.

Several age-comparative studies also have been reported with concept identification tasks in which the requirement is to identify the principle that serves to differentiate designated target stimulus items from other nontarget items. Most of these studies have found that older adults perform at lower levels than young adults (e.g., Arenberg, 1968, 1982, 1988; Brinley, Jovick, & McLaughlin, 1974; Hartley, 1981; Hayslip & Sterns, 1979; Kellogg, 1983; Offenbach, 1974).

A few studies were designed to investigate the specific nature of the difficulty experienced by older adults in concept identification tasks. For example, Arenberg (1968) instructed research participants to write information about the concept dimensions and classifications after each stimulus presentation and to indicate which dimensions were still viable solutions to the problem. Analysis of these records allowed him to determine that older adults made more errors than young adults after the presentation of redundant information. Older adults, to a greater extent than young adults, apparently interpreted the redundant information as though it were new, and hence used it to incorrectly eliminate alternatives that were still viable.

Age-related differences in dealing with redundant information also have been reported in studies using a selection procedure, in which the research participant rather than the experimenter controls the choice of the stimulus configurations to be examined (e.g., Arenberg, 1982, 1988). The information value of each selection is computed by determining how many of the remaining possibilities can be eliminated by the stimulus selection. Arenberg (1988) reported that these measures of the information value of the selections had correlations with age of between − .37 and − .40, values that were nearly as large as the − .45 correlation between age and overall solution accuracy. Much of the lower information value in the selections of older adults was apparently attributable to repetitions of previous selections, which are obviously uninformative because all the information was redundant with what had been provided earlier.

The Arenberg (1968, 1982, 1988) studies suggest that one of the factors contributing to poorer concept identification performance with increased age is a difficulty either in remembering old information or in integrating it with new information. Older individuals are apparently more likely than younger ones to fail to notice that the information is redundant with earlier information, and they also make repetitive selections more frequently than young adults.

Results from two other studies are also consistent with the interpretation that problems in memory, or possibly in information integration, contribute to the age differences in concept identification performance. The first study was by Offenbach (1974), who asked research participants to report the stimulus dimension they were considering as the possible solution after the presentation of each stimulus display. Examination of the sequence of responses revealed that older adults were more likely than young adults to repeat an unsuccessful hypothesis after negative or disconfirming feedback, and were less likely to retain a successful hypothesis after positive or confirming feedback. Offenbach suggested that older adults functioned as though they had poorer memory of prior hypotheses than young adults. Support for this speculation was provided by Kellogg (1983) in the finding that older adults were less accurate than young adults in reporting the hypotheses used on previous stimulus presentations.

Detailed analyses of the processes used by young and old adults in the performance of a reasoning task also were reported by Salthouse and Pril (1987). The task investigated in these studies was number series completion with three distinct kinds of problems. The simplest problems were

those in which the elements of the problem formed a continuous sequence, such as 2-4-6-8-10. A second category of problems involved two
alternating sequences, such as 2-9-4-8-6. Note that this problem is comprised of two distinct sequences, with the odd-numbered elements starting at 2 and increasing by 2, and the even-numbered elements starting
at 9 and decreasing by 1. The third problem type consisted of second-
order relations in which the invariance in the sequence occurred in the
relation among relations. An example is 2-4-7-11-16, in which the difference between the first two elements is $+2$, that between the second and
the third elements is $+3$, that between the third and the fourth is $+4$,
and so forth. The constant, in this case $+1$, is therefore evident at a
second level of abstraction in that it reflects the difference among
differences.

Both the pattern-alternation and the second-order abstraction problems
can be expected to place greater demands on memory than the simple
sequence problems because more of the earlier elements must be temporarily stored while attempting to identify the pattern relating the
elements. A common finding in both of the studies reported by Salthouse
and Prill (1987) was that the age differences in solution accuracy were
greater in the pattern-alternation and second-order relation problems than
in the simple continuation problems. An additional finding in the second
study of this project was that although both young and old adults devoted
more time to studying the elements at the position in the sequence where
the deviation from the simple continuation pattern was first apparent,
the increase in time was proportionally greater for older adults than for
young adults. A plausible inference from these results is that both memory
processes, and processes concerned with detecting patterns and abstrac-
ting relations, contribute to the difficulty experienced by older adults in
series completion problems.

Age differences also have been investigated in integrative reasoning
tasks such as syllogistic reasoning. The general finding has been that older
adults perform at lower levels of accuracy than young adults on these
kinds of tasks (e.g., Arenberg & Robertson-Tchabo, 1985; Foos, 1989;
Fullerton, 1988; Light, Zelinski, & Moore, 1982; Nehrke, 1972; Salthouse,
1991a; Salthouse, Legg, Palmon, & Mitchell, 1990; Salthouse, Mitchell,
Skovronek, & Babcock, 1989).

An interesting comparison in several integrative-reasoning studies has
involved contrasts of decisions based on information presented in a single
premise with decisions based on information presented in two or more
premises, and thus requiring some type of across-premise integration. For
example, if the terms were A, B, C, and D, and the relations were
presented in the sequence C-D, B-C, and A-B, then a question about the
relation between A and D would require information to be integrated

(i.e., across the A-B, B-C, and C-D premises), but a question about the relation between B and C would not require integration (because the B-C relation was specified in a single premise). Both Fullerton (1988) and Light et al. (1982) found that the age differences were greater when the problems required across-premise integration than when they did not.

Somewhat different results were reported by Arenberg and Robertson-Tchabo (1985) and by Salthouse and his colleagues (Salthouse, Legg, Palmon, & Mitchell, 1990; Salthouse, Mitchell, Skovronek, & Babcock, 1989) in that these investigators found the age differences to be of nearly the same magnitude for questions requiring integration as for those not requiring integration. In each of these studies, however, all questions required a transformation of the original information. For example, in the Salthouse, Legg, Palmon, & Mitchell (1990) and Salthouse, Mitchell, Skovronek, and Babcock (1989) studies the original information was presented in the form "A and B do the SAME," and the questions were in the form "If A increases, what will happen to B?" Because the questions in the Arenberg and Robertson-Tchabo, the Salthouse, Legg, Palmon, and Mitchell (1990), and the Salthouse, Mitchell, Skovronek, and Babcock (1989) studies all required that the original information be transformed, it is possible that the absence of differential age effects for questions requiring or not requiring integration was due to the constant requirement that the information be transformed and not simply preserved.

Performance in the Salthouse, Legg, Palmon, and Mitchell (1990) and Salthouse, Mitchell, Skovronek, and Babcock (1989) studies also was examined as a function of the number of premises presented in the problem for questions either requiring or not requiring across-premise integration. It was expected that decision accuracy would decrease with an increase in the number of presented premises, and that the magnitude of the decrease would be greater among older adults than among young adults. The role of integration processes in both the reduction in performance associated with additional premises and the influence of increased age on those reductions was investigated by comparing performance on trials with and without the information integration requirement.

The results of the Salthouse, Legg, Palmon, and Mitchell (1990) and Salthouse, Mitchell, Skovronek, Babcock (1989) studies confirmed the initial expectations of decreased accuracy with additional premises and of older adults exhibiting this pattern to a greater extent than young adults. Of particular interest was the further finding that performance was nearly identical when across-premise integration was required as when it was not. An implication of this pattern of results is that the requirement of integrating information across separate premises is apparently not a major factor contributing to poor performance on this type of reasoning task. The difficulty associated with the presentation of additional premises, and especially for older adults relative to young adults, seems to be related to the efficient preservation of relevant information from earlier premises during the presentation of later information and not to problems in information integration per se.

Another reasoning task that has been explored analytically is a complex, logical problem-solving task involving multiple elements with a variety of relations between each element. The goal for the participant in this task is to identify the relations between pairs of elements and then to devise an efficient sequence of operations that would take one from the initial position to the target position. The actual apparatus involved buttons and lights, and the operations consisted of pressing buttons in the correct combination and sequence to illuminate a target light. Arenberg (1974, 1988), Jerome (1962), and Young (1966) all reported that older adults have much more difficulty in this task than young adults. Each of these investigators also reported that many of the solution attempts of older adults are characterized by inefficient inquiries in the sense that the requested information (i.e., which light is activated by a particular button) is redundant with that already available. Arenberg (1988) further reported that this redundancy is evident both in the information-gathering or analysis phase of the problem (corresponding to the identification of the consequences of a button press) and in the sequence specification or synthesis phase (in which the buttons were pressed in the appropriate combination and sequence to cause the target light to be illuminated).

Many of the results just described seem to be interpretable as reflecting age-related impairments in working-memory functioning (e.g., Charness, 1985; Kausler, 1982; Welford, 1958). That is, working-memory deficits may be responsible for the findings that older adults frequently seek redundant information or make more mistakes with the presentation of redundant information in 20-questions and concept identification tasks, that they function as though they have little memory for previous presentations, responses, or feedback in concept identification tasks, and that they have particular difficulty with the integrative-reasoning and series-completion problems that seem to place the greatest demands on memory.

An apparent difficulty with the working-memory interpretation is that substantial age differences have been reported in tasks where all the relevant information is continuously available and when the participants are encouraged to take complete notes while performing the task (e.g., Arenberg, 1968, 1982, 1988; Hartley, 1981; Hybertson et al., 1982; Jerome, 1962). Although these characteristics seemingly would minimize the necessity of having to remember the relevant information, it is possible that the critical factor is the amount of information that is mentally available when integration is required. In other words, there may be severe limits on the amount of information that can be maintained internally, in one's working-memory system, and it may be those limits that place the greatest constraints on effective solutions, regardless of whether the information is externally available.

Tasks measuring spatial abilities, like those measuring reasoning abilities, can vary in both the number and the type of required processing operations. With respect to the variation in type of processing, some tasks seem to require analysis, in that target stimuli must be identified when they are embedded or hidden in a larger context, and others involve synthesis, in that the requirement is to identify fragmented or incomplete stimuli by integrating the discrete pieces into a coherent whole. Still others require various transformations like rotation, folding, or repositioning.

Disembedding or resistance to closure is measured in tests such as the Embedded Figures and Hidden Figures tests, and to some extent in the Wechsler Picture Completion Test. Synthesis or integration seems to be the primary operation required in the Gestalt Completion Test, the Hooper Visual Organization Test, various form boards tests, and the Wechsler Object Assembly Test. Results summarized in Tables 4.3 and 4.4 indicate that moderate to large age differences frequently are reported in each of these tests.

Not much analytical research has been conducted with embedded figures tasks, but a moderate amount of process-oriented research has been conducted with closure and synthesis tasks. An early study by Basowitz and Korchin (1957) noted that people who perform poorly on these tasks tend to concentrate on individual portions of the stimulus display and frequently report that they see unintegrated elements such as "rocks," "clouds," or a "flock of birds." The goal of the more recent process-oriented research has been to determine why some people apparently have such a difficult time integrating the elements into a coherent whole and consequently tend to produce these fragmentary and unconnected responses.

Experimental research with closure tasks has suggested that the age differences are not due to age-associated variations in cautiousness or reluctance to respond because roughly comparable age differences have been found across a variety of response methods, including forced-choice procedures (e.g., Danziger & Salthouse, 1978). Differential familiarity with the stimulus materials also seems to be relatively unimportant because the age differences are not substantially altered in magnitude when complete versions of the stimuli are presented before attempting to identify the incomplete versions (e.g., Danziger & Salthouse, 1978; Salthouse & Prill, 1988), or when performance is assessed after practice with other incomplete versions of the same stimulus objects (Salthouse & Prill, 1988).

The source of the age differences in closure tasks also does not appear to be related to a difficulty in identifying which portions of the stimulus display are the most informative because Danziger and Salthouse (1978) found that young and old adults were equivalent with respect to ratings of the informativeness of different portions of the display. Moreover, the phenomenon of less accurate identification with increased age is not restricted simply to highly degraded or impoverished stimuli because Cremer and Zeef (1987) and Salthouse (1988a) both found that the age differences remain relatively constant across a range of stimulus incompleteness levels.

A model of incomplete figure identification intended to be helpful in understanding the source of age differences in perceptual closure tasks was proposed and investigated by Salthouse and Prill (1988). The four major components in their model were (a) formulate hypothesis about the identity of the displayed item and derive implications, (b) test implications from the hypothesis, (c) preserve information from earlier viewed portions of the display, and (d) integrate discrete pieces into a coherent whole. Measures of each of these hypothesized components were obtained from specially constructed tasks. For example, the test-implications component was assessed by asking research participants to determine whether a portion of an incomplete stimulus could have been derived from a particular target object.

Although the availability of four conceptually distinct measures might have been expected to allow fairly precise localization of the source of age differences in perceptual closure tasks, older adults were found to perform significantly lower than young adults in each of the measures in the Salthouse and Prill (1988) project. At least based on the results of this project, therefore, it appears that age differences in perceptual closure are not attributable to a deficit in a single critical component, but instead seem to be manifested in several conceptually distinct components.

Integration processes also have been investigated with synthesis tasks in which discrete parts, separated either temporally or spatially, are to be integrated into a single composite figure. Most of the experimental research has involved line-segment stimulus patterns, with each of several stimulus frames containing fragments composed of one or more line segments. Two replicated findings with these kinds of tasks are that the age differences become greater as the number of separate stimulus frames increase and more integration operations are required, but that they remain invariant across increases in the number of discrete line segments (e.g., Salthouse, 1987a; Salthouse & Mitchell, 1989). Salthouse and Mitchell argued on the basis of this pattern of results for a distinction between structural and operational limits in working memory. They further suggested that aging may be associated with declines in operational capacity, as reflected in the number of operations that can be performed successfully, but not in structural capacity, when the latter is measured by the amount of information that can be handled in any given operation. (But see Salthouse, Babcock, and Shaw, 1991, for results indicating that young and old adults may not differ in operational capacity when it is measured in a different type of task.)

It is clear that integration of the complete pattern will be unsuccessful if early portions of the pattern are not available when the last portions have been encoded, and thus memory factors might be assumed to play an important role in the age differences in synthesis tasks. However, the currently available results are somewhat confusing regarding the involvement of memory factors in these age differences. Older adults have been found to be less accurate than young adults in memory for complete stimulus patterns (e.g., Ludwig, 1982; Salthouse & Mitchell, 1989), but age differences in synthesis accuracy have been found even after statistically adjusting for level of memory performance. Furthermore, although older adults were found to be less accurate than young adults in recognizing probes containing line segments presented in earlier frames in the trial in two studies reported by Salthouse and Mitchell, this pattern was statistically significant only among the better performing members of each age group. Finally, Salthouse, Mitchell, and Palmon (1989) found that the size of the age differences varied as a function of the specific context in which the recognition responses were required. Young and old adults were equivalent when the line segment patterns merely had to be recognized as same or different relative to an earlier stimulus, but the performance of older adults suffered more than that of young adults when the recognition task was embedded in a synthesis task requiring the integration of successively presented pattern fragments. These apparent inconsistencies must be explained adequately before a memory-based interpretation can be considered sufficient to account for all the age differences in perceptual closure or visual synthesis tasks.

Most measures of spatial ability require one or more spatial transformations to be performed on the stimulus material in order to reach a decision. One of the most common spatial transformations is rotation, and several age-comparative studies have been conducted using the mental rotation procedure introduced by Shepard and his colleagues (Cooper & Shepard, 1973; Shepard & Metzler, 1971). Shepard proposed that a decision regarding whether two stimuli presented at different orientations were the same or were mirror images of one another involved four discrete stages: encoding, rotation, comparison, and response. By manipulating the angular discrepancy between two stimuli (or between the target stimulus and the normal upright orientation), it was discovered that there was a remarkably linear relation between decision time and angular orientation. The slope of this function was hypothesized to correspond to the duration required to carry out a mental rotation of one of the stimulus objects, and the intercept was interpreted as representing the combined duration of encoding, comparison, and response processes.

Most studies employing the mental rotation procedure have found that older adults are slower than young adults in both the slope and the intercept of the function relating decision time to orientation discrepancy (e.g., Berg, Hertzog, & Hunt, 1982; Cerella, Poon, & Fozard, 1981; Clarkson-Smith & Halpern, 1983; Gaylord & Marsh, 1976; Hertzog & Rypma, 1991; Puglisi & Morrell, 1986). There are a few exceptions to this general finding, but they each involved small samples and very limited amounts of practice. For example, Jacewicz and Hartley (1979) examined 10 young adults and 10 middle-age adults for a total of 72 trials each. In contrast, Berg et al., Cerella et al., and Gaylord and Marsh all tested their participants for at least three sessions involving hundreds of trials.

Sharps and Gollin (1987) did not report separate analyses of slope and intercept parameters, but they claimed that there were no age differences in overall decision speed for groups of nine older adults and nine young adults performing 22 trials under a speed-emphasis condition. The accuracy of the older adults in this condition was quite close to chance, however, and thus these individuals may not even have been attempting to perform the task in the correct manner. Young adults in the other two conditions (accuracy-emphasis or equal-emphasis) in the Sharps and Gollin experiment were both faster and more accurate than the older adults in these conditions.

The bulk of the available research therefore suggests that older adults have larger slope parameters than young adults, implying that increased age is associated with slower rotation processes. Other processes are apparently also slowed with increased age, however, because in nearly every study significant age differences have been reported in the intercept parameter presumed to reflect processes of encoding, comparison, and response. It therefore cannot be concluded on the basis of the existing research that the age differences have been isolated to the rotation component because other potentially important components have not yet been differentiated. The rotation component is also not the only one important for prediction of performance on relevant spatial tests because Berg et al. (1982) reported similar correlations with performance on the PMA Space Test of from $-.54$ to $-.66$ for the slopes and from $-.46$ to $-.65$ for the intercepts.

A more complicated task that also seems to involve mental rotation processes is the perspective-taking task in which the research participant is requested to determine either the appearance or the location of objects when instructed to imagine viewing them from a different perspective or to make various types of judgments about an unfamiliar route. Although age differences favoring young adults frequently have been reported in miscellaneous variants of this task (e.g., Aubrey & Dobbs, 1989a, 1989b; Bruce & Herman, 1983; Del Vento Bielby & Papalia, 1975; Herman & Coyne, 1980; Kirasic, 1989, 1991; Kirasic & Bernicki, 1990; Lipman, 1991; Looft & Charles, 1971; Ohta, 1981, 1983; Ohta, Walsh, & Krauss, 1981; Rubin, 1974), relatively few analytical studies have been conducted that might allow inferences about the specific processes responsible for these differences. Some speculations have been offered, but they seldom were accompanied by convincing empirical evidence. For example, Ohta et al. suggested that ". . . cognitive systems associated with storing and retrieving spatial information may decline more rapidly across the adult life span than cognitive systems involved in the construction of unviewed spatial information" (p. 60). This inference was based on what appeared to be a different pattern of results across separate experiments; however, statistical support for this interpretation was lacking because no test of the relevant age × experiment interaction was reported.

The Block Design test used in the Wechsler batteries (e.g., Wechsler Adult Intelligence Scale, Wechsler Adult Intelligence Scale–Revised) also has been analyzed into distinct components. Examinees in this test are requested to arrange a set of colored blocks to match displayed stimulus designs as rapidly as possible. The major components that seem to be required for successful performance are segmentation of the target pattern into cells corresponding to individual blocks and manipulation of a block to match the pattern on the target cell of the to-be-reproduced pattern. Adult age differences in both of these components have been investigated in two independent projects.

Royer, Gilmore, and Gruhn (1984) investigated the segmentation component by manipulating what they termed the cohesiveness of stimulus patterns. Because it was hypothesized to be easier to segment the pattern when the boundaries between cells or blocks are distinguished by differences in color, cohesiveness was varied by altering the number of color changes at block boundaries. Solution times of older adults in the Royer et al. study increased more than those of young adults as the block boundaries became less distinct. This result leads to the inference that older adults have more difficulty than young adults in segmenting target designs. Confidence in this inference is increased by noting that it is consistent with the well-documented age differences reported in various embedded figures tests.

Salthouse (1987b) created a computer-administered version of the block design task in which representations of stimulus blocks were portrayed on a computer screen and then manipulated by the research participant through keyboard responses to reproduce the target design. This method of presentation allowed assessment of the efficiency of block manipulation, measured in terms of the number of keystrokes required to rotate the block until the target pattern was on the front face, independent of any individual differences that might exist in segmentation efficiency or manual dexterity.

In three separate experiments in the Salthouse (1987b) project, older adults were found to be less efficient than young adults at manipulating blocks to the desired positions. This was particularly true when the target pattern was not visible in the display of the block but instead was on one of its hidden faces. At least some of the difficulty of older adults in these situations therefore may have been due to inadequate internal representations of the configuration of patterns on the blocks.

Paper-folding tasks also have been analyzed to determine the source of the age differences in both speed and accuracy of performance. The principal experimental manipulation investigated has been the number of folds displayed prior to the representation of the hole punched through the folded paper. Both Salthouse (1988b) and Salthouse, Mitchell, Skovronek, and Babcock (1989) found that, relative to young adults, older adults had greater decreases in accuracy and greater increases in time with increases in the number of required folds.

An interesting question in light of this pattern of greater age differences with more folds is whether the difficulty is associated with the coordination and integration of successive folding operations or whether it is related to the necessity of preserving different pieces of information during other processing. Salthouse, Mitchell, Skovronek, and Babcock (1989) provided a preliminary answer to this question by contrasting performance on trials with only a single relevant fold and on trials with several relevant folds. For example, two trials both could involve four successive folds, but in one of the trials only a single fold might be relevant to the decision because the other, irrelevant, folds were in portions of the paper unaffected by the hole punch. If the decrease in accuracy with additional folds is attributable to a failure to coordinate and integrate the products of several successive folds, then one might expect performance on trials with only a single relevant fold to remain relatively constant as the number of folds increased. If the problem is one of preserving relevant information during the encoding and processing of other information, however, then one might expect declines in performance with additional folds to be similar for trials with one relevant fold and for trials with two or more relevant folds. The logic of these comparisons parallels that of the integrative reasoning task described earlier because the two tasks were designed to be structurally identical and were performed by the same individuals.

The primary result from the Salthouse, Mitchell, Skovronek, and Babcock (1989) study was that the magnitude of the accuracy decrease with additional folds was nearly the same for trials with only one and with more than one relevant fold. Furthermore, the same general pattern was evident across adults ranging between 20 and 80 years of age. These results suggest that a major factor contributing to poor performance on paper-folding tasks is the difficulty of preserving early information during the performance of other operations. Many of the age differences in the performance of paper-folding tasks therefore may be attributable to a decreased ability to preserve information while also carrying out other processing operations.

The cube comparison test served as the target task in a recent analytical project concerned with adult age differences in spatial abilities (Salthouse & Skovronek, in press). The major focus of the studies in this project was the influence of working memory on the performance of a moderately complex cognitive task. Three measures were identified as potential reflections of the operation of working memory during the performance of the task. The measures were (a) the magnitude of accuracy decline associated with increased angular deviation between the two to-be-compared cubes, (b) the number of redundant requests for information in a special, successive presentation, version of the task, and (c) the accuracy of recognizing probes of earlier presented information. As expected from previous research, substantial age differences were found in both the time and the accuracy of the overall decisions in the cube comparison task. No age differences were found in the measure of recognition of earlier information, but older adults had greater reductions in decision accuracy than young adults when working-memory demands were increased by the requirement of rotating one of the cubes, and they requested more redundant or repetitive information about the contents of the cube faces than young adults. This pattern of results was interpreted as suggesting that there may be little or no effects associated with increased age on the ability to preserve untransformed stimulus information, but that there is a loss in the ability to retain intermediate-level or abstract information generated or derived during the solution of the problem.

The research just reviewed indicates that the situation with respect to the analytical investigation of age-related differences in spatial abilities is similar to that noted with reasoning abilities. That is, there have been many attempts to examine age-related influences in particular processing components such as integration, mental rotation, and mental folding, but there also have been frequent speculations about the role of more general factors such as limitations of working memory. As with the research on reasoning, however, the available research does not yet appear either extensive enough or consistent enough to warrant strong conclusions about the proximal source of adult age differences in spatial ability.

HOW ARE AGE DIFFERENCES IN REASONING
AND SPATIAL ABILITIES BEST INVESTIGATED?

The goal of most of the research surveyed in the preceding two sections has been to explain the cause, at either a distal or a proximal level of analysis, of the well-documented age differences in reasoning and spatial abilities. Although a moderate amount of research has been conducted, the reasons for the age differences in these abilities are still poorly understood. For example, it is not yet known whether the average 65-year-old performs worse than the average 25-year-old because he or she was exposed to different experiences as a child or an adolescent, because of changes in the nature of the activities performed in one's daily life, or because, for whatever reason, a critical processing component has become impaired.

It seems likely that greater progress in understanding the causes of age-related differences in reasoning and spatial abilities will result from careful consideration of both the strengths and the weaknesses of alternative investigative strategies. This final section therefore consists of a brief discussion of the major advantages and disadvantages of research focusing on distal and proximal determinants of age-related differences in reasoning and spatial abilities.

The principal advantage of research oriented toward distal determinants is that it offers the potential of identifying the ultimate sources of age-related differences. However, much of the past research has been limited by vague and imprecise specification of the hypothesized distal determinants. If hypotheses based on these factors are to be investigated rigorously, it is essential to know what aspects of the environment or of the organism contribute to the developmental phenomena of interest, and to know what specific kinds of experience or organismic characteristics are presumed to be important in maintaining or increasing cognitive functioning across the life span.

It is also important that research concerned with distal causes examine interaction hypotheses in addition to hypotheses about the main effects of time-of-measurement, training, experience, and so forth. If these hypothesized determinants do function as mediators or moderators of the relations between age and cognitive performance, then interactions of the relevant variables with age actually may be of greater interest than the main effects. That is, a discovery that a measure of performance on a reasoning or spatial test is significantly related to factors such as time-of-measurement, deliberate training, or complexity of one's occupation is not necessarily relevant to the cause of age differences in those measures unless there is also evidence that these influences are greater at some ages than at others.

Another limitation of past research focusing on distal determinants is that the assessment of reasoning and spatial abilities often has been weak and narrow in scope. This is largely a consequence of relying upon single measures of the relevant abilities. More consistent results and stronger conclusions are likely to be possible if future researchers were to rely upon multiple measures of the important theoretical constructs. This practice would minimize the possibility that one's results merely reflect task-specific characteristics instead of the theoretical constructs of primary interest, and hence should serve to broaden the generality of the resulting inferences.

Research with a proximal focus has as its major strength the possibility of specifying the precise nature of the age differences that are observed. In some respects, however, this characteristic also can be considered a potential weakness of the analytical approach because there is seldom any assurance that the tasks or theoretical components chosen for investigation will be meaningful beyond the context of the particular project. This issue can be clarified by reference to Fig. 4.8.

Notice that each task is postulated to involve different combinations of processes or components. The components may correspond to

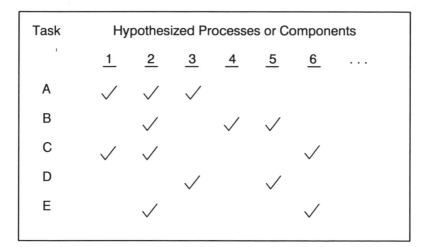

FIG. 4.8. Alternative compositions of theoretical processes or components in different cognitive tasks. A check mark indicates that the component is required for successful performance of the task.

theoretically important constructs, such as abstraction or mental rotation, or they may represent somewhat more mundane aspects, such as the sensory processes relevant to perceiving the material or the motoric processes involved in efficiently communicating the decision.

An intensive focus on one particular task eventually may indicate the relative magnitudes of the age-related influences on the specific processes or components in that task. For example, detailed study of Task B might reveal that the age differences were much larger in measures of Process 4 than in measures assumed to reflect Processes 2 or 5. A possible inference from this pattern of results might be that Process 4 is a major source of the age differences in Task B.

Although this localization strategy seems reasonable when applied to a single task, it can have severe limitations when considered in the context of several different tasks. A major problem is that the process or component identified as critical for the existence of age differences in that task may not be involved in other tasks in which age differences also are reported. This situation is represented in Fig. 4.8 in that Process 4 is portrayed as being unique to Task B. Moreover, even if the same theoretical process is present in another task, it cannot be assumed automatically that its importance, or its sensitivity to age-related influences, is independent of the context in which it occurs. In terms of Fig. 4.8, Process 2 may function quite differently in Task A, where it is combined with Processes 1 and 3, than in Task E, where it is combined with Process 6.

If either the processing component is not required in other tasks or if its relative importance or degree of age sensitivity varies according to the other processes with which it is combined, then there may be little or no generalizability of the results from one task to other tasks. As an example, assuming that all relevant processes were identified and assessed with equivalent sensitivity, one might be fairly confident that the source of the age differences in Task B are localized in Process 4. However, this information is unlikely to be helpful in understanding the source of the age differences in Tasks A, C, D, and E, because that process is not involved in any of those tasks.

One means of addressing the problem of restricted generalizability is to consider several tasks simultaneously. Careful selection of the tasks to be subjected to analytical investigation, together with detailed analyses of each task, should allow much broader inferences than those currently possible. For example, the only process common to Tasks A, B, and E in Fig. 4.8 is Process 2. One's confidence that this is a primary source of the age-related influences therefore would be strengthened if similar patterns of age differences are evident in each of these tasks. Even stronger support for this inference, and for the underlying task analyses, would be obtained if the measures of the common process were found to be highly correlated across the relevant tasks.

For the reasons just described, it seems desirable for researchers interested in analyzing the proximal determinants of age differences in cognition to expand the scope of their investigation to include at least two independent tasks. The aim of the research still can be the determination of the processing components primarily responsible for the age differences in those particular tasks, but the simultaneous consideration of several tasks provides at least some assurance that any conclusions are not restricted to a single task.

In addition to the recommendation that multiple measures or multiple tasks be employed in research concerned with both distal and proximal determinants of age differences in reasoning and spatial abilities, it is also desirable that the size of the samples used in future research be increased considerably relative to current practices in both types of research. Not only would this increase the statistical power to be able to detect any differences that might exist, but it should increase the ultimate generalizability of the results by reducing the likelihood of sampling biases. One of the easiest ways to improve a study based on a good idea is to ensure that the idea is investigated adequately by having a sufficient number of relevant observations, and therefore increasing the size of the samples is an important first step in improving the quality of age-comparative research concerned with reasoning and spatial abilities. More generally, strong inferences tend to require strong methods, and the power of one's methods is often directly proportional to the number and variety of relevant observations.

CONCLUSIONS

The purpose of this chapter has been to review both the empirical and the explanatory research concerned with the relations between age and reasoning and spatial abilities. The empirical evidence appears quite convincing in indicating robust age differences in these abilities in cross-sectional samples, as the age correlations average about $-.4$, and the average 60-year-old has been found to perform between .5 and 1.5 SDs below the level of the average 20-year-old. However, only limited success has been achieved in identifying the causes of these negative relations between age and reasoning and spatial abilities. One reason for the relative lack of progress is that only a small number of studies have been designed to investigate a specific hypothesis about the causes of age differences in the performance of reasoning and spatial tests. Characteristics intrinsic to each of the research approaches also contribute to the current inadequacy of explanations for age differences in reasoning and spatial abilities. Research investigating distal determinants of the age-related effects is hampered by the difficulty of obtaining measures of factors operating at earlier periods in one's life, and research with a proximal focus often suffers from questionable generalizability because of an emphasis on detailed analyses of specific tasks. Both types of research nevertheless need to be pursued because reasoning and spatial abilities are important determinants of the effectiveness of cognitive functioning outside the laboratory, and consequently satisfactory explanations for why increased age is associated with lower levels of these abilities are both desirable, and ultimately, necessary.

ACKNOWLEDGMENTS

Preparation of this chapter was facilitated by a National Institute on Aging Grant (AG06826). I would like to thank David Arenberg for helpful comments on an earlier draft of this manuscript.

REFERENCES

Adamowicz, J. K., & Hudson, B. R. (1978). Visual short-term memory, response delay and age. *Perceptual and Motor Skills, 46,* 267–270.

Aftanas, M. S., & Royce, J. R. (1969). Analysis of brain damage tests administered to normal subjects with factor score comparisons across ages. *Multivariate Behavioral Research, 4,* 459–481.

Alpaugh, P. K., & Birren, J. E. (1977). Variables affecting creative contributions across the adult life span. *Human Development, 20,* 240–248.

Alpaugh, P. K., Parham, I. A., Cole, K. D., & Birren, J. E. (1982). Creativity in adulthood and old age: An exploratory study. *Educational Gerontology, 8,* 101–116.

Arenberg, D. (1968). Concept problem solving in young and old adults. *Journal of Gerontology, 23,* 279–282.

Arenberg, D. (1974). A longitudinal study of problem solving in adults. *Journal of Gerontology, 29,* 650–658.

Arenberg, D. (1982). Changes with age in problem solving. In F. I. M. Craik & S. Trehub (Eds.), *Aging and cognitive processes* (pp. 221–235). New York: Plenum.

Arenberg, D. (1988). Analysis and synthesis in problem solving and aging. In M. L. Howe & C. J. Brainerd (Eds.), *Cognitive development in adulthood* (pp. 161–183). New York: Springer-Verlag.

Arenberg, D., & Robertson-Tchabo, E. A. (1985). Adult age differences in memory and linguistic integration revisited. *Experimental Aging Research, 11,* 187–191.

Arthur, W., Fuentes, R., & Doverspike, D. (1990). Relationships among personnel tests, age, and job performance. *Experimental Aging Research, 16,* 11–16.

Aubrey, J. B., & Dobbs, A. R. (1989a). Age and sex differences in the mental realignment of maps. *Experimental Aging Research, 16,* 133–139.

Aubrey, J. B., & Dobbs, A. R. (1989b). Age differences in extrapersonal orientation as measured by performance on the locomotor maze. *Canadian Journal on Aging, 8,* 333–342.

Babcock, R. L. (1991). Analysis of Adult Age Differences on the Raven's Advanced Progressive Matrices Test. Unpublished doctoral dissertation, Georgia Institute of Technology, Atlanta, Georgia.

Barr, R. A., & Giambra, L. M. (1990). Age-related decrement in auditory selective attention. *Psychology and Aging, 5,* 597–599.

Barrett, G. V., Mihal, W. L., Panek, P. E., Sterns, H. L., & Alexander, R. A. (1977). Information processing skills predictive of accident involvement for younger and older commercial drivers. *Industrial Gerontology, 4,* 173–182.

Basowitz, H., & Korchin, S. J. (1957). Age differences in the perception of closure. *Journal of Abnormal and Social Psychology, 54,* 93–97.

Berg, C., Hertzog, C., & Hunt, E. (1982). Age differences in the speed of mental rotation. *Developmental Psychology, 18,* 95–107.

Berkowitz, B. (1953). The Wechsler-Bellevue performance of white males past age 50. *Journal of Gerontology, 8,* 76–80.

Bigler, E., Steinman, D., & Newton, J. (1981). Clinical assessment of cognitive deficit in neurologic disorder: Effects of age and degenerative disease. *Clinical Neuropsychology, 3,* 5–13.

Birren, J. E. (1955). Age changes in speed of responses and perception and their significance for complex behavior. In *Old age in the modern world* (pp. 235–247). Edinburgh: Livingstone.

Birren, J. E., & Morrison, D. F. (1961). Analysis of the WAIS subtests in relation to age and education. *Journal of Gerontology, 16,* 363–369.

Birren, J. E., & Spieth, W. (1962). Age, response speed, and cardiovascular functions. *Journal of Gerontology, 17,* 390–391.

Botwinick, J., & Storandt, M. (1974). *Memory, related functions and age.* Springfield, IL: Thomas.

Brinley, J. F., Jovick, T. J., & McLaughlin, L. M. (1974). Age, reasoning and memory in adults. *Journal of Gerontology, 29,* 182–189.

Bromley, D. B. (1956). Some experimental tests of the effect of age on creative intellectual output. *Journal of Gerontology, 11,* 74–82.

Bromley, D. B. (1967). Age and sex differences in the serial production of creative conceptual responses. *Journal of Gerontology, 22,* 32–42.

Bruce, P. R., & Herman, J. F. (1983). Spatial knowledge of young and elderly adults: Scene recognition from familiar and novel perspectives. *Experimental Aging Research, 9,* 169–173.

Burke, H. R. (1972). Raven's Progressive Matrices: Validity, reliability and norms. *Journal of Psychology, 82,* 253–257.

Cerella, J., Poon, L. W., & Fozard, J. L. (1981). Mental rotation and age reconsidered. *Journal of Gerontology, 36,* 620–624.

Charness, N. (1985). Aging and problem-solving performance. In N. Charness (Ed.), *Aging and human performance* (pp. 225–229). Chichester, England: Wiley.

Charness, N. (1987). Component processes in bridge bidding and novel problem-solving tasks. *Canadian Journal of Psychology, 41,* 223–243.

Chown, S. M. (1961). Age and the rigidities. *Journal of Gerontology, 16,* 353–362.

Clark, J. W. (1960). The aging dimension: A factorial analysis of individual differences with age on psychological and physiological measurements. *Journal of Gerontology, 15,* 183–187.

Clarkson-Smith, L., & Halpern, D. F. (1983). Can age-related deficits in spatial memory be attenuated through the use of verbal coding? *Experimental Aging Research, 9,* 179–184.

Clayton, V., & Overton, W. F. (1976). Concrete and formal operational thought processes in young adulthood and old age. *International Journal of Aging and Human Development, 7,* 237–246.

Cobb, B. B., Lay, C. D., & Bourdet, N. M. (1971). *The relationship between chronological age and aptitude test measures of advanced-level air traffic control trainees* (Report No. FAA-AM-71-36). Oklahoma City: Federal Aviation Administration.

Cooper, L. A., & Shepard, R. N. (1973). Chronometric studies of the rotation of mental images. In W. Chase (Ed.), *Visual information processing* (pp. 75–176). New York: Academic.

Cornelius, S. W. (1984). Classic pattern of intellectual aging: Test familiarity, difficulty and performance. *Journal of Gerontology, 39,* 201–206.

Cremer, R., & Zeef, E. J. (1987). What kind of noise increases with age? *Journal of Gerontology, 42,* 515–518.

Crosson, C. W. (1984). Age and field independence among women. *Experimental Aging Research, 10,* 165–170.

Cunningham, W. R., Clayton, V., & Overton, W. (1975). Fluid and crystallized intelligence in young adulthood and old age. *Journal of Gerontology, 30,* 53–55.

Danziger, W. L., & Salthouse, T. A. (1978). Age and the perception of incomplete figures. *Experimental Aging Research, 4,* 67–80.

Davies, A. D., & Leytham, G. W. (1964). Perception of verticality in adult life. *British Journal of Psychology, 55,* 315–320.

Del Vento Bielby, D., & Papalia, D. (1975). Moral development and perceptual role-taking egocentrism: Their development and interrelationship across the life-span. *International Journal of Aging and Human Development, 6,* 293–308.

Denney, N. W. (1980). Task demands and problem-solving strategies in middle-aged and older adults. *Journal of Gerontology, 35,* 559–564.

Denney, N. W., & Denney, D. R. (1982). The relationship between classification and questioning strategies among adults. *Journal of Gerontology, 37,* 190–196.

Denney, N. W., & Palmer, A. M. (1981). Adult age differences on traditional and practical problem-solving measures. *Journal of Gerontology, 36,* 323–328.

Denney, N. W., Pearce, K. A., & Palmer, A. M. (1982). A developmental study of adults' performance on traditional and practical problem-solving tasks. *Experimental Aging Research, 8,* 115–118.

Dirken, J. M. (1972). *Functional age of industrial workers: A transversal survey of aging capacities and a method for assessing functional age.* Groningen, Netherlands: Wolters-Noordhoff.

Edwards, A. E., & Wine, D. B. (1963). Personality changes with age: Their dependency on concomitant intellectual decline. *Journal of Gerontology, 18,* 182–184.

Flynn, J. R. (1987). Massive IQ gains in 14 nations: What IQ tests really measure. *Psychological Bulletin, 101,* 171–191.

Foos, P. W. (1989). Adult age differences in working memory. *Psychology and Aging, 4,* 269–275.

Fullerton, A. M. (1988). Adult age differences in solving series problems requiring integration of new and old information. *International Journal of Aging and Human Development, 26,* 147–154.

Garfield, S. L., & Blek, L. (1952). Age, vocabulary level, and mental impairment. *Journal of Consulting Psychology, 16,* 395–398.

Gaylord, S. A., & Marsh, G. R. (1976). Age differences in the speed of a spatial cognitive process. *Journal of Gerontology, 30,* 674–678.

Gilbert, J. G. (1941). Memory loss in senescence. *Journal of Abnormal and Social Psychology, 36,* 73–86.

Glanzer, M., & Glaser, R. (1959). Cross-sectional and longitudinal results in a study of age-related changes. *Educational and Psychological Measurement, 19*, 89–101.

Goldfarb, W. (1941). *An investigation of reaction time in older adults* (Contributions to Education No. 831). New York: Teachers College, Columbia University Press.

Hartley, A. A. (1981). Adult age difference in deductive reasoning processes. *Journal of Gerontology, 36*, 700–706.

Hartley, A. A., & Anderson, J. W. (1983a). Task complexity and problem-solving performance in younger and older adults. *Journal of Gerontology, 38*, 72–77.

Hartley, A. A., & Anderson, J. W. (1973b). Task complexity, problem representation, and problem-solving performance by younger and older adults. *Journal of Gerontology, 38*, 78–80.

Hartley, A. A., & Anderson, J. W. (1986). Instruction, induction, generation, and evaluation of strategies for solving search problems. *Journal of Gerontology, 41*, 650–658.

Hayslip, B., & Sterns, H. L. (1979). Age differences in relationships between crystallized and fluid intelligences and problem solving. *Journal of Gerontology, 34*, 404–414.

Herman, J. F., & Coyne, A. C. (1980). Mental manipulation of spatial information in young and elderly adults. *Developmental Psychology, 16*, 537–538.

Heron, A., & Chown, S. M. (1967). *Age and function*. Boston: Little, Brown.

Hertzog, C., & Rypma, B. (1991). Age differences in components of mental-rotation task performance. *Bulletin of the Psychonomic Society, 29*, 209–212.

Hines, T. (1979). Information feedback, reaction time and error rates in young and old subjects. *Experimental Aging Research, 5*, 207–215.

Hooper, F. H., Hooper, J. O., & Colbert, K. C. (1984). *Personality and memory correlates of intellectual functioning: Young adulthood to old age*. Basel, Switzerland: Karger.

Hoyer, W. J., Rebok, G. W., & Sved, S. M. (1979). Effects of varying irrelevant information on adult age differences in problem solving. *Journal of Gerontology, 34*, 553–560.

Hybertson, E. D., Perdue, J., & Hybertson, D. (1982). Age differences in information acquisition strategies. *Experimental Aging Research, 8*, 109–113.

Jacewicz, M. M., & Hartley, A. A. (1979). Rotation of mental images by young and old college students: The effects of familiarity. *Journal of Gerontology, 34*, 396–403.

Jerome, E. A. (1962). Decay of heuristic processes in the aged. In C. Tibbitts & W. Donahue (Eds.), *Social and Psychological Aspects of Aging* (pp. 808–823). New York: Columbia University Press.

Kaufman, A. S., Reynolds, C. R., & McLean, J. E. (1989). Age and WAIS–R intelligence in a national sample of adults in the 20-to-74-year age range: A cross-sectional analysis with educational level controlled. *Intelligence, 13*, 235–253.

Kausler, D. H. (1982). *Experimental psychology and human aging*. New York: Wiley.

Kausler, D. H., Hakami, M. K., & Wright, R. E. (1982). Adult age differences in frequency judgments of categorical representations. *Journal of Gerontology, 37*, 365–371.

Kausler, D. H., & Puckett, J. M. (1980). Frequency judgments and correlated cognitive abilities in young and elderly adults. *Journal of Gerontology, 35*, 376–382.

Kausler, D. H., Wright, R., & Hakami, M. K. (1981). Variation in task complexity and adult age differences in frequency-of-occurrence judgments. *Bulletin of the Psychonomic Society, 18*, 195–197.

Kellogg, R. T. (1983). Age differences in hypothesis testing and frequency processing in concept learning. *Bulletin of the Psychonomic Society, 21*, 101–104.

Kesler, M. S., Denney, N. W., & Whitely, S. E. (1976). Factors influencing problem-solving in middle-aged and elderly adults. *Human Development, 19*, 310–320.

Kirasic, K. C. (1989). The effects of age and environmental familiarity on adults' spatial problem-solving performance: Evidence of a hometown advantage. *Experimental Aging Research, 15*, 181–187.

Kirasic, K. C. (1991). Spatial cognition and behavior in young and elderly adults: Implications for learning new environments. *Psychology and Aging, 6,* 10–18.

Kirasic, K. C., & Bernicki, M. R. (1990). Acquisition of spatial knowledge under conditions of temporospatial discontinuity in young and elderly adults. *Psychological Research, 52,* 76–79.

Kliegl, R., Smith, J., & Baltes, P. B. (1990). On the locus and process of magnification of age differences during mnemonic training. *Developmental Psychology, 26,* 894–904.

Kohn, M. L., & Schooler, C. (1983). *Work and personality.* Norwood, NJ: Ablex.

Koss, E., Haxby, J. V., DeCarli, C., Schapiro, M. B., Friedland, R. P., & Rapoport, S. I. (1991). Patterns of performance preservation and loss in healthy aging. *Developmental Neuropsychology, 7,* 99–113.

Kraus, J., Chalker, S., & Macindoe, I. (1967). Vocabulary and chronological age as predictors of "abstraction" on the Shipley-Hartford Retreat Scale. *Australian Journal of Psychology, 19,* 133–135.

Lachman, M. E., & Jelalian, E. (1984). Self-efficacy and attributions for intellectual performance in young and elderly adults. *Journal of Gerontology, 39,* 577–582.

Lee, J. A., & Pollack, R. A. (1978). The effects of age on perceptual problem-solving strategies. *Experimental Aging Research, 4,* 37–54.

Lee, J. S. (1991). *Abstraction and aging.* New York: Springer-Verlag.

Light, L. L., Zelinski, E. M., & Moore, M. M. (1982). Adult age differences in reasoning from new information. *Journal of Experimental Psychology: Learning, Memory, and Cognition, 8,* 435–447.

Lipman, P. D. (1991). Age and exposure differences in the acquisition of route information. *Psychology and Aging, 6,* 128–133.

Looft, W., & Charles, D. (1971). Egocentrism and social interaction in young and old adults. *International Journal of Aging and Human Development, 2,* 21–28.

Ludwig, T. E. (1982). Age differences in mental synthesis. *Journal of Gerontology, 37,* 182–189.

Mack, J. L., & Carlson, N. J. (1978). Conceptual deficits and aging: The category test. *Perceptual and Motor Skills, 46,* 123–128.

Mason, C. F., & Ganzler, H. (1964). Adult norms for the Shipley Institute of Living Scale and Hooper Visual Organization Test based on age and education. *Journal of Gerontology, 19,* 419–424.

McCrae, R. R., Arenberg, D., & Costa, P. T. (1987). Declines in divergent thinking with age: Cross-sectional, longitudinal and cross-sequential analyses. *Psychology and Aging, 2,* 130–137.

Mittenberg, W., Seidenberg, M., O'Leary, D. S., & DiGiulio, D. V. (1989). Changes in cerebral functioning associated with normal aging. *Journal of Clinical and Experimental Neuropsychology, 11,* 918–932.

Muhs, P. J., Hooper, E. H., & Papalia-Finlay, D. (1979–1980). Cross-sectional analysis of cognitive functioning across the life-span. *International Journal of Aging and Human Development,* 311–333.

Nehrke, M. F. (1972). Age, sex and educational differences in syllogistic reasoning. *Journal of Gerontology, 27,* 466–470.

Offenbach, S. I. (1974). A developmental study of hypothesis testing and cue selection strategies. *Developmental Psychology, 10,* 484–490.

Ohta, R. J. (1981). Spatial problem-solving: The response selection tendencies of young and elderly adults. *Experimental Aging Research, 7,* 81–84.

Ohta, R. J. (1983). Spatial orientation in the elderly: The current status of understanding. In H. L. Pick & L. P. Acredolo (Eds.), *Spatial orientation: Theory, research, and applications* (pp. 105–124). New York: Plenum.

Ohta, R. J., Walsh, D. A., & Krauss, I. K. (1981). Spatial perspective-taking ability in young and elderly adults. *Experimental Aging Research, 7*, 45–63.

Panek, P. E. (1985). Age differences in field-dependence/independence. *Experimental Aging Research, 11*, 97–99.

Panek, P. E., Barrett, G. V., Sterns, H. L., & Alexander, R. A. (1978). Age differences in perceptual style, selective attention, and perceptual motor reaction time. *Experimental Aging Research, 4*, 377–387.

Panek, P. E., & Stoner, S. B. (1980). Age differences on Raven's Coloured Progressive Matrices. *Perceptual and Motor Skills, 50*, 977–978.

Pierce, K., & Storandt, M. (1987). Similarities in visual imagery ability in young and old women. *Experimental Aging Research, 13*, 209–211.

Pierce, T. W., Elias, M. W., Keohane, P. J., Podraza, A. M., Robbins, M. A., & Schultz, N. R. (1989). Validity of a short form of the Category Test in relation to age, education, and gender. *Experimental Aging Research, 15*, 137–141.

Prigatano, G. P., & Parsons, O. A. (1976). Relationship of age and education to Halstead test performance in different patient populations. *Journal of Consulting and Clinical Psychology, 44*, 527–533.

Prohaska, T. R., Parham, I. A., & Teitelman, J. (1984). Age differences in attribution to causality: Implications for intellectual assessment. *Experimental Aging Research, 10*, 111–117.

Puglisi, J. T., & Morrell, R. W. (1986). Age-related slowing in mental rotation of three-dimensional objects. *Experimental Aging Research, 12*, 217–220.

Riege, W. H., & Inman, V. (1981). Age differences in nonverbal memory tasks. *Journal of Gerontology, 36*, 51–58.

Riege, W. H., Tomaszewski, R., Lantro, A., & Metter, E. J. (1984). Age and alcoholism: Independent memory decrements. *Alcoholism: Clinical and Experimental Research, 8*, 42–47.

Rimoldi, H., & Vander Woude, K. W. (1969). Aging and problem solving. *Archives of General Psychiatry, 20*, 215–225.

Royer, F. L., Gilmore, G. C., & Gruhn, J. J. (1984). Stimulus parameters that produce age differences in block design performance. *Journal of Clinical Psychology, 40*, 1474–1484.

Rubin, K. H. (1974). The relationship between spatial and communicative egocentrism in children and young and old adults. *Journal of Genetic Psychology, 125*, 295–301.

Ruff, R. M., Light, R. H., & Evans, R. W. (1987). The Ruff Figural Fluency Test: A normative study with adults. *Developmental Neuropsychology, 3*, 37–51.

Salthouse, T. A. (1987a). Adult age differences in integrative spatial ability. *Psychology and Aging, 2*, 254–260.

Salthouse, T. A. (1987b). Sources of age-related individual differences in block design tasks. *Intelligence, 11*, 245–262.

Salthouse, T. A. (1988a). Initializing the formalization of theories of cognitive aging. *Psychology and Aging, 3*, 3–16.

Salthouse, T. A. (1988b). The role of processing resources in cognitive aging. In M. L. Howe & C. J. Brainerd (Eds.), *Cognitive development in adulthood (pp. 185–239)*. New York: Springer-Verlag.

Salthouse, T. A. (1991a). Mediation of adult age differences in cognition by reduction in working memory and speed of processing. *Psychological Science, 2*, 179–183.

Salthouse, T. A. (1991b). *Theoretical perspectives in cognitive aging*. Hillsdale, NJ: Lawrence Erlbaum Associates.

Salthouse, T. A. (1991c). Age and experience effects on the interpretation of orthographic drawings of three-dimensional objects. *Psychology and Aging, 6*, 426–433.

Salthouse, T. A., Babcock, R., Mitchell, D. R., Skovronek, E., & Palmon, R. (1990). Age and experience effects in spatial visualization. *Developmental Psychology, 26*, 128–136.

Salthouse, T. A., Babcock, R., & Shaw, R. (1991). Effects of adult age on structural and operational capacities in working memory. *Psychology and Aging, 6,* 118–127.

Salthouse, T. A., Kausler, D. H., & Saults, J. S. (1988). Investigation of student status, background variables, and the feasibility of standard tasks in cognitive aging research. *Psychology and Aging, 3,* 29–37.

Salthouse, T. A., Legg, S., Palmon, R., & Mitchell, D. R. D. (1990). Memory factors in age-related differences in simple reasoning. *Psychology and Aging, 5,* 9–15.

Salthouse, T. A., & Mitchell, D. R. (1989). Structural and operational capacities in integrative spatial ability. *Psychology and Aging, 4,* 18–25.

Salthouse, T. A., & Mitchell, D. R. (1990). Effects of age and naturally occurring experience on spatial visualization performance. *Developmental Psychology, 26,* 845–854.

Salthouse, T. A., Mitchell, D. R., & Palmon, R. (1989). Memory and age differences in spatial manipulation ability. *Psychology and Aging, 4,* 480–486.

Salthouse, T. A., Mitchell, D. R., Skovronek, E., & Babcock, R. L. (1989). Effects of adult age and working memory on reasoning and spatial abilities. *Journal of Experimental Psychology: Learning, Memory, and Cognition, 15,* 507–516.

Salthouse, T. A., & Prill, K. A. (1987). Inferences about age impairments in inferential reasoning. *Psychology and Aging, 2,* 43–51.

Salthouse, T. A., & Prill, K. A. (1988). Effects of aging on perceptual closure. *American Journal of Psychology, 101,* 217–238.

Salthouse, T. A. & Skovronek, E. (in press). Within-context assessment of age differences in working memory. *Journals of Gerontology: Psychological Science.*

Schaie, K. W. (1958). Rigidity-flexibility and intelligence: A cross-sectional study of the adult life-span from 20 to 70. *Psychological Monographs, 72.*

Schaie, K. W. (1988). Internal validity threats in studies of adult cognitive development. In M. L. Howe & C. J. Brainerd (Eds.), *Cognitive development in adulthood* (pp. 241–272). New York: Springer-Verlag.

Schaie, K. W. (1989). Perceptual speed in adulthood: Cross-sectional and longitudinal studies. *Psychology and Aging, 4,* 443–453.

Schludermann, E. H., Schludermann, S. M., Merryman, P. W., & Brown, B. W. (1983). Halstead's studies in the neuropsychology of aging. *Archives of Gerontology and Geriatrics, 2,* 49–172.

Schultz, N. R., Kaye, D. B., & Hoyer, W. J. (1980). Intelligence and spontaneous flexibility in adulthood and old age. *Intelligence, 4,* 219–231.

Sharps, M. J., & Gollin, E. S. (1987). Speed and accuracy of mental image rotation in young and elderly adults. *Journal of Gerontology, 42,* 342–344.

Shepard, R. N., & Metzler, J. (1971). Mental rotation of three-dimensional objects. *Science, 171,* 701–703.

Sinnott, J. D. (1975). Everyday thinking and Piagetian operativity in adults. *Human Development, 18,* 430–443.

Spieth, W. (1965). Slowness of task performance and cardiovascular disease. In A. T. Welford & J. E. Birren (Eds.), *Behavior, aging and the nervous system* (pp. 366–400). Springfield, IL: Thomas.

Sterne, D. M. (1973). The Hooper Visual Organization Test and Trail Making Tests as discriminants of brain injury. *Journal of Clinical Psychology, 29,* 212–213.

Sward, K. (1945). Age and mental ability in superior men. *American Journal of Psychology, 58,* 443–479.

Tamkin, A. S., & Jacobsen, R. (1984). Age-related norms for the Hooper Visual Organization Test. *Journal of Clinical Psychology, 40,* 1459–1463.

Trembly, D., & O'Connor, J. (1966). Growth and decline of natural and acquired intellectual characteristics. *Journal of Gerontology, 21,* 9–12.

Trites, D. K., & Cobb, B. B. (1964). Problems in air traffic management: IV. Comparison of pre-employment, job-related experience with aptitude tests as predictors of training and job performance of air traffic control specialists. *Aerospace Medicine, 35,* 428–436.

Vega, A., & Parsons, O. A. (1967). Cross-validation of the Halstead-Reitan Tests for brain damage. *Journal of Consulting Psychology, 31,* 619–625.

Wasserstein, J., Zappulla, R., Rosen, J., & Gerstman, L. (1987). In search of closure: Subjective contour illusions, gestalt completion tests, and implications. *Brain and Cognition, 6,* 1–14.

Weisenburg, T., Roe, A., & McBride, K. E. (1936). *Adult intelligence.* New York: Commonwealth Fund.

Welford, A. T. (1958). *Aging and human skill.* London: Oxford University Press.

Wentworth-Rohr, I., Mackintosh, R. M., & Fialkoff, B. S. (1974). The relationship of Hooper VOT score to sex, education, intelligence and age. *Journal of Clinical Psychology, 30,* 73–75.

Willis, S. L., & Schaie, K. W. (1986). Training the elderly on the ability factors of spatial orientation and inductive reasoning. *Psychology and Aging, 1,* 239–247.

Wilson, T. R. (1963). Flicker fusion frequency, age and intelligence. *Gerontologia, 7,* 200–208.

Young, M. L. (1966). Problem-solving performance in two age groups. *Journal of Gerontology, 21,* 505–509.

CHAPTER FIVE

Language and Aging

Susan Kemper
University of Kansas

In 1979, Gillian Cohen surveyed research on the effects of aging on language and concluded that "Geriatric psycholinguistics is virtually an unexplored territory" (p. 412). In little more than a decade since she reached this conclusion, psycholinguists, sociolinguists, speech-language pathologists, and cognitive scientists have begun to explore this territory and to map a wide range of age-related changes to language. In some regions, age-related changes in language have been thoroughly mapped; in others, only the major landmarks have been charted.

This review examines what has been charted about the effects of aging on language. It begins by considering the regression hypothesis that language dissolution mirrors language acquisition and then goes on to survey different proposals regarding the effects of cognitive aging on language. The chapter concludes with a survey of contemporary research on language and aging, incorporating suggestions for future areas of study.

LANGUAGE AND COGNITION

The Regression Hypothesis

Periodically, the regression hypothesis has surfaced in an attempt to formulate a comprehensive theory of language development by linking language acquisition to language dissolution. This hypothesis claims that

213

the breakdown of language is the inverse of its acquisition (Jackson, 1958; Jakobson, 1941/1968). Typically, the regression hypothesis is put forth to account for aphasia disorders (Dennis & Wiegel-Crump, 1979; Grodzinsky, 1990; Lesser, 1978), although it also has been applied to the effects of normal aging and dementia (Emery, 1985) on language. Both strong and weak forms of the regression hypothesis have been suggested; in the strong form, language dissolution should be a mirror image of language acquisition involving the reverse pattern of cognitive and/or linguistic development. In the weak form, the stages or pattern of language dissolution merely should parallel those of language acquisition but for different reasons, reflecting different processing mechanisms and/or linguistic principles.

The regression hypothesis has been applied to phonology (Jakobson, 1941/1968), vocabulary (Rochford & Williams, 1962), morphology (Berko Gleason, 1978; de Villiers, 1974), and grammar (Crystal, Fletcher, & Garman, 1976; Lesser, 1974; Wepman & Jones, 1964; Whitaker & Selnes, 1978). Each of these studies used a similar approach: A rank ordering of the order of acquisition of phonological contrasts, vocabulary items, morphemes, or grammatical forms is established and then compared to a rank ordering obtained from aphasics. Although certain common patterns have emerged, significant differences have emerged as well. For example, Rochford and Williams reported a close parallel between the ages at which children were able to define a set of words and the probability that aphasics also would be able to define the words; however, the children and aphasics responded on the basis of different retrieval cues and produced different incorrect or partially correct definitions. The rank order of omission of grammatical morphemes by agrammatics does not parallel the order in which morphemes are acquired by children (de Villiers, 1974), although a common ordering of the difficulty of syntactic structures appears in child language and aphasic language (Crystal et al., 1976).

Most recently, a strong form of the regression hypothesis has been advanced as an adjunct to the government-binding theory of grammar (Chomsky, 1981, 1982, 1986; Hyams, 1986; Manzini & Wexler, 1987; Wexler & Chien, 1985). Grodzinsky (1990) articulated three, empirically testable, predictions based on the regression hypothesis: (a) A grammar of aphasic language should be a subset of that for normal language, (b) the smaller the grammar, the more severe the aphasia, and (c) grammars of aphasics must correspond to grammars of intermediate stages during acquisition.

In support of these claims, Grodzinsky (1990) noted that children must acquire, over time, certain principles of government-binding theory such as those that govern the interpretation (or binding) of anaphoric pronouns. For example, the anaphoric *her* cannot be coreferential with *Mary* in sentences such as *John wanted Mary to wash her* (e.g., it cannot be bound to *Mary*) but this government-binding principle must be acquired by English speakers. Hence, at some stage of development, children incorrectly interpret *her* as *Mary*, reflecting the rules of a smaller grammar, which lacks the binding principle, than that utilized by adult English speakers. This rule is lost by some aphasics, suggesting that the aphasics have reverted to this smaller grammar. Thus Conditions (a) and (c) are met; Grodzinsky acknowledged that the severity Condition (b) has not been met.

A strong form of the regression hypothesis also was advanced (Emery, 1985) as an account of the effects of normal aging and dementia on language. Emery's application of the regression hypothesis to normal aging is explicit:

> . . . our data show that there is an inverse relationship between sequence of language development and sequence of language deterioration, i.e., the syntactic forms mastered latest in development, and concomitantly the most complex, are the forms showing quickest and/or greatest processing deficits. Put another way, increasing linguistic complexity has a direct linear relationship with sequence in linguistic development; the data show an inverse relationship between the ontogenesis of complex linguistic forms and linguistic deterioration, i.e., the more complex, the later to develop, the earlier to deteriorate. (p. 34)

Hence, Emery claimed that the effects of aging on language meet Grodzinsky's (1990) three conditions: The language of older adults corresponds to a subset of that of young adults; the older the adults, the more restricted the language; and language dissolution retraces the steps of language acquisition.

Emery (1985) went on to extend the regression hypothesis to dementia. She argued that dementing adults "show evidence of regression toward the use of the most simple forms . . . of syntactic patterning" (p. 42). Hence, for Emery, the process of language development across the life span could be characterized as an inverted *u*-shaped curve: The language of very young children resembles that of severely demented adults, at least with regard to grammar, as in Fig. 5.1.

Emery's (1985) support for these claims is derived from studies of the adults' comprehension of different grammatical forms. The normal elderly adults had difficulty comprehending prepositions, as in *Do you put your stockings on after your shoes?*, passives, such as *The boy is called by the girl; who is called and who did the calling?*, and other complex constructions, including *What is the relationship of your brother's father to you?* Dementing adults rarely answered such questions correctly and they failed on word retrieval or naming tasks, as well. In addition, Emery

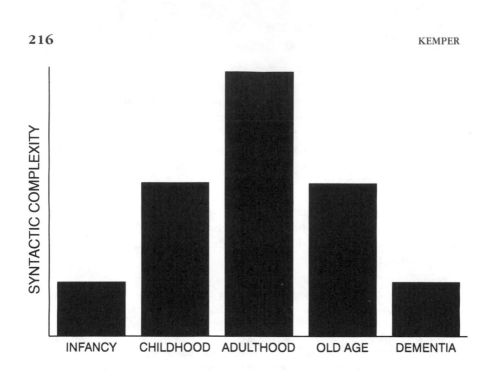

FIG. 5.1.   Hypothetical inverted u-shaped curve characterizing language development according to the regression hypothesis.

asked elderly adults and dementing adults to respond to questions such as *He found out that Mickey won the race. Who found out?* or to act out sentences such as *Mickey tells Donald to hop up and down. Make him hop.* Based, in part, on the work of C. Chomsky (1979), the questions and sentences were ordered on the basis of grammatical complexity and order of acquisition. Because Emery found that the elderly adults and the dementing adults performed most poorly on the most complex sentences, she concluded that language dissolution mirrors language acquisition.

Before evaluating Emery's (1985) claims, the status of the regression hypothesis must be weighed against competing models of the relationship of language to cognition. To the extent that aging affects cognition, by imposing limitations on working memory, reducing the speed of cognitive operations, impairing the allocation of attention, or by triggering the development of alternative information-processing styles and strategies, adults' language also will be affected. The effects of cognitive aging on language may mimic in reverse developmental patterns observed in children but for different reasons, which arise from alternative solutions to the problem of mapping cognition onto language and/or language onto cognition.

The Mapping Problem

Regardless of the status of the regression hypothesis, the basic questions addressed by studies of language and aging concern the nature of the relationship between language and cognition: "How is nonlinguistic knowledge mapped onto language?" and "How are linguistic expressions mapped onto nonlinguistic knowledge?" This mapping problem (Clark, 1977; Rice, 1983; Rice & Kemper, 1984; Slobin, 1979) can be expressed graphically, as in Fig. 5.2.

Figure 5.2 sketches five solutions to the mapping problem:

1. The strong cognition hypothesis is represented by the massive arrow from Cognition to Language to indicate that cognition in large part determines language.

2. The local homologies hypothesis is indicated by the small arrow from Cognition to Language to suggest that the linkages between cognition and language are localized with respect to specific aspects of cognition and language.

3. The linguistic determinism hypothesis is suggested by the arrow that reverses its direction going from Cognition to Language and back to Cognition; although cognition may account for the early course of

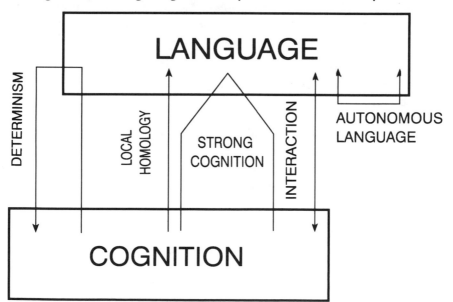

FIG. 5.2. Five solutions to the mapping problem showing the relationship between language and cognition. Adapted from Rice (1983), which later appeared in Rice & Kemper (1984).

language development, language constrains cognition by providing stable categories and contrasts.

4. The interaction hypothesis is represented by the double-headed arrow running between Cognition and Language to indicate that there are reciprocal influences of language on cognition and cognition on language.

5. The autonomous language hypothesis is suggested by the arrow that does not pass through Cognition to indicate that some aspects of language are independent of cognition.

These different solutions to the mapping problem arise because there is no one-to-one correspondence between language and cognition. Some aspects of cognition are immune to linguistic expression; for example, the procedural knowledge of how to ride a bicycle and the spatial knowledge as to the location of specific keys on a typewriter pose significant challenges when we are asked to map them onto linguistic expressions. Conversely, language itself contains many arbitrary conventions and constraints that do not appear to reflect nonlinguistic differences. For example, consider the following alternations. In English, full noun phrases, but not pronouns, can alternate with particles such as *on* in Example 1 (McCawley, 1971) and some verbs, such as *give*, can alternate between both double object and dative constructions whereas others, such as *donate* in Example 2, cannot (Bowerman, 1982). These alternations are purely linguistic because they do not correspond to nonlinguistic differences in meaning.

1. Particle Shift
    a. *Put the hat on* versus *Put on the hat*
    b. *Put it on* versus **Put on it*
2. Causatives
    a. *Mary gave the library a painting* versus
       Mary gave a painting to the library
    b. **Mary donated the library a painting* versus
       Mary donated a painting to the library

Such arbitrary linguistic conventions are not limited to English alone. Different languages impose different constraints on which aspects of cognition must be expressed linguistically. Languages utilize different formal devices for expressing nonlinguistic meanings including lexical choice, word order, and inflectional variation. Slobin (1979) illustrated these cross-linguistic complications to the mapping problem by contrasting the range of nonlinguistic information that must be linguistically expressed in order to say "Daddy gave me the ball" in different languages as given in Example 3:

3. Cross-Linguistic Mapping

a. English

Daddy	*gave*	*me*	*the*	*ball.*
actor	action past	recipient	definite	object

b. German

Der	*Vater*	*gab*	*mir*	*den*	*Ball*
definite singular masculine subject	actor	action past 3rd-person singular	recipient	definite singular masculine object	object

c. Hebrew

Aba	*natan*	*li*	*et*	*ha*	*kadur*
actor	action past 3rd-person singular masculine	recipient	objective	definite	object

d. Turkish

Babam	*bana*	*topu*	*verdi*
actor possessed by speaker	recipient	object definite	action past 3rd-person singular witnessed by speaker

Solving the mapping problem for language acquisition has proven to be a formidable challenge (Pinker, 1989; Pye, 1989), yet the study of language and aging has only begun to address this issue as research on the effects of advancing age on language processing has accumulated. In order to provide a framework for further studies of language and aging, five different hypotheses as to this mapping problem are outlined next; each is linked to research on language and aging.

Strong Cognition Hypothesis

The strong cognition hypothesis is an extension of Piaget's views on the relationship between language and cognition. According to the Piagetian perspective, language is simply one of several representational abilities, including symbolic play and deferred limitation. These representational abilities emerge and develop in parallel (Greenfield, Nelson, & Saltzman, 1972; Sinclair, 1971). For example, the development of object permanence at the end of the sensorimotor stage of development has been linked to the emergence of children's first words (Sugarman-Bell, 1978). Sinclair de Zwart (1973) showed that the shift from preoperational thinking to operational thinking is linked to a shift in how children use adjectives to describe arrays of objects. According to the strong cognition hypothesis, these examples show that the development of linguistic structures is contingent on the prior development of the appropriate cognitive structures.

When extended to the study of adult language and cognition, this account holds that adult development is characterized by the emergence of a period of postformal thinking (Kramer, 1983; Perry, 1968; Riegel, 1973, 1977; Rybash, Hoyer, & Roodin, 1986). The characteristics of postformal thinking contrast with those of formal thinking. Whereas formal thinking is absolute, analytic, fixed, rule governed, and logical, cognition during the period of postformal thinking is relativist, nonabsolute, synthetic, contextual, open to uncertainty, and tolerant of contradiction. Such as restructuring of thinking according to the strong cognition hypothesis ought to be paralleled by linguistic changes.

The association between postformal thinking and language processing has been articulated most strongly within the domain of discourse processing. Labouvie-Vief (1989) argued that there is a shift in discourse-processing style with age such that quantitative differences in recall arise from qualitative differences. Adams, Labouvie-Vief, Hobart, and Dorosz (1990) suggested that young adults adopt a detailed, text-based approach to recalling a narrative whereas older adults adopt an integrative or evaluative approach. Jepson and Labouvie-Vief (1992) found that young adults tend to recall the literal sequence of events and actions of a fable, whereas older adults tend to summarize the story's symbolic meaning and significance. Thus, the shift from formal to postformal thinking has been linked to a shift from literal to figurative language. Other manifestations of the effects of postformal thinking on language might include a shift from literal to symbolic responses to metaphors or other figurative expressions and an increasing preference for symbolic, metaphoric, or figurative language in, for example, poetry, rhetorical argument, scientific explanation, or literary prose. Dixon and Backman (in press) have begun to explore whether older adults can compensate for other prose-processing deficits by relying on metaphoric interpretation.

Emery (1985) suggested another variant of the strong cognition hypothesis to account for the language changes she has observed among healthy elderly adults and dementing adults. In addition to sentence comprehension tests (described earlier), the adults were given a wide range of tests including Piagetian tests of conservation. Emery linked the adults' syntactic processing problems to their performance on the Piagetian tasks; the elderly adults performed poorly on the conservation tasks and the dementing adults had near-zero performance on these tasks, indicating "regression to the pre-operational, and sometimes, even to the sensori-motor level of cognitive operations" (p. 43). Emery concluded that aging leads to the "de-socialization" of thought which in turn leads to the inability to process linguistically abstract, logical, and complex relationships. The near absence of language in the demented adults and their near-zero performance on the syntactic tests confirmed for Emery that "The progressive loss of capacity to use language as a rule governed system is synonymous with progressive de-socialization" (p. 43). Emery thus espoused both a strong form of the regression hypothesis and the strong cognition hypothesis with respect to the relationship between language and thought. Emery's empirical support for both hypotheses is, however, weak.

First, Emery's (1985) battery of syntactic tests included many items whose comprehension involves, not syntactic judgments, but semantic and pragmatic knowledge. An adult who is unable to retrieve the appropriate schema for dressing might incorrectly answer yes to *Do you put your stockings on after your shoes?*, whereas someone who is unable to retrieve the word *uncle*, or someone whose father did not have a brother, might not be able to respond to *What is the relationship of your father's brother to you?* Second, the task of acting out sentences such as *Make Mickey promise Donald to hop up and down* with hand puppets may have been too childish to elicit appropriate responses from the adults.

More critically, Emery's (1985) conclusions are not supported by other lines of research. Although studies of adults' speech production (Kemper, Kynette, Rash, Sprott, & O'Brien, 1989; Kynette & Kemper, 1986) and writing (Kemper, 1987a) reveal that older adults are unlikely to produce complex grammatical forms spontaneously, their speech does not evidence a progressive degeneration into "baby talk." Similarly, the analysis of speech samples produced by dementing adults has revealed that they are capable of correctly producing many different types of grammatical morphemes and syntactic constructions (Blanken, Dittman, Haas, & Wallesch, 1987; Kempler, Curtiss, & Jackson, 1987). Whereas the speech of young children might be considered to be "telegraphic" in that grammatical morphemes are lacking and word combinations based on agent-action-object concatenations predominate (Brown, 1973), the speech of elderly adults and dementing adults nonetheless includes obligatory grammatical morphemes and a wide range of grammatical forms. Thus, it is likely that the similarities Emery observed between the order of language acquisition in children and the order of language breakdown in elderly adults and dementing adults arise from different underlying mechanisms and principles, supporting only a weak version of the regression hypothesis and forcing the rejection of the strong cognition hypothesis.

Local Homologies Hypothesis

In contrast to the strong cognition hypothesis, the local homologies hypothesis does not look for global parallels between language and thought but for local linkages. Particular cognitive processes or structures, at some point during development, may be causally antecedent to specific aspects of language (Bates, 1979; Corrigan, 1979). Proponents of the strong cognition hypothesis had linked the sudden spurt in naming behavior commonly observed around age 15–18 months to the transition from sensorimotor thinking to preoperational thought. In contrast, Bates pointed out that not all characteristics of preoperational thought appear to be tied to the emergence of naming; whereas tool use and means–ends schemata are linked to early lexical development, object permanence is not. Thus, local linkages between some characteristics of thought and some characteristics of language may appear during the course of development.

The local homologies hypothesis also holds that the linkages between language and thought may vary over the course of development. Hence, cognitive structures or processes that may be relevant to the study of language acquisition may differ from those relevant to the study of language and aging. A prime example of this is the importance attached to the role of working-memory limitations in studies of language acquisition versus studies of language and aging. References to working memory in the language acquisition literature have been limited to occasional, and typically brief, suggestions that working-memory limitations may play some role in constraining the length of children's utterances (Bates, Bretherton, & Snyder, 1989; Bever, 1970; Bloom, 1970; Valian, 1986). Analogous concepts, such as short-term memory efficiency (Case, 1974; Case, Kurland, & Goldberg, 1982; Daneman & Case, 1981) and "m-space" (Pascual-Leone, 1974) have had little impact on theories of language acquisition. In contrast, working-memory limitations play a key role in studies of adult language processing crosscutting the domains of syntactic and discourse processing.

Within cognitive psychology, working memory is viewed as a limited-capacity storage and processing mechanism. Baddeley (1986) conceived of working memory as involving a central executive, which schedules and assigns processing tasks, and two temporary storage buffers—an

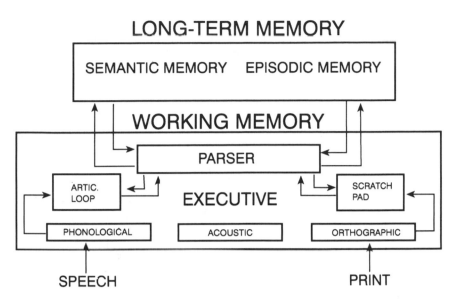

FIG. 5.3. Working-memory model of the locus of aging effects on language processing.

articulatory loop that retains phonological information for subsequent processing and a visual scratch pad that preserves visual information, as in Fig. 5.3. Similar limited-capacity components commonly are included in formal models of syntactic parsing mechanisms; linguistic analyses place great demands on working memory whenever the amount of information to be processed exceeds working memory's capacity, perhaps by overloading the articulatory loop, or whenever the processing operations themselves, such as those required to parse complex syntactic structures, are excessive and thus overload the central executive.

Working-memory limitations have been implicated in studies of adults' speech processing by Wingfield and Stine and their collaborators (Stine & Wingfield, 1990). In their task, adults listen to oral prose which may vary in linguistic complexity or rate of presentation. In some studies, the adults are tested on their immediate recall of sentences; in others, the adults are able to stop the tape recording at various points in order to recall the preceding material. Wingfield and Stine (1986) demonstrated that, at normal or slightly faster than normal presentation rates, elderly adults are able to segment speech appropriately at linguistic constituent boundaries and to recall these segments accurately. As presentation rates increased, the elderly adults still were able to segment the speech appropriately but their recall declined. Older adults are not differentially affected by propositionally dense speech (Stine, Wingfield, & Poon, 1986) but they are more dependent on linguistic prosody (Wingfield, Poon,

Lombardi, & Lowe, 1985) and redundancy (Stine & Wingfield, 1987) than young adults. Indeed, when prosody is disrupted, elderly adults have increased difficulty recalling speech (Wingfield, Lahar, & Stine, 1989). Thus, it appears that fast presentation rates and disruptions of prosody and redundancy impose performance limitations on elderly adults' ability to process speech by overloading the central executive. Conversely, the executive may be overloaded by other, simultaneous processing demands. Older adults are not able to benefit from bisensory augmentation from the simultaneous presentation of the audio and visual portions of a television news broadcast or the provision of a written transcript of the audio portion (Stine, Wingfield, & Myers, 1990). Apparently, the extra demands of processing the visual information offset any memory advantage the visual or textual information conferred on younger adults.

Kemper and her colleagues also are investigating the role of working memory in limiting adults' processing of complex syntactic constructions. For example, Kemper et al. (1989) reported that age-related declines in digit span, a measure of working memory, are associated with age-related differences in the syntactic complexity of adults' speech. Adults with smaller backward digit spans produce sentences with fewer embeddings, particularly left-branching embeddings, which impose high processing demands on working memory.

Working-memory limitations also affect adults' metalinguistic judgments about the grammaticality of sentences. Pye, Cheung, and Kemper (in press) found that adults of all ages are able to detect violations of grammatical rules as in *Whom did you see the woman from the apartment house next door and?* or *John is expected the woman from the city treasurer's office to help*. However, older adults, particularly those in their 80s, also rated some grammatical sentences as ungrammatical. For example, *You saw the woman from the apartment house next door and whom?* and *The woman from the city treasurer's office is expected to help John* are grammatical although the older adults typically rated these sentences as ungrammatical.

Other research also has implicated working-memory limitations as a primary determinant of language change across the life span. Kynette, Kemper, Norman, Cheung, and Anagnopoulos (1990) confirmed a link between adults' word-span and word-repetition rates (Hulme, Thomson, Muir, & Lawrence, 1984; Schweickert & Boruff, 1986). Elderly adults are able to recall as much as they can say in approximately 1.2 s; thus word-span as well as word-repetition rates for short one-syllable words exceed those for longer two- or three-syllable words. This relationship between word span and word repetition is stable across the life span and appears to be an accurate index of the capacity/duration of the articulatory loop component of working memory.

This finding suggests that at least part of the observed age-related decrements in language processing and working memory may be due to age-related slowing of phonological or articulatory processes. A similar account of some forms of childhood reading impairments recently was put forth by Crain and Shankweiler (1988, 1990) and Gathercole and Baddeley (1989, 1990). Crain and Shankweiler noted that poor readers lag behind good readers in their comprehension of complex syntactic structures, such as relative clauses, and that poor readers also evidence a variety of working-memory limitations, especially those involving phonological analysis. Language-processing deficits, including reading disorders in childhood and syntactic processing limitations in late adulthood, may arise whenever sentences impose severe processing demands on working memory.

Linguistic Determinism Hypothesis

Both the strong cognition and the local homologies hypotheses attempt to solve the mapping problem by allowing cognition to determine language. A third approach to the mapping problem is given by reversing the relationship under the hypothesis that language determines thought. Although most closely associated with the ''Whorfian hypothesis'' that grammatical and semantic differences between languages impose immutable barriers to mutual understanding (Whorf, 1956), this hypothesis can be applied within as well as between languages in less extreme forms. Languages provide their speakers with semantic and grammatical categories which may be used as productive tools in thinking. Verbal mediation in problem solving, verbal mnemonics for memory enhancement, and verbal metaphors in scientific explanation are examples of the use of language to aid thought. Semantic and grammatical categories also can be used to hinder and limit thought as in the use of verbal stereotypes, whether sexist, racist, or ageist.

One manifestation of linguistic determinism in the domain of language and aging is evident in studies of semantic processing and aging. Aging appears to affect the activation of semantic information during lexical decision tasks, naming tasks, and other word retrieval tasks (Bowles, Obler, & Poon, 1989; Light, 1990). Older adults have word-finding problems involving access to lexical information on the basis of orthographic or phonological cues. Such word-finding problems, in turn, may lead to other cognitive impairments affecting inferencing, reasoning, and problem solving.

Variations of this form of linguistic determinism have been common in the study of cognitive aging. Encoding deficits (Craik & Byrd, 1982; Craik & Rabinowitz, 1984; Eysenck, 1974) have been implicated in a variety of studies of adults' episodic and semantic memory. Linguistic determinism also is espoused by Bayles and Kaszniak (1987) who suggested that some types of dementia cause semantic processing limitations on verbal encoding and labeling which in turn cause further cognitive impairments to memory and reasoning.

Interaction Hypothesis

Unlike the first three accounts of the relationship between language and cognition, the interaction hypothesis allows for mutual influences. This hypothesis reflects the key role that language plays in structuring social interactions and cognitive processes and the effects of different patterns of social interaction and cognitive processes on language. One example of these mutual influences concerns the interaction of linguistic and cognitive notions of "agents." In many languages, agents are accorded special status; for example, agents typically are ordered before objects and exceptions to this rule are marked by special linguistic forms. So, for example in English, the agent typically precedes the verb as in *Mary wrote the book* and exceptions are marked by a variety of special forms including passive voicing, *The book was written by Mary*, or clefting, *It was the book that Mary wrote*. Proponents of the interaction hypothesis point out, however, that agents are not defined solely on the basis of nonlinguistic experiences but also by arbitrary linguistic conventions and regularities which are learned through social interactions (Schlesinger, 1982). The definition of agent for a speaker of English may differ from that of a speaker of another language such as Italian, reflecting different linguistic conventions despite common nonlinguistic experiences (MacWhinney, 1982). For example, English speakers choose *the pencil* as the agent in *The pencil kicks the cow*, on the basis of word order, ignoring animacy, whereas Italian speakers select *the cow* as the agent on the basis of animacy, overlooking word order.

The interaction hypothesis as applied to the study of language and aging is most evident in sociolinguistic studies of "elderspeak." Elderspeak is a simplified speech register directed toward elderly adults. It is elicited by the perception that the older adult is physically frail, cognitively impaired, and linguistically handicapped. Whether or not elderspeak facilitates comprehension, it may reinforce negative stereotypes of older adults, constrain their opportunities to communicate, and further their cognitive and physical decline. Thus, the language of elderspeak may act to limit the cognitive abilities of older adults and the perception of cognitive limitations in turn may trigger the use of elderspeak. Elderspeak is discussed more thoroughly later in the section on Communicative Competence.

Autonomous Language Hypothesis

The preceding hypotheses attempt to solve the mapping problem by fixing the relationship between language and thought; the strong cognition and local homologies hypotheses fix the relationship as unidirectional from cognition to language; the linguistic determinism hypothesis reverses this direction of influence and the interaction hypothesis permits bidirectional influences. An alternative approach is to reject the mapping problem by claiming that language is autonomous. This hypothesis is associated most closely with modularity theory (Fodor, 1982, 1987; Gardner, 1983; Garfield, 1987). As articulated by Fodor (1982), modularity theory distinguishes input-processing systems from central cognitive systems on the basis of seven criteria:

1. input systems are domain specific and operate only on information of the appropriate type,
2. their operation is mandatory and automatic,
3. modules are opaque to central processes, hence their operation is not influenced by, for example, desires or goals and their operation is not open to introspection;
4. modules are informationally encapsulated such that only the output of any module, not the products of intermediate computational steps, is available to other modules or the central system;
5. modules are fast as a consequence of the previous criteria,
6. the outputs of modules are shallow because they are insensitive to context, task demands, or background variation; and
7. modules have a fixed neurological architecture, hence they are subject to characteristic patterns of neurological pathology and ontological development.

Language is the prototypic module; other modules might include those for visual scene analysis and music processing, as in Fig. 5.4. Proponents of the autonomy hypothesis deny that there is a mapping problem and do not look for developmental parallels between language and cognition. Strong support for the separability of language and cognition comes from studies of two language disorders commonly associated with aging: aphasia and dementia. Aphasia is characterized by the impairment of language comprehension and/or production, in one or more modalities, without the concomitant impairment of cognition. Because aphasic disorders can be quite specific, these characteristic patterns of linguistic breakdown suggest that there are separate phonological, syntactic, and semantic submodules within the language module (Caplan, 1987; Grod-

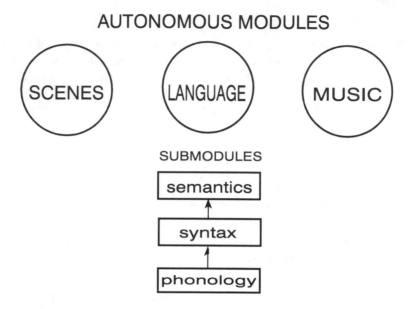

FIG. 5.4.   Modularity model of autonomous processing modules.

zinsky, 1990). Although dementia involves the general deterioration of cognition, the cognitive deterioration appears to spare grammatical and phonological aspects of language (Blanken et al., 1987; Kempler, 1990; Kempler et al., 1987, but see Lieberman, Friedman, & Feldman, 1990), again suggesting that there are encapsulated phonological and grammatical submodules within the language module.

Summary

No single solution to the mapping problem has received widespread support because each solution defines a particular orientation to the study of language and aging: The strong cognition hypothesis suggests that qualitative age-group differences in discourse processing arise from qualitatively different modes of thinking; the local homologies hypothesis has led to an emphasis on the effects of working-memory limitations on adults' language processing; linguistic determinism is reflected in the prevalence of research on semantic memory and word-finding problems; the interaction hypothesis underlines a concern with the effects of negative stereotypes of adults' linguistic competence; the autonomous language hypothesis is subsumed by modularity accounts of aphasias and dementia. These different orientations also are reflected in the wide range of methodologies that have been employed in the study of language and aging.

RESEARCH ON LANGUAGE AND AGING

The study of language and aging has evolved from a variety of different research traditions. Each tradition utilizes different methodologies to study language and aging. These traditions include the speech pathology tradition with its emphasis on aphasia tests and normative data, the developmental psycholinguistics' tradition of language sample analysis, and the psycholinguistic tradition of experimental research on syntactic processing, lexical and semantic processes, prose processing, and communicative competence.

Normative Studies

Global assessments of adults' language have been provided by a cluster of studies from speech pathology that sought normative data for the performance of older adults on aphasia diagnostic tests. Most aphasia tests do not include normative data from healthy, older adults; those that do so present a mixed picture of the effects of aging on language. Representative tests that do provide normative data from older adults include the Minnesota Test for the Differential Diagnosis of Aphasia (Schuell, 1965), the Boston Diagnostic Aphasia Examination (Goodglass & Kaplan, 1972), the Token Test (DeRenzi & Vignolo, 1962), the Auditory Comprehension Test for Sentences (Shewan, 1979), and the Porch Index of Communicative Ability (Porch, 1967).

In norming the Minnesota Test, Schuell (1965) reported that 62% of her sample of 50 nonaphasic adults were "50 + " (no upper bound was given). More errors were made by those over 50 years of age than those under 50 years on the reading, writing, and arithmetic subtests. Schuell suggested that these tests were sensitive to educational differences between the two groups of adults and did not reflect "true" effects of aging.

Normative data for the Boston Examination were obtained from 31 men aged 50–59 years, 31 men aged 60–69 years, and 25 men aged 70–85 years by Borod, Goodglass, and Kaplan (1980). Age-related declines are reported for many of the subtests; most of these age-group differences appear to reflect educational differences. Only two tests, repeating low-probability phrases, such as *The phantom soared across the foggy heath*, and naming animals, for example, the number of animal names produced in 60 s, produced clear-cut age-related declines.

The Token Test was developed to assess adults' auditory comprehension; adults are confronted with an array of colored circles and squares and asked to respond to commands such as *Touch the red circle* and *Put the red circle on top of the green square*. The commands are ordered roughly in length and difficulty, although the test was not systematically constructed, and Noll and Randolph (1978) demonstrated that errors increase with the difficulty of the commands. The Token Test is also sensitive to the effects of age (Bergman, 1980; Emery, 1985; Lesser, 1976; but see Noll & Randolph, 1978) such that older adults perform more poorly, especially on the more complex items, than young adults.

The Auditory Comprehension Test (Shewan, 1979) contrasts sentences of three lengths, three levels of vocabulary difficulty based on word frequency, and three levels of syntactic complexity. Syntactic complexity was based on the number of transformations required to generate the sentence according to early models of generative grammar (Fodor, Bever, & Garrett, 1974). With regard to syntactic complexity, the most difficult sentence on the test is *The milk was not drunk by her*, involving passive and negative transformations. Each sentence corresponds to one of four test pictures. The more complex sentences produced more errors but no effect of age on performance was reported over the age range 26–76 years.

The widely used Porch Index of Communicative Ability (PICA) was normed by Duffy, Keith, Shane, and Podraza (1976) on adults aged 20–96 years. Age was negatively correlated with performance, even when the positive effects of education were statistically controlled. Effects of age were reported for all subtests of the test, which includes subtests such as describing the functions of common objects, matching pictures to objects, completing sentences with object names, writing to dictation, and copying geometric forms.

It is not surprising that no clear picture of how aging affects language emerges from these aphasia tests. The tests themselves may not be sensitive to age-related differences in language processing. In general, few adults 65 years or older were included in the normative samples because the samples were biased toward the age range—for example, late 50s—of most aphasic patients. And the tests were biased linguistically toward those tasks most likely to be sensitive to aphasic impairments; the most difficult items may not pose sufficient challenges to elderly adults although they may exceed the abilities of neurologically impaired adults.

Language Sample Analysis

Motivated, in part, by these limitations of aphasia tests, and, in part, by the developmental psycholinguistics tradition of language sample analysis, a number of investigators have undertaken the detailed analysis of spontaneous oral and written language samples elicited from elderly adults. One research tradition uses a subtest from the Boston Examination, the Cookie Thief picture (Gleason, Goodglass, Obler, Green, Hyde, & Weintraub, 1980). Obler (1980) and Ulatowska, Cannito, Hayashi, and Fleming (1985) elicited written accounts of this picture from healthy elderly adults. Obler tested adults who were 50 and 60 years of age and contrasted the writing style of these two groups as "abbreviated" or "loquacious." The loquacious 60-year-olds used more words, especially grammatical function words such as pronouns and articles, and fewer but more complex sentences. However, these loquacious adults discussed fewer themes or idea units. When Obler extended this analysis to a broader age range of adults 30–80 years, a *u*-shaped pattern emerged: The speech patterns of the oldest and youngest groups were similarly loquacious, characterized by many words and many sentences. Ulatowska et al. elicited written descriptions of the same picture from children in the fourth and fifth grades and healthy elderly adults (whose ages were not reported). Of relevance was the description of the elderly adults' writing style as "a list of simple sentences with no overt cohesion apart from that resulting from mere juxtaposition of sentences" (p. 253). This description could apply equally to the example Obler provided of the abbreviated style "*Boy at cookie jar, passing them to girl, women drying dishes, sink overflowing, two cups and plate beside sink*" (p. 76).

A limiting factor in both studies may be the artificiality of the task. Many adults may not be motivated to compose well-structured essays composed of carefully crafted sentences in order to describe a picture of a boy stealing a cookie. A similar limitation may apply to other description tasks such as those employed by Bayles, Tomoeda, and Boone (1985), Shewan and Henderson (1988), Yorkston and Baukelman (1990), and Cooper (1990). A further limitation is that these studies are descriptive: The speech of older adults is characterized simply as "abbreviated" or "loquacious" and the investigators do not attempt to account for these changes in speech style in terms of cognitive or social factors.

Language sample analysis can be a useful technique for the investigation of aging and language when it is applied to spontaneous conversations and a broad range of linguistic measures are assessed. Walker, Hardiman, Hedrick, and Holbrook (1981) carried out an extensive series of analyses of speech samples elicited from college-age adults and adults 60–91 years of age. The older adults produced shorter sentences with fewer clauses, more varied vocabulary, and more revisions and interjections. Walker, Roberts, and Hedrick (1988) reported a similar decrease in sentence length and complexity and increases in hesitation phenomena including false starts and repetitions with age when conversations with nursing home residents were analyzed. These analyses suggest that the speech of older adults is less complex than that of younger adults and less fluent.

Kynette and Kemper (1986) compared adults 50–90 years of age on six different aspects of speech: simple and complex syntactic structures, verb tense constructions, grammatical forms, lexical diversity, and disfluencies including sentence fragments and lexical fillers. Across the age range, there was a reduction in the variability and accuracy of the adults' syntactic structures, verb tenses, and grammatical forms but no age-related changes to lexical diversity and speech disfluencies. Kynette and Kemper suggested that these age-group differences reflected a loss of syntactic complexity; the older adults produced few sentences with multiple clauses and made more errors when they attempted to do so.

Bromley (1991) analyzed a corpus of written language samples produced by 240 adults 20–86 years of age. The samples were self-descriptions of the writers' personalities. The analysis looked for age-related changes in a set of lexical measures, such as total word output and the use of long words of 10 or more letters, and a set of complexity measures, including the frequency of four categories of sentence types, ordered from least to most complex, and the incidence of subordinating conjunctions. There were no significant effects of age on the lexical measures, suggesting that semantic abilities are stable over the adult life span. Sentence complexity and the use of subordinating conjunctions did decline with age, indicating that normal aging is associated with a decline in linguistic complexity. Bromley also investigated how the adults' performance on a standardized vocabulary test and a nonverbal intelligence test correlated with the lexical and complexity measures. He found that vocabulary was positively correlated with word output, the use of long words, and word length but vocabulary was not correlated with any of the complexity measures. Nonverbal intelligence was not correlated with either set of measures.

The results of these language sample analyses must be evaluated cautiously because a variety of factors, some systematic and some random, can contribute to the fluency and complexity of speech. There has been no systematic evaluation of how dialect, education, sex, and health interact with age to affect adults' speech. Age-group differences in language may not be observed when exceptionally well-educated and healthy elderly adults are compared to young adults; conversely, age-group differences may be exacerbated when adults in poor health, those socially isolated in health-care facilities, or those with severe depression are studied. Nonetheless, these language sample analyses indicate that aging is associated with a variety of linguistic changes which affect the grammatical complexity and fluency of adults' speech.

Psycholinguistic Studies

Psycholinguistic studies of language and aging have been partitioned into four domains: syntactic processing, lexical and semantic processing, prose processing, and communicative competence. As indicated in the preceding discussion, exploration of these domains has been guided by different assumptions concerning the relationship of language and cognition. Neurobiological aspects of language and aging including the effects of aging on speech perception and production (for reviews, see Benjamin, 1988, Fozard, 1990, and Nerbonne, 1988) fall outside the scope of this review. The present review concludes by discussing two issues that have been neglected in the study of language and aging: second-language acquisition and cross-linguistic differences.

The partitioning of language into the four domains of syntactic processing, lexical and semantic processing, prose processing, and communicative competence does not resemble that traditionally made in linguistics or psycholinguistics. No level of morphological analysis is included because research on language and aging has not focused on age-related changes to morphology, or the componential analysis of words into stems, prefixes, affixes, or other meaningful units. Research on lexical and semantic processes is combined although lexical processes of word recognition typically are viewed as mediating between phonological and syntactic analyses whereas semantic processes concerned with the establishment of sentence meaning are typically postsyntactic. The domain of prose processing conflates a number of different approaches including text-based inferences, propositional analysis, and schema theory. The domain of communicative competence includes studies of adults' conversational interactions and discourse skills.

Syntactic Analysis

Investigations into how aging affects adults' syntactic processing have focused on the production and comprehension of complex syntactic structures. Various techniques have been used to probe adults' syntactic processing skills; these techniques range from the detailed analysis of language samples elicited from adults or obtained from adults' writings to the analysis of error patterns as adults act out sentences with toys.

Syntactic Complexity. Few studies have examined adults' processing of individual sentences. Feier and Gerstman (1980) asked adults 18–80 years of age to act out sentences with puppets. The sentences contained relative clauses. Although only 17% of the responses were errors, more errors were made by the older adults, 74–80 years of age, than by the young adults. The sentences varied in complexity according to two dimensions: locus of the embedding, contrasting subject embeddings or left-branching structures with object embeddings or right-branching structures, and type of embedding, contrasting subject and object relative clauses. These contrasts are illustrated in Example 4; surprisingly, Feier and Gertsman found no interaction of age with complexity, perhaps because the overall error rate was low:

4. Types of Relative Clauses
a. Branching direction
    Left-branching: The giraffe *that bumped into*
                       the cow kicked the hippo.
    Right-branching: The giraffe kicked the hippo
                       that bumped into the cow.
b. Type of embedding
    Subject embedding: The lion jumped over the horse
                         that pushed the elephant.
    Object embedding: The lion jumped over the horse
                         that the elephant pushed.

As a follow-up to the Kynette and Kemper (1986) study, Kemper (1986) tested adults' ability to imitate sentences containing different kinds of embedded sentences. The embedded clauses varied in length and locus. The sentences also varied in grammaticality; see Example 5.

5. Examples of Embedded Clauses
a. Left-branching
    Short: *Baking* tires me out.
    Long: *Baking ginger cookies for my grandchildren* tires me out.
b. Right-branching
    Short: My grandchildren watched *what I did.*
    Long: My grandchildren watched *what I took out of the oven.*

Whereas the elderly adults, 70–89 years of age, were able to imitate the short sentences correctly, they were unable to imitate the long sentences, especially when the embedding produced a left-branching structure or when the sentence was ungrammatical. The young, college-age adults were able to imitate the sentences correctly regardless of length, embedding, or grammaticality. Kemper suggested that aging impairs adults' syntactic processing by limiting how many different grammatical operations can be performed simultaneously.

This hypothesis received additional support from a series of detailed analyses of the syntactic structure of adults' speech and writing. Kemper (1987) analyzed the incidence of different types of embedded clauses in both a longitudinal sample and a cohort-sequential sample of adults' writings taken from diary entries. The longitudinal record spanned seven decades; the cohort-sequential sample contrasted adults born in the 1820s with those born in the 1860s for diary entries made when the adults were in their 40s versus in their 80s. The primary finding was the overall complexity of the adults' writing declined across the life span; 70- and 80-year-olds produced few sentences with embedded clauses, especially left-branching embeddings.

A similar finding emerged from the analysis of Kemper et al. (1989) of adults' speech. This analysis examined age-related changes to the length, clause embedding, and fluency of adults' speech. The initial analysis revealed that there is a gradual loss of complexity with advancing age; older adults in their 70s and 80s were less likely to produce sentences with embedded clauses, especially left-branching clauses, than young, college-age adults. This decline in linguistic complexity was attributed to a decline in working-memory capacity as indexed by a decline in digit span.

The analysis was extended over a 3-year span by Kemper, Kynette, and Norman (1992). Digit-span scores obtained in Years 1, 2, and 3 were intercorrelated, suggesting that they measure a common component of working memory. Two measures of linguistic complexity were analyzed: the average number of clauses per utterance and the incidence of left-branching clauses. Both complexity measures were intercorrelated across the 3-year span suggesting that the complexity of adults' speech is a stable characteristic. Further, digit span was significantly correlated with the complexity scores, even when the effect of age was statistically controlled.

Of particular interest was the finding that a loss of working-memory capacity, as measured by digit span, appears to be linked to a loss of linguistic complexity. When the digit spans obtained in Year 3 were regressed on those from Year 1, an analysis of the residuals revealed three groups of participants: those whose digit spans were relatively unchanged (74%), those who had experienced a digit-span gain of 3 or more points (5%), and those who had experienced a digit-span loss of 3 or more points (21%). A similar residual-gain score analysis of the linguistic complexity measures also identified three groups of participants: those who did not evidence a change in complexity (65%), those who evidenced a 30% or better gain in complexity (6%), and those who evidenced a 30% or worse loss in complexity (29%). Of those who experienced a loss of digit span after 3 years, most (91%) also evidenced a loss of linguistic complexity. The converse relationship did not hold; an increase in digit span was not associated with an increase in linguistic complexity. Although these results must be viewed cautiously, they do suggest that there is a link between working-memory capacity, as measured by digit span, and the production of complex, multiclause sentences.

Sentence Processing Models. A limited-capacity component is included in most models of sentence processing. Multiclause sentences, especially those with left-branching embeddings, increase the demand placed on this limited capacity component because multiple sentence constituents must be processed concurrently. For example, Yngve (1960) suggested that, during the production of a sentence, a burden is placed on working memory whenever multiple constituents must be anticipated as each word is uttered. The amount of structure that must be anticipated, Yngve suggested, can be measured by counting how many constituent nodes have yet to be realized. This measure, termed *Yngve depth*, correlates with other measures of linguistic complexity and Yngve depth declines across the lifespan (Kemper & Rash, 1988). During the production of a complex sentence with a left-branching embedding (Fig. 5.5), Yngve depth reaches a maximum of 4 when the speaker begins to utter the noun phrase *a nursery school*; at this point, the speaker must anticipate the constituent structure of the noun phrase, the remaining constituent—for example, the prepositional phrase—of the embedded gerund, and the predicate constituent of the main clause. In contrast, Yngve depth reaches a maximum of only 3 during the production of the right-branching variant of the sentence (Fig. 5.6). As the speaker begins to utter the noun phrase *a nursery school*, only the constituent structure of the noun phrase and the remaining constituent of the gerund must be anticipated.

Frazier (1985, 1988; Frazier & Rayner, 1988) challenged the notion of Yngve depth and suggested an alternative metric, "local node count," which differs from Yngve depth in two regards: (a) Sentence embeddings are acknowledged explicitly as sources of complexity and hence count more heavily than other constituents in the node count calculation and (b) complexity is computed from three-word sequences such that a cluster of many constituent nodes within a three-word sequence will count more

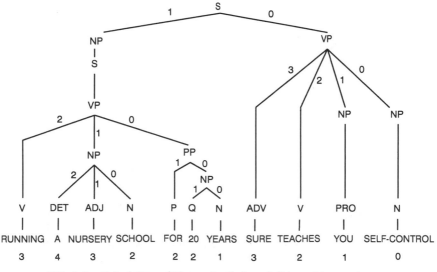

FIG. 5.5.   Calculation of Yngve depth for a left-branching sentence.

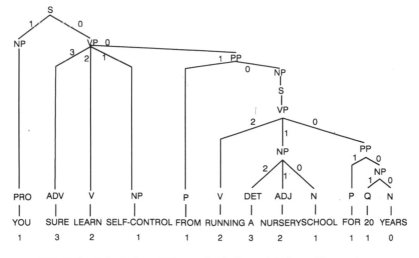

FIG. 5.6. Calculation of Yngve depth for a right-branching sentence.

heavily than a distributed sequence of nodes. In general, Frazier node count is strongly correlated with Yngve depth and produces a similar asymmetry in sentence complexity for left- and right-branching sentences.

Left-branching clauses are also more difficult to comprehend than right-branching ones. One parsing model, the so-called Sausage Machine, of Frazier and Fodor (1978) involves two parsing stages: a limited-capacity first-stage parser and an unlimited second-stage parser. The model explains the asymmetry in the processing left- and right-branching clauses as arising from the restriction of the first-stage parser to the analysis of six or so words at a time. The first-stage parser attempts to form meaningful grammatical constituents from each group of six words. These constituents then are assembled into clauses by the second-stage parser. Sometimes the first-stage parser is not successful or the constituents it forms are not correct; the second-stage parser then must reanalyze the words into the correct constituents. Left-branching clauses that exceed the capacity of the first-stage parser will trigger such reanalysis. For example, the first-stage parser initially will (incorrectly) analyze the doubly embedded left-branching sentence in Fig. 5.7 as a six-word coordinate noun phrase followed by a six-word coordinate verb phrase. The second-stage parser must break up these constituents and reanalyze the input in order to correctly pair each noun phrase with the appropriate verb. No such reanalysis is required for the right-branching sentence in Fig. 5.8. The first-stage parser will supply the correct constituents, segmenting the first group of words into two noun phrases and a verb and the second group of six words into three noun phrases and two verbs. These consti-

The woman the man the girl loved met died.

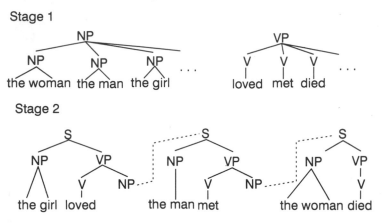

FIG. 5.7.   Two-stage analysis of a left-branching sentence.

The girl loved the man who met the woman who died.

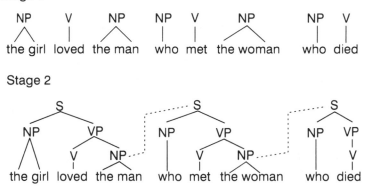

FIG. 5.8.   Two-stage analysis of a right-branching sentence.

tuents then can be assembled readily into clauses by the second-stage parser.

These models of sentence production and comprehension can be extended naturally to account for the effects of aging on syntactic processing. Yngve (1960) suggested Miller's (1962) "7 ± 2" as a candidate for the maximum depth of spoken sentences and that "a depth factor in language change should be easily observable . . ." (p. 452). Aging may provide just such a "depth factor" by imposing a lower limit on the depth of constituent structures that can be produced. Reducing maximum depth to "5 ± 2" effectively would restrict the production of most left-branching constructions as well as limit the production of other constructions involving, for example, elaborated noun phrases, prepositional phrases, and auxiliary verb sequences. Reducing the capacity of the first-stage parser in the Frazier and Fodor (1978) model would produce a similar effect on sentence comprehension. If the first-stage parser were restricted to operating, not on six words at a time, but on four words at a time, comprehension of most left-branching constructions would be disrupted.

New Directions. Research on adults' on-line processing of complex sentences clearly is indicated by the preceding discussion. A variety of techniques, ranging from monitoring word-by-word reading times to tracking eye movements, exists for studying the effects of transient processing load during sentence comprehension. Parallel techniques, including syntactic priming tasks and dual-task procedures, are available for studying transient syntactic effects during sentence production. Such studies would help to map out the effects of aging on the mechanics of sentence production and comprehension by tracing how aging alters syntactic processing.

A promising beginning to such on-line studies is Stine's (1990) study of word-by-word reading times. Stine collected word-by-word reading times from both young and older adults and used regression procedures to determine if there were age-group differences in how the adults allocated reading time to individual words. The major finding was that young adults' reading times increased at sentence boundaries as well as at the boundaries between grammatical constituents whereas the older adults' reading times increased at constituent boundaries only. Stine interpreted these different patterns of reading times as reflecting ''a change in reading strategy by the older adults in response to WM [working memory] limitations . . . the sentence may be too big a unit . . . when WM capacity is limited . . .'' (p. 17).

Lexical and Semantic Analysis

The study of aging and lexical and semantic processing spans two different research traditions. On the one hand, researchers have attempted to understand the sources of adults' word-finding problems. Word-finding problems are a frequent complaint among elderly adults and the incidence of such problems increases with age. On the other hand, largely motivated by studies of age-group differences in memory encoding and retrieval, other researchers have attempted to understand how aging might affect the organization or utilization of semantic information. Vocabulary definitions, word associations, and word recognition processes have been scrutinized carefully for age-group differences. Representative research on lexical retrieval and semantic activation is reviewed next. Further discussion of these issues can be found in chapters 2 and 3 in this volume.

Lexical Retrieval. Burke, Worthley, and Martin (1988) and Burke, MacKay, Worthley, and Wade (1991) confirmed the incidence of word-finding problems, or tip-of-the-tongue (TOT) experiences, among elderly adults. Burke et al. suggested that TOTs result whenever the phonological information about a word is inaccessible as a result of infrequent access. Most TOTs involve proper names of persons, places, or movies. Whereas young adults also have occasional difficulty retrieving abstract words, midage and elderly adults have increased difficulty in retrieving the names of common objects. Although Burke et al. did note that word-finding problems typically occur with proper names and names of common objects, they did not attach any significance to the relative rarity of word-finding problems for other parts of speech, including adjectives, adverbs, grammatical function words, and verbs. It is likely that the distributions of word-finding problems across these categories reflect the frequency with which specific words (tokens) are accessed.

Word-finding problems are evident on a variety of other naming tasks. Although most of this research has focused on the retrieval of nouns, Nicholas, Obler, Albert, and Goodglass (1985) demonstrated that verb naming, as well as noun naming, is disrupted by aging. In this study, adults were timed as they attempted to name the object depicted in a line drawing from the Boston Naming Test (Kaplan, Goodglass, & Weintraub, 1976) or to name the action depicted in other line drawings. Responses were scored as correct or incorrect; errors were further classified as semantically related, as in responding *harness* for yoke or *courting* for proposing; perceptually related, such as *flower* for pinwheel or *playing music* for measuring; part–whole substitutions, as in *clock* for pendulum or *kneeling* for proposing; circumlocutions such as *artistic thing for flowers* for trellis or *down on his hands and knees* for crawling; or into other, less frequent categories. Actions were named more accurately than objects by all age groups, confirming Burke et al.'s observations about the relative incidence of noun TOTs and TOTs for "abstract" words including verbs. However, there were age-group differences in naming. Not only were the young adults faster at naming the objects or actions, but they were more accurate and produced a different pattern of errors than older adults. Semantic confusions decreased with advancing age whereas circumlocutions increased with age, indicating a general disruption of word retrieval processes.

In a similar study, Albert, Heller, and Milberg (1988) found an age-related increase in both semantic confusions and circumlocutions but the changes in naming ability were not evident until the adults reached their 70s. Naming ability for 50-year-olds was similar to that for 20-year-olds. Albert et al. suggested that older adults have difficulty using semantic information for word retrieval, as evidenced by the incidence of semantic confusions and circumlocutions.

The disruption of word retrieval was also evident when Bowles and Poon (1985) asked adults to retrieve a word to correspond to a dictionary definition such as "a mythical animal with one straight horn on its head." The definitions were preceded by different types of cues including the correct target word *unicorn*, the orthographically similar word *uniform*, the semantically related word *dragon*, the unrelated word *candle*, the initial letters of the target word *un*, and the neutral string *xxxxx*. Whereas older adults were able to respond as rapidly and accurately as young adults after the correct word and initial-letter primes, they responded less accurately and less rapidly following the other cues. The older adults benefited less from perceptually related and semantically related words than did the young adults. Bowles and Poon thus concluded that aging affects word retrieval by disrupting the semantic activation or utilization of orthographic and phonological information.

This disruption of lexical retrieval processes is also evident in adults' oral discourse. A number of investigators have noted that adults' conversations and stories are disrupted by word retrieval problems which affect their ability to establish and maintain reference. Ulatowska and her collaborators (Ulatowska et al., 1985; Ulatowska, Hayashi, Cannito, & Fleming, 1986) documented an increase in referential ambiguity with advancing age. This increase is evident in a decrease in the ratio of nouns to pronouns, an increase in ambiguous referring expressions, and a decrease in the use of proper nouns. The disruption of reference occurs in spontaneous speech, question answering, and story retelling as in the following extract involving ambiguous pronominal reference: ". . . So the policeman talked to him for a short time. And then *he* went on *his* way . . ." (Ulatowska et al., 1986, p. 38). Kemper (1990) and Kemper, Rash, Kynette, and Norman (1990) also observed that the cohesion of adults' stories varies with age; older adults use fewer cohesive ties, particularly the repetition of nouns and definite descriptions, and produce more ambiguous references than do young adults. Pratt, Boyes, Robins, and Manchester (1989) observed that older adults also make more referential errors in story retelling than do young adults. Further, they noted that adults with larger working-memory spans made fewer referential errors than adults with smaller spans, regardless of age.

Semantic Activation.　　Memory impairments in old age commonly have been linked to age-related changes in explicit memory processes involving the "richness, extensiveness, and depth" (Craik & Byrd, 1982,

p. 208) to which to-be-remembered information is processed. This research has been conducted within the framework of network theories of semantic memory (Anderson, 1983; Colins & Loftus, 1975), which assume that lexical entries or concepts are nodes in an interconnected network based on associations and similarities of meaning. When a concept is accessed, its node is activated and this activation begins to spread throughout the network to related concepts. Spreading activation facilitates access to related concepts and can inhibit access to unrelated concepts. Semantic network theories dominate studies of word recognition processes; consequently, cognitive aging researchers have focused on age-related impairments of the activation of semantic information. Age-group differences in the automaticity of semantic activation among related concepts, the speed or spread of activation, and changes in the content or organization of semantic information all have been examined extensively. Although this research was motivated by age-group differences in recall and recognition, it documents the age constancy of semantic activation (Burke & Harrold, 1988; Howard, 1988).

The spread of semantic activation also appears to be age constant. Howard, McAndrews, and Lasaga (1981) examined spreading activation using a lexical decision task. On each trial, a pair of letter strings was presented; pairs of unrelated words such as *rain–bright* were presented on some trials, pairs of semantically related words such as *rain–snow* or *rain–wet* were presented on other trials, whereas word–nonword pairs were presented on yet other trials. "Yes" responses to word–word pairs and "no" responses to word–nonword pairs were timed; the spread of semantic activation is determined by comparing response latencies for related word pairs to those for unrelated word pairs. Although elderly adults do respond more slowly than young adults (but see Howard, Shaw, & Heisey, 1986), both groups benefited from the spread of semantic activation from one word to related words, and the magnitude of the spreading activation effect was similar for both groups.

Balota and Duchek (1988) also concluded that the time course of spreading activation is similar in young and older adults but that lexical access is slowed in older adults. They compared young and older adults using a delayed pronunciation task in which a word is presented and then, after a delay of 150–1,200 ms, a cue to pronounce the word is given. Pronunciation latencies decrease with delay, indicating that time is required to recognize the word, access its lexical and phonological representation, and prepare the articulatory response. More important, Balota and Duchek found that there was an age-group difference in pronunciation latency, favoring the young adults, and that this difference decreased with delay. The greatest difference between young and old adults was obtained after the shortest delay. Thus, the older adults benefited more from the delay than the young adults. Balota and Duchek concluded that the process of word recognition, including accessing lexical and phonological representations, is slower in older adults.

Further evidence for age constancy in the nature and automaticity of semantic activation comes from Burke and Yee's (1984) study. Adults were asked to make a lexical decision to a letter string following a sentence. Responses to nonwords, for example, *lat*, were compared to responses to lexical items that varied in their relationship to the preceding sentence. Some target lexical items were unrelated to the sentence whereas other targets were either (a) implied by the sentence as a whole, for example, *bone* following *She gave her hungry dog something to chew*; (b) associated with a noun from the sentence, for example, *chair* following *That round table is usually in the kitchen*; or (c) associated instrumentally with the sentence, for example, *knife* following *The cook cut the meat*. Although lexical decision times for young adults were faster than those for older adults, older and young adults exhibited equivalent facilitative effects: Only instrumental associations, for example, *The cook cut the meat*, facilitated lexical decisions for related words, for example, *knife*. The older adults, however, did have more difficulty remembering the sentences on a subsequent recall test.

Evidence for age constancy in the formation and organization of new word associations is provided by Rabinowitz (1986) and Howard (1988). In Howard's study, adults first were shown a series of sentences and then later given a word recognition test. During the sequence of word recognition trials, nouns from the same sentence sometimes occurred on successive trials whereas nouns from different sentences occurred on other successive trials. For example, word associations formed while reading the sentence *The meat fried in the skillet while the author rubbed his stomach* might be tested later by comparing word recognition latencies for *stomach* immediately following a recognition trial for *author* versus a recognition trial for an unrelated word. Both young and older adults benefited from the sentence primes and the magnitude of the priming effect was constant across age groups. In contrast, older adults performed less accurately than young adults when they were asked to judge whether or not two nouns occurred in the same sentence or when they were given one noun from the sentence and asked to recall the others.

New Directions.   The study of aging and lexical and semantic processing largely has used lexical decision tasks, naming tasks, and relatedness judgment tasks to determine whether there are age differences in the activation of semantic information. In general, this work has not documented age-related differences in the activation of semantic information but has shown that older adults have word-finding problems involving access to lexical information on the basis of orthographic or phonological cues. Thus, although older adults show parallel priming effects in lexical decision tasks when compared to young adults, they perform less well on naming tasks and have more word-finding problems than young adults. These word-finding problems are evident in spontaneous speech and contribute to the disruption of cohesion and reference.

Recently, these two lines of research have been integrated in a common framework as a contrast between explicit memory processes—for example, word retrieval—and implicit memory processes—for example, semantic activation (Howard, 1988; see also chapter 3 of this volume). Whereas implicit memory processes may be age constant, explicit memory processes exhibit age-related declines.

Prose Processing

Cohen (1979) launched the study of aging and prose processing and in so doing established a research agenda that continues to dominate this domain of study. In Experiment 1, Cohen contrasted young and older adults who were highly educated or less well educated; she tested the adults' ability to answer factual questions based on verbatim memory and inference questions which required integrating factual information. The results were clear-cut: Regardless of age or educational level, the participants were able to answer the factual questions, and both advanced age and limited education hindered answering the inference questions. In Experiment 3, Cohen tested the participants' ability to recall a prose passage. Recall was scored by counting how many specific propositions, or facts, were recalled, how many general propositions were used to summarize the gist of the story, and how many detailed modifiers, including temporal and causal connections between propositions, were preserved. Again, the results were clear-cut: Older adults and less educated adults recalled fewer propositions, used fewer summary propositions, and retained fewer modifiers than younger and better educated adults. Cohen concluded: ". . . in old age comprehension . . . is handicapped by diminished ability to perform simultaneously the task of registering the surface meaning and also carrying out further processes involving integration, construction, or reorganization of different elements of meaning" (p. 426).

Since Cohen's (1979) pioneering research, the study of adults' prose processing has been influenced significantly by the Kintsch and van Dijk model of prose processing as propositional analysis (Kintsch & van Dijk, 1978; van Dijk & Kintsch, 1983). This approach sees a text as an integrated hierarchy of propositions. A proposition is a fact expressed by a predicate and one or more arguments. Predicates are usually verbs, adjectives, or adverbs whereas arguments are usually concepts, or nouns, or other propositions. Prose processing, according to this account, involves recovering individual propositions, establishing the interconnections among these propositions, which may be explicitly stated or inferred, and constructing a propositional hierarchy in order to identify the main points and supporting details. Propositions are interconnected via argument repetition; one proposition is subordinate to another if the second proposition repeats an argument of the first. Recursively applied, argument overlap yields a hierarchy such that the higher a proposition is in the hierarchy, the more arguments it shares with other propositions. The top-most propositions represent the main ideas of the text; low-level propositions are supporting details. Verbatim prose memory involves the storage of this propositional hierarchy including stated and inferred propositions whereas gist memory involves the construction of a summary of this propositional hierarchy from the main points and relevant background knowledge. Prose recall can emphasize either verbatim recall of the propositional hierarchy or gist recall of the main points and relevant background information.

For example, the text in Fig. 5.9 has been analyzed as a sequence of propositions, these propositions have been interconnected via argument overlap in order to form a propositional hierarchy, the main point of the text has been determined from this hierarchy, and a gist summary has been given based on the main point and relevant background knowledge.

Propositional analysis has dominated the study of aging and prose processing. It has generated two lines of research to account for age-group differences in prose processing. One line attributes age-group differences to an interaction between reader parameters and text parameters. Reader parameters include education and verbal ability; text parameters include genre differences, such as those between narrative and expository texts. A second line of research has sought to link adults' prose-processing problems to other cognitive aging deficits. These studies have explored how variations in processing demands and working-memory capacity affect adults' prose processing by contrasting young and older adults' recall of main points versus details and by examining age-group differences in the recall of facts versus inferences. Representative research is summarized next. Cohen (1988), Hultsch and Dixon (1984), Light and Burke (1988), and Zelinski and Gilewski (1988) all provided extensive reviews of these issues.

Reader and Text Interactions. Age-related differences in prose processing commonly are attributed to different prose-processing skills employed by younger and older adults (Simon, Dixon, Nowak, & Hultsch,

A. Text:
An earthquake devastated the remote villages. It left hundreds
without food, water, and shelter for weeks.

B: Propositions:
 1: (devastated, earthquake, village)
 2: (remote, village)
 3: (mountain, village)
 4: (left, earthquake, hundreds) [inferred: it = earthquake]
 5: (without, hundreds, food)
 6: (without, hundreds, water)
 7: (without, hundreds, shelter)
 8: (for, p7, weeks)

C: Propositional hierarchy:

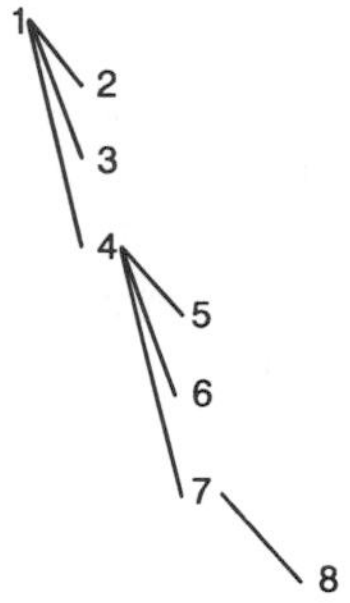

D: Main point:
An earthquake devastated a village.

E: Summary:
Hundreds suffered from an earthquake's devastation.

FIG. 5.9.   Propositional analysis of a text.

1982; Spilich & Voss, 1982). Strong evidence to support this view initially came from research showing that age-group differences are attenuated when educational level and/or verbal ability, as measured by reading,
vocabulary, or intelligence tests, are controlled. For example, Dixon,
Hultsch, Simon, and von Eye (1984) contrasted high- and low-verbal ability adults on a prose-recall task; young, middle-age, and older adults were
tested. Young adults recalled more than older adults, high-verbal adults
recalled more than low-verbal adults, and more main ideas were recalled than details. More significantly, there was a three-way interaction
between age, verbal ability, and propositional importance. For high-verbal
ability adults, there were large age-group differences for recall of details
from low levels of the propositional hierarchy, and the age-group differences decreased with propositional level so that there were no age-
group differences in recall of main ideas from the top level of the propositional hierarchy. The reverse pattern held for low-verbal ability adults:

Age-group differences were greater for main ideas than for low-level details.

Other intellectual abilities also may contribute to differences in prose processing. Hultsch, Hertzog, and Dixon (1984) examined the relationship between prose recall and a wide range of ability tests. Verbal comprehension, general intelligence, verbal productive thinking, and associative memory were all correlated with text recall and age differences in text recall were reduced, although not eliminated, when age-group differences on these measures of intellectual ability were statistically controlled. Hultsch et al. also found that there were different patterns of correlations between text recall and intellectual abilities for young, middle-age, and elderly adults. The best predictors of text recall for young and middle-age adults were general intelligence and verbal comprehension. This suggests that young adults utilize a wide range of semantic and prose-processing skills to aid text recall. In contrast, general intelligence did not predict text recall for the older adults but specific intellectual abilities did so; these included verbal productive thinking, verbal comprehension, and associate memory. Hultsch et al. suggested that the poor text recall of older adults reflects two distinct phenomena: the poor performance of chronically low-ability adults and the poor performance of adults who have lost specific intellectual skills necessary for prose processing.

Another line of research also supports the interpretation of age-group differences as reflecting differences in young and older adults' reading skills by emphasizing the effects of schooling on prose recall. Meyer and Rice (1981, 1983) suggested that older adults do not employ the same text organizational strategies as those used by young adults who are or have recently been in school. Schooling, they suggested, emphasizes outlining, attention to "advance organizers" such as titles and other signals, verbatim recall, and the identification of main points and supporting details. Hence, young adults may adopt a different processing strategy than that spontaneously used by older adults. This account was supported by Meyer and Rice's (1981) finding that middle-age and older adults recalled as many propositions from a text as did young adults although they recalled different propositions. Whereas the young adults showed a "levels" effect such that their recall was best for topics and main points and worse for low-level details, middle-age and older adults did not. Hence, Meyer and Rice concluded that the young adults were more sensitive to the hierarchical organization of the text than were the middle-age and older adults, perhaps because of schooling practices.

These effects of schooling on prose processing may not apply to all prose genres, especially narratives. Meyer and Rice (1981) suggested that narratives may be more difficult for older adults to recall because they are less familiar with this genre, as they encounter stories less often than expository prose. Although this claim is not supported by empirical evidence, the research literature is generally consistent with the hypothesis: Large age-group differences in prose recall have been found when young and older adults are tested on narrative stories (Cohen, 1979; Gordon, 1975; Gordon & Clark, 1974; Tun, 1989; Zelinski, Light, & Gilewski, 1984; but see Mandel & Johnson, 1984, and Petros, Norgaard, Olson, & Tabor, 1989).

Zelinski and Gilewski (1988) conducted a meta-analytic study of 36 different studies of prose processing. Their analysis yielded three reliable effects: (a) overall age deficits in recall, (b) which may be attenuated by high levels of education and/or verbal ability, and (c) genre differences such that larger age effects occur with narratives than with expository prose. As Zelinski and Gilewski pointed out, education and/or verbal ability and prose genre may reduce, but not completely eliminate, age-group differences in prose processing.

Prose-Processing Deficits. The persistence of age-related differences in prose processing has been attributed to cognitive aging deficits arising from prose-processing demands and working-memory limitations. Typical of this approach is the work of Spilich (1983) who compared young and elderly adults' (as well as demented adults') recall using the Kintsch and van Dijk (1978) model. A key finding was an age group by propositional level interaction: The elderly adults recalled as many high-level propositions as did the young adults but they recalled significantly fewer low-level propositions.

Within the Kintsch and van Dijk (1978) model, there are two alternative explanations of such a result. Both explanations reflect the assumption that prose processing occurs within a limited-capacity working-memory system. Under this assumption, not all of the propositions in a text are processed simultaneously; propositions are processed in sentence-by-sentence cycles such that (a) some old propositions are carried over from the previous cycle and (b) new propositions are recovered from the next sentence and added to the old propositions. The number of propositions that can be retained from one cycle to the next (termed the carry-over buffer) and the selection of which propositions to be carried over are crucial parameters of this model. Spilich (1983) used parameter-estimation procedures derived from those of Kintsch and van Dijk to evaluate two alternative explanations of his results: First, older adults may have a smaller carry-over buffer than young adults. If so, some propositions will not be integrated with others in the propositional hierarchy because the process of detecting argument overlaps will be impaired. Alternatively, older adults may not use the same strategy as young adults to select propositions for retention from one cycle to the next. If so, they will not form the same propositional hierarchy of main points and subordinate details. Spilich's analysis indicated that the older adults used the same selection strategy as the young adults but with a smaller carry-over buffer. Both young and older adults use a selection strategy that favors the retention of high-level propositions. Thus, given a smaller buffer, the older adults were less likely to retain low-level propositions from one processing cycle to the next; hence, they were unable to recall these propositions because the low-level propositions were not stored as part of the propositional hierarchy.

A natural implication of the assumption that older adults' prose processing is hindered by working-memory limitations is that older adults not only will forget low-level details but they will be less likely to make and retain text-based inferences. This hypothesis is supported by a variety of findings: Cohen (1981) found that older adults are less likely to infer a causal connection (c) between sentences (a and b) as in Example 6. Light and Capps (1986) found that older adults are less likely to establish the referent of a pronoun as in (7b) although they can do so in (7a).

6. Causal Inferences
    a. A burning cigarette was carelessly discarded.
    b. The fire destroyed many acres of virgin forest.
    c. A discarded cigarette started a fire.
7. Pronominal Reference
    a. Henry spoke at a meeting while John drove to the beach.
       He brought along a surfboard.
    b. John stood watching while Henry jumped across a ravine.
       The ground was so rocky and uneven that only goats used
       this path. There were no flowers but a few weeds grew
       here and there. He fell in the river.

Support for a direct link between working-memory capacity and text-processing limitations, however, has been mixed in studies utilizing an individual differences approach to prose processing. There is no consensus about how working-memory capacity is best measured and span measures of working-memory capacity do not correlate consistently with measures of prose processing (Cohen & Faulkner, 1981; Hartley, 1986, 1988; Light & Anderson, 1985; Pratt et al., 1989; Zacks & Hasher, 1988; Zelinski, 1988).

Hasher and Zacks (1988) reconceptualized working-memory limitations as arising from the intrusion of interfering thoughts and ideas. Hasher and Zacks proposed that inhibitory mechanisms limit the access of information into working memory. Information that is irrelevant or peripheral to the task, such as personal preoccupations, idiosyncratic interpretations or associations of words or phrases, musings or daydreams, are normally inhibited. They proposed that older adults' prose processing is impaired because the inhibitory mechanisms weaken with age, permitting the intrusion into working memory of "irrelevant environmental details, personalistic memories or concerns, and off goal path interpretations" (p. 221). They further suggested "a person with reduced inhibitory functioning can be expected to show more distractibility, to make more inappropriate responses and/or to take longer to make competing appropriate responses, and finally, to be more forgetful than others . . . the increased presence of irrelevant thoughts in working memory (and the attendant consequences) may well be the factors that produce the behaviors that have made it appear as if older adults have reduced capacity . . ." (p. 221).

New Directions.   Although aging and prose processing has been researched extensively, a number of issues have been largely neglected. Chief among these is investigating the link between prose-processing deficits and deficits in syntactic and semantic analysis. The study of aging and prose processing also could benefit from a broadening of its research agenda to include the following. First, the investigation of other aspects of prose processing than rote recall; question answering and prose summarization and interpretation may be more relevant to daily reading and listening activities and, hence, less vulnerable to aging declines (Labouvie-Vief, 1989). Second, the adoption of other methods of text analysis such as the question-answering procedures of Graesser (1981) and the causal networks of Trabasso and van den Broek (1985); these methods may help to clarify whether prose-processing deficits arise during initial comprehension or during memory encoding or retrieval. Third, further work on the role of knowledge schemata in prose processing; the investigations by Light and Anderson (1983) and Zelinski and Miura (1988) of scripted activities, by Radvansky, Gerard, Zacks, and Hasher (1990) of mental models, and by Hultsch and Dixon (1983) on topic familiarity suggest that older adults may be able to compensate for low-level deficits through the use of high-level knowledge schemata. Fourth, further specification of techniques for enhancing adults' prose processing, including techniques to improve listening ability, are warranted in light of the success of the training program developed by Meyer, Young, and Bartlett (1989).

Communicative Competence

Ryan, Giles, Bartolucci, and Henwood (1986) proposed the term *communication predicament of aging* to refer to the impact of negative expectations, held by others and, perhaps, echoed by older adults them-

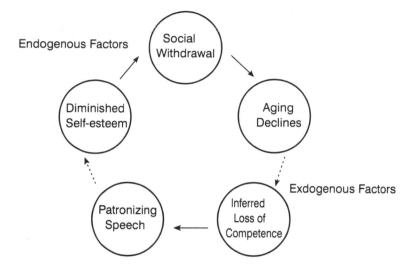

FIG. 5.10. The cycle of endogenous and exdogenous factors leading to the communicative predicament of aging. Adapted from Ryan et al. (1986).

selves, about the communicative competence of older adults. This predicament leads to "a vicious cycle in which the changes of aging (e.g., physical appearance, voice quality, hearing difficulties, slowness of move-ment, loss of role) elicit [exdogenous] interpretations from others of diminished competence; and these inferences then lead to constraining conditions in which the older person has less opportunity to communi-cate effectively . . . diminished self-esteem and withdrawal from social interactions . . . [and further] physiological, psychological, and social declines" (pp. 16–17). This cycle of endogenous change leading to ex-dogenous change which in turn leads to further endogenous change is portrayed in Fig. 5.10. The communicative predicament of aging affects how effective and competent speakers are judged to be on the basis of voice cues (Ryan & Johnson, 1987; Ryan & Laurie, 1990; Stewart & Ryan, 1982), how elderly drivers are questioned after traffic accidents (Franklyn-Stokes, Harriman, Giles, & Coupland, 1988), and the nature of instruc-tions given to elderly adults by young adults (Rubin & Brown, 1975) and elderly peers (Molfese, Hoffman, & Yuen, 1981) during referential com-munication tasks.

Elderspeak. An invidious manifestation of this predicament is the use of baby talk by caregivers to institutionalized elderly. In this context, baby talk has been rechristened elderspeak (Snow & Ferguson, 1977). Caporael and her colleagues (Caporael, 1981; Caporael & Culbertson, 1986; Caporael, Lucaszewski, & Culbertson, 1983) found that caregivers assume elderly adults will prefer to be addressed in a simplified register with exaggerated pitch and intonation and that elderspeak will enhance elderly adults' attention and comprehension. Such overaccommodations to stereotyped expectations about the communicative needs of older adults often are judged by elderly adults to be demeaning and disrespectful (Coupland & Coupland, 1990; Ryan et al., 1986), although they may be received positively and facilitate communication under some circumstances (Caporael et al., 1983; Cohen & Faulkner, 1986; Coupland, Grainger, & Coupland, 1988; Wingfield et al., 1989).

There is some evidence that speech accommodations can aid elderly adults. As part of a test of listening comprehension, Cohen and Faulkner (1986) manipulated stress; presumably this manipulation involved changes to word durations, pitch, and amplitude. Whereas heavy stress on semantically important words improved older adults' comprehension, misleading stress on irrelevant words hindered their comprehension. The young adults' performance was not affected by the stress manipulation. A similar outcome was obtained when Wingfield et al. (1989) manipulated prosody during a prose-recall task. Normal prosody was contrasted with "list" prosody in which each word received equal stress, pitch, and amplitude. Although the young adults' recall declined somewhat in the list condition, the elderly adults' recall accuracy was severely impaired when they attempted to recall list prosody material. Both studies indicate that elderly adults are more dependent on prosody than are young adults because disruptions of normal stress and prosody impaired their performance and exaggerated stress enhanced their performance.

Apart from these studies, too little attention has been paid to the psycholinguistics of elderspeak. No formal, systematic evaluations of the psycholinguistic properties of elderspeak have been conducted. What is needed is research that systematically varies, alone and in combination, those aspects of elderspeak that are presumed to be facilitative, for example, presentation rate, prosody, word stress, word duration, pitch, amplitude, use of contrastive intonation, use of simple versus complex grammar, use of familiar versus unfamiliar vocabulary. For example, word stress is determined typically by word duration, pitch, and amplitude. Prosody includes word stress but also includes intonation contour, intrasentential pauses, and vowel prolongation. Whether all these acoustic properties must be manipulated to facilitate elderly adults' listening comprehension is not clear. It may be that elderly adults benefit only from manipulations of the timing of speech segments—for example, word durations, vowel prolongation, intrasentential pauses—and not from the other aspects of prosody. Additionally, elderly adults might benefit from written accommodations as well as from spoken ones; manipulations of the grammar, vocabulary, or style of text materials might differentially improve adults' reading comprehension and memory.

Another promising area for further research is the development of effective speech accommodations as elderly adults and their families, physicians, and caregivers learn to accommodate to physical limitations and disabilities. Some have advocated the adoption of simplified speech styles for communicating with elderly adults, such as Blazer (1969) who recommended that physicians "speak clearly and slowly . . . clarity of speech and the effective use of single sentences is most effective in communicating with an elderly patient" (p. 83). More positively, Beisecker (1988, 1989) studied how effective communication among elderly adults and health professionals evolves through the use of companions who serve as spokespersons for the elderly patients by relaying medical information to the physician and as translators by conveying medical recommendations to the elderly patients. These companions have learned to communicate effectively with the elderly adults, perhaps through the use of speech accommodations. A parallel line of research is the study of how family members learn to accommodate to the linguistic impairments of aphasic adults by adopting speech modifications (Gravel & LaPointe, 1982; Linebaugh, Margulies, & Macisack, 1984; Linebaugh, Pryor, & Margulies, 1983). Effective modifications included slower speaking rates, increased redundancy, and more frequent and longer pauses.

Discourse Patterns. An alternative approach to the study of aging and communication competence emphasizes elderly adults' use and mastery of specific discourse patterns. This approach focuses on elderly adults as skilled conversationalists and storytellers who are able to use complex discourse patterns. Most of this research on aging and communication competence has focused on autobiographical reminiscences, suggesting that communicative competence is maintained across the lifespan as a corollary of older adults' concern with assessing and evaluating the meaning and significance of their lives.

Kemper et al. (1990) and Pratt and Robins (1991) analyzed the personal narratives told by elderly adults; Kemper (1990) analyzed a seven-decade longitudinal record of diary entries. All three studies found that elderly adults employed elaborate narrative structures that included hierarchically elaborated episodes with beginnings describing initiating events and motivating states, developments detailing the protagonists' goals and actions, and endings summarizing the outcomes of the protagonists' efforts. The elderly adults provided background information regarding the setting and story protagonists through the use of sequential and embedded episodes. The elderly adults also attached evaluative codas to their narratives which assessed the contemporary significance of these episodes. The elderly adults may have used more complex narrative structures, perhaps because they had learned how to capture and maintain the attention of their audience by establishing the setting, describing the goals and motives of the characters, and structuring their stories as hierarchies of events and episodes.

These studies also consistently obtained positive correlations between the age of the storyteller and ratings of the quality of the narratives. Naive raters as well as English teachers apparently agree on what makes a "good" story: Good stories involve complex plots with multiple episodes and evaluative codas. Whether older adults have learned through experience to tell stories or whether they simply have more interesting experiences and points of view to relate, their stories conform more closely to this ideal than those of young adults. It is not surprising, therefore, that Mergler, Faust, and Goldstein (1985) found that not only are stories told by older adults' preferred by listeners but also that their stories are more memorable than those told by young adults.

Dyadic conversations between older adults and their peers and older adults and young adults also have been examined for the effects of aging on communicative competence. Boden and Bielby (1983, 1986) showed how dyads of elderly adults utilize talk about the past along with talk about the present to achieve a shared sense of meaning and personal worth which is lacking in the discourse of young adults. Elderly adult conversationalists weave together autobiographical details with references to historical events and descriptions of their former lifestyles to establish their own identities and a shared identity.

Because intergenerational talk cannot exploit such shared reminiscences, it consequently gives rise to conflicting discourse patterns. One such pattern is verbosity, or sustained off-target speech that is not focused on the current context. Gold, Andres, Arbuckle, and Schwartzman (1988) documented the occurrence of verbosity in interviews with elderly men. Verbosity correlates positively with age, extroversion, social activity, and declining nonverbal intelligence. Gold et al. suggested that "the failure to maintain focus in speech could reflect the particular combination of a significant loss of nonverbal intellectual ability and intact, well-developed, and practiced verbal skills" (p. P32).

Verbosity, with its focus on autobiographic details, may contribute to a second discourse pattern which also has negative interpersonal and intergenerational consequences. The Couplands and their collaborators (Coupland & Coupland, 1990; Coupland, Coupland, Giles, & Henwood, 1988) focused on the structure of intergenerational conversation. A salient component of these conversations was the older adults' "painful self-disclosures" of bereavement, ill-health, immobility, and assorted personal and family troubles. Painful self-disclosures are cathartic; they may promote positive self-appraisal by contrasting personal strengths and competencies with problems and limitations. Yet self-disclosures also maintain negative age stereotypes and reinforce age stereotypes about weaknesses and disabilities. Consequently, self-disclosures can suppress conversational interactions and limit intergenerational talk.

New Directions. The study of aging and communicative competence is thus paradoxical. On the one hand, some studies have documented the positive development of communicative competence whereas, on the other hand, further studies have documented an age-related decline in communicative competence. Whereas the studies of the structure of personal narratives demonstrate that elderly adults are skilled storytellers, the studies of verbosity and intergenerational conversation suggest that their stories will not be listened to and appreciated. Discourse analytic research bridging these two paradigms clearly is warranted.

Neglected Issues

There are a number of issues pertaining to the study of language and aging that largely have been neglected. Some have been identified in the preceding review. Two additional neglected issues are first, the study of aging and second-language acquisition and proficiency; and second, investigations into cross-linguistic differences. These issues are summarized briefly below along with some suggestions for future lines of research on these topics.

Second-Language Acquisition

Tran (1990) reported that the English-language proficiency of Vietnamese immigrants is significantly related to their age. He concluded that "many older Vietnamese adults do not have a good command of the English language . . ." (p. 99) and suggested that this may be because they were "too old" to learn English.

This has been a recurrent theme in the psychology of language. Since Lenneberg (1967) suggested that there was a critical period for first-language acquisition, for the recovery from childhood aphasia, and for second-language acquisition, debate has focused on whether children are better second-language learners than are adults (for reviews, see Hyltenstam & Obler, 1989; Krashen, Long, & Scarcella, 1979). Most recent attempts to test this hypothesis have examined adults' second-language proficiency, correlating proficiency with age of second-language acquisition and attempting to partial out the effects of length of exposure to the second language and any transfer effects due to the first language (Braine, 1987; Hakuta, 1987). A recent example of this sort of research is that of Johnson and Newport (1989).

Johnson and Newport (1989) administered a test of metalinguistic judgments to a panel of adults who learned English as a second language (their first language was either Chinese or Korean). The adults varied in their age of arrival in the United States (determining age at first exposure to English) and years of exposure to English. The results indicated that there was a strong negative correlation between age at acquisition and second-language proficiency, $r = -.77$. Native speakers of English and those who acquired English between ages 3 years and 7 years performed equally well on the metalinguistic judgment test whereas those who acquired English after ages 8–10 years performed significantly less well on the metalinguistic judgment test. Johnson and Newport also considered whether the age at which formal instruction in English was begun, total years of exposure to English, years of formal instruction in English, and motivational and attitudinal variables, such as level of self-consciousness, cultural identification, and motivation to learn English, affected second-language proficiency. Based on a series of correlational analyses, they concluded that age of arrival has a strong effect on second-language proficiency.

A similar conclusion was reached by Bachi (1956) who used Israeli census data to evaluate the effects of age of immigration on adults' use of Hebrew, by Oyama (1978) who examined adults' ability to repeat sentences presented in white noise, and by Patkowski (1980) who examined ratings of the syntactic complexity of spontaneous speech samples. In each case, those who acquired English as children outperformed those who acquired English as adults.

Most of this research assumes that adults are less efficient second-language learners than children because there is a critical period (Lenneberg, 1967) for language acquisition. This assumption holds that the "window" for language acquisition closes in late childhood or adolescence as a result of neurological changes to cortical or subcortical areas of the brain. Other interpretations are possible. For example, Newport (1990) suggested that "the very limitations of the young child's information processing abilities provide the basis on which successful language acquisition occurs" (pp. 22–23). She suggested that young children must process linguistic inputs in a piecemeal fashion whereas adults process linguistic inputs holistically because adults have larger working memories. Consequently, young children are able to perform a componential analysis by detecting morphological and grammatical patterns holding among the linguistic pieces and thereby gain productive control over these regularities; adults must rely on holistic forms, hence their output will not be productive but limited to formulaic expressions.

Observations of second-language learning strategies provide some support for Newport's (1990) hypothesis. Wong Fillmore (1989) studied how preschool and kindergarten children initially may rely on the rote imitation of formulatic expressions to communicate with others with whom they do not share a common language. But these children go on to develop variable formulas, slotting different words into the rote framework, in order to expand their linguistic repertoire. Wong Fillmore suggested that basic grammar and morphology may develop from such variable formulas as the children gradually learn more phrase and sentence patterns. Observations of adult second-language learners suggest that they typically do not develop variable formulas or productive morphology and grammar (Newport, 1990).

However, as pointed out by Hyltenstam and Obler (1989), this research assumes that adult second-language proficiency in adulthood is not affected by aging per se. Young and old adults are assumed to be equally disadvantaged with regard to second-language learning. Newport (1990) argued "once the organism is fully mature (that is, during adulthood), there should no longer be a systematic relationship between age of arrival and performance" (p. 20). That is, Newport assumed that second-language proficiency is affected only by age at acquisition, such that those who learn a second language during childhood (i.e., before age 15 years) attain a higher level of proficiency than those who learn a second language as an adult (i.e., after age 15 years), regardless of length of exposure to the second language or age at testing for second-language proficiency.

This assumption may not be warranted. No one has attempted to disentangle the effects of age at acquisition from those of age at testing as well as years of exposure. Johnson and Newport (1989) do not report the age at testing for their subjects. They do report that their subjects had been exposed to English from ages 3 years to 26 years and they were between 3 years and 39 years of age at the time they first arrived in the United States; hence, their oldest subjects could have been only 65 years old at the time of testing. The Vietnamese refugees in Tran's (1990) study were between ages 40 years and 92 years; 10.9% were over age 60 years. These observations suggest that the second-language acquisition of older adults rarely has been evaluated. It may be that second-language acquisition, like first-language proficiency, declines across the life span even when age at acquisition and years of exposure are held constant. Braine (1987), in reviewing Bachi's (1956) data, suggested that they reveal a "loss of language learning ability associated with middle age" (p. 125).

Aging may affect second-language acquisition in two ways. First, older adults may not be able to perform the sorts of distributional and componential analyses used by young, native learners to acquire morphological and grammatical rules. Older adults may rely on rote imitation and formulatic expressions such as those employed by younger adult learners as well as on other less efficient learning strategies. Second, not only may older adults be less able to acquire a second language than are young adults but, having once acquired a second language, older adults may have more difficulty, compared to young adults, in retaining or utilizing their second language due to the effects of aging on language use. Older adults' second-language proficiency, like their first-language proficiency, may be affected by such factors as working-memory limitations, cognitive slowing, or attentional deficits.

Cross-Linguistic Differences

Because languages differ in important ways, aging may affect different languages in different ways. English is a word-order language in that English makes minimal use of grammatical inflections whereas English word order is largely fixed. Other languages, for example Russian, rely heavily on inflections and allow word order to vary. Word order itself is subject to variation: English prefers subject-verb-object order producing right-branching structures whereas Dutch and German prefer subject-object-verb order. Further, as pointed out by Bach, Brown, and Marslen-Wilson (1986), word order can interact with the mechanics of clause embedding as in Fig. 5.11. In Dutch and German, a string of noun phrases will precede a string of verbs and each noun phrase must be retained until it can be assigned its proper grammatical role as the subject or object of a verb. Dutch verb-final sentences typically involve crossed dependencies among the subjects, objects, and verbs of one clause and those of another whereas German verb-final sentences typically involve nested dependencies.

Bach et al. (1986) demonstrated that German nested dependencies are more difficult for native speakers to process than are Dutch crossed dependencies; presumably English right-branching dependencies are easier yet to process. Such an ordering of processing difficulty suggests that syntactic parsing proceeds left to right through a sentence, temporarily storing the sequence of noun phrases until each can be assigned as the subject or object of a verb. Crossed dependencies (Dutch) are easier to process than nested dependencies (German) because the innermost clause (i.e., *Hans to feed the horses*) can be completely assembled and temporarily stored while the main clause is still being assembled (i.e., *the men have taught Hans*) whereas in the case of nested dependencies, the complete sequence of verbs must be processed before the individual clauses can be assembled.

Obviously, any age-related reduction of the capacity of the temporary store will affect the retention and interpretation of such complex syn-

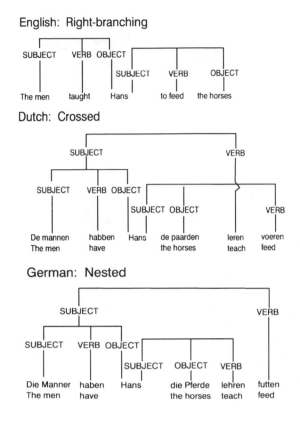

FIG. 5.11.   Right-branching, crossed, and nested dependencies in English, Dutch, and German.

tactic constructions. Age-related working-memory impairments might be expected to have more serious effects on German speakers than on Dutch or English speakers. Of course, other properties of a language may override such syntactic complexities. For example, Japanese and English differ in preferred branching direction (Frazier & Rayner, 1988). The contrast in branching direction is illustrated in Fig. 5.12.

In Japanese, the embedded clause (i.e., *John married yesterday*) precedes the main clause, whereas in English the embedded clause follows the main clause. Although Japanese is a predominantly left-branching language and Kemper (1988) argued that left-branching structures are difficult for older adults to process, other properties of Japanese may aid older adults' comprehension. Japanese is a highly inflected language and case markings on the nouns may be exploited during the parsing process to aid in the assignment of clause structure. Second, informal, spoken Japanese is highly elliptical; nouns, verbs, case markings, and other in-

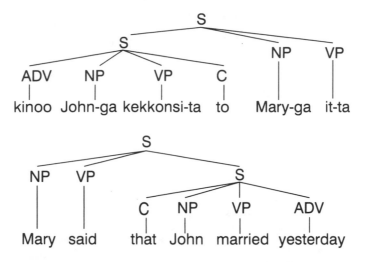

FIG. 5.12.   Branching direction in Japanese and English.

flections can be omitted. This frequent use of ellipsis may work to the advantage of older speakers who are able to use contextual cues to the speaker's meanings but unable to process long or complex spoken sentences. Consequently, elderly Japanese speakers may be able to bypass syntactic processing problems arising from working-memory limitations due to left-branching constructions.

CONCLUSIONS

The study of language and aging falls at the intersection of two areas of research: cognitive aging and developmental psycholinguistics. As a result, the area could draw upon the sophisticated theories and methodologies of each discipline in order to formulate precise hypotheses about the relationship of language and cognition across the life span and to formally describe the linguistic skills of older adults. This has not yet happened, although new directions for research on language and aging hold the promise that global accounts of language dissolution in old age will be replaced by detailed accounts of how aging affects syntactic processing, lexical and semantic analysis, prose processing, and communicative competence.

ACKNOWLEDGMENTS

Preparation of this chapter was supported by Grants R01 AG06319 and K04 AG0043 from the National Institute on Aging. I thank Cheryl Anagnopoulos, Hintat Cheung, James Jackson, Donna Kynette, and

Suzanne Norman for their assistance, and the members of the KU Child Language Program, especially Mabel Rice and Cliff Pye, for their indulgence.

REFERENCES

— Adams, C., Labouvie-Vief, G., Hobart, C., & Dorosz, M. (1990). Adult age group differences in story recall style. *Journals of Gerontology: Psychological Sciences, 45*, P17–27.

Albert, M. S., Heller, H. S., & Milberg, W. (1988). Changes in naming ability with age. *Psychology and Aging, 3*, 173–178.

— Anderson, J. A. (1983). A spreading activation theory of memory. *Journal of Verbal Learning and Verbal Behavior, 22*, 261–295.

Bach, E., Brown, C., & Marslen-Wilson, W. (1986). Crossed and nested dependencies in German and Dutch: A psycholinguistic study. *Language and Cognitive Processes, 1*, 249–262.

Bachi, R. (1956). A statistical analysis of the revival of Hebrew in Israel. *Scripta Hierosolymitana, 3*, 179–247.

Baddeley, A. (1986). *Working memory*. Oxford: Clarendon.

Balota, D. A., & Duchek, J. M. (1988). Age-related differences in lexical access, spreading activation, and simple pronunciation time. *Psychology and Aging, 3*, 84–93.

Bates, E. (1979). *The emergence of symbols: Cognition and communication in infancy*. New York: Academic.

Bates, E., Bretherton, I., & Snyder, L. (1989). *From first words to grammar: Individual differences and dissociable mechanisms*. New York: Cambridge University Press.

Bayles, K. A., & Kaszniak, A. W. (1987). *Communication and cognition in normal aging and dementia*. Boston: Little, Brown.

Bayles, K. A., Tomoeda, C., & Boone, D. R. (1985). A view of age-related changes in language function. *Developmental Neuropsychology, 1*, 231–264.

Beisecker, A. E. (1988). Aging and the desire for information and input in medical decisions: Patient consumerism in medical encounters. *The Gerontologist, 28*, 330–335.

Beisecker, A. E. (1989). The influence of a companion on the doctor—Elderly patient interaction. *Health Communication, 1*, 55–70.

Benjamin, B. J. (1988). Changes in speech production and linguistic behavior with aging. In B. Shadden (Ed.), *Communication behavior and aging* (pp. 163–181). Baltimore: Williams & Wilkins.

Bergman, M. (1980). *Aging and the perception of speech*. Baltimore: University Park Press.

Berko Gleason, J. (1978). The acquisition and dissolution of the English inflectional system. In A. Caramazza & E. B. Zurif (Eds.), *Language acquisition and language breakdown* (pp. 109–120). Baltimore: Johns Hopkins University Press.

Bever, T. G. (1970). The cognitive basis of linguistic structures. In J. B. Hayes (Ed.), *Cognition: The development of language* (pp. 279–352). New York: Wiley.

Blanken, G., Dittman, J., Haas, J-C., & Wallesch, C-W. (1987). Spontaneous speech in senile dementia and aphasia: Implications for a neurolinguistic model of language production. *Cognition, 27*, 247–275.

Blazer, D. (1969). Techniques for communicating with your elderly patient. *Geriatrics, 33*, 79–84.

Bloom, L. (1970). *Language development: Form and function in emerging grammars*. Cambridge, MA: MIT Press.

Boden, D., & Bielby, D. D. (1983). The past as resource. *Human Development, 26*, 308–319.

Boden, D., & Bielby, D. D. (1986). The way it was: Topical organization in elderly conversation. *Language and Communication, 6,* 73–89.

Borod, J. C., Goodglass, H., & Kaplan, E. (1980). Normative data on the Boston Diagnostic Aphasic Examination, Parietal Lobe Battery, and the Boston Naming Test. *Journal of Clinical Neuropsychology, 2,* 209–215.

Bowerman, M. (1982). Reorganizational processes in lexical and syntactic development. In E. Waner & L. Gleitman (Eds.), *Language acquisition: The state of the art* (pp. 319–346). New York: Cambridge University Press.

Bowles, N. L., Obler, L. K., & Poon, L. W. (1989). Aging and word retrieval: Naturalistic, clinical, and laboratory data. In L. W. Poon, D. C. Rubin, & B. A. Wilson (Eds.), *Everyday cognition in adulthood and late life* (pp. 244–264). New York: Cambridge University Press.

Bowles, N. L., & Poon, L. W. (1985). Aging and the retrieval of words in semantic memory. *Journal of Gerontology, 40,* 71–77.

Braine, M. D. S. (1987). Acquiring and processing first and second languages: Comments on Hakuta, Cummins, and Aaronson and Ferres. In P. Homel, M. Palij, & D. Aaronson (Eds.), *Childhood bilingualism: Aspects of linguistic, cognitive, and social development* (pp. 121–128). Hillsdale, NJ: Lawrence Erlbaum Associates.

Bromley, D. B. (1991). Aspects of written language production over adult years. *Psychology and Aging, 6,* 296–308.

Brown, R. (1973). *A first language.* Cambridge, MA: Harvard University Press.

Burke, D. M., & Harrold, R. M. (1988). Automatic and effortful semantic processes in old age; Experimental and naturalistic approaches. In L. L. Light & D. M. Burke (Eds.), *Language, memory, and aging* (pp. 100–116). New York: Cambridge University Press.

Burke, D. M., MacKay, D. G., Worthley, J., & Wade, E. (1991). On the tip of the tongue: What causes word finding failures in young and older adults? *Journal of Memory and Language, 30,* 542–579.

Burke, D., Worthley, J., & Martin, J. (1988). I'll never forget what's-her-name: Aging and tip of the tongue experiences in everyday life. In M. M. Gruneberg, P. Morris, & R. N. Sykes (Eds.), *Practical aspects of memory: Current research and issues* (Vol. 2, pp. 113–118). Chichester, England: Wiley.

Burke, D. M., & Yee, P. L. (1984). Semantic priming during sentence processing by young and older adults. *Developmental Psychology, 20,* 903–910.

Caplan, D. (1987). *Neurolinguistics and linguistic aphasiology: An introduction.* Cambridge, England: Cambridge University Press.

Caporael, L. (1981). The paralanguage of caregiving: Baby talk to the institutionalized aged. *Journal of Personality and Social Psychology, 40,* 876–884.

Caporael, L. R., & Culbertson, G. H. (1986). Verbal response modes of baby talk and other speech at institutions for the aged. *Language and Communication, 6,* 99–112.

Caporael, L. R., Lucaszewski, M. P., & Culbertson, G. H. (1983). Secondary babytalk: Judgments of institutionalized elderly and their caregivers. *Journal of Personality and Social Psychology, 44,* 746–754.

Case, R. (1974). Structures and strictures: Some functional limitations on the course of cognitive growth. *Cognitive Psychology, 6,* 544–573.

Case, R., Kurland, D. M., & Goldberg, J. (1982). Operational efficiency and the growth of short term memory span. *Journal of Experimental Child Psychology, 33,* 386–404.

Chomsky, C. (1979). *The acquisition of syntax in children from 5 to 10.* Cambridge, MA: MIT Press.

Chomsky, N. (1981). *Lectures on government and binding.* Dordrecht, Netherlands: Foris.

Chomsky, N. (1982). *Concepts and consequences of the theory of government and binding.* Cambridge, MA: MIT Press.

Chomsky, N. (1986). *Barriers*. Cambridge, MA: MIT Press.

Clark, E. V. (1977). Strategies and the mapping problem in first language acquisition. In J. Macnamara (Ed.), *Language learning and thought* (pp. 147–168). New York: Academic.

Cohen, G. (1979). Language comprehension in old age. *Cognitive Psychology, 11*, 412–429.

Cohen, G. (1981). Inferential reasoning in old age. *Cognition, 9*, 59–72.

Cohen, G. (1988). Age differences in memory for texts: Production deficiency or processing limitations? In L. L. Light & D. M. Burke (Eds.), *Language, memory, and aging* (pp. 171–190). New York: Cambridge University Press.

Cohen, G., & Faulkner, D. (1981). Memory for discourse in old age. *Discourse Processes, 4*, 253–265.

Cohen, G., & Faulkner, D. (1986). Does "elderspeak" work? The effect of intonation and stress on comprehension and recall of spoken discourse in old age. *Language and Communication, 6*, 91–98.

Collins, A. M., & Loftus, E. F. (1975). A spreading activation theory of semantic memory. *Psychological Review, 82*, 407–428.

Cooper, P. V. (1990). Discourse production and normal aging: Performance on oral picture description tasks. *Journals of Gerontology: Psychological Sciences, 45*, P210–P214.

Corrigan, R. (1979). Cognitive correlates of language: Differential criteria yield differential results. *Child Development, 50*, 617–631.

Coupland, N., & Coupland, J. (1990). Language and later life: The diachrony and decrement predicament. In H. Giles & P. Robinson (Eds.), *Handbook of language and social psychology* (pp. 201–251). London: Wiley.

Coupland, N., Coupland, J., Giles, H., & Henwood, K. (1988). Accommodating the elderly: Invoking and extending a theory. *Language in Society, 17*, 1–14.

Coupland, N., Grainger, K., & Coupland, J. (1988). Politeness in context: Intergenerational issues. *Language in Society, 17*, 253–262.

Craik, F. I. M., & Byrd, M. (1982). Aging and cognitive deficits: The role of attentional resources. In F. I. M. Craik & S. Trehub (Eds.), *Aging and cognitive processes* (pp. 191–211). New York: Plenum.

Craik, F. I. M., & Rabinowitz, J. C. (1984). Age differences in the acquisition and use of verbal information: A tutorial review. In H. Bouma & D. G. Bouwhuis (Eds.), *Attention and performance* (Vol. 10, pp. 471–499). Hillsdale, NJ: Lawrence Erlbaum Associates.

Crain, S., & Shankweiler, D. (1988). Syntactic complexity and reading acquisition. In A. Davison & G. Green (Eds.), *Critical approaches to readability* (pp. 167–192). Hillsdale, NJ: Lawrence Erlbaum Associates.

Crain, S., & Shankweiler, D. (1990). Explaining failures in spoken language comprehension by children with reading disability. In D. A. Balota, G. B. Flores d'Arcais, & K. Rayner (Eds.), *Comprehension processes in reading* (pp. 539–556). Hillsdale, NJ: Lawrence Erlbaum Associates.

Crystal, D., Fletcher, P., & Garman, M. (1976). *The grammatical analysis of language disability*. London: Edward Arnold.

Daneman, M., & Case, R. (1981). Syntactic form, semantic complexity, and short-term memory influences on children's acquisition of new linguistic structures. *Developmental Psychology, 17*, 367–378.

Dennis, M., & Wiegel-Crump, C. A. (1979). Aphasic dissolution and language acquisition. *Studies in Neurolinguistics, 4*, 211–224.

DeRenzi, E., & Vignolo, L. A. (1962). The Token Test. *Brain, 85*, 665–678.

de Villiers, J. G. (1974). Quantitative aspects of agrammatism in aphasia. *Cortex, 10*, 36–54.

Dixon, R. A., & Backman, L. (in press). Reading and memory for prose in adulthood: Issues of expertise and compensation. In S. R. Yussen & M. C. Smith (Eds.), *Reading across the life span*. New York: Springer-Verlag.

Dixon, R. A., Hultsch, D. F., Simon, E. W., & von Eye, A. (1984). Verbal ability and text structure effects on adult age differences in recall. *Journal of Verbal Learning and Verbal Behavior, 23*, 569–578.

Duffy, J. A., Keith, R. L., Shane, H., & Podraza, B. L. (1976). Performance of normal (non-brain-injured) adults on the Porch Index of Communicative Ability. In R. H. Brookshire (Ed.), *Clinical aphasiology conference proceedings* (pp. 32–42). Minneapolis: BRK.

Emery, O. (1985). Language and aging. *Experimental Aging Research, 11*, 3–60.

Eysenck, M. W. (1974). Age differences in incidental learning. *Developmental Psychology, 10*, 936–941.

Feier, C. D., & Gerstman, L. J. (1980). Sentence comprehension abilities throughout the adult life span. *Journal of Gerontology, 35*, 722–728.

Fodor, J. A. (1982). *Modularity of mind.* Cambridge, MA: MIT Press.

Fodor, J. A. (1987). Modules, frames, fridgeons, sleeping dogs, and the music of the spheres. In J. L. Garfield (Ed.), *Modularity in knowledge representation and natural-language understanding* (pp. 25–36). Cambridge, MA: MIT Press.

Fodor, J. A., Bever, T. G., & Garrett, M. (1974). *The psychology of language.* New York: McGraw-Hill.

Fozard, J. L. (1990). Vision and hearing in aging. In J. E. Birren & K. Warner Schaie (Eds.), *Handbook of the psychology of aging* (pp. 150–171). New York: Academic.

Franklyn-Stokes, A., Harriman, J., Giles, H., & Coupland, N. (1988). Information seeking across the life span. *Journal of Social Psychology, 128*, 419–421.

Frazier, L. (1985). Syntactic complexity. In D. R. Dowty, L. Karttunen, & A. M. Zwicky (Eds.), *Natural language parsing: Psychological, computation, and theoretical perspectives* (pp. 129–189). New York: Cambridge University Press.

Frazier, L. (1988). The study of linguistic complexity. In A. Davison & G. Green (Eds.), *Critical approaches to readability* (pp. 193–223). Hillsdale, NJ: Lawrence Erlbaum Associates.

Frazier, L., & Fodor, J. D. (1978). The sausage machine: A new two-stage parsing model. *Cognition, 6*, 291–325.

Frazier, L., & Rayner, K. (1988). Parameterizing the language processing system: Left- versus right-branching within and across languages. In J. A. Hawkins (Ed.), *Explaining language universals* (pp. 247–279). Oxford: Basil Blackwell.

Gardner, H. (1983). *Frames of mind.* New York: Basic.

Garfield, J. L. (1987). Introduction: Carving the mind at its joints. In J. L. Garfield (Ed.), *Modularity in knowledge representation and natural-language understanding* (pp. 17–24). Cambridge, MA: MIT Press.

Gathercole, S. E., & Baddeley, A. D. (1989). Evaluation of the role of phonological STM in the development of vocabulary in children: A longitudinal study. *Journal of Memory and Language, 28*, 200–213.

Gathercole, S. E., & Baddeley, A. D. (1990). Phonological memory deficits in language disordered children—Is there a causal connection? *Journal of Memory and Language, 29*, 336–360.

Gleason, J. B., Goodglass, H., Obler, L., Green, E., Hyde, M. R., & Weintraub, S. (1980). Narrative strategies of aphasic and normal-speaking subjects. *Journal of Speech and Hearing Research, 23*, 370–382.

Gold, D., Andres, D., Arbuckle, T., & Schwartzman, A. (1988). Measurement and correlates of verbosity in elderly people. *Journals of Gerontology: Psychological Sciences, 43*, 27–33.

Goodglass, H., & Kaplan, E. (1972). *The assessment of aphasia and related disorders.* Philadelphia: Lea & Febiger.

Gordon, S. K. (1975). Organization and recall of related sentences by elderly and young adults. *Experimental Aging Research, 1*, 71–80.

Gordon, S. K., & Clark, W. C. (1974). Application of signal detection theory to prose recall and recognition in elderly and young adults. *Journal of Gerontology, 29,* 64–72.

Graesser, A. C. (1981). *Prose comprehension beyond the word.* New York: Springer-Verlag.

Gravel, J. S., & LaPointe, L. L. (1982). Rate of speech of health care providers during interactions with aphasic and nonaphasic individuals. In R. H. Brookshire (Ed.), *Clinical aphasiology conference proceedings* (pp. 208–211). Minneapolis: BRK.

Greenfield, P., Nelson, K., & Saltzman, E. (1972). The development of rulebound strategies for manipulating seriated cups: A parallel between action and grammar. *Cognitive Psychology, 3,* 291–310.

Grodzinsky, Y. (1990). *Theoretical perspectives on language deficits.* Cambridge, MA: MIT Press.

Hakuta, K. (1987). The second-language learner in the context of the study of language acquisition. In P. Homel, M. Palij, & D. Aaronson (Eds.), *Childhood bilingualism: Aspects of linguistic, cognitive, and social development* (pp. 31–56). Hillsdale, NJ: Lawrence Erlbaum Associates.

Hartley, J. T. (1986). Reader and text variables as determinants of discourse memory in adulthood. *Psychology and Aging, 1,* 150–158.

Hartley, J. T. (1988). Aging and individual differences in discourse memory. In L. Light & D. Burke (Eds.), *Language, memory, and aging* (pp. 36–57). New York: Cambridge University Press.

Hasher, L., & Zacks, R. T. (1988). Working memory, comprehension, and aging: A review and a new view. In G. H. Bower (Ed.), *The psychology of learning and motivation* (Vol. 22, pp. 193–226). New York: Academic.

Howard, D. V. (1988). Aging and memory activation: The priming of semantic and episodic memories. In L. Light & D. M. Burke (Eds.), *Language, memory, and aging* (pp. 77–99). New York: Cambridge University Press.

Howard, D. V., McAndrews, M. P., & Lasaga, M. I. (1981). Semantic priming of lexical decisions in young and old adults. *Journal of Gerontology, 35,* 884–890.

Howard, D. V., Shaw, R. J., & Heisey, J. G. (1986). Aging and the time course of semantic activation. *Journal of Gerontology, 41,* 195–203.

Hulme, C., Thomson, N., Muir, C., & Lawrence, A. (1984). Speech rate and the development of short-term memory span. *Journal of Experimental Child Psychology, 38,* 241–253.

Hultsch, D. F., & Dixon, R. A. (1983). The role of pre-experimental knowledge in text processing in adulthood. *Experimental Aging Research, 9,* 17–22.

Hultsch, D. F., & Dixon, R. A. (1984). Memory for text materials in adulthood. In P. B. Baltes & O. G. Brim, Jr. (Eds.), *Life-span development and behavior* (Vol. 6, pp. 77–108). New York: Academic.

Hultsch, D. F., Hertzog, C., & Dixon, R. A. (1984). Text recall in adulthood: The role of intellectual abilities. *Developmental Psychology, 20,* 1192–1209.

Hyams, N. M. (1986). *Language acquisition and the theory of parameters.* Dordrecht, Netherlands: D. Reidel.

Hyltenstam, K., & Obler, L. K. (1989). Introduction. In K. Hyltenstam & L. K. Obler (Eds.), *Bilingualism across the lifespan* (pp. 1–12). New York: Cambridge University Press.

Jackson, J. H. (1958). Evolution and dissolution of the nervous system. In J. Taylor (Ed.), *Selected writings of John Hughlings Jackson* (pp. 191–212). New York: Basic.

Jakobson, R. (1941/1968). *Child language, aphasia, and phonological universals.* The Hague, Netherlands: Mouton.

Jepson, K. L., & Labouvie-Vief, G. (1992). Symbolic processing in the elderly. In R. L. West & J. D. Sinnott (Eds.), *Everyday memory and aging: Current research and methodology* (pp. 124–137). New York: Springer-Verlag.

Johnson, J. S., & Newport, E. L. (1989). Critical period effects in second language learning: The influence of maturational state on the acquisition of English as a second language. *Cognitive Psychology, 21*, 60–99.

Kaplan, E., Goodglass, H., & Weintraub, S. (1976). *The Boston Naming Test*. Philadelphia: Lea & Febiger.

Kemper, S. (1986). Imitation of complex syntactic constructions by elderly adults. *Applied Psycholinguistics, 7*, 277–287.

Kemper, S. (1987). Life-span changes in syntactic complexity. *Journal of Gerontology, 42*, 323–328.

Kemper, S. (1988). Geriatric psycholinguistics: Syntactic limitations of oral and written language. In L. Light & D. Burke (Eds.), *Language, memory, and aging* (pp. 58–76). New York: Cambridge University Press.

Kemper, S. (1990). Adults' diaries: Changes made to written narratives across the life-span. *Discourse Processes, 13*, 207–223.

Kemper, S., Kynette, D., & Norman, S. (1992). Age differences in spoken language. In R. West & J. Sinnott (Eds.), *Everyday memory and aging: Current research and methodology* (pp. 138–152). New York: Springer-Verlag.

Kemper, S., Kynette, D., Rash, S., Sprott, R., & O'Brien, K. (1989). Life-span changes to adults' language: Effects of memory and genre. *Applied Psycholinguistics, 10*, 49–66.

Kemper, S., & Rash, S. (1988). Speech and writing across the life-span. In M. M. Gruneberg, P. E. Morris, & R. N. Sykes (Eds.), *Practical aspects of memory: Current research and issues* (pp. 107–112). Chichester, England: Wiley.

Kemper, S., Rash, S. R., Kynette, D., & Norman, S. (1990). Telling stories: The structure of adults' narratives. *European Journal of Cognitive Psychology, 2*, 205–228.

Kempler, D. (1990). Language changes in dementia of the Alzheimer type. In R. Lubinski (Ed.), *Dementia and communication* (pp. 98–113). Philadelphia: Decker.

Kempler, D., Curtiss, S., & Jackson, C. (1987). Syntactic preservation in Alzheimer's disease. *Journal of Speech and Hearing Research, 30*, 343–350.

Kintsch, W., & van Dijk, T. (1978). Towards a model of text comprehension and production. *Psychological Review, 85*, 363–394.

Kramer, D. (1983). Post-formal operations? A need for further conceptualization. *Human Development, 26*, 91–105.

Krashen, S., Long, M., & Scarcella, R. (1979). Age, rate, and eventual attainment in second language attainment. *TESOL Quarterly, 13*, 573–582.

Kynette, D., & Kemper, S. (1986). Aging and the loss of grammatical forms: A cross-sectional study of language performance. *Language and Communication, 6*, 43–49.

Kynette, D., Kemper, S., Norman, S., Cheung, H., & Anagnopoulos, C. (1990). Adults' word recall and word repetition. *Experimental Aging Research, 16*, 117–121.

Labouvie-Vief, G. (1989). Modes of knowledge and the organization of development. In M. L. Commons, C. Armon, F. A. Richards, & J. Sinnott (Eds.), *Beyond formal operations 2*. New York: Praeger.

Lenneberg, E. (1967). *Biological foundations of language*. New York: Wiley.

Lesser, R. (1974). Verbal comprehension in aphasia: An English version of three Italian tests. *Cortex, 10*, 247–263.

Lesser, R. (1976). Verbal and non-verbal components in the Token Test. *Neuropsychologia, 14*, 79–85.

Lesser, R. (1978). *Linguistic investigations in aphasia*. New York: Elsevier.

Lieberman, P., Friedman, J., & Feldman, L. S. (1990). Syntax comprehension deficits in Parkinson's disease. *Journal of Nervous and Mental Disease, 178*, 360–365.

Light, L. (1990). Interactions between memory and language in old age. In J. E. Birren & K. W. Schaie (Eds.), *Handbook of the psychology of aging* (pp. 275–290). New York: Academic.

Light, L., & Anderson, P. A. (1983). Memory for scripts in young and older adults. *Memory & Cognition, 11*, 435–444.

† Light, L., & Anderson, P. A. (1985). Working memory capacity, age, and memory for discourse. *Journal of Gerontology, 40*, 737–747.

Light, L., & Burke, D. (1988). Patterns of language and memory in old age. In L. Light & D. Burke (Eds.), *Language, memory, and aging* (pp. 244–272). New York: Cambridge University Press.

Light, L., & Capps, J. L. (1986). Comprehension of pronouns in younger and older adults. *Developmental Psychology, 22*, 580–585.

Linebaugh, C. W., Margulies, C. P., & Macisack, S. L. (1984). The effectiveness of comprehension-enhancing strategies employed by spouses of aphasic patients. In R. H. Brookshire (Ed.), *Clinical aphasiology conference proceedings* (pp. 188–197). Minneapolis: BRK.

Linebaugh, C. W., Pryor, A. P., & Margulies, C. P. (1983). A comparison of picture descriptions by family members of aphasic patients to aphasic and nonaphasic listeners. In R. H. Brookshire (Ed.), *Clinical aphasiology conference proceedings* (pp. 218–226). Minneapolis: BRK.

MacWhinney, B. (1982). Basic syntactic processes. In S. A. Kuczaj (Ed.), *Language development* (Vol. 1, pp. 73–136). Hillsdale, NJ: Lawrence Erlbaum Associates.

† Mandel, R. G., & Johnson, N. S. (1984). A developmental analysis of story recall and comprehension in adulthood. *Journal of Verbal Learning and Verbal Behavior, 23*, 643–659.

Manzini, M. R., & Wexler, K. (1987). Parameters, binding theory, and learnability. *Linguistic Inquiry, 18*, 413–444.

McCawley, J. D. (1971). Prelexical syntax. In R. J. O'Brien (Ed.), *Monograph series on language and linguistics*. Washington, DC: Georgetown University Press.

Mergler, N., Faust, M., & Goldstein, M. (1985). Storytelling as an age-dependent skill. *International Journal of Aging and Human Development, 20*, 205–228.

Meyer, B. J. F., & Rice, G. E. (1981). Information recalled from prose by young, middle, and old readers. *Experimental Aging Research, 7*, 253–269.

Meyer, B. J. F., & Rice, G. E. (1983). Learning and memory from text across the adult life span. In J. Fine & R. O. Freedle (Eds.), *Developmental issues in discourse* (pp. 291–306). Norwood, NJ: Ablex.

Meyer, B. J. F., Young, C. J., & Bartlett, B. J. (1989). *Memory improved: Reading and memory enhancement across the life span through strategic text structures.* Hillsdale, NJ: Lawrence Erlbaum Associates.

Miller, G. (1962). Some psychological studies of grammar. *American Psychologist, 17*, 748–762.

Molfese, V. J., Hoffman, S., & Yuen, R. (1981). The influence of setting and task partner on the performance of adults over 65 on a communication task. *International Journal of Aging and Human development, 14*, 45–53.

Nerbonne, M. A. (1988). The effects of aging on auditory structures and functions. In B. Shadden (Ed.), *Communication behavior and aging* (pp. 137–162). Baltimore: Williams & Wilkins.

Newport, E. L. (1990). Maturational constraints on language learning. *Cognitive Science, 14*, 11–28.

Nicholas, M., Obler, L., Albert, M., & Goodglass, H. (1985). Lexical retrieval in healthy aging. *Cortex, 21*, 595–606.

Noll, J. D., & Randolph, S. R. (1978). Auditory semantic, syntactic, and retention errors made by aphasic subjects on the Token Test. *Journal of Communication Disorders, 11*, 543–553.

Obler, L. K. (1980). Narrative discourse style in the elderly. In L. K. Obler & M. L. Albert (Eds.), *Language and communication in the elderly* (pp. 75–90). Lexington, MA: Heath.

Oyama, S. (1978). The sensitive period and comprehension of speech. *Working Papers on Bilingualism, 16*, 1–17.

Pascual-Leone, J. (1974). *Cognitive development and cognitive style*. Lexington, MA: Heath.

Patkowski, M. (1980). The sensitive period for the acquisition of syntax in a second language. *Language Learning, 30*, 449–472.

Perry, W. G. (1968). *Forms of intellectual and ethical development in the college years*. New York: Holt, Rinehart & Winston.

Petros, T. V., Norgaard, L., Olson, K., & Tabor, L. (1989). Effects of text-genre and verbal ability on adult age differences in sensitivity to text structure. *Psychology and Aging, 4*, 247–250.

Pinker, S. (1989). *Learnability and cognition: The acquisition of argument structure*. Cambridge, MA: MIT Press.

Porch, B. E. (1967). *The Porch Index of Communicative Ability*. Palo Alto, CA: Consulting Psychologists Press.

Pratt, M. W., Boyes, C., Robins, S., & Manchester, J. (1989). Telling tales: Aging, working memory, and the narrative cohesion of storytellers. *Developmental Psychology, 25*, 628–635.

Pratt, M. W., & Robins, S. L. (1991). That's the way it was: Age differences in the structure and quality of adults' personal narratives. *Discourse Processes, 14*, 73–85.

Pye, C. (1989). The nature of language. In M. L. Rice & R. L. Schiefelbusch (Eds.), *Teachability of language* (pp. 127–132). New York: Brooks.

Pye, C., Cheung, H., & Kemper, S. (in press). Islands at eighty. In H. Goodluck (Ed.), *Psycholinguistic studies of island constraints*. New York: D. Reidel.

Rabinowitz, J. C. (1986). Priming in episodic memory. *Journal of Gerontology, 41*, 204–213.

Radvansky, G. A., Gerard, L. D., Zacks, R. T., & Hasher, L. (1990). Younger and older adults' use of mental models as representations of text materials. *Psychology and Aging, 5*, 209–214.

Rice, M. L. (1983). Contemporary accounts of the cognition/language relationship. *Journal of Speech and Hearing Disorders, 48*, 347–359.

Rice, M. L., & Kemper, S. (1984). *Child language and cognition*. Baltimore: University Park Press.

Riegel, K. (1973). Dialectical operations: The final period of cognitive development. *Human Development, 16*, 346–370.

Riegel, K. (1977). The dialectics of time. In N. Datan & L. Ginsberg (Eds.), *Life-span developmental psychology: Normative life crises* (pp. 99–128). New York: Academic.

Rochford, J., & Williams, M. (1962). Studies in the development and breakdown of the use of names: 1. The relationship between nominal dysphasia and acquisition of vocabulary in childhood. *Journal of Neurology, Neurosurgery, and Psychiatry, 25*, 222–227.

Rubin, K. H., & Brown, I. D. R. (1975). A life-span look at person perception and its relationship to communicative interaction. *Journal of Gerontology, 30*, 461–468.

Ryan, E. B., Giles, H., Bartolucci, G., & Henwood, K. (1986). Psycholinguistic and social psychological components of communication by and with the elderly. *Language and Communication, 6*, 1–24.

Ryan, E. B., & Johnson, D. G. (1987). The influence of communication effectiveness on evaluations of younger and older adult speakers. *Journal of Gerontology, 42*, 163–164.

Ryan, E. B., & Laurie, S. (1990). Evaluations of older and younger adult speakers: Influence of communication effectiveness and noise. *Psychology and Aging, 5*, 514–519.

Rybash, J. M., Hoyer, W. J., & Roodin, P. A. (1986). *Adult cognition and aging: Developmental changes in processing, knowing, and thinking*. New York: Pergamon.

Schlesinger, I. M. (1982). *Steps to language: Toward a theory of native language acquisition*. Hillsdale, NJ: Lawrence Erlbaum Associates.

Schuell, H. M. (1965). *Minnesota test for differential diagnosis of aphasia*. Minneapolis: University of Minnesota Press.

Schweickert, R., & Boruff, B. (1986). Short-term memory capacity: Magic number or magic stuff? *Journal of Experimental Psychology: Learning, Memory, and Cognition, 12*, 419–425.

Shewan, C. M. (1979). *Auditory comprehension test for sentences*. Chicago: Biolinguistics Clinical Institutes.

Shewan, C. M., & Henderson, V. L. (1988). Analysis of spontaneous language in the older normal population. *Journal of Communication Disorders, 21*, 139–154.

Simon, E. W., Dixon, R. A., Nowak, C. A., & Hultsch, D. F. (1982). Orienting task effects on text recall in adulthood. *Journal of Gerontology, 37*, 575–580.

Sinclair, H. J. (1971). Sensorimotor action patterns as a condition for the acquisition of syntax. In R. Huxley & D. Ingram (Eds.), *Language acquisition: Models and methods* (pp. 121–130). New York: Academic.

Sinclair de Zwart, H. J. (1973). Language acquisition and cognitive development. In T. E. Moore (Ed.), *Cognitive development and the acquisition of language* (pp. 315–336). New York: Academic.

Slobin, D. I. (1979). *Psycholinguistics* (2nd ed.). Glenview, IL: Scott, Foresman.

Snow, C. E., & Ferguson, C. A. (1977). *Talking to children: Language input and acquisition*. New York: Cambridge University Press.

Spilich, G. J. (1983). Life-span components of text processing: Structural and procedural changes. *Journal of Verbal Learning and Verbal Behavior, 22*, 231–244.

Spilich, G. J., & Voss, J. F. (1982). Contextual effects upon text memory for young, aged-normal, and aged-impaired individuals. *Experimental Aging Research, 8*, 147–151.

Stewart, M. A., & Ryan, E. B. (1982). Attitudes toward younger and older adult speakers: Effects of varying speech rates. *Journal of Language and Social Psychology, 1*, 91–109.

Stine, E. L. (1990). Online processing of written text by younger and older adults. *Psychology and Aging, 5*, 68–78.

Stine, E. A. L., & Wingfield, A. (1987). Process and strategy in memory for speech among younger and older adults. *Psychology and Aging, 2*, 272–279.

Stine, E. A. L., & Wingfield, A. (1990). How much do working memory deficits contribute to age differences in discourse memory? *European Journal of Cognitive Psychology, 2*, 289–304.

Stine, E. A. L., Wingfield, A., & Myers, S. D. (1990). Age differences in processing information from television news: The effects of bisensory augmentation. *Journals of Gerontology: Psychological Sciences, 45*, P1–P8.

Stine, E. A. L., Wingfield, A., & Poon, L. W. (1986). How much and how fast: Rapid processing of spoken language in later adulthood. *Psychology and Aging, 1*, 303–311.

Sugarman-Bell, S. (1978). A description of communicative development in the prelanguage child. In I. Markova (Ed.), *The social context of language* (pp. 49–66). London: Wiley.

Trabasso, T., & van den Broek, P. (1985). Causal thinking and the representation of narrative events. *Journal of Memory and Language, 24*, 612–630.

Tran, T. V. (1990). Language acculturation among old Vietnamese refugee adults. *The Gerontologist, 30*, 94–99.

Tun, P. A. (1989). Age differences in processing expository and narrative text. *Journals of Gerontology: Psychological Sciences, 44*, P9–P15.

Ulatowska, H. K., Cannito, M. P., Hayashi, M. M., & Fleming, S. G. (1985). Language abilities in the elderly. In H. K. Ulatowska (Ed.), *The aging brain: Communication in the elderly* (pp. 125–139). San Diego: College-Hill.

Ulatowska, H. K., Hayashi, M. M., Cannito, M. P., & Fleming, S. (1986). Disruption of reference in aging. *Brain and Language, 28*, 24–41.

Valian, V. (1986). Syntactic categories in the speech of young children. *Developmental Psychology, 22*, 562–579.

van Dijk, T., & Kintsch, W. (1983). *Strategies of discourse comprehension.* New York: Academic.

Walker, V. G., Hardiman, C. J., Hedrick, D. L., & Holbrook, A. (1981). Speech and language characteristics of an aging population. In J. J. Lass (Ed.), *Advances in basic research and practice* (Vol. 6, pp. 143–202). New York: Academic.

Walker, V. G., Roberts, P. M., & Hedrick, D. L. (1988). Linguistic analyses of the discourse narratives of young and aged women. *Folia Phoniatica, 40*, 58–64.

Wepman, J. M., & Jones, L. V. (1964). Five aphasias: A commentary on aphasia as a regressive linguistic phenomenon. In D. M. Rioch & E. A. Weinstein (Eds.), *Disorders of communication* (pp. 190–203). Baltimore: Williams & Wilkins.

Wexler, K., & Chien, Y.-C. (1985). The development of lexical anaphors and pronouns. *Papers and Reports on Child Language Development, 24*, 138–149.

Whitaker, H. A., & Selnes, O. A. (1978). Token Test measures of language comprehension in normal children and aphasic patients. In A. Caramazzo & E. B. Zurif (Eds.), *Language acquisition and language breakdown* (pp. 195–210). Baltimore: Johns Hopkins University Press.

Whorf, B. L. (1956). *Language, thought, and reality.* Cambridge, MA: MIT Press.

Wingfield, A., Lahar, C. J., & Stine, E. L. (1989). Age and decision strategies in running memory for speech: Effects of prosody and linguistic structure. *Journal of Gerontology: Psychological Sciences, 44*, P106–P113.

Wingfield, A., Poon, L. W., Lombardi, L., & Lowe, D. (1985). Speed of processing in normal aging: Effects of speech rate, linguistic structure, and processing time. *Journal of Gerontology, 40*, 579–585.

Wingfield, A., & Stine, E. L. (1986). Organizational strategies in immediate recall of rapid speech by young and elderly adults. *Experimental Aging Research, 12*, 79–83.

Wong Fillmore, L. (1989). Teachability and second language acquisition. In M. L. Rice & R. L. Schiefelbusch (Eds.), *Teachability of language* (pp. 311–332). New York: Brooks.

Yngve, V. (1960). A model and a hypothesis for language structure. *Proceedings of the American Philosophical Society, 104*, 444–466.

Yorkston, K. M., & Beukelman, D. R. (1980). An analysis of connected speech samples of aphasic and normal speakers. *Journal of Speech and Hearing Disorders, 45*, 27–36.

Zacks, R. T., & Hasher, L. (1988). Capacity theory and the processing of inferences. In L. Light & D. Burke (Eds.), *Language, memory, and aging* (pp. 154–170). New York: Cambridge University Press.

Zelinski, E. (1988). Integrating information from discourse: Do older adults show deficits? In L. L. Light & D. Burke (Eds.), *Language, memory, and aging* (pp. 133–160). New York: Cambridge University Press.

Zelinski, E. M., & Gilewski, M. J. (1988). Memory for prose and aging. A meta-analysis. In M. L. Howe & C. J. Brainerd (Eds.), *Cognitive development in adulthood* (pp. 133–160). New York: Springer-Verlag.

Zelinski, E. M., Light, L. L., & Gilewski, J. J. (1984). Adult age differences in memory for prose: The question of sensitivity to passage structure. *Developmental Psychology, 20*, 1181–1192.

Zelinski, E. M., & Miura, S. A. (1988). Effects of thematic information on script memory in young and older adults. *Psychology and Aging, 3*, 292–299.

PART TWO

NEUROPSYCHOLOGY AND NEUROSCIENCE

CHAPTER SIX

A Physiological Framework for Perceptual and Cognitive Changes in Aging

Gwen O. Ivy
Colin M. MacLeod
Ted L. Petit
Etan J. Markus
University of Toronto

Physiological change with age is widespread, from such readily observed changes as wrinkling skin to less apparent changes like hardening arteries. Perhaps most compelling are the transformations that take place throughout the nervous system, which is far from exempt from the toll of time. At virtually every level—from peripheral sensory and motor systems to the brain itself—transformations take place that make us different organisms and that require us to adapt continuously. Some of these alterations are relatively easy to accommodate, but many demand quite dramatic adaptation. It is a worthy goal to try to identify these changes, to describe the challenge that we are facing. This leads to the primary question we want to address in this chapter: What are the changes that occur in the aging nervous system?

A catalog of changes is hardly a satisfying end point, however. Consequently, the second goal of the chapter is to provide, where possible, some idea of the causes of these changes with age. After all, time alone does not cause these changes; it is the cellular and molecular events that happen gradually over time that are responsible. To the extent that those events can be understood, we can begin to develop techniques for treating and perhaps even slowing or reversing the more negative repercussions of aging. A third goal, given that this is a Handbook of Cognitive Aging, is to make connections, wherever possible, between age-related changes in the nervous system and age-related changes in cognitive performance. It should be noted at the outset, though, that our knowledge of the causative connections between biological structures and behavioral functions is still quite speculative and fragmentary.

In discussing the aging nervous system, we have adopted the following organizational plan. To begin, we consider anatomical and functional changes in sense organs, changes that generally reduce the contact of the aging individual with his or her environment. We then turn to some larger scale changes in the anatomy of the brain, from which we move down to changes at the cellular and intracellular level. From there, we shift the focus to the changes that take place in the plasticity of the nervous system as it ages.

We cannot hope to capture all the richness of the changing nervous system, but we do hope to characterize the main influences of age. Along the way, we offer occasional speculations as to how the underlying neural transformations might relate to observed cognitive and behavioral changes with age. There is a great deal that we do not know about how the brain and the rest of the nervous system develop throughout the life span, but increasingly there is also a good deal that we do know, beginning with how we acquire information from the world around us.

AGE CHANGES IN PERIPHERAL SENSORY SYSTEMS

A major concern with regard to some aging individuals is their increasing degree of apparent sensory isolation. Failing sensation can lead to a kind of severing of the ties that link the present to the past. An individual unable to process what is going on in the environment begins to lose touch, which can be frightening to all those concerned. What are the normal changes in the sensory systems that occur with aging? What kinds of extraordinary changes can occur? At least some of the apparent decline in cognitive ability with aging may be not in the higher mental processes but in the inputs to those higher processes from the sensory world. Of course, the implications for how best to deal with such declines will be quite different depending on their source.

Vision

A number of changes that occur with age in the visual system adversely affect our ability to see clearly. Around the age of 50 years, various alterations in the lens begin to affect the transmission of light to the retina. For example, the lens becomes more compact and so loses its flexibility for focusing on objects that are close to it. This explains why we become more farsighted as we get older, a change that actually may be compensatory for the many individuals who have been shortsighted from a younger age.

We also require more light for a given task due to yellowing of the lens, which both decreases the light transmitted to the retina and alters its spectral qualities. All lens yellowing causes a rather selective loss of sensitivity to the shorter (blue and violet) wavelengths with age (Said & Weale, 1959), but a general loss of sensitivity over the entire color spectrum also has been reported (Gilbert, 1957). With advanced aging, cataracts (or lens clouding) may develop due to cross-linking of lens proteins, again obscuring the outside world. This condition is present in approximately 25% of 70-year-olds (Corso, 1981). In addition to blockage of light to the retina, this condition also causes glare due to increased scattering of the light. Individuals with cataracts thus face the frustration of needing more light to see but receiving more glare when light is increased.

Fortunately, most of the age-related decrements in the performance of the lens can be alleviated or even completely corrected. For example, glasses with bifocal lenses usually can compensate fully for decreased lens flexibility, whereas cataracts are operable and these cloudy lenses often can be replaced with clear synthetic ones. Correction for yellowing of the lens generally requires a behavioral adaptation for color perception, but the extended time course permits relatively smooth gradual adaptation.

A decline in both visual acuity and depth perception begins as early as the fourth decade of life, but is still very modest in most individuals by 60 years of age. However, a rapid decline in these functions often occurs between 60 and 80 years of age (Anderson & Palmore, 1974). Visual acuity problems are often the result of a decreased amount of light reaching the retina through a yellowing lens and a pupil that is both smaller and slower to adapt to changing light situations. Depth perception is affected by all of the changes just mentioned, because ability to discriminate details affects an individual's perception of texture gradient. Fortunately, distance cues are usually redundant, given the existence of both primary and secondary cues, and thus provide a means of compensating for physical problems.

The retina also undergoes age-related deterioration that adversely affects vision. A portion of essentially every cell type in the retina is lost with age, most notably the receptors and the retinal ganglion cells. Loss of ganglion cells may well contribute to decreased visual acuity in the elderly because these are the primary cells that project visual information into the central nervous system. Unfortunately, these neurons cannot regenerate.

Additional age-related changes in vision, such as spatial and temporal resolution, light and contrast sensitivity, decreased visual fields, and others have been reviewed extensively by Fozard (1990) and by Cohen and Lessel (1984). The physiological reasons for these changes are still rather speculative at present and are not dealt with here.

Audition

Although only about 19% of 54-year-olds experience hearing difficulties, fully 75% of 79-year-olds have this problem (Schaie & Geiwitz, 1982). Most human and nonhuman primate hearing deficits that occur with age involve an inability to hear high-frequency sounds (Bennett, Davis, & Miller, 1983). The several types of auditory presbycusis that occur with age—sensory, neural, mechanical, and metabolic—are considered next. Sensory presbycusis, an atrophy of hair cells in the basal coil of the organ of Corti in the cochlea, leads to loss of ability to hear high frequencies with negligible effects on speech range frequencies (Ordy & Brizzee, 1979). Neural presbycusis, which also occurs in aging, is characterized by atrophy of cochlear nerve fibers and degeneration in the auditory pathway. This can result in impaired speech comprehension, due to decreased ability to hear high-frequency sounds, but does not cause a parallel impairment of pure-tone discrimination (Ordy & Brizzee, 1979).

Mechanical presbycusis results from reduced basilar membrane elasticity, which occurs with aging. Again, high-frequency tone perception is affected most adversely. Finally, there is a deficit called metabolic presbycusis—a loss of hearing at all frequencies. This stems from atrophy of the stria vascularis of the cochlea, which causes biochemical and bioelectrical deficiencies in the fluids bathing the cochlea (Kermis, 1984).

Thus, several different physical changes with age contribute to hearing loss, especially to loss of high-frequency sound perception. This can lead quite directly to behavioral problems that may not be recognized as outgrowths of hearing loss. For example, people hard of hearing may avoid social interaction (or be excluded from it) and so become socially isolated, or may even develop a paranoia that everyone is intentionally whispering to exclude them (Schaie & Geiwitz, 1982). Although hearing aids are beneficial in many individuals, most such devices do not selectively boost the higher frequencies, but boost the lower ones as well, creating a distracting "booming" effect in the sound landscape.

As was the case in the visual system, there are prosthetic devices to assist the aging individual with auditory difficulties, although they are less socially acceptable and considerably more expensive. However, unlike in vision, where the problem typically is reduced light over the whole spectrum, the high-frequency loss in audition creates a somewhat more difficult technological problem. Already, great strides are being made in developing hearing aids that selectively enhance the higher frequencies; no doubt the future will see much more work along these lines. We now turn our attention to the senses about which less is known—the senses of touch, smell, and taste.

Somatosensation

Although the sensation of touch is extremely important in the ability to manually locate, manipulate, and identify objects, there are very few systematic investigations of changes in tactile sensitivity as a function of age. Thornbury and Mistretta (1981) measured touch thresholds on the pad of the index finger in 55 male and female adults ranging in age from 19 to 88 years. Using a forced-choice method, which is more reliable in repeated tests and does not require the subject to establish a response criterion, the study revealed that tactile thresholds increase significantly with age and that older people vary widely in sensitivity. Other investigators also have reported both decreased and variable tactile sensitivity in old age (e.g., Schimriqk & Ruttinger, 1980). Schaumburg, Spencer, and Ochoa (1983) studied the sense of touch by applying a vibrating tuning fork to various areas of subjects' bodies and found that reduced vibratory perception in the lower extremities was prevalent after 50 years of age. Evidence also points to a progressive age-related decrease in vibration sensitivity at high frequencies (80–250 Hz) but not at low frequencies (25–40 Hz) (Verriollo, 1980). Taken together, then, the data seem to indicate that in the normal process of aging there is a rather general loss of tactile sensitivity.

Attempts have been made to correlate age-based sensitivity loss to changes in mechanoreceptors, such as Meissner corpuscles in glabrous skin. These corpuscles, which are rapidly adapting and responsive to low-frequency vibration and light touch (Johannson, 1979), decrease in number during aging and those that remain undergo morphological alterations (Bruce, 1980; Schimriqk & Ruttinger, 1980). Evidence also indicates that the quantity of corpuscle neural surface exposed to stimuli may change with age, presumably causing an alteration in mechanoreception. Mathewson and Nava (1985) examined 53 albino mice and found that from young (2–7 months) to middle age (9–15 months), the neurites innervating Meissner corpuscles became more coarse, tortuous, and ramified. In old age (18–24 months), neurites seemed attenuated and tangled, and they innervated significantly fewer receptors. Similar age-related alterations have been reported in the Meissner's corpuscle neural surface in humans (Bruce, 1980; Corso, 1981; Schimriqk & Ruttinger, 1980). Thus, loss of corpuscle neural surface also should be considered an important factor in tactile sensitivity loss during normal aging. Because Meissner's corpuscles are sensory receptors that respond to mechanical stimulation of the skin (both light touch and pressure), a reduction in their number or a change in their morphology could lead to a reduced perception of touch and a consequent failure to immediately recognize contact with objects. The severity of the perceptual loss would be expected to be in proportion to the extent of receptor loss at the periphery.

The third major domain of research on somatosensation is that of pain. Studies on pain are contradictory, both for humans and for rats. A decreasing perception of pain with increasing age has been reported (Ordy & Brizzee, 1975; Schaie & Geiwitz, 1982). In this regard, Ordy and Brizzee noted that there is a progressive loss of myelinated axons in the peripheral nervous system as aging occurs and they hypothesized that this loss lowers pain sensitivity because fewer reports of pain will reach the central nervous system (CNS).

Because endogenous opiates are our natural analgesics, Hamm and Knisely (1985) studied pain and aging in relation to these morphine like compounds. Enhanced secretion of these opioids decreases pain sensation; blockage of their secretion increases pain sensation. Rats were divided into 3 groups: young (5–7 months), middle-age (15–17 months), and old (22–24 months). Each subject was administered front-paw shock, and the degree of analgesia experienced was quantified by measuring latency to lift the paw, assuming latency to be a direct indicant of degree of analgesia. It was found that as age increased, the degree of displayed analgesia decreased. It thus seems that the endogenous opioid pain modulatory system (the raphe nuclei and a descending pathway within the dorsolateral funiculus of the spinal cord) undergoes a functional decline as age increases, at least in rats. This should result in a greater perception of pain as a subject gets older. A decline of opioid binding affinity and a decreased opioid receptor density also have been reported in several areas of the CNS (Hamm & Knisely, 1985). These two decreases could cause a further lessening of the analgesic effect—and thus further heightening of pain perception with age—by reducing the amount of opioid binding to a decreased number of receptors.

In summary, somatosensory research indicates that sensitivity to vibration and touch tend to decrease with age. This could put aging individuals in discomfort in certain situations as, for example, after failing to shift position frequently enough while standing, sitting, or sleeping. In contrast to the clear loss of touch information, the change in the perception of pain is more complicated. Certain changes may lead to a loss in pain sensitivity whereas others actually may heighten perception of pain when the pain signal finally gets through. The ratio of these two types of change will differ across individuals, preventing a straightforward generalization.

Gustation

Perhaps the sensory modality least affected by aging is taste, although its overlap with the other chemical sense, smell, makes identification of their unique contributions difficult. The surface of the tongue contains numerous taste buds, each of which consists of anywhere from 50 to 200 sensory receptor cells. Although taste sensations generally are divided into four categories—sweet, salty, sour, and bitter—based on differential localization on the tongue, there do not seem to be specific receptor subtypes for each taste. Rather, a given receptor appears to be responsive to several of the taste categories, although it may be tuned more to one than to another. Miller (1988) investigated human taste-bud density across adult age groups and found that intersubject variation was greater than any difference among age groups. Indeed, taste-bud densities on the tips of human male cadaver tongues were found to vary by more than 100-fold (Miller, 1986).

In rats, the number of fungiform papillae—the bumplike structures visible on the surface of the tongue that contain cell clusters, or taste buds—was found to decrease by only 5% for individuals older than 30 months (Mistretta & Oakley, 1986), which is approximately 90 years old in human terms. In humans, the papillae decrease only slightly between the ages of 5 years and 55 years (Moses et al., 1967). The functional concomitants of these rather small decreases have not been measured but are not likely to have an appreciable effect on neural responses to taste (Mistretta & Oakley, 1986). The number of taste buds per papilla also have been examined and no significant age-related effects have been detected either in rhesus monkeys (Bradley, Stedman, & Mistretta, 1985) or in rats (Mistretta & Baum, 1984).

Perhaps not surprisingly, given the foregoing analysis of the physical changes, behavioral studies in humans have detected little, if any, decrement with age in the ability to perceive taste. However, the threshold for salt appears to rise more rapidly with age than does that for sucrose (Grzegorczyk, Jones, & Mistretta, 1979; Moore, Nielson, & Mistretta, 1982; Weiffenbach, Baum, & Burghauser, 1982), although the bitter threshold appears to decrease (Kermis, 1984).

The foregoing notwithstanding, it is well established that elderly subjects, when blindfolded, do have more trouble identifying tastes than do younger subjects (Schiffman, 1977). Simple salt and sucrose could be perceived easily at all ages, but more complex taste stimuli presented difficulties for the elderly. These findings have been interpreted as suggesting that olfactory rather than taste perception might be impaired with age, given that much of what generally is considered to be taste also involves olfaction. Of course, it could be argued that this phenomenon results from difficulties with attention and memory, rather than from perceptual deficits. Indeed, these possibilities represent general confounding factors in studies of taste perception in the aged.

In any case, taste detection is not notably impaired with age. In part, this may be due to the fact that, unlike most other neural cells, taste receptors have life spans of only a few days and are replaced continually throughout the life of the individual. Even if the rate of replacement of receptors declines with age, this appears to have little observable effect on taste perception.

Olfaction

Unlike taste, smell seems quite affected by aging. Consider how the sense of smell works. Olfactory receptors are the ciliated peripheral processes of primary olfactory neurons. The central processes of these primary neurons form the olfactory nerve and project directly to the olfactory bulb. The primary olfactory neurons thus provide a direct link between the environment and the brain, a fact that has led to the proposal that certain diseases, such as Alzheimer's disease, may be transmitted by viruses or toxins along the olfactory nerve to the brain (Doty, Reyes, & Gregor, 1987; Rezek, 1987; Roberts, 1986). Although there is no direct evidence for this, there is evidence that olfactory abilities are impaired in patients with Alzheimer's disease. What remains to be clarified is the locus of the impairment.

Both smell threshold and identification were found to be impaired in one study (Doty et al., 1987), suggesting a peripheral detection problem. However, only identification of odors was found to be impaired in a second study (Koss, Weiffenbach, Haxby, & Friedland, 1988), suggesting that the cues reached the brain but were not processed properly. This is consistent with the fact that the regions known to be most affected in Alzheimer's disease are largely centers that receive heavy olfactory input. As is discussed in more detail later in this chapter, several regions involved in processing olfactory information are subject to severe pathology in the disease, including the anterior olfactory nucleus, prepyriform cortex, entorhinal cortex, and olfactory epithelium.

Several measures of olfactory ability also have been shown to be impaired in normal aging. For example, Doty et al. (1984) examined smell identification ability on a 40 odorant forced-choice test in 1,955 subjects ranging in age from 5 years to 99 years. Women significantly outperformed men at all ages, and nonsmokers outperformed smokers. Best performance for both sexes was reached during the third and fourth decades, followed by a slow decrease to the seventh decade and a marked decline after that. Major olfactory impairment was seen in over half of the subjects aged 65 to 80 years (25% of these subjects were anosmic) and in over three quarters of the subjects aged over 80 years (50% of these subjects were anosmic).

Perhaps the largest study of olfactory discrimination ever conducted was the *National Geographic* study, performed on 26,200 volunteers (Gilbert & Wysocki, 1987). The September 1986 issue of the magazine contained six "scratch and sniff" samples of different odors. The participants were asked if they could detect the odor, identify its major quality (floral, woody, etc.), and discern its relative intensity. Participants had no trouble detecting most of the odors until after age 70 years, but detection of one odor (mercaptans, the odorants added to natural gas to aid its detection) declined at about age 50 years whereas detection of another (rose) remained high into the 90s. Clearly, a decline in the sense of smell, as in the case of hearing, seems to be selective, although the causes of the selective loss have not been pinpointed.

Possible causes for impaired olfactory ability with age include atrophy of up to 73% of the olfactory bulb in subjects 76–91 years old (Ordy & Brizzee, 1975), reduction in the volume of layers in the bulb (Bhatnagar, Kennedy, Baron, & Greenberg, 1987), and decreased numbers of primary and secondary olfactory neurons (Hinds & McNelly, 1981). It is probably the case that olfactory abilities would show an even greater age-related decline were it not for the fact that, like taste receptors, olfactory receptors (primary olfactory neurons) are replaced continually (Graziadei & Graziadei, 1978).

In conclusion, according to both smell threshold and odor identification experiments, the data strongly suggest that the average, healthy elderly person's odor world significantly differs from that of the young adult. In fact, it probably could be concluded that more than 50% of elderly persons 65 years and older evidence substantial olfactory impairment, which may be why the elderly account for a disproportionate number of accidental gas poisoning cases each year (Doty et al., 1984).

Summary

It is not altogether unexpected to find that all senses change with age, or that, with the possible exception of taste, all senses appear to show a decline with advanced age. In vision, the loss is caused by a number of structural changes that reduce the full-spectrum light (but especially the violet and blue light) reaching the receptor surface, and perhaps also the transmission beyond the retina. In smell and hearing, the decline would appear to be selective, attacking some dimensions (such as high frequencies in hearing) more than others. In touch, there are contrasting changes: At the same time as sensitivity to proprioceptive inputs appears to be diminishing, sensitivity to pain may be increasing.

Overall, sensory changes are evident in most modalities, but in no case are the normal changes extremely debilitating and often they can be largely overcome with the assistance of prosthetic devices. Except in the case of extreme damage to a sensory system—not the result of normal aging—there is no apparent reason for sensory loss to bring about serious perceptual or cognitive dysfunction.

GROSS CHANGES IN BRAIN ANATOMY

Developmental changes in the brain itself are, of course, the focus of much of the work in the neuroscience of aging. Can we understand the perceptual and especially the cognitive changes we notice with aging in terms of modifications taking place in the brain? What are the neurological changes? This area of research is thriving, and we reasonably can expect considerable progress over the next decade. Much of the work involves animal models of aging, but there is considerable work with humans as well. We try to examine both and to paint—in broad strokes—a picture of how and why the brain is altered by the advancement of age.

Brain Weight and Tissue Loss

An obvious place to begin any examination of gross changes in brain anatomy is with the overall weight of the brain. In the rat, whereas body weight increases until middle age and then declines during aging, there is a life-span increase in brain weight (Campbell & Gaddy, 1987; Markus, Petit, & LeBoutillier, 1987; Rogers & Styren, 1987). As is seen in later sections, this is not surprising because neuronal loss is minimal in the aged rat brain whereas glial growth (both by growth of individual cells and by proliferation of some glial cell subtypes) is common, resulting in a total net stability (or even increase) of brain volume with age in this species.

In the human, however, there is a progressive loss of brain tissue with advancing age. This is characterized in particular by a marked atrophy of neocortical gyri and a widening of sulci, with a corresponding secondary dilation of the ventricular system (Andrew, 1971; Ordy, Kaack, & Brizzee, 1975; Scheibel & Scheibel, 1975). Total brain mass shrinks by approximately 5%–10% per decade in the normal aged individual, leading to losses of 5% by age 70 years, 10% by age 80 years, and 20% by age 90 years (Minckler & Boyd, 1968; Wisniewski & Terry, 1976).

In the rat, several studies have observed that the thickness of the neocortex remains stable as the animal gets older (Curcio & Coleman, 1982; Markus, Petit, & LeBoutillier, 1991; Pcters, Feldman, & Vaughan, 1983; Peters, Harriman, & West, 1987). Examinations of the rat hippocampus also reveal either life-span stability or increases in structural size. Similarly, examinations of the dentate gyrus of the hippocampus have revealed little or no consistent age-related change in the thickness of the inner or outer leaf (Bondareff & Geinisman, 1976; Markus, Petit, & LeBoutillier, 1991). Coleman, Flood, and West (1987) reported an initial increase in almost all hippocampal dimensions (4 months vs. 12 months) followed by stability throughout middle age and into aging. On the other hand, the hippocampal CA4 region seems to show a lifelong increase in size. This is based on findings that the angle at which the granule cell layer broadens increases over the life span, as does the ratio of total mossy fiber system to perforant path volume (Coleman et al., 1987; Markus, Petit, & LeBoutillier, 1991). Ricci, Ramacci, Ghiraidi, and Amenta (1989) also reported an increase in the dimensions of the mossy fiber tract between 4- and 12-month-old rats, although they observed a reduction in their 24-month-old group.

The majority of the tissue loss in normal human aging is in the cerebral cortex. Focusing just on the cortex, Corsellis (1976) found a 2% (female) to 3.5% (male) drop per decade from age 20 years. The atrophy is most marked over the frontal lobes, although parietal and temporal lobes suffer considerable losses as well. Several investigators have attempted to correlate declines in overall human brain mass with behavioral indices, particularly in cases of dementia. There does not appear to be a clear correlation between these two factors in the human (Corsellis, 1976; Terry & Davies, 1980; Tomlinson, Blessed, & Roth, 1970; Wisniewski & Terry, 1976). Terry and Davies did not find differences in overall brain weight or in more specific measures of cortical thickness in the frontal and superior temporal regions when they compared demented and age-matched controls. However, it should be noted that most studies attempting to correlate declines in brain mass with loss of cognitive abilities have not focused on the mass of individual structures as, for example, hippocampus.

In sum, the existing work on gross brain mass would lead to the conclusion that, despite the clear decline of this mass with age in the human, there is no correspondingly clear behavioral consequence. However, as we see in several upcoming sections, a finer grained analysis of regionally specific pathologies holds more promise for yielding anatomical substrates for cognitive decline.

The Vascular System and Cerebral Blood Flow

Blood vessels transport oxygen and glucose, as well as other nutrients, growth factors, and hormones, to virtually all of the cells of the body. Like other tissues, blood vessels show signs of aging that may impair their function and impact heavily on the tissues supplied. In the case of non-proliferative populations such as neurons, decreased oxygen (ischemia) leads to a frank loss of cells. Brain microvasculature is specialized both morphologically and with active transport mechanisms to maintain a blood-brain barrier, which it does at some energy cost. Age-related changes to brain circulatory systems may have the added consequence of permitting entry into the neural tissues of substances not normally found there, such as amyloid, to be discussed later. Erosion of the blood-brain barrier is of special concern because increased permeability permits the entry into the brain of blood-borne toxic or infectious substances.

In fact, a number of morphological changes have been noted in brain microvasculature during normal aging. Fang (1976) demonstrated a significant increase with age in the "winding" or "coursing" effects of cerebral blood vessels in normal human brain. Whereas intercerebral arteries, arterioles, and venules in young cortex are relatively straight and evenly dispersed, those in aged cortex become more coiled, tortuous, and differentially dispersed. For example, there is a pronounced decrease in vascularity in deeper laminae of the cortex in areas where there is also cell loss. Fang proposed that this areal rearrangement of microvasculature is related to neuron dropout and concomitant glial infiltration of cortical regions, although neither the initial cause nor the effect of such changes is known. Certainly, such dramatic cell loss and vascular reorganization in the cortex would be expected to result in some type of functional or cognitive deficit, but the nature of this deficit would hinge critically on the cortical region(s) affected.

Some morphological changes with age may well reflect altered blood-brain barrier function. In aged monkeys, both thickened basement lamina of cortical capillaries and aberrant interendothelial tight junctions—anatomical substrates of main portions of the blood-brain barrier—have been observed (Burns, Kruckeberg, Comerford, & Buschmann, 1979; Burns, Kruckeberg, Gaetano, & Shulman, 1983). A similar thickening of the basement lamina was observed in cortical capillaries of Alzheimer's disease and was thought to be involved in altered blood-brain barrier permeability (Mancardi, Perdelli, Rivano, Leonarde, & Bugiani, 1980). The number of mitochondria per cerebral capillary profile also was shown to decline with increasing age in both rat (Burns et al., 1983) and monkey (Burns et al., 1979). Such a decrease in energy-producing mitochondria, coupled with changes in interendothelial tight junctions and the overall thinning of the endothelial component of the capillary wall, suggests a decline in the work capability of these capillaries with serious perturbations in ionic homeostasis between blood and brain (Burns et al., 1983). Once again, this puts the brain at risk from factors present in the blood that normally are blocked from access to the brain. For example, a current theory of Alzheimer's disease pathogenesis is that a protein that is the precursor to amyloid plaque formation leaks from the cerebral vasculature into the immediate vicinity of otherwise healthy neurons. This in turn causes neuronal degeneration and the formation of amyloid (or senile) plaques, the major anatomical hallmark of Alzheimer's disease.

The aforementioned microscopic changes in cerebral vasculature with age may contribute to decreased cerebral blood flow. Cerebral blood flow and oxygen uptake in a normal elderly population (mean age 71 years) was found to be lower than the values for a young group (mean age 21 years), and cerebral oxygen consumption was 6%–10% lower in the elderly (Dastur et al., 1963; Lassen, Feinberg, & Lane, 1960). The reduction in metabolic rate was found to be greater on the left side than on the right side (Lassen et al., 1960), suggesting implications for language in particular. In contrast to normal aged individuals, both cerebral blood flow and oxygen consumption are reduced markedly in patients with presenile and senile dementia; most important, this is in general proportion to intellectual deterioration (Lassen, 1959; Schmidt, 1950).

Specific subsystems of the clinical picture also correlate with both decreased cerebral blood flow and neuronal degeneration. For example, decreased blood flow occurs in the temporal region of demented patients who display primarily memory deficits, in occipitoparietotemporal regions of patients displaying agnosia and disorientation, and in both frontal and post-central-temporal regions of patients with severe mental deterioration (Hagberg & Ingvar, 1976). The regions with lowest blood flow were also those with the most pronounced degenerative changes at autopsy (Brun, Gustafson, & Ingvar, 1975), although the direction of causality has not been established. Further, it should be emphasized that it is not known if the loss of neurons or the decreased blood flow is the primary pathogenetic factor in the various subtypes of dementia.

The importance of cerebral blood flow to abstract thinking also is emphasized by studies where presenile and senile patients performed tests requiring abstract thinking. We know that induced neural activity in both the sensorimotor and more abstract realms gives rise to both localized and generalized increases in cerebral blood flow in normal individuals (Ingvar, 1975). In contrast, patients did not show an elevation in cerebral blood flow in frontal and postcentral association areas (Ingvar, Risberg, & Schwartz, 1975).

This section has focused on vascular system and cerebral blood flow, and has suggested that reduced blood flow is a likely concomitant of aging. The provocative question that remains is whether neurons die because of decreased oxygen and nutrient supply or whether neuronal death leads to deterioration of the local microvasculature because there is no longer a source of growth and maintenance factors. It is tempting to speculate that the social-psychological isolation that many elderly experience leads to decreased activity of certain neuronal populations, which in turn leads to locally decreased cerebral blood flow and, consequently, to neuronal death in these brain regions.

Neuron Loss

It is quite common to hear students talking about how many neurons they lost at a party on the weekend. Is there, in fact, significant neuron loss with age and, if so, what are the consequences of this loss? Given that CNS neurons typically do not undergo mitosis during adulthood, lost cells are not replaced, making some degree of neuronal loss a necessary feature of aging.

In humans, neuronal dropout appears to be a consistent feature of the aging brain, although some brain regions are more affected than others. This complex and conflicting literature has been reviewed extensively by Coleman and Flood (1987), who pointed out that numerous technical difficulties plague such quantitative studies. For example, neurons not only die, but shrink in size, and the smallest ones soon become practically indistinguishable from glial cells. To complicate matters further, glial cells themselves proliferate, thus replenishing cell density (though not cell volume, because glial cells are smaller than most neurons). These changes then are superimposed upon a generally shrinking brain (due mainly to loss of neurons and their extensive dendritic arbors), with shrinkage affecting neocortex in particular. Nonetheless, when all factors are considered, the bulk of the evidence indicates a substantial decrease in neuron density, as well as in absolute numbers, in a variety of brain regions.

In neocortex, Brody (1955, 1970) reported a 50%–60% decrease in neuron density in superior temporal gyrus, a 50% decrease in superior frontal gyrus, a 20%–30% decrease in precentral gyrus and area striata, and a 10%–20% decrease in postcentral and inferior temporal gyri between young to middle adulthood and the 9th to 10th decades of life. Other authors (reviewed in Coleman & Flood, 1987) find decreases in neuron density from 10%–60% in different neocortical areas, thus corroborating the general finding that neuron numbers decrease from youth to old age and that some neocortical areas are more susceptible than others.

A number of studies (Henderson, Tomlinson, & Gibson, 1980; Terry & DeTeresa, 1982; Terry, DeTeresa, & Hansen, 1987) have found a greater decrease in the density of large as opposed to small neurons, which would seem to indicate that large neurons are selectively dying off. However, Terry et al. attributed this to neuronal shrinkage, not loss, because they found a relative increase in density of small neurons. These authors concluded, then, that neurons do not actually die; rather, the large ones just shrink. However, if their data on shrinkage are valid and are combined with data from numerous other investigators who find an actual decrease in neuron number with age, small neurons would have to be the ones that are selectively dying off. What could be the theoretical consequence of this? In general, the smaller cortical neurons tend to be local circuit neurons, with projections within a cortical column or to adjacent columns, whereas larger neurons project to more distant cortical regions or subcortically. The loss of small neurons thus would cause decreased processing of information within cortical columns and between adjacent or nearby columns.

It remains possible that Terry and DeTeresa (1982) did not effectively distinguish small neurons from glial cells, which are increased in number in the aging brain. Given the bulk of evidence indicating decreases with age in both cortical volume and neuronal density in the human cerebral cortex, it seems most likely that the larger neurons are the ones actually dying off with age, although the remaining neurons also may be shrinking (discussed in Coleman & Flood, 1987). The functional implications of a selective loss of large pyramidal cells would be a decrease in both incoming and outgoing information in neocortex, thus curtailing communication between the higher brain regions and the rest of the nervous system. Certainly, more careful studies designed to unambiguously differentiate small neurons from glial cells are required to firmly resolve this important issue.

Neuron counts in neocortex of nonhuman primates generally corroborate findings in humans. Yet rodent data, as was the case with measures of tissue thickness, indicate few or no age-related changes. Neuronal density in neocortical layers II and III has been reported to remain stable (Curcio, McNelly, & Hinds, 1985) and in several studies no changes in total cortical neuronal density have been observed (Curcio & Coleman, 1982; Diamond, Johnson, Protti, Ott, & Kajisa, 1985; Peters et al., 1983). Although these findings show that neocortical neuron density remains constant throughout most of the rat's life span, there is some evidence that neuronal numbers decrease during very old age. Peters et al. (1987) determined that both decreased cortical thickness and neuron loss were present in deep cortical layers (where the larger pyramidal cells reside) in 47-month-old diet-restricted Sprague Dawley rats. Because diet restriction extends life span and promotes health by a number of measures, these data may indicate that rodents also are afflicted with neuron death in neocortex if given the conditions to live long enough.

There is also substantial evidence that cells are lost with age in human hippocampus and subiculum, structures intimately involved in learning and memory processes. Although specific estimates of loss vary across studies, most hippocampal regions appear to undergo a moderate loss of approximately 20% with age (for a review, see Coleman & Flood, 1987). In aged nonhuman primates, there is a substantial reduction of both the depth of the CA1 pyramidal cell layer and the density of neurons in this layer (by about 40%), indicating a high degree of neuronal loss in this hippocampal region (Brizzee & Ordy, 1979). Data on neuronal density and volume in various regions of rat hippocampus similarly reflect neuronal loss with age (reviewed in Coleman & Flood, 1987).

Subcortical brain regions display variable neuron loss with age. For example, the olfactory bulbs and some hypothalamic nuclei show neuronal loss, whereas other hypothalamic nuclei display stable numbers of neurons (Rogers & Styren, 1987; Sartin & Lamperti, 1985). Specifically, the supraoptic and paraventricular nuclei of the hypothalamus do not show neuronal loss with age in either humans or rodents although, at least in humans, the medial preoptic nucleus shows pronounced loss throughout life in both sexes. It is presently not known how neuron loss in this sexually dimorphic brain region might correlate with gonadal aging or with sexual behavior, but questions such as these are worth asking because they will help to link brain and behavior.

In cerebellum, there is substantial evidence that at least 20%–30% of Purkinje cells are lost with age in humans (Ellis, 1920; Hall, Miller, & Corsellis, 1975), nonhuman primates (Nandy, 1981), and rodents (Inukai, 1928; Rogers, Silver, Shoemaker, & Bloom, 1980). Although this may lead to motor disturbances, such as uneven gait, any effects of such loss on cognitive processes are not obvious.

Despite conflicting reports on loss of cholinergic neurons in human nucleus basalis during normal aging, there does seem to be real loss if the preadult period of life is compared with the senescent period (reviewed in Coleman & Flood, 1987). However, given that the death of some cholinergic neurons probably is compensated for by increased transmitter production by neighboring neurons, we might not expect this loss to result in cognitive deficits unless it proceeds to pathological levels such as are found in Alzheimer's disease (see chapter 8 in this volume).

Finally, there is an approximate 30%–40% decline in numbers of pigmented neurons in both locus coeruleus (Mann, Yates, & Hawkes, 1983; Vijayashankar & Brody, 1979) and in substantia nigra (McGeer, McGeer, & Suzuki, 1977) of humans. Although the exact time of the neuron loss is not clear, it is apparent after 50 years of age. Similar loss has been well documented in rodents (Sabel & Stein, 1981; Tatton et al., in press). A severe loss of locus coeruleus neurons that project to neocortex has been related to intellectual impairment in both Alzheimer's and Parkinson's diseases (Agid, Javoy-Agid, & Ruberg, 1987; Bondareff

& Mountjoy, 1986; Cash et al., 1987), and a severe loss of substantia nigra neurons that project to the striatum has been linked to motor disturbances in Parkinson's disease (Chui et al., 1986; Jellinger, 1987).

Changes in Glial Cells

There are three types of glial cells in the CNS: astrocytes, oligodendrocytes, and microglia. These cells perform a wide variety of support functions in the nervous system. For example, astrocytes are known to function in the removal of degenerative debris in the nervous system, as well as in maintaining ion homeostasis (particularly by taking up potassium from the extracellular fluid) and in metabolism of putative neurotransmitters. In response to practically any form of neural insult, astrocytes become hypertrophic, displaying a response that includes enlargement of the cell body and increases in both the number and length of astrocytic processes. In fact, these are the cells that form glial scars after brain or spinal cord injury. Oligodendrocytes provide the insulating myelin sheath for many CNS axons and are responsible for maintaining this sheath, as well as for control of the local ionic environment of the axon. The functions of microglia are not as well understood but, like astrocytes, these cells are thought to play a role in phagocytosis, the cellular engulfment and digestion of neural debris following brain trauma.

Changes in glial cells with age have not been widely investigated, probably due both to past difficulties in distinguishing the different glial subtypes in the same region and to our lack of understanding of specific glial functions. It is generally accepted that most glial cells retain the ability to proliferate throughout an animal's life span, but it is not known if all glial subtypes do, or whether they do to the same extent. Korr (1980, 1982) showed that several nonneuronal cell types can proliferate in brains of aged rodents. These proliferative cells include astrocytes, oligodendrocytes, cells of the subependymal layer (thought to contain undifferentiated glioblast cells), and endothelial cells, which line the vascular system. Extensive data have been reported on two of these subtypes, astrocytes and microglia, and are reviewed in Finch and Morgan (1990).

Briefly, the density of astrocytes has been shown to increase in hippocampus, neocortex, and striatum of senescent rats, and the density of microglia was found to increase in neocortex (Landfield, Rose, Sandles, Wohlstadter, & Lynch, 1977; Sturrock, 1980; Vaughan & Peters, 1974). Further, the volume fraction of astrocyte processes increased by 45% in rat hippocampus (Geinisman, Bondareff, & Dodge, 1978), indicating hypertrophy of these cells with age. Astrocyte hypertrophy also has been seen in rat striatum and neocortex (Lindsey, Landfield, & Lynch, 1979) as well as in primate hippocampus (Knox, Jirge, Brizzee, Ordy, & Bartus, 1979) and the cellular laminae of human frontal cortex (Hansen, Armstrong, & Terry, 1987). Hypertrophied astrocytes are a prominent feature of neuritic plaques in aged humans (Terry & Wisniewski, 1972) and in affected areas of neocortex in Alzheimer's disease (Schechter, Yen, & Terry, 1981).

These findings, along with those showing decreased numbers of neurons with age, are consistent with the idea that more and/or bigger glial cells are created to handle the increased incidence of neural trauma with age. These data also imply that there should be an increase in the glia to neuron ratio with age. This could be important because glia and neurons play mutually supportive roles in maintenance of brain homeostasis, and any disruption of the normal ratio would have negative consequences for nervous system function. In the future, it will be important to determine which subtypes of glial cells proliferate during normal aging—and which merely increase in size.

As was the case with astrocytes, high concentrations of proliferative microglia are seen in the brains of Alzheimer's patients in regions that have a high density of amyloid (or senile) plaques and other Alzheimer's pathology. These regions include the subiculum, area CA1 of hippocampus, and various neocortical association areas (e.g., Cras et al., 1990). It has been proposed that microglia process neuronally derived amyloid precursor protein in an aberrant manner, leading to toxic beta-amyloid protein deposition and amyloid plaque formation in the affected regions (Cras et al., 1990). Because amyloid plaques also are seen, though to a much lesser extent, in normal aged brains, it is possible that similar pathogenetic mechanisms for plaque formation are involved. However, it is also possible that the increased numbers of microglia associated with amyloid plaques are a response to existing pathology rather than a cause of it.

In sum, increased numbers of glial cells are a common feature of aging brains and probably reflect the accumulation of neural traumatic incidents throughout the life span. Without this proliferation and glial scar formation, the brain could not effectively heal its various wounds.

CHANGES AT THE CELLULAR LEVEL

Lipofuscin

One of the most consistent age-related morphological changes to occur in cells is an approximately linear accumulation of age pigment, or lipofuscin. Although lipofuscin accumulates in virtually all organisms and all cell types, neurons accumulate larger amounts of the pigment because they do not divide. The term lipofuscin derives from the Greek *lipo* (fat) and *fuscus* (dark or dusty) and was first given to the pigment due to its staining with lipidic dyes and its brownish color in unstained sections (Hueck, 1912). It is now known, however, that a major portion of the pigment is proteinaceous rather than lipidic.

Under ultraviolet light, the lipofuscin pigment emits a characteristic yellowish autofluorescence. Lipofuscin granules as seen under the electron microscope have several emblematic morphological properties. The granules are surrounded by a single limiting membrane of lysosomal origin and contain an electron-dense matrix which may be fine or rough granular and may contain lamellar (membranous) bodies and/or vacuoles (previously containing lipid).

It should be emphasized that lipofuscin is a normal component of the cell cytoplasm; it represents the normal process of cellular catabolism taking place in digestive organelles called lysosomes. Thus, even young, healthy neurons and glial cells contain some lipofuscin; the amount present represents the balance between anabolic and catabolic processes in the cell. The increased amount of cellular lipofuscin seen with age is thought to be due to decreased efficiency of the lysosomal system. This, in turn, may be caused by decreased synthesis of enzymes or by decreased efficiency of enzymes due to free radical damage to either the enzymes themselves or their substrates (Harman, 1990; Ivy et al., 1990).

The accumulation of lipofuscin is not uniform throughout the brain, but displays regional differences. In a nonhuman primate (*Macaca mulatta*), the rank order of lipofuscin accumulation from highest to lowest was found to be: medulla, hippocampus, midbrain, pons, neocortex, and cerebellum, as determined by percentage of neurons in a region displaying aggregates of lipofuscin (Brizzee, Ordy, & Kaack, 1974). Further, within a given brain region, some cell types accumulate more lipofuscin than do others. For example, in neocortical association areas, medium and large pyramidal neurons of layers II–III and V accumulate more pigment than do stellate or small pyramidal cells of layer IV, and the large cells of the brainstem acquire more pigment than do the small cells.

Cell volume alone does not seem to determine susceptibility to pigment accumulation: Neurons of the human cerebellar dentate nucleus accumulate about seven times the amount of lipofuscin as Purkinje neurons and three times that of hippocampal pyramidal cells, even though the cytoplasmic volumes of these three cells is about the same (Mann, Yates, & Stamp, 1979). Brizzee et al. (1974) pointed out that most of the lipofuscin in the Purkinje cell layer and dentate nucleus actually is located in adjacent glial cells and suggested that glia may remove or modulate the amount of lipofuscin in adjacent neurons. Thus, some neuron populations may be "saved" from catabolic overload by neighboring glial cells.

There is some evidence that increased amounts of lipofuscin in neuronal cytoplasm result in decreased RNA content and nucleolar volume (Mann, Yates, & Barton, 1977), as well as in cell death (Hinds & McNelly, 1979). It is thus possible that a critical mass of lipofuscin in the cytoplasm may result in a fundamental breakdown in cellular homeostasis and ultimately lead to death of the neuron. If so, it is likely that different cell types have their own critical levels of sensitivity to pigment accumulation. For instance, it is known that fibroblasts in culture die when 30% of their cytoplasm is occupied by lipofuscin (Collins & Brunk, 1978). Yet although neurons in the primate inferior olive have more lipofuscin than neurons of any other brain region (Brizzee et al., 1974), two out of three studies found no cell death in this region with age (Moatamed, 1966; Monagle & Brody, 1974; Sandoz, 1977). Clearly, the association of lipofuscin with impaired cellular function or cell death is not simple.

Brizzee, Ordy, Hansche, and Kaack (1976) examined the relation between age, neuron loss, glial cell number, and lipofuscin accumulation in five neocortical laminae of Brodman's area 3 (somatosensory cortex) in the rhesus monkey. Although lipofuscin content and glial cell number increased with age in all laminae, lamina IV exhibited the highest correlations with age of increased lipofuscin content and decreased neuron number.

Similar correlations have been observed in pyramidal neurons of area CA1 of hippocampus in both rats and monkeys. Brizzee and Ordy (1979) found an age-related decline in short-term memory in Fischer 344 rats that was significantly correlated with decreased numbers of CA1 neurons and increased lipofuscin content in remaining neurons. This was corroborated by Kadar, Silbermann, Brandeis, and Levy (1990), who showed that aged rats exhibited increased errors in the eight-arm radial maze task, a short-term memory task for spatial information. These rats also displayed significant amounts of lipofuscin in CA1 and CA3 pyramidal cells. Likewise, a series of studies in rhesus monkeys demonstrated age-related impairments in short-term memory, susceptibility to sensory interference, and ability to modify previously reinforced habits, which were significantly correlated with a decrease in mean depth of the CA1 zone, loss of CA1 neurons, and increased lipofuscin content per neuron (Bartus, 1979; Brizzee, Ordy, & Bartus, 1980). Of course, such correlations do not prove causality and instead may reflect different manifestations of a common pathogenetic mechanism.

Aside from potentially causing the death of neurons, little is known about the significance of lipofuscin to cellular performance. Davies and Fotheringham (1981) attempted to answer this question in cells of the supraoptic nucleus, which produce hormone-containing organelles called neurosecretory granules. They found the presence of lipofuscin did not interfere with this primary cell function in either normally hydrated or in osmotically stressed old mice. Also, Rogers et al. (1980) attempted to assess functional impairment in lipofuscin-laden Purkinje cells of aged rats more directly by single-unit electrophysiological recording techniques. Purkinje cells were found to exhibit significant changes in firing pattern with age, but these were more highly correlated with cell death and dendritic spine loss than with proportion of cells containing lipofuscin. No data were given on the relation of firing pattern to lipofuscin content per cell.

A specialized form of lipofuscin in neurons is neuromelanin. The ultrastructure and composition of neuromelanin are closely related to those of lipofuscin, with the exception that neuromelanin contains an extra electron-dense component that is believed to consist of catecholamine degradation products. Neuromelanin is a prominent component of lipofuscin in neurons of substantia nigra and locus coeruleus, in particular, as well as in nucleus paranigralis, nucleus subcoeruleus, the dorsal motor nucleus of the vagus, and a few other nuclei (Bazelon, Fenichel, & Randall, 1967; Fix, 1980). Although neurons in substantia nigra and locus coeruleus are especially susceptible to death during normal aging and (particularly) in Parkinson's disease, only a correlation exists between pigment accumulation and death of these neurons.

AMYLOID PLAQUES

A typical amyloid (or senile) plaque is approximately 70 microns in diameter (a neuron is about 10–30 microns) and consists of a central core of amyloid protein surrounded by reactive astrocytes, microglia, degenerating axons, and macrophages. Plaques are thought to originate from defective proteolytic processing of an amyloid precursor protein, though the source of this protein is still in dispute (microglia, the neurons themselves, and the cerebrovascular system are the hottest contenders). Plaques are a major pathological hallmark of Alzheimer's disease and are found in a number of other disease states (Pick's disease, Creutzfeldt–Jakob disease, Kuru, and Guam–Parkinson dementia) as well as in normal aging.

Brain regions susceptible to plaque formation appear to be the same in Alzheimer's disease and normal aging, involving most regions of neocortex, with a predilection for occipitotemporal gyrus, the amygdala, and hippocampus (especially CA1, followed by subiculum and CA2/CA3) (Gellerstedt, 1933; Meencke et al., 1983; Tomlinson, Blessed, & Roth,

1968). However, patients with Alzheimer's disease have both an increased plaque density in these brain regions and a more extensive brain distribution of plaques than do normal aged individuals. It is generally agreed that the density of plaques correlates fairly well with the degree of dementia (Morimatzu, 1975; Simchowicz, 1907; Spielmeyer, 1922; Tomlinson et al., 1968, 1970).

NEUROFIBRILLARY TANGLES

With increasing age, pyramidal cells in certain brain regions have a predilection for accumulating tangled masses of filaments in their cytoplasm. In humans, the filaments are often, but not always, paired and twisted into a double helix of approximately 10 nanometers diameter, undefined length, and a periodicity of 80 nanometers (Kidd, 1964; Terry & Davies, 1980; Terry & Wisniewski, 1972; Wisniewski, Johnson, Raine, Kay, & Terry, 1970). As the filaments accumulate, they gradually fill the cytoplasm and extend into the dendritic and axonal processes, pushing the nucleus to one side. This results in an apparent loss of mitochondria and ribosomes, the respective energy and protein synthesis factories of the cell. Such tangle-bearing neurons will have difficulty functioning normally.

Paired helical filaments are known to be composed largely of abnormally phosphorylated tau molecules and to be associated with ubiquitin (Delacourte & Defossez, 1986; Grunde-Iqbal et al., 1986; Ihara, Nukina, Miura, & Ogawara, 1986; Wood, Mirra, Pollock, & Binder, 1986). Tau is a protein involved in stabilizing microtubules, the part of the neuronal cytoskeleton responsible for rapid transport of materials between the cell body and its axonal and dendritic processes. The presence of ubiquitin, which is a molecular tag that signals which proteins should be degraded, probably indicates that the cell recognizes the presence of these abnormal tau proteins, but that the proteolytic system is incapable of degrading them.

The brain regions most susceptible to neurofibrillary tangles are the hippocampus (especially CA1), the subiculum, and the entorhinal cortex (Ball, 1978; Hirano & Zimmerman, 1962; Kemper, 1978; Matsuyama & Nakamura, 1978; Tomlinson et al., 1968). Neurofibrillary tangles are rare in the neocortex of normal aged individuals, but are found in locus coeruleus as early as the fourth decade and in substantia nigra in the sixth decade (Forno & Alvord, 1971). Some neurons are resistant to this pathology, including Betz cells of the motor cortex, the basal ganglia, most cerebellar circuits and Purkinje cells, specific cortical projection nuclei of the thalamus, and the spinal cord (Hirano & Zimmerman, 1962; reviewed in Kemper, 1984).

There is evidence that degree of tangle formation in neurons correlates with the degree of cognitive impairment in patients with senile dementia of the Alzheimer's type (Ball, 1976, 1978; Tomlinson et al., 1970;
Tomlinson & Henderson, 1976). It is likely that neurofibrillary tangles
disrupt many features of neuronal metabolism and activity and that the
degree of impairment in normal aging also will relate to the numbers of
neurons so affected.

GRANULOVACUOLAR DEGENERATION

Pyramidal neurons in human hippocampus are uniquely susceptible to
a form of neuronal pathology termed granulovacuolar degeneration
(GVD), in which the cytoplasm of the cells fills up with clear membrane-
bound vesicles, each of which contains a single small, dense granule. The
vesicles may fill the neuron, distorting its shape and undoubtedly interfering with its normal cellular functions. GVD is most prominent in area
CA1 of hippocampus, followed by CA2, the subiculum, and CA4 (Meencke
et al., 1983; Tomlinson, 1979). GVD is not common before age 60 years
(Tomlinson & Kitshner, 1972) but appears in approximately 20% of brains
after that age (Dayan, 1970). After age 80 years, 75% of brains have this
pathology (Tomlinson & Kitshner, 1972).

There is no clear relation of GVD to the neurofibrillary tangle or the
senile plaque. Although tangles and GVD may both exist in the same cell,
this is not the rule (Woodard, 1962). Further, high concentrations of GVD
may occur without any plaques or tangles (Tomlinson & Kitshner, 1972).
The only evidence that GVD may impair cognitive function comes from
its high incidence in the brains of patients with senile dementia of the
Alzheimer's type (Ball & Lo, 1977; Woodard, 1962). Of course, these
brains also are plagued with plaques and tangles.

A recent study by Hyman, van Hoesen, and Damasio (1990) analyzed
the pathology in memory-related neural systems that deteriorate in Alzheimer's disease and related this to known connectivity between these
structures. Because these same brain regions are affected (though to a lesser extent) in normal aging by plaques, tangles, GVD, and neuron dropout,
their findings are relevant here. The neurons in laminae II and IV of
entorhinal cortex, which project to hippocampus/amygdala and limbic/
association cortex, respectively, are also the most susceptible to neurofibrillary tangle formation. Hippocampal projections to entorhinal cortex, subiculum, limbic, and association cortex, and mamillary bodies arise
from CA1, subiculum, and the intervening prosubicular area, which are
highly prone to tangles as well as to GVD. Likewise, the amygdaloid nuclei
that are most prone to tangle formation are also the ones that send

efferents to entorhinal cortex and hippocampus. Further, the terminal zones of many of the projections of this memory-related neural system are prone to plaque formation.

Such pathology would disrupt severely neural transmission between entorhinal cortex, hippocampus, and amygdala, as well as between these key memory structures and their cortical and subcortical targets. Although pathology in normal aging is not of the magnitude seen in Alzheimer's disease, it is not unlikely that many of the cognitive changes seen in aging are due to the relatively higher degree of pathology in these specific memory-related structures than in other brain regions.

DENDRITIC STRUCTURE

A number of researchers have examined dendritic structure in the aging rat (Feldman, 1974, 1977; Geinisman & Bondareff, 1976; Geinisman, Bondareff, & Dodge, 1977; Vaughan, 1977), and have reported reduced branching complexity of basal and oblique dendrites of layer V pyramidal cells, as well as a thinning of dendritic spines in the visual and auditory cortex. In the rat and mouse occipital cortex, layer III pyramidal cells also show a decrease in dendritic arborization with age; this is especially evident in the distal apical dendritic branches of the oldest animals (Feldman, 1977; Leuba, 1983; Markus, Petit, & LeBoutillier, 1991). A similar reduction has been observed in layer III pyramidal cells in the auditory cortex (Vaughan, 1977). However, examinations of layer II pyramidal cells in entorhinal cortex (Coleman & Buell, 1983) and of layer IV stellate cells in mouse somatosensory cortex (Coleman, Buell, Magagna, Flood, & Curcio, 1986) revealed no dendritic changes over the life span.

Based on these findings, it would seem that life-span changes in dendritic configuration may be related closely to cortical region and cell type. More specifically, it appears that cells in laminae and cortical regions related to cortico-cortical processing of information are those most susceptible to dendritic deterioration with age. A behavioral implication is that sensory input would arrive fairly intact but that the impairment of higher cognitive operations would affect adversely both associational processes and any resultant motor output.

In the hippocampus, dentate gyrus granule cells show a slight decline in proximal dendrites with age (Markus, Petit, & LeBoutillier, 1991). Similar observations were made earlier by Geinisman et al. (1978) who, based on an electron microscopic analysis of the supragranular (i.e., proximal) dendritic zone, found a decrease in dentate dendritic shaft profiles in aged rats. This indicates that hippocampal commissural input to this zone is declining, most likely leading to decreased communication between the two hemispheres. Studies of hemispheric communication in aged organisms would seem to be called for.

In contrast to findings of dendritic decline with age in certain rat brain regions, in others an age-related increase in dendrites actually is found (Connor, Diamond, & Johnson, 1980; Flood, Beull, DeFiore, Horwitz, & Coleman, 1985; Hinds & McNelly, 1977). Flood and Coleman (1988) viewed these apparently discrepant age-related changes as a manifestation of the shifting balance between degenerative processes and compensatory proliferation of both synapses and dendritic branches. Thus, although some brain regions initially show compensatory dendritic proliferation to age-related neuronal loss, ultimately in old age a regression is found.

SYNAPTIC NUMBER AND STRUCTURE

As would be expected with dendritic atrophy, there appears to be an age-related decline in the number of synapses in the cerebral cortex of the rat. This has been observed as decreased synaptic density in the molecular layers of both the occipital and the parietal cortex (Adams & Jones, 1982; Markus, Petit, & LeBoutillier, 1991). In addition, the number of synapses per neuron has been estimated to decline following young adulthood and then to level off into old age (Markus, Petit, & LeBoutillier, 1991).

In the hippocampal dentate gyrus, decreases with age in synaptic density and in estimated number of synapses per neuron have been reported (Bertoni-Freddari, Giuli, Pieri, & Paci, 1986; Bertoni-Freddari, Giuli, Pieri, Paci, & Dravid, 1985; Bondareff & Geinisman, 1976; Geinisman & Bondareff, 1976; Geinisman et al., 1977; McWilliams & Lynch, 1984), although there are reports of synaptic stability in this region (Cotman & Scheff, 1979; Curcio & Hinds, 1983; Hoff, Scheff, Bernardo, & Cotman, 1982). In the CA4 region of the rat hippocampus, however, no age-related changes in synaptic density were observed (Markus, Petit, & LeBoutillier, 1991). Thus, as was found to be the case with dendritic branching, synaptic density and number vary according to the specific brain region examined, but generally appear to decline with age.

Several researchers also have attempted to determine if there are any age-related changes in the structure of the individual synapse itself. Adams and Jones (1982) found a decrease in the number of synaptic vesicles per presynaptic terminal in the rat parietal cortex, and Markus, Petit, and LeBoutillier (1991) recently observed a decrease in number of vesicles per unit length of occipital cortex synapses. Adams and Jones also observed a reduction in the area of the presynaptic and postsynaptic terminals. Quantitative measurements of the synapse itself indicate that both synaptic length and postsynaptic density area remain stable in the occipital and sensory motor cortex with age (Markus et al., 1987; Markus, Petit, Le-Boutillier, Brooks, & Winocur, 1991). Further, despite decreases in post-synaptic density width in occipital cortex, none were observed in motor cortex. Therefore, several parameters of synaptic size have been shown to decrease in many (but perhaps not all) neocortical regions.

Turning to the hippocampus, examination of synapses in the rat generally have shown no age-related changes in synaptic size or structure in the dentate gyrus (Bondareff & Geinisman, 1976; Markus, Petit, LeBoutillier, Brooks, & Winocur, 1991) or in CA1 pyramidal cell synapses (Scheff, Anderson, & DeKosky, 1984). However, in a more extensive study, Bertoni-Freddari et al. (1986) reported a decrease in synaptic length between young- and midadulthood followed by an actual increase in length during aging. Thus the status of change in hippocampal synapses with age is not clear at present. Consistent with findings in the cerebral cortex, though, aged animals were found to have fewer synaptic vesicles in the CA1 region of the hippocampus. Thus, whereas some aspects of synaptic change in hippocampus are analogous to those in neocortex, others may not be.

ANATOMICAL PLASTICITY

During development, there is a proliferation of dendrites and synapses, and even after reaching a mature configuration, the dendritic tree and synaptic component of the neuron continue to be plastic. The capacity of the neuron to respond anatomically by producing new dendritic and synaptic material is assumed to underlie learning and memory processes (see Petit, 1988, for review). Therefore, an examination of these plastic capacities of the neuron is of particular significance.

Plasticity has been induced or examined in aging using techniques such as environmental enrichment, lesion-induced synaptogenesis, and naturally occurring reactions to age-associated synaptic loss. Increases in dendrites and synapses can be induced through environmental stimulation (Turner & Greenough, 1985) or by the elimination of neighboring afferents (Hoff et al., 1982; McWilliams & Lynch, 1978, 1979; Steward & Vinsant, 1983). Studies examining environmental enrichment effects on general brain features have found changes during early adulthood that include increased occipital cortex thickness (Katz & Davies, 1984; Rosenzweig, Bennet, & Krech, 1964) and decreased neuronal packing density (Katz & Davies, 1984). In later adulthood and aging, these enrichment effects are reduced, with reports of increased cortical weight or thickness in middle-age (Riege, 1971) and aged rats (Diamond et al., 1985), as well as reports of no significant enrichment effects in middle-age (Connor et al., 1980; van Gool, Pronker, Mirmiram, & Uylings, 1987) and aged rats (Markus, Petit, & LeBoutillier, 1991; van Gool et al., 1987). Coinciding with these findings, examinations of neuronal packing density also have uncovered no effects of enrichment in old rats (Diamond et al., 1985; Markus, Petit, & LeBoutillier, 1991).

Enrichment-induced changes in neocortical dendritic structure also appear to become more difficult to produce with advancing age. Despite the dendritic plasticity found in adulthood (young, layers IV & V: Greenough, Juraska, & Volkmar, 1979; young, layers III & IV: Juraska, Greenough, Elliott, Mack, & Berkowitz, 1980; middle-age, layer III: Connor, Melone, Yuen, & Diamond, 1981; Green, Greenough, & Schlumpf, 1983), there are also reports of no enrichment effect (middle-age: Connor et al., 1980; old: Markus, Petit, & LeBoutillier, 1991; Markus, Petit, LeBoutillier, & Johnson, 1991).

Similar dendritic effects have been found in the hippocampus. Although enrichment during rearing causes significant dendritic proliferation in granule cells (Fiala, Joyce, & Greenough, 1978; only in females: Juraska, Fitch, Henderson, & Rivers, 1985) and CA3 pyramidal cells (Juraska, Fitch, & Washburne, 1989), the small amount of proliferation found with enrichment during adulthood was not significant (Fiala et al., 1978). An increased medial and distal dendritic branching of dentate granule cells has been observed following enrichment in aged animals (Markus, Petit, & LeBoutillier, 1991; Markus, Petit, LeBoutillier, & Johnson, 1991).

In terms of synapses, although rearing in an enriched environment has been reported to increase the number of synapses per unit area and per neuron in the superficial third (layers I to IV) of the occipital cortex (Turner & Greenough, 1985), Markus, Petit, and LeBoutillier (1991) and Markus, Petit, LeBoutillier, and Johnson (1991) did not observe any effects of enrichment on occipital cortex synaptic density in aged animals. Once again, brain region seems to be important; the effects of enrichment are not uniform.

In addition to age-related alterations in enrichment-induced synaptogenesis, researchers also have examined the response of the aged brain to lesion-induced synaptogenesis. During aging, synaptic sprouting seems to decline (Jones, 1988; McWilliams, 1988). This has been shown most clearly as a reduced sprouting response in the hippocampus following entorhinal damage (see McWilliams, 1988, for review).

Some researchers also have observed a compensatory plasticity in response to the "naturally occurring" synaptic and dendritic loss or denervation seen during aging. For example, although dendrites in general decrease in size during aging (Rogers & Styren, 1987), in some regions an age-related proliferation is found (Connor et al., 1980; Flood & Coleman, 1988; Flood et al., 1985; Hinds & McNelly, 1977). As mentioned earlier, Flood and Coleman suggested that although certain populations of neurons are undergoing atrophy during aging, others are undergoing a compensatory plastic proliferatory response. A similar suggestion has been made at the synaptic level, where increased synaptic size has been noted in humans in areas where synapses are decreasing in number (Dyson & Jones, 1980). These researchers suggested that the remaining synapses are increasing in size as a plastic compensatory response to adjacent synaptic loss.

It seems, therefore, that neuronal connections are quite dynamic even during aging, with a continuous interplay between growth and regression processes. Initial cell loss appears to be compensated for by a growth of dendrites and/or synapses. During aging, however, in addition to the increased cell loss, there is a reduction in the capacity or speed of compensatory growth processes, leading to only a partial compensation or recovery. Although retaining plasticity, the brain cannot completely accommodate the changes caused by age.

ELECTROPHYSIOLOGY AND PHYSIOLOGICAL PLASTICITY

A number of physiological parameters in neurons are known to change with age and any or all of these have potentially severe effects on the processing and integration of information in the brain. In some regions of the CNS, age-related reductions are found in conduction velocities (rat: Aston-Jones, Rogers, Shaver, Dinan, & Moss, 1985; Rogers, Zornetzer, & Bloom, 1981; human: Dorfman & Bosley, 1979; Hume, Cant, Shaw, & Cowen, 1982), and spontaneous firing rates of neurons (rat: Rogers et al., 1981; cat: Levine, Lloyd, Fischer, Hull, & Buchwald, 1987). Such evidence may be relevant to the hypothesis of overall cognitive slowing with age advanced by Salthouse (chapter 4 of this volume), a link worth pursuing. Consider some of the other relevant evidence.

Detailed examinations have shown aged cat caudate nucleus neurons are harder to drive, the duration of their inhibitory response to cortical and substantia nigra stimulation is decreased, and they are less able to respond at short intervals to a second stimulus (Levine, Lloyd, Hull, Fischer, & Buchwald, 1987). In the cerebellum of old rats, parallel fibers have a longer refractory period and a lower volley amplitude (Rogers et al., 1981). However, despite innervation by fewer fibers, the threshold for dentate nucleus activation does not change in old rats. Examining this question in hippocampus, Barnes and McNaughton (1980) found an increase in the excitability of the dentate gyrus granule cells. This results in hippocampal complex spike cells showing similar overall activity in young and old rats, but with a critical difference: The place-specific firing of cells in old rats is less precise (Barnes, McNaughton, & O'Keefe, 1983). The deficits seen in old rats on spatial tasks (e.g., Barnes, 1979) probably derive from these age-related changes in the firing properties of place cells.

Another factor contributing to age-related deficits in spatial learning is changes in hippocampal physiological plasticity. Frequency potentiation, which lasts for seconds (Landfield, McGaugh, & Lynch, 1978), long-term potentiation (LTP), which lasts for days (Landfield et al., 1978), and kindling, which lasts for months (deToledo-Morrell & Morrell, 1984) are all harder to induce in old rats with poor spatial memory than in young rats. In addition, LTP decays faster in old rats with poor spatial abilities than in unimpaired old rats (Barnes & McNaughton, 1985). It will be important to determine why poor spatial ability is the signature of such harder to induce and maintain neural processes.

SPATIAL LEARNING AND LONG-TERM RETENTION

Because age-related changes in human cognition are the focus of most chapters in this book, we focus instead on behavioral changes in experimental animals, and their correlation with the observed neural changes. An age-related decline in the number of neurons reduces the number of basic elements that the organism can use in the process of acquiring and storing information. Because neuronal communication takes place primarily at synaptic junctions, most of which occur on the dendritic component of the neuron, age-related changes in dendritic and synaptic configuration could have a profound effect on information processing.

A large body of research exists documenting spatial learning deficits in aged animals. Aged rats make more errors learning 4- and 14-choice maze problems (Goodrick, 1972; Ingram, 1988), a complex sequential T-maze (Goldman, Berman, Gershon, Murphy, & Altman, 1987; Warren, Zerweck, & Auletta, 1982), and Hebb–Williams type mazes (Markus, Petit, LeBoutillier, & Johnson, 1991). They also take longer or make more errors learning a radial arm maze (Beatty, Bierley, & Boyd, 1985; Geinisman, de Toledo-Morrell, & Morrell, 1986; Jucker, Oettinger, & Battig, 1988; Willig et al., 1987), a water maze (Rapp, Rosenberg, & Gallagher, 1987), and a circular platform maze (Barnes & McNaughton, 1985). Interestingly, though, little or no aging effects are found on tasks requiring non-spatial ability or a limited amount of discrimination learning (e.g., Goodrick, 1972; Winocur, 1986).

The foregoing strongly suggests that a prime instance of age-related deficits is spatial learning, which requires the animal to integrate information on spatial relations between objects and its own position. This ability is found to be extremely impaired in aged animals (Barnes, 1988; Rapp et al., 1987). In fact, a series of studies by Barnes and co-workers (Barnes, Green, Baldwin, & Johnson, 1987; Barnes, Nadel, & Honig, 1980; see also Rapp et al., 1987) revealed that aged rats, more than young rats, tend to use nonspatial strategies, perhaps to compensate for their declining spatial abilities. This spatial deficiency may well account for the deficits found in working memory.

Long-term retention also seems to be impaired in aged rats. Long-term retention deficits have been found in active and passive avoidance (e.g., Gold, McGaugh, Hankins, Rose, & Vasquez, 1981), as well as in spatial memory tasks (e.g., Barnes & McNaughton, 1985; Rapp et al., 1987). Highlighting that the problem is primarily over the long term, Markus, Petit, LeBoutillier, and Johnson (1991) observed that over the life span animals are increasingly impaired in their long-term (3-month) retention of a Hebb–Williams type maze, but that on an immediate retention task (passive avoidance: 10 s), no age-related effects appeared. Of course, although suggestive of retention deficits with aging, data on long-term retention inevitably are confounded with the acquisition process. Consequently such results may reflect a weaker or less reliable initial acquisition, the impact of which is revealed over time, rather than a memory trace that is decaying faster in the aged animal. As in the human literature, separating acquisition processes from retention processes is very difficult.

By comparing animals across the life span, researchers have tried to determine whether declines in cognition are seen across the entire life span or emerge only as the animal becomes old. Using a radial arm maze, Jucker et al. (1988) found a lifelong decline in working memory. Gold et al. (1981), comparing young to 1- and 2-year-old rats, found a decline in passive and active avoidance retention (3 weeks) as the age of animals increased. Similarly, in mice, Forster, Popper, Retz, and Lal (1988) found a decline in 48-hr retention of an active avoidance task from 3.5 months of age through adulthood and into old age. Markus, Petit, LeBoutillier, and Johnson (1991) observed a lifelong decrease in long-term retention, whereas difficulties in perseveration and deficits in maze learning were found only during old age. Taken together, these findings suggest a lifelong age-related decline in retention, but a possible "old-age only" decline in other behavioral capacities.

As just suggested, aging also appears to be associated with an increase in perseverative behavior. Aged rats are more susceptible to carry-over effects and show increased sensitivity to both proactive and retroactive interference (see Winocur, 1984). This perseveration is manifested in behaviors such as increased returns to the start box in a maze (Markus, Petit, LeBoutillier, & Johnson, 1991), increased entering of blind alleys in old animals (Jucker et al., 1988), deficits in extinction and reversal tasks in aged rats (Goodrick, 1972), and increased sensitivity to the intertrial interval (Winocur, 1986). Such perseverative behaviors may underlie in part deficits observed in learning and memory tasks.

BEHAVIORAL PLASTICITY

Similar to examining the effects of environmental enrichment on the neural plasticity of the brain, researchers also have examined the effects of enrichment on the behavioral capacities of aged animals. Goldman et al. (1987) showed that the degree of enrichment-related improvement was greater in young adult rats than in the middle-age and 24-month-old animals. Similar results were observed in maze learning by Markus, Petit, LeBoutillier, and Johnson (1991), where the primary improvements were observed in young enriched animals, with little or no improvement seen in aged enriched animals. Thus, behavioral plasticity appears to decline with age in at least some situations, and once again spatial tasks are strongly affected.

Motor activity, however, may be an exception. Markus, Petit, LeBoutillier, and Johnson (1991) observed a dramatic improvement in motor ability of enriched middle-age and old rats; their results are in agreement with similar research in young-adult rats (Gentile & Beheshti, 1987) and in middle-age rats (Riege, 1971), as well as in old mice (Warren et al., 1982). The Gentile and Beheshti study indicates that the significant factor may not be the amount of motor activity per se, but rather the type of activity: They showed a greater effect of enriched housing than of an exercise regime. Because exercise has been shown to have no effect on synaptic function at the neuromuscular junction of old mice (Herscovich & Gershon, 1987), it seems that the improvement in motor ability in the middle-age and old animals stems from changes at a central rather than a peripheral locus.

CONCLUSION

In this chapter, we have outlined the many and varied changes that occur in the nervous system as a result of aging. This is a focal research area in neuroscience, with new findings emerging at a very rapid rate. In some domains, a great deal is already known; in others, the surface barely has been scratched. We have tried to consider all of these areas and, in so doing, to speculate on the functional implications of age-related changes in the nervous system. Of course, such implications are not always evident, and in those cases we simply have described what is known at present. In all cases, the challenge will be to build the necessary bridges between changes in the neural substrate and changes in behavior with age. Here, as always, behavioral and physiological research should inform each other. Ultimately, a complete understanding of age changes will require the collaboration of these two approaches.

ACKNOWLEDGMENTS

The authors are deeply indebted to Judith Smith and Laurel Wheeler for their patience in typing this manuscript.

REFERENCES

Adams, I., & Jones, D. G. (1982). Quantitative ultrastructural changes in rat cortical synapses during early-, mid- and late-adulthood. *Brain Research, 239*, 349–363.

Agid, Y., Javoy-Agid, F., & Ruberg, M. (1987). Biochemistry of neurotransmitters in Parkinson's disease. In C. D. Marsden & S. T. Fahn (Eds.), *Movement disorders 2* (pp. 166–230). London: Butterworths.

Anderson, B., & Palmore, E. (1974). Longitudinal evaluation of ocular function. In E. Palmore (Ed.), *Normal aging II, Reports from the Duke longitudinal studies, 1970–1973* (pp. 24–32). Durham, NC: Duke University Press.

Andrew, S. (1971). *The anatomy of aging in man and animals.* New York: Grune & Stratton.

Aston-Jones, G., Rogers, J., Shaver, R. D., Dinan, T. G., & Moss, D. E. (1985). Age-impaired impulse flow from nucleus basalis to cortex. *Nature, 318*, 462–464.

Ball, M. J. (1976). Neurofibrillary tangles and the pathogenesis of dementia: A quantitative study. *Neuropathology and Applied Neurobiology, 2*, 395–410.

Ball, M. J. (1978). Topographic distribution nerve fibrillary tangles and granulovacuolar degeneration in hippocampal cortex of aging and demented patients: A quantitative study. *Acta Neuropathologica, 42*, 73–80.

Ball, M. J., & Lo, P. (1977). Granulovacuolar degeneration in the aging brain and in dementia. *Journal of Neuropathology and Experimental Neurology, 36*, 474–487.

Barnes, C. A. (1979). Memory deficits associated with senescence: A neurophysiological and behavioral study in the rat. *Journal of Comparative and Physiological Psychology, 93*, 74–104.

Barnes, C. A. (1988). Selectivity of neurological and mnemonic deficits in aged rats. In T. L. Petit & G. O. Ivy (Eds.), *Neural plasticity: A lifespan approach* (pp. 235–264). New York: Liss.

Barnes, C. A., Green, E. J., Baldwin, J., & Johnson, W. E. (1987). Behavioral and neurophysiological examples of functional sparing in senescent rat. *Canadian Journal of Psychology, 41*, 131–140.

Barnes, C. A., & McNaughton, B. L. (1980). Physiological compensation for loss of afferent synapses in the hippocampal granule cells during senescence. *Journal of Physiology (London), 309*, 473–485.

Barnes, C. A., & McNaughton, B. L. (1985). An age comparison of the rates of acquisition and forgetting of spatial information in relationship to long-term enhancement of hippocampal synapses. *Behavioral Neuroscience, 99*, 1040–1048.

Barnes, C. A., McNaughton, B. L., & O'Keefe, J. (1983). Loss of place specificity in hippocampal complex spike cells of the senescent rat. *Neurobiology of Aging, 4*, 113–119.

Barnes, C. A., Nadel, L., & Honig, W. K. (1980). Spatial memory deficit in senescent rats. *Canadian Journal of Psychology, 34*, 29–39.

Bartus, R. T. (1979). Effects of aging on visual memory, sensory processing, and discrimination learning in a nonhuman primate. *Aging, 10*, 85–114.

Bazelon, M., Fenichel, G. M., & Randall, J. (1967). Studies on neuromelanin. I. A melanin system in the human adult brain stem. *Neurology, 17*, 512–519.

Beatty, W. W., Bierley, R. A., & Boyd, J. G. (1985). Preservation of accurate spatial memory in aged rats. *Neurobiology of Aging, 6*, 219–225.

Bennett, C. L., Davis, R. T., & Miller, J. M. (1983). Demonstration of presbycusis across repeated measures in a non-human primate species. *Behavioural Neuroscience, 97*(4), 602–607.

Bertoni-Freddari, C., Giuli, R. F., Pieri, C., & Paci, D. (1986). Age-related morphological rearrangements of synaptic junctions in the rat cerebellum and hippocampus. *Archives of Gerontology and Geriatrics, 5*, 297–304.

Bertoni-Freddari, C., Giuli, R. F., Pieri, C., Paci, D., & Dravid, A. (1985). A modulating effect of Hydergine on the synaptic plasticity of old rats. *Journal of Pharmacology, 16*, 33–38.

Bhatnagar, K. P., Kennedy, R. C., Baron, G., & Greenberg, R. A. (1987). Number of mitral cells and the bulb volume in the aging human olfactory bulb: A quantitative morphological study. *Anatomical Record, 218*, 73–87.

Bondareff, W., & Geinisman, Y. (1976). Loss of synapses in the dentate gyrus of the senescent rat. *American Journal of Anatomy, 145*, 129–136.

Bondareff, W., & Mountjoy, C. Q. (1986). Number of neurons in nucleus locus ceruleus in demented and non-demented patients: Rapid estimation and correlated parameters. *Neurobiology of Aging, 7*, 297–300.

Bradley, R. M., Stedman, H. M., & Mistretta, C. M. (1985). Age does not affect numbers of taste buds and papillae in adult rhesus monkeys. *Anatomical Record, 212*, 246–249.

Brizzee, K. R., & Ordy, J. M. (1979). Age pigments, cell loss and hippocampal function. *Mechanisms of Aging and Development, 9*, 143–162.

Brizzee, K. R., Ordy, J. M., & Bartus, R. T. (1980). Localization of cellular changes within multimodal sensory regions in aged monkey brain: Possible implications for age-related cognitive loss. *Neurobiology of Aging, 1*, 45–52.

Brizzee, K. R., Ordy, J. M., Hansche, J., & Kaack, B. (1976). Quantitative assessment of changes in neuron and glia cell packing density and lipofuscin accumulation with age in the cerebral cortex of a nonhuman primate (*Macaca mulatta*). In R. D. Terry & S. Gershon (Eds.), *Neurobiology of aging* (pp. 229–244). New York: Raven.

Brizzee, K. R., Ordy, J. M., & Kaack, B. (1974). Early appearance and regional differences in intraneuronal and extraneuronal lipofuscin accumulation with age in the brain of a nonhuman primate (*Macaca mulatta*). *Journal of Gerontology, 29*(4), 366–381.

Brody, H. (1955). Organization of the cerebral cortex: 3. A study of aging in the human cerebral cortex. *Journal of Comparative Neurology, 102*, 511–556.

Brody, H. (1970). Structural changes in the aging nervous system. In H. T. Blumenthal (Ed.), *The regulatory role of the nervous system in aging: Vol. 7. Interdisciplinary topics in gerontology* (pp. 9–21). Basel, Switzerland: Karger.

Bruce, M. F. (1980). The relation of tactile thresholds to histology in the fingers of elderly people. *Journal of Neurology, Neurosurgery and Psychiatry, 43*, 730–734.

Brun, A., Gustafson, L., & Ingvar, D. H. (1975). *Neuropathological findings related to neuropsychiatric symptoms and regional cerebral blood flow in presenile dementia.* VIIth International Congress of Neuropathology, Budapest, 1974. Excerpta Medica, Amsterdam, pp. 101–105.

Burns, E. M., Kruckeberg, T. W., Comerford, L. E., & Buschmann, M. B. T. (1979). Thinning of capillary walls and declining numbers of endothelial mitochondria in the cerebral cortex of the aging primate, *Macaca nemestrina. Journal of Gerontology, 34,* 642–650.

Burns, E. M., Kruckeberg, T. W., Gaetano, P. K., & Shulman, L. M. (1983). Morphological changes in cerebral capillaries with age. In J. Cervos-Navarro & H. - I. Sarkander (Eds.), *Brain aging: Neuropathology and neuropharmacology (Aging,* Vol. 21, pp. 115–132). New York: Raven.

Campbell, B. A., & Gaddy, J. R. (1987). Rate of aging and dietary restriction: Sensory and motor function in the Fischer 344 rat. *Journal of Gerontology, 42,* 154–159.

Cash, R., Dennis, R., L'Heureux, R., Raiseman, R., Javoy-Agid, F., & Scatton, B. (1987). Parkinson's disease and dementia: Norepinephrine and dopamine in locus coeruleus. *Neurology, 37,* 42–46.

Chui, H. C., Mortimer, J. A., Slager, U. T., Barrow, C., Bondareff, W., & Webster, D. D. (1986). Pathological correlates of dementia in Parkinson's disease. *Archives of Neurology, 43,* 991–995.

Cohen, M. M., & Lessell, S. (1984). The neuro-ophthalmology of aging. In M. L. Albert (Ed.), *Clinical neurology of aging* (pp. 313–344). New York: Oxford University Press.

Coleman, P. D., & Buell, S. J. (1983). Dendritic extent of layer II pyramids in entorhinal cortex of aging F344 rat. *Society of Neuroscience Abstracts, 9,* 930.

Coleman, P. D., Buell, S. J., Magagna, L., Flood, D. G., & Curcio, C. A. (1986). Stability of dendrites in cortical barrels of C57BL/6N mice between 4 and 45 months. *Neurobiology of Aging, 7,* 101–105.

Coleman, P. D., & Flood, D. G. (1987). Neuron numbers and dendritic extent in normal aging and Alzheimer's disease. *Neurobiology of Aging, 8,* 521–545.

Coleman, P. D., Flood, D. G., & West, M. J. (1987). Volumes of the components of the hippocampus in the aging F344 rat. *Journal of Comparative Neurology, 266,* 300–306.

Collins, V. P., & Brunk, U. (1978). Quantitation of residual bodies in cultured human glial cells during stationary and logarithmic growth phases. *Mechanisms of Aging and Development, 8,* 139–152.

Connor, J. C., Diamond, M. C., & Johnson, R. E. (1980). Occipital cortical morphology of the rat: Alterations with age and environment. *Experimental Neurology, 68,* 158–170.

Connor, J. C., Melone, J. H., Yuen, A. R., & Diamond, M. C. (1981). Dendritic length in aged rats' occipital cortex: An environmentally induced response. *Experimental Neurology, 73,* 827–830.

Corsellis, J. A. W. (1976). Some observations on the Purkinje cell population and on brain volume in human aging. In R. D. Terry & S. Gershon (Eds.), *Neurobiology of aging* (pp. 205–209). New York: Raven.

Corso, J. F. (1981). *Aging sensory systems and perception.* New York: Praeger.

Cotman, C. W., & Scheff, S. W. (1979). Compensatory synapse growth in aged animals after neuronal death. *Mechanisms of Aging and Development, 9,* 103–117.

Cras, P., Kawai, M., Siedlak, S., Mulvihill, P., Gambetti, P., Lowery, D., Gonzalez-DeWhitt, P., Greenberg, B., & Perry, G. (1990). Rapid communication: Neuronal and microglial involvement in β-amyloid protein deposition in Alzheimer's disease. *American Journal of Pathology, 137,* 241–246.

Curcio, C. A., & Coleman, P. D. (1982). Stability of neuron number in cortical barrels of aging mice. *Journal of Comparative Neurology, 212,* 158–172.

Curcio, C. A., & Hinds, J. W. (1983). Stability of synaptic density and spine volume in dentate gyrus of aged rats. *Neurobiology of Aging, 4,* 77–87.

Curcio, C. A., McNelly, N. A., & Hinds, J. W. (1985). Aging in the rat olfactory system: Relative stability of piriform cortex contrasts with changes in olfactory bulb and olfactory epithelium. *Journal of Comparative Neurology, 235,* 519–528.

Dastur, D. K., Lane, M. H., Hansen, D. B., Kety, S. S., Butler, R. N., Perlin, S., & Sokoloff, L. (1963). Effects of aging on cerebral circulation and metabolism. In J. E. Birren, R. N. Butler, S. W. Greenhouse, L. Sokoloff, & M. R. Yarrow (Eds.), *Human aging* (pp. 59–76). Public Health Service Publication No. 986.

Davies, I., & Fotheringham, A. P. (1981). Lipofuscin—Does it affect cellular performance? *Experimental Gerontology, 16,* 119–125.

Dayan, A. D. (1970). Quantitative histological studies on the aged human brain. *Acta Neuropathologica (Berlin), 16,* 85–94.

Delacourte, A., & Defossez, A. (1986). Alzheimer's disease: Tau proteins, the promoting factors of microtubule assembly, are major components of paired helical filaments. *Journal of Neurological Science, 76,* 173–186.

deToledo-Morrell, L., & Morrell, F. (1984). Age dependent deficits in spatial memory are related to impaired hippocampal kindling. *Behavioral Neuroscience, 98,* 902–907.

Diamond, M. C., Johnson, R. E., Protti, A. M., Ott, C., & Kajisa, L. (1985). Plasticity in the 904-day-old male rat cerebral cortex. *Experimental Neurology, 87,* 309–317.

Dorfman, L. J., & Bosley, T. M. (1979). Age-related changes in peripheral and central nerve conduction in man. *Neurology, 29,* 38–44.

Doty, R. L., Reyes, P. F., & Gregor, T. (1987). Presence of both odor identification and detection deficits in Alzheimer's disease. *Brain Research Bulletin, 18,* 597–600.

Doty, R. L., Shaman, P., Applebaum, S. L., Giberson, R., Siksorski, L., & Rosenberg, L. (1984). Smell identification ability: Changes with age. *Science, 226,* 1441–1443.

Dyson, S. E., & Jones, D. G. (1980). Quantitation of terminal parameters and their interrelationships in maturing central synapses: A perspective for experimental studies. *Brain Research, 183,* 43–59.

Ellis, R. S. (1920). Norms for some structural changes in the human cerebellum from birth to old age. *Journal of Comparative Neurology, 32,* 1–33.

Fang, H. C. H. (1976). Observation of aging characteristics of cerebral blood vessels: Macroscopic and microscopic features. In R. D. Terry & S. Gershon (Eds.), *Neurobiology of aging* (pp. 240–247). New York: Raven.

Feldman, M. L. (1974). Degenerative changes in aging dendritis. *Gerontologist, 14*(Suppl.), 36–38.

Feldman, M. L. (1977). Dendritic changes in aging rat brain: Pyramidal cell dendrite length and ultrastructure. In K. Nandy & I. Sherwin (Eds.), *The aging brain and senile dementia: Advances in behavioral biology* (Vol. 23, pp. 117–123). New York: Plenum.

Fiala, B. A., Joyce, J. N., & Greenough, W. T. (1978). Environmental complexity modulates growth of granula cell dendrites in developing but not adult hippocampus of rats. *Experimental Neurology, 59,* 372–383.

Finch, C. E., & Morgan, D. G. (1990). RNA and protein metabolism in the aging brain. *Annual Review of Neuroscience, 13,* 75–87.

Fix, J. D. (1980). A melanin-containing nucleus associated with the superior cerebellar peduncle in man. *Journal für Hirnforschung, 21,* 429–436.

Flood, D. G., Beull, S. J., DeFiore, C. H., Horwitz, G. J., & Coleman, P. D. (1985). Age-related dendritic growth in dentate gyrus of human brain is followed by regression in the 'oldest old'. *Brain Research, 345,* 366–368.

Flood, D. G., & Coleman, P. D. (1988). Cell type heterogeneity of changes in dendritic extent in the hippocampal region of the human brain in normal aging and in Alzheimer's disease. In T. L. Petit & G. O. Ivy (Eds.), *Neural plasticity: A lifespan approach* (pp. 265–281). New York: Liss.

Forno, L. S., & Alvord, E. C., Jr. (1971). Some new observations and correlations. In F. H. McDowell & C. H. Markham (Eds.), *Recent advances in Parkinson's disease (Contemporary neurology series, No. 8)* (pp. 120–130). Philadelphia: Davis.

Forster, M. J., Popper, M. D., Retz, K. C., & Lal, H. (1988). Age differences in acquisition and retention of one-way avoidance learning in C57BL/6NNia and autoimmune mice. *Behavioral and Neural Biology, 49*, 139–151.

Fozard, J. L. (1990). Vision and hearing in aging. In J. E. Birren & K. W. Shaie (Eds.), *Handbook of the psychology of aging* (3rd ed., pp. 50–83). New York: Academic.

Geinisman, Y., & Bondareff, W. (1976). Decrease in the number of synapses in the senescent brain: A quantitative electron microscopic analysis of the dentate gyrus molecular layer in the rat. *Mechanisms of Aging and Development, 5*, 11–23.

Geinisman, Y., Bondareff, W., & Dodge, J. T. (1977). Partial deafferentation of neurons in the dentate gyrus of the senescent rat. *Brain Research, 134*, 541–545.

Geinisman, Y., Bondareff, W., & Dodge, J. T. (1978). Dendritic atrophy in the dentate gyrus of the senescent rat. *American Journal of Anatomy, 152*, 321–330.

Geinisman, Y., de Toledo-Morrell, L., & Morrell, F. (1986). Aged rats need a preserved complement of perforated axospinous synapses per hippocampal neuron to maintain good spatial memory. *Brain Research, 398*, 266–275.

Gellerstedt, N. (1933). *Zur kenntnis der Hirnveranderungen bei der Normalen Altersunvolution* [(Contributions) to the knowledge of brain changes during normal aging]. Uppsala, Sweden: Almquist & Wiksells Boktryckeri -A -B.

Gentile, A. M., & Beheshti, Z. (1987). Enrichment versus exercise effects on motor impairments following cortical removals in rats. *Behavioral and Neural Biology, 47*, 321–332.

Gilbert, A. N., & Wysocki, C. J. (1987). The smell survey results. *National Geographic, 170*, 324–361.

Gilbert, J. G. (1957). Age changes in color matching. *Journal of Gerontology, 12*, 210–215.

Gold, P. E., McGaugh, J. L., Hankins, L. L., Rose, R. P., & Vasquez, B. J. (1981). Age dependent changes in retention in rats. *Experimental Aging Research, 8*, 53–58.

Goldman, H., Berman, R. F., Gershon, S., Murphy, S. L., & Altman, H. J. (1987). Correlation of behavioral and cerebrovascular functions in the aging rat. *Neurobiology of Aging, 8*, 409–416.

Goodrick, C. L. (1972). Learning by mature-young and aged Wistar albino rats as a function of test complexity. *Journal of Gerontology, 27*, 353–357.

Graziadei, P. P. C., & Graziadei, G. A. M. (1978). The olfactory system: A model for the study of neurogenesis and axon regeneration in mammals. In C. Cotman (Ed.), *Neuronal plasticity* (pp. 131–154). New York: Raven.

Green, E. J., Greenough, W. T., & Schlumpf, B. E. (1983). Effects of complex or isolated environments on cortical dendrites of middle aged rats. *Brain Research, 264*, 233–240.

Greenough, W. T., Juraska, J. M., & Volkmar, F. R. (1979). Maze training effects on dendritic branching in occipital cortex of adult rats. *Behavioral and Neural Biology, 26*, 287–297.

Grundke-Iqbal, I., Iqbal, K., Quinlan, M., Tung, Y. -C., Wang, G., & Wisniewski, H. M. (1986). Microtubule associated protein tau: A component of Alzheimer paired helical filaments. *Journal of Biological Chemistry, 261*, 6084–6089.

Grzegorczyk, P. B., Jones, S. W., & Mistretta, C. M. (1979). Age-related differences in salt taste acuity. *Journal of Gerontology, 34*, 834–840.

Hagberg, B., & Ingvar, D. H. (1976). Cognitive reduction in presenile dementia related to regional abnormalities of the cerebral blood flow. *British Journal of Psychiatry, 128*, 209–222.

Hall, T. C., Miller, A. K. H., & Corsellis, J. A. N. (1975). Variations in the human Purkinje cell population according to age and sex. *Neuropathology and Applied Neurobiology, 1*, 267–292.

Hamm, R. J., & Knisely, J. S. (1985). Environmentally induced analgesia: An age related decline in an endogenous opioid system. *Journal of Gerontology, 40,* 268–274.

Hansen, L. A., Armstrong, D. M., & Terry, R. D. (1987). An immunohistochemical quantification of fibrous astrocytes in the aging human cerebral cortex. *Neurobiology of Aging, 8,* 1–6.

Harman, D. (1990). Lipofuscin and ceroid formation: The cellular recycling system. In E. A. Porta (Ed.), *Lipofuscin and ceroid pigments* (pp. 3–15). New York: Plenum.

Henderson, G., Tomlinson, B. E., & Gibson, P. H. (1980). Cell counts in human cerebral cortex in normal adults throughout life using an image analysing computer. *Journal of Neurological Science, 46,* 113–136.

Herscovich, S., & Gershon, D. (1987). Effects of aging and physical training on the neuromuscular junction of the mouse. *Gerontology, 33,* 7–13.

Hinds, J. W., & McNelly, N. A. (1977). Aging of the rat olfactory bulb: Growth and atrophy of constituent layers and changes in size and number of mitral cells. *Journal of Comparative Neurology, 171,* 345–368.

Hinds, J. W., & McNelly, N. A. (1979). Aging in the rat olfactory bulb: Quantitative changes in mitral cell organelles and somato-dendritic synapses. *Journal of Comparative Neurology, 184,* 811–820.

Hinds, J. W., & McNelly, N. A. (1981). Aging in the rat olfactory system: Correlation of changes in the olfactory epithelium and olfactory bulb. *Journal of Comparative Neurology, 203,* 441–453.

Hirano, A., & Zimmerman, H. M. (1962). Alzheimer's neurofibrillary changes. *Archives of Neurology, 7,* 73–88.

Hoff, S. F., Scheff, S. W., Bernardo, L. S., & Cotman, C. W. (1982). Lesion-induced synaptogenesis in the dentate gyrus of aged rats: 1. Loss and reacquisition of normal synaptic density. *Journal of Comparative Neurology, 205,* 246–252.

Hueck, W. (1912). Pigmentstudien [Pigment Studies]. *Beitraege zur Pathologischen Anatomie und zur Allgemeinen Pathologie, 54,* 68–232.

Hume, A. L., Cant, B. R., Shaw, N. A., & Cowen, J. C. (1982). Central somatosensory conduction time from 10 to 79 years. *Electroencephalography and Clinical Neurophysiology, 54,* 49–54.

Hyman, B. T., van Hoesen, G. W., & Damasio, A. R. (1990). Memory-related neural systems in Alzheimer's disease: An anatomic study. *Neurology, 40,* 1721–1730.

Ihara, Y., Nukina, N., Miura, R., & Ogawara, M. (1986). Phosphorylated Tau protein is integrated into paired helical filaments in Alzheimer's disease. *Journal of Biochemistry, 99,* 1807–1810.

Ingram, D. (1988). Complex maze learning in rodents as a model of age-related memory impairment. *Neurobiology of Aging, 9,* 475–485.

Ingvar, D. H. (1975). Brain work in presenile dementia and in chronic schizophrenia. In *Brain work* (pp. 478–492). Copenhagen: Munksgaard.

Ingvar, D. H., Risberg, J., & Schwartz, M. S. (1975). Evidence of subnormal function of association cortex in presenile dementia. *Neurology, 10,* 964–974.

Inukai, T. (1928). On the loss of Purkinje cells, with advancing age, from the cerebellar cortex of the albino rat. *Journal of Comparative Neurology, 45,* 1–31.

Ivy, G. O., Kanai, S., Ohta, M., Smith, G., Sato, Y., Kobayashi, M., & Kitani, K. (1990). Lipofuscin-like substances accumulate rapidly in brain, retina and internal organs with cysteine protease inhibition. In E. A. Porta (Ed.), *Lipofuscin and ceroid pigments* (pp. 31–47). New York: Plenum.

Jellinger, K. (1987). The pathology of parkinsonism. In C. D. Marsden & S. T. Fahn (Eds.), *Movement disorders 2* (pp. 124–165). London: Butterworths.

Johansson, R. S. (1979). Tactile sensibility in the human hand: Receptive field characteristics of mechanoreceptive units in the glabrous skin area. *Journal of Physiology, 281,* 101–123.

Jones, D. G. (1988). Synaptic trends and synaptic remodelling in the developing and mature neocortex. In T. L. Petit & G. O. Ivy (Eds.), *Neural plasticity: A lifespan approach* (pp. 21–42). New York: Liss.

Jucker, M., Oettinger, R., & Battig, K. (1988). Age-related changes in working and reference memory performance and locomotor activity. *Behavioral and Neural Biology, 50*, 24–36.

Juraska, J. M., Fitch, J. M., Henderson, C., & Rivers, N. (1985). Sex differences in the dendritic branching of dentate granule cells following differential experience. *Brain Research, 333*, 73–80.

Juraska, J. M., Fitch, J. M., & Washburne, D. L. (1989). The dendritic morphology of pyramidal neurons in the hippocampal CA3 area: 2. Effects of gender and the environment. *Brain Research, 479*, 115–119.

Kadar, T., Silbermann, M., Brandeis, R., & Levy, A. (1990). Age-related structural changes in the rat hippocampus: Correlation with working memory deficiency. *Brain Research, 512*, 113–120.

Katz, H. B., & Davies, C. A. (1984). Effects of different environments on the cerebral anatomy of rats as a function of previous and subsequent housing conditions. *Experimental Neurology, 83*, 274–287.

Kemper, T. L. (1978). Senile dementia: A focal disease in the temporal lobe. In K. Nandy (Ed.), *Senile dementia: A biomedical approach* (pp. 105–113). Amsterdam: Elsevier.

Kemper, T. (1984). Neuroanatomical and neuropathological changes in normal aging and in dementia. In M. L. Albert (Ed.), *Clinical neurology of aging* (pp. 9–52). New York: Oxford University Press.

Kermis, M. D. (1984). *Psychology of human aging: Theory, research, and practice*. Toronto: Allyn & Bacon.

Kidd, M. (1964). Alzheimer's disease. An electronmicroscope study. *Brain, 87*, 307–327.

Knox, C. A., Jirge, S. K., Brizzee, K. R., Ordy, J. M., & Bartus, R. T. (1979). Quantitative analysis of synaptic junctions, axon preterminals and astroglial processes in the hippocampus of young and old rhesus monkeys. *Society for Neuroscience Abstracts, 5*, 18.

Korr, H. (1980). Proliferation of different cell types in the brain. *Advances in Anatomy, and Embryology and Cell Biology, 61*, 1–72.

Korr, H. (1982). Proliferation of different cell types in the brain of senile mice: Autoradiographic studies with ^{3}H- and ^{14}C-Thymidine. *Experimental Brain Research*, (Suppl. 5), 51–57.

Koss, E., Weiffenbach, J., Haxby, J., & Friedland, R. (1988). Olfactory detection and identification performance are dissociated in early Alzheimer's disease. *Neurology, 38*, 1228–1232.

Landfield, P. W., McGaugh, J. L., & Lynch, G. (1978). Impaired synaptic potentiation processes in the hippocampus of aged, memory-deficient rats. *Brain Research, 150*, 85–101.

Landfield, P. W., Rose, G., Sandles, L., Wohlstadter, T. C., & Lynch, G. S. (1977). Patterns of astroglial hypertrophy and neuronal degeneration in the hippocampus of aged, memory-deficient rats. *Journal of Gerontology, 32*, 3–12.

Lassen, N. A. (1959). Cerebral blood flow and oxygen consumption in man. *Physiological Review, 39*, 183–238.

Lassen, N. A., Feinberg, J., & Lane, M. H. (1960). Bilateral studies of cerebral oxygen uptake in young and aged normal subjects and in patients with organic dementia. *Journal of Clinical Investigation, 39*, 491–500.

Leuba, G. (1983). Aging of dendrites in the cerebral cortex of the mouse. *Neuropathology and Applied Neurobiology, 9*, 467–475.

Levine, M. S., Lloyd, R. L., Fischer, R. S., Hull, C. D., & Buchwald, N. A. (1987). Sensory, motor and cognitive alterations in aged cats. *Neurobiology of Aging, 8*, 253–263.

Levine, M. S., Lloyd, R. L., Hull, C. D., Fischer, R. S., & Buchwald, N. A. (1987). Neurophysiological alterations in caudate neurons in aged cats. *Brain Research, 401*, 213–230.

Lindsey, J. D., Landfield, P. W., & Lynch, G. (1979). Early onset and topographical distribution of hypertrophied astrocytes in hippocampus of aging rats: A quantitative study. *Journal of Gerontology, 34*, 661–671.

Mancardi, G. L., Perdelli, F., Rivano, C., Leonarde, A., & Bugiani, O. (1980). Thickening of the basement membrane of cortical capillaries in Alzheimer's disease. *Acta Neuropathologica, 49*, 79–85.

Mann, D. M. A., Yates, P. O., & Barton, C. M. (1977). Neuromelanin and RNA in cells of substantia nigra. *Journal of Neuropathology and Experimental Neurology, 36*, 379–383.

Mann, D. M. A., Yates, P. O., & Hawkes, J. (1983). The pathology of the human locus coeruleus. *Clinical Neuropathology, 2*, 1–7.

Mann, D. M., Yates, P. O., & Stamp, J. E. (1979). The relationship between lipofuscin pigment and aging in the human nervous system. *Journal of Neurological Science, 37*, 83–93.

Markus, E. J., Petit, T. L., & LeBoutillier, J. C. (1987). Synaptic structural change during development and aging. *Developmental Brain Research, 35*, 239–248.

Markus, E. J., Petit, T. L., & LeBoutillier, J. C. (1991). *Lifespan plasticity in the rat: 2. Occipital and hippocampal neuronal dendritic and synaptic morphology.* Manuscript submitted for publication.

Markus, E. J., Petit, T. L., LeBoutillier, J. C., Brooks, W. J., & Winocur, G. (1991). *Morphological characteristics of the synapse: Relationship to synaptic change.* Manuscript submitted for publication.

Markus, E. J., Petit, T. L., LeBoutillier, J. C., & Johnson, S. (1991). *Lifespan plasticity in the rat: I. Learning and memory.* Manuscript submitted for publication.

Mathewson, R. C., & Nava, P. B. (1985). Effects of age on Meissner corpuscles: A study of silver-impregnated neurites in mouse digital pads. *Journal of Comparative Neurology, 231*, 250–259.

Matsuyama, H., & Nakamura, S. (1978). Senile changes in the brain in the Japanese: Incidence of Alzheimer's neurofibrillary change and senile plaques. *Aging (New York), 7*, 287–297.

McGeer, P. L., McGeer, E. G., & Suzuki, J. S. (1977). Aging and extrapyramidal function. *Archives of Neurology, 34*, 33–35.

McWilliams, J. R. R. (1988). Age related declines in anatomical plasticity and axonal sprouting. In T. L. Petit & G. O. Ivy (Eds.), *Neural plasticity: A lifespan approach* (pp. 329–349). New York: Liss.

McWilliams, J. R. R., & Lynch, G. (1978). Terminal proliferation and synaptogenesis following partial deafferentation: The reinnervation of the inner molecular layer of the dentate gyrus following removal of its inner commissural afferents. *Journal of Comparative Neurology, 180*, 581–616.

McWilliams, J. R. R., & Lynch, G. (1979). Terminal proliferation in the partially deafferentated dentate gyrus: Time course for the appearance and removal of degeneration and replacement of lost terminals. *Journal of Comparative Neurology, 187*, 191–198.

McWilliams, J. R. R., & Lynch, G. (1984). Synaptic density and axonal sprouting in rat hippocampus: Stability in adulthood and decline in late adulthood. *Brain Research, 294*, 152–156.

Meencke, H. -J., Ferszt, R., Gertz, H. -J., & Cervos-Navarro, J. (1983). Hippocampal pathology in normal aging and dementia. In J. Cervos-Navarro & H. -I. Sarkander (Eds.), *Brain aging: Neuropathology and neuropharmacology* (*Aging*, Vol. 21, pp. 13–26). New York: Raven.

Miller, I. J. (1986). Variation in human fungiform taste bud densities among regions and subjects. *Anatomical Record, 216*, 474–482.

Miller, I. J. (1988). Human taste bud density across adult age groups. *Journal of Gerontology, 143*, 26–30.

Minckler, T. M., & Boyd, E. (1968). Physical growth. In J. Minckler (Ed.), *Pathology of the nervous system* (Vol. 1, pp. 98–122). New York: McGraw-Hill.

Mistretta, C. M., & Baum, B. J. (1984). Quantitative study of taste buds in fungiform and circumvallate papillae of young and aged rats. *Journal of Anatomy, 138*, 323–332.

Mistretta, C. M., & Oakley, I. A. (1986). Quantitative anatomical study of taste buds in fungiform papillae of young and old Fischer rats. *Journal of Gerontology, 41*, 315–318.

Moatamed, F. (1966). Cell frequencies in the human inferior olivary nuclear complex. *Journal of Comparative Neurology, 128*, 109–116.

Monagle, R. D., & Brody, H. (1974). The effects of age upon the main nucleus of the inferior olive in the human. *Journal of Comparative Neurology, 155*, 61.

Moore, L. M., Nielson, C. R., & Mistretta, C. M. (1982). Sucrose taste thresholds: Age-related differences. *Journal of Gerontology, 37*, 64–69.

Morimatzu, W. M. (1975). On some involutional changes in the hippocampal changes of elderly brains. *Japanese Journal of Geriatrics, 21*, 30–40.

Moses, S., Rotem, Y., Jagoda, N., Talmor, N., Eichhorn, F., & Levin, S. (1967). A clinical, genetic and biochemical study of familial dysautonomia in Israel. *1st. J. Med. Sci., 3*, 358–371.

Nandy, K. (1981). Morphological changes in the cerebellar cortex of aging *Macaca nemestrina. Neurobiology of Aging, 2*, 61–64.

Ordy, J. M., & Brizzee, K. R. (1975). *Advances in behavioural biology* (Vol. 16). London: Plenum.

Ordy, J. M., & Brizzee, K. R. (1979). *Sensory systems and communication in the elderly* (Vol. 10). New York: Raven.

Ordy, J. M., Kaack, B., & Brizzee, K. R. (1975). Life-span neurochemical changes in the human and non-human primate brain. In H. Brody, D. Harman, & J. M. Ordy (Eds.), *Aging* (Vol. 1, pp. 133–190). New York: Raven.

Peters, A., Feldman, M. L., & Vaughan, D. W. (1983). The effects of aging on the neuronal population within area 17 of adult rat cerebral cortex. *Neurobiology of Aging, 4*, 273–282.

Peters, A., Harriman, K. M., & West, C. D. (1987). The effects of increased longevity, produced by dietary restriction, on the neuronal population of area 17 in rat cerebral cortex. *Neurobiology of Aging, 8*, 7–20.

Petit, T. L. (1988). Synaptic plasticity and the structural basis of learning and memory. In T. L. Petit & G. O. Ivy (Eds.), *Neural plasticity: A lifespan approach* (pp. 201–234). New York: Liss.

Rapp, P. R., Rosenberg, R. A., & Gallagher, M. (1987). An evaluation of spatial information processing in aged rats. *Behavioral Neuroscience, 101*, 3–12.

Rezek, D. J. (1987). Olfactory deficits as a neurologic sign in dementia of the Alzheimer type. *Archives of Neurology, 44*, 1030–1032.

Ricci, A., Ramacci, M. T., Ghirardi, O., & Amenta, F. (1989). Age-related changes of the mossy fibre system in rat hippocampus: Effects of long term acetyl-L-carnitine treatment. *Archives of Gerontology Geriatrics, 8*, 63–71.

Riege, W. H. (1971). Environmental influences on brain and behavior of year-old rats. *Developmental Psychobiology, 4*, 157–167.

Roberts, E. (1986). Alzheimer's disease may begin in the nose and may be caused by aluminosilicates. *Neurobiology of Aging, 7*, 561–567.

Rogers, J., Silver, M. A., Shoemaker, W. J., & Bloom, F. E. (1980). Senescent changes in a neurobiological model system: Cerebellar Purkinje cell electrophysiology and correlative anatomy. *Neurobiology of Aging, 1*, 3–11.

Rogers, J., & Styren, S. D. (1987). Neuroanatomy of aging and dementia. *Review of Biological Research on Aging, 3,* 223–253.

Rogers, J., Zornetzer, S. F., & Bloom, F. E. (1981). Senescent pathology of cerebellum: Purkinje neurons and their parallel fiber afferents. *Neurobiology of Aging, 2,* 15–25.

Rosenzweig, M. R., Bennet, E. L., & Krech, D. (1964). Cerebellar effects of environmental complexity and training among adult rats. *Journal of Comparative and Physiological Psychology, 57,* 438–439.

Sabel, B. A., & Stein, D. G. (1981). Extensive loss of subcortical neurons in the aging rat brain. *Experimental Neurology, 73,* 507–516.

Said, F. S., & Weale, R. A. (1959). The variation with age of the spectral transmissivity of the living human crystalline lens. *Gerontologia, 3,* 213–231.

Sandoz, P. (1977). Age-related loss of nerve cells from the human inferior olive and unchanged volume of its grey matter. *IRCS Journal of Medical Science, 5,* 376.

Sartin, J. L., & Lamperti, A. A. (1985). Neuron numbers in the hypothalamic nuclei of young, middle-aged and aged male rats. *Experientia, 41,* 109–111.

Schaie, K. W., & Geiwitz, J. (1982). *Adult development and aging.* Toronto: Little, Brown.

Schaumburg, H. H., Spencer, P. S., & Ochoa, J. (1983). The aging human peripheral nervous system. In R. Katzman & R. Terry (Eds.), *The neurology of aging* (pp. 111–122). Philadelphia: Davis.

Schechter, R., Yen, S. -H. C., & Terry, R. D. (1981). Fibrous astrocytes in senile dementia of the Alzheimer type. *Journal of Neuropathology and Experimental Neurology, 40,* 95–101.

Scheff, S. W., Anderson, K. J., & DeKosky, S. T. (1984). Strain comparison of synaptic density in hippocampal CA1 of aged rats. *Neurobiology of Aging, 41,* 109–111.

Scheibel, M. E., & Scheibel, A. B. (1975). Structural changes in the aging brain. In H. Brody, D. Harman, & J. M. Ordy (Eds.), *Aging* (Vol. 1, pp. 11–37). New York: Raven.

Schiffman, S. (1977). Food recognition by the elderly. *Journal of Gerontology, 32,* 586–592.

Schimriqk, K., & Ruttinger, H. (1980). The touch corpuscles of the plantar surface of the big toe: Histological and histometrical investigations with respect to age. *European Neurology, 19,* 49–60.

Schmidt, C. F. (1950). *The cerebral circulation in health and disease.* Springfield, IL: Thomas.

Simchowicz, R. (1907). Histologische studien über senile demenz [Histological studies on senile dementia]. *Nissl-Alzheimers Arb. IV,* 1.

Spielmeyer, W. (1922). *Histopathologie des nervensystems* [Histopathology of nervous system]. Berlin: Springer-Verlag.

Steward, O., & Vinsant, S. L. (1983). The process of reinnervation in the dentate gyrus of the adult rat: A quantitative electron microscopic analysis of terminal proliferation and reactive synaptogenesis. *Journal of Comparative Neurology, 214,* 370–386.

Sturrock, R. R. (1980). A comparative quantitative and morphological study of ageing in the mouse neostriatum, indusium griseum and anterior commissure. *Neuropathology and Applied Neurobiology, 6,* 51–68.

Tatton, W. G., Greenwood, C. E., Verrier, M. C., Holland, D. P., Kwan, M. M., & Biddle, F. G. (in press). Different rates of age-related loss for four murine monoaminergic neuronal populations. *Neurobiology of Aging, 12.*

Terry, R. D., & Davies, P. (1980). Dementia of the Alzheimer type. *Annual Review of Neuroscience, 3,* 77–95.

Terry, R. D., & DeTeresa, R. (1982). The importance of video editing in automated image analysis in studies of the cerebral cortex. *Journal of Neurological Science, 53,* 413–421.

Terry, R. D., DeTeresa, R., & Hansen, L. A. (1987). Neocortical cell counts in normal human adult aging. *Annals of Neurology, 21,* 530–539.

Terry, R. D., & Wisniewski, H. M. (1972). Ultrastructure of senile dementia and of experimental analogs. In C. M. Gaitz (Ed.), *Aging and the brain*. New York: Plenum.

Thornbury, J. M., & Mistretta, C. M. (1981). Tactile sensitivity as a function of age. *Journal of Gerontology, 36*, 34–39.

Tomlinson, B. E. (1979). The ageing brain. In W. T. Smith & J. B. Cavanagh (Eds.), *Recent advances in neuropathology* (pp. 129–159). Amsterdam: Elsevier.

Tomlinson, B. E., Blessed, G., & Roth, M. (1968). Observations on the brain of non-demented old people. *Journal of Neurological Science, 7*, 331–356.

Tomlinson, B. E., Blessed, G., & Roth, M. (1970). Observations of the brain of demented old people. *Journal of Neurological Science, 11*, 205–242.

Tomlinson, B. E., & Henderson, G. (1976). Some quantitative cerebral findings in normal and demented old people. In R. D. Terry & S. Gershon (Eds.), *Neurobiology of aging* (pp. 183–204). New York: Raven.

Tomlinson, B. E., & Kitshner, D. (1972). Granulovacuolar degeneration of hippocampal pyramidal cells. *Journal of Pathology, 106*, 165–185.

Turner, A. M., & Greenough, W. T. (1985). Differential rearing effects on rat visual cortex synapses: 1. Synaptic and neuronal density and synapses per neuron. *Brain Research, 329*, 195–203.

van Gool, W. A., Pronker, H. F., Mirmiram, M., & Uylings, H. B. M. (1987). Effects of housing in an enriched environment on the size of the cerebral cortex in young and old rats. *Experimental Neurology, 6*, 225–232.

Vaughan, D. W. (1977). Age related deterioration of pyramidal cell basal dendrites in rat auditory cortex. *Journal of Comparative Neurology, 171*, 501–516.

Vaughan, D. W., & Peters, A. (1974). Neuroglial cells in the cerebral cortex of rats from young adulthood to old age: An electron microscope study. *Journal of Neurocytology, 3*, 405–429.

Verriollo, R. T. (1980). Age-related changes in the sensitivity to vibration. *Journal of Gerontology, 35*, 185–193.

Vijayashankar, N., & Brody, H. (1979). A quantitative study of the pigmented neurons in the nuclei locus coeruleus and subcoeruleus in man as related to aging. *Journal of Neuropathology and Experimental Neurology, 38*, 490–497.

Warren, J. M., Zerweck, C., & Auletta, M. (1982). Effects of environmental enrichment on old mice. *Developmental Psychobiology, 15*, 13–18.

Weiffenbach, J. M., Baum, B. J., & Burghauser, R. (1982). Taste thresholds: Quality specific variation with human aging. *Journal of Gerontology, 37*, 372–377.

Willig, F., Palacios, A., Monmaur, P., M'harzi, M., Laurent, J., & Delacour, J. (1987). Short-term memory, exploration and locomotor activity in aged rats. *Neurobiology of Aging, 8*, 393–402.

Winocur, G. (1984). The effect of retroactive and proactive interference on learning and memory in old and young rats. *Developmental Psychobiology, 17*, 537–545.

Winocur, G. (1986). Memory decline in aged rats: A neuropsychological interpretation. *Journal of Gerontology, 41*, 758–763.

Wisniewski, A., Johnson, A. B., Raine, C. S., Kay, W. J., & Terry, R. D. (1970). Senile plaques and cerebral amyloidosis in aged dogs: A histochemical and ultrastructural study. *Laboratory Investigation, 23*, 287.

Wisniewski, H. M., & Terry, R. D. (1976). Neuropathology of the aging brain. In R. D. Terry & S. Gershon (Eds.), *Neurobiology of aging* (pp. 65–78). New York: Raven.

Wood, J. G., Mirra, S. S., Pollock, N. J., & Binder, L. I. (1986). Neurofibrillary tangles of Alzheimer's disease share antigenic determinants with the axonal microtubule-associated protein tau. *Proceedings of the National Academy of Sciences (USA), 83*, 4040–4043.

Woodard, J. S. (1962). Clinicopathological significance of granulovacuolar degeneration in Alzheimer's disease. *Journal of Neuropathology and Experimental Neurology, 21*, 85–91.

CHAPTER SEVEN

The Neuropsychology of Memory and Aging

Morris Moscovitch
University of Toronto
Rotman Research Institute

Gordon Winocur
Trent University
Rotman Research Institute

Research in the neuropsychology of aging is concerned with changes in behavior with age that are related to corresponding changes in the nervous system. In recent years, this field of research has become so vast as to encompass the full range of behaviors and their presumed neurological substrates. A comprehensive coverage of the current status of this field is well beyond the scope of this chapter. Our plan, instead, is to focus on a single function, memory. Failing memory is one of the chief complaints of elderly people. Indeed, the decline of memory with age is a robust phenomenon that has been documented extensively in the literature. We also can draw on a large theoretical and empirical literature on memory in younger adults as well as a rapidly growing literature on memory disorders in a neurological population.

Research on neurological patients has identified a number of structures that, when damaged, lead to a variety of memory disorders. Principal among these is the hippocampus and associated medial temporal cortex as well as anatomically related structures in the limbic system and diencephalon.[1] Damage to any of these structures can lead to a deficit in encoding and retention of new information and, perhaps, to impairment of some aspects of retrieval. There also has been a growing appreciation

---

[1]Although a variety of structures are involved, for the purpose of this chapter we will typically not distinguish among them but consider them as part of the hippocampal or medial temporal lobe system. The latter two terms are used interchangeably.

of the contribution of the frontal lobes and its related structures to memory. Unlike the hippocampus, the frontal lobes contribute to organizational aspects of memory at encoding and retrieval—the use to which memory is put rather than its mere storage and reactivation.

Age-related changes in hippocampal and frontal systems are likely to be associated with failing memory in the elderly. However, memory is a complex function that consists of a number of separable components, each likely to be mediated by structures in addition to the hippocampal and frontal systems. Support for this idea is based on evidence from studies of normal and brain-damaged people that different memory functions are dissociable one from another. Our knowledge of these dissociations can inform our search for patterns of impaired and preserved memory functions in the elderly that correspond to those observed in patients with a variety of different brain lesions.

Although we are reasonably certain as to which structures are involved, we are less certain as to which morphological changes in the neural substrate are the ones associated with memory failure. Is it cell loss, dendritic loss, changes in neurotransmitters, changes in membrane structures, or intracellular changes? These issues are discussed at length in chapter 6 of this volume. Our present concern is only with gross structural changes related to memory decline in old age. Traditionally, such changes were verified by histological postmortem analysis and then were related to the psychological performance of elderly people. Where both the psychological and histological data were derived from the same individuals, the postmortems typically occurred long after the psychological tests had been conducted (Huppert, 1991). The possibility remains that some of the neurological changes occurred after the cognitive assessment and were not an accurate reflection of the cognitive changes that were measured. Major advances in neuroimaging techniques eventually may compensate for the limitations of postmortem examination. Neuroimaging allows for examination of brain structure through computerized tomography (CT) and magnetic resonance imaging (MRI) scans, and brain function through measures of blood flow and cerebral metabolism (regional cerebral blood flow [rCBF], positron emission tomography [PET], and single photon emission computerized tomography [SPECT]). The goal of relating neuropsychological performance to brain structure and function in living normal people is brought much closer with these techniques and even greater progress will be made as they become more sensitive. We review first those studies that already have made a contribution, though at the moment they are relatively few in number. The focus of our chapter, therefore, is on information obtained from traditional neuropsychological research.

Before we review this literature, we wish to comment on two methodological procedures, double and single dissociation experiments, that have been used extensively and successfully in neuropsychological investigations of brain function. Although in principle these procedures may be applied to neuropsychological studies of aging, in practice this has proved difficult because of the special problems associated with this area of research.

Double Dissociation

Since the 1950s, double dissociation experiments have served as the ideal paradigm for localizing function in the brain (Shallice, 1988; Teuber & Milner, 1968; Teuber, 1955). The aim of double dissociation experiments is to show that loss of a particular function is associated with damage to a particular structure and is not the result of generalized neurological or functional deterioration that accompanies brain damage. This is accomplished by comparing subjects with circumscribed damage to different brain areas and showing that functional loss is directly related to the site of the lesion. In a successful double dissociation experiment, damage to area A produces deficits in function A while sparing function B, whereas the opposite applies when area B is damaged. This paradigm enabled investigators to conclude that damage to particular structures had predictable deficits; the knowledge also was used to infer the functions of the damaged region of the brain.

There are two problems in applying this approach to the study of aging. The first is that no discrete lesions are found in the brains of normal elderly people. Instead, various degrees of structural deterioration may be detected. Adapting the double dissociation approach to this population would involve comparing deficits in people with atrophy in different regions. Age-related change, however, occurs in many structures; to complicate matters it is usually the same structures that are affected in most elderly people. Regional variations do occur both within and across individuals but our ability to compare deterioration in different structures is imperfect. What is needed is the establishment of normal baselines against which deterioration can be evaluated.

With appropriate baselines, it becomes possible to assess structural variation across individuals and relate it to functional decline. Modified double dissociation experiments can then be conducted on normal, old people. In the modified procedure, correlations are computed between two psychological tests (or groups of tests) and the extent of deterioration to two brain structures (Jernigan, 1986). A double dissociation is said to exist when performance on one test is correlated with the extent of deterioration to one region but not the other, whereas the reverse holds for the other test.

The development of sophisticated neuroimaging procedures makes it possible to conduct these studies. CT and MRI scanning techniques have already been used successfully to document age-related changes in a variety of brain regions. Consistently, disproportionate changes have been found in frontal and medial temporal lobe areas, although other regions have been implicated (for reviews see Albert and Stafford, 1980; Jernigan, Archibald, Berhow, Sowell, Foster, & Hesselink, 1991). These findings are in general accord with those reported after postmortem examination (Terry, Deteresa, & Hansen, 1987). Evidence of age-related changes using rCBF and PET techniques is less reliable (deLeon, George, & Ferris, 1986).

Investigators have also begun to correlate the structural changes on CT and MRI with neuropsychological function in normal aging. Though few in number, and often lacking the structural and functional precision of focal lesion work, these pioneering studies are very encouraging. They indicate that performance on certain neuropsychological tests can be correlated differentially with evidence of atrophy in frontal and temporal lobes. For example, Albert and her colleagues (Albert & Stafford, 1986; Stafford, Albert, Naesa, Sandro, & Garvey, 1988) report that naming, abstraction, and memory are highly correlated with fluid volume and CT density number in a CT slice that contains frontal and temporal lobe tissue. Similarly, Jernigan (1986), using a mixed group of high functioning and demented old people, has found that performance on visual reproduction and naming were correlated with temporal and frontal-lobe deterioration, respectively.

Development of more precise neuroimaging techniques that can sample all areas with equal proficiency will allow for the precise localization of age-related changes in normal people. These, along with improved neuropsychological tests with better localizing value, promise to raise the caliber of *in vivo* studies of brain-behavior relations in normal aging to that now attained only in the best studies of patients with focal lesions.

Single Dissociation

When double dissociation experiments are not feasible, single dissociation experiments may be conducted. In single dissociation experiments the effects of lesions to only one area of the brain are examined. These experiments attempt to show that damage to a particular region affects performance on certain tests but not on others. Generally, single dissociation experiments are not preferred because the results are open to the interpretation that the observed deficits arise from nonspecific effects of the lesion rather than from selective disruption of functions associated with the damaged region. That is, the test on which performance is impaired may be simply the one that is most difficult, not necessarily the one that is mediated by the region in question. Moreover, by focusing on only a single region, single dissociation experiments fail to take into account contributions of other structures in mediating different components of a particular task. For example, many patients with anterior communicating artery aneurysms that damage the ventromedial aspect of the frontal lobes are usually far more impaired on tests of free recall than on recognition (Moscovitch, 1989). It would be tempting to conclude that the damaged region mediates performance on tests of free recall. Although this could be the case, the alternative interpretation is that free recall is simply the more "difficult" of the two tests and that damage to other brain regions implicated in memory, like the hippocampus and dorsomedial thalamus, also might produce the same pattern of preserved and impaired functions. It is only when patients with damage to those regions also are tested and found to have impaired recognition as well as recall that we can conclude that the ventromedial frontal region is critical for free recall.

When applied to studies of normal elderly people, single dissociation experiments are translated into ones in which the extent of deterioration to a particular region is correlated with performance on some tests but not others. Typically, the performance of young and old people is compared on a particular test, believed on other grounds to be mediated by a particular structure. The results then are related to postmortem analysis of brains belonging to other individuals who presumably share common characteristics with the subjects that are being studied (Huppert, 1991). Not surprisingly, deterioration is found in the designated structure. Because many cognitive functions deteriorate with age, it is likely that the elderly will be impaired on many tests. Moreover, because other regions are also likely to deteriorate with age, one cannot conclude that impairment on the target task arises from damage to a specific region. To ascribe the deficit on the target test to deterioration of a particular region of the brain clearly is not warranted.

A Functional Analogue of Double and Single Dissociations

An approach that continues to be useful and informative is one that relies purely on performance on standardized neuropsychological tests to infer the integrity of brain structures. To the extent that scores on these tests are valid measures of localized deterioration, they can substitute, at least to a first approximation, for direct evidence of structural change obtained by neuroimaging or histological techniques. The procedure thus permits a functional analogue of double and single dissociation experiments. In the case of double dissociation, performance on Target Test A would be correlated with scores on the standardized neuropsychological Test A, but not on Test B, whereas the reverse pattern would be obtained for Target Test B.

The limitations of this technique are well known. The standardized tests were developed in studies of patients with focal brain lesions. Their localizing value is better suited to populations with clearly defined brain lesions than those, like normal old people, with more diffuse brain deterioration. Also, neuropsychological tests are at best imperfect measures of the structural integrity of specific brain regions. Moreover, performance on the tests may be influenced by factors unrelated to brain damage, such as the clinical or psychological state of the individual, for example, mood and education. For these reasons correlations among tests that are sensitive to damage to the same general region are often low, even in patients with focal lesions. Failure to find a correlation among neuropsychological tests does not mean necessarily that the functions they measure are not mediated by a common structure. It might imply, instead, that supportive functions are sufficiently different that they obscure the correlation that may exist between the principal components. Consequently, only significant correlations on functional double or single dissociation tests are informative. They indicate that a constellation of deficits probably can be ascribed to deterioration of a specific region that mediates a function or functions common to all the tests.

An example of the successful application of the functional single dissociation procedure comes from studies of source amnesia in patients with frontal lesions and in elderly people. Source amnesia refers to memory loss for the source from which information was acquired (e.g., where one learned a particular fact) when the content itself is preserved. Schacter, Harbluk, and McLachlan (1984) showed that extent of source amnesia in patients with memory disorders was correlated with their performance on the Wisconsin Card Sorting Test (WCST), a test sensitive to frontal dysfunction, but was unrelated to the severity of their general amnesia, a finding confirmed by Shimamura and Squire (1987). As a direct test of the prediction that frontal lesions lead to source amnesia, Janowsky, Shimamura, and Squire (1989b) showed that patients with frontal lesions who are not amnesic have source amnesia whereas amnesic patients with intact frontal lobes do not show this deficit. Craik, Morris, Morris, and Loewen (1990) used this functional dissociation approach to show that the extent of source amnesia in elderly people (McIntyre & Craik, 1987) also is related to their performance on the WCST and, by implication, to the extent of their frontal dysfunction. It now remains to be shown by neuroimaging techniques that this deficit indeed is related to the degree of structural deterioration in the frontal lobes in elderly people and not to deterioration in other regions. Ideally, one would hope to convert studies of this type, single dissociation, to studies of double dissociation in the functional and structural domains.

GENERAL OUTLINE

The general framework driving research in the neuropsychology of aging, whether stated explicitly or implicitly, is that cognitive decline in the elderly results from neural deterioration in structures presumed to mediate performance on particular tests. With respect to the hippocampus and frontal lobes, the hypothesis is that decline in memory and executive functions with age are related to changes in these two structures (Mittenberg, Seidenberg, O'Leary, & DiGiulio, 1989). The major purpose of our chapter is to evaluate the evidence with respect to this hypothesis. Clearly, other areas also may be affected by the aging process, in particular subcortical areas such as the basal ganglia and the thalamus (Hang et al., 1983), but the approach used in our article should be applicable to them too.

In our attempt to understand the neuropsychology of memory impairment in aging with an emphasis on hippocampal and frontal-lobe functions, we review the brain-damage literature pertaining to the respective contributions of these structures to memory and learning. We first turn our attention to the hippocampus with an emphasis on patients with focal lesions to that structure. Having identified the type of tests that are sensitive to hippocampal damage, we then examine the literature on normal aging to test the hypothesis that elderly people are selectively impaired on those tests. Structural and functional double dissociation experiments of the sort discussed in the previous section are rare. More common are studies in which performance of elderly people is examined on tests known to be sensitive to hippocampal system dysfunction and we review this literature. We then follow a similar plan with respect to the frontal lobes. From these reviews, it will become apparent that the frontal lobe's contribution to memory is distinct from that of the hippocampus but complementary to it.

One of our objectives is to determine whether conclusions derived from studies of people with focal lesions can be applied meaningfully to elderly people in whom brain structure deteriorates gradually. If this is indeed possible, then properly designed studies of elderly people can be used to advance our general knowledge of neuro-cognitive function.

Neuropsychological research on humans often is limited by a lack of precise knowledge of the structures involved and also by lack of control over the neural and environmental conditions. We, therefore, also turn to animal studies to see if they conform to our findings in the human literature and to fill gaps in that literature.

Our working assumption is that the cognitive deficits that typically accompany old age are related to dysfunction of the neural substrates that mediate cognitive performance in adulthood. Although the primary cause of dysfunction is presumed to be age-related changes in neural structures, these do not always occur in isolation from environmental influences. Environmental or psychosocial factors may precipitate, enhance, retard, or perhaps even reverse the neural degeneration and cognitive decline that accompanies old age. This point must be kept in mind to guard against the view that only biological factors are important. We will return to this point towards the end of our chapter to note some recent research in this area.

Before we proceed with our review, we sketch a model of hippocampal and frontal functions that can serve as a framework for organizing the literature and as a guide for later discussion.

Theoretical Model

Historically, the structures most widely identified with memory function are the hippocampus and associated cortex in the medial temporal lobes (Scoville & Milner, 1957; Milner, 1966) as well as anatomically related structures that include the mammillary bodies and dorsomedial nucleus of the thalamus (Victor, Adams, & Collins, 1971). Since Milner's work on patients with memory disorders following neurosurgical excisions of the medial temporal lobes, particular attention has been focused on the hippocampus. Damage to this region (Zola-Morgan, Squire, & Amaral, 1986) and its input and output pathways (Hyman, Van Hoesen, & Damasio, 1990) leads to a profound memory loss for new experiences (anterograde amnesia) accompanied by a temporally graded loss of memory for events immediately preceding lesion onset (retrograde amnesia). More remote memories typically are spared.

There have been numerous attempts to capture more precisely the functions of the hippocampus and the nature of the memory deficits that produce amnesia. These efforts have been complicated by the growing realization that, despite their profound amnesia, patients can acquire and retain new information although they lack any conscious awareness of having done so. Similar developments have occurred in research on animal models in which hippocampal system damage was found to affect performance on some memory tests but not on others (for review, see Hirsh, 1974; O'Keefe & Nadel, 1978; Olton, Becker, & Handelmann, 1979; Weiskrantz, 1978). These studies, as well as extensive research on normal people, led to an important distinction between two types of memory tests (Cohen & Squire, 1980; Graf & Schacter, 1985; Jacoby & Witherspoon, 1982; Moscovitch, 1982a, 1984). Explicit tests of memory are those, such as recognition and recall, that depend on recollection of previously experienced events in their spatiotemporal contexts. Implicit tests are those in which there is no need to refer intentionally to the past during performance; memory is inferred from the effects of experience or practice on behavior.

Our view (see Moscovitch, 1989; Moscovitch & Umilta, 1990, 1991), which is shared by other investigators (see Mishkin & Appenzeller, 1987; Squire, 1987; Tulving & Schacter, 1990), is that only performance on explicit tests of memory is mediated by the hippocampal system whereas performance on implicit tests is mediated by other cortical and subcortical structures. Sensory information is received and interpreted initially by specialized cortical (and perhaps subcortical) structures. The act of processing this information modifies the cortical structures so that they store a long-term *perceptual* and *semantic record* (Kirsner & Dunn, 1985) of the input and its interpretation (see Fig. 7.1).

These records constitute nonconscious mnemonic representations that mediate performance on implicit tests of memory. The output of these structures can affect action systems directly or can be delivered to consciousness. Information in consciousness is then channelled automatically to the hippocampus. The hippocampus then integrates or binds the consciously apprehended information with the perceptual and semantic

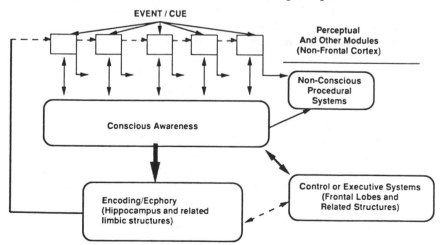

FIG. 7.1.   A schematic model of memory (from Moscovitch, 1989).

records that contributed to it to form a long-lasting *memory trace*. This is achieved via reciprocal pathways between the hippocampus and the cortex. The formation of this memory trace is termed *consolidation*. The duration of the consolidation process varies with the type and complexity of the information and may last for months or years in animals and humans, respectively. Once consolidation is complete the hippocampus no longer is needed and the memory trace is stored and accessed through other structures. During the consolidation period, however, conscious recollection of an event occurs when an external, or internally generated, cue gains access to consciousness and interacts effectively with the memory trace. The product of that interaction, termed *ecphory* (Semon, 1922, cited in Schacter, Eich, & Tulving, 1978), contributes to the conscious memory of past experiences. Once initiated, the ecphoric process runs off automatically and is not subject to voluntary control (Tulving, 1983).

In order to use the hippocampal system effectively, controlled, strategic processes are necessary at both input and output. At input, strategic processes are involved in selecting and organizing the information that receives conscious attention and that serves as the initial stimulus or retrieval cue. At output, strategic operations are involved in verifying the information retrieved from the hippocampal system, placing it in the proper spatiotemporal context, and in using it to plan subsequent behavior or initiate additional memory search.

These considerations highlight the need for mechanisms that work with memory in addition to ones that are involved in consolidating, storing, and reactivating memory traces. *Working with memory,* we believe, is mediated by the frontal lobes (Moscovitch & Winocur, 1992). It is a basic feature of this structure's contribution to other behavioral processes and arises from the structure's inherent organizational and planning functions. Damage to the frontal lobes, therefore, typically does not lead to memory loss if the cues are sufficient to specify the target event. Damage, however, leads to impairment on tests in which extra-cue organizational factors are important, in which complex search strategies must be initiated and executed, and in which the retrieval information must be ordered temporally and spatially with respect to other events.

The working-with-memory function of the frontal lobes may not be restricted only to consciously recollected information. The same function may be necessary for the organization of unconscious memory processes that drive performance on implicit tests of memory, particularly those involved in learning and applying rules and procedures.

The Hippocampus and Memory.   Patients with medial temporal-lobe lesions that include extensive damage to the hippocampus can be characterized by the following dissociations (Moscovitch, 1982a):

1. Memory is impaired but intellectual and general cognitive functions are preserved.

2. Memory loss is restricted primarily to long-term or secondary memory. Short-term or primary memory is relatively spared.

3. Anterograde amnesia is severe and is frequently accompanied by a limited, temporally graded retrograde amnesia. Memory for more remote events appears to be spared in most patients with lesions confined to the medial temporal lobes and hippocampus.

4. Despite the severe anterograde memory loss for consciously recollected information, many amnesic patients can acquire and retain much new information, often at a normal level. Amnesics can perform normally on implicit tests of memory where there is no need to recollect the past but where memory is assessed by changes in behavior that reflect past experience. For example, a patient may not remember having studied a word or learned a motor task if tested explicitly. Yet savings for previously studied words can be demonstrated by showing that patients read or perceive them better than new words (for reviews see Moscovitch, 1984; Richardson-Klavehn & Bjork, 1988; Schacter, 1987a). Similarly, patients execute previously practiced motor tasks better than new ones (Corkin, 1965; Milner, 1966).

5. In addition to these defining features or obligatory symptoms of medial temporal-lobe amnesia, the literature suggests that other features also may form part of the syndrome. Amnesic patients are disproportionately susceptible to interference in memory, as are rats and monkeys with hippocampal lesions (Iverson, 1977; Winocur, 1982). Interference in memory occurs when an experience adversely impairs new learning or recollection of previously acquired information. It has been suggested on the basis of animal studies that hippocampal lesions uniquely affect spatial memory (O'Keefe & Nadel, 1978). It always has been clear in the literature on human amnesics, and is becoming accepted in the animal literature, that the memory deficit extends beyond the spatial domain. Nevertheless, it still may be the case that spatial memory is more vulnerable to effects of hippocampal damage than memory without a spatial component.

Memory and the Hippocampus in the Elderly

In this section we examine memory decline in the elderly to see if the pattern of preserved and impaired abilities is similar to that of patients with focal, medial-temporal lesions. Although we are aware of the dangers of generalizing from studies that were in many cases not specifically designed to test this hypothesis, nevertheless we were struck by numerous points of convergence. By identifying similar functional dissociations in the elderly, this review demonstrates the value of the neuropsychological approach to the study of aging and memory.

Dissociation of Intelligence and Memory. Perhaps the most salient feature of amnesia is that severe memory loss occurs against a background of intact intelligence. This stark dissociation cannot be found in the elderly population. As memory declines, so does intelligence. The drop in intelligence test scores does not imply that the elderly are demented, because IQ scores are corrected for age. A person between 65 and 75 years of age who is considered to be of average intelligence for his or her cohort has an absolute score that is significantly lower than that of a subject who is between 20 and 30 years of age. Indeed, when applied to the young subject, an average score for the elderly would indicate an IQ below the normal range.

It is important, however, not to create the impression that memory loss always results from intellectual decline. More likely, brain structures mediating performance on intelligence tests are as affected by the aging processes as are medial temporal-lobe structures involved in memory. It is not easy to distinguish between these alternatives but a closer examination of the pattern of performance on various subtests of the intelligence scale may help us understand what is at issue.

Large declines with age are found on subtests that have a timed component (see Botwinick, 1978; Salthouse, 1982, 1985; Storandt, 1977). When allowances are made for the elderly person's slowness on timed tests, the decline is not as sharp, though it is still noticeable. Moreover, a drop in performance with age is found even on tests where speed is not a factor. The greatest decline occurs on tests of fluid intelligence, which require a novel or creative approach to problem solving (e.g., Raven's matrices). Age differences are minimal on tests of crystallized intelligence, which assess old knowledge or the application of well-learned intellectual skills (Horn, 1982).

Against this background, one would expect that age-related decline in memory would correlate with fluid, rather than with crystallized, intelligence. Indeed, this observation has been made by several investigators (Salthouse, 1982, 1985). It is noteworthy, however, that in at least one study, aging affected memory even when the effects of intelligence were factored out (Cockburn & Smith, 1991).

To argue for a causal relationship between fluid intelligence and memory at a neuropsychological level one would have to show that the same structures are involved in both functions. Alternatively, if the relation is not causal, one should be able to find a double (or at least single) dissociation between deterioration to different structures and performance on tests of intelligence and memory, as suggested in the previous section. For example, performance on tests of episodic memory might vary more directly with structural deterioration of the hippocampal system whereas performance on tests of fluid intelligence might correlate more closely with deterioration of other neocortical structures. Failure to find a double or single dissociation does not logically imply that the decline in memory and intelligence are related causally. It does, however, undermine the argument that they are independent of each other. Unfortunately, the appropriate structural double dissociation studies have not yet been conducted, though some functional, single dissociation experiments have been reported.

Until the evidence is in, we still can proceed to investigate whether the memory decline is related to hippocampal deterioration regardless of whether it is also related to intelligence. The critical issue is whether memory decline in the elderly, apart from its relation to intelligence, has features in common with the pattern of memory loss following hippocampal lesions. It should be emphasized that this type of damage will account for only some aspects of memory loss in the elderly. Because of the widespread effects of age on brain function, elderly people may exhibit additional problems with memory that are related to deterioration in regions other than the hippocampus and medial temporal lobes. The challenge is to determine if the other salient features of the medial temporal-lobe amnesia can be identified reliably in the memory performance of old people.

Dissociation of Short-Term and Long-Term Memory. In elderly people, as in amnesic patients with medial temporal-lobe/hippocampal lesions, short-term memory as measured by digit span is relatively spared whereas long-term memory as measured by free recall and by tests of paired-associate learning is impaired. Studies conducted in the 1960s showed that immediate free recall of supraspan word lists gave rise to a serial position effect whose shape was determined by the contribution of short-term or primary memory and long-term or secondary memory (Glanzer & Cunitz, 1966). The recency portion of the serial position curve reflects recall from short-term memory whereas the primacy and middle portion reflects recall from long-term memory. Various procedures and formulas were devised to distinguish more precisely between the two components (Watkins, 1974). Consistent with the hypothesis that medial temporal-lobe/hippocampal damage affects only long-term memory, patients with such lesions have a reduced primacy effect with normal recency (Baddeley & Warrington, 1970; Moscovitch, 1982a; see also Corsi, cited in Milner, 1974). Using Tulving and Colotla's (1970) formula for distinguishing primary (short-term) from secondary (long-term) memory,

Moscovitch (1982a) showed no effect of left hippocampal lesions on primary memory but a substantial deficit in secondary memory. Interestingly, patients with left frontal-lobe lesions also showed a slight decline in primary memory, a finding consistent with others in the literature (Janowsky, Shimamura, Kritchevsky, & Squire, 1989).

Like medial temporal-lobe/hippocampal lesions, age consistently and primarily affects the long-term-memory component of free recall (for reviews see Craik, 1977, and chapter 2 of this volume). Significant deficits in short-term memory occasionally have been reported but they are typically mild and may be related to deterioration of other cortical structures such as the frontal lobes. Here, too, correlations of short-term and long-term memory in the elderly with neuroimaging data from various structures, and with behavioral measures sensitive to the integrity of these structures, would be valuable.

The relation between amnesia and other purported measures of short-term memory is more controversial. On the Brown–Peterson test, some investigators report no difference between controls and amnesic patients of various etiologies (Baddeley & Warrington, 1970; Warrington, 1982), some report more rapid decay for the patients (see references in Butters & Cermak, 1974; Winocur et al., 1985), and still others report parallel decay rates but lower overall performance for amnesics (Kinsbourne & Wood, 1975). Corsi (cited in Milner, 1974) found that performance on the Brown–Peterson task was related to the amount of hippocampal removal. Because only the Corsi study used patients with known lesions to the medial temporal cortex, perhaps that should serve as our prototype. Interestingly, although Corsi found no significant defect associated with frontal lesions, Stuss, Kaplan, Benson, Weir, Chiuli, and Sarazin (1982) did report that schizophrenic patients with frontal lobectomies are impaired on the Brown–Peterson test relative to controls.

Despite indications of the possible involvement of both the frontal lobes and the hippocampus on the Brown–Peterson test, no reliable age-related differences have been reported (see Craik, 1977, and chapter 2 of this volume).

Yet another way of distinguishing between short- and long-term memory is by examining performance on variable delayed match-to-sample tests with samples that are difficult to verbalize and rehearse. Patients with bilateral, medial temporal-lobe/hippocampal lesions perform well at short delays, when performance presumably can be supported by primary memory and secondary memory but deteriorate noticeably at long delays when success depends only on secondary memory (Milner, Corkin, & Teuber, 1968; Sidman, Stoddard, & Mohr, 1968; Wickelgren, 1968). A similar pattern of performance had been noted in elderly people on comparable tasks. Poon and Fozard (1980), using a continuous recognition task, found that age differences are more pronounced at long than at short intervals. Smith (1975) also reported that age differences in recall are greater at long than at short delays (but see Salthouse, 1982).

Memory loss for specific events following hippocampal lesions is time-dependent in animals as in humans. This observation has been reliably observed in rats and monkeys in several paradigms. The hippocampal deficit in nonmatch to sample in monkeys is apparent only at relatively long delays (Roberts, Dember, & Brodwick, 1962; Zola-Morgan & Squire, 1986). In rats, increasing delays on spatial and on nonspatial (Winocur, 1985) alternation, as well as on runway passive avoidance (Winocur, 1985), and on differential reinforcement of low rates of responding (DRL), accentuates the hippocampal deficit (Rawlins, Winocur, & Gray, 1983). In many of these tests, the deficit is further exacerbated if an interfering interpolated activity is introduced during the delay interval.

In humans, more rapid forgetting in patients with hippocampal damage also was observed by Huppert and Piercy (1976a), Corsi (cited in Milner, 1974), and Frisk and Milner (1990). Other investigators, however, claimed that the rate of forgetting in hippocampal patients is similar to that of normal people (Freed, Corkin, & Cohen, 1987). The discrepancy among these different findings has yet to be resolved, but it is likely to hinge on the type of memory tests that are used to assess forgetting and perhaps on the extent to which implicit memory factors influence performance on those tests. It is significant, in this regard, that it is only on tests of recognition, in which perceptual familiarity can come into play, that for-getting rate is normal in patients with confirmed (Freed, Corkin, & Co-hen, 1987) or suspected hippocampal lesions (Kopelman, 1985). This interpretation is consistent with the observation that forgetting on im-plicit tests of memory seems to be unaffected by amnesia (Diamond & Rozin, 1984; Graf, Squire, & Mandler, 1984; Milner et al., 1968; War-rington & Weiskrantz, 1970).

Memory at short and long delays also has been studied in various animal models. Rats and monkeys with medial temporal-lobe/hippocampal le-sions typically perform normally when information has to be retained over short intervals but are impaired progressively as the interval length-ens. For example, on variations of nonmatch-to-sample tasks (Mahut, Zola-Morgan, & Moss, 1982; Mishkin, 1978; Zola-Morgan & Squire, 1986), monkeys with lesions to the hippocampus are impaired only at long de-lays, the impairment being greater as the lesion encroaches on cortex con-taining hippocampal input and output pathways (Squire & Zola-Morgan, 1988). Rats have been tested on delayed alternation (Thompson, 1981; Winocur, 1985), conditional discrimination learning (Winocur, 1991b), and choice behavior in the radial arm maze (Kesner & Novak, 1982); in all cases, the results point consistently to a deficit that was related to the length of the delay interval (but see Aggleton, Hunt, & Rawlins, 1986). Versions of some of these tests also have been administered to old monkeys (Bartus, Fleming, & Johnson, 1978) and to rats (Winocur, 1992; Zornetzer, Thompson, & Rogers, 1982) with results that are similar to those observed with humans and with hippocampally lesioned rats; namely, the greatest deficit typically occurs at long delays. When deficits have been found at short delays, they have been related to frontal-lobe, rather than to hippocampal, damage or deterioration (see below, section on frontal lobes).

Dissociation Between Anterograde and Retrograde Memory.
Traditionally, the amnesic syndrome has been defined in terms of anterograde memory loss. Retrograde amnesia is a more variable component of the syndrome. In some patients it is restricted to a short period immediately preceding the onset of trauma whereas in others it may extend as far back as childhood. There is no consistent evidence that the amount of retrograde amnesia is related to the severity of anterograde amnesia (Kopelman, 1989; Mayes, 1988; Parkin, 1987; Shimamura & Squire, 1986; Stuss & Guzman, 1988). However, retrograde amnesia does seem to be associated more often with some etiologies than others. Retrograde memory loss has been found reliably in patients with Korsakoff's syndrome but the form it takes is in dispute. Sanders and Warrington (1971) found a severe memory loss that was equivalent across the patient's entire lifetime. Others have found a temporally graded memory loss with severity greatest for events immediately preceding the trauma (Albert, Butters, & Levin, 1979; Squire & Cohen, 1982).

Patients with lesions restricted to diencephalic areas thought to be central to amnesia in Korsakoff's syndrome show an entirely different pattern of retrograde memory loss. Although they are amnesic for events immediately preceding the lesion, their memory for more remote events is typically in the normal range (Squire & Cohen, 1982; Winocur et al., 1984). In patients with medial temporal-lobe lesions, remote memories generally are spared, though the period of retrograde amnesia may extend back from trauma onset by as much as 3 years (Scoville & Milner, 1957). The difference between diencephalic and hippocampal retrograde amnesia may reflect the different contributions of these structures in learning and retention. In a recent study, Kopelman (1991) showed that the frontal lobes also may be involved in mediating remote memory. He found that remote memory loss in Korsakoff amnesic patients was correlated with their performance on frontal-lobe tests but was independent of their deficit on tests of episodic memory for recently studied material.

Gauging the extent and severity of retrograde amnesia is difficult and may contribute to some of the variability found in the literature. Whereas it is possible to control all aspects of the learning situation in tests for anterograde memory, such control is absent in testing for premorbid memories. The patient's memory for a particular event may be determined by several factors including the saliency of the event, its relevance to the patient, the amount of exposure (for discussion, see Butters & Albert, 1982; Squire & Cohen, 1982).

The ideal study of retrograde amnesia would involve memory for controlled learning episodes that occurred at regularly spaced intervals throughout an individual's life span. Although this type of study is unlikely ever to be conducted in humans, something approximating it has been conducted in monkeys and rats. Winocur (1990) compared the effects of hippocampal and diencephalic lesions in rats on a food preference that was learned at intervals ranging from a few minutes to 8 days before surgery. Only hippocampal lesions produced a temporally graded amnesia extending back for 2 days. Testing memory for location in a water maze, Sutherland and Arnold (1987) reported a similar pattern of results. A temporally graded retrograde amnesia in monkeys for object discriminations learned at various intervals prior to surgery also was reported by Zola-Morgan and Squire (1990).

The differential effects of hippocampal and diencephalic lesions in animals are consistent with those observed in humans with lesions to the two structures. The results support the hypothesis that the hippocampus and thalamus contribute differently to learning and memory. In line with other observations, Winocur (1990) proposed that the thalamus is critical for encoding whereas the hippocampus is necessary for consolidation and retention of recent information (see also Signoret, 1974; Squire, 1987).

Studies on the effects of age on memory for remote events have produced contradictory results. Investigators have reported effects ranging from impaired to superior performance in the elderly compared to the young (for review see Rubin, Wetzler, & Nebes, 1986).

Apart from the methodological problems inherent in testing remote memory in general, there are also problems peculiar to studying the effects of age on remote memory from a neuropsychological perspective. First, it is likely that structures other than the medial temporal lobes/hippocampus deteriorate with age. Our knowledge of the effects of damage to those structures on remote memory is minimal. Even if the hippocampus were the only critical structure, we do not know precisely when the hippocampus begins to deteriorate, although it is probable that some deterioration occurs before age 65 years. Learning is likely to be affected from the time deterioration sets in and (if the animal and human literature on amnesia is an indication) some temporally graded remote memory loss also should accompany hippocampal deterioration. A person tested for remote memory at age 65 years or older is therefore someone with a history of minor but cumulative remote memory loss that may have begun in middle age and that may have been compounded by slight learning deficits that can be traced to the same period.

If one could overcome some of the methodological problems, we would expect a temporally graded memory loss that dates back to the onset of hippocampal decline. Based on behavioral data of loss on secondary-memory, we assume this decline begins in middle age but we know of no corroborating neuroanatomical evidence. For example, when compared to someone who is 50 years of age, a 70-year-old person should show the greatest relative loss for events that occurred 5 years ago but a smaller deficit for events that occurred 30 years ago. For 70-year-olds, the number of memories that can be recovered declines noticeably for those memories that were acquired in the 25 years preceding testing, reaches an asymptote for memories acquired when the subject was between 35 and 45 years of age, and even rises for memories that were acquired between the ages of 20 and 35 years. The results reported in Fitzgerald and Lawrence (1984) and discussed by Rubin et al. (1986) are generally consistent with this idea (see Fig. 7.2). Comparisons of 70-year-olds with 50-year-old people yield differences in favor of the 50-year-olds for memories acquired in the last 20 years, but not for those acquired earlier.

Another approach to studying retrograde memory involves the examination of age of acquisition effects for words and pictures. The question addressed is whether words or pictures to which one is exposed early in life are identified, understood, or remembered better than words or pictures that are encountered at a later age (Carroll & White, 1973; Gilhooly & Gilhooly, 1980; Gilhooly & Logie, 1980). Worden and Sherman-Brown (1983) and Moscovitch and Ladowsky (1988) looked at cohort effects for words that changed in frequency from a person's childhood to old age. They were interested in whether performance on tests of memory, on lexical decision, and on naming was determined by the frequency the target words had in the person's youth (dated) or in his or her old (contemporary) age. As a control, words that remained high (common) or low (rare) in frequency throughout the lifetime were used. Estimated frequency was based on published word frequency norms from the 1920s (Thorndike, 1921), 1940s (Thorndike & Lorge, 1944), 1960s (Kucera & Francis, 1967), and 1980s (Francis & Kucera, 1982).

It is well established that performance in young adults is better for low- than for high-frequency words when recognition is tested, whereas the reverse is true of tests of recall, lexical decision, and naming. The results from both Worden and Sherman-Brown's (1983) and Moscovitch and Ladowsky's (1988) studies showed that in all tests performance of people over 65 years of age was determined by dated, rather than contemporary,

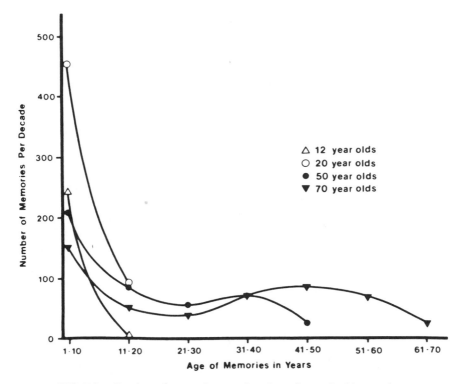

FIG. 7.2.   Number of memories as a function of age of subject and age of memories (from Fitzgerald & Lawrence, 1984, as modified by Rubin, Wetzler, & Nebes, 1986).

word frequencies whereas the reverse was found for young people. The pattern of performance with respect to common and rare words, however, was equivalent for the two groups (see Figs. 7.3 and 7.4).

The results of these studies, as well as similar ones using less well-controlled material (Botwinick & Storandt, 1980; Poon & Fozard, 1978), offer the best support for Ribot's (1882) original hypothesis that memory is best for material acquired early in life. Although we favor a memory interpretation, we cannot rule out the possibility that greater familiarity with early-acquired words partially accounts for the effects. These results are consistent with the view that old people have a temporally-graded, retrograde remote memory loss.

Dissociations Between Memory With and Without Awareness

Brain Lesion Studies.   Memory with awareness involves conscious recollection of the past and usually is measured by explicit tests such as recognition and recall. Memory without awareness does not require conscious reflection on the past. Instead, retention of the past is inferred

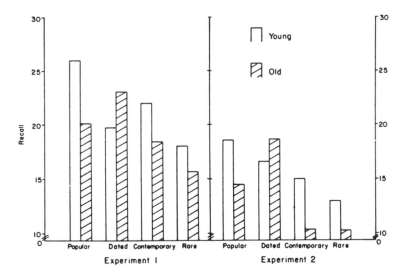

FIG. 7.3. Number of words recognized and recalled by young and old people as a function of changing (contemporary and dated) or stable (popular and rare) word frequencies (from Worden and Sherman-Brown, 1983).

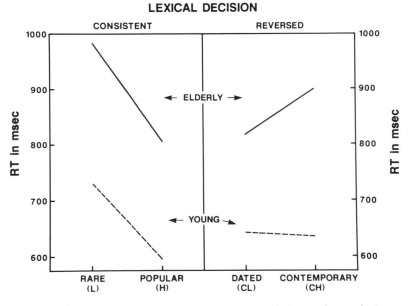

FIG. 7.4. Reaction time in msec by young and elderly people on a lexical decision task for words. *Consistent* refers to rare and popular words whose frequency of usage remained unchanged during an elderly person's lifetime. Dated and contemporary words are those whose current frequencies are the *reverse* of those that existed during the elderly person's youth.

from performance on implicit tests that measure changes in behavior with experience or practice. For example, having read a word or seen a face, the subject is likely to identify either one more quickly on subsequent viewing, often without consciously remembering the initial presentation.

The distinction between implicit and explicit tests of memory is an old one, but it is only recently that the significance of the distinction for theories of memory has been appreciated. Concern with dissociations among different forms or tests of memory has fueled empirical and theoretical work which, in turn, has led to major advances in our understanding of normal memory and of memory disorders. Major reviews on the topic have appeared in recent years (Hintzman, 1990; Johnson & Hasher, 1987; Richardson-Klavehn & Bjork, 1988; Schacter, 1987a) and the interested reader is referred to them. Our purpose is not to adjudicate among the various theories or among some of the controversies in the empirical literature. Instead we review some of the basic, reliable findings on normal young adults and relate them to neuropsychological research on memory disorders in humans and animals. Taken together, the observed dissociation among different tests of memory suggests that different critical components, at both the functional and structural level, are involved in each of the tests. An examination of the neuropsychological literature helps us identify some of these components. We then discuss these findings in relation to the corresponding literature on normal aging.

There is general agreement that damage to the medial temporal lobe and related structures causes severe impairment on explicit tests of memory while leaving performance on implicit tests relatively intact. For example, amnesic patients with severe deficits in recall and recognition of single words and pictures nonetheless perform normally on implicit tests of perceptual identification (Cermak, Talbot, Chandler, & Wolburst, 1985; Warrington & Weiskrantz, 1970), word-stem completion (Graf & Schacter, 1985; Graf, Squire, & Mandler, 1984; Rozin & Diamond, 1984), fragment completion (Tulving, Hayman, & MacDonald, 1991), speeded reading of transformed and normal text (Moscovitch, Winocur, & McLachlan, 1986; Musen, Shimamura, & Squire, 1990), and lexical decision tasks (Moscovitch, 1985).

The ease with which amnesic patients learn related as compared to unrelated word pairs in the Wechsler Memory Scale (WMS) also may be attributed to their preserved ability on implicit tests. Performance on the related-pair trials may not be governed by explicit recall of the appropriate response but by activation of old word associations, which is an implicit test of memory (see also, Winocur & Weiskrantz, 1976). Whether amnesics also can be shown to retain unrelated word pairs on implicit tests of learning is currently controversial. On tests of word-stem completion, Graf and Schacter (1985) reported that only mild amnesic patients performed better on unrelated pairs (see also, Shimamura & Squire, 1987). However, Mayes and Gooding (1989), using different amnesic patients, claimed that performance on that test was correlated with the extent of frontal-lobe dysfunction rather than with the severity of amnesia. Using speeded reading as the implicit test, Moscovitch et al. (1986) found that even severely amnesic patients read old sentences and unrelated pairs more quickly, but Musen and Squire (1990) failed to replicate the results on word pairs.

Analogues of implicit and explicit tests of memory also can be found in the animal literature. In the 1950s when investigators first began to create animal models of the amnesic syndrome by lesioning the hippocampus in nonhuman species, they were initially surprised to discover that lesioned animals continued to perform well on a large variety of learning and memory tasks (Douglas, 1967; Kimble, 1968). It took almost two decades before theoretical and empirical developments in the animal and human literatures began to converge on each other. In general, animals with hippocampal lesions, like humans, were found to be deficient on tests in which successful performance depended on their making reference to a particular past event or episode. For example, rats were impaired on the standard radial arm maze in which they must keep track of the arms already entered (Olton et al., 1979); hippocampally-damaged rats (Eichenbaum, Parikh, & Cohen, 1985) and monkeys (Zola-Morgan & Squire, 1986) were impaired on nonmatching-to-sample tasks, which required subjects to remember particular stimuli at long delays. Other examples included spatial (Jarrard, 1975) and nonspatial (Walker & Means, 1973; Winocur, 1985) delayed alternation, and memory for specific contexts (Winocur & Olds, 1978). When animals can learn habitual responses or rules that do not require reference to a particular past episode, performance is spared following hippocampal lesions. Thus, they perform normally on tests of simultaneous discrimination learning tasks, on certain active and passive avoidance conditioning tasks, and on reference memory tasks (O'Keefe & Nadel, 1978; Olton et al., 1979).

The picture that emerges is that the cortical or subcortical region involved in processing a certain type of information also mediates performance on implicit tests of memory that pertain to that information. This suggests that these regions are modified by the information they have processed and have stored a representation of it. For many implicit tests, particularly those that are perceptual, reactivation of that representation or some aspects of it is both a necessary and sufficient condition for eliciting strong repetition-priming effects (Moscovitch, 1989; Moscovitch & Umilta, 1990, 1991; Schacter, 1990; Squire, 1987; Tulving & Schacter, 1990).

For some implicit tests, however, an additional strategic or organiza-

tional component comes into play. For example, improvement with practice at solving puzzles such as the Tower of Hanoi requires planning, organization of response sequences, and monitoring of responses in addition
to mere repetition. Other tests may fall between these two poles. Shallice (1982) and St. Cyr, Taylor, and Lang (1988) showed that mastering
the Tower of Hanoi depends, in part, on the integrity of the frontal lobes
and related structures in the basal ganglia. Even improvement in learning simple jigsaw puzzles may be impaired in patients with frontal dysfunction (Wilson & Baddeley, 1988).

There is suggestive evidence that the frontal lobes may contribute to
performance on still other implicit tests of memory. Work on normal people has indicated that repetition effects on reading transformed script and
word-stem completion are influenced by semantic or lexical variables as
well as perceptual ones (Roediger, 1990; Tardif & Craik, 1989). It is significant that patients with considerable frontal dysfunction, such as Huntington's disease patients (Martone, Butters, Payne, Becker, & Sax, 1984)
or patients with severe closed head injury (Wilson & Baddeley, 1988),
show little improvement in learning to read transformed script. Working
with Korsakoff amnesic patients who also frequently have frontal-lobe
deficits, Mayes and Gooding (1989) used stem-completion to test implicit
learning of associates. They found that performance correlated significantly with frontal-lobe impairment but not with severity of amnesia. Howard,
Fry, and Brune (1991) reported deficits on similar implicit paired-associate
tests in old people, but did not examine whether performance was correlated with frontal dysfunction. In light of these observations, a hypothesis worth pursuing is that the frontal lobes contribute to those implicit
tests that require organizational skills or have a strategic, lexical, or semantic search component.

Successful performance on implicit tests that have a prominent sensorimotor component depend on the integrity of the basal ganglia, particularly the caudate nucleus, which have prominent connections to the frontal
lobes. For example, Butters, Heindel, and Salmon (1990) showed that patients with Huntington's or Parkinson's diseases are impaired on pursuit-
rotor and on weight-biasing tasks, but not on perceptual or semantic repetition-priming tests. Patients with Alzheimer's disease, on the other hand,
with suspected degeneration in the temporal-parietal region, perform normally on the implicit, sensorimotor tasks but show some impairment on
implicit, semantic tasks. Consistent with the hypothesis that the lateral
temporal cortex is necessary for successful performance on such tasks,
patients with surgical excisions of the left temporal lobe showed reduced
conceptual repetition effects (Blaxton, 1991). Because the visual cortex
was relatively spared in all these patients, visual perceptual repetition effects were normal (Keane, Gabrieli, Fennema, Growdon, & Corkin, 1991).

Using experimental animal models, Mishkin (Mishkin & Appenzeller, 1987) provided the most detailed analysis of neuroanatomical structures mediating performance on implicit and explicit tests of memory. Mishkin referred to the structures necessary for implicit memory as the "habit system." In line with evidence from the human literature, the critical regions in Mishkin's habit system include the basal ganglia and related cortical structures.

Aging Studies

Experiments have been conducted in the elderly on a variety of implicit tests of memory (for reviews, see Graf, 1990; Howard, 1988, 1991). Our working assumption is that age-related deficits will appear only on those tests that involve the hippocampus and frontal lobes. Performance on many implicit tests of memory, therefore, should be unaffected by age. In line with our hypothesis, no age differences in repetition effects were found on lexical decision tasks (Moscovitch, 1982b), picture naming (Mitchell, 1989; Mitchell, Brown, & Murphy, 1990), speeded reading (Moscovitch et al., 1986), category judgment tasks (Rabbitt, 1982), word-fragment completion (Light, Singh, & Capps, 1986; but see below, p. 339), perceptual identification of words (Light & Singh, 1987) and pictures (Snodgrass & Corwin, 1988), homophone spelling (see Davis et al., 1990; Howard, 1988; but see Rose, Yesavage, Hill, & Bower, 1986), category exemplar generation (Light & Albertson, 1989), preferences for novel patterns (Wiggs, 1990; cited in Howard, 1991), and skin conductance responses to studied versus new words (Reese-Nishio, 1984; cited in Moscovitch, 1985). All these tests can be considered to be primarily perceptual repetition-priming tests that do not involve the hippocampus. The absence of a significant semantic search component precludes frontal-lobe involvement on these tests.

However, age-related changes have been reported on implicit tests of memory that are thought to have a substantial frontal contribution. Moscovitch et al. (1986) reported that institutionalized elderly people whose frontal dysfunction is prominent in comparison to community-dwelling elderly people (Winocur & Moscovitch, 1990a) have difficulty learning to read transformed script and show little repetition effects for that material. Even normal elderly people show an impaired ability to acquire this reading skill, a finding confirmed by Hashtroudi, Chrosniak, and Schwartz (in press). Age-related deficits were reported in a pursuit-rotor task and a mirror-tracing task (Wright & Payne, 1985), both of which are known to be impaired in patients with basal ganglia pathology and frontal dysfunction (Butters et al., 1990).

Dywan and Jacoby (1990) found age-related changes on a fame-judgment task. In that implicit test of memory, subjects were shown a study list of names of famous and nonfamous people. On the subsequent fame-judgment test, elderly people were much more likely than young people to classify nonfamous names that appeared on the study list as famous. The authors speculated that this tendency may be related to impaired frontal-lobe function in the elderly.

A similar "frontal" explanation likely accounts for the discrepancies in the literature on age-related deficits on word-stem completion. Initial reports by Light and Singh (1987) claimed that there was a slight, but statistically nonsignificant, age-related deficit on word-stem completion. In subsequent research, Chiarello and Hoyer (1988), Davis et al. (1990), and Hultsch, Masson, and Small (1991) found significant deficits on the same tests in the elderly. Indeed, both authors argued, and Hultsch et al. demonstrated, that the initial failure to find a significant deficit was related to the weak statistical power of the Light and Singh study. Moreover, stem completion was the only one among a number of perceptual repetition-priming tests on which Hultsch et al. found an age-related decline. Winocur and Diesman (unpublished observations) confirmed these age differences on stem completion. In line with our hypothesis, the deficits were correlated with performance on verbal fluency and the WCST, two standard psychometric tests of frontal function. The elderly also were impaired on recognition but their performance on that explicit test of memory was not significantly correlated with performance on frontal-lobe tests. Although not a double dissociation experiment, it is one of the few studies that does meet the criteria for a correlational test of single dissociation. Similar correlations between stem-completion and WCST were reported by Davis et al. (1991).

It is interesting to note that implicit memory for a recurring serial pattern (Nissen & Bullemer, 1987) is not impaired in old people, though explicit memory for that pattern is (Howard & Howard, 1989). One might have expected, given the sequential nature of the task, that the frontal lobes would be involved and that elderly people therefore might be impaired (see Kay, 1951). One possibility worth investigating is the type of organization involved in acquiring and executing the task. In the typical test, an asterisk appears in one of four locations on a screen and the task is to push the button under the asterisk as soon as possible. The recurring sequence can be learned by simple associations or by forming hierarchies that organize the input and output components of the task. As Cohen, Ivry, and Keele (1990) recently demonstrated, it is only the hierarchical component of the implicit test that is disrupted by a concurrent, attention-demanding task. It is also this component that is most likely to require frontal involvement and be sensitive to the effects of aging.

In the animal literature, performance on analogues of implicit tests of memory that have no frontal component is not impaired with age. Thus, performance in aged rats is normal on discrimination learning (Kay & Sime, 1962; Winocur, 1984), operant conditioning tasks such as learning to press a lever on a continuous reinforcement schedule (Campbell & Haroutunian, 1981; Winocur, 1986), and one-way active avoidance learning (Doty, 1966). On the other hand, there is growing evidence that old rats, like old people, are impaired on implicit tests that do have a frontal component. Acquisition of a maze-learning skill and conditional rule learning can be considered two such tests, because rats with hippocampal lesions perform normally on them. Performance on both tests, however, is impaired by prefrontal lesions indicating a strong frontal contribution to them. Consistent with our hypothesis, old rats are deficient on these tests (Winocur, 1992; Winocur & Moscovitch, 1990b).

Summary

Damage to the hippocampal system produces a memory disorder that has the following four defining features: (a) Memory is affected independently of intelligence, (b) long-term memory is impaired relative to short-term memory, (c) the memory deficit is greater for recent than for remote events, and (d) memory with awareness is affected whereas memory without awareness, as revealed by implicit tests of memory, generally is spared. By and large, these same four features are characteristic of the memory loss that accompanies old age in both humans and experimental animals such as rats and monkeys. Though the loss is not as severe in the elderly as in amnesics with focal hippocampal system lesions, the common pattern observed in both supports our hypothesis that progressive deterioration of the hippocampal system with age accounts for some of the age-related memory deficits. Because evidence of double or single dissociation (either structural or functional) is not typically available in the aged population, we cannot say for certain that the pattern of memory loss is caused by hippocampal system deterioration. Gathering such evidence is a top priority of research in this area. However, the neural deterioration that accompanies the aging process is not confined only to the hippocampal system. The involvement of other structures leads to additional memory deficits in the elderly. These additional deficits, we hypothesize, will resemble those of patients with focal lesions to the affected structures. Because the frontal lobes are especially vulnerable to the aging process, age-related memory deficits also should be similar to those observed in patients with frontal lesions. This hypothesis is examined in the next section.

FRONTAL LOBES

The functions of the frontal lobes are more diverse and elusive than those of the hippocampus. Structurally, the frontal cortex is heterogeneous consisting of a number of anatomically distinct areas that have different phylogenetic and ontogenetic histories. Whereas it has been known for some time that two large subdivisions of the prefrontal cortex, the orbitofrontal and dorsolateral regions, have different functions (Goldman-Rakic, 1987; Milner, 1964; Mishkin, 1964), recent evidence suggests that even smaller regions within these subdivisions have specialized functions that can be distinguished from one another. Given this apparent diversity, it is understandable that there is little agreement about the functions of the frontal lobes. Although there have been some constructive and commendable attempts at presenting unifying theories of frontal-lobe function (e.g., Fuster, 1989; Goldman-Rakic, 1987; Luria, 1966), none has been comprehensive enough to accommodate the range of findings in the literature. Two camps or points of view can be identified. One camp believes that there is a common underlying function that expresses itself in diverse ways determined by the anatomical connections in each region and their respective domains; Goldman-Rakic's (1987) view that frontal lobes are involved in working memory falls into this camp. The other camp does not assume a functional link among the various regions but rather argues for greater functional independence among them (Petrides, 1989). Until one can formulate with greater clarity and precision what the functions of the prefrontal cortex are, it will remain difficult to adjudicate between these two general viewpoints.

The organization of this section reflects these two points of view. In the first part, we catalog the deficits associated with focal damage to the frontal cortex, specifying the affected subregions when we can. We then examine the literature on aging to determine if comparable deficits are found in elderly people. In the second part, we consider unifying frameworks that attempt to integrate the available evidence, and suggest directions for future research and theoretical development.

Psychometric Tests of Frontal Functions

There are a number of psychometric test batteries that contain tests purported to be sensitive to frontal-lobe lesions. We do not review them in detail (see Stuss & Benson, 1986), but instead simply describe briefly those that are used most commonly. Among these are tests of verbal fluency and the WCST, which is a test of hypothesis formation and set shifting. Milner (1963, 1964) showed that lesions of the dorsolateral prefrontal cortex, usually on the left side, lead to a difficulty in shifting sets (or hypotheses) that is marked by perseveration on previously correct, but currently incorrect, responses. Deficits in the fluency with which words can be generated from a given initial letter are associated with left or-bitofrontal lesions (see also Benton, 1968). Generating category names, however, is more likely to be affected by left-temporal-lobe lesions (New-combe, 1969). Tests of nonverbal fluency, in which subjects are required to generate meaningless designs, is affected more by right than left fron-tal lesions (Jones-Gotman & Milner, 1977).

Recently, a number of investigators have shown that diffuse damage or damage to other structures including the left and right temporal lobe can lead to deficits on verbal fluency (Joanette & Goulet, 1986; Martin, Loring, Meador, & Lee, 1990; Miceli, Caltagirone, Gainotti, Massulo, & Silveri, 1981; Pendelton, Heaton, Lehman, & Hulihan, 1982) and on WCST (Anderson, Jones, Tranel, Tranel, & Damasio, 1990; Heaton, 1981; Robinson, Heaton, Lehman, & Stilson, 1980). It is difficult to adjudicate between these different claims. The procedures used for testing verbal fluency and WCST in the various studies were different as, in some cases, were the etiology of the patients' damage. Because performance on ver-bal fluency and WCST, like that on other psychometric tests, may be de-termined by multiple factors, changes in some aspects of the test may alter the critical components of the test so that the contribution of non-frontal structures becomes more prominent (Heaton, 1981; Nelson, 1976; Teuber, Battersby & Bender, 1951). Frontal deficits most clearly emerge when strong response sets are developed and set shifting is dependent on internal monitoring of outcomes. This conclusion is supported by the predominance of perseverative responses in frontal, as compared to other patients, in all the studies (Anderson et al., 1980; Heaton, 1981; Milner, 1964).

With regard to letter fluency, if patients with diffuse damage or epilepsy without surgical intervention are removed from the sample (Martin et al., 1990), then the findings show that deficits are greatest in patients with left frontal lesions, though patients with right frontal lesions are also impaired.

Age-related deficits have been observed on both WCST and tests of verbal fluency, but not consistently. There seems to be some agreement that the likelihood of finding such deficits increases greatly as individu-als enter their eighth decade. The performance of adults in their 60s and 70s may be more variable, which may account for reports of normal (Ben-ton, Eslinger, & Damasio, 1981) and of impaired (Leach, Warner, Hotz-Sud, Kaplan, & Freedman, 1991) performance in the elderly. In addition, as with studies of brain-damaged patients, the methodological differences in the design and administration of the tests may influence their outcome. For example, a modified version of the WCST was developed by Nelson (1976) specifically to enable normal elderly people to cope with its demands. Ostensibly, the "frontal" component of the test was left intact, but there is no assurance that the modified test was sensitive to the type of mild frontal dysfunction that is expected to be found in the elderly. The same may be true of different forms of verbal fluency tests.

Another test that has gained some popularity is the Stroop test (MacLeod, 1991; Stroop, 1935), which has recently been standardized for use with clinical populations (Golden, 1978). In this test, subjects are shown a list of color patches and two lists of color names. One list is written in black, the other in a color that does not correspond to the name (the word *red* written in blue). The subject's task is to name the color patches, read the black list, and then name the color in which the word is written in the colored list. Successful performance with the colored list requires that the subject overcome the interfering effect of the word in order to name the color. Even in normal young adults, naming times are longer and errors are greater for the colored list than for the other two. This increase in errors and latency is known as the Stroop effect.

As might be expected, patients with frontal lesions show a larger Stroop effect than do intact controls, presumably because frontal patients have greater difficulty in suppressing the interfering effects of the written color name (*red*) (Golden, 1978; Perret, 1974). Likewise, elderly people show greater Stroop interference than do young adults (Cohn, Dustman, & Bradford, 1984; Comalli, Wapner, & Werner, 1962; MacLeod, 1991).

Experimental Tests of Frontal Functions

In addition to psychometric tests, a number of experimental tests have been developed that are sensitive to frontal-lobe lesions. Unfortunately, many of the tests also involve a memory component that may be affected by temporal-lobe/hippocampal lesions. Because frontal- and temporal-lobe/hippocampal lesions are presumed to affect different components of the test, the nature of the impairment should be different in the two cases. In evaluating the performance of patients with cortical lesions, it is important, where possible, to note the pattern of deficits in an attempt to distinguish between lesions to the frontal lobes and lesions to other cortical structures. For example, patients with frontal lesions are impaired at judging which of two stimuli appeared more recently even though they remember having seen both stimuli earlier. Patients with temporal-lobe lesions, on the other hand, fail the recency judgments only when their memory of the stimuli themselves is impaired. When they recognize the stimuli as "old," they can determine as well as normal people which of the two occurred more recently (Milner, 1974; Milner, Petrides, & Smith, 1985).

Temporal Order.   Judgments of temporal order also are affected by frontal- and hippocampal lesions. Shimamura, Janowsky, and Squire (1990) showed that both amnesic patients and patients with frontal lesions are impaired in reproducing the order of a recently presented list of words and of world events that occurred during the last 30 years. What is important from our perspective is that the deficit in temporal ordering was not related to the severity of the amnesia.

This is consistent with Milner's (1974) finding regarding the contribution of frontal lobes and hippocampus to judgments of temporal recency. Interestingly, if the stimuli are manipulated instead of merely observed, recency judgment is intact following frontal lesions (McAndrews & Milner, in press).

Studies of Parkinsonian patients, whose profile of cognitive deficits includes frontal dysfunction, are similarly impaired on tests of temporal order (Vriezen & Moscovitch, 1990) and of dating (Sagar, Cohen, Sullivan, Corkin, & Growdon, 1988; Sagar, Sullivan, Gabrieli, Corkin, & Growdon, 1988). Patients with Alzheimer's disease, on the other hand, who have a profound memory loss due to medial temporal-lobe degeneration, tend to be less impaired on similar tests if they can recognize the material.

Memory for temporal order is worse in old than in young adults. Old adults have greater difficulty than do young adults in reconstructing the order of a list of words, pictures, activities (Kinsbourne, 1973; Kausler, Lichty & Davis, 1985; Naveh-Benjamin, 1990; Vriezen & Moscovitch, 1992), and in judging the relative recency of two items (McCormack, 1982), though on some studies the effect fails to reach significance (McCormack, 1981; Perlmutter, Metzger, Nezworsti, & Miller, 1981). Since temporal ordering depends on frontal and hippocampal involvement, it is not completely certain whether the deficit in elderly people can be attributed solely to frontal dysfunction or whether there is also a medical temporal-lobe component to it (Vriezen & Moscovitch, 1992).

Judgments of temporal order or recency also may figure in tests such as delayed response, spatial alternation, object reversal, and spatial reversal. In delayed response, subjects must match one of two items to a previously presented target. When the targets and test items are chosen from a small set of recurring items, successful performance involves the temporal segregation of the current target from targets presented on previous trials that are no longer relevant. On the spatial alternation task, the subject must alternate responses from one side to the other on each trial. On object and spatial reversal tasks responses to one object or spatial location are rewarded until a criterion is reached and then the formerly unrewarded response is reinforced. To perform well on the alternation and reversal tasks, the subject again must focus on the immediately preceding trial to guide performance and ignore the prior targets' responses. Frontal lesions produced deficits on these tests in humans (Freedman & Oscar-Berman, 1986), monkeys (Goldman-Rakic, 1987; Jacobsen, 1935; Mishkin, 1964; Mishkin & Pribram, 1965; Nissen, Riesen, & Nowlis, 1938), and rats (Kolb, 1984) that are exacerbated when the subject must overcome a strong, prepotent response. As demonstrated in the reversal studies (Mishkin, 1964), no deficits are found in establishing the initial prereversal response but large deficits are seen in animals with frontal lesions on the reversal condition. Lesions of medial temporal lobes also will lead to impaired performance on these tests. The temporal-lobe deficits, however, are linked more to the delay between the target and test items or to the delay between trials rather than to the size of the stimulus set or to the establishment of prepotent responses.

Tasks with a spatial component, such as spatial alternation, are difficult for animals with hippocampal lesions even if no delay is involved. However, their error pattern is different from that of animals with frontal lesions. Whereas hippocampal animals either choose randomly (Diamond, Zola-Morgan, & Squire, 1989) or develop a position preference, frontal animals tend to perseverate on the previously correct response (Diamond & Goldman-Rakic, 1989).

Aged rats and monkeys are impaired on a variety of alternation and reversal tasks that are sensitive to both hippocampal and frontal lesions. On the reversal tasks, aged monkeys, like monkeys with frontal lesions, perseverate on the previously correct response, but like monkeys with hippocampal lesions they also have difficulty in learning a new response once the perseverative tendency is overcome (Bartus, Dean, & Fleming, 1979; Bartus, Fleming, & Johnson, 1978). In most studies, therefore, it is difficult to know the source of the poorer performance in aged rats. An exception is the study by Winocur (1986) on delayed, go–no-go alternation with rats. In these tests, we see a decrement in performance of aged rats that is indicative of both frontal and hippocampal dysfunction. Their performance, impaired even at short delays as a result of frontal dysfunction, becomes worse at longer delays due to impaired hippocampal function.

Conditional Associative Learning. Investigators also have used conditional associative learning to investigate the effects of frontal and medial temporal-lobe lesions in animals and humans. In this paradigm, the subject must learn to associate by trial and error a set of responses say, hand-movements, to a set of stimuli, such as different lights. In humans, damage to either the right or left frontal lobes produces impairment on verbal and nonverbal versions of this test (Petrides, 1985). In contrast, patients with unilateral temporal-lobe lesions with large hippocampal removals in the left hemisphere are impaired only on the verbal versions of the test, whereas those with removals on the right hemisphere, are impaired on the pictorial, nonverbal version. These results confirm the hypothesis that hippocampal removals interfere with encoding of hemisphere-specific information into long-term memory and not with the conditional aspects of the task. In work with monkeys, Petrides (1989) identified Brodmann's areas 6 and 8 as the frontal regions that are critical for conditional associative learning. Recent work with positron emission tomography (PET) scans has shown that the homologous region is involved in this test in humans (Petrides, 1991).

Impaired performance on the conditional associative learning test also has been found in normal elderly people, but it is difficult to determine with certainty whether the deficit is related to frontal or hippocampal dysfunction or to both. Vriezen and Moscovitch (1992) administered two versions of this test: a trial-and-error version similar to the one used by Petrides (1985) and a correction version in which the correct answer was supplied if an error was made. The latter version, we believe, may be more sensitive to hippocampal than to frontal dysfunction. The elderly people were equally impaired on both. Unfortunately, the study was not designed to assess predictions about the respective contributions of the two brain regions. Double dissociation studies along the lines discussed in the introduction would be helpful in this case.

The distinction between frontal-lobe and hippocampal involvement in conditional associative learning also was demonstrated in rats (Winocur, 1991b). Rats were taught to press a bar on the left or right depending on the side on which a light appeared. The amount of time between light onset and the opportunity to respond was varied. Rats with hippocampal lesions were not impaired in learning the basic conditional discrimination at short intervals, but their performance deteriorated as the interval between stimulus and response was increased. However, rats with frontal-lobe lesions were severely and equally impaired at all intervals. These results support the hypothesis that the hippocampus is critical for retention whereas the frontal lobes are necessary for the conditional aspects of the task. Again, as predicted, old rats performed more poorly than did young rats on this test. The pattern of the old rats' performance was indicative of both frontal and hippocampal dysfunction. Some deficit was noted at short delays (frontal), which was exacerbated at long delays (hippocampal) (Winocur, 1992).

Self-Ordered Pointing and Radial Arm Mazes. In self-ordered pointing, patients are required to select an item from an array of items pictured on a page (Petrides & Milner, 1982). Having done so, the patient turns to the next page in which the same array appears, although the items are arranged differently. The task is to select a different item on every page. This procedure is repeated for as many pages as there are items. Patients with frontal-lobe damage, in the vicinity of areas 46 and 9, are impaired on this test with left and right frontal lesions producing the greatest impairment on a verbal and nonverbal version of this test, respectively. Comparisons between old and young people are not available for the self-ordered pointing task.

Analogues of this test were developed for use with monkeys (Passingham, 1985; Petrides, 1985). In these tests, animals are presented with several stimuli and are rewarded for responding to a different stimulus on each trial. Frontal lesions in areas homologous to those in humans produce deficits on these tests, but again no data are available on the performance of old monkeys.

The radial arm maze, used extensively with rats, can be considered to be a spatial analogue of the self-ordered pointing task. The rat is rewarded for selecting a new arm on each trial. Deficits again are observed following frontal lesions (Kolb, Sutherland, & Whishaw, 1983). As expected, aged rats perform more poorly than young rats (Barnes, 1988; De Toledo-Morrell & Morrell, 1985).

It should be noted that in humans, monkeys, and rats, damage to the medial temporal lobes also will lead to impaired performance on the various versions of self-ordered tests. As yet, it is not always possible to distinguish between the effects of the two lesions on the basis of performance measures.

Learning Other Complex Mazes. Aged rats are impaired at learning complex mazes, tasks that are also sensitive to frontal and hippocampal lesions (Ingram, 1988; Winocur & Moscovitch, 1990b). Winocur and Moscovitch showed that hippocampal and frontal contribution to maze learning can be dissociated, with the former implicated in retaining maze-specific information and the latter in acquiring a general maze-learning skill. Aged rats are impaired on both components. Studies of maze learning in people have shown that patients with right hippocampal lesions are impaired on this task because they fail to remember the path traced (Corkin, 1965), whereas patients with right frontal lesions perform poorly because they do not adhere to the rules. Although elderly people also have difficulty in learning complex mazes, no studies have been reported that dissociate frontal from hippocampal effects.

Source Amnesia and List Differentiation.   Event monitoring, a component of self-ordered pointing and radial arm maze tasks, is also a component on tests that require the subject to identify the source of the information they remember. For example, subjects are taught a set of facts, some by one experimenter and the remainder by another. Their task is to remember the facts as well as how they acquired the information. As expected, amnesic patients with various etiologies have difficulty remembering both facts and sources. When the amnesic patients' fact memory was equated with that of normal people by testing the amnesics at much shorter delays, the extent of their deficit on memory for sources varied according to the degree of frontal dysfunction as measured by WCST and verbal fluency (Schacter et al., 1984), and not according to the severity of their amnesia. Moreover, whereas normal people and nonfrontal amnesic patients often forgot which of the two experimenters taught them a particular fact (source attribution errors or source forgetting), they rarely, if ever, attributed their knowledge to an extraexperimental source. The term *source amnesia* was used to describe this more extreme form of the deficit, which was a much more common error for the amnesic patients with frontal dysfunction. The results were replicated by Shimamura and Squire (1987) (see also Parkin, Leng, & Stanhope, 1988). As a direct test of the hypothesis that source amnesia is related to frontal-lobe damage, Janowsky, Shimamura, and Squire (1989a) tested nonamnesic patients with focal frontal-lobe lesions. Their patients demonstrated the predicted source amnesia.

Deficits on tests of list differentiation in Korsakoff patients also may be related to the frontal dysfunction that is associated with the syndrome. Huppert and Piercy (1976b) showed that even when Korsakoff patients recognized the words they studied, they were poor at reporting whether they had studied the words recently or 24 hours earlier, or whether the words came from the first or second list they had studied. Deficits in memory for temporal order and for monitoring sources may underlie impaired performance on these tests (Moscovitch, 1982a; Schacter, 1987b).

Elderly adults, like frontal patients, are deficient in identifying the source of the events they have experienced (McIntyre & Craik, 1987). Thus, elderly people are poor at recognizing the physical attributes of the target—for example, whether it was heard in a male or female voice (Kausler & Puckett, 1981) or whether it was seen in capital or small letters (Kausler & Puckett, 1980); they even have difficulty remembering whether they saw or generated the target. In other experiments elderly people were found to be impaired in discriminating between having performed an act, intending to do so, or merely imagining it (Cohen & Faulkner, 1989; Guttentag & Hunt, 1988; Koriat, Ben-Zur, & Scheffer,

1988; for further references, see Light, 1991). In short, elderly people are prone to source forgetting and occasionally even show source amnesia.

Studies by Craik et al. (1990) provide supportive evidence of a link between age-related deficits on these tests and frontal dysfunction. As noted earlier, Craik et al. showed that performance on the source attribution test in elderly people is correlated with the number of perseverative errors on the WCST, a test of frontal function.

In highlighting the elderly person's difficulties with source attribution, one should not lose sight of the fact that in all likelihood the same subjects also will have poorer memory than the young for the targets. Our point is that these are different deficits attributable to disruption of different mechanisms. Source memory failure results from a decline in frontal-lobe function whereas target memory failure is related to hippocampal dysfunction. To underscore this point, amnesic patients without frontal damage, who are typically poor at remembering both types of information, can perform normally on the source attribution test if their target memory is equated with that of controls. However, elderly people (like patients with frontal damage) are not as good as the young in recollecting the context of an event even when their memory for the event itself is intact (Kliegl & Lindenberger, 1988, cited in Light, 1991; Schacter, Kaszniak, Khilstrom, & Valoliserri, in press).

Frequency Estimation. Another example of a deficit that may be related to monitoring is found in tests of frequency estimation. Here subjects are presented with a series of items, some of which are repeated various numbers of times. The subject's task is to estimate the frequency with which an item was presented. Smith and Milner (1988) found that at high frequencies, patients with left or right frontal lesions underestimated the number of presentations more than normal people and patients with temporal-lobe lesions. The evidence on age-related deficits in frequency estimation is contradictory (Hasher & Zacks, 1979, 1984). Whereas many investigators report that elderly people are worse at estimating frequency than the young (Freund & Witte, 1986; Kausler, Hakami, & Wright, 1982; Kausler, Lichty, & Hakami, 1984), others found no age differences (Attig & Hasher, 1980; Ellis, Palmer, & Reeves, 1988; Hasher and Zacks, 1979; Kausler, Lichty, & Davis, 1985). It should be noted that frontal patients were impaired most noticeably at high frequencies when performance even among normal people was inaccurate. The deficits in the elderly, therefore, also are expected to occur primarily when the frequency estimation task is sufficiently difficult to challenge their frontal lobes. The contradictory findings in the literature on normal aging may be reconciled if this factor is taken into account. As Freund and Witte (1986) elegantly demonstrated, age-related deficits in frequency estimation emerge only at high frequencies (above five) when presentation rate is slow but at lower frequencies as presentation is increased.

Release from Proactive Inhibition. The effects of frontal-lobe lesions also have been examined on a number of other tests that include release from proactive inhibition (PI), metamemory, free recall, and recognition. Although some investigators have reported deficits on these tests, the results have not been conclusive.

In release from PI, subjects are presented with lists of words from a single taxonomic category followed by a list from a different category. Recall, tested after each list, declines as PI builds up in the same category condition but recall improves when the category shifts thereby showing a release from PI. Korsakoff patients typically fail to release from PI (Cermak, Butters, & Moreines, 1974; Winocur, Kinsbourne, & Moscovitch, 1981), a condition attributed to frontal dysfunction in many of these amnesics. As a direct test of this hypothesis, Moscovitch (1982a) found that patients with left unilateral frontal lobectomies also failed to show normal release from PI, especially if they were impaired on the WCST. Using a different test, Janowsky et al. (1989a) found no differences between frontal-lobe patients and normal controls. Based on their findings that only those frontal patients who were also amnesic failed to show normal release from PI, Freedman and Cermak (1986) suggested that PI release failure is likely to occur in frontal patients only if there is an accompanying memory disorder.

Failure to release from PI with the elderly has been reported by some investigators but not by others (Elias & Hirasuna, 1976; Puglisi, 1981). Here, too, the neurological literature is instructive in helping to resolve the contradictory evidence. As noted, release from PI is typically normal in community-dwelling elderly but is consistently impaired in institutionalized, but nondemented, elderly people (Moscovitch & Winocur, 1983). Deficits on both frontal and hippocampal tests are even more widespread, and certainly more severe, in institutionalized elderly people than among the community-dwelling elderly (Winocur, 1982; Winocur & Moscovitch, 1990a). As in patients, failure to release from PI seems to occur most reliably in elderly people who have frontal dysfunction superimposed on a memory disorder.

Metamemory. Metamemory refers to a self-monitoring process whereby individuals gain insight into the operation and capacity of their own memory. Although it often is reported that patients with frontal-lobe lesions lack such insight, being unaware of even severe amnesia, few studies have tested metamemory directly. An exception is the study by Janowsky et al. (1989a) on "feeling of knowing." In their test, subjects had to recall obscure facts in response to questions. For facts they failed to recall, they were asked to gauge their feeling of knowing the forgotten fact by estimating whether a cue might help them recall or recognize it. The patients were tested immediately or after a delay of 1–3 days. They also were tested for feeling of knowing of factual information that they had acquired premorbidly. Janowsky et al. reported that patients with frontal lesions were impaired on the metamemory task only when tested 1–3 days later. In contrast, Korsakoff amnesic patients were impaired at all intervals. Non-Korsakoff amnesic patients performed normally on the metamemory task, suggesting that the Korsakoff deficit on this test was related to the frontal dysfunction that commonly accompanies their memory disorder. These results suggest that both memory and frontal disorders must be present to obtain reliable "feeling of knowing" deficits. In this regard, "feeling of knowing" resembles release from PI.

Many more studies on metamemory have been conducted in elderly people than in patients with frontal damage. A variety of paradigms and abilities have been subsumed under the label of metamemory. These include test of peoples' ability to choose appropriate mnemonic strategies, to reflect on their memory performance in everyday life, to predict their performance on memory tests, to evaluate how well they have done and to adjust study times according to the difficulty of the memory test. Not surprisingly, given the diversity of the techniques, the results have been mixed. Sometimes old people are not as good as the young, but in most cases there are no age differences. In a test of feeling of knowing, for which there are comparable data on patients with frontal-lobe lesions, Butterfield, Nelson, and Peck (1988) and Lachman, Lachman, and Thronesbery (1979) found no age-related decline if metamemory was tested shortly after study, consistent with the finding that deficits are absent in immediate tests even with frontal patients.

Metamemory tests may vary in their sensitivity to frontal damage (Janowsky et al., 1989a). Even for those that are sensitive, clear deficits emerge only in subjects who have pronounced frontal dysfunction with a superimposed memory disorder. This may account for the relatively few studies that report age differences in metamemory in normal elderly people. What is needed are independent measures of frontal and hippocampal function in the elderly that can be correlated with their performance on metamemory tests. It would be desirable in this regard to compare community-dwelling elderly with healthy, institutionalized elderly because the latter group is known to have memory loss compounded by conspicuous signs of frontal dysfunction.

Free Recall and Recognition. In contrast to metamemory, age-related deficits in free recall are among the most robust and reliable findings in the psychological literature. Smaller but reliable age-related deficits in recognition also have been reported. Comparing the extent of age-related deficits on the two tasks is problematic because baseline conditions, difficulty, and scales of measurement are dissimilar. Nonetheless, a number of investigators (see chapter 2 of this volume) have argued that aging affects recall more than recognition. Because encoding and retention processes are presumably equivalent in recall and recognition, what distinguishes one from the other must be the processes involved at retrieval. Whereas recognition benefits from presentation of the target item, which acts as a retrieval cue that can automatically reactivate the stored information, free recall is dependent on self-initiated retrieval processes that must search and generate the appropriate cue before the automatic retrieval process is triggered. According to Craik (1983, 1986) recognition receives much greater environmental support than recall and, as a result, makes fewer demands on cognitive resources. Because, according to Craik, cognitive resources are diminished with age, recall is likely to suffer more than recognition as one gets older.

From a neuropsychological perspective, the memory processes common to recognition and recall are those likely to be mediated by the hippocampal system, which is involved in consolidation, retention, and the automatic aspects of retrieval (ecphory; Tulving, 1983) that are triggered by the appropriate cue (Moscovitch, 1989; Moscovitch & Umilta, 1990, 1991). Strategic, self-initiated retrieval, however, is a hallmark of many tests of recall but not of most tests of recognition. We believe that this strategic retrieval component is mediated by the frontal lobes and its related structures (Moscovitch, 1989; Moscovitch & Umilta, 1990, 1991). The greater deficit in recall than in recognition in elderly people is therefore likely to be a function of both hippocampal and frontal system deterioration that occurs with age.

Patients with lesions restricted to the lateral or orbital surface of the frontal lobes are typically unimpaired on many tests of recall and recognition that measure learning and retention.[2] However, an impairment is noted when organizational abilities at encoding or retrieval are required for successful performance. Thus, impaired performance in frontal-lobe patients has been reported on recall of stories and of categorized lists of words (Incisa della Rochetta, 1986; Janowsky et al., 1989; Mayes, 1988). In both cases the material is structured and allows for organizational factors to come into play and aid recall. On the other hand, both free recall of

---

[2]It is worth noting that bilateral lesions of the ventromedial surface of the frontal lobes, which often includes damage to the adjacent basal forebrain, can cause severe memory disturbances even on recall and recognition. A closer examination of the nature of the memory disorder indicates that this memory loss, though more severe, resembles that of frontal patients and is distinguishable on many grounds from that of patients with lesions to the medial temporal/hippocampus and other limbic structures (Delbecq-Desrouesne, Beauvois, & Shallice, 1990; Moscovitch, 1989; Stuss & Benson, 1986).

unstructured word lists and learning of pairs of randomly associated words are intact after frontal lesions but impaired after hippocampal damage.

It follows, therefore, that memory differences in favor of the young over the old should be greater on tests that benefit from organizational factors than on those that do not. When older adults were matched with young on memory span for difficult-to-organize material, such as color names, random letters, or nonsense words, they performed significantly worse than did the young when more meaningful materials were used (Craik, 1968; Heron & Craik, 1964; Craik & Masani, 1967; Taub, 1974). Greater age differences were also found for high-frequency versus low-frequency words (Kausler & Puckett, 1979) and for blocked versus random arrangements of related words (Laurence & Trottere, 1971). Age differences in mnemonic organization at recall, whether clustering or other measures are used as an index, also have been reported in many studies (Denney, 1980; Horn, Donaldson, & Egstrom, 1981; Hultsch, 1974; Sanders, Murphy, Schmitt, & Walsh, 1980; Smith, 1980). Salthouse (1982) suggested that the organizational effects originate at encoding. There is reason to believe that many organizational problems also occur at retrieval (Burke & Light, 1981; Craik & Birtwistle, 1971; Tulving & Pearlstone, 1966). The possibility that organizational factors exert their influence at both encoding and retrieval is consistent with effects observed in patients with frontal lesions (Incisa della Rochetta, 1986). As Salthouse (1982) noted in a review of the literature on the effects of organization on memory, "A reasonable conclusion with respect to aging and organizational processes in memory is that older adults engage less frequently, and perhaps less successfully, in the types of organization that facilitate memory performance. No one source of evidence is completely compelling [see pp. 135–187 for some contradictory findings], but the consistency with which age differences in organization are reported makes it quite likely that a real difference in organization exists" (p. 137).

Summary

There is a remarkable consistency between the memory deficits seen in human patients and experimental animals with frontal lesions and those seen in normal aging. Indeed, there is not one instance where a significant discrepancy is found. Moreover, in a number of instances, performance on the frontal memory tests correlated significantly with performance on nonmnemonic tests of frontal function in the elderly but not with performance on non-frontal tests, thereby satisfying the criterion of at least functional, single dissociation. As with studies of hippocampal memory functions, evidence of functional and structural double dissociation is necessary to establish unequivocally that decline in performance with age on the various frontal memory tests is indeed related to the deterioration of the frontal cortex.

A NOTE ON PSYCHOSOCIAL INFLUENCES

This chapter has focused on decline in learning and memory function in the brain and, specifically, the prefrontal cortex and hippocampus. It is important to emphasize that cognitive function does not decline in one-to-one fashion with chronological age. Numerous factors (e.g., medical history, educational level, lifestyle) can contribute to significant differences in cognitive abilities among individuals within the same age range. In one study, Arbuckle, Gold, and Andres (1986) assessed the relative contributions of chronological age, and social and personality factors to memory function in normal old people. Chronological age was found to be the least influential factor, accounting for only a small part of the total variance in memory performance.

Our own work has shown that environmental influences and psychological factors can significantly affect cognitive function in old age. In several studies (Winocur & Moscovitch, 1983, 1990; Winocur, Moscovitch, & Witherspoon, 1987; Winocur, Moscovitch, & Freedman, 1987; Moscovitch & Winocur, 1985), groups of old people living in the community or in institutions were compared on a wide range of clinical and experimental neuropsychological tests. Despite being carefully matched for age, IQ, health, and other factors, the community group consistently outperformed their counterparts in residences. Subsequent experimentation showed that these differences could be attributed to poor adjustment to the demands of institutional life. For example, old people in institutions, who were as healthy as the community-dwelling individuals, were generally less active and perceived themselves as having little control over decisions that affected their lives. Within our institutionalized sample, performance on tests of learning and memory was found to correlate significantly with measures of psychosocial function. Further, in comparisons over time, changes in activity level and perceived control correlated with changes in cognitive performance.

A significant feature of our results that bears directly on the theme of this chapter is that the neuropsychological tests that were most sensitive to extraneous factors also measured hippocampal and prefrontal lobe function. This suggests that biological aging, environmental influences, and psychosocial variables interact in important ways to affect cognitive decline in the elderly. Future research must take greater account of these factors, while adopting a more global approach to the neuropsychology of aging (see also Poon, 1985).

MEMORY AND WORKING WITH MEMORY: A FRAMEWORK FOR UNDERSTANDING THE EFFECTS OF HIPPOCAMPAL AND FRONTAL SYSTEM DETERIORATION WITH AGE

As is clear from this review, memory is not a unitary process. A number of separable components have been identified at both the functional and structural levels. We have distinguished two broad classes of memory tests, explicit and implicit, performance on which is mediated by different neural structures. Explicit tests of memory such as recognition and recall depend on the conscious recollection of previously experienced events. On implicit tests, the subject is not required to refer intentionally to the past in performing the test; memory is inferred from the effects of experience or practice on behavior. Indeed, in the case of amnesic patients, explicit conscious recollection of the target event may be absent even as its retained trace implicitly affects performance. As we noted, performance on implicit tests likely is mediated by perceptual and semantic input modules, located in the posterior neocortex, and by motor output modules in the basal ganglia (and probably other regions as well).

Conscious recollection also can be separated into two components, associative and strategic. The associative component involves the mandatory and relatively automatic encoding, storage, and retrieval of information that is consciously apprehended. This process is dependent on the hippocampus and its related structures. According to our model (see Fig. 7.1), the hippocampus facilitates the formation and retrieval of a cross-modular associative trace. An event, or the stimulus information that is connected with it, is picked up by perceptual modules that are located in the posterior neocortex. These perceptual structures are modified in the process of decoding the information, thereby creating an *engram* or perceptual record (Kirsner & Dunn, 1985), which then is represented in the input modules.

The output of the perceptual modules are delivered to consciousness and to central systems that are involved in interpreting them. This consciously experienced, semantically interpreted event then is relayed automatically to the hippocampus and its related limbic structures. The hippocampus in turn mandatorily binds the information it receives with the engrams in the various modules and central systems that recorded the experience. This constitutes the memory trace. Simultaneously the hippocampus encodes all the bound information in the memory trace as a file entry. We propose that consolidation is the process of establishing a long-lasting record or file entry of the memory trace (see Moscovitch, 1989, in press; Moscovitch & Umilta, 1990, 1991).

At retrieval, an externally presented or internally generated cue enters consciousness and automatically interacts with the memory trace via the file entry in the hippocampal system. The product of that interaction yields an output that enters consciousness and forms the basis of our conscious experience of remembering. The information thus retrieved is a product of the cue-engram interaction and may or may not be veridical. The processes of consolidation and automatic retrieval are all subsumed under associative memory processes.

The associative system, with the hippocampus at its core, is a system that automatically encodes consciously apprehended information and, in response to the appropriate cue, automatically delivers aspects of the stored information back to consciousness as a memory. The system lacks intelligence. Sometimes the memories that are delivered are veridical; sometimes they are not. How can one be distinguished from the other? Sometimes the memories are delivered in a haphazard fashion without temporal order or contextual information. How are they organized? Sometimes the initial cue is adequate; at other times an appropriate cue must be found if the initial one fails. What guides this search?

Strategic processes associated with the prefrontal cortex are necessary to perform these functions and, thereby, confer "intelligence" and control on the associative system. These strategic processes coordinate, interpret, and elaborate the information in consciousness to provide the hippocampal-associative-memory system with the appropriate encoding information and retrieval cues that it takes as its input. Comparable processes are involved in evaluating the hippocampal system's output and placing those retrieved memories in a proper spatiotemporal context. In short, it is a working-with-memory system. What makes us aware of the various processes involved in memory search are not the operations of the hippocampal-associative system, but rather the operations of the strategic frontal system that occupy consciousness. We are aware of the questions we deliver to the hippocampus, the answers we get from it, and the evaluation of the answers, but we are not aware of the ecphoric operations of the hippocampus itself (Moscovitch, 1989; Tulving, 1983).

The model of frontal-lobe function that we propose is, therefore, closer to the camp that believes that the frontal lobes have a common underlying function, though each subregion specializes in the domain in which it executes this function. The strategic, organizational role of the frontal lobes in memory is no different from its role in problem solving, ordering motor sequences, and so on. Even with respect to memory, different regions of the frontal lobes may be allocated to handle information from different domains (spatial vs. verbal: Milner et al., 1985) or from different regions or aspects of the same domain (upper or lower visual field: Goldman-Rakic, 1987). But in each case the same type or types of underlying functions will be involved.

As this brief account indicates, at least three distinguishable neurological components underlie performance on implicit and explicit tests of memory: (a) a neocortical component that is involved in engram formation and reactivation and that mediates performance on some implicit tests of memory; (b) an associative/hippocampal component that operates only on consciously apprehended information by binding engrams that are associated with conscious experience into a memory trace, and that delivers aspects of the memory traces back to consciousness in response to appropriate retrieval cues; and (c) a strategic/frontal system that operates on the input to the hippocampal component and the output from it. The frontal system also may be involved in engram formation and reactivation in the neocortex.

The posterior neocortex and the hippocampus are the structures involved in encoding, retention, and automatic retrieval of the contents of memory. They constitute the "memory" part of the system. To judge from the preserved performance on many implicit tests in old people and in older animals, aging has little influence on the formation of engrams. It is the hippocampal component that is susceptible to the effects of aging and, consequently, accounts for the decline in consolidation and long-term retention with age. Because we believe that the functions of the hippocampus and its related structures are relatively automatic, age-related loss in associative memory should be resistant to mnemonic strategies and to the depletion of cognitive resources.

The frontal lobes operate on the input to the hippocampal system and the output from it. It is the working-with-memory component. We prefer the term working with memory to the related term *working memory* to describe frontal functions for a number of reasons.

First, it captures the essence of what we believe the frontal system does. It works with engrams and memory traces, but does not form or store them. The hippocampal system provides the grist for the frontal mill.

Second, it eliminates the confusion that is associated with working memory, which has one meaning for human cognitive psychologists and another for experimental animal psychologists. For animal psychologists it refers to tasks that typically are associated with hippocampal rather than frontal damage (Olton et al., 1979), whereas the reverse is true of the human literature (Baddeley, 1986).

Third, even if we adopt the human cognitive sense of the word (as some animal neuropsychologists have done; e.g., Goldman-Rakic, 1987, 1991), the problem is not solved. As defined by Baddeley (1986) and others in human cognitive psychology, working memory is "a temporary storage of information that is being processed in any range of cognitive tasks" (p. 34). This definition is much too broad to capture only the functions of the frontal lobes. Further, working memory itself is divisible into a number of subcomponents: There are at least two slave systems, one verbal and one nonverbal, whose operations are controlled by a central executive. But it is only the central executive that is identified with the frontal lobes by Baddeley and others (Shallice, 1988).

Even if we accept Baddeley's (1986) modified proposal that frontal damage impairs the operation of the central executive and leads to a "dysexecutive syndrome," we have not solved the problem of retaining the concept of a working-memory deficit to describe the effects on frontal damage or dysfunction. Is the deficit noted only on those tasks in which the central executive operates, or that involve input from the two slave systems? If so, how then are we to account for deficits in temporal ordering, even of very remote events? Or for source amnesia? Or for frequency judgments? Thus, in its old usage, the term working-memory deficit is too broad, and in its modified form as a type of dysexecutive syndrome related to working memory, it is too narrow (see also critique in Moscovitch & Umilta, 1990).

A working-with-memory deficit seems to capture the essence of the impairment associated with frontal lesions. As we noted throughout this chapter, what is impaired after frontal damage or dysfunction is not memory itself but the uses to which memory is put, the inferences based on memory, the temporal ordering of remembered episodes, their placement in proper contexts, and the implementation of encoding and retrieval strategies with respect to particular events. In other words, what is impaired is the application of remembered events to the organization of behaviors in a current context. Indeed, deficits on these types of test are often striking and are found consistently in patients with frontal lesions and in elderly people with presumed frontal dysfunction, whereas performance on more traditional working-memory tests, such as backward digit span and reading span, is sometimes unimpaired in elderly people (see chapter 2 of this volume; see also Frisk & Milner, 1990).

Based on our description of the distinguishing characteristics of hippocampal and frontal systems, it follows that it is the frontal system that should be more prone to depletion of cognitive resources. The hippocampal system, being modular (see Fodor, 1983; Moscovitch & Umilta, 1990, 1991), operates in a relatively automatic fashion with little expenditure of cognitive resources. According to our model, an account of memory decline in the elderly that appeals to depletion of cognitive resources with age as a causal agent (Craik & Byrd, 1982; Hasher & Zacks, 1979, 1988; see also chapters 2 & 4 of this volume) is only applicable to those memory functions that are mediated by the frontal lobes. As yet, we know of no evidence in favor of or against this hypothesis. In fact, it may be in principle impossible to test it properly unless a measure of cognitive resources is devised that does not interfere with primary-task performance (see

Navon, 1984, and Salthouse, 1982, for critiques of theoretical and empirical aspects of the concept of cognitive resources).

The advantage of a neuropsychological model of aging is that it has no need to appeal to the concept of cognitive resources: It is sufficient, from a neuropsychological view, to ascribe memory decline in the elderly to deteriorating frontal and hippocampal functions. At the same time, the neuropsychological framework is capable of accommodating the concept of cognitive resources and of suggesting some counterintuitive, but neuropsychologically appealing, predictions about the type of deficits that might be observed if cognitive resources were reduced with age.

ACKNOWLEDGMENTS

Preparation of this chapter was supported by a Medical Research Council of Canada Grant to Gordon Winocur and Morris Moscovitch and an Ontario Mental Health Foundation Research Associateship to MM. We thank Gus Craik and Tim Salthouse for their excellent editorial comments.

REFERENCES

Aggleton, J. P., Hunt, P. R., & Rawlins, J. N. P. (1986). The effects of hippocampal lesions upon spatial and non-spatial tests of working memory. *Behavioral Brain Research, 19,* 133–146.

Albert, M. S., Butters, N., & Levin, J. (1979). Temporal gradients in the retrograde amnesia of patients with alcoholic Korsakoff's disease. *Archives of Neurology, 36,* 211–216.

Albert, M., & Stafford, J. L. (1986). CT scan and neuropsychological relationships in aging and dementia. In G. Goldstein & R. E. Tasker (Eds.), *Advances in Clinical Neuropsychology, Vol. 3* (pp. 31–53). New York: Plenum.

Anderson, S. W., Jones, R. D., Tranel, A. P., Tranel, D., & Damasio, H. (1990). Is the Wisconsin Card Sorting Test an index of frontal lobe damage? *Journal of Clinical and Experimental Neuropsychology, 12,* 80.

Arbuckle, T. Y., Gold, D., & Andres, D. (1986). Cognitive functioning of older people in relation to social and personality variables. *Psychology and Aging, 1,* 55–62.

Baddeley, A. D. (1986). *Working memory.* Oxford, England: Oxford University Press.

Baddeley, A. D., & Warrington, E. K. (1970). Amnesia and the distinction between long- and short-term memory. *Journal of Verbal Learning and Verbal Behavior, 9,* 575–589.

Barnes, C. A. (1988). Aging in the physiology of spatial memory. *Neurobiology of Aging, 9,* 563–568.

Bartus, R. T., Dean, R. L., & Fleming, D. L. (1979). Aging in the rhesus monkey: Effects on visual discrimination learning and reversal learning. *Journal of Gerontology, 34,* 209–219.

Bartus, R. T., Fleming, D., & Johnson, H. R. (1978). Aging in the rhesus monkey: Debilitating effects on short-term memory. *Journal of Gerontology, 33,* 858–871.

Benton, A. L. (1968). Differential effects of frontal lobe disease. *Neuropsychologia, 6,* 53–60.

Benton, A. L., Eslinger, P. J., & Damasio, A. R. (1981). Normative observations on neuro-psychological test performance in old age. *Journal of Clinical Neuropsychology, 3,* 33–42.

Blaxton, T. A. (1991). *Dissociations among memory measures in both normal and memory impaired subjects.* Manuscript submitted for publication.

Botwinick, J. (1978). *Aging and behavior* (2nd ed.). New York: Spring.

Botwinick, J., & Storandt, M. (1980). Recall and recognition of old information in relation to age and sex. *Journal of Gerontology, 35,* 70–75.

Burke, D. M., & Light, L. L. (1981). Memory and aging: The role of retrieval processes. *Psychological Bulletin, 90,* 513–516.

Butterfield, E. C., Nelson, T. O., & Peck, V. (1988). Developmental aspects of the feeling of knowing. *Developmental Psychology, 24,* 654–663.

Butters, N., & Albert, M. S. (1982). Processes underlying failures to recall remote events. In L. S. Cermak (Ed.), *Human memory and amnesia* (pp. 275–303). Hillsdale, NJ: Lawrence Erlbaum Associates.

Butters, N., & Cermak, L. (1974). Some comments on Warrington and Baddeley's report of normal short-term memory in amnesic patients. *Neuropsychologia, 12,* 283–285.

Butters, N., Heindel, W. C., & Salmon, D. P. (1990). Dissociation of implicit memory in dementia: Neurological implications. *Bulletin of the Psychonomic Society, 28,* 359–366.

Campbell, B. A., & Haroutunian, V. (1981). Effects of age on long-term memory: Retention of fixed-interval responding. *Journal of Gerontology, 36,* 338–341.

Carroll, J. B., & White, M. N. (1973). Word frequency and age of acquisition as determiners of picture-naming latency. *Quarterly Journal of Experimental Psychology, 25,* 85–95.

Cermak, L. S., Butters, N., & Moreines, J. (1974). Some analyses of the verbal encoding deficit of alcoholic Korsakoff patients. *Brain and Language, 1,* 141–150.

Cermak, L. S., Talbot, N., Chandler, K., & Wolburst, L. R. (1985). The perceptual priming phenomenon in amnesia. *Neuropsychologia, 23,* 615–622.

Chiarello, C., & Hoyer, W. J. (1988). Adult age differences in implicit and explicit memory: Time course and encoding effects. *Psychology and Aging, 3,* 358–366.

Cockburn, J., & Smith, P. T. (1991). The relative influence of intelligence and age on everyday memory. *Journal of Gerontology: Psychological Sciences, 46,* 31–36.

Cohen, A., Ivry, R. I., & Keele, S. W. (1990). Attentional structure in sequence learning. *Journal of Experimental Psychology: Learning, Memory, and Cognition, 16,* 17–30.

Cohen, G., & Faulkner, D. (1989). Age differences in source forgetting: Effects on reality monitoring and eyewitness testimony. *Psychology and Aging, 4,* 10–17.

Cohen, N. J., & Squire, L. R. (1980). Preserved learning and retention of pattern analysing skill in amnesia: Dissociation of "knowing how" and "knowing that." *Science, 210,* 207–209.

Cohn, N. B., Dustman, R. E., & Bradford, D. C. (1984). Age-related decrements in Stroop color test performance. *Journal of Clinical Psychology, 40,* 1244–1250.

Comalli, P. E., Jr., Wapner, S., & Werner, H. (1962). Interference effects of Stroop color-word test in childhood, adulthood, and aging. *Journal of the Genetic Psychology, 100,* 47–53.

Corkin, S. (1965). Tactually-guided maze learning in man: Effects of unilateral cortical excisions and bilateral hippocampal lesions. *Neuropsychologia, 3,* 339–351.

Craik, F. I. M. (1968). Short-term memory and the aging process. In G. A. Talland (Ed.), *Human aging and behaviour.* New York: Academic.

Craik, F. I. M. (1977). Age differences in human memory. In J. E. Birren & K. W. Schaie (Eds.), *Handbook of the psychology of aging* (pp. 384–420). New York: Van Nostrand Reinhold.

Craik, F. I. M. (1983). On the transfer of information from temporary to permanent storage. *Philosophical Transactions of the Royal Society of London, Series B, 302,* 341–359.

Craik, F. I. M. (1986). A functional account of age differences in memory. In F. Klix & H. Hagendorf (Eds.), *Human memory and cognitive capabilities* (pp. 409–422). Amsterdam: Elsevier.

Craik, F. I. M., & Birtwistle, J. (1971). Proactive inhibition in free recall. *Journal of Experimental Psychology, 91*, 120–123.

Craik, F. I. M., & Byrd, M. (1982). Aging and cognitive deficits: The role of attentional resources. In F. I. M. Craik & S. Trehub (Eds.), *Aging and cognitive processes.* New York: Plenum.

Craik, F. I. M., & Masani, P. A. (1967). Age differences in the temporal integration of language. *British Journal of Psychology, 38*, 291–299.

Craik, F. I. M., Morris, L. W., Morris, R. G., & Loewen, E. R. (1990). Relations between source amnesia and frontal lobe functioning in older adults. *Psychological Aging, 5*, 148–151.

Davis, H. P., Cohen, A., Gundy, M., Colombo, P., Van Dusseldorp, G., Simolke, N., & Romano, J. (1990). Lexical priming deficits as a function of age. *Behavioral Neuroscience, 104*, 288–297.

de Leon, M. J., George, A. E., & Ferris, S. H. (1984). Computed tomography and positron emission tomography correlates of cognitive decline in aging and senile dementia. In L. W. Poon (Ed.), *Handbook for clinical memory assessment of older adults* (pp. 353–358). Washington, DC: American Psychological Association.

Delbecq-Derouesne, J., Beauvois, M. F., & Shallice, T. (1990). Preserved recall versus impaired recognition: A case study. *Brain, 113*, 1045–1074.

Denney, N. W. (1980). Task demands and problem solving strategies in middle-aged and older adults. *Journal of Gerontology, 35*, 559–564.

De Toledo-Morrell, L., & Morrell, F. (1985). Electrophysiological markers of aging and memory loss in rats. *Annals of the New York Academy of Sciences, 444*, 296–311.

Diamond, A., & Goldman-Rakic, P. S. (1989). Comparison of human infants and rhesus monkeys on Piaget's AB̄ task: Evidence for dependence on dorsolateral prefrontal cortex. *Experimental Brain Research, 74*, 24–40.

Diamond, R., & Rozin, P. (1984). Activation of existing memories in anterograde amnesia. *Journal of Abnormal Psychology, 93*, 98–105.

Diamond, A., Zola-Morgan, S., & Squire, L. R. (1989). Successful performance by monkeys with hippocampal lesions on AB̄ and object retrieval, two tasks that work developmental changes in human infants. *Behavioral Neuroscience, 103*, 526–537.

Doty, B. A. (1966). Age and avoidance conditioning in rats. *Journal of Gerontology, 21*, 287–290.

Douglas, R. J. (1967). The hippocampus and behavior. *Psychological Bulletin, 67*, 416–442.

Dywan, J., & Jacoby, L. L. (1990). Effects of aging on source monitoring: Differences in susceptibility to false fame. *Psychology and Aging, 5*, 379–387.

Eichenbaum, H., Parikh, T., & Cohen, N. J. (1985). Delayed non-match to sample with trial-unique odor stimuli in intact and fornix-damaged rats: A new test for recognition memory and model of temporal-lobe amnesia. *Society for Neurosciences* (Abstract), *11*, 875.

Elias, C. S., & Hirasuna, N. (1976). Age and semantic and phonological encoding. *Developmental Psychology, 12*, 497–503.

Ellis, N. R., Palmer, R. L., & Reeves, C. L. (1988). Developmental and intellectual differences in frequency processing. *Developmental Psychology, 24*, 38–45.

Fitzgerald, J. M., & Lawrence, R. (1984). Autobiographical memory across the life-span. *Journal of Gerontology, 39*, 692–699.

Fodor, J. (1983). *The modularity of mind.* Cambridge, MA: MIT Press.

Francis, W. N., & Kucera, H. (1982). *Frequency analysis of English usage: lexicon and grammar.* Boston: Haughton Mifflin.

Freed, D. M., Corkin, S., & Cohen, N. J. (1987). Forgetting in H.M.: A second look. *Neuropsychologia, 25*, 461–471.

Freedman, M., & Cermak, L. S. (1986). Semantic encoding deficits in frontal lobe disease and amnesia. *Brain and Cognition, 5,* 108–114.

Freedman, M., & Oscar-Berman, M. (1986). Bilateral frontal lobe disease and selective delayed response deficits in humans. *Behavioral Neuroscience, 100,* 337–342.

Frisk, V., & Milner, B. (1990). The role of the left hippocampal region in the acquisition and retention of story content. *Neuropsychologia, 28,* 349–359.

Fuster, J. M. (1989). *The prefrontal cortex* (2nd ed.). New York: Raven.

Gilhooly, K. J., & Gilhooly, M. L. (1980). The validity of age-of-acquisition ratings. *British Journal of Psychology, 72,* 105–110.

Gilhooly, K. J., & Logie, R. H. (1980). Age-of-acquisition, imagery, concreteness, familiarity, and ambiguity measures for 1,944 words. *Behavior Research Methods & Instrumentation, 12,* 395–427.

Glanzer, M., & Cunitz, A. R. (1966). Two storage mechanisms in free recall. *Journal of Verbal Learning and Verbal Behavior, 5,* 351–360.

Golden, C. J. (1978). *Stroop color and word test.* Chicago: Stoelting.

Goldman-Rakic, P. S. (1987). Circuitry of primate prefrontal cortex and regulation of behavior by representational memory. In F. Plum (Ed.), *Handbook of physiology—The nervous system* (Vol. 5). Bethesda, MD: American Physiological Society.

Goldman-Rakic, P. S. (1991). The circuitry of working memory revealed by anatomy and metabolic imaging. In H. Levin & H. M. Eisenberg (Eds.), *Frontal lobe function and injury* (pp. –). Oxford, England: Oxford University Press.

Graf, P. (1990). Life-span changes in implicit and explicit memory. *Bulletin of the Psychonomic Society, 28,* 353–358.

Graf, P., & Schacter, D. L. (1985). Implicit and explicit memory for new associations in normal and amnesic subjects. *Journal of Experimental Psychology: Learning, Memory, and Cognition, 11,* 501–518.

Graf, P., Squire, R. L., & Mandler, G. (1984). The information that amnesic patients do not forget. *Journal of Experimental Psychology: Learning, Memory, and Cognition, 11,* 501–518.

Guttentag, R. E., & Hunt, R. R. (1988). Adult age differences in memory for imagined and performed actions. *Journals of Gerontology: Psychological Sciences, 43,* P107–P108.

Hasher, L., & Zacks, R. T. (1979). Automatic and effortful processes in memory. *Journal of Experimental Psychology: General, 108,* 356–388.

Hasher, L., & Zacks, R. T. (1984). Automatic processing of fundamental information: The case of frequency of occurrence. *American Psychology, 39,* 1372–1388.

Hasher, L., & Zacks, R. T. (1988). Working memory, comprehension, and aging: A review and a new view. In G. H. Bower (Ed.), *The psychology of learning and motivation* (Vol. 22, pp. 193–225). New York: Academic.

Hashtroudi, S., Chrosniak, L. D., & Schwartz, B. L. (in press). A comparison of the effects of aging on priming and skill learning. *Psychology and Aging.*

Haug, H., Barmwater, U., Eggers, R., Fischer, D., Kuhl, S., & Sass, N. L. (1983). Anatomical changes in aging brain: Morphometric analysis of the human prosencephalon. In J. Cervos-Navarro & H. I. Sarkander (Eds.), *Neuropharmacology* (Aging, Vol. 21, pp. 1–12). New York: Plenum.

Heaton, R. K. (1981). *Wisconsin Card Sorting Test Manual.* Odessa, FL: Psychological Assessment Resources, Inc.

Heron, A., & Craik, F. I. M. (1964). Age differences in cumulative learning of meaningful and meaningless material. *Scandinavian Journal of Psychology, 5,* 209–217.

Hintzman, D. L. (1990). Human learning and memory: Connections and dissociations. *Annual Review of Psychology, 41,* 109–139.

Hirsh, R. (1974). The hippocampus and contextual retrieval of information from memory: A theory. *Behavioral Biology, 12,* 421–444.

Horn, J. L. (1982). The theory of fluid and crystallized intelligence in relation to concepts of cognitive psychology and aging in adulthood. In F. I. M. Craik & S. Trehub (Eds.), *Aging and cognitive processes* (pp. 237–278). New York: Plenum.

Horn, J. L., Donaldson, G., & Engstrom, R. (1981). Apprehension, memory, and fluid intelligence decline in adulthood. *Research on Aging, 3,* 33–84.

Howard, D. V. (1988). Implicit and explicit assessment of cognitive aging. In M. L. Howe & C. J. Brainerd (Eds.), *Cognitive development in adulthood: Progress in cognitive development research* (pp. 3–37). New York: Springer-Verlag.

Howard, D. V. (1991). Implicit memory: An expanding picture of cognitive aging. *Annual Review of Gerontology and Geriatrics, 11.*

Howard, D. V., Fry, A. F., & Brune, C. M. (1991). Aging and memory for new associations: Direct versus indirect measures. *Journal of Experimental Psychology: Memory, Learning, and Cognition, 17,* 779–792.

Howard, D. V., & Howard, J. H., Jr. (1989). Age differences in learning serial patterns: Direct versus indirect measures. *Psychology and Aging, 4,* 357–364.

Hultsch, D. F. (1974). Learning how to learn in adulthood. *Journal of Gerontology, 29,* 302–308.

Hultsch, D. F., Masson, M. E. J., & Small, B. J. (1991). Adult age differences in direct and indirect tests of memory. *Journals of Gerontology: Psychological Sciences, 46,* P22–30.

Huppert, F. A. (1991). Memory function in older adults: Remembering new information. In F. Boller & J. Grafman (Eds.), *Handbook of neuropsychology.* Amsterdam: Elsevier.

Huppert, F. A., & Kopelman, M. D. (1989). Rates of forgetting in normal aging: A comparison with dementia. *Neuropsychologia, 27,* 849–860.

Huppert, F. A., & Piercy, M. (1976a). Recognition memory in amnesic patients. *Cortex, 12,* 3–20.

Huppert, F. A., & Piercy, M. (1976b). Recognition memory in amnesic patients: Effects of temporal context and familiarity of material. *Cortex, 4,* 3–28.

Hyman, B. T., Van Hoesen, G. W., & Damasio, A. R. (1990). Memory-related neural systems in Alzheimer's disease: An anatomic study. *Neurology, 40,* 1721–1730.

Incisa della Rochetta, A. (1986). Classification and recall of pictures after unilateral frontal or temporal lobectomy. *Cortex, 22,* 189–211.

Ingram, D. K. (1988). Complex maze learning in rodents as a model of age-related memory impairment. *Neurobiology of Aging, 9,* 475–485.

Iverson, S. D. (1977). Temporal lobe amnesia. In C. W. M. Whitty & O. L. Zangwill (Eds.), *Amnesia* (2nd ed.). London: Butterworth.

Jacobsen, C. F. (1935). Functions of the frontal association in primates. *Archives of Neurology and Psychiatry, 33,* 558–569.

Jacoby, L. L., & Witherspoon, D. (1982). Remembering without awareness. *Canadian Journal of Psychology, 32,* 300–324.

Janowsky, J. S., Shimamura, A. P., Kritchevsky, M., & Squire, L. R. (1989). Cognitive impairment following frontal lobe damage and its relevance to human amnesia. *Behavioral Neuroscience, 103,* 548–560.

Janowsky, J. S., Shimamura, A. P., & Squire, L. R. (1989a). Memory and metamemory: Comparison between patients with frontal lobe lesions and amnesic patients. *Psychobiology, 17,* 3–11.

Janowsky, J. S., Shimamura, A. P., & Squire, L. R. (1989b). Source memory impairment in patients with frontal lobe lesions. *Neuropsychologia, 27,* 1043–1056.

Jarrard, L. E. (1975). Role of interference in retention by rats with hippocampal lesions. *Journal of Comparative and Physiological Psychology, 89,* 400–408.

Jernigan, T. L. (1986). Anatomical validation: Issues in the use of computed tomography. In L. W. Poon (Ed.), *Handbook for clinical memory assessment of older adults* (pp. 353–358). Washington, DC: American Psychological Association.

Jernigan, T. L., Archibald, S. L., Berhow, M. T., Sowell, E. R., Foster, D. S., & Hesselink, J. R. (1991). Cerebral structure on MRI, Part I: Localization of age-related changes. *Biological Psychiatry, 29,* 55–67.

Joanette, Y., & Goulet, P. (1986). Criterion-specific reduction of verbal fluency in right brain-damaged right-handers. *Neuropsychologia, 24,* 875–879.

Johnson, M. K., & Hasher, L. (1987). Human learning and memory. *Annual Review of Psychology, 38,* 631–668.

Jones-Gotman, M., & Milner, B. (1977). Design fluency: The invention of nonsense drawings after focal lesions. *Neuropsychologia, 15,* 653–674.

Kausler, D. H., & Puckett, J. M. (1979). Effects of word frequency on adult age differences in word memory span. *Experimental Aging Research, 5,* 161–169.

Kausler, D. H., & Puckett, J. M. (1980). Adult age differences in recognition memory for a nonsemantic attribute. *Experimental Aging Research, 6,* 349–355.

Kausler, D. H., & Puckett, J. M. (1981). Adult age differences in memory for sex of voice. *Journal of Gerontology, 36,* 44–50.

Kausler, D. H., Lichty, W., & Davis, T. M. (1985). Temporal memory for performed activities: Intentionality and adult age differences. *Developmental Psychology, 211,* 1132–1138.

Kay, H. (1951). Learning of a serial task by different age groups. *Quarterly Journal of Experimental Psychology, 3,* 166–183.

Kay, H., & Sime, M. (1962). Discrimination with old and young rats. *Journal of Gerontology, 17,* 75–80.

Keane, M. M., Gabrieli, J. D., Fennema, A. C., Growdon, J. H., & Corkin, S. (1991). Evidence for a dissociation between perceptual and conceptual priming in Alzheimer's disease. *Behavioral Neuroscience, 105,* 326–342.

Kesner, R. P., & Novak, J. M. (1982). Serial position curve in rats: Role of the dorsal hippocampus. *Science, 218,* 173–175.

Kimble, D. P. (1968). Hippocampus and internal inhibition. *Psychological Bulletin, 70,* 285–290.

Kinsbourne, M. (1973). Age effects on letter span related to rate and sequential dependency. *Journal of Gerontology, 28,* 317–319.

Kinsbourne, M., & Wood, F. (1975). Short-term memory processes and the amnesic syndrome. In D. Deutsch & J. A. Deutsch (Eds.), *Short-term memory.* New York: Academic.

Kirsner, K., & Dunn, D. (1985). The perceptual record: A common factor in repetition priming and attribute retention. In M. I. Posner & O. S. M. Marin (Eds.), *Attention and performance* (Vol. 11, pp. 547–566). Hillsdale, NJ: Lawrence Erlbaum Associates.

Kliegl, R., & Lindenberger, U. (1988). *A mathematical model of proactive interferences in cues recall: Localizing adult age differences in memory functions.* Paper presented at the Cognitive Aging Conference, Atlanta.

Kolb, B. (1984). Functions of the frontal cortex of the rat: A comparative review. *Brain Research Reviews, 8,* 65–98.

Kolb, B., Sutherland, R. J., & Whishaw, I. (1983). A comparison of the contributions of the frontal and parietal association cortex to spatial localization in rats. *Behavioral Neuroscience, 97,* 13–27.

Kopelman, M. D. (1985). Rates of forgetting in Alzheimer-type dementia and Korsakoff syndrome. *Neuropsychologia, 23,* 623–638.

Kopelman, M. D. (1989). Remote and autobiographical memory, temporal context memory and frontal atrophy in Korsakoff and Alzheimer patients. *Neuropsychologia, 27,* 437–460.

Kopelman, M. D. (1991). Frontal dysfunction and memory deficits in the alcoholic Korsakoff Syndrome and Alzheimer-type dementia. *Brain, 114,* 117–137.

Koriat, A., Ben-Zur, H., & Sheffer, D. (1988). Telling the same story twice: Output monitoring and age. *Journal of Memory Language, 27,* 23–39.

Kucera, M., & Francis, W. (1967). *Computational analysis of present-day American English.* Providence, RI: Brown University Press.

Kucera, M., & Francis, W. (1982). *Computational analysis of present-day American English.* Providence, RI: Brown University Press.

Lachman, J. L., Lachman, R., & Thronesbery, C. (1979). Metamemory through the adult life span. *Developmental Psychology, 15,* 543–551.

Laurence, M. W., & Trottere, M. (1971). Effect of acoustic factors and list organization in multi-trial free-recall learning of college-age and elderly adults. *Developmental Psychology, 5,* 202–210.

Leach, L. R., Warner, C. M., Hotz-Sud, R., Kaplan, E., & Freedman, M. (1991). The effects of age on Wisconsin Card Sorting Variables. *Journal of Clinical and Experimental Neuropsychology, 13,* 28 (Abstract).

Lhermitte, F., & Signoret, J.-L. (1974). The amnesic syndromes and the hippocampal-mamillary system. In M. R. Rosenzweig & E. L. Bennett (Eds.), *Neural mechanisms of learning and memory.* Cambridge, MA: MIT Press.

Light, L. L. (1991). Memory and aging. *Annual Review of Psychology, 42,* 333–376.

Light, L. L., & Albertson, S. A. (1989). Direct and indirect tests of memory for category exemplars in young and older adults. *Psychology and Aging, 4,* 487–492.

Light, L. L., & Singh, A. (1987). Implicit and explicit memory in young and older adults. *Journal of Experimental Psychology: Learning, Memory, and Cognition, 13,* 531–541.

Light, L. L., Singh, A., & Capps, J. L. (1986). Dissociation of memory and awareness in young and older adults. *Journal of Clinical Experimental Neuropsychology, 8,* 62–74.

Luria, A. R. (1966). *Higher cortical functions in man.* New York: Basic.

MacLeod, C. M. (1991). Half a century of research on the Stroop effect: An integrative review. *Psychological Bulletin, 109,* 163–203.

Mahut, H., Zola-Morgan, S., & Moss, U. (1982). Hippocampal resections impair associative learning and recognition memory in the monkey. *Journal of Neuroscience, 2,* 1214–1229.

Martin, R. C., Loring, D. W., Meador, K. J., & Lee, G. P. (1990). The effects of lateralized temporal lobe dysfunction on formal and semantic word fluency. *Neuropsychologia, 28,* 823–829.

Martone, M., Butters, N., Payne, M., Becker, J. T., & Sax, D. S. (1984). Dissociation between skill learning and verbal recognition in amnesia and dementia. *Archives of Neurology, 41,* 965–970.

Mayes, A. R. (1988). *Human organic memory disorders.* Cambridge, England: Cambridge University Press.

Mayes, A. R., & Gooding, P. (1989). Enhancement of word completion priming in amnesics by cueing with previously novel associates. *Neuropsychologia, 27,* 1057–1072.

McAndrews, M. P. & Milner, B. (in press). The frontal cortex and memory for temporal order. *Neuropsychologia.*

McCormack, P. D. (1981). Temporal coding by young and elderly adults: A test of the Hasher-Zacks model. *Developmental Psychology, 17,* 80–86.

McCormack, P. D. (1982). Temporal coding and study-phase retrieval in young and elderly adults. *Bulletin of the Psychonomic Society, 20,* 242–244.

McIntyre, J. S., & Craik, F. I. M. (1987). Age differences in memory for item and source information. *Canadian Journal of Psychology, 41,* 175–192.

Miceli, G., Caltagirone, C., Gainotti, G., Masullo, C., & Silveri, M. C. (1981). Neuropsychological correlates of localized cerebral lesions in non-aphasic brain-damaged patients. *Journal of Clinical Neuropsychology, 3,* 53–63.

Milner, B. (1963). Effects of different brain lesions on card sorting. *Archives of Neurology, 9,* 90–100.

Milner, B. (1964). Some effects of frontal lobectomy in man. In J. M. Warren & K. Akert (Eds.), *The frontal granular cortex and behavior* (pp. 313–331). New York: McGraw-Hill.

Milner, B. (1966). Amnesia following operation on the temporal lobe. In C. W. M. Whitty & O. L. Zangwill (Eds.), *Amnesia.* London: Butterworths.

Milner, B. (1974). Hemispheric specialization: Scope and limits. In F. O. Schmitt & F. G. Worden (Eds.), *The neurosciences: Third research program.* Cambridge, MA: MIT Press.

Milner, B., Corkin, S., & Teuber, H. -L. (1968). Further analysis of the hippocampal amnesic syndrome. *Neuropsychologia, 6,* 267–282.

Milner, B., Petrides, M., & Smith, M. L. (1985). Frontal lobes and the temporal organization of memory. *Human Neurobiology, 4,* 137–142.

Mishkin, M. (1964). Preservation of central sets after frontal lesions in monkeys. In J. M. Warren & K. Akert (Eds.), *The frontal granular cortex and behavior.* New York: McGraw-Hill.

Mishkin, M. (1978). Memory in monkeys severely impaired by combined but not by separate removal of amygdala and hippocampus. *Nature, 273,* 297–298.

Mishkin, M., & Appenzeller, T. (1987). The anatomy of memory. *Scientific American, 256,* 80–89.

Mishkin, M., & Pribram, K. H. (1965). Analysis of the effects of frontal lesions in the monkey: 2. Variations of delayed response. *Journal of Comparative and Physiological Psychology, 49,* 36–40.

Mitchell, D. B. (1989). How many memory systems? Evidence from aging. *Journal of Experimental Psychology: Learning, Memory, and Cognition, 15,* 31–49.

Mitchell, D. B., Brown, A. S., & Murphy, D. R. (1990). Dissociations between procedural and episodic memory: Effects of time and aging. *Psychology and Aging, 5,* 264–276.

Mitchell, D. B., Hunt, R. R., & Schmitt, F. A. (1986). The generation effect and reality monitoring: Evidence from dementia and normal aging. *Journal of Gerontology, 41,* 79–84.

Mittenberg, W., Seidenberg, M., O'Leary, D. S., & DiGiulio, D. V. (1989). Changes in cerebral functioning associated with normal aging. *Journal of Clinical and Experimental Neuropsychology, 11,* 918–932.

Moscovitch, M. (1982a). Multiple dissociations of function in amnesia. In L. S. Cermak (Ed.), *Human memory and amnesia.* Hillsdale, NJ: Lawrence Erlbaum Associates.

Moscovitch, M. (1982b). A neuropsychological approach to perception and memory in normal and pathological aging. In F. I. M. Craik & S. Trehub (Eds.) *Aging and cognitive processes.* New York: Plenum.

Moscovitch, M. (1984). The sufficient conditions for demonstrating preserved memory in amnesia. A task analysis. In N. Butters & L. R. Squre (Eds.), *The neuropsychology of memory.* New York: Guilford.

Moscovitch, M. (1985). Memory from infancy to old age: Implications for theories of normal and pathological memory. *Annals of the New York Academy of Sciences, 444,* 78–96.

Moscovitch, M. (1989). Confabulation and the frontal system: Strategic vs. associative retrieval in neuropsychological theories of memory. In H. L. Roediger III & F. I. M. Craik (Eds.), *Varieties of memory and consciousness: Essays in honor of Endel Tulving.* Hillsdale, NJ: Lawrence Erlbaum Associates.

Moscovitch, M. (in press). A neuropsychological model of memory and consciousness. In L. R. Squire and N. Butters (Eds.), *The neuropsychology of memory* (2nd ed.). New York: Guilford Press.

Moscovitch, M., & Ladowsky, R. (1988, November). *Implicit and explicit tests of semantic memory: The frequency effect for words that change in frequency.* Paper presented at the meeting of the Psychonomics Society, Chicago.

Moscovitch, M., & Umilta, C. (1990). Modularity and neuropsychology: Implications for the organization of attention and memory in normal and brain-damaged people. In M. E. Schwartz (Ed.), *Modular processes in dementia.* Cambridge, MA: MIT Press/Bradford.

Moscovitch, M., & Umilta, C. (1991). Conscious and nonconscious aspects of memory: A neuropsychological framework of modules and central systems. In R. G. Lister & H. J. Weingartner (Eds.), *Perspectives on cognitive neuroscience.* Oxford, England: Oxford University Press.

Moscovitch, M., & Winocur, G. (1983). Contextual cues and release from proactive inhibition in old and young people. *Canadian Journal of Psychology, 37,* 331–344.

Moscovitch, M., & Winocur, G. (1992). The frontal lobes and memory. In L. R. Squire (Ed.), *The encyclopedia of learning and memory: Neuropsychology* (D. L. Schacter, section editor). New York: Macmillan & Co.

Moscovitch, M., & Winocur, G., & McLachlan, D. (1986). Memory as assessed by recognition and reading time in normal and memory impaired people with Alzheimer's disease and other neurological disorders. *Journal of Experimental Psychology: General, 115,* 331–347.

Musen, G., Shimamura, A. P., & Squire, L. R. (1990). Intact text-specific reading skill in amnesia. *Journal of Experimental Psychology: Learning, Memory, and Cognition, 16,* 1068–1076.

Musen, G., & Squire, L. R. (1990). Implicit memory. No evidence for rapid acquisition of new associations in amnesic patients or normal subjects. *Society for Neuroscience Abstracts, 16,* 287.

Naveh-Benjamin, M. (1990). Coding of temporal order information: An automatic process? *Journal of Experimental Psychology: Learning, Memory, and Cognition, 16,* 117–126.

Navon, D. (1984). Resources—A theoretical soup stone? *Psychological Review, 91,* 216–234.

Nelson, H. E. (1976). A modified card sorting test sensitive to frontal lobe defects. *Cortex, 12,* 313–324.

Newcombe, F. (1969). *Missile wounds of the brain.* London: Oxford University Press.

Nissen, M. J., & Bullemer, P. C. (1987). Attentional requirements of learning: Evidence from performance measures. *Cognitive Psychology, 19,* 1–32.

Nissen, H. W., Riesen, A. H., & Nowlis, V. (1938). Delayed response and discrimination learning by chimpanzees. *Journal of Comparative Psychology, 26,* 316–386.

O'Keefe, J., & Nadel, L. (1978). *The hippocampus as a cognitive map.* Oxford, England: Oxford University Press.

Olton, D. S., Becker, J. T., & Handelmann, G. E. (1979). Hippocampus, space, and memory. *The Behavioral and Brain Sciences, 2,* 313–365.

Packard, M. G., & White, N. M. (1991). Dissociation of hippocampus and caudate nucleus memory systems by post-training intracerebral injection of dopamine agonists. *Behavioral Neuroscience, 105,* 73–84.

Parkin, A. J. (1987). *Memory and amnesia.* Oxford, England: Blackwell.

Parkin, A. J., Leng, N. R. C., & Stanhope, N. (1988). Memory impairment following ruptured aneurysm of the anterior communicating artery. *Brain and Cognition, 7,* 231–243.

Passingham, R. E. (1985). Memory of monkeys *(Macaca Mulatta)* with lesions in prefrontal cortex. *Behavioral Neuroscience, U99,* 3–21.

Pendelton, M. G., Heaton, R. K., Lehman, R. A. W., & Hulihan, D. (1982). Diagnostic utility of the Thurstone Word Fluency Test in neuropsychological evaluations. *Journal of Clinical Neuropsychology, 4,* 307–317.

Perlmutter, M., Metzger, R., Nezworski, T., & Miller, K. (1981). Spatial and temporal memory in 20 and 60 year olds. *Journal of Gerontology, 36,* 59–65.

Perret, E. (1974). The left frontal lobe of man and the suppression of habitual responses in verbal categorical behavior. *Neuropsychologia, 12,* 323–330.

Petrides, M. (1985). Deficits in conditional associative learning tasks after frontal- and temporal-lobe lesions in man. *Neuropsychologia, 23,* 249–262.

Petrides, M. (1989). Frontal lobes and memory. In F. Boller & J. Grafman (Eds.), *Handbook of neuropsychology* (Vol. 3) North Holland: Elsevier.

Petrides, M. (1991). Paper presented at the International Neuropsychological Symposium, Taormina, Sicily.

Petrides, M., & Milner, B. (1982). Deficits on subject-ordered tasks after frontal and temporal-lobe lesions in man. *Neuropsychologia, 20,* 249–262.

Poon, L. W. (1985). Differences in human memory with aging: Nature, causes, and clinical implications. In J. E. Birren & K. W. Schaie (Eds.), *Handbook of the psychology of aging* (Vol. 2). New York: Van Nostrand.

Poon, L. W., & Fozard, J. L. (1978). Speed of retrieval from long-term memory in relation to age, familiarity, and datedness of information. *Journal of Gerontology, 33,* 711–717.

Poon, L. W., & Fozard, J. L. (1980). Age and word frequency effects in continuous recognition memory. *Journal of Gerontology, 35,* 77–86.

Puglisi, J. T. (1981). Semantic encoding in older adults as evidence by release from proactive inhibition. *Journal of Gerontology, 36,* 743–745.

Rabbitt, P. M. A. (1982). How do old people know what to do next? In F. I. M. Craik & S. Trehub (Eds.), *Aging and cognitive processes.* New York: Plenum.

Rabinowitz, J. C. (1989). Judgments of origin and generation effects: Comparisons between young and elderly adults. *Psychological Aging, 4,* 259–268.

Rawlins, J. N. P., Winocur, G., & Gray, J. (1983). Hippocampal lesions and timing behavior in the rat. *Behavioral Neuroscience, 97,* 857–872.

Rees-Nishio, M. (1984). *Memory, emotion, and skin conductance responses in young and elderly normal and memory-impaired people.* Unpublished doctoral dissertation, University of Toronto.

Ribot, T. (1882). *Diseases of memory.* New York: Appleton.

Richardson-Klavehn, A., & Bjork, R. A. (1988). Measures of memory. *Annual Review of Psychology, 39,* 475–543.

Roberts, W. W., Dember, W. N., & Brodwick, M. (1962). Alternation and exploration in rats with hippocampal lesions. *Journal of Comparative and Physiological Psychology, 55,* 695–700.

Robinson, A. L., Heaton, R. K., Lehman, R. A. W., & Stilson, D. W. (1980). The utility of the Wisconsin Card Sorting Test in detecting and localizing frontal lobe lesions. *Journal of Consulting and Clinical Psychology, 48,* 605–614.

Roediger, H. L. (1990). Implicit memory: Retention without remembering. *American Psychologist, 45,* 1043–1056.

Rose, T. L., Yesavage, J. A., Hill, R. D., & Bower, G. H. (1986). Priming effects and recognition memory in young and elderly adults. *Experimental Aging Research, 12,* 31–37.

Rubin, D. C., Wetzler, S. E., & Nebes, R. D. (1986). Autobiographical memory across the life span. In D. C. Rubin (Ed.), *Autobiographical memory.* Cambridge, England: Cambridge University Press.

Sagar, J. J., Cohen, N. J., Sullivan, E. V., Corkin, S., & Growdon, J. H. (1988). Remote memory in Alzheimer's disease and Parkinson's disease. *Brain, 111,* 185–206.

Sagar, J. J., Sullivan, E. V., Gabrieli, J. D. E., Corkin, S., & Growdon, J. H. (1988). Temporal ordering and short-term memory deficits in Parkinson's disease. *Brain, 111,* 525–540.

Salthouse, T. A. (1982). *Adult cognition.* New York: Springer-Verlag.

Salthouse, T. A. (1985). *A theory of cognitive aging.* Amsterdam: North-Holland.

Sanders, H., & Warrington, E. K. (1971). Memory for remote events in amnesic patients. *Brain, 94,* 661–668.

Sanders, R. E., Murphy, M. D., Schmitt, F. A., & Walsh, K. K. (1980). Age differences in free-recall rehearsal strategies. *Journal of Gerontology, 35,* 550–558.

Schacter, D. L. (1987a). Implicit memory: History and current status. *Journal of Experimental Psychology: Learning, Memory, and Cognition, 13,* 501–518.

Schacter, D. L. (1987b). Memory, amnesia, and frontal lobe dysfunction. *Psychobiology, 15,* 21–36.

Schacter, D. L. (1990). Perceptual representational systems and implicit memory: Toward a resolution of the multiple memory systems debate. In A. Diamond (Ed.) *Development and neural bases of higher cognition: Annals of the New York Academy of Sciences.*

Schacter, D. L., Eich, J. E., & Tulving, E. (1978). Richard Semon's theory of memory. *Journal of Verbal Learning and Verbal Behavior, 17*, 721–743.

Schacter, D. L., Harbluk, J. L., & McLachlan, D. R. (1984). Retrieval without recollection: An experimental analysis of source amnesia. *Journal of Verbal Learning and Verbal Behavior, 23*, 593–611.

Schacter, D. L., Kaszniak, A. W., Kihlstrom, J. F., & Valdiserri, M. (1991). On the relation between source memory and aging. *Psychology and Aging, 6*, 559–568.

Scoville, W. B., & Milner, B. (1957). Loss of recent memory following bilateral hippocampal lesion. *Journal of Neurology, Neurosurgery & Psychiatry, 20*, 11–21.

Shallice, T. (1982). Specific impairments of planning. *Philosophical Transactions of the Royal Society of London, Series B, 298*, 199–209.

Shallice, T. (1988). *From neuropsychology to mental structure.* Cambridge, England: Cambridge University Press.

Shimamura, A. P., Janowsky, J. S., & Squire, L. R. (1990). Memory for temporal order in patients with frontal lobe lesions and patients with amnesia. *Neuropsychologia, 28*, 803–813.

Shimamura, A. P., & Squire, L. R. (1986). Korsakoff's Syndrome: A study of the relationship between anterograde amnesia and remote memory impairment. *Behavioral Neuroscience, 100*, 165–170.

Shimamura, A. P., & Squire, L. R. (1987). A neuropsychological study of fact memory and source amnesia. *Journal of Experimental Psychology: Learning, Memory, and Cognition, 13*, 464–473.

Sidman, M., Stoddard, L. T., & Mohr, J. P. (1968). Some additional quantitative observations of immediate memory in a patient with bilateral hippocampal lesions. *Neuropsychologia, 6*, 245–254.

Smith, A. D. (1975). Aging and interference with memory. *Journal of Gerontology, 30*, 319–325.

Smith, A. D. (1980). Age differences in encoding, storage, and retrieval. In L. W. Poon, J. L. Fozard, L. S. Cermak, D. Arenberg, & L. W. Thompson (Eds.), *New directions in memory and aging.* Hillsdale, NJ: Lawrence Erlbaum Associates.

Smith, M. L., & Milner, B. (1988). Estimation of frequency of occurrence of abstract designs after frontal or temporal lobectomy. *Neuropsychologia, 26*, 297–306.

Snodgrass, J. G., & Corwin, J. (1988). Pragmatics of measuring recognition memory: Applications to dementia and amnesia. *Journal of Experimental Psychology: General, 117*, 34–50.

Squire, L. R. (1987). *Memory and brain.* New York: Oxford University Press.

Squire, L. R., & Cohen, N. J. (1982). Remote memory, retrograde amnesia, and the neuropsychology of memory. In L. S. Cermak (Ed.), *Human memory and amnesia* (pp. 275–303). Hillsdale, NJ: Lawrence Erlbaum Associates.

Squire, L. R., & Zola-Morgan, S. (1988). Memory: Brain systems and behavior. *Trends in Neuroscience, 22*, 170–175.

Stafford, J. L., Albert, M. S., Nreja, M. A., Sandor, T., & Garvey, A. J. (1988). Age-related differences in computed tomographic scan measurements. *Archives of Neurology, 45*, 409–415.

Storandt, M. (1977). Age, ability level, and method of administering and scoring the WAIS. *Journal of Gerontology, 32*, 175–178.

Stroop, J. R. (1935). Studies of interference in serial verbal reactions. *Journal of Experimental Psychology, 18*, 643–662.

Stuss, D. T., & Benson, D. F. (1986). *The frontal lobes.* New York: Raven.

Stuss, D. T., & Guzman, D. A. (1988). General remote memory loss with minimal anterograde amnesia: A clinical note. *Brain and Cognition, 8*, 21–30.

Stuss, D. T., Kaplan, E. F., Benson, D. F., Weir, W. S., Chiuli, S., & Sarazin, F. F. (1982). Evidence for the involvement of orbitofrontal cortex in memory functions: An interference effect. *Journal of Comparative and Physiological Psychology, 96,* 913–925.

Sutherland, R. J., & Arnold, K. A. (1987). Hippocampal damage produces temporally-graded retrograde amnesia in rats. *Society for Neurosciences* (Abstract), *13,* 1066.

Tardif, T., & Craik, F. I. M. (1989). Reading a week later: Perceptual and conceptual factors. *Journal of Memory and Language, 28,* 107–125.

Taub, H. A. (1974). Coding for short-term memory as a function of age. *Journal of Genetic Psychology, 125,* 309–314.

Teuber, H. -L. (1955). Physiological psychology. *Annual Review of Psychology, 9,* 267–296.

Teuber, H. -L., Battersby, W. S., & Bender, M. B. (1951). Performance of complex visual tasks after cerebral lesions. *Journal of Nervous and Mental Diseases, 114,* 413–429.

Teuber, H. -L., & Milner, B. (1968). Alteration of perception and memory in man: Reflections on methods. In L. Weiskrantz (Ed.), *Analysis of behavioral change.* New York: Harper & Row.

Thompson, R., Langer, S. K., & Rich, I. (1964). Lesions of the limbic system and short-term memory in albino rats. *Brain, 87,* 537–542.

Thompson, R. (1981). Rapid forgetting of a spatial habit in rats with hippocampal lesions. *Science, 212,* 959–960.

Thorndike, E. L. (1921). *The teacher's word book.* New York: Teachers College, Columbia University Press.

Thorndike, E. L., & Lorge, I. (1944). *The teacher's word book of 30,000 words.* New York: Teachers College, Columbia University Press.

Tulving, E. (1983). *Elements of episodic memory.* Oxford, England: Clarendon.

Tulving, E., & Colotla, V. (1970). Free recall of trilingual lists. *Cognitive Psychology, 1,* 86–98.

Tulving, E., Hayman, C. A. G., & MacDonald, C. A. (1991). Long-lasting perceptual priming and semantic learning in amnesia: A case experiment. *Journal of Experimental Psychology: Learning, Memory, and Cognition, 17,* 595–617.

Tulving, E., & Pearlstone, Z. (1966). Availability versus accessibility of information in memory for words. *Journal of Verbal Learning and Verbal Behavior, 5,* 381–391.

Tulving, E., & Schacter, D. L. (1990). Priming and human memory systems. *Science, 247,* 301–306.

Victor, M., Adams, R. D., & Collins, G. H. (1971). *The Wernicke-Korsakoff Syndrome.* Philadelphia: Davis.

Vriezen, E., & Moscovitch, M. (1990). Temporal ordering and conditional associative learning in Parkinson's disease. *Neuropsychologia,* 1283–1294.

Vriezen, E., & Moscovitch, M. (1991). *Age differences in memory for temporal order and conditional associative learning: A hippocampal or frontal effect?* Manuscript submitted for publication.

Walker, D. W., & Means, L. W. (1973). Single alternation performance in rats with hippocampal lesions: Disruption by an irrelevant task interposed during the intertrial interval. *Behavioral Biology, 9,* 93–104.

Warrington, E. K. (1982). The double dissociation of short- and long-term memory deficits. In L. S. Cermak (Ed.), *Human memory and amnesia.* Hillsdale, NJ: Lawrence Erlbaum Associates.

Warrington, E. K., & Weiskrantz, L. (1970). Amnesic syndrome: Consolidation or retrieval? *Nature, 228,* 629–630.

Watkins, M. J. (1974). Concept and measurement of primary memory. *Psychological Bulletin, 81,* 695–711.

Weiskrantz, L. (1978). A comparison of hippocampal pathology in man and other animals. In *Functions of the septo-hippocampal system,* Ciba Foundation Symposium 58 (pp. 373–387). Amsterdam: Elsevier.

Wickelgren, W. A. (1968). Sparing of short-term memory in an amnesic patient: Implications for the strength theory of memory. *Neuropsychologia, 6,* 239–244.

Wiggs, C. L. (1990). *Aging and memory for frequency of occurrence of novel visual stimuli: Direct and indirect measures.* Unpublished doctoral dissertation, Georgetown University, Washington, DC.

Wilson, B., & Baddeley, A. (1988). Semantic, episodic, and autobiographical memory in a post meningitic amnesic patient. *Brain and Cognition, 8,* 31–46.

Winocur, G. (1982). The amnesic syndrome: A deficit in cue utilization. In L. S. Cermak (Ed.), *Human memory and amnesia* (pp. 139–166). Hillsdale, NJ: Lawrence Erlbaum Associates.

Winocur, G. (1984). The effects of retroactive and proactive interference on learning and memory in old and young rats. *Developmental Psychobiology, 17,* 537–545.

Winocur, G. (1985). The hippocampus and thalamus: Their roles in short- and long-term memory and the effects of interference. *Behavioral Brain Research, 16,* 135–152.

Winocur, G. (1986). Memory decline in aged rats: A neuropsychological interpretation. *Journal of Gerontology, 41,* 758–761.

Winocur, G. (1990). Anterograde and retrograde amnesia in rats with dorsal hippocampal or dorsomedial thalamic lesions. *Behavioral Brain Research, 30,* 145–154.

Winocur, G. (1991a). *A comparison of normal old rats and young rats with lesions to the hippocampus or prefrontal cortex on a test of matching-to-sample.* Manuscript submitted for publication.

Winocur, G. (1991b). Functional dissociation of the hippocampus and prefrontal cortex in learning and memory. *Psychobiology, 19,* 11–20.

Winocur, G. (1992). Conditional learning in aged rats: Evidence of hippocampal and prefrontal cortex impairment. *Neurobiology of Aging, 13,* 131–135.

Winocur, G., Kinsbourne, M., & Moscovitch, M. (1981). The effect of cuing on release form proactive interference in Korsakoff amnesic patients. *Journal of Experimental Psychology: Human Learning and Memory, 7,* 56–65.

Winocur, G., & Moscovitch, M. (1984). Paired-associate learning in institutionalized and non-institutionalized old people. *Journal of Gerontology, 38,* 455–464.

Winocur, G., & Moscovitch, M. (1990a). A comparison of cognitive function in institutionalized and community-dwelling old people of normal intelligence. *Canadian Journal of Psychology, 44,* 435–444.

Winocur, G., & Moscovitch, M. (1990b). Hippocampal and prefrontal cortex contributions to learning and memory: Analysis of lesion and aging effects on maze learning in rats. *Behavioral Neuroscience, 104,* 544–551.

Winocur, G., Moscovitch, M., & Freedman, J. (1987). An investigation of cognitive function in relation to psychosocial variables in institutionalized old people. *Canadian Journal of Psychology, 41,* 257–269.

Winocur, G., Moscovitch, M., & Witherspoon, D. (1987). Contextual cuing and memory performance in brain-damaged amnesics and old people. *Brain & Cognition, 6,* 129–141.

Winocur, G., & Olds, J. (1978). Effects of context manipulation on memory and reversal learning in rats with hippocampal lesions. *Journal of Comparative and Physiological Psychology, 92,* 312–321.

Winocur, G., Oxbury, S., Roberts, R., Agnetti, V., & Davis, C. (1984). Amnesia in a patient with bilateral lesions to the thalamus. *Neuropsychologia, 22,* 123–143.

Winocur, G., & Weiskrantz, L. (1976). An investigation of paired-associate learning in amnesic patients. *Neuropsychologia, 14,* 97–110.

Worden, P. E., & Sherman-Brown, S. (1983). A word-frequency cohort effect in young versus elderly adults' memory for words. *Developmental Psychology, 19,* 521–530.

Wright, B. M., & Payne, R. B. (1985). Effects of aging on sex differences in psychomotor reminiscence and tracking proficiency. *Journal of Gerontology, 40,* 179–184.

Zola-Morgan, S., & Squire, L. R. (1986). Memory impairment in monkeys following lesions limited to the hippocampus. *Behavioral Neuroscience, 100,* 155–160.

Zola-Morgan, S. M., & Squire, L. R. (1990). The primate hippocampal formation: Evidence for a time-limited role in memory storage. *Science, 250,* 288–290.

Zola-Morgan, S., Squire, L. R., & Amaral, D. G. (1986). Human amnesia and the medial temporal region: Enduring memory impairment following a bilateral lesion limited to field CA1 of the hippocampus. *Journal of Neuroscience, 6,* 2950–2967.

Zornetzer, S. F., Thompson, R., & Rogers, J. (1982). Rapid forgetting in aged rats. *Behavioral and Neural Biology, 36,* 49–60.

CHAPTER EIGHT

Cognitive Dysfunction in Alzheimer's Disease

Robert D. Nebes
University of Pittsburgh

As humans age, not only do they suffer the myriad cognitive changes detailed in the other chapters in this volume, but also they are at increased risk for a variety of physical and mental diseases, many of which severely impair their cognitive functioning. The present chapter examines the effects produced by the most common cause of severe cognitive dysfunction in the aged—Alzheimer's disease (AD). After providing some background information on this disease, the rest of the chapter reviews what we know of the underlying nature of the cognitive impairments seen in AD. Although there is a large literature on the behavioral impairments produced by AD, most of it merely documents the presence of these impairments to determine whether they are useful in diagnosing AD or in charting its course. The present chapter has a different emphasis, focusing on those studies that investigate the underlying cognitive dysfunctions responsible for the behavioral impairments. Thus, for example, when discussing verbal memory, we review those papers that go beyond showing that AD patients have difficulty recalling words, and instead investigate whether the underlying problems lie in semantic encoding or in retrieval, and so forth.

Alzheimer's disease is a progressive degenerative disease of the brain whose most prominent symptoms are behavioral, in that patients develop a dementia that worsens gradually over time. Although there are a multitude of other diseases and disorders that produce dementia (e.g., Multi-infarct disease, Huntington's disease, etc.), AD is by far the most common cause, being responsible for up to 80% of the dementias in the older population (Evans et al., 1989). Its prevalence increases dramatically with age. The most recent community epidemiological study (Evans et al., 1989) found that approximately 10% of the population over age 65 years has AD, with the prevalence rising from 3% in individuals in their 60s to 47% in those over the age of 75 years. Given the growing number of persons surviving into their 80s in our population, this disease is sure to have an increasing effect on our society and it consequently has become a major focus of both clinical and basic research.

Despite a massive amount of recent research, AD remains a diagnostic problem, in that there are no definitive biological markers. In the living patient, the diagnosis is still a clinical one based to a great extent on excluding other known causes of cognitive impairment (e.g., depression, metabolic diseases, alcoholism, etc.). Even though some very sophisticated technologies recently have been applied to the diagnosis of AD (e.g., Positron Emission Tomography), the principal diagnostic criteria are still behavioral. Although a definitive diagnosis of AD requires microscopic examination of brain tissue, most clinicians would hesitate to diagnose AD even in the presence of the neuropathological changes typically found in AD, unless there was also significant cognitive impairment. AD is one disease where knowledge of a patient's cognitive status always has been a major concern. However, there is at present no distinctive pattern of cognitive deficit that can reliably distinguish AD from other diseases. The onset of the behavioral deficits is insidious and easily confused with the cognitive changes associated with many conditions such as depression and even normal aging. With all the clinical information a research-oriented dementia center can muster, up to 10% of patients clinically diagnosed as having AD turn out at autopsy to be suffering from some other condition (Katzman, Lasker, & Bernstein, 1988). This hit rate is actually quite good, given clinical performance just 10–15 years ago, but it still means that when a research study reports testing 20 AD patients, it is likely that several of those individuals do not actually have AD. Interpretation of intersubject variability is, therefore, even more of a concern in AD research than it is in the study of normal aging, as it may indicate the presence of a number of inappropriate subjects. Readers wishing more detail on the medical and the clinical-neuropsychological aspects of AD should see Katzman (1986), Katzman et al. (1988), and Kaszniak (1986).

The primary behavioral deficit that characterizes AD is a progressive dementia. To be called demented, an individual must show a progressive decline in multiple areas of cognition. The most commonly used research criteria (the NINCDS-ADRDA criteria—McKhann et al., 1984) require that in order to receive a diagnosis of "probable" AD a patient must have deficits (defined as performance below the fifth percentile for the patient's age and education) in two or more areas of cognition. The relevant areas of cognition include:

1. orientation to place and time,
2. memory,
3. language,
4. praxis,
5. attention,
6. visual perception,
7. problem solving and
8. social functioning.

Unfortunately, at the present time there is no standard set of psychological tests used to diagnose AD, and those tests that are commonly given usually do not have education and age norms available. Special emphasis always has been given to a memory impairment in the diagnosis of AD. In the overwhelming majority of patients with AD a memory impairment is one of the earliest and most prominent symptoms (Chenoweth & Spencer, 1986). If a patient does not have a memory deficit, the question always arises as to whether the patient truly has AD, or at least, whether it is an atypical presentation.

What type of patients typically are used in research on the cognitive effects of dementia? When reading studies in this area, it is important to examine carefully the description of the patient population because studies vary in the types of patients they use. In some studies, patients are selected solely because they are demented. The disease thought to be responsible for the dementia may not be mentioned or the diagnosis may just be "organic brain syndrome," which effectively means that the dementia is thought to result from a brain disease and not from a psychiatric disorder such as depression. However, many different diseases produce a dementia (e.g., Huntington's disease, Multi-infarct dementia, etc.) and, to the degree that these various diseases produce different patterns of cognitive impairment, results from such studies will be difficult to interpret. However, even in such a mixed series of patients, given the predominance of AD as a cause of dementia it is likely that the majority of the patients will have AD. Other studies also use a mixture of demented patients, although actual diagnoses are given (e.g., 10 patients with AD, 8 with Multi-infarct dementia). However, these studies also combine data from patients regardless of etiology because the authors do not have any a priori reason to predict that the etiology of the dementia would affect the results (e.g., Grober, Buschke, Kawas, & Fuld, 1985). In most recent studies, however, the demented population is either made up solely of patients of one diagnostic type or, if patients with different diseases are present, the different patient groups are directly compared (e.g., Bayles & Tomoeda, 1983). In most studies of AD, patients carry a diagnosis of "probable" AD, because in order to get a diagnosis of "definite" AD neuropathological examination of brain tissue from either an autopsy or a biopsy is necessary, and this is rarely available. To gain a diagnosis of probable AD according to the NINCDS-ADRDA criteria (McKhann et al., 1984), a patient must have a dementia including deficits in two or more areas of cognition, a progressive worsening of memory and other cognitive functions, no disturbance of consciousness (i.e., no delirium), and an absence of other possible causes of a progressive decline in cognition. Some psychological studies of AD also will use patients who carry a diagnosis of "possible AD." Such patients have either an atypical clinical presentation or a second disorder that could cause a dementia (e.g., thyroid disease), although it is not considered to be the cause of the dementia in this particular patient. Some investigations use patients who carry a diagnosis of primary degenerative dementia based on criteria from the *Diagnostic and Statistical Manual of Mental Disorders* of the American Psychiatric Association. Generally, patients with this diagnosis will meet criteria for an NINCDS-ADRDA diagnosis of AD (Katzman et al., 1988). It also should be kept in mind that AD has a very heterogeneous presentation. Although most patients show a similar pattern of deficits, behaviorally distinct subgroups of AD patients have been found (e.g., Freed, Corkin, Growdon, & Nissen, 1989; Martin et al., 1986). At the present time it is not clear whether these represent distinct diseases that we cannot now distinguish diagnostically or whether they represent random variations in a diffuse disease process.

In most cognitive studies of AD, the patients will have a dementia of a mild to moderate level of severity. At the milder end, such individuals may function fairly well in their own home, although typically they receive help with finances and with some household work. They may or may not be aware of their increasing cognitive decline. Usually, if not already retired, they will be forced to stop work, especially if they have an intellectually demanding job. These persons often withdraw from activities where their increasing deficits are a problem—for example, a bridge club. They are also usually dependent on others for transportation as they are forced to stop driving due to either lapses in judgment or problems with becoming lost. By the time they are moderately demented, AD patients need a caretaker in order to survive in everyday life, as they may become easily confused and disoriented and cannot be trusted to take their own medicines, cook, and so on, unless supervised. More severely demented patients are usually untestable on most cognitive tasks because they cannot understand or reliably follow task directions. It should be emphasized that although most studies examine AD patients who are mildly to moderately demented, this leaves a great deal of room for interstudy variability in patient severity. Because the pattern of behavioral symptoms can change dramatically (and perhaps even qualitatively) as the disease progresses, differences in dementia severity often may serve as a major source of experimental disagreements (see, e.g., the Primary Memory section).

The remainder of this chapter examines the cognitive dysfunctions responsible for the various behavioral deficits found in AD. Given the organization of this book, the literature is discussed under the general headings of attention, memory, language, spatial abilities, and reasoning/conceptualization. It is obvious from the length of the sections devoted to these five topics that certain areas have been researched much more extensively than have others. Because of the dramatic nature of the memory deficit in AD, the vast majority of research in this disease has concentrated on memory, with most of the rest being devoted to language. The sections on attention, visuospatial abilities, and reasoning are, therefore, relatively brief. This is not only because few studies have been carried out in these areas, but also because most of the studies that do exist have focused on demonstrating that there are problems rather than on determining the underlying nature of cognitive impairment. The goal of the present chapter is not only to concisely review research findings, but also to examine whether the various theoretical constructs commonly used to explain the pattern of age effects on cognition (e.g., cognitive slowing, automaticity, etc.) are useful in accounting for the pattern of deficits seen in AD patients. A number of broader issues also will be examined briefly. For example, are there qualitative differences between the cognitive impairments produced by AD and those associated with normal aging, or are the differences only quantitative?

ATTENTION

As mentioned previously, attentional deficits are part of the dementia associated with AD and so most dementia test batteries include tasks that claim to measure attentional abilities. For example, the Dementia Rating Scale (Mattis, 1976) has a subscale called attention. The tests contributing to this subscale include digit span, following simple verbal commands, imitating motions, determining the number of *As* present in a small array of letters (untimed), reading a list of words aloud, and a multiple-choice visual matching test using nonsense shapes. Other common clinical tests of attention involve measuring simple response time and the time subjects take to cancel all instances of a given letter in a large array of letters (Huff et al., 1987). Although attention undoubtedly is involved in all of the aforementioned tasks, these tasks certainly differ from the paradigms commonly used in the cognitive literature to assess specific attentional abilities. Most clinical-neuropsychological measures of attention are designed to detect decrements in an individual's ability to maintain concentration and to resist distraction (Lezak, 1983), rather than to determine the actual nature of the attentional dysfunction. There have been, however, a few studies of attention in AD patients using paradigms from the experimental-psychology literature.

It is clear from reading the cognitive literature that the term attention has been applied to a number of very different mental operations. However, almost all of the cognitive studies investigating attention in AD have dealt with selective attention. Selection is necessary because under many conditions humans have a limited ability to process information. In this sense, then, attention is the mechanism by which a subject allocates a limited processing capacity to certain information or to certain mental operations. Limitations of selective attention are of two main types: divided attention and focused attention (Schneider, Dumais, & Shiffrin, 1984). To the degree that individuals cannot simultaneously process multiple sources of independent information as efficiently as they can one source, or carry out multiple mental operations as efficiently as they can one operation, they show a limitation in divided attention. Similarly, to the extent that individuals find it difficult to ignore (i.e., not process) information they know is irrelevant (thus impairing their performance in comparison to a situation where no irrelevant information is present), they show a limitation in focused attention.

Focused Attention

Several studies have examined the ability of AD patients to focus their attention on relevant sources of information. Nebes and Brady (1989) asked subjects to search an array of six letters for a target letter. In half the arrays, all six letters were black, whereas in the rest two letters were black and four were red. The subjects were told that the target, if it was present, would always be black. This meant that in the two-color arrays, color effectively segregated the array into two relevant (i.e., black) and four irrelevant (i.e., red) letters. To the degree that subjects can focus their processing on the relevant information, they should search the two-color arrays faster than the all-black arrays because there are fewer relevant letters to examine. The results showed that although the AD patients generally were slower than the normal old or young, all three groups responded faster to the two-color arrays than to the all-black arrays. More important, the magnitude of this response-time advantage for the two-color arrays over the all-black arrays did not differ in the three groups. These results were interpreted as indicating that AD patients are as effective as the normal young or old in using a physical feature to restrict their processing to the relevant information present in a stimulus display.

A different conclusion was reached by two studies that used a dichotic listening task to examine attentional focusing. In dichotic listening, two different auditory messages (usually lists of words) are presented simultaneously through earphones, with one message going to each ear. When no constraints are placed on the order in which subjects recall the words, right-handed normals are biased toward first reporting all the words they can recall from their right ear and then those from their left ear. They also tend to show a significant right-ear advantage in recall accuracy. In order to examine focused attention using dichotic listening, Mohr, Cox, Williams, Chase, and Fedio (1990) told subjects which ear to report first. When told to report first those words heard in their left ear, the normal old in the Mohr et al. study reported more left- than right-ear words, whereas when told to report first those words heard in their right ear, they reported more right- than left-ear words. In fact, in this latter condition, they showed an even greater right-ear superiority than when their order of report was unconstrained. By contrast, the performance of the AD patients was insensitive to instructions. They showed a strong right-ear superiority even when instructed to report left-ear words first. Also their right-ear superiority did not increase when instructed to report right-ear words first. Mohr et al. interpreted these findings as evidence that AD patients have difficulty intentionally shifting their attention to the specified ear, that is, in intentionally allocating their attention to one source of information. AD patients, therefore, are unable to modify the right-ear bias typically found in the free-report situation. However, an identical pattern of dichotic performance was interpreted by Bouma and Van Silfhout (1989) in quite a different way. They suggested that this overwhelming right-ear superiority in AD patients demonstrated an impairment of right-hemisphere attentional mechanisms. They used Kinsbourne's model of the cortical control of attention (for a recent description, see Reuter-Lorenz, Kinsbourne, & Moscovitch, 1990) in which each cerebral hemisphere directs attention toward the opposite side of space. These two directional biases are normally in a dynamic balance allowing individuals to easily shift the spatial focus of their attention. However, if one hemisphere is injured, an imbalance is created, with the intact hemisphere overpowering the injured one, causing the spatial focus of attention to shift strongly away from the intact hemisphere. Bouma and Van Silfhout argued that the strong unmodifiable right-ear advantage found in dichotic listening in AD reflects an underlying dysfunction of right-hemisphere attentional mechanisms.

However, if this were the case, then we might expect to see an abnormal distribution of attention in other situations, but no such strong right-sided attentional bias has been reported in tasks such as visual search.

Finally, there is a recent report by Freed et al. (1989) suggesting that although most AD patients show adequate focused attention, there is a subpopulation who have a major problem. This study used a task devised by Posner (1980). The subject pressed a button when an "X" appeared to the right or left of a central fixation point. Before each trial, subjects were given a visual cue—an arrow pointing to the left, to the right, or in both directions. Following a unidirectional arrow, most of the time (80%) the "X" appeared on the side indicated by the arrow (i.e., the cue was valid). However, the other 20% of the time the "X" appeared on the other side (i.e., the cue was invalid). The bidirectional arrow was neutral giving no information about where the stimulus was likely to occur. As typically is found, the normals in the Freed et al. study responded faster when given a valid cue than when given an invalid cue. This was also true of many of the AD patients. However, a substantial subgroup of AD patients showed "anomalous" performance on this task, meaning that their response time to invalid cues was faster than to valid cues. The authors argued that this is not just random variability in the AD population because patients with this anomalous attention result were also likely to show an unusual pattern of memory performance in which their recognition accuracy for pictures was actually better at 72 hr after presentation than at 24 hr. The authors felt that these individuals represent a distinct subgroup of AD patients with a focused-attention deficit due to the presence of a lesion in a particular brain stem nucleus. The poorer performance at 24 hr than at 72 hr is hypothesized to reflect an attentional disorder producing a heightened response to novel stimuli at 24 hr. It is unfortunate that the focused-attention task was not itself analyzed in more detail in this report. For example, no mention is made of the results from the bidirectional arrow cues, which could serve as a neutral condition allowing separate examination of the benefit and cost produced by the cues. There is also no discussion of what sort of attentional deficit might produce a negative cue effect (i.e., faster response to invalid cues). The results do demonstrate, however, the possibility that apparent inconsistencies in cognitive test results either between subjects or between studies may reflect a deficit present in only a subpopulation of AD patients.

Given the few studies that have investigated focused attention in AD, it is difficult to interpret the inconsistency in the results to date. The experimental procedures vary in the sensory modality used, the nature of the task (i.e., search vs. recall vs. detection), the nature and salience of the cue (i.e., spatial position of the relevant stimulus vs. a physical feature of the stimulus), and even in the type of data collected (i.e., response time vs. accuracy). There is also the possibility that a deficit may exist only in a subgroup of AD patients with a substantial neuronal loss in a particular nucleus. Certainly, more study of this important area of cognition is warranted, especially because focused-attention abilities do not appear to deteriorate with normal aging (Plude & Hoyer, 1986). If there is actually a focused-attention deficit in AD, this would represent a qualitatively different pattern of deficit from that seen in normal aging.

Divided Attention

The literature on divided attention in AD is somewhat larger and more consistent than that on focused attention. Several studies have used the dichotic listening paradigm to examine subjects' ability to divide their attention between two concurrent streams of information. Both Mohr et al. (1990) and Grady et al. (1989) found AD patients to be very poor in reporting words heard under dichotic conditions. To determine whether this might be merely a problem with processing degraded auditory information, Grady et al. used two types of stimuli: dichotically presented words and degraded words presented monotically. They found that AD patients' performance was disrupted much more by dichotic presentation than by degradation of the auditory input. This led them to argue that AD patients have an even greater problem than do the normal old in dividing their attention between different sources of information. Nebes and Brady (1989) also examined the ability of AD patients to divide their attention among multiple inputs. They examined how decision time in a visual-search task was affected by increasing the number of items in the array. Subjects were shown two, four, or six letters and asked whether a target letter was present. In comparison to young and normal-old individuals, AD patients showed a substantially greater increase in search time as the number of items in the array increased. That is, increasing the amount of information over which subjects had to divide their attention impaired the performance of AD patients much more than it did that of normals. The rise in the AD patients' response time with increasing array size was larger than that found in the normals both in terms of absolute response time and percentage change. This result is consistent with data from a shape cancellation task (Foldi, Davidoff, Jutagir, & Gould, 1987) in which the density of the array (number of items among which the subject had to search) was varied from 20 to 50 items. Foldi et al. found that as the density increased, the accuracy difference between normals and AD patients increased, with AD patients tending to miss more items (there was no increase in false positives).

Although the studies just described required division of attention across sources of information, others have examined AD patients' ability to divide their attention between concurrent cognitive operations or tasks. Baddeley, Logie, Bressi, Della Sala, and Spinnler (1986) postulated that the central executive system of working memory (see upcoming Primary Memory section) is dysfunctional in AD patients. Such an impairment would make it difficult for these individuals to coordinate multiple tasks or cognitive operations (i.e., a divided-attention deficit). To test this hypothesis, they administered a dual-task procedure to normal young and old subjects and patients with AD. As a primary task, the subject performed on a pursuit rotor, which was set individually for each subject such that at baseline the subject was on target 60% of the time. Baddeley et al. then determined the effect that three different secondary tasks had on performance of the primary task. The secondary tasks were (a) counting from one to five over and over, (b) responding to a tone by pressing a footswitch, and (c) recalling strings of digits. This latter task was equated in difficulty for each subject by using digit strings of a length equal to that subject's digit span. Because of their memory deficit, AD patients typically would have to remember shorter strings than the normals. Counting aloud did not affect the pursuit-rotor performance of any of the groups. Tone detection did not affect the normals, but did impair the performance of the AD patients. Finally, digit recall affected pursuit-rotor performance in all three groups, but dramatically more so in the AD patients. At least for the digit-recall task, this greater dual-task deficit cannot be attributed to the secondary task being more difficult for AD patients than for the normals, and so these results suggest that AD patients have substantially more difficulty than normals in integrating the performance of two concurrent tasks (i.e., in dividing their attention). Morris (1986) conducted a similar dual-task study in which the primary task was short-term memory for a consonant trigram (Brown–Peterson task). The subject was given a trigram and had to recall the letters after a delay of between 5 s and 20 s. During this delay, subjects either did nothing or engaged in one of four different secondary tasks. These tasks required the subject to (a) tap regularly on the table with their finger, (b) say "the" repeatedly (articulatory suppression), (c) reverse the order of two presented digits, and (d) add together two digits. Results showed that with an unfilled interval there was little forgetting across 20 s in either the AD patients or the normal old. However, when required to either tap and/or say "the," the memory performance of the AD patients was severely disrupted, whereas that of the normals was unaffected. Reversing digit order or adding the digits impaired the memory performance of both groups, but the AD patients were affected more than were the normals. Morris argued that these results demonstrate a decrease in the processing capacity of the central executive system in AD patients. In normals, tapping and articulation take up so little capacity that they have no effect on subjects' ability to simultaneously rehearse items in short-term memory. However, the capacity of AD patients is so reduced that even the small additional demand imposed by tapping or articulation produces a major disruption in memory performance as the subject is unable to cope with the simultaneous demands of the distractor task and rehearsal of the trigrams. It is noteworthy that even the simple act of tapping caused an impairment in memory for letters, because the effect of this motor task cannot be due to a material-specific interference effect with the to-be-remembered letters.

All of the studies just described conclude that AD patients have a major impairment in their ability to divide their attention, both among multiple sources of information and among concurrently running cognitive operations. This deficit is above and beyond any such limitation found in the normal old (see chapter 1 of this volume). However, presently there is no evidence that this increased divided-attention deficit in AD represents anything more than a quantitative difference from that present in the normal old. This conclusion must be considered tentative at best, however, as so few divided-attention tasks and manipulations actually have been carried out in the AD population.

EPISODIC MEMORY

Although AD causes major deficits in most areas of cognition, the symptom that people usually associate with this disease is a loss of memory. This is a fairly accurate perception, because an impairment in episodic memory (i.e., memory for events) is often the symptom that brings an individual's incipient dementia to the notice of family and friends. Individuals with AD may ask the same question over and over, forget to pay their bills or take their medications, forget important recent events in their life such as the death of a family member, and so forth. However, episodic memory performance also declines over the course of normal aging, making memory deterioration a fairly nonspecific symptom. There also may be a subpopulation of elderly individuals who show a substantial memory impairment not associated with declines in other areas of cognition. Called in the past, benign senescent forgetfulness (Kral, 1978), a newer term, *Age Associated Memory Impairment* (AAMI), is beginning to appear in the literature (Crook et al., 1986). It can be argued that AAMI simply represents an attempt by the medical community to find a diagnosis to give to persons who have the typical memory impairments associated with normal aging but who complain about it to a doctor. Nevertheless, it does appear that there are nondemented older individuals who show substantially greater memory impairments than do the majority of the elderly population. Whether this represents just one tail of the normal distribution of memory abilities in the elderly, or a presently unknown pathological condition, the existence of major memory problems in nondemented older individuals does complicate the diagnosis of AD. This is especially true because memory deficits are often the only sign of a dementia that may be evident for some time. Also, cognitive decline in AD is usually insidious, and the gradual worsening of memory may not be apparent until it leads to some dramatic event, or until it has become moderately severe. It is not surprising, therefore, that a great deal of research has focused on using memory tests to clinically differentiate normal aging from dementia (e.g., Erickson, Poon, & Walsh-Sweeney, 1980). However, given the focus of this chapter, the present section concentrates on those studies that have sought to investigate the information-processing deficits underlying the memory impairment of AD.

All of the studies described in this section investigate what Tulving (1984) called episodic memory. Episodic memory is an autobiographical record of unique events in an individual's experience encoded in relation to a spatiotemporal context. Tulving contrasted this with what he called semantic memory—an organized body of knowledge regarding words and concepts, their meanings and associations. Because of its heavy emphasis on concept meaning, semantic memory is examined in the upcoming section Language and Semantic Knowledge. Given the diversity of (or often lack of) theoretical models underlying the episodic memory studies carried out with AD patients, there is no obvious way to organize this large literature. However, to give the present review some kind of structure, I discuss findings with respect to both putative types of episodic memory (e.g., primary memory, secondary memory, etc.), as well as putative memory operations (e.g., encoding, retrieval, etc.).

Primary Memory

Although the division of episodic memory into primary memory and secondary memory (or short-term and long-term memory) has been questioned, it is a theoretical distinction that has guided a great deal of neuropsychological research on memory. This is due mainly to evidence that primary-memory performance remains relatively intact in many amnesic patients, despite their severe secondary-memory impairment. A number of studies, therefore, have examined whether primary memory is similarly spared in AD. Primary memory typically is viewed as a limited-capacity, temporary store of information held in consciousness, whereas secondary memory is an unlimited permanent store of information.

Several procedures have been devised to measure the storage capacity of primary memory. One approach has been to give subjects lists of words and to examine their free-recall accuracy as a function of the serial position of the stimulus words. Typically, normals, both old and young, show a u-shaped function in which recall is better for items presented early in the list (primacy effect) and for those presented late in the list (recency effect), than it is for those falling in the middle of the list. The recency effect is postulated to reflect the number of items that the subject has stored in primary memory, whereas the primacy effect is considered a measure of secondary-memory performance. Another commonly used measure of primary-memory capacity is the memory span—the largest number of items (e.g., letters, numbers, spatial positions, etc.) a subject simultaneously can hold in mind at one time.

Wilson, Bacon, Fox, and Kaszniak (1983) used a free-recall task and examined the serial-position effect in normals and AD patients. Results showed a mild decrease in the recency portion of the curve and a major decrease in the primacy portion. This suggests that primary memory is much less impaired by AD than is secondary memory, although Wilson et al. emphasized that the primary-memory performance of their AD patients was definitely not normal. Spinnler, Della Sala, Bandera, and Baddeley (1988) corrected each subject's primary and recency scores on the basis of that subject's performance on items in the middle portion of the serial-position function and found no difference in the size of the recency effect in normals and AD patients, but a large difference in the primacy effect, again suggesting a relative preservation of primary memory in AD. By contrast, Martin, Brouwers, Cox, and Fedio (1985) did not find a differential impairment in either primacy or recency, the shape of the serial-position curve being the same for both normal and demented subjects. Instead, the whole serial-position curve was just shifted down (i.e., the AD patients recalled less at all serial positions). Thus, there was no evidence for a differential impairment of secondary as compared to primary memory in their data. Why the difference in results? One possible explanation is variability between the studies in the severity of the dementia present in their patients. Pepin and Eslinger (1989) recently showed that the shape of the serial-position curve changes with dementia severity. More mildly demented patients showed a normal serial position curve, whereas moderately demented patients showed a normal recency effect but decreased primacy. This is an excellent example of how the pattern of cognitive impairment present in AD can change with increasing severity of dementia.

Studies that have measured memory span in AD patients almost uniformly have found AD patients to have smaller spans. Corkin (1982) found AD patients to have a smaller span both for verbal (lists of words) and nonverbal (a series of spatial positions) information. Spinnler et al. (1988) and Dannenbaum, Parkinson, and Inman (1988) also found decreased span in AD.

Another approach used to compare primary- and secondary-memory abilities is the selective-reminding procedure of Buschke, in which it is theoretically possible to determine whether subjects are retrieving information from primary or from secondary memory. Subjects are given a series of alternating study and recall trials of a 10-word list. On each study trial (after the first), subjects are reminded only of those items they failed to recall on the preceding recall trial, and then are asked to recall all 10 words again. If subjects recall an item of which they have just been reminded, it is considered to be retrieved from primary memory, whereas if they recall an item that they also had recalled on the previous trial (and so it had not been presented again), retrieval is considered to be from secondary memory. Across 10 trials, Ober, Koss, Friedland, and Delis (1985) found that most of their normal subjects' recall came from secondary memory (i.e., they were recalling items they had not heard on that study trial), especially as the number of repetitions increased. By contrast, most of the AD patients' recall came from primary memory as defined by this procedure. This reflected the fact that the AD patients were unlikely to recall any item that had not been presented to them immediately before recall.

Overall, it would appear that although AD patients are impaired on measures purported to measure the magnitude of primary-memory capacity, their primary-memory deficit is substantially less than their secondary-memory deficit.

Another model of short-term memory that recently has been applied to the study of AD is that of working memory—the temporary storage of information for use in the performance of other tasks and operations. In the Baddeley version of this model (Morris & Baddeley, 1988), short-term memory is composed of three distinct components: two slave systems (an articulatory loop and a visuo-spatial scratchpad) and a controlling central executive system (CES). The articulatory loop is a limited duration buffer that has both a passive store of phonologically encoded information, as well as an active articulatory rehearsal operation used to process input into the phonological store and to refresh this store. The visuo-spatial scratchpad is a similar limited duration buffer used to maintain and manipulate visual images. The crucial component of this model is the CES, a limited-capacity attentional system that coordinates and schedules the various operating processes and strategies necessary to carry out ongoing cognitive tasks. Evidence for a CES impairment in AD comes mainly from the severe problems that these patients have in coordinating simultaneous mental operations that make competing demands on attentional capacity. For example, the work of Morris (1986), reported in the Divided Attention section, showed that the addition of even a simple concurrent distractor task was sufficient to produce a major deficit in short-term memory, probably by interfering with maintenance rehearsal. Similarly, the studies of Baddeley et al. (1986) using dual concurrent tasks also can be interpreted as evidence for a CES impairment in AD. As for the two slave systems, at present the scratchpad component remains uninvestigated. What evidence exists about the articulatory loop suggests that this component of working memory remains intact in AD. Morris (1984) showed that the pattern of experimental results used to support the evidence of the articulatory loop in normals also occurs in AD patients. Like normals, the immediate recall of AD patients is worse for phonologically similar words than for dissimilar words. Also like normals, the memory span of AD patients is smaller for multisyllable words than for monosyllable words, and this difference is abolished by concurrent articulation of an interference word which would act to suppress the articulatory loop. Morris concluded that the articulatory loop remains intact in AD patients, and that any problems these patients experience on primary-memory tasks spring from the demands these tasks make on the patients' CES. Similarly, Spinnler et al. (1988) suggested that the reason their AD patients show a normal recency effect, but impaired performance on memory span, is that the recency portion of the serial-position curve reflects operations of the passive phonological store, which remains intact in AD, whereas the memory-span task makes a substantial demand on the CES, which is impaired in these individuals.

Secondary Memory

A major impairment of secondary memory is probably the most prominent symptom of the dementia associated with AD. Some of the evidence for this secondary-memory deficit was just discussed in the Primary Memory section. Other evidence can be found in the upcoming sections Encoding, Storage, and Retrieval, as most of the studies on these memory processes have used secondary-memory tasks. Instead of summarizing this information, the present section highlights one aspect of secondary memory—memory for text. AD patients are grossly impaired in recalling even short pieces of text, such as a four- or five-sentence story, even if no delay is imposed. With a delay, these patients often do not even remember having been given the story. This has made tests of story memory an important clinical tool. However, only one study has seriously examined the fundamental cognitive dysfunction responsible for this deficit in textual memory. Spilich (1983) compared text recall in normal young subjects, and in a group of older persons living in a residential nursing facility. He used a standardized memory test (Wechsler Memory Scale) to divide the older individuals into those with a normal memory and those with a memory impairment. Obviously, from the viewpoint of understanding the cognitive effects of dementia, and especially of AD, this sort of classification is less than ideal. However, given that most of the individuals in the memory-impaired group are probably demented and have AD, it is definitely worth examining his results, especially in view of the sophisticated behavioral analyses he carried out. The subjects were shown two lengthy (four long paragraphs) stories which they were to read aloud. Then they were asked to recall the stories. A propositional analysis carried out on their recall showed that young subjects remembered more propositions than did the normal old, who in turn, remembered more than the memory-impaired old. This is not surprising given the selection criteria. However, when proposition recall was examined as a function of the relative importance of the propositions in the text, some interesting differences emerged. Both the young and normal old recalled more high-order propositions (i.e., those expressing important superordinate information) than lower order propositions. By contrast, proposition importance did not appear to affect the recall of the impaired elderly, although a floor effect complicated interpretation of the impaired subjects' results. Spilich then calculated the parameters affecting text recall using the model of Kintsch and van Dijk (1978). This model assumes that subjects carry over some propositions from one part of the text to the next in a working-memory buffer, allowing them to establish local and global coherence of the text. Typically, the more important the proposition, the more likely it is to be carried over. The results of the analysis showed that although the normal old had a smaller memory buffer (i.e., they carried over fewer propositions), like the young they tended to carry over the more important propositions. A smaller buffer would mean that any decrease in the recall accuracy of the normal old from that seen in the young should be in the less important propositions, and it was. Thus, the difference between the normal old and the young appeared quantitative. By contrast, the memory-impaired subjects did not have a smaller buffer than the normals, but rather, the propositions they carried over appeared to be selected without regard for their significance. Therefore, although both young and normal old were sensitive to the overall thematic structure of the text, the impaired elderly were not, and in this respect they differed qualitatively from the normals in their processing of text. Because the information the impaired old carried over from one part of the text to the next was chosen relatively at random, this would devastate their ability both to comprehend and to recall the text. Information from outside the text also often intruded into the recall of the impaired elderly, suggesting that associations or thoughts that the impaired subjects had while reading the text often were carried over and incorporated into their recall structure, further degrading their memory. Although there are a number of potential problems with this study, especially in terms of the subject population and the presence of a floor effect, this is the type of fine-grained cognitive analysis that is necessary if we are to understand the cognitive mechanisms responsible for the behavioral deficits found in normal aging and in AD.

Remote Memory

Amnesic patients (e.g., patients with Korsakoff syndrome) often show a temporal gradient in their memory deficit. That is, their memory for information from their distant past appears better preserved than their memory for more recent information. A number of studies have examined whether this is also true in AD. Several approaches have been used to investigate this apparent preservation of remote memory. One technique (cued autobiographical memory) involves giving subjects a cue word (e.g., *song*) and asking them to produce a memory of a specific event in their life related to that cue and then to date that event. Generally, in this situation most memories produced by normals come from their recent past with a scattering from earlier times in their life, especially in the case of older individuals (Sagar, 1990). Although this approach has been used to investigate memory for remote versus more recent information, it is obviously a big jump to infer that the relative number of memories that subjects produce from different times in their life reflects differences in the number of available memories of different ages. At best, this approach demonstrates subjects' recall preferences. Also, it is usually impossible to verify the accuracy of any such memories.

A second experimental approach has been to test subjects' knowledge of externally verifiable information. Subjects are asked questions about public events that took place in different decades, or are asked to name pictures of famous faces—individuals who became famous at a particular time in the past. Moscovitch (1982) showed AD patients a set of famous faces and found a temporal gradient in their memory (i.e., they recalled the names of the older faces better than the newer faces) across the entire range of decades tested. By contrast, Wilson, Kaszniak, and Fox (1981), using the same set of famous faces as well as a recognition test of public-event memory, found AD patients to be worse than the normal old on information from all decades, with no temporal gradient in their level of accuracy. More recently, Sagar, Cohen, Sullivan, Corkin, and Growdon (1988) gave AD patients the cued-autobiographical-memory task and a famous-scenes test in which subjects were shown a photo of a famous event (e.g., Oswald being assassinated) and were asked both to identify the event and to date it. In both tasks, although AD patients performed more poorly than did normals, they recalled proportionately more information (both public and personal) from their more remote past than from their more recent past. Similarly, Kopelman (1989) administered tests of memory for famous faces and public events as well as a test of cued autobiographical memory and a personal-events interview. In the latter task, a subject was asked to recall specific information from various decades in his or her life (e.g., names of schools attended, addresses lived at, etc.). Recall accuracy then was verified independently. Although AD patients performed more poorly than normals on all of these tasks, they also showed a different pattern of results. The normals were most accurate in remembering recent information, whereas this was the time period for which the AD patients performed worst. The AD patients instead showed a temporal gradient in which the older the information, the better their performance.

Overall, it appears that in AD patients older memories are better preserved than are more recent memories. The question then becomes why? One obvious possibility is that this temporal gradient reflects the increasing memory encoding and storage deficits experienced by AD patients as the disease progresses. However, as Sagar (1990) pointed out in his recent review of this area, a temporal gradient in memory performance is found even for events that took place long before the onset of the dementia. That is, a patient whose dementia became evident in the 1980s still will recall information from the 1940s better than that from the 1950s, which in turn is recalled better than that from the 1960s. Another possibility is that older memory traces are strengthened across time either due to reminiscence or to the formation of linkages with newly acquired information, which enrich the set of retrieval cues available for the older memories (Sagar, 1990). Alternatively, there may be some qualitative change in the form of the memory trace across time. Cermak (1984) suggested that over time the memory trace of an episode loses its associations to time and context and assumes the character of semantic memory. If, for some reason, semantic information were more resistant to degradation or easier to access in AD patients, this could explain the relative preservation of their older memories. However, at present, this is merely speculation.

Implicit Memory

Up to this point, all of the studies discussed have required subjects to intentionally recall, reproduce, or recognize previously presented stimuli. Recently, however, it has become clear that it is also possible to demonstrate the effect of prior experience through changes in subjects' behavior that do not involve intentional recollection. A distinction has been drawn between explicit-memory measures and implicit-memory measures. Explicit-memory tasks require subjects to deliberately remember previously presented information (i.e., typical recall and recognition tests). By contrast, implicit-memory tasks measure the facilitation that prior experience has on subjects' performance when they do not have to intentionally recollect those experiences (Schacter, 1987). One of the most dramatic examples is the comparison between cued-recall and stem-completion tasks. In both tasks, subjects are shown a list of stimulus words and asked to process them in some way (e.g., make some decision about them). In the cued-recall task, subjects later are given the first few letters (the word stem) of the words in the stimulus list and told to complete each stem with one of the words from the previous list. This requires that they explicitly search for their memory of the prior event. By contrast, in the stem-completion task, subjects also are given the word stem, but no mention is made of the prior stimulus list. Instead, subjects are told to complete the stem with the first word that comes to mind. In this task, the effect of the subjects' previous experience with the stimulus list is evidenced by an increased likelihood that they will complete the stems with words from the stimulus list (in comparison to a baseline condition where they did not experience these stimuli). The effect of prior experience thus is measured implicitly by a change in the subjects' behavior. This distinction between implicit and explicit measures of memory has produced a great deal of interest because patients with organic amnesias (e.g., Korsakoff syndrome) with major deficits on explicit-memory measures, often perform normally on implicit-memory measures. Although amnesics may not even remember having seen the stimulus list, like normals they tend to complete the stems with words from the stimulus list when told to produce the first word that comes to mind. Similarly, it appears that implicit memory also remains intact in the normal old, despite their obvious explicit-memory loss (see Graf, 1990, for a recent review). At present, it is not clear whether this pattern of results reflects the action of two distinct memory systems, or whether it results from differences in the encoding/retrieval demands of the two types of task (Schacter, 1987). Therefore, the terms implicit and explicit have been used to refer to both hypothesized memory systems as well as types of task. In the present review, the terms explicit/implicit will be used without implying the existence of separate (either psychologically or neuroanatomically) memory systems. Although less theoretically loaded terminology, such as direct and indirect measures of memory, might be more appropriate, most of the studies discussed have used the explicit/implicit terminology, and therefore I do also.

There are a number of studies that have shown substantial deficits on implicit-memory measures in AD patients. Several of these used the word-stem completion task described earlier. Both Shimamura, Salmon, Squire, and Butters (1987) and Salmon, Shimamura, Butters, and Smith (1988) found the implicit-memory performance of AD patients on a stem-completion task to be much lower than that of normals, even though patients with another type of dementia (Huntington's disease) showed normal implicit memory. However, a recent report by Grosse, Wilson, and Fox (1990) suggests that AD patients do show normal priming in word-stem completion under certain conditions. Grosse et al. argued that because AD patients have a severe deficit in memory encoding (see the next section of this chapter), in order to examine implicit memory it is necessary to maximize the original encoding of the stimuli by these patients. In their task, subjects were given incomplete sentences which they were to complete with a single word. The context of each sentence was very constraining, such that normals almost always completed it with the same word ("He hit the nail with a __"). The typical ending for each of these sentences served as the target word both for a later recognition test (explicit memory) and for a word-stem completion task (implicit memory). Grosse et al. found that although recognition was poorer in AD patients than in normals, the two groups did not differ on word-stem completion. The AD patients were just as likely as normals to complete the stems with words they had generated as part of the sentence-completion task. Grosse et al. argued that the failure of previous studies to demonstrate normal word-stem completion in AD patients really reflects inadequate semantic encoding by the patients in these studies, rather than an actual implicit-memory deficit. It should be noted that the explicit-recognition performance of the AD patients was still deficient even with these self-generated stimuli. This agrees with the results of Mitchell, Hunt, and Schmitt (1986) who found that having AD subjects generate an ending to an incomplete sentence did not improve their later recall of that ending, whereas in normals it did. Thus, although self-generation of stimuli facilitates AD patients' performance on tests of implicit memory for those stimuli, it does not facilitate their performance on tests of explicit memory, such as recall or recognition.

Brandt, Spencer, McSorley, and Folstein (1988) found evidence of abnormal performance by AD patients on a quite different implicit-memory task. Subjects were read a list of 10 stimulus nouns. Later, in what to the subjects was a totally independent task, they were given a word-association test in which they heard a probe word and were to say the first word that came to mind. Some of the probes were chosen such that the previously presented stimulus words were the third most common associate of the probes (as determined from norms). The question here was whether prior exposure to the stimulus words would make AD patients more apt to emit those stimulus words on the word-association task. It did, but the effect was not as great as that found in normals. Of course, the question raised by Grosse et al. (1990) also could apply here: Is the initial encoding into memory of the stimulus words by AD patients in this study sufficient to support even implicit-memory performance?

Heindel, Salmon, and Butters (in press) used a very different approach to examine implicit-memory performance in AD and Huntington's disease patients. Subjects were shown 30 line drawings of objects and asked to name them. Later, in what the subjects thought was a totally different task, they were asked to identify perceptually degraded drawings of objects. The degradation was accomplished by removing portions of the drawings' contours. Subjects initially were given the most degraded version of the drawings, and then increasingly more and more complete versions. The dependent measure here was the degree of degradation at which the subjects first identified the drawings. Some of the object drawings were the same items that the subject had seen in the earlier naming task. Here, implicit memory would be evident as enhanced identification (identification of a more degraded version) of previously encountered drawings in comparison to novel drawings. Results showed that although demented Huntington's disease patients showed normal implicit memory, AD patients were definitely impaired.

There are, however, a number of other implicit-memory tasks on which AD patients perform normally. Three studies have examined repetition priming in AD patients. Repetition priming is a phenomenon in which subjects more rapidly process a stimulus the second time they encounter it in a task. For example, when subjects make lexical decisions about a series of words, if a given word is repeated, normal subjects' decision time for that word drops substantially. This approach does not require that subjects explicitly recall their prior experience with the stimuli, but rather, their memory for the stimulus is evident in the facilitation that occurs the second time they process the stimulus. Both normal old and AD patients show as much repetition priming on a lexical decision task as do the young, even with lags as long as 30 words between presentations of the same stimulus (Moscovitch, 1982; Ober & Shenaut, 1988). Moscovitch, Winocur, and McLachlan (1986) used a somewhat different task in which subjects were asked to read sentences presented in mirror-image form. They were given three sessions on this task over the course of several weeks, and all subjects (i.e., young, normal old, and the cognitively impaired old) showed improvement in their reading speed over the sessions. This was more than just general skill learning, however, as some of the same sentences were repeated (without the subjects' knowledge), and the decrease in reading time was especially great for these repeated sentences, both in normal and cognitively impaired older subjects. That is, like the normals, the cognitively impaired subjects showed item-specific facilitation of their reading time on sentences they had seen before. However, when direct recognition for these repeated sentences was tested, the impaired elderly performed quite poorly. So, when memory for text was tested indirectly by changes in the subjects' performance, impaired older individuals were affected as much by prior experience with specific stimuli as were the normal old or normal young. However, when their memory for these stimuli was examined by explicit-memory measures such as recognition, they were impaired.

Knopman and Nissen (1987) used a different implicit-memory measure, but also found normal performance in AD patients. They administered a serial reaction-time task in which subjects were to respond to an asterisk appearing on a screen by pressing one of four buttons depending on the spatial position of the asterisk. Unknown to the subjects, the order in which the asterisk appeared in the various positions was not random, but rather, repeated itself every 10 trials. Over the course of 400 trials, the response time of both normal old and AD subjects decreased steadily. To test whether this increased speed of response was due to learning of the repetitive sequence of stimulus positions or just to general skill learning, a series of trials then was given in which the sequence of stimulus positions was randomized. The response times of both normal and AD subjects rose dramatically, indicating that they had learned the sequence of the repeating stimuli. However, unlike the normals, almost all of the AD patients were unaware that there had been a repeating sequence in the first 400 trials.

Overall, it appears that under certain conditions, AD patients do perform relatively normally on implicit-memory measures, whereas under other conditions their performance is obviously deficient. What might explain this variability? One possibility, suggested by Grosse et al. (1990), is that the implicit-memory performance of AD patients may be limited by their severe encoding deficit, and only when the task ensures adequate initial encoding of the stimuli will their normal implicit memory become evident. Another possibility is that the implicit-memory performance of AD patients is abnormal only when the task requires a memory search. All of the reports of abnormal implicit-memory performance in AD have used as their dependent measure a change in the likelihood that subjects will emit a given word—that is, a change in the probability that one of the previously presented stimuli will be used to complete a word stem or will be given as an associate or as a picture name. By contrast, most reports of normal performance on implicit-memory tasks (except for Grosse et al.) have used as their dependent measure a change in the speed with which subjects process a presented word. Nelson, Canas, Bajo, and Keelean (1987) showed that stem completion involves a lexically based search process similar to that involved in cued recall. Thus, it is possible that a deficit in lexical search rather than in implicit memory may be responsible for the problems AD patients have on the stem-completion and associate-generation tasks. Schacter (1987) also raised the possibility that different implicit-memory phenomena have different sources—that word completion may depend on the same system involved in recall and recognition, whereas repetition-priming and motor-learning tasks reflect the action of a distinctly different memory system. Another potentially important factor for explaining the variability in the implicit-memory results is the severity of the AD patients' dementia. A recent study (Landrum & Radtke, 1990) found that although mildly demented patients performed normally on a stem-completion task, more severely demented patients did not. Of course, with severely demented patients it is often difficult to determine why they are doing poorly. Is it due to a deficit in the cognitive operation your test was designed to measure, or is it due to a failure to comprehend instructions or to maintain an attentional set?

Encoding

A major determinant of how well a stimulus will be remembered is how well it is encoded. It is therefore not surprising that many of the investigations into the source of the memory problems in AD have focused on the encoding operation. A number of investigators have argued that the initial processing of information into memory by AD patients is grossly defective. One line of support for this hypothesis is that certain stimulus factors known to influence encoding in normals have no effect on the performance of AD patients. For example, it is well established that in a word-recognition task, the performance of normal individuals is affected by the frequency in the language of the stimulus words. The less common the stimulus word, the more likely normal subjects are to recognize it later. Wilson, Bacon, Kramer, Fox, and Kaszniak (1983) found that although normal-old subjects recognized previously shown rare words more accurately than they did common words, the performance of AD patients was unaffected by word frequency. Because the AD patients were much less accurate on this task than were the normals, it is possible that the lack of the rare-word effect in AD is due merely to the weakness of their memory traces rather than to some specific encoding problem (Meudell & Mayes, 1981). To test this possibility, Wilson et al. also measured the recognition memory of their normal subjects after a 1-week delay, at a time when the normals' overall accuracy level was similar to that of the AD patients. If the lack of a rare-word superiority in AD patients was due solely to an impoverished or weak memory trace, then after a 1-week delay, the older normals should perform similarly to the

AD patients. They did not; the normals still showed a rare-word recognition superiority. Wilson et al. therefore concluded that the lack of a rare-word superiority in the recognition performance of AD patients reflected a basic problem in their initial processing of the stimuli.

Another stimulus factor known to affect memory performance is the imageability of the stimuli. Normals typically recall high-imagery nouns more accurately than they do low-imagery nouns. A common interpretation of this finding is that normal subjects encode high-imagery words both in terms of their verbal label and also as an image. This dual encoding is postulated to increase the likelihood that the stimulus information later will be retrieved. Hart, Kwentus, Taylor, and Hamer (1987) found that the recall performance of AD patients did not vary as a function of the imageability of the stimulus words, suggesting that they did not dually encode high-imagery words. Rissenberg and Glanzer (1987) also examined the dual-encoding hypothesis; however, they used words that differed in their concreteness, a dimension related to imageability. They found that the difference in recall accuracy between concrete and abstract words was actually greater for AD patients than for normals, suggesting AD patients might engage in dual encoding. However, Rissenberg and Glanzer instead argued that this result reflected a greater retrieval deficit for abstract words in AD patients. They supported this assertion with data showing that when asked to name a concept upon hearing its definition, AD patients had more trouble with abstract concepts than with concrete concepts. But, because it is likely that the definitions of abstract concepts are more complex than those of concrete ones, this interpretation is debatable.

There is one study in which AD patients do appear to show a type of dual encoding. Karlsson et al. (1989) compared the performance of normal and demented patients on two conditions. In one, the subjects were shown a series of sentences that were commands (e.g., "Lift the cup.") and were told to remember them. In the other condition, they were given the actual object mentioned in each command and had to carry out the action described. At the end of each condition, the subjects were asked to recall all the sentences. Both the normals and the AD patients (including severely demented patients) recalled more of the sentences in which they actually had carried out the action, than those in which they had just read the sentence. Also, if the semantic category of the object in the sentence was given as a recall cue, the recall of both the normal and demented subjects was facilitated. This was especially true of those sentences that the subject had enacted. It appears that enriching the encoding situation by having the subject carry out the motor movement described by the stimulus sentence can facilitate the recall and cued-recall performance of such sentences by AD patients. However, a very similar study by Dick, Kean, and Sands (1989) found no memory advantage in AD patients for actions the subjects had performed over those they had just heard described. The reason for this disagreement is not clear, but at least in this case it is unlikely to be due to a difference between the studies in the severity of patient dementia, as Karlsson et al. found the same pattern even in severely demented patients.

Much of the work on encoding in AD has examined whether these individuals benefit from contextual support provided either by the experimenter or by the stimulus material itself. Studies have examined whether AD patients can use experimenter-provided verbal mediators, or stimulus organization to improve their encoding. Butters et al. (1983) found that AD patients did not use a verbal context provided at encoding to improve their memory. Subjects were shown a series of drawings each consisting of three animal or human figures on a background scene. On some trials, the drawings were presented without comment, whereas on others, a short verbal passage was read aloud to the subject. This passage provided a story linking the figures to the background. Subjects then were shown a background scene and had to decide which of two figures had been present in that scene in the original drawing. Although patients with other types of brain damage, including Huntington's dementia, showed superior recognition for those scene-figure pairings presented with a verbal context, the AD patients did not. It appeared that AD patients were unable to use the verbal mediators provided to them in order to facilitate their encoding of the visual stimuli. Other interpretations of these results are, however, possible. In order to use these stories to improve their memory, it was necessary for subjects to comprehend and remember a multisentence text. They also had to divide their attention between the story and the drawing during encoding. Any difficulty with text comprehension, division of attention, or any reduction in overall attentional capacity would severely limit AD patients' ability to make use of the provided verbal context. Their failure to use such context does not, therefore, necessarily imply that AD patients have a problem with using context to facilitate encoding.

However, these confounds were not present in a study by Backman and Herlitz (1990), which also concluded that the memory of AD patients does not benefit from contextual information. Here, context was seen in terms of subjects' degree of prior knowledge about the stimuli. Rather than providing additional information at the time of study, Backman and Herlitz took advantage of the fact that, due to their prior experience, subjects possess more information about some stimuli than about others. Backman and Herlitz showed subjects a series of pictures of 20 public figures (10 of whom had been famous in the 1940s, whereas the other 10 became famous in the 1980s) and then asked the subjects to pick them out in a recognition test. The normal old were more accurate in recognizing the dated (i.e., the 1940s faces) than the more recent faces; the AD patients, by contrast, showed no such difference in recognition accuracy. Backman and Herlitz went on to demonstrate that both the normal old and the AD patients in this study knew more about the dated than about the more recent public figures. Both groups rated the dated public figures as more familiar than the recent ones, and both groups were more accurate in recognizing (from among four choices) the names of dated than of recent public figures. Although both the demented patients and the normal old possessed more knowledge about dated public figures than about more recent ones, only the normals appeared to use this additional information to enrich their encoding of the stimuli. Like Butters et al. (1983), Backman and Herlitz concluded that AD patients have difficulty encoding contextual information into memory in order to produce a richer memory trace (see also chapter 2 of this volume).

A similar hypothesis is that AD patients are unable to encode semantic information about stimuli into memory (Martin et al., 1985), because they either no longer know or cannot access information about the specific semantic attributes that make up stimulus meaning (see the Language and Semantic Knowledge section for more detail on semantic attributes). The evidence in favor of this hypothesis comes from a variety of studies showing that AD patients do not take advantage of the semantic structure present in stimuli and that their performance is not affected by the semantic aspects of stimulus material. For example, Weingartner et al. (1981) showed that normals remembered a list of words substantially better if the words were selected from several distinct semantic categories (e.g., furniture and fruits) then if they were chosen randomly so as to have no relationship to one another. By contrast, AD patients performed equally poorly on both types of list, even when the lists were given multiple times and the items from each category were presented as a group so as to emphasize their relationship. Also, unlike normals, AD patients did not group items from the same category together in their recall—that is, they showed no evidence of response clustering based on the categorical relationship between items. Because of these findings, and the fact that AD patients' episodic-memory performance was highly correlated with their performance on semantic tasks, such as verbal fluency, Weingartner et al. concluded that AD patients cannot access the semantic information about stimuli that would allow them to effectively encode these stimuli into memory.

Another line of evidence regarding AD patients' ability to encode stimuli semantically comes from studies using the depth of processing model of Craik and Tulving (1975). This model suggests that how well a stimulus is remembered is a function of how "deeply" it is processed, with the deepest level involving meaning. In a study by Corkin (1982), subjects heard a series of words and were asked questions that oriented them toward processing either the sensory aspects of a word (Was it said in a male or female voice?), its phonetic aspects (Does it rhyme with __?), or its semantic aspects (Is it a type of __?). The subjects then were asked to pick out these stimuli in a recognition test. As expected, normals recognized more of the words about which they had answered semantic questions, than words about which they had answered sensory or phonetic questions. By contrast, the AD patients showed no such superiority for semantically processed stimuli. A different result was found by Martin et al. (1985) who presented subjects with lists of object names under four different conditions. In one condition they were given no instructions (free encoding), whereas in the others they were to either generate a rhyme for each word, tell where it could be found, or pantomime an action involving the object. The latter two conditions were considered to involve semantic processing. Martin et al. found that although AD patients recalled fewer words than did the normal old, both subject groups recalled more of the words that they had processed with respect to meaning. This suggests that both normal and AD subjects spontaneously encoded words with respect to their semantic attributes. However, despite these results, other findings led Martin et al. to conclude that there is a semantic encoding deficit in AD. This conclusion was based on evidence from another study suggesting that AD patients may not encode as many semantic features as do normals. They found that when AD patients made an error on a recognition task, they usually chose a distractor that was semantically related to the target. Martin et al. argued that, whereas AD patients may encode semantic features into memory, they may not encode the most salient features or may not encode enough features to allow them to discriminate closely related semantic concepts. Thus, the problem in AD may be more one of insufficient semantic elaboration than of a total lack of semantic encoding.

The question remains, however, as to why Martin et al. (1985) found relatively normal depth of processing in AD patients whereas Corkin (1982) did not. One possibility is that the processing required by Martin et al. was more extensive that that required by Corkin. In Corkin's procedure, the subject had only to answer a yes/no question about the stimuli, whereas in Martin et al.'s study they had to actually generate a rhyme, search their memory for information about the typical location of an item, or pantomime its use. These procedures would appear to involve more extensive processing of the stimuli than that required by Corkin's procedures.

A recent study by Cushman, Como, Booth, and Caine (1988) also produced impressive evidence for a semantic deficit in encoding. In their first experiment, subjects were given 12 words along with a number of semantic cues (e.g., for *penny*, the associated cue was *a piece of money*). They were required to pick out the cue that went with each stimulus word and therefore had to process the meaning of the stimulus. Cued recall of the 12 words was then tested using the semantic cues. Because the AD patients were able to match the cue to the stimulus word for only three quarters of the stimuli (unlike normals who matched them all), cued-recall performance was measured only for those items correctly matched to their cue initially. As would be expected, the free recall of the AD patients was grossly impaired. However, the recall of these patients improved relatively more than did that of the normal old when the semantic cues were given (20% vs. 3%). Most of the improvement in recall with cues came, however, in the less demented patients, many of whom performed normally on cued recall (although not on free recall). If semantic cues were provided to guide initial encoding as well as being presented at recall, the memory performance of the AD patients did benefit, but only in the mildly demented patients. An even more impressive semantic deficit was found in Cushman et al.'s second experiment which examined release from proactive interference (PI). In this paradigm, subjects' recall is tested across a series of word lists. If all the words used in these lists are drawn from the same semantic category, then the recall accuracy of normals tends to decrease as the number of lists they have encountered increases, presumably due to a buildup in PI. However, the recall of normals improves immediately if a list of words from a different semantic category then is presented. In this task, evidence for spontaneous semantic encoding can be seen both in the increasing PI across lists drawn from the same semantic category and in the release from PI with a switch in category. In Cushman et al. (1988), AD patients showed neither an increase in PI nor a release from PI. Overall, this pattern of results led Cushman et al. to conclude that at least one of the major causes of AD patients' poor episodic memory is an impairment in their use of semantic information at encoding and recall.

Although the studies described to this point have argued that AD patients are unable to use context or the semantic aspects of stimulus material in encoding, there is some evidence suggesting that under certain circumstances AD patients encode semantic context quite normally. Nebes, Martin, and Horn (1984) examined the effect that the *approximation-to-text* of various word strings had on subjects' recall of those strings. Approximation-to-text is a measure of the degree to which a sequence of words conforms to the syntactic and semantic patterns of English. The word lists used in their study varied from random strings of words (e.g., *dress, awake, hammer, tide, empty, play, hill*) to strings of a moderate approximation (e.g., *to, ask, for, is, to, earn, our, living*) to actual sentences (e.g., *I, first, saw, him, as, he, jumped, from*). The higher the order of approximation, the easier it is for normals to recall the string, presumably because in the higher approximations, the words are more likely to form meaningful groupings (i.e., chunks), which are easier to encode than are unrelated words. Nebes et al. found that as approximation-to-text increased, memory performance increased equally in both normals and AD patients. This suggested that AD patients are capable of using the language structure present in strings of words to facilitate encoding. However, because both syntactic and semantic structure increase with increasing approximation, it was not clear whether AD patients were actually using semantic structure. This was clarified in a subsequent study (Nebes, Brady, & Jackson, 1989) in which subjects were given seven-word sentences that were either (a) normal, (b) semantically anomalous but syntactically correct (e.g., *His hotel arrived at the governor's bark*), (c) syntactically anomalous (sentence word order was scrambled), or (d) both semantically and syntactically anomalous (e.g., *Softly liquid the many scrambled husbands prizes*). Results indicated that AD patients were as effective as normal subjects in using both the syntactic and the semantic structure present in sentences to improve their memory. There was also evidence that the mechanism by which semantic structure facilitated encoding (i.e., the formation of multiword chunks) was the same in the AD patients as it was in the normals. In normals, chunk size (the number of words the subject remembered in the same order as they had been presented) increased with increasing semantic structure. This was equally true of AD patients. Not only did semantic structure facilitate the memory of AD patients as much as that of normals, but the mechanism of action appeared to be the same as in normals.

What can we conclude from the studies just described? First, the ability of AD patients to encode information into memory appears to be severely impaired. Most of the experimental paradigms used to investigate encoding have demonstrated major deficits in AD patients. Also, there seems to be substantial evidence that AD patients do not take advantage of the semantic aspects of stimuli or the semantic structure present in stimulus context to improve their encoding. However, there do seem to be situations in which the encoding of semantic information by AD patients is relatively normal. The question now becomes what determines the success or failure of semantic encoding in AD patients? Why is it that AD patients are unable to use the categorical structure present in lists of words (Weingartner et al., 1981) but are able to use the semantic information provided by connected text (Nebes, Brady, & Jackson, 1989)? One possible explanation is that AD patients can use the semantic information inherent in text to encode sentences because reading text is such an overlearned skill in most persons. Encoding of the words in a sentence into memory is strongly guided by preceding context, perhaps through some kind of automatic priming mechanism (Stanovich & West, 1983). It is possible that demented patients may be able to effectively encode semantic information only to the extent that their encoding is induced and directed by the stimulus material itself and is not an intentional act (Craik, 1984). However, when demented patients must self-initiate a novel coding scheme such as encoding words by membership in a semantic category or linking up a story to a visual scene, they may not encode semantic information into episodic memory.

There are several problems with this explanation, however. First, as noted in the Implicit Memory section, when an incomplete sentence was used to guide subjects' generation of a word, although it may have helped their implicit memory for that word, it did not help their explicit memory (Grosse et al., 1990; Mitchell et al., 1986). However, in these cases, the subject was attempting to remember a word without the context that had surrounded it at encoding. By contrast, in the two Nebes et al. (1984, 1989) studies, subjects were recalling meaningful groupings of words (i.e., chunks). Another obvious problem with this explanation is the Cushman et al. (1988) data on release from PI. Use of semantic information in this task does not appear to require an intentional or self-initiated use of semantic information and yet AD patients were impaired. Obviously, a great deal more work is needed to clarify why semantic context can facilitate encoding of stimuli in some situations, but not in others (see also chapter 2 of this volume).

Storage

Most of the studies investigating memory storage in AD have examined whether information is lost from secondary memory at a faster rate in demented patients than it is in normals. Given the encoding problems just described, it is of course necessary to equate normal and demented subjects for the degree of their initial learning to the extent that can be done. Kopelman (1985) showed subjects 120 pictures of scenes. The exposure duration was individually set such that after a 10-min delay, each subject correctly recognized approximately 75% of the pictures. This naturally required a longer presentation time for the AD patients than for the normal old (an average of 9 s vs. ½ s). The subjects' retention of the pictures was then retested at 24 hr and at 1 week. The rationale here was that a recognition measure should reduce the retrieval demands of the task, whereas equating the performance of normals and AD patients soon after stimulus presentation should eliminate any group differences due to encoding. Any group difference in later memory performance would show that normal old and AD patients varied in their rate of forgetting (i.e., loss from storage). Kopelman found that under these conditions information was lost from secondary memory at the same rate in his AD patients as it was in his normals. Interestingly, when Huppert and Kopelman (1989) used this same approach to compare normals of different ages, the normal old forgot information more rapidly than did the young. It should be noted, however, that typically young and normal old subjects show parallel rates of forgetting (Craik, 1977).

It is possible to criticize this approach in that the normals and the AD patients were permitted widely different encoding times. Normals were allowed only about ½ s to see the picture and this may have qualitatively changed how they encoded the stimuli because of the time pressure created. However, this is not true of another study (Becker, Boller, Saxton, & McGonigle-Gibson, 1987), which, rather than equating for the degree of initial learning in normals and AD patients, used the difference in accuracy between immediate and delayed (30 min) recall as their measure of the rate of forgetting for a short story and a complex picture (Rey figure). As expected, the AD patients recalled substantially less than did the normals at immediate recall. However, when Becker et al. examined how much more information was lost over the next 30 min, there was no difference between the normals and the AD patients. Again, the conclusion was that the memory problem of AD is due to encoding deficits, rather than to an abnormally rapid loss of information from memory. It should be noted that this study measured memory recall rather than recognition and so involved a substantial retrieval demand. Despite this, the decrease in memory was the same in the normal old and AD patients, at least over the course of 30 min.

There is, however, one study that found evidence of an increased rate of forgetting in AD patients (Hart, Kwentus, Taylor, & Harkins, 1987). This study also examined recognition of visual stimuli, but used a different technique to equate the initial performance of AD and normal subjects. Subjects were shown 130 line drawings of objects. The normals were shown the drawings for 2 s each, whereas the AD patients were allowed 4 s each. The subjects then were given a criterion test in which they were shown a series of 16 drawings (8 old and 8 new) and were to indicate for each drawing whether they had seen it before. If they failed to get $^{13}/_{16}$ correct, all 130 figures were shown to them again, for durations of between 4 s and 12 s each, depending on how poorly they had performed on the criterion test. After this, they received a second criterion test. All of the normals reached criterion on the first testing, whereas many of the AD needed a second presentation, at which time they all reached criterion. Subjects' recognition memory then was tested at delays of 10 min, 2 hr, and 48 hr. The results showed that by 10 min postcriterion testing, there was a large difference in recognition accuracy between the normals and the AD patients. This difference increased at 2 hr, at which point the forgetting of the AD patients reached asymptote, whereas that of the normal old continued to decline, although their memory performance never declined to that of the AD. Hart et al. concluded that there is a greater loss of information from secondary memory in AD than there is in normal old individuals.

One possible reason for this disagreement may lie in the time periods over which forgetting was examined. Hart, Kwentus, Taylor, and Hawkins (1987) tested at 10 min, 2 hr, and 48 hr, and found that normals and AD patients differed in their rate of forgetting mainly over the first 2 hr. Kopelman's (1985) technique did not allow for any measurement of decline until 24 hr, by which time the decline of the AD patients in Hart et al.'s data was reaching asymptote. Actually, if you look just at the 10-min and the 48-hr points in Hart et al.'s data (making the comparison similar to that of Kopelman), the percentage decrease in recognition performance is very similar for the normals and the AD patients. It may be that AD patients do show abnormally fast forgetting, but the majority of this forgetting takes place soon after they acquire the information. After this rapid initial loss, the rate at which they lose further information is similar to that of the normals. This, of course, would not explain Becker et al.'s (1987) data, which examined the rate of forgetting over the course of 30 min. However, given differences in the type of material, the type of test, and the fact that the performances of the normal and AD subjects were not actually equated in this study, there are many possible reasons for this disagreement.

One other line of evidence suggesting AD patients experience a faster than normal initial loss of information comes from studies that have used the Brown–Peterson task to investigate the forgetting from primary memory caused by an interference task. Corkin (1982) gave subjects consonant trigrams followed by interference periods of between 3 s and 30 s during which they counted backward from a given number. The normal old and AD patients performed similarly at a zero-second delay, but as the interference period was lengthened, AD patients showed a much greater decrease in recall than did normals, until at about 15 s, they essentially recalled nothing. Kopelman (1985) used a similar design, with interference periods of 0 s, 2 s, 5 s, 10 s, or 20 s. The normal old showed the usual gradual drop in recall accuracy over time, but still recalled approximately half the letters at 20 s. By contrast, the AD patients' recall dropped much more rapidly, being obviously worse than the normals with delays as short as 2 s to 5 s. By the end of 20 s the AD patients remembered nothing. As described in the Attention section, Morris (1986), using a variety of interference tasks, also found a more rapid loss of information from primary memory in AD patients than in the normal old.

However, Dannenbaum et al. (1988) argued that all these studies are flawed because they did not match for the initial level of acquisition. They argued that just because both normal and AD patients can remember a three-letter array perfectly with a zero-second delay does not mean that they have learned it equally well. To equate initial level of acquisition, Dannenbaum et al. found each subject's digit span with no delay, and then, using a list length equal to their span, examined what percentage of the span was lost with an interference period. Their approach differed from the other studies in that rather than using various time periods filled with an interference task, they had just a single "delayed" condition, which consisted of recall after the subject had counted the number of squares present in three arrays. Therefore, there was no set delay, but rather the period over which loss was measured varied depending on how quickly subjects counted the squares. Effectively, this procedure is looking at memory loss over a given amount of interference activity rather than over a given amount of time. They found that even after equating the initial levels of acquisition, AD patients still lost information from primary memory at a faster rate than did the normal old.

Retrieval

One way of determining whether a memory decrement results from a retrieval deficit is to compare the magnitude of the impairment found on recall tasks with that on cued-recall and recognition tasks. The rationale is that recognition and cued recall place much less of a demand on retrieval operations than does free recall and so, if the memory impairment is lessened in these tasks, there is a deficit in retrieval. For example, because the magnitude of the memory difference between young and normal older persons is typically less in cued-recall or recognition tasks than it is in free-recall tasks, some of the memory deficit found in the normal old has been attributed to a retrieval problem (see Craik, 1977, for a review of this literature). What about AD? There is no question that AD patients do poorly on recognition tests (e.g., Shimamura et al., 1987). However, the real question is whether in comparison to the normal old, their memory deficit on a recognition test is less than that on a free-recall test. Unfortunately, I have been unable to find a study that directly compared recall and recognition performance, with all the appropriate controls, in normal old and AD patients. This may reflect the difficulty of avoiding ceiling and floor effects with two groups performing at such different accuracy levels. There are, however, a few issues regarding retrieval that have emerged from studies using recognition. Miller (1977) suggested that demented patients have a specific retrieval deficit based on his finding that the difference in recognition accuracy between normals and demented subjects was substantially greater when there were eight choices than when there were only two. However, Meudell and Mayes (1981) showed that differentially poorer recognition with eight than with two choices is also found in normals if their level of accuracy is reduced to that of demented patients by placing a 1-week delay between stimulus presentation and testing. This pattern of results, therefore, would seem more a function of a weak memory trace than of a specific retrieval deficit. This finding points out the difficulty of drawing conclusions about qualitative differences in processing based on group-condition interactions when the two subject groups are performing at very different levels of accuracy. Finally, it should be noted that recognition tests tend to be more sensitive than are recall measures in differentiating normal from mildly demented individuals (Branconnier, Cole, Spera, & De Vitt, 1982). This certainly does not suggest that using a recognition measure tends to reduce the difference in memory performance between normals and demented patients.

AD patients also perform more poorly than do normals on tests of cued recall. However, again the issue is whether use of memory cues differentially aids AD patients, thus decreasing the difference in memory performance between normals and demented patients. Martin et al. (1985), in the context of their depth of processing study reported in the Encoding section, examined the effect of using the subject's own responses as memory cues. In this task, the subject had been given object names and asked to either produce a rhyme, tell where the object could be found, or pantomime its use. After testing the subject's free recall, Martin et al. used the subject's own rhymes and so on as recall cues for the object names. Although the cues did help the AD patients, there was no evidence that the cues helped them more than they helped the normal old, despite the fact that the normals were operating near ceiling. Davis and Mumford (1984) compared free recall with cued recall using either the word's first letter or its category name. Again, the AD patients showed no evidence that cues improved their memory performance more than that of the normals. In fact, unlike normals, who benefited from both types of cue, the AD patients only benefited from the letter cues. Grober and Buschke (1987) reported a similar pattern with a category cue—no evidence that the cues help the AD patients more than the normals.

Overall, these studies do not demonstrate a retrieval deficit in AD any greater than that found with normal aging. However, in interpreting the results from the recognition and cued-recall studies, one thing to keep in mind is that a severe encoding deficit in AD could result in a memory trace so impoverished that neither recognition nor memory cues would be able to activate it. In this case, even if AD patients did have a major retrieval deficit, it might not be evident as improved performance on recognition or cued-recall tasks.

Several studies have examined the interaction between encoding and retrieval in AD. The approach here is to minimize both the encoding and retrieval demands to see if this reduces the memory impairment in AD. As mentioned before, Cushman et al. (1988) found some evidence that if encoding was guided by having patients match up a stimulus with a semantic cue and if that cue also was presented at retrieval, the memory of mildly demented AD patients improved. However, this was not true of more demented patients. Another recent study gives an even more negative picture of AD patients' performance in a situation where both encoding and retrieval are supported. Granholm and Butters (1988) used the encoding specificity model, which postulates that the most successful memory-retrieval cues are those cues that serve to reinstate the stimulus situation present at encoding. Thus, a word weakly associated with a to-be-remembered stimulus, if it is present both at encoding and at retrieval, will be a better retrieval cue for that stimulus than will a strongly associated word that is present only at retrieval. Granholm and Butters compared the recall performance of subjects on conditions in which (a) there was no associate present (typical free recall), (b) the same associate was present at both encoding and retrieval (i.e., either the same strong or the same weak associate), and (c) different associates were present at encoding and retrieval (weak then strong or vice versa). Normals and patients with a dementia due to Huntington's disease performed best when the same cues were present at encoding and retrieval, whether or not the cue was strongly associated with the stimulus. By contrast, the AD patients performed better when the retrieval cue was strong, regardless of whether it also had appeared at the time of encoding. However, the AD patients were not helped by consistent presentation of the same weak cue at encoding and retrieval. The fact that strong associates helped even when they had not appeared at encoding (i.e., the weak–strong condition) suggested that the AD patients had not encoded any specific linkages between the associates and the stimuli. Instead, when presented with a cue, they free associated to it, rather than relying on the product of specific encoding to guide retrieval.

Finally, one line of evidence that may support the presence of a retrieval deficit in AD is that these patients are much more likely than normals to show a high rate of intrusions on memory tests. Kramer et al. (1988) presented subjects with a 16-word list composed of four items from each of four different categories. This was followed by immediate and delayed recall and cued recall (with category names) of the list. AD patients were over three times more likely than normals or patients with another form of dementia (Huntington's disease) to have items from outside the list intrude into their responses. Many of these intrusions were semantically related words; that is, they were members of one of the four categories from which the stimulus items had been drawn. This was especially the case in cued recall. A number of other memory studies (e.g., Cushman et al., 1988; Granholm & Butters, 1988; Wilson, Bacon, Fox, & Kaszniak, 1983) also have demonstrated an increased rate of intrusions in AD and these are usually extratask intrusions. That is, they are items that have not occurred anywhere else in the task. Whether increased intrusions really represent a failure in memory retrieval is debatable. Another possible mechanism for this increased rate of intrusions would be that AD patients are poor at discriminating the memory strength of items that they are considering as potential responses. Especially with cued recall, a number of potential responses may be generated during retrieval and the subject must discriminate among these on the basis of some measure of memory strength. Any disruption of this discrimination ability would lead to increased extralist intrusions, even if the retrieval mechanism itself remained intact.

Overall, the evidence for a major role of a retrieval deficit in the memory impairment of AD is, at best, marginal. Efforts to attenuate the memory deficit in AD by using tasks that minimize retrieval demands have not been successful. Similarly, attempts to facilitate the interaction of encoding and retrieval operations have failed to improve memory performance in AD, apparently because of encoding deficiencies. The only real evidence for a retrieval deficit in AD (above whatever exists in normal aging) consists of an increased rate of intrusions.

LANGUAGE AND SEMANTIC KNOWLEDGE

This section on language in Alzheimer's disease is relatively brief given the amount of material that is available. However, much of this area recently was reviewed in depth (Nebes, 1989) and, therefore, I attempt to summarize concisely what is known about the language deficits found in AD, concentrating on current theoretical issues and on relevant studies published since the previous review.

Language deficits commonly are found in AD patients, and in some cases, may be the most prominent early symptom of the disease (Martin, 1987). Clinically, the presence of major language deficits distinguishes the dementia found in AD from that seen in other dementing diseases such as Huntington's disease (Butters, Granholm, Salmon, Grant, & Wolfe, 1987), and so there has been a great deal of interest in this aspect of dementia. If we divide language into syntax and semantics, the overwhelming majority of the work on AD deals with semantics. This is because AD appears to produce only minor impairments in patients' syntax while causing major deficits on tests of semantic abilities. Studies investigating syntax in AD typically have examined patients' spontaneous speech. Although the speech of AD patients tends to be relatively incoherent, it generally remains grammatically correct. Syntactic errors are rare (at least until late in the course of the disease) and the frequency with which various syntactic constructions (e.g., propositional phrases, subordinate clauses) are used is the same in normal and demented individuals, as is the length and grammatical complexity of their utterances (Hier, Hagenlocker, & Shindler, 1985; Kempler, Curtiss, & Jackson, 1987). The syntactic aspects of language appear, therefore, to be relatively preserved in AD patients.

By contrast, the presence of a semantic impairment has become commonly accepted as a central or core deficit in the dementia of AD (Bayles & Kaszniak, 1987; Butters, Heindel, & Salmon, 1990; Martin & Fedio, 1983). It even has been suggested (e.g., Weingartner et al., 1981) that AD patients' semantic impairment may underlie many of the other cognitive deficits (e.g., memory encoding) found in these patients. Many of the recent studies into semantic functioning in AD have adopted the Collins and Loftus (1975) network model of semantic memory in which various semantic concepts are represented by nodes interconnected by a variety of associative relationships such as membership in a common category, functional relationships (e.g., knife-cut), and property relationships (e.g., knife-sharp). It has been proposed that the semantic-memory system of AD patients suffers from a variety of different dysfunctions including insufficient activation of concept nodes, breakdown of the associational links between concepts, and, more specifically, disruption of the links between concepts and their specific attributes or properties. In this section of the chapter I first review the studies in this area, grouped into three major topics (word-finding ability, knowledge of concept meaning, and the use of semantic context), and then examine how these results relate to possible mechanisms of semantic dysfunction.

Word-Finding Ability

AD patients often have problems finding appropriate words both in their everyday speech and on standardized tests for aphasia. Their spontaneous speech is frequently full of pronouns without preceding referents, empty phrases, and indefinite terms such as *stuff* or *things* (Nicholas, Obler, Albert, & Helm-Estabrooks, 1985). The speech of moderately demented patients becomes semantically empty, conveying little information. Their word-finding problem can be quantified by a verbal-fluency task in which they are given a category and asked to generate as many members of that category as they can in a brief period. Categories may be semantic (e.g., furniture) or lexical (words beginning with a particular letter). Typically, AD patients generate many fewer items (e.g., five or six words over the course of 60 s) than do normals (Ober, Dronkers, Koss, Delis, & Friedland, 1986). Interestingly, despite the difficulty AD patients have generating appropriate members of a category, there is evidence that the structure of the categories remains generally intact in AD patients. The same structural factors that affect the fluency of normals also affect the fluency of AD patients. When given a semantic category, AD patients, like normals, are more likely to generate a high dominant item than a less dominant item (e.g., for the category "bird," they are more likely to say "robin" than "penguin"). Similarly, for lexical categories, both AD patients and normals are more likely to emit words of high frequency in the language than low-frequency words, although like normals they do produce a scattering of less frequent words (Ober et al., 1986). However, on another type of fluency task, the pattern of responses in AD patients is quite different from that seen in normals. This task asks subjects to name items they might find in a supermarket. Although normals typically name four or more items from each of a number of categories (e.g., fruit, meat), AD patients often give only a single category member, or give the category name itself (vegetables) rather than actual members of the category (Ober, Koss, Friedland, & Delis, 1985; Tröster, Salmon, McCullough, & Butters, 1989). Thus, the strategic use of category structure to guide retrieval is much less evident in AD patients than it is in normals. Tröster et al. (1989) argued that this reflects a breakdown in the actual structure of semantic knowledge of AD patients.

Another major source of evidence for word-finding problems in AD comes from studies on object naming. Although the normal old have some difficulty naming objects (Albert, Heller, & Milberg, 1988), it is minor compared to that seen in AD. Object-naming problems occur early in the course of AD and steadily worsen as the disease progresses. The source of this naming problem has been attributed to (a) perceptual misidentification of the stimulus, (b) impairment of the semantic representation of the object concept, or (c) a failure in lexical access. Evidence for the role of perceptual problems comes from two sources. First, the more realistic the representation of the object, the more successful AD patients are in naming it. They are more likely to name an actual physical object than they are a colored picture of the object, which in turn they are more likely to name than a line drawing, especially if its contours are disrupted (Kirshner, Webb, & Kelly, 1984; Shuttleworth & Huber, 1988). The second line of evidence is that when AD patients misname an object, they sometimes call it by the name of a visually similar, but unrelated, item (Rochford, 1971). However, it has been shown that such perceptual errors are not that common (Bayles & Tomoeda, 1983) and, in fact, are no more common proportionately than they are in normals (Shuttleworth & Huber,

1988). The second hypothesis suggests that AD patients have lost (or lost access to) knowledge of the semantic attributes of object concepts, thus making it difficult for them to match the perceived item to its semantic representation (Bayles & Tomoeda, 1983; Huff, Corkin, & Growdon, 1986; Martin & Fedio, 1983). Evidence for this hypothesis comes again from the nature of the naming errors (Albert et al., 1988). AD patients often call an object either by the name of its superordinate category (e.g., a trumpet is called a musical instrument) or by the name of a semantically related object (e.g., a hammer is called a saw). They also have special difficulty picking out the name of a pictured object if the distractors are the names of other items from the same category as the object (Huff et al., 1986). Similarly, AD patients are poor at selecting the picture of a named object if the distractors are other members of the same semantic category, but not if they are from different categories (Chertkow, Bub, & Seidenberg, 1989). The explanation often given for this pattern of results is that AD patients have lost (or cannot access) the specific features and attributes of semantic concepts and so can no longer distinguish closely related semantic concepts. Finally, the naming problem in AD has been attributed to a difficulty in accessing the appropriate lexical node from the semantic representation. Evidence for this hypothesis is that the higher the frequency of an object's name in the language, the more likely AD patients are to name the object (e.g., Kirshner et al., 1984; Shuttleworth & Huber, 1988). Because word frequency is a function of the name rather than of the object, this suggests a role for a lexical access problem in the naming deficit of AD. Other evidence for this hypothesis is the effectiveness of phonemic cuing in facilitating naming in AD (Martin & Fedio, 1983). However, it should be noted that AD patients have great difficulty recognizing the correct name of a given object or recognizing an object upon hearing its name, which argues against their naming problem being due solely to a lexical access problem.

There is evidence both for and against all three of these potential causes of the naming deficit in AD. One possible reason for these conflicting results simply may be that deficits in perceptual analysis, lexical access, and semantic knowledge all contribute to the naming problem in AD, but in different patients. That is, this could be an example of a final common behavioral failure produced by different cognitive deficits in different patients. Support for such a multideterminant source of the naming problem of AD can be found in the results of Barker and Lawson (1968), who showed that allowing AD patients to handle an object and see its use demonstrated greatly increased the likelihood that they would name it. This suggests that enriching the perceptual information ameliorated their naming problem. However, the naming performance of the same group of AD patients also varied with the frequency of the object's name in the language, suggesting a lexical access problem. Most important, these two effects did not interact indicating that these two factors acted independently to determine the naming performance of AD patients. The results of a recent study also provide evidence that the naming disorder in different AD patients may have different causes. Kempler, Andersen, Hunt, and Henderson (1990) examined the consistency with which subjects misnamed objects across repeated testing sessions. If subjects are inconsistent in which items they misname from time to time, this would support an access problem, whereas if they are consistent it would suggest an actual loss of information. Kempler et al. found that although some patients consistently failed to name the same items from session to session, other patients were inconsistent, failing to name an object in one session that they had named in another. It is possible that the underlying cognitive dysfunction responsible for the failure of AD patients to name an object may be different in different patients.

Knowledge of Concept Meaning

It has become commonly accepted that AD produces a cognitive deficit not found in other dementing diseases or in the normal old—a disruption of concept meaning. More specifically, a number of investigators have argued that semantic information about concepts is organized hierarchically, with a concept's relation to its superordinate category at the top of the hierarchy and its specific attributes (e.g., the functions and physical features that distinguish it from closely related members of its category) at the bottom. They suggest that early in the course of AD, knowledge of these specific attributes either is lost or becomes inaccessible, whereas category knowledge is maintained until late in the disease·(Chertkow et al., 1989; Huff et al., 1986; Martin & Fedio, 1983; Tröster et al., 1989). That is, there is a bottom-up deterioration in semantic knowledge. Such a loss of specific attributes is seen to effectively strip concepts of most of their meaning, making it difficult for AD patients to name pictures, encode stimuli into memory, understand language, and so forth. What is the evidence for this hypothesis?

Warrington (1975) intensively studied three demented patients and found that although they could answer yes/no questions about the category of pictured objects (e.g., "Is it an animal?"), they had difficulty answering questions about physical attributes (e.g., "Is it bigger than a cat?"). Martin and Fedio (1983) showed that although their AD patients could sort objects by category and could answer questions about an object's category, they had great difficulty answering questions about an object's physical features or functions. When shown a picture of a saw, AD patients knew that it was a tool, but had trouble deciding whether it was made of metal and whether it could be used for cutting. Martin and Fedio suggested that in AD, the semantic attributes determining word meaning either are lost or becomes less accessible. Chertkow et al. (1989) replicated Martin and Fedio using a much larger number of objects and an extensive examination of their knowledge of attributes, functions, functional context, and category. They minimized the retrieval demands of the task by giving the subjects a choice (e.g., for a saw—"Do you cut things with it or lift things with it?"). Although AD patients performed normally on questions about semantic category, they were impaired on questions regarding attributes and functions. Interestingly, they had substantially more difficulty answering questions about items they were unable to name, suggesting a deterioration of semantic knowledge for some specific items.

However, Grober et al. (1985) found evidence on a different task that concept attributes are not lost in demented patients. They presented subjects with a target concept followed by a list of words, some of which were attributes of the target. The subjects were asked to check off those words related to the target. AD patients were quite accurate on this task (95% correct) and so Grober et al. concluded that demented patients retain their knowledge of specific concept attributes. Nebes and Brady (1988) came to the same conclusion based on a task that measured the time subjects took to decide whether or not a given stimulus word was related to a target concept. AD patients' ability to detect four different types of relationship between target and stimulus was examined. On those trials in which the stimulus word was actually related to the target, it was either (a) the name of its category, (b) a general associate, (c) a distinctive physical feature of the target, or (d) a verb describing a characteristic action or function involving the target. If AD patients have lost knowledge of the physical features and functions of objects or find this information differentially difficult to access, they should be slower and less accurate to make decisions about a target's feature or function than about its associate and category. Results showed that AD patients were actually worse making decisions about the category and associate relationship than they were making decisions about specific features or functions—the opposite of the hypothesis described earlier. A recent study (Bayles, Tomoeda, & Trosset, 1990) also found attribute knowledge to be less affected than category knowledge. Bayles et al. compared the ability of AD patients both to name objects and to make category judgments about the same objects. The rationale was that because object naming is dependent on knowledge of specific attributes, as the severity of the dementia increases, AD patients' accuracy in naming objects should decline at a faster rate than should their accuracy in making decisions about the objects' category. However, after statistically controlling for differences in task difficulty (on the basis of the performance of normals), Bayles et al. found that object-naming performance actually declined less with increasing dementia severity than did category judgment, again suggesting that knowledge of the specific attributes of concepts is not differentially impaired in AD.

Given that AD patients retain their knowledge of the specific semantic attributes of concepts, could there be some disruption of attribute organization? In the study described previously, Grober et al. (1985) noticed that although AD patients were very accurate in deciding which words went with a concept, when they did miss an attribute it was as likely to be an important attribute as it was an unimportant one. They followed up on this observation in an experiment in which they gave subjects a target and three words that, according to norms, varied in their importance to the meaning of the concept. The subject was to choose the word most important to the target's meaning and then the next most important one. If given the concept "airplane" and the words *radar, fly,* and *luggage,* the patient should choose *fly* and then *radar.* Grober et al. found that their demented patients were much less likely than normals to select the most important attributes first. They concluded that, although AD patients retain knowledge of concept attributes, they do not know the relative importance (i.e., salience) these attributes have for the meaning of the concepts. Such a disruption of the organization of semantic attributes could produce much the same sort of cognitive impairment (in naming, etc.) as an actual loss of attributes. However, the findings of a recent study by Nebes and Brady (1990) do not support this conclusion. Like Nebes and Brady (1988), they measured the time subjects took to make a decision about whether a given stimulus word was related to a target concept, but here the stimulus words varied in their normed importance to the meaning of the target. Rather than directly asking subjects to decide which attribute is most important, knowledge of attribute importance was measured indirectly. Subjects were given a series of target concepts, each of which was followed by a single stimulus word. Sometimes this stimulus was an attribute of the concept; other times it was not. If AD patients no longer know the relative importance of concept attributes, then, unlike normals, their decision time should not be influenced by attribute importance. However, results showed that the more important the attribute, the less time subjects needed to decide that it was related to the concept and that this was equally true of normal and demented subjects. That is, when AD patients' knowledge of the comparative importance of semantic attributes was measured indirectly, they performed normally. Nebes and Brady (1990) therefore concluded that the organization of the concept attributes was not disrupted by AD.

How are we to understand this variability in results with respect to attribute knowledge in AD? First, why do Warrington (1975), Martin and Fedio (1983), and Chertkow et al. (1989) find evidence for a loss of specific attributes in AD patients, whereas Grober et al. (1985) and Nebes and Brady (1988) do not? It is clear that the demands of the experimental task are crucial. When AD subjects are asked a direct question about an object's attributes (e.g., "Is it made of metal?") they do poorly, although when asked merely to decide whether a concept is related to an attribute, they perform comparatively normally. This pattern of results can be viewed in the context of the Collins and Loftus (1975) spreading-activation model of semantic memory. In this model, the properties of a concept are represented by pathways from that concept to its attributes, pathways that are labeled with the nature of the relationship (e.g., has, is, can, etc.). When a subject is asked a question about the relationship of two concepts, activation spreads out along the network in parallel from each concept (i.e., here, the target and the attribute). If these two waves of activation intersect and the resultant activation at this intersection exceeds some threshold, a pathway connecting the two concepts has been found. The nature of this pathway then must be evaluated to determine whether it satisfies the constraints of the question. In terms of this model, therefore, it would appear that the tasks in the Grober et al. and Nebes and Brady studies required only that AD patients determine whether a pathway exists connecting the target and its attribute. By contrast, the Warrington, Martin and Fedio, and Chertkow et al. studies required that the patients also evaluate the nature of this pathway and decide whether it met the constraints posed by a direct question. These results may indicate that the pathways connecting concepts and their attributes remain intact in AD, but that these patients have difficulty consciously evaluating the nature of the pathways. Similarly, the discrepancy between Grober et al. and Nebes and Brady (1990) as to whether AD patients know the relative importance of attributes also may be explained by differing task requirements. When this knowledge is assessed by having AD patients directly compare the relative importance of multiple attributes they fail, whereas when this knowledge is assessed indirectly the patients perform normally. Again, this can be viewed in the context of the Collins and Loftus model in which the pathways between a concept and its attributes vary in their "criteriality" (i.e., their importance to overall concept meaning). In this model, the time it takes to determine that a path exists between a concept and an attribute is a function of its criteriality. The present pattern of results suggests that the concept-attribute pathways in AD patients retain their relative criterialities, because attribute-decision time was affected as much by attribute importance in AD patients as it was in normals. The problem for AD patients appears to be more one of consciously comparing levels of attribute importance than it does a loss of knowledge of attribute salience.

As mentioned earlier, one area of semantic information thought to remain intact in AD is knowledge of the superordinate category of a concept. However, the actual results are not totally consistent. AD patients are extremely impaired on tasks, such as the Similarities subtest of the Wechsler Adult Intelligence Scale, that ask them to say how two items are related (Martin & Fedio, 1983). For example, when asked how a table and a chair are alike, AD patients often will mention superficial similarities (e.g., they both have legs) or tell you how they are different (e.g., you sit on one and eat off the other). Even when you point out to them that the two items belong to the same category (e.g., furniture) and tell them that this is the type of response they should give, it does not help them with future items. As mentioned in the section Word-Finding Ability, AD patients have major problems retrieving members of a specified semantic category (Ober et al., 1986). They also are impaired on a test of abstract concept formation (Flicker, Ferris, Crook, & Bartus, 1986). In this study, subjects were shown an array of 25 common objects. In each set of trials, 8 of the 25 items came from the same category (e.g., clothing). In one condition, the experimenter gave the subject a selection principle (pick out the items you would use to get dressed), whereas in another set of trials, the subject was told just to pick out the items that were most alike. None of the subjects, including mildly to moderately demented AD patients, had trouble with the first condition. Even AD patients could recognize items that fit a specified category. By contrast, in the second condition, the normal old as well as the AD patients showed a deficit. That is, they were less likely than the young to pick out all the items that fell in the same category when that category was not specified but left for them to determine. This decrement was fairly small in the normal old, and increased in the AD patients with the severity of their dementia. Flicker et al. felt that this result shows defective concept formation both in the normal old and in AD patients. They argued that this is not the result of deficits in other cognitive areas, such as attention, language, or memory, as any such deficits also should have affected performance in the first condition, where neither the normal old nor demented individuals had problems. This result, however, does conflict with the findings of Martin and Fedio (1983) and Weingartner et al. (1981), who found that when given a variety of objects AD patients could sort them into appropriate categories. The source of this disagreement is not clear, because the Martin and Fedio and the Weingartner et al. studies did not describe their methodology in any detail. There are, however, other studies that do show relatively normal performance by AD patients on tasks testing knowledge of semantic categories. When asked to decide whether a provided object is a member of a specified category, AD patients perform normally (Huff et al., 1986; Martin & Fedio,

1983). Nebes, Boller, and Holland (1986) found similar results in a response-time task, and also showed that, like normals, the category-decision time of AD patients was affected by category dominance or typicality. That is, the more dominant an item was in that category, the faster AD patients decided that it was a category member. This suggests that the internal structure of semantic categories, in terms of the relative dominance of their various members, is maintained in AD. This is consistent with the verbal fluency results of Ober et al. (1986) mentioned earlier, which showed that dominance also determined the likelihood that AD patients would generate a particular member of a category.

Is knowledge about the relationship between a superordinate semantic category and its members preserved in AD? The answer appears to depend on how you test the subjects. If AD patients are presented with an object or its name, they can verify whether it belongs to a specified category. Similarly, when given an assortment of objects, they may be able to sort out members of a category (Martin & Fedio, 1983; Weingartner et al., 1981), although this recently was challenged (Flicker et al., 1986). However, when AD patients must systematically search a category or must generate the name of the category that encompasses several stimuli (i.e., similarities test), they do quite poorly. Thus, AD patients have difficulty demonstrating category knowledge if the task requires them to carry out a search operation. This conclusion is supported by the recent study of Bayles et al. (1990). They found that the ability of their AD patients to name the category of a pictured object declined much faster with increasing dementia than did their ability to recognize its category name, again suggesting a problem with accessing information about an object's category.

Effect of Semantic Context

In normals, the semantic context in which a stimulus occurs has a strong influence on the processing of that stimulus. Is this also true of AD or does the semantic impairment in these patients leave them unaffected by stimulus context? Both intentional use of semantic context and more indirect effects have been studied in AD patients using a variety of procedures. The effect that context has on episodic memory already has been covered, and so this section reviews how context influences such cognitive operations as lexical access and comprehension as well as the priming of semantic concepts.

One major role of semantic context is to disambiguate words. Most words have a variety of meanings, and which one is appropriate depends on the context in which the word is found (e.g., *bank*). Two studies (Cushman & Caine, 1987; Kempler et al., 1987) examined the ability of subjects to use context to disambiguate spoken homophones—words that sound identical but have different meanings (e.g., *him* and *hymn*). In both, the subjects were asked to write down a series of words dictated to them, the final word of which was a homophone. The ability of the preceding words (i.e., context) to influence spelling was examined. For example, how would a subject spell *him/hymn* if the preceding two words were *church* and *music*. Both studies found that AD patients were less responsive to context. That is, the word they wrote down was less likely to be consistent with the preceding context.

In normals, semantic context also appears to guide lexical access. The speed with which a normal individual can generate the last word of an incomplete sentence varies as a function of the context provided by the sentence frame. If the sentence is highly constraining, in that few words fit the semantic and syntactic constraints imposed by the sentence context (e.g., "Father carved the turkey with a __"), normals complete the sentence much faster than if there is little constraint (e.g., "They went to see the famous __"). Subjects are thought to generate a set of specific features that a concept must possess in order to be an acceptable ending to the sentence. The more constraining the sentence, the more restrictive a set of features is generated (Schwanenflugel & LaCount, 1988). Because AD patients have major word-finding problems, and may have lost specific concept attributes, we might expect that their word-finding performance would be insensitive to contextual constraint. However, results show that AD patients are actually affected more by sentence context than are normals (Nebes et al., 1986). AD patients performed fairly normally (both in terms of the appropriateness of the endings they generated and in terms of their response time) when their lexical search was highly constrained and guided by sentence context. When only minimal contextual guidance was provided, however, they showed the word-finding problems typically present in such patients.

Recently, the semantic-priming paradigm has been used to study how context influences cognitive processing in AD. This approach is based on the network model of semantic memory (Collins & Loftus, 1975) described earlier. It assumes that when a concept is presented, its representation in semantic memory is activated and this activation then spreads automatically to related concepts, briefly increasing their accessibility. Experimental evidence for such a spread of activation comes from priming studies in which the time it takes a subject to process a stimulus (e.g., to name it or to make a decision about it) is measured under two conditions: In one, the preceding item (i.e., the context or prime) is semantically related to the stimulus being processed (i.e., target), whereas in the other the prime is unrelated. Any decrease in the time subjects take to process a target when it is preceded by a related prime as compared to an unrelated prime is considered to reflect facilitation due to the spread of activation from the related prime to the target concept. For example, the word *doctor* is processed faster if it is preceded by a related prime such as *nurse* than if it is preceded by an unrelated prime such as *pencil.* Nebes et al. (1984) reasoned that if the network of semantic associations was in fact disrupted by AD, then unlike normals, AD patients should not show semantic priming. Actually, they found that although AD patients were slower than normals, the magnitude of the priming effect in these patients was no less than that seen in the normal old. Nebes et al. interpreted this as evidence that the structure of semantic memory remains intact in AD patients. Because semantic priming was assumed to result from an automatic spread of activation, they suggested that the problems AD patients have on some semantic tasks (e.g., verbal fluency) are due to the demands those tasks place on attentional capacity rather than to a true semantic deficit.

One problem with this interpretation is that semantic context can affect performance not only through the automatic spread of activation described earlier, but also through an attention-dependent mechanism (Neely, 1977). These two mechanisms can be distinguished by examining the pattern of the priming effect. Because only related concepts are affected by automatic spreading activation, the prime acts solely to facilitate performance. By contrast, the attention-dependent mechanism involves the subject consciously directing a limited-capacity processor to a location in semantic memory based on an expectancy generated by the prime. In attention-dependent priming, not only does a related prime facilitate processing (in comparison to a neutral condition), but an unrelated prime inhibits it. Because Nebes et al. (1984) did not use a neutral condition, they could not distinguish automatic from attention-dependent priming. However, in a follow-up study (Nebes et al., 1986), incomplete sentences served as related, unrelated, and neutral primes. The results showed evidence of both facilitation and inhibition of performance by semantic context in AD patients. In fact, AD patients showed even more inhibition than did normals. This result suggests that AD patients are able to use semantic context even when this requires attentional capacity. However, Hartman (in press) found, with single-word primes, a pattern of results suggestive of a purely automatic use of semantic context by AD patients—that is, she found facilitation without inhibition. The relationship between semantic priming and attentional processing is, therefore, still unclear (for more on this issue see the Discussion section of this chapter).

The studies just described used as their primary measure the time it took subjects to read a target word aloud. Another task commonly used with semantic priming is lexical decision. The subject is shown a string of letters and has to decide whether it forms an actual English word. This procedure may be more likely to produce attention-depending priming than is word naming (Seidenberg, Waters, Sanders, & Langer, 1984). Here, the evidence for semantic priming in AD is conflicting. Although Nebes, Brady, and Huff (1989) actually found larger priming effects with lexical decision in AD patients than in normals, Ober and Shenaut (1988) found no significant priming. A possibly important methodological difference between the two studies may be the time between the presentation of the prime and the stimulus. The Nebes et al. study used a very short interval, whereas the interval in the Ober and Shenaut study was substantially longer. This pattern of results could mean that the activation produced by the prime fades more rapidly in AD patients. This would be consistent with a recent study by Ober and Shenaut (1989), which used a short interval and found normal priming in AD patients for both word naming and lexical decision. Thus, it is possible that some parameters of semantic priming (e.g., the rate of spread of activation or its persistence) may be abnormal, although there is, as yet, no conclusive evidence for this.

Chertkow et al. (1989) recently suggested that the semantic priming results actually demonstrate a semantic anomaly in AD because the priming seen in AD patients often is larger than that seen in normals, a phenomenon they call hyperpriming. On a lexical decision task they found that the priming effect was larger in AD patients than in the normal old, both in terms of absolute time (141 ms vs. 25 ms) and in terms of the percentage of response time to unprimed stimuli (10% vs. 3%). Most important, those particular items for which the patients had problems answering questions about their attributes (see preceding section Knowledge of Concept Meaning) were the ones that showed the greatest priming effect. They therefore argue that the presence of priming and especially hyperpriming effects reflect the breakdown of semantic memory.

However, Ober and Shenaut (1990) offered a very different explanation for the presence of greater than normal priming in AD. They noted that those studies that found hyperpriming used procedures that maximized the opportunity for attention-dependent priming. That is, these studies used a lexical-decision task with a long interval between prime and target, and also had a high number of related prime-target pairings. These same studies also were associated with longer overall response times in AD patients than were studies showing normal levels of priming (i.e., they were more difficult). Ober and Shenaut argued that because of their decreased attentional capacity, AD patients are especially dependent on context in situations involving effortful processing. Rather than showing a dysfunctional semantic network, the hyperpriming seen in AD patients just may reflect a greater reliance on environmental support in situations where processing is very difficult for these patients. Stanovich and West (1983) showed that even in the normal young, longer processing time is associated with a larger priming effect, theoretically because more time is available for semantic context to affect ongoing processing. If processing is slowed in normals by using infrequent words as stimuli or by perceptually degrading the stimuli, this greatly increases the magnitude of the priming effect. In fact, if the priming effect in Stanovich and West (Experiment 1) is expressed as a percentage of subjects' response time to unprimed stimuli (as was done by Chertkow et al., 1989), the difference in percentages between the frequent and infrequent word stimuli is very similar to the difference in percentages between normals and AD patients reported by Chertkow et al. Thus, it is not clear that the hyperpriming seen in AD patients necessarily does result from some specific semantic impairment.

There is another contextual priming paradigm, associative priming, that has produced evidence for deterioration of the semantic network in AD patients. Here, subjects are given a series of weakly related word pairs and are asked to make some judgment about the pairs. Later, in what the subjects think is a different task, they are given a set of stimulus words and for each one must say the first word that comes to mind (i.e., free associate). Some of these stimulus words are the first word of one of the pairs they had seen earlier in the judgment task. Priming is demonstrated by an increase in the likelihood (over a control condition) that the subject will respond by giving as an associate the word that had been paired with that stimulus in the judgment task. This is an implicit measure of whether prior experience can prime (i.e., activate) a preexisting weak association between two concepts. Two different studies (Huff, Mack, Mahlmann, & Greenberg, 1988; Salmon et al., 1988) found decreased associative priming in AD patients. They interpreted this as evidence for a deterioration in the network of semantic associations in AD. How can we reconcile this apparent decreased ability to prime associative links with the semantic-priming results reviewed earlier? One important difference between the semantic-priming and the associative-priming tasks is the demand for lexical search in the latter. In semantic priming, the effect of the prime is measured by a change in the speed or accuracy with which a subject processes a presented stimulus, whereas in associative priming, it is measured by a change in the likelihood that a subject will emit a given word. Thus, successful associative priming requires a lexical search and it is this operation that may be responsible for the impairment in associative priming in AD, not a dissolution of the associational network itself.

Source of the Semantic Impairment in AD

The semantic impairment produced by AD has been attributed to a variety of underlying deficits. Some investigators have proposed that presentation of a stimulus does not adequately activate the representation of that stimulus concept in the semantic memory of AD patients or that this activation fails to spread to the preexisting associations of the stimulus. For example, Salmon et al. (1988) suggested that AD patients fail to show normal amounts of implicit memory on a stem-completion task because prior exposure to a stimulus word does not activate the semantic representation of that word sufficiently to increase the likelihood that that word will be used to complete a stem. Heindel et al. (in press) offered a similar explanation for why prior exposure to an object picture failed to facilitate later recognition by AD patients of a degraded version of that picture. The poor associative priming found by Salmon et al. (1988) and by Brandt et al. (1988) has been attributed to activation failing to spread from the stimulus to associated concepts. Similarly, Rissenberg and Glanzer (1987) proposed that many of the problems AD patients have on memory tasks are due to the failure of the stimulus to activate the phonemic and semantic information associated with the stimulus, thereby producing a defective memory trace. Such a failure of activation to spread to associated concepts could reflect a weakening of the associative network, or even an actual loss of the associations, thus producing an effective dissolution of the semantic network (Huff et al., 1988; Salmon et al., 1988). However, there is other evidence suggesting that the activation of semantic nodes is adequate in AD patients. For example, the finding of normal repetition priming in AD (Moscovitch, 1982; Ober & Shenaut, 1988) suggests that presentation of a stimulus does activate its representation in semantic memory, and that this activation is maintained for some time. Similarly, results from studies using semantic priming (Hartman, in press; Nebes et al., 1984, 1986, 1989) suggest that the network of associations between concepts remains intact and that activation spreads along it in a relatively normal fashion. Although work by Ober and Shenaut (1989) suggests that some aspects of semantic priming (e.g., duration of activation) may be abnormal in AD patients.

Other investigators (e.g., Chertkow et al., 1989; Huff et al., 1988) feel that AD patients actually have lost knowledge they once possessed about semantic concepts. The most impressive evidence for this view comes from Chertkow et al. who showed item-specific loss of information in AD patients. If an AD patient was unable to select a picture of an object upon hearing its name, then he or she usually also was unable to name that object. Similarly, if an AD patient was unable to name an object, the patient was usually quite poor at answering direct questions about the object's specific attributes. Such item-specific consistency of deficit across different tasks strongly suggests that AD patients actually have lost semantic knowledge about certain concepts.

An alternative view of the semantic defect in AD is that these patients are impaired on tasks that require them to conduct a directed search of their semantic memory. If we look at studies that appear to tap the same semantic information but that vary in their retrieval demands, AD patients do much worse on procedures that require an intentional memory search. For example, AD patients show normal contextual priming if priming is measured by changes in the speed with which they process a presented word (Nebes et al., 1984), but impaired priming if priming is measured by changes in the likelihood that a particular word will be retrieved (Huff et al., 1988). Similarly, AD patients can decide correctly whether a presented attribute is related to a particular concept, but are very poor at generating the attributes of a given concept (Nebes & Brady, 1988). AD patients also have much more difficulty recalling the name of an object's category than they do recognizing the category name (Bayles et al., 1990), again suggesting a retrieval problem. However, there are semantic tasks on which AD patients do poorly but that do not require an intentional directed search of semantic memory. For example, the disambiguation of a spoken word by context does not involve any intentional search of memory and yet AD patients perform abnormally. Also the item-specific decrements demonstrated by Chertkow et al. (1989) argue against the problems in AD being due solely to an access problem. Overall, there does not seem to be any simple explanation for why AD patients are severely impaired on some semantic tasks, whereas performing quite normally on others. Given the importance of this topic for distinguishing between AD and other dementing disorders and between AD and normal aging, this area of research deserves a great deal more work to clarify the underlying source of the semantic impairment of AD.

VISUOSPATIAL ABILITIES

As noted in the introduction, in order to qualify for a diagnosis of AD an individual must have deficits in at least two areas of cognition. Visuospatial abilities are involved in several of these cognitive areas, particularly visual perception and constructional praxis (i.e., the manipulation of objects in space). In some AD patients a visuospatial impairment is actually the most prominent behavioral symptom seen early in the disease (Becker, Huff, Nebes, Holland, & Boller, 1988; Martin, 1987). Even in those AD patients who do not have a disproportionately severe spatial impairment, visuospatial deficits still may underlie a number of the principal behavioral symptoms present. For example, Kirshner et al. (1984) argued that at least some of the difficulty AD patients have in naming objects results from an inadequate perceptual analysis of the stimuli. This conclusion was based on their finding that the accuracy with which AD patients named objects increased as the perceptual difficulty of the object's representation decreased. Their AD patients were least successful in naming line drawings of objects, somewhat better with color photos, and best with the actual objects. Kirshner et al. also argued that at least some of the naming errors made by demented patients resulted from perceptual misidentification; that is, patients called the stimulus by the name of a perceptually similar object (however, see contradictory findings in the section Language and Semantic Knowledge). Similarly, the facial-recognition deficit found in many AD patients may result from a basic visuospatial impairment (Eslinger & Benton, 1983), as may the difficulty many AD patients have in finding their way around even familiar environments (Henderson, Mack, & Williams, 1989). However, despite the obvious importance of visuospatial skills, there has been relatively little research into how visuospatial impairments might contribute to the pattern of behavioral symptoms found in AD. Although we know that AD patients tend to get lost, are poor in drawing, and have difficulty discriminating complex figures, we really do not know what cognitive operations are dysfunctional.

In terms of visuoperceptual performance, it is clear that AD patients do not perform well when asked to discriminate complex visual forms such as faces (Eslinger & Benton, 1983), checkerboard patterns (Brouwers, Cox, Martin, Chase, & Fedio, 1984), random shapes (Huff et al., 1986), or spatially organized arrays of geometric shapes (Becker et al., 1988; Mendez, Mendez, Martin, Smyth, & Whitehouse, 1990). They also perform poorly when required to discriminate small differences in the orientation of lines in space (Eslinger & Benton, 1983). These perceptual studies typically involve multiple choice, match-to-sample tasks, which place a minimal demand on the patients' memory. The spatial problems seen in AD patients also extend to visuoconstructive performance (i.e., manipulating objects in space). A test of drawing has become a fairly standard part of most dementia batteries because of its sensitivity to early dementia. AD patients are impaired both in spontaneous drawing (e.g., drawing a clock face to command) and in copying such items as a line drawing of a house (Brouwers et al., 1984; Henderson et al., 1989; Moore & Wyke, 1984). Demented patients also have difficulty manipulating objects in three-dimensional space to reproduce a given pattern, as is evident in their poor performance on the block design subtest of the WAIS (Storandt, Botwinick, Danziger, Berg, & Hughes, 1984) and on a three-dimensional block construction test (Becker et al., 1988).

When we look for information about the nature of the cognitive dysfunctions responsible for these perceptual and constructional performance decrements, however, there are few relevant studies. Several experiments have examined basic visual and spatial skills to determine whether they might contribute to the behavioral symptoms of AD. Schlotterer, Moscovitch, and Crapper-McLachlan (1983) found no evidence in AD patients for decrements in peripheral information processing such as visual acuity, or spatial frequency contrast sensitivity. When they examined the effect that homogeneous and patterned visual masks had on the ability of subjects to identify a letter, Schlotterer et al. found that AD patients required no more time than did the normal old to escape the effects of a homogeneous mask. These patients, however, did require more time than normals to escape the effects of a patterned mask. Given the currently accepted interpretation (Kline & Schieber, 1985) of such masking effects, these results again suggest that peripheral visual processing remains relatively intact in AD, but that more "central" visual processing may be impaired. Mendez et al. (1990) looked at a variety of basic visual skills in the normal old and AD patients. They found that although their AD patients and normals were similar in visual acuity and color identification performance, the AD patients were impaired on a number of other basic visual skills. A subgroup of their AD patients had substantial difficulty localizing objects in space, and all of their patients were impaired in differentiating figure from ground (identifying line drawings of objects whose contours overlapped). A number of the patients in the Mendez et al. study were also poor at identifying visual objects, even though these patients later could identify these same objects when they were presented tactually. This suggests that the patients' identification problem resulted from impaired visuoperceptual processing. Capitani, Della Sala, Lucchelli, Soave, and Spinnler (1988) also found AD patients to have difficulty disentangling figure from ground. They used the Gottschaldt test in which subjects have to find a simple geometric shape hidden in a more complex shape. Again, a portion of the AD patients performed dramatically worse than age- and education-matched normal subjects. Interestingly, they interpreted this as a failure of selective or focused attention rather than a problem with visual processing. This again illustrates the difficulty of determining the underlying cognitive dysfunction from tasks with complex cognitive demands.

One limitation of the studies just described is that there was little emphasis on directly relating the visuoperceptual impairments of AD patients to their behavioral problems. For example, to what degree is a given AD patient's failure to differentiate figure from ground in the Mendez et al. (1990) study responsible for his or her problem in discriminating objects or faces? One study that did attempt to relate underlying spatial and cognitive deficits to behavioral problems in AD patients was carried out by Henderson et al. (1989). From each patient's caretaker they obtained a rating of how commonly the patient became lost, wandered away, or became spatially disoriented. These ratings were analyzed with respect to that patient's performance on tests of spatial ability (object drawing), attention (digit span), language (object naming), memory (delayed recall of five words), as well as on a measure of general dementia severity (Mini-Mental State Exam [MMS]). When these results were entered into a step-wise regression, scores on the drawing test and on the memory test were significant predictors of spatial disorientation in the everyday life of AD patients. The other measures, including the MMS, were not significant predictors. Henderson et al. concluded that the spatial orientation problems (e.g., becoming lost) experienced by many demented patients are not merely a function of overall dementia severity, but rather result from the combination of a specific spatial impairment with a memory deficit. However, as the authors admitted, because their cognitive testing was somewhat limited, this study may underestimate the role that other cognitive operations (e.g., attention) play in spatial disorientation.

Another recent paper sought to determine whether a specific problem in mental rotation might be responsible for some of the impairments that AD patients show on visuospatial tasks. This is certainly a reasonable hypothesis because tasks such as drawing objects, orienting oneself to the environment, or reproducing three-dimensional designs may require a mental manipulation either of objects in space or of the viewer with respect to a spatial frame. Flicker, Ferris, Crook, Reisberg, and Bartus (1988) examined the ability of normal and AD patients to mentally rotate objects in space (extrapersonal orientation) and to mentally rotate themselves in space (personal or egocentric orientation). As a test of egocentric orientation, subjects were shown a streetmap on which was drawn a route. The subject was to mentally follow the route and at each turn to say whether a right or left turn was required. On approximately half of these turns, subjects had to mentally walk back toward themselves and so, in order to decide which way to turn, they had to mentally rotate themselves in space. On the rest of the turns, no such mental rotation was needed. As a measure of extrapersonal orientation, subjects were asked to name objects both in their normal orientation and when the objects were rotated 180°. The assumption here is that to name upside-down objects, the subject has to mentally rotate them to their normal orientation. The results of the streetmap test showed that although both the normal old and AD patients made more errors on turns that required a mental rotation, there was no evidence that the performance of AD patients was more disrupted than that of the normal old by the need for such a spatial transformation. On the object-naming task, AD patients named fewer objects than the normal old, as would be expected. However, both demented and normal older subjects showed a similar effect of rotation in that both named fewer rotated than unrotated objects. More important, the size of this difference in naming accuracy between rotated and unrotated objects was the same in the two groups. Therefore, on both tasks, AD subjects had no more difficulty than the normal old in performing a mental rotation. This was true regardless of whether subjects had to mentally manipulate objects in extrapersonal space or mentally rotate themselves. This is certainly an unexpected finding, as there are relatively few complex cognitive operations for which AD patients show preserved function. If this conclusion is correct, then it would mean that the visuospatial performance deficits associated with AD are not caused by an impairment in these patients' ability to carry out mental manipulations of objects in space. However, it should be noted that this study did not directly relate individual AD patients' performance on the mental rotation tasks to the presence of any behavioral problems. It would be very interesting to know if there were any patients among this sample who had prominent problems with, for example, wandering or visual recognition, and how these persons performed on the rotation tasks.

Another approach to understanding the various visuospatial impairments in dementia has been to compare them to those seen in patients with a focal lesion in different areas of the brain. Eslinger and Benton (1983) compared demented patients on two tasks that may tap different spatial abilities (analysis of visual features and spatial orientation). Evidence that these two abilities are independent and discrete comes from findings that a focal lesion in one brain region disrupts one ability without harming the other, whereas a lesion in a different brain region has the opposite effect (i.e., there is a double dissociation of lesion site and deficit). In one task, subjects were asked to judge line orientation. They were given a line of a certain slope and asked to pick out a line of the same slope from an array of 11 lines differing in orientation. In the second task, they were shown a photo of a target face and had to pick it out from among a number of choices. On some trials, the orientation of the face or the lighting conditions differed between the target and the correct choice. Although AD patients were impaired on both tasks, performance on the two tasks was often dissociated. That is, some patients did much worse on one task than on the other, whereas other patients showed the opposite pattern. Eslinger and Benton concluded that there are multiple visuospatial abilities and that, rather than disrupting all abilities equally, dementia is a multifocal process that randomly affects different cortical areas, impairing different spatial abilities in different people.

In a similar vein, Moore and Wyke (1984) examined the nature of the drawing errors made by AD patients, comparing them to the errors seen in patients with focal right- or left-hemispheric damage. Patients with injury lateralized to the right cerebral hemisphere typically produce drawings that, although full of appropriate details, are fragmented and spatially disorganized. By contrast, patients with focal left-hemispheric injury usually produce drawings that, although having an appropriate spatial organization, are greatly simplified. This pattern of results generally has been interpreted (e.g., Warrington, 1969) as indicating that left-hemisphere damage causes a deficit in patients' ability to plan and execute motor sequences, producing a simplified drawing. By contrast, right-hemisphere damage causes a deficit in patients' ability to articulate the parts of the drawing in space. When Moore and Wyke (1984) analyzed the drawings made by AD patients, they saw elements of both these types of drawing deficit. When asked to draw an object to command, AD patients tended to omit details (e.g., when drawing a house, they might leave out the windows). By contrast, when copying from a model, AD patients did include more details, but often placed them in inappropriate positions. However, Moore and Wyke argued that the AD patients' problem is more than just a combination of the two types of cognitive deficit seen in focally brain-injured patients. For example, the lack of detail in drawings made to command was often much more extreme in AD patients than in left-hemisphere-injured patients. Over 40% of AD patients did not even include a roof in their drawing of a house, something that is rarely seen in left-hemisphere-lesioned patients. Moore and Wyke therefore argued that other concurrent cognitive deficits (e.g., in memory) may play a major role in the visuoconstructional problems seen in AD.

It is clear from these studies that we have barely begun to understand the effects that AD has on visuoperceptual and spatial abilities. Even so, the results of these studies do point out some major experimental issues that need to be examined. First, do the more complex behavioral problems found in AD (e.g., a failure to recognize faces) reflect an underlying deficit in basic visuoperceptual processing (e.g., discriminating figure from ground)? Are we mistakenly attributing the source of behavioral problems to higher order cognitive deficits, when in fact they spring from basic problems early in the course of information processing? Second, to what extent are all visuospatial abilities impaired in AD? There is evidence that some visuospatial skills (e.g., rotation) may be totally spared (Flicker et al., 1988), or may be impaired only in a subpopulation of AD patients (Eslinger & Benton, 1983). This means that we cannot restrict our testing to just one aspect of spatial abilities, but must examine a variety of spatial skills. Also, we should not base our interpretations only on group means, but rather, we must also examine individual patterns of performance. Finally, there is the issue of the interaction of visuospatial deficits with other cognitive deficits in AD. Unlike subjects with focal brain injury, any interpretation of the visuospatial deficits seen in AD must take into account the multiple other cognitive impairments present in these patients. How do these other deficits interact with and alter the expression of the visuospatial impairment (Henderson et al., 1989; Moore & Wyke, 1984)?

REASONING AND CONCEPTUALIZATION

If the literature on visuospatial abilities in AD is limited, that on reasoning and concept formation is practically nonexistent. There are a number of obvious reasons for this lack. First, most of the tasks developed to investigate these processes in normals are, even at their simplest, impossibly difficult for AD patients (e.g., poisoned food version of a concept identification task). Second, it is very difficult to interpret AD patients' failure to perform a reasoning or conceptualization task. Are they failing because they lack a particular problem-solving skill or conceptual ability, or does their failure spring from extraneous factors that limit their performance? For example, does an AD patient's inability to solve an item on the Ravens Progressive Matrices reflect a deficit in nonverbal reasoning or is it due to a failure to understand and remember the instructions, to analyze the visuospatial nature of the stimuli, or even to maintain attention? Given the multiplicity of cognitive deficits present in demented patients, it is especially difficult to pinpoint the nature of the particular cognitive dysfunction responsible for failure on such complex tasks. This is not to say that tasks, or at least items, involving reasoning and conceptualization are not found in test batteries given to AD patients. They are quite common. It is just that there have been practically no studies examining why AD patients perform so poorly on such tasks.

A number of measures of reasoning and problem solving have been used with AD patients. For example, the Ravens Progressive Matrices is a nonverbal reasoning test in which the subject is presented with a visual pattern from which a piece is missing. The subject has to decide which of several choices correctly completes the pattern. The early problems involve geometric pattern matching, whereas later problems require analogical reasoning. AD patients do very poorly on this task, especially when reasoning is required (Grady et al., 1988; Pillon, Dubois, Lhermitte, & Agid, 1986). Another commonly given clinical test is the Wisconsin Card Sorting task. Here, the subject has to sort cards, each of which contains between one and four identical shapes, either stars, triangles, crosses, or circles; all of the shapes on a card are either red, green, yellow, or blue. Subjects sort the cards by placing each card beneath one of four stimulus cards containing (a) one red triangle, (b) two green stars, (c) three yellow crosses, or (d) four blue circles. A subject can sort a particular card (e.g., a card with two red crosses) either by its color (in the case of the example putting it under Item a), its shape (putting it under Item c) or its number (putting it under Item b). Subjects are not told how to sort the cards, but are given feedback (the experimenter says correct or incorrect) after placing each card. From this feedback subjects have to form a hypothesis as to which of the card's physical features is relevant and then have to test their hypothesis by sorting the cards. Again, even mildly demented AD patients do very poorly (Pillon et al., 1986) in this problem-solving task.

Another area of complex cognitive processing disrupted in patients with AD is the ability to form, comprehend, and manipulate abstract concepts. There is a large literature demonstrating that abstract conceptualization is disrupted by injury to many different regions of the cortex (Lezak, 1983). It is not surprising, therefore, that diffuse brain disease such as that associated with AD produces substantial deficits in processing abstract concepts. As a result, most test batteries designed to assess dementia typically include measures of proverb interpretation or conceptualization. Again, however, the emphasis is usually on detecting deficits in order to aid diagnosis, rather than on understanding the underlying nature of the deficits, although there are a few exceptions. In proverb interpretation, subjects typically are given a common proverb or idiom (i.e., "People who live in glass houses shouldn't throw stones") and asked to say what it means. If someone interprets the proverb in terms of its literal meaning (e.g., "Because the stone might break the glass"), it is assumed that he or she is unable to comprehend the abstract meaning of the phrase. However, as Kempler, Van Lancker, and Read (1988) pointed out, the answers given by AD patients are not always easily classifiable. Also, it is difficult to know whether a patient's poor performance reflects a true problem in understanding abstract concepts or whether it result from other cognitive deficits. That is, patients might fail because they are unable to find the appropriate words to explain the saying, or because they misunderstand the saying due to a problem in decoding the meaning of individual words, or because of memory or attentional decrements. Kempler et al. therefore devised a task that compared the performance of normals and AD patients in understanding both idioms (e.g., "He is living high on the hog") and control sentences—novel concrete sentences (e.g., "He is sitting deep in the bubbles"). The control sentences were matched to the idioms in length, word frequency, and grammatical structure. Any deficits in AD patients' memory, attention, language skills, and so on, should affect their performance on the control sentences and idioms similarly, and therefore if AD patients perform worse on the idioms, this would suggest that they have particular difficulty in understanding the abstract message of the idiom. Subjects responded by pointing to a picture (four choices) that correctly represented the meaning of the sentence. This pointing response avoided confounding a problem in understanding idioms with a language production deficit. Results showed that AD patients had substantially more difficulty pointing to a picture that represented the abstract meaning of an idiom than they did pointing to a picture that represented the meaning of a novel concrete sentence. When AD patients made errors on the idioms, they tended to choose pictures that represented the literal meaning of the idiom (e.g., choosing the picture of a man sitting above a pig, for the aforementioned example). Kempler et al. suggested two possible cognitive dysfunctions that might account for AD patients' failure to understand idioms and proverbs. They argued that the relevant difference between idioms and novel sentences is that an idiom constitutes a meaningful unit or chunk and is perceived as a whole. By contrast, concrete sentences are processed as a series of words whose literal meanings must be retrieved and the grammatical structure of the sentence analyzed. One possibility, therefore, is that AD patients do not recognize the group of words making up an idiom as representing an integrated unit. Another possibility is that having identified the idiom as a unit, they may have difficulty retrieving the complex abstract meaning associated with the phrase, relying instead on their ability to process the literal meaning of the words making up the idiom.

DISCUSSION

From the preceding review it is clear that although AD patients show decrements on most cognitive tasks, there is considerable variability in the severity of their deficits on different measures. Can this variability be understood within any of the various theoretical frameworks proposed to deal with similar variability in the effects of normal aging?

Effortful Versus Automatic Processing

Several investigators (e.g., Jorm, 1986; Nebes et al., 1984) have proposed that AD patients are severely impaired on tasks that require effortful processing, but perform relatively normally on tasks that involve automatic processes. Automatic processes are those that require neither conscious awareness nor intention, and place minimal demands on a person's limited attentional capacity. If this hypothesis is true, then many of AD patients' impairments on cognitive tasks might result not from deficits in specific cognitive operations per se (e.g., encoding), but rather from decreased attentional capacity that limits their ability to carry out effort-ful processing. Situations in which access to, and use of, information is automatic should be associated then with minimal deficits in AD patients.

What is the evidence supporting this hypothesis? Certainly AD patients are severely impaired on tasks that require effortful processing (e.g., memory recall, verbal fluency, problem solving, etc.) and the deficits AD patients show on a variety of cognitive tasks have been attributed to decreased attentional capacity (e.g., Hart, Kwentus, Taylor, & Hamer, 1987). However, AD patients are impaired on most tasks and so the presence of deficits on tasks requiring effortful processing is not that en-lightening. The more important prediction from this hypothesis is that AD patients will perform relatively normally on tasks that involve auto-matic processes. Unfortunately, criteria distinguishing effortful from au-tomatic processes have been operationalized for only three limited areas of cognition: visual/memory search (Schneider & Shiffrin, 1977), memory encoding (Hasher & Zacks, 1979), and semantic priming (Neely, 1977). Results from experimental measures in other areas of cognition or from clinical tasks are, therefore, difficult to evaluate in terms of the effortful-automatic distinction. For example, Jorm (1986) argued that the reason AD patients do better on the verbal than on the performance subtests of the WAIS is that the mental skills involved in the verbal subtests are com-paratively automatic. However, we have no criteria to evaluate the rela-tive contribution of effortful and automatic processes to the performance of such complex tasks. Thus, it becomes a judgment call as to whether automatic processes are more involved in verbal subtests such as Arith-metic or Similarities, than they are in performance subtests such as Block Design. If we are to rigorously test this automaticity hypothesis, we need paradigms for which there are at least some explicit criteria (however uncertain) that will allow us to distinguish effortful from automatic processing. This leaves us with only two relevant sets of data: memory encoding and semantic priming. Hasher and Zacks (1979) proposed a number of criteria for determining whether information is encoded au-tomatically. Among the types of encoding they argued fit these criteria is the encoding of information about the frequency with which a partic-ular stimulus had been encountered and the modality in which it ap-peared. Strauss, Weingartner, and Thompson (1985) examined encoding of frequency information in AD patients. Subjects were read a list of words, some of which were repeated a variable number of times. After receiving all the words, subjects were shown each word from the list and asked to judge how many times it had appeared in the list. AD patients did not show any ability to judge the frequency with which different words had occurred. Similar results were found by Grafman et al. (1990). The latter study also examined whether, like normals, AD patients automatically encode information about the modality in which stimuli appear. They found that AD patients were severely impaired in a test of incidental memory for the sensory modality (visual vs. auditory) in which stimuli had been presented. If we assume that information about frequency of occurrence and modality of presentation is encoded automatically, as suggested by Hasher and Zacks, then the AD patients in these studies were impaired on automatic processes. However, this assumption has been challenged by a number of studies (e.g., Fisk & Schneider, 1984), which have produced evidence that this type of encoding is not necessarily automatic. Thus, this result may not tell us anything about the status of automatic processing in AD. Also, even if frequency information is encoded automatically, the task used in the Strauss et al. study (i.e., judgment of relative frequency) would certainly seem to require effortful processes.

The second set of data relevant to the automaticity hypothesis is that on semantic priming. Neely (1977) argued that automatic priming results from a spread of activation from one node to another along the semantic network. Presentation of a prime automatically will facilitate processing of semantically related concepts, but will have no effect, positive or negative, upon unrelated concepts. By contrast, attention-dependent priming is seen to result from the subject directing a limited-capacity processor to a location in semantic memory on the basis of an expectancy generated by the prime. On those trials in which a prime is not actually related to the following stimulus, the prime actually will inhibit processing of the stimulus (in comparison to a neutral condition). If AD patients show only the automatic version of semantic priming, they will show a pattern of facilitation, with no inhibition. The evidence with this procedure is conflicting. Nebes et al. (1986), using a sentence-priming procedure, found inhibition by unrelated primes in AD patients that was even larger than that found in normals. By contrast, Hartman (in press) found evidence for purely automatic priming (semantic facilitation, with no inhibition). Thus, at present, there is no strong and consistent evidence that the automatic-effortful distinction can explain the pattern of cognitive deficits in AD. However, the amount of available data is still rather limited, and this picture may change with future research.

Central Executive System

Another theoretical construct that shows promise for explaining the pattern of cognitive deficits in AD is the Central Executive System (CES). The CES is conceived of as scheduling and coordinating processing programs that are simultaneously active, functioning to resolve scheduling conflicts and to integrate the operation of concurrent processing activities

(Baddeley et al., 1986). Although the CES has been used primarily to explain working-memory results in AD patients (e.g., Morris, 1986), it certainly has wider potential. Spinnler et al. (1988) argued that a CES dysfunction makes it difficult for AD patients to carry out the active manipulation and processing of stimulus information necessary for successful secondary memory. Becker (1988) also proposed that it is possible to differentiate multiple causes for the memory deficit of AD, and that one of the major causes is a defect in CES function. Obviously, the concept of a CES deficit also can be applied to the divided-attention results in AD (Baddeley et al., 1986), as well as to other areas of cognition. For example, the problems that AD patients have in comprehending and remembering texts could be due to a CES impairment making it difficult for them to coordinate the simultaneous decoding of language symbols with the encoding of this information into memory. However, in order for the CES concept to be more widely useful, several problems will have to be overcome. First, it will be necessary to show how the results of a dysfunctional CES can be operationally distinguished from a decrease in attentional capacity in AD. Second, in order to relate a CES deficit to problems in other cognitive areas in AD, comparatively pure measures of CES function are needed. At present, it is not clear what these would be.

Mental Slowing

Recently, there has been a great deal of interest in whether a slowing of information processing might account for the pattern of cognitive decrements seen with advancing age. This view, championed by Birren (Birren, Woods, & Williams, 1980), argues that normal aging is associated with a nearly uniform slowing in the rate at which all mental operations are carried out. Supporting evidence for this hypothesis has come from a number of meta-analyses (Cerella, 1985; Salthouse, 1985) that have regressed the response times of the old against those of the young across a wide variety of tasks differing in psychological complexity. These analyses have found that the relationship between the response times of young and normal-old subjects is well described by a linear function of the form: Old (time) = A + B Young (time), where B is a constant proportion equal to approximately 1.5. This function typically accounts for over 90% of the variance despite the diverse nature of the experimental data represented. An important aspect of this function is that the magnitude of the absolute difference in response time between the young and old increases with task difficulty. The more processing a given condition requires (i.e., the longer it takes), the larger will be the difference in absolute response time between the young and old. However, proportionately this group difference remains constant across different tasks, the old taking approximately 1.5 times longer than the young.

We have shown in a similar meta-analysis (Nebes & Madden, 1988) that AD also is associated with a generalized cognitive slowing. That is, a linear function described the relationship between the response times of young subjects and AD patients on 37 different experimental conditions. This function differed from that for the normal old on these same conditions in that the multiplicative factor was substantially larger (B = 2.2). This suggests that a generalized mental slowing is also present in patients with AD, albeit in a more exaggerated form. We recently increased the number of conditions in our analysis to 61 and confirmed this generalized slowing. We also now have evidence that as the severity of the dementia in AD increases, so too does the degree of mental slowing, the multiplicative factor in the function rising from 1.9 in mildly demented patients to 2.9 in moderately demented individuals.

The implications of a generalized mental slowing for the interpretation of response-time results is the same for Alzheimer-disease research as it is for studies of normal aging. Salthouse (1985) argued that if one is to interpret an interaction between age and condition as showing a specific cognitive deficit in the elderly, it is necessary to demonstrate that the magnitude of this interaction is disproportionately large. That is, it is not enough to show that there is a larger increase in response time across conditions in the old than in the young. You must also show that the size of this increase is greater than that predicted by the linear function describing generalized cognitive slowing. We would suggest that the same is true of studies examining Alzheimer's disease. For example, we earlier described a study by Nebes and Brady (1989) that found visual search time to rise with increasing array size at a greater rate in AD patients than in normal old or young subjects. The interpretation of these results was that AD patients suffered a greater divided-attention deficit than did normals. However, if we examine these results in the framework of our latest meta-analysis, this interaction between group and array size is not disproportionately greater than that predicted by a generalized slowing. Therefore, these results may not actually reflect a greater divided-attention deficit in AD after all. Similarly, Ferris, Crook, Sathananthan, & Gershon (1976) found a larger difference in response time between AD patients and normals on a choice response-time task than on a simple response-time task. They argued that this pattern was due to their AD patients having more difficulty with the increased information-processing demands of the choice task. However, again their results might reflect nothing more than generalized slowing.

It seems therefore, that just as cognitive-aging research has had to take generalized slowing into account in its attempts to demonstrate specific cognitive deficits, so too will Alzheimer-disease research. Although response-time studies of AD are still fairly rare, such studies should become more common given the current interest in using the methodology and theories of cognitive aging to understand the mental impairments associated with AD. We would hope that Alzheimer-disease research will benefit from the recent findings in cognitive aging and will not blindly interpret condition by group interactions in response time as showing the presence of specific deficits without taking into account the presence of a generalized mental slowing in AD, a slowing that appears to be even greater than that found in normal aging.

Heterogeneity of Impairment in AD

Finally, there are several conceptual issues that transcend the specific cognitive deficits seen in AD patients. The first of these is the heterogeneity of the cognitive impairment in AD. Although most of the studies reviewed have dealt with AD patients as if they constituted a homogeneous group, there is, in fact, a considerable amount of intersubject variability. Whereas the majority of AD patients undergo a global deterioration of cognitive function, a substantial minority show more focal symptoms, especially early in the course of the disease. For example, some individuals may have a disproportionately severe visuospatial deficit or language deficit, with only mild impairments in other areas of cognition (Becker et al., 1988; Martin, 1987; Martin et al., 1986). There are several possible explanations for this variability. It may be that these varying patterns of deficit reflect the presence of a number of distinct diseases that we are unknowingly lumping together under the name AD. Or, if they are not distinct diseases, they may at least be qualitatively distinct subgroups (i.e., major variants of AD) that differ in important clinical features. For example, Seltzer and Sherwin (1983) contended that AD patients with major language deficits are more likely to have become demented early in their life (i.e., presenile dementia) and to show a more rapid deterioration. Similarly, Breitner and Folstein (1984) claimed that patients with prominent agraphia (i.e., problems writing a spontaneous sentence) are more likely to have a family history of AD, suggesting a genetic basis for their disease. However, other studies (e.g., Becker et al., 1988; Martin et al., 1986) have failed to replicate such associations between behavioral patterns and clinical symptoms.

Another possible source for the behavioral heterogeneity in AD is variation in which particular brain regions happen to be most affected in a given patient. That is, there could be some individual variability in which brain regions have the most severe neuropathology. Alternatively, there may be an interaction of a diffuse neuronal loss with the patient's own existing level of ability. For example, in someone with relatively poor spatial abilities, it may not take much damage to right parietal cortex to produce a major visuospatial dysfunction. Certainly there is evidence that brain regions may be impaired differentially in individual AD patients. For example, Eslinger and Benton (1983) found that the deficits shown by AD patients on two distinct spatial operations (known to be disrupted by focal damage to different brain areas) were strongly dissociated. That is, some patients performed relatively worse on one operation than on the other, whereas other patients showed the reverse pattern, suggesting individual variability in the locus of the neuropathology. Similarly, Shuttleworth and Huber (1988) found that object-naming deficits in AD could result from either visuospatial or linguistic dysfunction, which again are known to follow damage to different brain regions. However, the most impressive evidence is that of Martin et al. (1986), who found that different profiles of cognitive deficit were associated with regional changes in brain physiology consistent with the results of studies on focal brain lesions. AD patients with a prominent language deficit showed decreased metabolism on Positron Emission Tomography primarily in their left hemisphere, whereas those with a prominent spatial deficit showed decreased metabolism in their right hemisphere. Obviously, variations in the regional distribution of brain dysfunction also could reflect the action of different diseases, and so, at the present time, the ultimate source of this intersubject variability in the pattern of cognitive deficits in AD is still very much in doubt.

Relationship Between AD and Normal Aging

The last issue is the relationship between normal aging and AD. The present orthodoxy is that AD represents a disease process of unknown etiology that is distinct from the normal aging process, although it is more common in older persons. However, as Drachman (1983) pointed out, there are other possibilities, and at present we do not have definitive evidence that would allow us to exclude them. For example, it is possible that persons diagnosed as having AD represent merely one extreme of the normal distribution of cognitive loss produced by normal aging. Another possibility is that AD represents an exaggeration or acceleration of normal aging due to other factors (e.g., cardiovascular disease) that interact with the aging process (Drachman, 1983). A question central to this issue is whether AD differs from normal aging qualitatively (suggesting, although not proving, that it is a distinct disease), or only quantitatively. At present, there is relatively little evidence, either behavioral, neuropathological, or neurochemical, that AD differs qualitatively from normal aging. In terms of cognition, it has not proved easy to distinguish qualitative from quantitative differences. If a particular cognitive process becomes severely impaired (i.e., a quantitative change), it may force a dramatic shift in the way subjects carry out a particular task, or even make the task impossible to perform (a qualitative change). An excellent example of this was described in the Retrieval section, in which an apparent qualitative difference in retrieval (Miller, 1977) turned out to be due to a quantitative difference in memory strength (Meudell & Mayes, 1981). Right now, the best we can do is point to a few possible areas of cognition that might show qualitative differences between the performance of the normal old and AD patients. First is the literature suggesting that AD patients, unlike the normal old, show abnormal implicit-memory performance. However, this evidence is not compelling, as AD patients actually perform normally on some implicit-memory tasks (Moscovitch et al., 1986) and the normal old, in turn, perform abnormally on some implicit-memory tasks (Howard, 1988). A similar statement can be made about semantic memory, which is supposed to be unimpaired in normal aging but disrupted in AD. Again, as described in the section Language and Semantic Knowledge, this distinction is not so clear and simple. Still, these may be productive areas in which to pursue the search for qualitative differences between normal aging and AD. Another possible source of evidence may lie in studies of cognitive slowing. If the normal old show a uniform proportional slowing in all aspects of cognition, whereas AD patients are disproportionately slowed on certain cognitive operations, as suggested by Nebes and Madden (1988), this could be interpreted as evidence for a qualitative difference in the nature of the cognitive impairment of the two groups. However, this is only one study, and before leaping to any such generalization, the nature of the slowing in AD needs to be determined for a much broader array of tasks. Overall, it is clear that before we can make any confident statement about the qualitative/quantitative nature of cognitive differences between AD and normal aging, we will require a great deal more information about the cognitive effects of Alzheimer's disease than we possess at the present time.

ACKNOWLEDGMENTS

The preparation of this chapter was supported by Grant AG 04791 from the National Institute of Aging. Correspondence concerning this chapter should be addressed to Dr. Robert Nebes, Western Psychiatric Institute and Clinic, 3811 O'Hara St., Pittsburgh, PA 15213, USA.

REFERENCES

Albert, M. S., Heller, H. S., & Milberg, W. (1988). Changes in naming ability with age. *Psychology and Aging, 3,* 173–178.

Backman, L., & Herlitz, A. (1990). The relationship between prior knowledge and face recognition memory in normal aging and Alzheimer's disease. *Journals of Gerontology: Psychological Sciences, 45,* P94–P100.

Baddeley, A., Logie, R., Bressi, S., Della Sala, S., & Spinnler, H. (1986). Dementia and working memory. *Quarterly Journal of Experimental Psychology, 38A,* 603–618.

Barker, M. G., & Lawson, J. S. (1968). Nominal aphasia in dementia. *British Journal of Psychiatry, 114,* 1351–1356.

Bayles, K. A., & Kaszniak, A. W. (1987). *Communication and cognition in normal aging and dementia.* Boston: College-Hill.

Bayles, K. A., & Tomoeda, C. K. (1983). Confrontation naming in dementia. *Brain and Language, 19,* 98–114.

Bayles, K. A., Tomoeda, C. K., & Trosset, M. W. (1990). Naming and categorical knowledge in Alzheimer's disease. *Brain and Language, 39,* 498–510.

Becker, J. T. (1988). Working memory and secondary memory deficits in Alzheimer's disease. *Journal of Clinical and Experimental Neuropsychology, 6,* 739–753.

Becker, J. T., Boller, F., Saxton, J., & McGonigle-Gibson, K. L. (1987). Normal rates of forgetting of verbal and non-verbal material in Alzheimer's disease. *Cortex, 23,* 59–72.

Becker, J. T., Huff, F. J., Nebes, R. D., Holland, A., & Boller, F. (1988). Neuropsychological function in Alzheimer's disease: Pattern of impairment and rates of progression. *Archives of Neurology, 45,* 263–268.

Birren, J. E., Woods, A. M., & Williams, M. V. (1980). Behavioral slowing with age: Causes, organization and consequences. In L. W. Poon (Ed.), *Aging in the 1980's* (pp. 293–308). Washington DC: American Psychological Association.

Bouma, A., & Van Silfhout, B. (1989). Dichotic listening in patients with Alzheimer's disease. *Journal of Clinical and Experimental Neuropsychology, 11,* 369.

Branconnier, R. J., Cole, J. O., Spera, K. F., & De Vitt, D. R. (1982). Recall and recognition as diagnostic indices of malignant memory loss in senile dementia: A bayesian analysis. *Experimental Aging Research, 8,* 189–193.

Brandt, J., Spencer, M., McSorley, P., & Folstein, M. F. (1988). Semantic activation and implicit memory in Alzheimer disease. *Alzheimer Disease and Associated Disorders, 2,* 112–119.

Breitner, J. C. S., & Folstein, M. F. (1984). Familial Alzheimer dementia: A prevalent disorder with specific clinical features. *Psychological Medicine, 14,* 63–80.

Brouwers, P., Cox, C., Martin, A., Chase, T., & Fedio, P. (1984). Differential perceptual-spatial impairment in Huntington's and Alzheimer's dementias. *Archives of Neurology, 41,* 1073–1076.

Butters, N., Albert, M. S., Sax, D. S., Miliotis, P., Nagode, J., & Sterste, A. (1983). The effect of verbal mediators on the pictorial memory of brain-damaged patients. *Neuropsychologia, 21,* 307–332.

Butters, N., Granholm, E., Salmon, D. P., Grant, I., & Wolfe, J. (1987). Episodic and semantic memory: A comparison of amnesic and demented patients. *Journal of Clinical and Experimental Neuropsychology, 9,* 479–497.

Butters, N., Heindel, W. C., & Salmon, D. P. (1990). Dissociation of implicit memory in dementia: Neurological implications. *Bulletin of the Psychonomic Society, 28,* 359–366.

Capitani, E., Della Sala, S., Lucchelli, F., Soave, P., & Spinnler, H. (1988). Perceptual attention in aging and dementia measured by Gottschaldt's hidden figure test. *Journals of Gerontology: Psychological Sciences, 43,* P157–P163.

Cerella, J. (1985). Information processing rates in the elderly. *Psychological Bulletin, 98,* 67–83.

Cermak, L. A. (1984). The episodic/semantic distinction in amnesia. In N. Butters & L. R. Squire (Eds.), *The neuropsychology of memory* (pp. 55–62). New York: Guilford.

Chenoweth, B., & Spencer, B. (1986). Dementia: The experience of family caregivers. *The Gerontologist, 26,* 267–272.

Chertkow, H., Bub, D., & Seidenberg, M. (1989). Priming and semantic memory loss in Alzheimer's disease. *Brain and Language, 36,* 420–446.

Collins, A. M., & Loftus, E. F. (1975). A spreading-activation theory of semantic processing. *Psychological Review, 82,* 407–428.

Corkin, S. (1982). Some relationships between global amnesias and the memory impairments in Alzheimer's disease. In S. Corkin, K. L. Davis, J. H. Growdon, E. Usdin, & R. J. Wurtman (Eds.), *Alzheimer's disease: A report of progress in research* (pp. 149–164). New York: Raven.

Craik, F. I. M. (1977). Age differences in human memory. In J. E. Birren & K. W. Schaie (Eds.), *The handbook of the psychology of aging* (pp. 384–420). New York: Van Nostrand Reinhold.

Craik, F. I. M. (1984). Age differences in remembering. In L. R. Squire & N. Butters (Eds.), *Neuropsychology of memory* (pp. 3–12). New York: Guilford.

Craik, F. I. M., & Tulving, E. (1975). Depth of processing and the retention of words in episodic memory. *Journal of Experimental Psychology: General, 104,* 268–294.

Crook, T., Bartus, R. T., Ferris, S. H., Whitehouse, P., Cohen, G. D., & Gershon, S. (1986). Age-associated memory impairment: Proposed diagnostic criteria and measures of clinical change. *Developmental Neuropsychology, 2,* 261–276.

Cushman, L. A., & Caine, E. D. (1987). A controlled study of processing of semantic and syntactic information in Alzheimer's disease. *Archives of Clinical Neuropsychology, 2,* 283–292.

Cushman, L., Como, P. G., Booth, H., & Caine, E. D. (1988). Cued recall and release from proactive interference in Alzheimer's disease. *Journal of Clinical and Experimental Neuropsychology, 10,* 687–692.

Dannenbaum, S. E., Parkinson, S. R., & Inman, V. W. (1988). Short-term forgetting: Comparisons between patients with dementia of the Alzheimer type, depressed and normal elderly. *Cognitive Neuropsychology, 5,* 213–233.

Davis, P. E., & Mumford, S. J. (1984). Cued recall and the nature of the memory disorder in dementia. *British Journal of Psychiatry, 144,* 383–386.

Dick, M. B., Kean, M. -L., & Sands, D. (1989). Memory for action events in Alzheimer-type dementia: Further evidence of an encoding failure. *Brain and Cognition, 9,* 71–87.

Drachman, D. A. (1983). How normal aging relates to dementia: A critique and classification. In D. Samuel, S. Algeri, S. Gershon, V. E. Grimm, & G. Toffano (Eds.), *Aging of the brain* (pp. 19–31). New York: Raven.

Erickson, R. C., Poon, L. W., & Walsh-Sweeney, L. (1980). Clinical memory testing of the elderly. In L. W. Poon, J. L. Fozard, L. S. Cermak, D. Arenberg, & L. W. Thompson (Eds.), *New directions in memory and aging* (pp. 379–402). Hillsdale, NJ: Lawrence Erlbaum Associates.

Eslinger, P. J., & Benton, A. L. (1983). Visuoperceptual performance in aging and dementia: Clinical and theoretical observations. *Journal of Clinical Neuropsychology, 5,* 213–220.

Evans, D. A., Funkenstein, H. H., Albert, M. S., Scherr, P. A., Cook, N. R., Chown, M. J., Hebert, L. E., Hennekens, C. H., & Taylor, J. O. (1989). Prevalence of Alzheimer's disease in a community population of older persons. *Journal of the American Medical Association, 262,* 2551–2556.

Ferris, S., Crook, T., Sathananthan, G., & Gershon, S. (1976). Reaction time as a diagnostic measure in senility. *Journal of the American Geriatrics Society, 24,* 529–533.

Fisk, A. D., & Schneider, W. (1984). Memory as a function of attention, level of processing and automatization. *Journal of Experimental Psychology: Learning, Memory, and Cognition, 10,* 181–197.

Flicker, C., Ferris, S. H., Crook, T., & Bartus, R. T. (1986). The effects of aging and dementia on concept formation as measured on an object-sorting task. *Developmental Neuropsychology, 2,* 65–72.

Flicker, C., Ferris, S. H., Crook, T., Reisberg, B., & Bartus, R. T. (1988). Equivalent spatial-rotation deficits in normal aging and Alzheimer's disease. *Journal of Clinical and Experimental Neuropsychology, 10,* 387–399.

Foldi, N. S., Davidoff, D., Jutagir, R., & Gould, T. (1987). Influences on selective attention in Alzheimer's patients and healthy elderly. *Journal of Clinical and Experimental Neuropsychology, 9,* 63.

Freed, D. M., Corkin, S., Growdon, J. H., & Nissen, M. J. (1989). Selective attention in Alzheimer's disease: Characterizing cognitive subgroups of Alzheimer's disease. *Neuropsychologia, 27,* 325–339.

Grady, C. L., Grimes, A. M., Patronas, N., Sunderland, T., Foster, N. L., & Rapoport, S. I. (1989). Divided attention, as measured by dichotic speech performance in dementia of the Alzheimer type. *Archives of Neurology, 46,* 317–320.

Grady, C. L., Haxby, J. V., Horwitz, B., Sundaram, M., Berg, G., Schapiro, M., Friedland, R. P., & Rapoport, S. I. (1988). Longitudinal study of the early neuropsychological and cerebral metabolic changes in dementia of the Alzheimer type. *Journal of Clinical and Experimental Neuropsychology, 10,* 576–596.

Graf, P. (1990). Life-span changes in implicit and explicit memory. *Bulletin of the Psychonomic Society, 28,* 353–358.

Grafman, J., Weingartner, H., Lawlor, B., Mellow, A. M., Thompsen-Putnam, K., & Sunderland, T. (1990). Automatic memory processes in patients with dementia—Alzheimer's type. *Cortex, 26,* 361–371.

Granholm, E., & Butters, N. (1988). Associative encoding and retrieval in Alzheimer's and Huntington's disease. *Brain and Cognition, 7,* 335–347.

Grober, E., & Buschke, H. (1987). Genuine memory deficits in dementia. *Developmental Neuropsychology, 3,* 13–36.

Grober, E., Buschke, H., Kawas, C., & Fuld, P. (1985). Impaired ranking of semantic attributes in dementia. *Brain and Language, 26,* 276–286.

Grosse, D. A., Wilson, R. S., & Fox, J. H. (1990). Preserved word-stem-completion priming of semantically encoded information in Alzheimer's disease. *Psychology and Aging, 5,* 304–306.

Hart, R. P., Kwentus, J. A., Taylor, J. R., & Hamer, R. M. (1987). Selective reminding procedure in depression and dementia. *Psychology and Aging, 2,* 111–115.

Hart, R. P., Kwentus, J. A., Taylor, J. R., & Harkins, S. W. (1987). Rate of forgetting in dementia and depression. *Journal of Consulting and Clinical Psychology, 55,* 101–105.

Hartman, M. D. (in press). The use of semantic knowledge in Alzheimer's disease: Evidence for impairments of attention. *Neuropsychologia.*

Hasher, L., & Zacks, R. T. (1979). Automatic and effortful processes in memory. *Journal of Experimental Psychology: General, 108,* 356–388.

Heindel, W. C., Salmon, D. P., & Butters, N. (in press). Pictorial priming and cued recall in Alzheimer's disease and Huntington's disease. *Brain and Cognition.*

Henderson, V. W., Mack, W., & Williams, B. W. (1989). Spatial disorientation in Alzheimer's disease. *Archives of Neurology, 46,* 391–394.

Hier, D. B., Hagenlocker, K., & Shindler, A. G. (1985). Language disintegration in dementia: Effects of etiology and severity. *Brain and Language, 25,* 117–133.

Howard, D. V. (1988). Implicit and explicit assessment of cognitive aging. In M. L. Howe & C. J. Brainerd (Eds.), *Cognitive development in adulthood* (pp. 3–37). New York: Springer-Verlag.

Huff, F. J., Becker, J. T., Belle, S. H., Nebes, R. D., Holland, A. L., & Boller, F. (1987). Cognitive deficits and clinical diagnosis of Alzheimer's disease. *Neurology, 37,* 1119–1124.

Huff, F. J., Corkin, S., & Growdon, J. H. (1986). Semantic impairment and anomia in Alzheimer's disease. *Brain and Language, 28,* 235–249.

Huff, F. J., Mack, L., Mahlmann, J., & Greenberg, S. (1988). A comparison of lexical-semantic impairments in left hemisphere stroke and Alzheimer's disease. *Brain and Language, 34,* 262–278.

Huppert, F. A., & Kopelman, M. D. (1989). Rates of forgetting in normal aging: a comparison with dementia. *Neuropsychologia, 27,* 849–860.

Jorm, A. F. (1986). Controlled and automatic information processing in senile dementia: A review. *Psychological Medicine, 16,* 77–88.

Karlsson, T., Backman, L., Herlitz, A., Nilsson, L., Winblad, B., & Osterlind, P. (1989). Memory improvement at different stages of Alzheimer's disease. *Neuropsychologia, 27,* 737–742.

Kaszniak, A. W. (1986). The neuropsychology of dementia. In I. Grant & K. M. Adams (Eds.), *Neuropsychological assessment of neuropsychiatric disorders* (pp. 172–220). New York: Oxford University Press.

Katzman, R. (1986). Alzheimer's disease. *New England Journal of Medicine, 314,* 964–973.

Katzman, R., Lasker, B., & Bernstein, N. (1988). Advances in the diagnosis of dementia: Accuracy of diagnosis and consequences of misdiagnosis of disorders causing dementia. In R. D. Terry (Ed.), *Aging and the brain* (pp. 17–62). New York: Raven.

Kempler, D., Andersen, E., Hunt, M., & Henderson, V. (1990). Linguistic and attentional contributions to anomia in Alzheimer's disease. *Journal of Clinical and Experimental Neuropsychology, 12,* 398.

Kempler, D., Curtiss, S., & Jackson, C. (1987). Syntactic preservation in Alzheimer's disease. *Journal of Speech and Hearing Research, 30,* 343–350.

Kempler, D., Van Lancker, D., & Read, S. (1988). Proverb and idiom comprehension in Alzheimer disease. *Alzheimer Disease and Associated Disorders, 2,* 38–49.

Kintsch, W., & van Dijk, T. A. (1978). Toward a model of text comprehension and production. *Psychological Review, 85,* 363–394.

Kirshner, H. S., Webb, W. G., & Kelly, M. P. (1984). The naming disorder of dementia. *Neuropsychologia, 22,* 23–30.

Kline, D. W., & Schieber, F. (1985). Vision and aging. In J. E. Birren & K. W. Schaie (Eds.), *Handbook of the psychology of aging* (2nd ed., pp. 296–331). New York: Van Nostrand Reinhold.

Knopman, D. S., & Nissen, M. J. (1987). Implicit learning in patients with probable Alzheimer's disease. *Neurology, 37,* 784–788.

Kopelman, M. D. (1985). Rates of forgetting in Alzheimer-type dementia and Korsakoff syndrome. *Neuropsychologia, 23,* 623–638.

Kopelman, M. D. (1989). Remote and autobiographical memory, temporal context memory and frontal atrophy in Korsakoff and Alzheimer patients. *Neuropsychologia, 27,* 437–460.

Kral, V. A. (1978). Benign senile forgetfulness. In R. Katzman, R. D. Terry, & K. L. Blick (Eds.), *Alzheimer's disease: Senile dementia and related disorders* (Aging series, Vol. 7, pp. 47–51). New York: Raven.

Kramer, J. H., Delis, D. C., Blusewicz, M. J., Brandt, J., Ober, B. A., & Strauss, M. (1988). Verbal memory errors in Alzheimer's and Huntington's dementias. *Developmental Neuropsychology, 4,* 1–15.

Landrum, R. E., & Radtke, R. C. (1990). Degree of cognitive impairment and the dissociation of implicit and explicit memory. *Journal of General Psychology, 117,* 187–196.

Lezak, M. D. (1983). *Neuropsychological assessment.* New York: Oxford University Press.

Martin, A. (1987). Representation of semantic and spatial knowledge in Alzheimer's patients: Implications for models of preserved learning in amnesia. *Journal of Clinical and Experimental Neuropsychology, 9,* 191–224.

Martin, A., Brouwers, P., Cox, C., & Fedio, P. (1985). On the nature of the verbal memory deficit in Alzheimer's disease. *Brain and Language, 25,* 323–341.

Martin, A., Brouwers, P., Lalonde, F., Cox, C., Teleska, P., & Fedio, P. (1986). Towards a behavioral typology of Alzheimer patients. *Journal of Clinical and Experimental Neuropsychology, 8,* 594–610.

Martin, A., & Fedio, P. (1983). Word production and comprehension in Alzheimer's disease: The breakdown of semantic knowledge. *Brain and Language, 19,* 124–141.

Mattis, S. (1976). Mental status examination for organic mental syndrome in the elderly patient. In L. Bellak & T. B. Karasu (Eds.), *Geriatric psychiatry* (pp. 77–121). New York: Grune & Stratton.

McKhann, G., Drachman, D., Folstein, M., Katzman, R., Price, D., & Stadlan, E. (1984). Clinical diagnosis of Alzheimer's disease: Report of the NINCDS-ADRDA Work Group. *Neurology, 34,* 939–949.

Mendez, M. F., Mendez, M. A., Martin, R. N., Smyth, K. A., & Whitehouse, p. J. (1990). Complex visual disturbances in Alzheimer's disease. *Neurology, 40,* 439–443.

Meudell, P., & Mayes, A. (1981). A similarity between weak normal memory and amnesia with two and eight choice word recognition: A signal detection analysis. *Cortex, 17,* 19–29.

Miller, E. (1977). *Abnormal ageing.* London: Wiley.

Mitchell, D. B., Hunt, R. R., & Schmitt, F. A. (1986). The generation effect and reality monitoring: Evidence from dementia and normal aging. *Journal of Gerontology, 41,* 79–84.

Mohr, E., Cox, C., Williams, J., Chase, T. N., & Fedio, P. (1990). Impairment of central auditory function in Alzheimer's disease. *Journal of Clinical and Experimental Neuropsychology, 12,* 235–246.

Moore, V., & Wyke, M. A. (1984). Drawing disability in patients with senile dementia. *Psychological Medicine, 14,* 97–105.

Morris, R. G. (1984). Dementia and functioning of the articulatory loop system. *Cognitive Neuropsychology, 1,* 143–157.

Morris, R. G. (1986). Short-term forgetting in senile dementia of the Alzheimer's type. *Cognitive Neuropsychology, 3,* 77–97.

Morris, R. G., & Baddeley, A. D. (1988). Primary and working memory functioning in Alzheimer-type dementia. *Journal of Clinical and Experimental Neuropsychology, 10,* 279–296.

Moscovitch, M. (1982). A neuropsychological approach to perception and memory in normal and pathological aging. In F. I. M. Craik & S. Trehub (Eds.), *Aging and cognitive processes* (pp. 55–78). New York: Plenum.

Moscovitch, M., Winocur, G., & McLachlan, D. (1986). Memory as assessed by recognition and reading time in normal and memory-impaired people with Alzheimer's disease and other neurological disorders. *Journal of Experimental Psychology: General, 115,* 331–347.

Nebes, R. D. (1989). Semantic memory in Alzheimer's disease. *Psychological Bulletin, 106,* 377–394.

Nebes, R. D., Boller, F., & Holland, A. (1986). Use of semantic context by patients with Alzheimer's disease. *Psychology and Aging, 1,* 261–269.

Nebes, R. D., & Brady, C. B. (1988). Integrity of semantic fields in Alzheimer's disease. *Cortex, 24,* 291–300.

Nebes, R. D., & Brady, C. B. (1989). Focused and divided attention in Alzheimer's disease. *Cortex, 25,* 305–315.

Nebes, R. D., & Brady, C. B. (1990). Preserved organization of semantic attributes in Alzheimer's disease. *Psychology and Aging, 5,* 574–579.

Nebes, R. D., Brady, C. B., & Huff, F. J. (1989). Automatic and attentional mechanisms of semantic priming in Alzheimer's disease. *Journal of Clinical and Experimental Neuropsychology, 11,* 219–230.

Nebes, R. D., Brady, C. B., & Jackson, S. T. (1989). The effect of semantic and syntactic structure on verbal memory in Alzheimer's disease. *Brain and Language, 36,* 301–313.

Nebes, R. D., & Madden, D. J. (1988). Different patterns of cognitive slowing produced by Alzheimer's disease and normal aging. *Psychology and Aging, 3,* 102–104.

Nebes, R. D., Martin, D. C., & Horn, L. C. (1984). Sparing of semantic memory in Alzheimer's disease. *Journal of Abnormal Psychology, 93,* 321–330.

Neely, J. H. (1977). Semantic priming and retrieval from lexical memory: Roles of inhibitionless spreading activation and limited-capacity attention. *Journal of Experimental Psychology: General, 106,* 226–254.

Nelson, D. L., Canas, J. J., Bajo, M. T., & Keelean, P. D. (1987). Comparing word fragment completion and cued recall with letter cues. *Journal of Experimental Psychology: Learning, Memory, and Cognition, 13,* 542–552.

Nicholas, M., Obler, L. K., Albert, M. L., & Helm-Estabrooks, N. (1985). Empty speech in Alzheimer's disease and fluent aphasia. *Journal of Speech and Hearing Research, 28,* 405–410.

Ober, B. A., Dronkers, N. F., Koss, E., Delis, D. C., & Friedland, R. P. (1986). Retrieval from semantic memory in Alzheimer-type dementia. *Journal of Clinical and Experimental Neuropsychology, 8,* 75–92.

Ober, B. A., Koss, E., Friedland, R. P., & Delis, D. C. (1985). Processes of verbal memory failure in Alzheimer-type dementia. *Brain and Cognition, 4,* 90–103.

Ober, B. A., & Shenaut, G. K. (1988). Lexical decision and priming in Alzheimer's disease. *Neuropsychologia, 26,* 273–286.

Ober, B. A., & Shenaut, G. K. (1989, February). *Abnormalities of semantic priming in Alzheimer's disease.* Paper presented at the meeting of the International Neuropsychological Society, Vancouver.

Ober, B. A., & Shenaut, G. K. (1990). Automatic versus controlled priming in Alzheimer's disease: A synthesis of current findings. *Journal of Clinical and Experimental Neuropsychology, 12,* 79.

Pepin, E. P., & Eslinger, P. J. (1989). Verbal memory decline in Alzheimer's disease: A multiple-process deficit. *Neurology, 39,* 1477–1482.

Pillon, B., Dubois, B., Lhermitte, F., & Agid, Y. (1986). Heterogeneity of cognitive impairment in progressive supranuclear palsy, Parkinson's disease and Alzheimer's disease. *Neurology 36,* 1179–1185.

Plude, D. J., & Hoyer, W. J. (1986). Age and the selectivity of visual information processing. *Psychology and Aging, 1,* 4–10.

Posner, M. I. (1980). Orienting of attention. *Quarterly Journal of Experimental Psychology, 32,* 3–25.

Reuter-Lorenz, P. A., Kinsbourne, M., & Moscovitch, M. (1990). Hemispheric control of spatial attention. *Brain and Cognition, 12,* 240–266.

Rissenberg, M., & Glanzer, M. (1987). Free recall and word-finding ability in normal aging and senile dementia of the Alzheimer's type: The effect of item concreteness. *Journal of Gerontology, 42,* 318–322.

Rochford, G. (1971). Study of naming errors in dysphasic and in demented patients. *Neuropsychologia, 9,* 437–443.

Sagar, H. J. (1990). Aging and age-related neurological disease: Remote memory. In F. Boller & J. Grafman (Eds.), *Handbook of neuropsychology: Vol. 4, Aging and dementia* (pp. 311–324). Amsterdam: Elsevier.

Sagar, H. J., Cohen, N. J., Sullivan, E. V., Corkin, S., & Growdon, J. H. (1988). Remote memory function in Alzheimer's disease and Parkinson's disease. *Brain, 111,* 185–206.

Salmon, D. P., Shimamura, A. P., Butters, N., & Smith, S. (1988). Lexical and semantic priming deficits in patients with Alzheimer's disease. *Journal of Clinical and Experimental Neuropsychology, 10,* 477–494.

Salthouse, T. A. (1985). Speed of behavior and its implications for cognition. In J. E. Birren & K. W. Schaie (Eds.), *Handbook of the psychology of aging* (2nd ed. pp. 400–426) New York: Von Nostrand Reinhold.

Schacter, D. L. (1987). Implicit memory: History and current status. *Journal of Experimental Psychology: Learning, Memory, and Cognition, 13,* 501–518.

Schlotterer, G., Moscovitch, M., & Crapper-McLachlan, D. (1983). Visual processing deficits as assessed by spatial frequency contrast sensitivity and backward masking in normal ageing and Alzheimer's disease. *Brain, 107,* 309–325.

Schneider, W., Dumais, S. T., & Shiffrin, R. M. (1984). Automatic and control processing and attention. In R. Parasuraman & D. R. Davies (Eds.), *Varieties of attention* (pp. 1–24). New York: Academic.

Schneider, W., & Shiffrin, R. M. (1977). Controlled and automatic human information processing: 1. Detection, search and attention. *Psychological Review, 84,* 1–66.

Schwanenflugel, P. J., & LaCount, K. L. (1988). Semantic relatedness and the scope of facilitation for upcoming words in sentences. *Journal of Experimental Psychology: Learning, Memory, and Cognition, 14,* 344–354.

Seidenberg, M. S., Waters, G. S., Sanders, M., & Langer, P. (1984). Pre- and postlexical loci of contextual effects on word recognition. *Memory & Cognition, 12,* 315–328.

Seltzer, B., & Sherwin, I. (1983). A comparison of clinical features in early- and late-onset primary degenerative dementia. *Archives of Neurology, 40,* 143–146.

Shimamura, A. P., Salmon, D. P., Squire, L. R., & Butters, N. (1987). Memory dysfunction and word priming in dementia and amnesia. *Behavioral Neuroscience, 101,* 347–351.

Shuttleworth, E. C., & Huber, S. J. (1988). The naming disorder of dementia of Alzheimer type. *Brain and Language, 34,* 222–234.

Spilich, G. J. (1983). Life-span components of text processing: structural and procedural differences. *Journal of Verbal Learning and Verbal Behavior, 22,* 231–244.

Spinnler, H., Della Sala, S., Bandera, R., & Baddeley, A. (1988). Dementia, ageing, and the structure of human memory. *Cognitive Neuropsychology, 5,* 193–211.

Stanovich, K. E., & West, R. F. (1983). On priming by a sentence context. *Journal of Experimental Psychology: General, 112,* 1–36.

Storandt, M., Botwinick, J., Danziger, W. L., Berg, L., & Hughes, C. P. (1984). Psychometric differentiation of mild senile dementia of the Alzheimer type. *Archives of Neurology, 41,* 497–499.

Strauss, M. E., Weingartner, H., & Thompson, K. (1985). Remembering words and how often they occurred in memory-impaired patients. *Memory & Cognition, 13,* 507–510.

Tröster, A. I., Salmon, D. P., McCullough, D., & Butters, N. (1989). A comparison of category fluency deficits associated with Alzheimer's and Huntington's disease. *Brain and Language, 37,* 500–513.

Tulving, E. (1984). Precis of "Elements of episodic memory." *The Behavioral and Brain Sciences, 7,* 223–268.

Warrington, E. K. (1969). Constructional apraxia. In P. J. Vinken & G. W. Bruyn (Eds.), *Handbook of clinical neurology: Vol. 4, Disorders of speech, perception and symbolic behavior* (pp. 67–83). Amsterdam: North Holland.

Warrington, E. K. (1975). The selective impairment of semantic memory. *Quarterly Journal of Experimental Psychology, 27,* 635–657.

Weingartner, H., Kaye, W., Smallberg, S. A., Ebert, M. H., Gillin, J. C., & Sitaram, N. (1981). Memory failures in progressive idiopathic dementia. *Journal of Abnormal Psychology, 90,* 187–196.

Wilson, R. S., Bacon, L. D., Fox, J. H., & Kaszniak, A. W. (1983). Primary memory and secondary memory in dementia of the Alzheimer type. *Journal of Clinical Neuropsychology, 5,* 337–344.

Wilson, R. S., Bacon, L. D., Kramer, R. L., Fox, J. H., & Kaszniak, A. F. (1983). Word frequency effect and recognition memory in dementia of the Alzheimer's type. *Journal
of Clinical Neuropsychology, 5,* 97–104.
Wilson, R. S., Kaszniak, A. W., & Fox, J. H. (1981). Remote memory in senile dementia.
Cortex, 17, 41–48.

PART THREE

APPLICATIONS

CHAPTER NINE

Applied Cognitive Aging Research

Denise C. Park
University of Georgia

THE DOMAIN OF APPLIED COGNITIVE AGING RESEARCH

The emergence of applied adult cognition as a substantive research area is an exciting and well-timed development in the study of cognitive aging. Although the cognitive aging knowledge base is far from complete, basic researchers have begun to develop a sufficient understanding of the aging cognitive system that this knowledge now can be used to enhance productivity and to improve quality of life for older adults. The application of theoretical principles to issues of practical significance for older adults can provide a means for testing the generality and accuracy of theoretical constructs and experimental hypotheses in the real world. Finally, a cross-fertilization between basic and applied research is likely to develop as findings from applied cognitive aging research result in further development and differentiation of basic theoretical constructs.

There are a broad range of important issues that applied cognitive aging researchers might address in their work. Cognitive aging psychologists have conducted basic laboratory studies and developed theoretical frameworks which might be useful in a variety of real-world contexts. For example, studies could be done to determine the most effective way to present information in the news and television media to young adults compared to older adults or how one might design maps that would enhance route following in older adults. Other studies might examine how to structure text so that it is easy for old adults to comprehend and remember, or determine what components of driving behavior decline most precipitously with age. In the domain of health behaviors, cognitive aging researchers are developing frameworks to understand how adults of different ages represent illness and how that may affect their subsequent illness behavior; they are relating age differences in cognitive function to older adults' ability to understand and carry out a complex medication-taking regimen, and determining how electronic memory systems can be used to facilitate appropriate health-seeking behaviors. With respect to work and productivity in older adults, our understanding of automatization of cognitive processes and expert cognition is helping us to explain how well-practiced, expert behaviors maintained into late adulthood may offset or compensate for declines in component behaviors like speeded responding or memory. We are able to predict how age might impact on the acquisition of new work skills, such as computer training, as well as how to design software and training programs to be compatible with the cognitive changes that occur with age. The field of applied cognitive aging research is relatively new and there has been little systematic treatment of the implications of basic research for applied problems to date or the potential applied research has to contribute to our theoretical understanding of cognition and aging. In recognition of this, the present chapter focuses on basics by (a) examining the implications of present theoretical frameworks for the development of this research, (b) addressing methodological issues of particular importance to the applied cognitive aging researcher, and (c) providing frameworks to guide research as well as describing progress to date in two important domains of applied cognitive aging research.

Before beginning, it would be useful to propose a definition for applied cognitive aging research. Broadly defined, applied cognitive aging research is research that adopts the use of a cognitive aging framework to solve real-world problems for older adults. The problem solution dictated by the applied cognitive aging perspective could involve a training intervention, a restructuring of cognitive information, or molar changes in the older adult's environment. Most readers will recognize that there is already a fair amount of such research, but much of it has not adopted an explicit cognitive aging framework. This picture, however, is changing rapidly, such that mainstream researchers who have focused on theoretical and/or basic empirical problems in the cognitive laboratory are now beginning to examine the implications of their findings for applied problems of the elderly. I believe that this has occurred for several reasons: (a) Most important, theory-based basic research on cognition and aging has developed sufficiently that solutions to real-world problems are beginning to be suggested; (b) it is possible to design applied research that contributes to basic theoretical conceptualizations of aging and cognition; and (c) funding agencies are becoming increasingly concerned that scientific research show promise for contributing directly to the solution of real-world problems. In the present chapter, I focus on both the potential and realized contributions that basic cognitive aging science can make or has made to resolving challenges that confront older citizens.

In developing this topic, it also may be worthwhile to differentiate applied cognitive aging research from human factors research and from the study of everyday memory. As Charness and Bosman (1990) noted, human factors typically involves manipulating or changing components of the environment or changing tools used to operate upon the environment to facilitate behavior. With this in mind, it appears that human factors differs from applied cognitive aging research along two dimensions. First, human factors includes cognitive manipulations but also encompasses a broader range of modifications to tools and the environment than just cognition. For example, an applied cognitive aging researcher probably would not be interested in designing handrails or a staircase suited for use by frail elderly. These problems would fall partially within the purview of human factors psychologists, as design would require knowledge of both motor and perceptual behaviors in the elderly. The intersection of applied cognitive psychology and human factors would occur, however, when one considered how to design graphic or verbal instructions to direct people through the building in which the handrail and steps existed. To summarize, human factors psychologists operate upon perceptual, cognitive, and motor behaviors whereas the applied cognitive psychologist is primarily interested in cognition.

The second dimension on which the two areas can be discriminated has to do with the nature of the object that is modified. The human factors psychologist operates primarily upon tools and the environment, using his or her knowledge of the perceptual, motor, and cognitive systems to make them friendlier or easier to use. The applied cognitive aging psychologist, unlike the human factors psychologist, does not restrict him or herself to operating only on tools and the environment. Fozard and Popkin (1978) over a decade ago noted that the applied aging psychologist can operate to change either the environment or the individual to optimize the situation of the elderly. The tradition of changing the individual rather than the environment is a robust one with respect to applied cognition and aging, as exemplified by the interest in memory and cognitive abilities training (see reviews by West, 1989; Willis, 1989; Yesavage, Lapp, & Sheikh, 1989).

Applied cognitive aging research also shares some overlap with the study of everyday memory and cognition, but important distinctions exist between the two areas. The study of ecologically valid memory processes outside the laboratory using a cognitive aging theoretical framework is not applied cognitive aging research unless it is conducted in an effort to understand how to solve a particular problem confronting older adults. For example, a recent study designed to understand everyday memory differences in processing the visual and verbal components of a newscast (Stine, Wingfield, & Myers, 1990) does not attempt to solve a problem for older adults and thus it is not an applied study. At the same time, the Stine et al. study certainly identified an everyday memory problem of consequence for older adults and is likely to serve as the empirical base for future applied cognitive aging research. In contrast, training studies designed to determine how to improve memory for names and other information that might be in the newscasts would exemplify applied cognitive aging research (West, 1989; Yesavage, Rose, & Bower, 1983).

Theoretical Perspectives

The characterization of processes and structures associated with later life cognitive development are of great significance for the applied cognitive aging researcher who wishes to select techniques and interventions to improve the components of a behavior. If, for example, basic research indicated that cognitive behaviors of older adults could not be modified by experience (lack of plasticity), then the focus of applied cognitive aging research necessarily would be on intervention strategies that emphasized passive supports for cognition. Similarly, if advanced age is characterized by unlimited plasticity, then active cognitive training and other experiential interventions should be the focus of applied cognitive aging researchers. These two extreme positions are theoretical endpoints for different views of cognition and aging.

As Salthouse (1987a) noted, the general decrementalist view which suggests unrelenting decline across all areas of micro- and macrocognitive function with advanced age is "no longer held by most contemporary researchers in the area of cognitive aging" (p. 141). Similarly, the unlimited plasticity/disuse model also has fallen into disfavor, as there is substantial evidence for age-related decline in most component processes of cognitive function (Charness & Bosman, 1990; Plude & Hoyer, 1985; Salthouse, Kausler, & Saults, 1988). Furthermore, there is convincing evidence that alleged differences in experience or unfamiliarity with stimulus materials cannot account for these age differences (Salthouse, 1987a, 1987b, 1990a, 1990b). Thus, the prevailing view of cognitive development in adulthood is one of both growth and decline. Perhaps the most integrative and comprehensive view of growth and decline in cognitive function has been articulated by Baltes and colleagues (Baltes, Dittmann-

Kohli, & Dixon, 1984; Baltes & Schaie, 1976; Baltes & Willis, 1982). Baltes et al. noted that although fluid intelligence abilities do decline with advanced age, there is a certain amount of cognitive energy or capacity held in reserve by both young and elderly adults. With optimal training or under suitable conditions, this reserve capacity can be expressed as plasticity and used, increasing cognitive performance above some observed baseline level. Just as older adults have smaller physical reserves of capacity or energy (Fries & Crapo, 1981), Baltes et al. suggested that older adults also have less cognitive or intellectual reserve capacity than the young. These differences, however, are manifested only when the cognitive system is maximally stressed, that is, the limits of a person's cognitive capacity (both baseline and reserve) are reached or exceeded (Kliegel & Baltes, 1987).

Reserve Capacity and the Potential for Intraindividual Change

The concept of reserve capacity has major implications for the conduct of applied cognitive aging research, as an important focus of such research might be to determine how to actualize reserve capacities to effect desired intraindividual changes in cognitive behaviors. The cognitive training literature, which has focused primarily, but not exclusively, on psychometric abilities (see Willis, 1989, for an excellent review), frequently is cited as a demonstration of the actualization of reserve capacity (plasticity) in older adults. Willis, Blieszner, and Baltes (1981) and Baltes and Willis (1982) demonstrated improvement in figural relations with training, with long-term maintenance over periods up to 10 months. Schaie and Willis (1986), using a longitudinal design, demonstrated improvement in inductive reasoning and spatial orientation both for elderly subjects who had declined from their earlier level of ability and also for those who had not declined, so that the performance increase for these latter subjects represented an improvement over previously observed levels. Improvements were noted at the level of ability factor scores, using multiple measures, suggesting that a primary ability had been affected. In general, the cognitive training literature presents impressive and methodologically sophisticated evidence that relatively brief training sessions (10 hr or less) positively affect both speed and error rates. Salthouse (1987a, 1989) expressed concern that this research fails to contribute to our understanding of age differences due to the exclusion of young adult control subjects and also suggested (Salthouse, 1987a, 1990b) that the plasticity (potential to improve) of young adults is greater than that of older adults. Baltes, Dittmann-Kohli, and Kliegl (1986) acknowledged these concerns but emphasized that the important point about the cognitive training work is the focus on the substantial amounts of plasticity shown by elderly subjects with respect to cognitive skills—perhaps the issue of primary importance to applied cognitive aging researchers.

The cognitive training work has focused primarily on psychometric abilities, although the construct of reserve capacity has been theoretically framed to include other substantive areas of cognitive research. In fact, Baltes et al. (1984) noted that, although the construct has been confined largely to discussions of psychometric intelligence, an integration of this approach with mainstream views of the component processes of adult cognition would be welcome. In order to be useful to applied cognitive aging researchers, as well as to be integrated with other aspects of cognitive aging, the construct of reserve capacity requires more elaboration.

One problem is that little is known about how to measure plasticity or other qualities associated with reserve capacity. Thus far, the finding that individual behavior can be modified substantially in the elderly through cognitive training (Kliegl & Baltes, 1987; Willis et al., 1981; Willis & Schaie, 1986) has been used largely to demonstrate the existence of reserve capacity. Such a post hoc measurement strategy results in a circularity that precludes a definition of the construct that is independent of the behavior it allegedly predicts. Moreover, it is clear that there are substantial individual differences in modifiability of behavior in older adults, as Willis and Schaie reported. Willis and Schaie categorized subjects as being either "decliners" who showed a decrease in performance on inductive or spatial reasoning tasks over a 14-year period or "stables" who did not show declines over the same period. They found that a substantial number of both types of subjects failed to profit from extensive training. Thirty-four percent of the stables and 25.5% of the decliners did not improve on inductive reasoning after training, whereas 52.9% of stable subjects and 37.3% of decliner subjects showed no significant improvement from training on spatial orientation ($ns > 50$ for all conditions). This study points to how important it may be to determine residual plasticity in individuals as a measure of who is likely to be affected positively by training. Perhaps those individuals who did not improve had less reserve capacity or had actualized all that they had, or maybe there are manipulations that could have been effective, but the particular ones selected for these individuals were inadequate. In any case, the ability to successfully measure and predict who will profit from attempts to modify the cognitive system through training is of great pragmatic importance for applied cognitive aging research, as the resources required to implement cognitive training programs are substantial. As a caveat, measurement of such plasticity may prove to be an elusive goal, as have attempts to measure processing resources (Salthouse, 1988).

A second concern has to do with the structural and control aspects of reserve capacity. The usage of the construct to date has implied that reserve capacity is a fixed and stable general pool of untapped cognitive resources, typically available in lesser quantities in elderly compared to young adults (Kliegl & Baltes, 1987). At the same time, it is possible that reserve capacity is characterized by a number of specific multiple-ability pools, much as a number of domain-specific resource pools have been hypothesized to exist in working memory (Davies, Jones, & Taylor, 1984; Navon, 1984). If the multiple-reserves argument is correct, one might expect low correlations among the magnitude of improvement after training for different abilities or domains within individual subjects. Given a multiple-reserves scenario, the applied aging psychologist would need to be able to measure and differentiate specific reserves to determine if a particular older adult were a suitable candidate for modification of a particular cognitive behavior.

There are other issues that need to be elaborated for the construct of reserve capacity to reach fruition in an applied setting. These include specifying the relationship of reserve capacity to working memory, as well as ascertaining the stability of reserve capacity, which conceivably could fluctuate as a function of illness, arousal, and other variables, as Kahneman (1973) and Hasher and Zacks (1988) suggested to be the case for working memory. Indeed, Baltes and colleagues (Baltes et al., 1984; Baltes & Willes, 1982) emphasized repeatedly in their work that their results apply only to the healthy elderly, indirectly suggesting that illness (chronic or short-term) may reduce reserves. It also might be useful to explore the possibility that reserve capacity is some fixed proportion of overall cognitive ability. Indirect support for this hypothesis could be construed from the findings of age invariance for high-ability older adults on some text processing (Hultsch & Dixon, 1984), inference (Zacks, Hasher, Doren, Hamm, & Attig, 1987), and memory studies (Hess, 1984). If reserve capacity were in proportion to overall cognitive ability, the absolute amount of extra resources available to high-ability elderly to utilize in demanding situations would be greater, resulting in age invariance on moderately difficult tasks, such as those just noted. (The prediction of age decrements on very difficult tasks would remain, because reserves might not be sufficient to overcome such task requirements.) Also note that the aforementioned argument cannot be differentiated from evidence that high-ability older people have greater capacity in working memory (Hasher & Zacks, 1988).

Finally, the implication of training older adults routinely to maximize their use of reserve cognitive resources for health and well-being needs to be explored. Presumably cognitive reserves exist to permit the individual to adapt appropriately to cognitively stressful situations (much as physical reserves exist), so that training elderly adults to maximize cognitive resources for prolonged periods on a regular basis conceivably could have adverse consequences. Consider that many stressful situations in our daily environments are those that demand maximal cognitive resources for a prolonged period, and thus extended activation of reserve capacities (e.g., negotiating a complex traffic route in a foreign city in an unfamiliar rental car; presenting a new and important scientific talk to a highly critical audience; bringing a mildly sick toddler to work who requires attention and simultaneously attempting to carry out demanding professional duties). It seems improbable that repeatedly subjecting oneself to these types of cognitively demanding situations would be desirable or adaptive. Thus, it may be important to determine the relationship, if any, between the sustained use of reserve capacity in elderly adults to physical health and mental well-being. Alternatively, however, one could argue that the prolonged activation of reserve capacities might increase reserve capacities, much as regular cardiovascular workouts improve cardiovascular function. Either argument seems plausible. Studies addressing many of these issues would not be too difficult to design and implement and also would help to integrate the aging literature in psychometric/cognitive abilities with more traditional work on aging, comprehension, and memory. Baltes et al. (1984) suggested that this integration has been neglected. There are many recent attempts to improve specific memory behaviors through cognitive training (West, 1989; Yesavage et al., 1989), although as yet there has been little explicit linkage between the memory-training work and the issues raised in the present chapter. Given that a well-developed data base on memory training exists, this may be a logical place to begin the integration of these theoretical and practical issues with an area of applied cognitive aging research.

Age-Related Decline in Cognitive Function: Environmental Supports and Intraindividual Interventions

Although the cognitive training literature and the construct of reserve capacity emphasizes the residual plasticity that remains in the cognitive system with advanced age, mainstream theoretical views of cognitive and aging have emphasized various components of the cognitive system that have declined relative to young adults. In contrast to the cognitive training literature, research on the component processes of cognition has focused primarily on the understanding of age-related differences in processes and structures. As a result of this focus, there are several different theoretical accounts of underlying causes of age differences in cognitive function. Major theoretical frameworks suggest age decrements in cognition occur as a result of (a) limited mental energy or processing resources (Craik & Byrd, 1982), (b) age-related slowing (Salthouse, 1985a), or (c) dysfunctional inhibitory mechanisms (Hasher & Zacks, 1988). Each of these theoretical accounts provides clear directions for the applied cognitive aging psychologist, and they are considered in turn.

Before turning to theoretical explanations of age differences in cognition, however, it may be worthwhile to provide a broadbrush sketch of the empirical findings that generally characterize the aging cognitive system. As Plude and Hoyer (1985), Charness and Bosman (1990), Salthouse et al. (1988), and others noted, there is convincing evidence that most component processes of cognition decline with advanced age when the difficulty level is sufficient for effects to emerge. Processes that decline include attentional processes (Plude & Hoyer, 1985), working-memory capabilities (Foos, 1989), discourse comprehension (Light & Albertson, 1988), inference formation and interpretation (Cohen, 1979, 1981), and encoding and retrieval processes in memory (Kausler, 1982). At the same time, there are other areas that show age invariance or only small age differences, including semantic priming tasks (Howard, McAndrews, & Lasaga, 1981), picture recognition (Park, Puglisi, & Smith, 1986; Park, Royal, Dudley, & Morrell, 1988), implicit memory (Light & Singh, 1987), and prospective memory (Einstein & McDaniel, 1990). There are various explanations for such invariance. For example, Howard (1988) suggested priming is age invariant due to intact organizational structures, whereas Smith and Park (1990) suggested that it is the combined support of perceptual detail and semantic meaning that results in age invariance in memory for complex scenes. Tulving and Schacter (1990) argued that age invariance in implicit memory reflects the operation of an independent memory system. In addition to these basic memory tasks, there is evidence that older adults' performance on highly practiced expert skills can match that of young adults on tasks that include typing (Salthouse, 1984), bridge playing (Charness, 1983), and chess playing (Charness, 1981a, 1981b). The underlying mechanisms responsible for the preserved functioning on these very different tasks are not well understood and almost certainly differ across tasks. The resistance of highly practiced or expert behaviors to age-related decline is discussed in detail by Salthouse (1987a, 1987b, 1990b). Empirical findings of age invariance are of potential importance to applied cognitive aging researchers in directing them toward effective interventions, an issue that is discussed further later on.

Limited Processing Resources. This hypothesis (Craik & Byrd, 1982) suggests that elderly adults show declines on cognitive tasks when compared to young adult controls due to a diminished pool of mental energy that governs controlled (Schneider & Shiffrin, 1977) or effortful (Hasher & Zacks, 1979) cognitive processes in working memory. Age differences become manifest on cognitive tasks that require a substantial amount of cognitive resources, or self-initiated processing (Craik, 1986; Rabinowitz, Craik, & Ackerman, 1982). Examples of tasks that require a high commitment of resources would be those in which the encoding or retrieving of information occurs when there is little contextual support present. Of particular interest to applied cognitive aging researchers is the environmental support hypothesis (Craik, 1983, 1986) which, based on the limited resource account, suggests that age differences are smallest on cognitive tasks when encoding and retrieval support is provided, typically either in the form of contextual cues or through a resource limiting encoding or retrieval operation (e.g., recognition is less resource intensive than recall). The environmental support hypothesis has received some confirmation in the experimental literature. Craik and McDowd (1987) reported that as the amount of mental effort required at retrieval decreased from cued recall to recognition, age differences decreased. Moreover, other work has suggested that contextual or environmental cues can be highly supportive of memory in older adults. For example, Shaw and Craik (1989) found increasingly elaborate verbal contextual cues resulted in smaller age differences in memory for target items associated with the cues. Also, Park, Smith, Morrell, Puglisi, and Dudley (1990) found that older adults' memory for pictures benefited more than young adults when the pictures were presented with highly integrative semantic cues when compared to an unrelated cuing condition. Sharps and Gollin (1987, 1988) reported that both spatial and object memory was facilitated more in older adults than young adults by a distinctive context, although Park, Cherry, Smith, and Lafronza (1990) were unable to replicate this age-by-context interaction for either spatial or object memory (however, see Sharps [1991] for follow-up work that provides partial confirmation of his original finding).

Craik and Simon (1980) and Rabinowitz et al.(1982) also proposed that, due to limited processing resources, older adults are less sensitive to highly specific contextual stimuli, resulting in the breakdown of the encoding specificity principle (Tulving & Thomson, 1973) for older adults. If correct, this hypothesis would suggest that only a certain type of context (general, semantically related cues) could be used to support the memories of older adults. However, several studies have provided evidence for equivalent facilitation for young and old by both specific and general semantic contexts (Park, Puglisi, Smith, & Dudley, 1987; Puglisi, Park, Smith, & Dudley, 1988), confirming the validity of the encoding specificity principle for both young and elderly. It seems clear that context can provide potent support for cognitive processes in young and elderly adults and likely provides a means of facilitating cognitive processes in applied settings.

Thus, the environmental support hypothesis suggests that provision of cognitive supports or aids that minimize the use of processing resources is likely to be an effective means of reducing differences in cognition between young and elderly adults. Moreover, the findings of age invariance cited earlier may provide important clues as to the nature or form that supportive interventions might take. For example, the finding of age invariance for complex picture recognition (Park et al., 1986; Smith, Park, Cherry, & Berkovsky, 1990) suggests that information presented in a pictorial format, when possible, would be likely to provide effective memory support for elderly adults, possibly because fewer processing resources are required to encode and retrieve complex pictures relative to their verbal analogs. The finding that older adults can comprehend discourse without difficulty when inferences are stated directly (Zacks et al., 1987), but have problems when they must form the inferences, suggests that instructions that explicitly present material rather than requiring subtle inferences would better support processing of complex verbal material by older adults. Many other examples will suggest themselves to readers who are familiar with basic research findings in the cognitive aging literature. In general, little attention has been devoted to studying ways to reduce processing-resource requirements in the everyday environment to facilitate comprehension and memory of elderly adults. Because environmental interventions to support cognitions of the type described provide a passive form of support, and typically require no training of any type to be of use to older adults, they are inexpensive and broadly applicable interventions. It is unlikely that young or older adults even would notice the use of such subtle support systems.

The resources account of age-related deficits also suggests that an alternative way to improve some categories of cognitive behaviors in older adults might be through automatization of the components of complex behaviors (Plude & Hoyer, 1985), so that fewer resources then are required to perform the behaviors or to remember the information (Hasher & Zacks, 1979; Schneider & Shiffrin, 1977). The findings regarding age differences in the automatization of component behaviors, however, are mixed. Plude and Hoyer concluded that "elderly adults are capable of developing automatic target detection responses at a rate comparable to that of young adults" (p. 68). Recently, however, Fisk, McGee, and Giambra (1988) presented evidence suggesting that older adults are much slower than young people to acquire automatization of even consistent mapping responses, despite more than 8,000 trials of practice. In a consistent mapping paradigm, the same items are presented repeatedly and maintain their identity as targets or nontargets. Fisk et al. suggested that a primary cause of age differences in cognitive function may be the disproportionately slowed rate at which the cognitive components of a task become automatized for old compared to young adults. Certainly, further study is required in this area. If it is the case that the elderly do experience slowed automatization of responses, it will require relatively more training for an elderly adult to free up limited processing resources through automatizing a behavior with practice. At the same time, the potential gain to be realized by automatizing and thus freeing up scarce resources could be greater for older than for younger adults.

It also should be noted that there are many problems with resource accounts of cognitive aging. The most vexing aspect of this approach has been the difficulty that researchers have had in specifying and measuring cognitive resources, and then relating this measured quantity to performance. Salthouse (1985b) and Light (1991) provided particularly cogent discussions of these issues. Despite the problem with this approach, the resources analogy has been a useful construct in directing cognitive aging research and may be of particular importance in the early development of applied cognitive aging research.

Age-Related Slowing. A second major theoretical perspective with implications for applied cognitive aging research is the hypothesis that age-related cognitive declines are a result of a reduction in the speed at which information is processed in the cognitive system with advanced age (Salthouse, 1985a). The phenomenon of age-related slowing of behavior is perhaps the best documented and least contested of any in the field of cognition and aging, although different mechanisms have been suggested as the underlying cause of slowing (see Salthouse, 1985a). Regardless of the underlying cause, the slowing phenomenon does lend itself to recommendations for interventions and training programs. It is obvious that the hypothesis suggests that it may be of critical importance to allow sufficient time for older adults to process events or information, and that this could minimize age differences in applied settings. Age differences only would be minimized with this approach, however, when there was a well-specified criterion that older adults had been unable to meet primarily due to time limitations. In situations involving difficult, ill-defined problems, providing unlimited time for solution could result in young adults' speeded cognitive operations, maximizing, rather than minimizing, age differences. In support of this point, it should be noted that age differences remain on many cognitive tasks, even when pacing is slowed (Arenberg, 1967) or when subjects have been permitted unlimited time to learn (Morrell, Park, & Poon, 1989, 1990). Thus, it is improbable that slowed stimulus pacing or permitting unlimited time for cognitive operations will eliminate entirely age-related changes in cognitive function.

Of particular interest to applied cognitive aging research, is the complexity hypothesis proposed by Cerella, Poon, and Williams (1980). They suggested that, due to central slowing, age differences increase as the complexity of a cognitive task increases. This suggests that great attention must be paid to the timing aspects when elderly adults are placed in complex situations where speeded responding is required. One everyday situation with such requirements occurs when one approaches a complex traffic interchange on a freeway at a relatively high speed. Little time is allotted to make appropriate choices so that particular care must be devoted to the signage and design of such intersections if they are to be successfully negotiated by elderly adults. Charness and Bosman (1990; see also chapter 10 in this volume) presented a comprehensive set of estimated values for many components of information-processing tasks that will contribute greatly to the development of appropriate interfaces between elderly and their environment, particularly when speeded decisions are required or only a limited amount of time to process information is available (as in signage).

The alternative to adapting the environment to accommodate the slowed behavior of elderly adults is to attempt to effect intraindividual change by enhancing speed in the elderly. There are a number of studies that have demonstrated that training improves reaction times in older adults (Berg, Hertzog, & Hunt, 1982; Madden, 1983; Madden & Nebes, 1980; Salthouse & Somberg, 1982). (Consult Salthouse, 1990b, for a summary table of the effects of practice on speeded behaviors in young and old.) Nevertheless, in these studies, age differences in speed have remained, after even 50 hr of practice (Salthouse & Somberg, 1982). Thus, it seems clear that practice is unlikely to reduce age differences in speed to the point that old adults begin to perform like young adults who also have received training. Once again, however, the important point for applied work may be merely that practice or training improves speed in older adults.

Failure to Inhibit. The final theoretical framework to be considered was proposed recently by Hasher and Zacks (1988). Hasher and Zacks suggested that, rather than suffering from decreased processing resources, older adults have faulty inhibitory mechanisms in working memory. Due to these inefficient inhibitory processes, older adults attend to irrelevant contextual detail and have faulty interpretations of context; they also engage in more personal internal musings peripherally related to context and target events. As a result, the content of working memory is different for old compared to young adults, with the working memories of older adults containing more irrelevant information which detracts from the processing of target information. Evidence for this view is demonstrated by the increase in Stroop interference effects with age (Cohn, Dustman, & Bradford, 1984), and larger age differences for inconsistent or varied mapping paradigms where stimulus and response choices are unpredictable compared to predictable or consistent mapping (Plude & Hoyer, 1985). Also, Hasher, Stoltzfus, Zacks, and Rypma (1991) recently found that older adults showed less inhibition in a negative priming paradigm when compared to young adults. Due to the relative recency of this hypothesis, there is not a large amount of research that directly addresses Hasher and Zacks's hypothesis or the conditions under which the hypothesis applies. If correct, the failure to inhibit hypothesis has many implications for applied settings. In designing environments for older adults or designing information to be presented to them, it should be assumed that the older adult will be highly distractible and easily captured by competing sources of information.

There is some evidence that older adults find irrelevant information in the memory environment more distracting than do young adults (Kausler & Kleim, 1978) and also that irrelevant information inhibits performance on a card-sorting task (Rabbitt, 1965) and on concept formation problems (Hoyer, Rebok, & Sved, 1979). Studies are needed to investigate whether irrelevant sources of information (such as might occur in a busy office environment with a number of workers using computers and telephones) are in fact especially disruptive to elderly adults. One study that addressed such issues in the laboratory was conducted by Park, Smith, Dudley, and Lafronza (1989). They investigated the effects of requiring subjects to process distracting digits while encoding or retrieving words, using free recall and cued recall. They found evidence for an interaction between age and encoding but not age and retrieval. In other words, the requirement that older subjects attend to an irrelevant task at encoding disrupted their memory disproportionately, but their retrieval performance was no more disrupted by distraction than it was in young adults. This study did not provide a direct test of the Hasher and Zacks (1988) argument, however, because, unlike the real world where we attempt to ignore irrelevant information, subjects were required to attend to the distraction. Future basic research on age differences in the effects of truly irrelevant distraction on various component behaviors of cognition is required before further extrapolation to the applied level can occur. It may be particularly informative to determine how different types of distracting information may interact with age and encoding and retrieval operations. For example, young adults may be distracted at encoding only by stimuli that are highly related or integrated with the target information, whereas old adults may be distracted by any type of irrelevant information, even material presented in different modalities or that is unrelated to the target. Finally, the implications of the Hasher and Zacks argument for the structuring of signage, instructions, and other written materials (in terms of both structural and semantic aspects of the information presented) is substantial, but little is known about what types of information and formats would improperly focus older adults' attention (although, see Mergler & Zandi, 1983; also see Kline, Ghali, Kline, & Brown, 1990). Because the failure to inhibit hypothesis makes many predictions that have applicability to real-world problems and it requires much further empirical work, this theoretical framework may be a fertile ground for conducting applied cognitive aging research with both theoretical and practical implications.

METHODOLOGICAL ISSUES

Control Groups

Whether or not one should include a young adult control group in an applied cognitive aging study should be determined by the question the study is designed to answer. The failure to include a range of ages in a study will limit the contributions of the study toward a theoretical understanding of age differences. At the same time, the applied researcher should recognize that the classic young adult–old adult cross-sectional comparison may not be the most useful life-span comparison. Comparisons between young-old and old-old adults may be more informative and could have the advantage of minimizing the magnitude of cohort effects (if one assumes cohort effects are greater with larger period differences), as age comparisons would span approximately 20 years as opposed to 50 years. Understanding changes into late adulthood may be of particular interest to the applied psychologist as declines in behaviors that dip below some critical level for adequate functioning in the community are more likely to occur in the old-old. Moreover, little is known about differentiation of behavior in very late adulthood from earlier phases. Applied cognitive aging research should be viewed as successful to the extent that it moves older adults closer to some target or criterion behavior, independent of where younger adults fall on this criterion behavior. Thus, including a young adult control group may not enhance our understanding of the solution of real-world problems with cognitive components for the elderly. The important issue is not whether an older adult can be improved to the level of young adulthood, but whether functioning can be maintained at a sufficient level to maintain productivity of the older adult and to permit self-care and prevent institutionalization.

Sampling Issues

Charness and Bosman (1990) pointed out that it is frequently the frail elderly who are most in need of cognitive interventions to help them perform tasks such as understanding instructions, remembering to take medications, learning how to do banking by a computer, and so forth. Thus, the findings from the basic literature on typically healthy, elderly samples may not generalize to this group. The frail elderly are likely to evidence increased variability relative to healthier samples, and for this reason, larger samples of these groups may be required. Moreover, the particular type of intervention a researcher decides to implement may vary as a function of the elderly sample under consideration. In support of these points, Craik, Byrd, and Swanson (1987) reported a series of important findings. They collected data on free-recall, paired-associate learning, and word generation from young adults and three groups of elderly adults—affluent, active elderly; vigorous, active low-income elderly; and less active, low-income elderly. They also varied the degree of contextual support available to subjects on the memory tasks. The results are shown in Table 9.1 and can be used to make a number of important points. First, there is a monotonic increase in performance on all of the tasks as a function of sample type, with the less active elderly performing most poorly, followed by the affluent, active elderly, and then young groups. Second, on word recall, as environmental support increases (from free-free to cued-cued), performance increases. Of most interest is the interaction of sample type with environmental support. The magnitude of facilitation of the support is largest for the disadvantaged, inactive elderly (from 2.4 to 5.5 words, more than a 100% increase) and smallest for young adults (6.0 to 7.8 words). The finding that passive intervention (contextual support) is of greatest help to groups that initially are performing most poorly is of great practical importance for applied research, particularly given that the cognitive training work has focused primarily on high-functioning healthy elderly people. An important applied study would be to compare the effects of training active, internal strategies to the effects of passive, contextual supports on groups of advantaged compared to disadvantaged and/or frail elderly adults. One might predict greater effectiveness of active internal strategies for the active, healthy, financially secure elderly, and that environmental support strategies might be more effective for those older adults less advantaged on these dimensions.

Mechanisms for Facilitation

It is important to be clear on how a researcher expects that the training or environmental intervention introduced will improve cognitive performance. Passive environmental supports are likely to be compensatory in nature; that is, they will reduce cognitive demands rather than improve the declining component behavior within the individual. Another approach may be to improve a behavior through remediation, that is, by training a declining behavior back to its original level by acting on the

TABLE 9.1
Mean Recall as a Function of Sample and Support

	Low-Income Inactive Elderly	Low-Income Active Elderly	Upper Income Active Elderly	Young Active Adult
Cued-Cued	5.5	7.3	8.1	7.8
Cued-Free	2.2	5.4	5.8	5.6
Free-Cued	2.2	4.5	5.3	5.8
Free-Free	2.4	4.6	4.7	6.0

component processes accounting for the decline. If a researcher were to select remediation as a strategy, it would likely involve a methodology that operated on the component processes of cognition rather than focused on a molar behavior. Encapsulation or compilation is another approach (Hoyer, 1985) that involves the automatization of large, complex chunks of behavior. Little research exists on whether encapsulation can be used for acquisition of complex novel behaviors in the elderly, although it appears from the data of Fisk et al. (1988) and others that the greatly increased time required to encapsulate complex behaviors in the elderly might make this an unlikely strategy for new behavior. In any case, clarity on the part of the researcher with respect to the underlying mechanism of improvement will help specify and refine intervention designs. Salthouse (1987a, 1987b) discussed these issues in some detail, particularly the difficulty of determining the underlying mechanisms affected by improvements in performance through interventions.

Generalization of Effects

Does the researcher expect to influence behavior at the level of a general ability factor, or is the improvement in cognition expected to be task specific? A researcher who selects passive environmental support as an intervention should recognize that because such intervention typically is tied to a specific stimulus context, it is likely that the intervention will exert an effect only on a particular behavior. A researcher who wants to generalize a behavior (e.g., improving general way-finding abilities) might be advised to select a training design. In the event that an experimenter wishes to effect a change in general cognitive ability, there are many complex theoretical and methodological issues to consider. Willis (1989) discussed the importance of collecting multiple measures of behavior to demonstrate the training influence on a latent ability, as well as the implications of demonstrating near and far transfer in such designs. Some researchers do use training designs to improve only a specific skill, such as improvement of remembering names and faces (Yesavage et al., 1983), so that multiple measurement of behavior to demonstrate change in a latent ability factor is unnecessary. Nevertheless, because older adults appear to be highly sensitive to contextual manipulations, researchers should take care to demonstrate that training effects demonstrated in the laboratory do generalize beyond the boundaries of the laboratory. If older adults are unable to manifest improvements in everyday social situations (where processing resources may be more limited due to distractions and high levels of arousal), contextually bound improvements in cognitive behaviors would not be very useful.

Laboratory Effects in the Real World

A variable that exerts a powerful influence in a relatively sterile laboratory situation, where an elderly individual's processing resources likely are focused exclusively on the cognitive task at hand, may have a much weaker effect in the real world. A classic demonstration of this occurs with the principle of encoding specificity (Tulving & Thomson, 1973), which states that compatibility between encoding and retrieval contexts produces better memory than different contexts. Although encoding specificity is demonstrated easily with word or picture pairs in the laboratory (Park, Puglisi, & Sovacool, 1984; Puglisi et al., 1988; Rabinowitz et al., 1982), attempts to produce encoding specificity by manipulating aspects of the room in which the material is encoded and retrieved have been comparatively unsuccessful (Bjork & Richardson-Klavehn, 1989; Fernandez & Glenberg, 1985). Bjork and Richardson-Klavehn outlined a number of reasons for this, but one particularly important point relevant to applied cognitive research is that contextual variables that are highly salient in the laboratory may be less salient when translated into the real world. The cognitive aging researcher, therefore, may wish to use larger samples to offset power problems, as well as to consider carefully what level of facilitation would be practically significant. The amount of variability controlled by manipulations considered to be powerful by cognitive psychologists may not be of sufficient magnitude to have meaningful effects on real-world behaviors.

MODELS OF APPLIED COGNITIVE AGING RESEARCH

In the next two sections, the evolution and development of applied research in specific domains are detailed to present a concrete example of many of the issues and problems faced by applied cognitive aging researchers. The first topic is highly focused and addresses the cognitive components associated with taking medications; it also emphasizes the contributions that applied cognitive aging work can make to understanding health behaviors in the elderly. The second domain is directed toward productivity and vitality, focusing on cognitive factors affecting the older adult in the workplace. In this second section, the implications of different theoretical frameworks for work and productivity are discussed, and diverse areas of applied cognitive research that have implications for the workplace are integrated.

MEDICATION ADHERENCE: A PROBLEM FOR APPLIED COGNITIVE AGING RESEARCHERS

The Problem of Medication Nonadherence

Medication nonadherence can be defined as using medication incorrectly—taking extra doses, taking the wrong dosage, taking medication at the wrong time, or omitting dosages entirely. The statistics regarding medication adherence leave little doubt that it is a substantial problem for older adults. Data from the World Health Organization (1981) indicate that approximately 50% of all prescription drugs are consumed by elderly adults, with 34% of older people taking three or more prescriptions on a daily basis. Estimates of nonadherence rates for medication in the elderly are high. Kendrick and Bayne (1982) reported a nonadherence rate of 43% whereas Kiernan and Isaacs (1981) estimated nonadherence in the elderly to be 40%. Recent data collected with electronic monitoring techniques suggest that no more than 70%–75% of medication is taken, regardless of how convenient the dosage schedule (Cramer, Scheyer, & Mattson, 1990). Although medication nonadherence rates are high and equal in both young and old, it is likely that the underlying causes of nonadherence may be different for the two age groups (Morrell et al., 1989), with cognitive factors playing a more substantial role for old compared to young adults. One way to approach the study of medication adherence is to consider the cognitive components of the behavior and to examine age differences in each component. It would appear that adherence to a medication regimen has four major cognitive components, as adherence requires that the individual (a) understand the instructions presented on the individual prescription containers for taking the medication (comprehension); (b) be able to integrate the instructions and timing of dosages for each of the different prescriptions across the 24-hour day period (a working-memory task); (c) remember (or write down) the schedule for the daily regimen (long-term memory); and (d) actually remember to take the medication at the appropriate time (prospective memory).

A Conceptual Model for Understanding Adherence Behaviors

It is also important to recognize that a thorough understanding of adherence behaviors can occur only if patients' beliefs and attitudes are taken into account regarding both their illness and the efficacy of the medication. Because we are dealing with a complex real-world behavior, studying the cognitive system independent of a patient's beliefs will yield an incomplete understanding of this multifaceted behavior. It seems reasonable to postulate that individuals who do not think they are sick, or who do not believe a medication will help a particular illness, are unlikely to adhere to the regimen, regardless of how well their cognitive system functions. Leventhal and Cameron (1987), in recognition of the importance of beliefs and attitudes, proposed a self-regulatory model to understand adherence behaviors. The patient is viewed as a problem solver in a dynamic environment who develops a representation of his or her illness. The patient develops a plan of action for dealing with the illness (which may include adherence to medications), and then appraises the success of this effort and readjusts behavior as appropriate. Memory/comprehension variables play an important role in predicting adherence behaviors, once an illness representation has been generated, particularly for older adults. A research group (consisting of D. Park, D. Birchmore, C. Hertzog, H. Leventhal, and R. Morrell) developed a conceptual model for understanding the interplay among disease, psychosocial, and cognitive factors in predicting adherence (see Fig. 9.1). The conceptual model suggests that a number of psychosocial variables, disease, and medication factors predict the nature of an individual's illness representation. Once this representation has been developed, appropriate cognitive abilities (hypothesized to be of disproportionate importance for the elderly) are necessary to implement a decision to adhere. Social support also may affect adherence directly, as significant others may serve as effective memory aids. The model also suggests that there is a positive relationship between adherence and subjective well-being. The dynamic nature of the adherence process is represented by the arrows leading from adherence and well-being back to patient beliefs, as unsatisfactory health and well-being may result in a readjustment of the illness representation. This proposed conceptual model was developed with the hope of facilitating specific, theory-based multidisciplinary hypotheses and research that ultimately will test the adequacy of the whole model.

Cognition, Aging, and Adherence

For the purposes of the present discussion on applied cognitive aging, we focus on the part of the model that describes relationships among aging, cognitive variables, and adherence. In order to understand the cog-

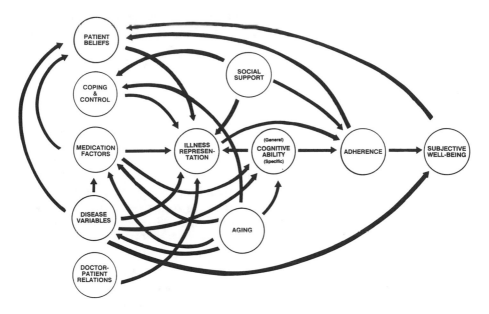

FIG. 9.1. A conceptual model for medication adherence that integrates illness representation with age and cognition function.

nitive aging component of medication adherence, it is useful to begin in the laboratory to determine if there are age-related differences in the four components of medication cognition.

Long-Term Memory for Medication Information.   The earliest work on memory for medication information was conducted by Ley and colleagues (Ley, 1979; Ley et al., 1976). Ley concluded that recall of medication information can be improved by the use of simple language, categorization, repetition, and the use of concrete advice statements. Information that is perceived to be important is remembered better, as is information presented early on. Ley et al. also reported that age did correlate with increased forgetting of information. In a similar vein, Page, Verstraete, Robb, and Etzwiler (1981) found that of seven recommendations made to diabetic patients, only two were remembered on average. Morrell et al. (1989) demonstrated substantial age effects in memory for medication information, regardless of whether subjects had unlimited or experimenter-controlled study time. When permitted unlimited study time, older adults studied for shorter periods (although not a significant difference) than did young, suggesting that they did not compensate for age-related declines in the component processes of cognition by studying longer. Little is known about older adults' long-term memory for their personal drug regimen. It is possible that the age effects observed in the laboratory might be smaller or entirely absent if personal medications had been studied.

Prospective Memory and Adherence.   The literature is sparse on age differences in prospective memory—remembering to perform future actions. There is some debate as to whether age differences in prospective memory exist at all. A recent, laboratory-based study conducted by Einstein and McDaniel (1990) showed a lack of age differences in prospective memory, even when multiple measures of memory were obtained. Until recently, it has been difficult to accurately measure the relatively private act of taking medication outside the laboratory in order to study the prospective component of medication adherence. In the past, the most commonly relied-upon measures for studying adherence behaviors have been verbal reports and pill counting, both of which are unreliable measures and do not permit inferences as to the timing of doses, nor can occasional omissions compensated for by later commissions be detected. Correcting for some of these problems, Leirer, Morrow, Pariante, and Sheikh (1988) monitored elderly adults' adherence behaviors on a pseudodrug regimen using microelectronic barcoding technology. Subjects were given small credit-card size scanning devices along with bar codes for four different imaginary drugs. Each drug had instructions about how and when to take the medications and subjects were told to scan the bar code for each medication at the time they were to take this pseudodrug. The results indicated that a significant number of adherence errors were made, but those subjects who had received specific medication training performed better than a group that received general memory training. In a later study that used similar techniques, Leirer, Morrow, Tanke, and Pariante (1991) found that adherence performance was significantly related to recognition vocabulary performance, suggesting cognitive ability factors may be important in understanding adherence. Because only old adults were tested in both studies, age hypotheses were not addressed. It is also not clear from these studies whether the nonadherence was due to prospective failures in memory, or to problems in comprehension and working or long-term memory. Prospective remembering could be isolated in future studies by examining subsets of subjects who show comprehension and memory for a drug regimen and who also indicate that they intend to take all of their medication if they can remember to do so.

Improvement of Medication Adherence

The approach that one might take to improving adherence depends on the particular component of medication cognition that the experimenter wishes to improve, as well as on the theoretical orientation with respect to training and environmental supports. Medication cognition research is still in its infancy, but various interventions recently have been explored. The most favored approach to date has emphasized the use of passive techniques that require little or no training to use, primarily in the form of restructured information or cognitive prostheses that minimize for elderly subjects the comprehension, working-memory, and long-term memory components of medication adherence.

Restructuring Information. One obvious way to facilitate memory and comprehension of medication information for the older adult is to restructure the information appropriately so that it is more readily understood and remembered, relying on knowledge from basic laboratory research to direct the nature of the restructuring. Morrow, Leirer, and Sheikh (1988) provided a virtual blueprint for researchers interested in addressing these issues. They argued that instructions should be designed to facilitate the development of a mental model for the steps involved in taking medications. Their recommendations include organizing the information in a standard list format, use of graphics when appropriate, use of simple language, avoidance of negatives and inferences, and other such recommendations that logically follow from the cognitive aging literature.

In line with Morrow et al.'s (1988) recommendations, Morrell et al. (1989) reported that standardized labels that presented information explicitly with no inferences required were comprehended and remembered better by both young and elderly adults than was information taken from an actual patient's chart in a hospital pharmacy. Given the finding of age invariance for picture recognition (Park et al., 1986; Smith, Park, Cherry, & Berkovsky, in press), Morrell et al. (1990) hypothesized that labels that presented medication pictorially might differentially improve older adults' memory for the information. Two previous studies had reported that labels with pictorial components were facilitative for individuals with limited education or vision (Eustace, Johnson, & Gault, 1982; Meisel & Kiely, 1981). In the Morrell et al. study, young and old adults were presented with well-organized verbal labels (similar to those used in Morrell et al., 1989) or labels that presented medication information in a mixed pictorial/verbal format and were asked to remember the information (shown in Fig. 9.2). The main finding was that label format interacted with age, but in an unexpected manner. Young adults made more mistakes on the verbal labels (.30) compared to the pictorial (.14), whereas older adults showed more forgetting with pictorial labels (.63) than with verbal labels (.55). Comprehension was poorer for older adults but did not interact with label condition. These findings suggest that the mixed format is not an efficient way to present the information for older adults.

EXAMPLES OF VERBAL AND MIXED LABELS

VERBAL LABEL   MIXED LABEL

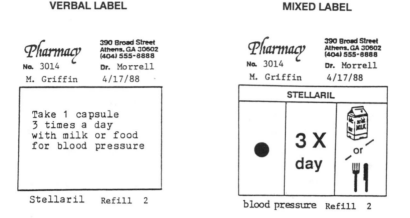

FIG. 9.2.   Examples of verbal and verbal/pictorial labels. Adapted from Morrell, Park, & Poon (1990), with permission.

Perhaps the transformation of the picture/word format into a single compatible representation required sufficient processing resources that older adults were disadvantaged. Nevertheless, the finding that label format does interact with age suggests that this line of research may be worth pursuing further. Moreover, the study does not address the issue of whether the mixed labels are superior to labels as they are dispensed from a typical pharmacy (which seems likely), as performance was compared in this condition to optimally designed verbal labels used in the 1989 study.

One question that remains from the research on improved structuring of information is whether there is a direct relationship between adherence behaviors and improved instructions. It is important to show this direct linkage if major changes are to be effected in the wording of drug prescriptions and instructions that accompany medications.

External Cognitive Prostheses.   There have been other attempts to improve medication adherence in elderly adults by providing them with external supports for various aspects of medication or health cognition. Such external aids do not alter the cognitive system but provide support for one or more of the components of medications cognition specified earlier. Leirer, Morrow, Pariante, and Doksum (1989) focused on the prospective component of adherence. They compared postcard reminders about an influenza vaccine to other reminder techniques, using an older adult sample. Computer voice mail increased adherence from 1.5% in the postcard condition to 11.8%. Subjects who received voice mail as well as additional verbal and posted reminders showed an adherence rate of 37.5%. It is difficult to separate the effects of multiple reminders from voice-mail reminders in these data, but the data do indicate that computer-generated reminders, particularly used in combination with other reminders, are an effective memory support to improve health-seeking behaviors in older adults. In a later study which used the barcoding techniques to measure adherence, Leirer et al. 1991 reported that a teleminder system substantially improved adherence for pseudomedications in the elderly, but it was not entirely clear if this was due to improving prospective or organizational/comprehension components of cognition.

As most readers undoubtedly have noted, there are a number of memory aids for taking medication that are available without prescription at most drugstores. These typically take the form of partitioned containers of various shapes and complexity in which medications can be organized and loaded. Presumably, these containers are marketed to facilitate adherence, particularly to complex regimens. It is essential, however, for safe usage of the medication organizers, that consumers be able to load them correctly. To determine if this was likely, Park, Morrell, Frieske, Blackburn, and Birchmore (1991) tested the ability of arthritis patients (aged 35–75 years) to correctly load their own medication in three types of containers, displayed in Fig. 9.3. The main results, shown in Fig. 9.4, indicated that errors were particularly high for the 7-day organizer without times. This organizer merely has seven slots (one for each day of the week) for a patient to drop in all pills for a day's medication. Consider that once the pills are placed in such an organizer, a subject no longer has any information about the pill's name or instructions on when or how to take them. Thus, initial errors in loading are likely to be compounded by additional errors in recognition of medication, long-term, and prospective memory. Although further investigation certainly is warranted, the data suggest that only the 7-day organizer with times appears to be loaded correctly by arthritis patients, and thus has the potential to be an effective environmental support. This organizer, after it is correctly loaded, supports three of the four components of medication cognition. Subjects' comprehension and organization of their medication regimen would be facilitated by a loaded organizer. In addition, by physically presenting the medication in the order it is to be taken, the organizer also relieves subjects of remembering the medication-taking plan that they develop.

To pursue more directly the effects of the 7-day with times organizer on adherence behaviors, Park, Morrell, Blackburn, Frieske, and Birch-

SCHEMATICS OF THREE TYPES OF
ORGANIZERS USED IN STUDY

7-Day with Times Organizer

SUN	•	MON	•	TUE	•	WED	•	THU	•	FRI	•	SAT
MORN	MORN	MORN	MORN	MORN	MORN	MORN
NOON	NOON	NOON	NOON	NOON	NOON	NOON
EVE	EVE	EVE	EVE	EVE	EVE	EVE
BED	BED	BED	BED	BED	BED	BED

7-Day without Times Organizer

S M T W T F S

Wheel Organizer

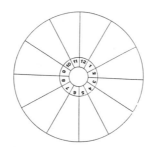

FIG. 9.3.   Examples of different medication organizers. Adapted from Park,
Morrell, Frieske, Blackburn, & Birchmore (1990) with permission.

more (1989) followed the actual medication-taking behaviors of 15 rheumatoid arthritis patients (mean age of 52.5 years) for 3 weeks. They used
the barcode-monitoring technique of Leirer et al. (1988, in press) and
provided some evidence that a 7-day with times organizer facilitated adherence to subjects' personal medication-taking strategies. In a later study
with 64 older adults, Park, Morrell, Frieske, and Kincaid (in press) reported that the medication organizers when combined with organizational
charts significantly facilitated adherence behaviors of old-old adults.
Young-old adults did not improve their already high degree of adherence.
Of particular interest was the finding that old-old adults made significantly
more adherence errors than did young-old adults. The data from both
of these studies also indicated that a substantial number of older adults

The Effect of type of Organizer
On Errors Loading Organizer

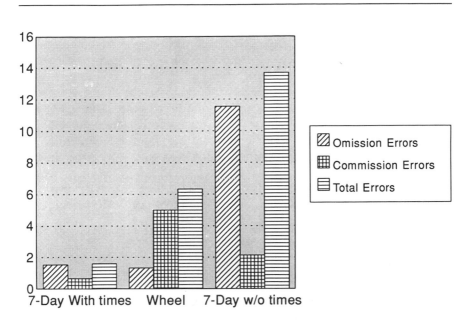

FIG. 9.4. Omission, commission, and total errors made in loading organizer as a function of type medication organizer. Adapted from Park et al. (1991) with permission.

are highly adherent, even with complex medication regimens, so that it may be wise to restrict the examination of interventions in future studies to only those evidencing some criterion level of nonadherence.

There are many cognitive prostheses that could be introduced to improve adherence behaviors beyond the ones discussed here. Most would require little training for patients to use and little is known about their effectiveness. Wristwatch devices programmed to beep when medication should be taken would affect only the prospective component—perhaps these would be equally helpful to young and older adults. The effects of written, organized regimens that integrate information across a 24-hour period, alleviating working-memory concerns, are not well understood. There is much potential for sound applied cognitive aging research to be conducted in this area, particularly given the recent advances in measurement of adherence behaviors that have occurred.

Training Interventions. There are a number of studies that have examined the effects of providing patients with more detailed knowledge about their illness and medications on adherence behaviors (Feinberg,

1988; Winfield & Task Force on Arthritis Patient Education, 1989). In general, the literature suggests that such patient education improves adherence, but the measurement of adherence has not been rigorous. Leirer et al. (1988), using rigorous measurement techniques, did demonstrate improvement in remembering a pseudodrug regimen with a multifaceted training program that emphasized understanding and organizing the regimen, as well as prospective memory training. It is not possible to determine what aspect of the training was most important and which cognitive components were particularly affected, but the study does seem to indicate that such training would be helpful to older adults. There is little additional research of this nature that has approached the problem from a theoretical cognitive perspective. It may be that training is a less fruitful approach for improving medication cognition due to the time involved and individualized instruction required compared to providing subjects with personal organizers, charts, and other cognitive prostheses. On the other hand, the relative costs/benefits of such interventions remain unknown due to the lack of available research.

COGNITION AND PRODUCTIVITY IN THE OLDER WORKER: MAINTENANCE AND ACQUISITION OF SKILLS

Let us now focus our discussion on the relationships among aging, cognition, and productivity in the workplace. There is little doubt that the component behaviors comprising cognition decline across the life span. Yet as Salthouse (1990a) and others have noted, older adults frequently hold positions where great demands are placed upon them, particularly in the area of public office and statesmanship. In this next section, I examine the relationship between aging and productivity and then develop a conceptual framework for studying aging, cognition, and work. Following this, theoretical views of cognitive aging are related to the framework, mechanisms for general facilitation of cognition are discussed, and methodological considerations are reviewed.

Age, Experience, and Productivity in the Workplace

There is some evidence that older adults' work behaviors are perceived more negatively than those of young adults (Avolio & Waldman, 1989; Rosen & Jerdee, 1976), and that the age of the rater may interact with the age of the ratee (Cleveland & Landy, 1981). Of even greater importance is the relationship between age and actual job performance. Rhodes (1983) reviewed 183 studies and found evidence for positive, negative, and no relationships between age and job performance. She was unable to determine a mediating variable for these relationships, such as differences in occupations, or differences in experience. Waldman and Avolio (1986) adopted a meta-analytic as opposed to a qualitative approach in an effort to determine the relationship more precisely. Using data from 13 studies, they reported that productivity was weakly but positively related to age for both professional and nonprofessional positions. This was particularly the case when objective rather than rating measures of productivity were used, although their data did not permit them to examine the moderating role of experience. McEvoy and Cascio (1989) carried out a meta-analysis on 96 studies, representing over 38,000 subjects. They reported no significant relationship between age and performance, even when type of performance measure and type of job was examined.

As Griew (1970) noted, however, the conclusion that there is no relationship between age and job performance in these studies may be unwarranted due to selective attrition of less able subjects from the sample at the older ages, a point also made by McEvoy and Cascio (1989). According to Griew, it is likely that any studies of this sort underestimate the negative effects of aging on work behavior. Because age is confounded with experience, determining the relationship between these variables and performance is difficult, a point cogently discussed by Salthouse (1990b). Nevertheless, Avolio, Waldman, and McDaniel (1990) presented evidence that experience is a better predictor of performance than is age for five different occupations. However, McDaniel, Schmidt, and Hunter (1988) indicated that the correlation between experience and performance is most predictive for lower amounts of experience. In other words, they found that the relationship between performance and experience was highest for individuals employed 0–3 years, and lowest for individuals employed 9–12 years. Additionally, the relationship between performance and experience was stronger for low-complexity compared to high-complexity jobs. Avolio et al. suggested that the relative gains from experience may diminish as the absolute amount of experience increases, possibly because the relevant components of job performance reach asymptote at an early stage. Because the more experienced workers are older, cognitive mechanisms may at least partially mediate this relationship. That is, experience produces less improvement over the years because as individuals age, their cognitive system is less plastic and they profit less from experience than younger adults. Separating subjects into age cohorts with differing levels of experience would permit a direct test of this hypothesis. Sparrow and Davies (1988) suggested the relationship between age and performance is nonlinear, with best performance occurring in late, young adulthood to early middle age, a finding similar to that reported for creativity and productivity of scientists and musicians (Horner, Rushton, & Vernon, 1986; Lehman, 1953), although see Over (1989) and Simonton (1989) for a different viewpoint.

Of critical interest to the applied cognitive aging researcher is the relationship of cognitive ability to job performance, because of the age-related declines observed in cognition. Schmidt, Hunter, Outerbridge, and Goff (1988) provided careful evidence that cognitive ability differences are related to both job knowledge and job performance over a period of 5 years, with evidence that the predictive validity of the cognitive ability measures is maintained over this 5-year period. Because the age range of subjects in this study is limited, and the observation period is insufficient for age-related decline to become manifest, no inferences regarding age, ability, and performance can be made from this study. Nevertheless, the finding that cognitive ability does appear to predict job performance leads to the hypothesis that age-related changes in cognition may have a decremental effect in work behaviors of older adults. Moreover, Murphy (1989) noted that there are many lines of evidence suggesting that cognitive ability is related to job performance.

A Model for Understanding Cognitive Aging and Work Behavior

Murphy (1989) proposed a model for understanding the relationship of cognitive ability to job performance that has particular implications for a cognitive aging model of work behavior. He proposed that cognitive ability may be the best predictor of work performance in conditions of "transition" where the worker must acquire new information or learn new procedures in order to perform appropriately. At the same time, there are also periods of "maintenance" in a job when the demands of the job remain stable, and when the worker relies on already-acquired procedures and knowledge. Murphy suggested that transition periods may be analogous to varied mapping paradigms whereas maintenance is analogous to a consistent mapping task. In line with Murphy's reasoning, Ackerman (1987) proposed that cognitive ability variables predict performance only on behaviors that have qualities of varied mapping (require active engagement of cognitive resources), an area in which older adults have been demonstrated to be particularly deficient.

This model provides at least a partial solution to the puzzle of high competence in the workplace of older workers coupled with diminishing measures of cognitive performance outlined by Salthouse (1990a, 1990b). The model predicts that older adults would not manifest deficits in performance in the workplace to the extent that they were in jobs that required primarily maintenance with few periods of transitions. When placed in a transitional situation, or in jobs generally characterized by a high amount of transition, older adults would be disadvantaged, however, due to the higher demands for cognitive resources.

Several studies have demonstrated performance declines in aging managers, despite the evidence reviewed earlier suggesting that there is not a strong relationship between age and job performance. In each case, the studies have involved simulations of complex management decisions rather than performance in actual work situations. Thus, these studies could appropriately be viewed as simulating transition components of work, where age differences are to be expected. For example, Meyer (1970) gave managers a basket of work that required them to solve problems presented in letters, memos, and reports. He found age correlated unfavorably with in-basket test performance. Taylor (1975) partialed out the effects of experience on performance; nevertheless he reported that older managers took longer to make decisions and had difficulty integrating information. Older managers were better at evaluating the value of information (a potentially good example of wisdom; see Birren & Fisher, 1990, for a treatment of this important topic). Streufert, Pogash, Piasecki, and Post (1990) noted that groups of elderly management teams performed more poorly on a number of molecular management tasks, with poor performance particularly marked on complex tasks. In both the Taylor and Streufert et al. studies, poor performance was noted on particularly resource-demanding components (integration of information and complex decision components).

Resource/Working-Memory Perspectives on Work

The views of cognitive aging reviewed earlier fit nicely into Murphy's (1989) job performance model. The resource perspective suggests that as long as older adults are in jobs that are comprised predominantly of maintenance tasks, few age deficits will be observed. Even highly complex behaviors acquired earlier would remain stable, based on processes of encapsulation described by Hoyer (1985) and Salthouse (1990b). Moreover, because these older workers would have acquired highly elaborated and complex schemata for work information (similar to the schemata master chess and bridge players acquire for these games; Charness, 1981a, 1981b, 1983), they also might be able to accommodate complex new information during transition periods without great use of resources, if the information or skill readily fits into already-existing schemas. According to a resource view, it would not be the complexity of the skill or information to be acquired that would determine difficulty of adaptation in transition, but rather the resources required to process that information into existing schemata. Acquisition of new skills for which older adults did not possess elaborated schemata would be particularly problematic for older as compared to younger workers. In support of this hypothesis, Elias, Elias, Robbins, and Gage (1987) and Zandri and Charness (1989) demonstrated that training time for elderly adults to learn standard software packages with which they were quite unfamiliar was 50% to 200% longer than for young adults. At the same time, the older adults did ultimately achieve a proficiency equal to that of younger adults. Thus, it may be more important to allow additional time for acquisition of new skills in older adult workers, but there is no evidence that older adults will be unable to acquire new work skills.

A resource perspective also would suggest the automatization of a skill or process (encapsulation) would reduce the working-memory load on older adults, freeing up resources for other uses during periods of transition. At the same time, the data of Fisk et al. (1988) suggest that attempting to automatize new responses in older adults may prove to be difficult. The development of training strategies for elderly workers might best be built on skills or processes already automatized in the individual's cognitive/performance repertoire, rather than attempting to limit resource demands by automatizing an entirely new process or procedure.

A resource perspective appears to suggest that older adults should have special difficulty in jobs of higher complexity. There is considerable evidence on this topic, but little of it supports the hypothesized age × complexity interaction. Waldman and Avolio (1986) reported positive correlations of age with performance, with the relationship more strongly positive for more complex jobs, whereas McEvoy and Cascio (1989) in a later meta-analysis reported no relationship between performance, age, and job complexity. Sparrow and Davies (1988) in a careful study of copy machine repairmen found no interaction of age with the complexity of the repair job for either quality of work or speed of completion. Finally, Avolio et al. (1990) found evidence for better managerial performance on complex tasks with increased age compared to simpler tasks, the opposite prediction of a resource view of aging. None of these studies permits a ready characterization of the tasks performed as maintenance or transitional. The findings would be predicted by the Murphy (1989) framework if one presumed the behaviors studied were largely maintenance behaviors, as one might expect the age × complexity interaction only on transitional tasks, an issue worthy of future research.

Finally, a resource perspective suggests that successful elderly workers might increasingly learn to rely on environmental supports to maintain performance. One might argue that the job tasks of a high-powered executive, a U.S. senator, or a top-level university administrator involve considerably less self-initiated processing than those of more junior colleagues. Any information that the individual requires can be searched for by staff members; prospective memory functions and integration of activities would largely be assumed by clerical/administrative staff. The primary task in high-level positions is to exercise judgment, organize procedures, and select appropriate environmental supports (staff) who can compensate for any deficiencies, technical or otherwise, in the leadership. Birren (1969) presented striking anecdotal accounts of business executives' self-reported hiring of personnel for the purpose of environmental supports. A better understanding of how members of a work team or even a spouse can be used to support various cognitive functions in which an older worker might be deficient will be important in understanding aging, cognition, and work behavior.

Age-Related Slowing and Work

The slowing hypothesis suggests that component processes of cognition will be slowed and thus less efficient in older adults. The slowing could result in older adults requiring more time to add new skills or behavior to their repertoire. New tasks that required speeded responding might be better suited for young adults. In general, acquisition of new skills in self-paced situations would be ideal for the older worker, although self-pacing would not guarantee older adults would reach proficiency levels of the young. Interestingly, in both the Taylor (1975) and Streufert et al. (1990) studies, there was no evidence that older managers processed information more slowly. At the same time, Streufert et al. noted inefficient strategy use and Taylor reported that older managers took longer to make a decision. Therefore, slowing appears to be selective and related conceivably to working-memory functions, an area in which age-related declines are well documented (Babcock & Salthouse, 1990; Foos, 1989; Salthouse, Mitchell, & Palmon, 1989).

Failure to Inhibit and Work

The failure to inhibit hypothesis would suggest that older adults may not select the most appropriate information for further processing and that they may focus on irrelevant aspects of information. Streufert et al. (1990) noted that "older teams . . . spent inordinate amounts of time discussing issues before implementing decisions, often ignoring current information, even when that information was highly relevant to issues being discussed," providing evidence for the off goal-path behaviors discussed by Hasher and Zacks (1988). In addition, the Hasher and Zacks hypothesis suggests that older adults may be more captured than young by irrelevant stimulation in the work environment. If the failure to inhibit hypothesis is correct, care should be taken to ensure that older adults work in an environment free from distractions and disruptions. For example, "landscaped" offices created by the placement of mobile partitions that occlude views of other workers but permit conversations and background noise from machines to intrude may be a particular problem for older adults.

Exercise: A General Mechanism for Facilitation?

Before leaving the topic of cognition, aging,and productivity in the workplace, it seems worthwhile to address the intriguing notion that a general facilitator of cognitive performance might exist—something that would enhance cognitive performance both within and outside of the workplace. One hypothesis that has been explored is that cognitive processes are improved in older adults who engage in regular physical activity. Clarkson-Smith and Hartley (1989) speculated that the cardiovascular benefit of exercise enhances central nervous system function and thus attenuates age-related slowing which may contribute to age-related cognitive decline. Following this line of reasoning, one option for general improvement of cognitive function in the workplace might be to maintain a high level of fitness in the work force, a very direct and relatively inexpensive method to improve cognitive function. There is a lengthy list of findings relating higher levels of aerobic fitness to improved reaction time (Dustman et al., 1984; Rikli & Busch, 1986; Spirduso, 1980), to superior reasoning (Powell & Pohndorf, 1971), as well as to improved mental health (Blumenthal, Williams, Needles, & Wallace, 1982; Hilyer & Mitchell, 1979). Clarkson-Smith and Hartley (1989) found differences between older adults with a high level of physical activity and those who were more sedentary, on reasoning measures, working-memory measures, and reaction times, even when controlling for health and intelligence.   Recognizing the correlational nature of their work, Clarkson-Smith and Hartley (1990) used structural equation modeling techniques to examine causal relationships. They found age and exercise directly influenced reaction time, working memory, and reasoning—with a positive valence for exercise and a negative one for age, thus suggesting that exercise improves cognitive function. They did not find evidence that deficits in cognitive function were attributable directly to health status nor evidence that physical inactivity directly contributed to cognitive deficits. Blumenthal and Madden (1988) and Madden, Blumenthal, Allen, and Emery (1989) conducted two careful prospective studies and reported different findings from Clarkson-Smith and Hartley (1989, 1990). Subjects were assigned randomly to exercise or no-exercise groups and experimental subjects then were subjected to a rigorous program of exercise for 12 weeks or more. Substantial improvements of 11.2% to 15% were noted in oxygen uptake (VO_2max) in exercised subjects. Despite this improvement, measures of memory search performance and word comparison yielded no significant benefits attributable to exercise. It is important to note that subjects in these studies were not selected for a particularly sedentary life style and the improvements in VO_2max are less than observed in prospective studies by Dustman et al. (1984) where cognitive improvements were observed. Moreover, they used measures of cognitive function that differed and were narrower than those used by Clarkson-Smith and Hartley (1989, 1990). In general, the work of Clarkson-Smith and Hartley seems to suggest that providing opportunities to exercise in the work environment may be a legitimate way to maintain if not enhance cognitive skills of older workers. Because Clarkson-Smith and Hartley (1990) did not find a causal relationship of exercise to morale, nor of morale to work performance, it is implausible that their findings were mediated by subjects being relieved of depression and concomitant psychomotor slowing. A prospective exercise study in the workplace with subjects of widely varying ages and lifestyles (sedentary vs. active) would be most informative. It would be of particular importance to measure both component and molar behaviors of cognition and work.

Methodological Issues

The study of age and cognition in the workplace results in methodological problems unique to this topic. Perhaps they were best summarized by Griew (1970). First, he noted that determining how productivity or performance is measured is an issue. This becomes a particular issue for aging research because the literature suggests that there is some evidence that ratings of worker productivity are affected or related to both the age of the rater and ratee. Second, Griew was concerned about demonstrating reliable age effects on target behaviors. He recommended using extreme age groups to solve this problem. A preferable alternative in many cases, however, would be for the experimenter to use subjects of all ages and then to treat age as a continuous variable. The use of extreme groups will cause the sometimes-hypothesized curvilinear relationship between age and productivity to be obscured.

Another sampling concern is that an adequate range of ages be represented, particularly at the upper end of the age continuum. In early research on age and work, older adults were conceptualized to be those over 40 years of age (Entwistle, 1959; Murrell, 1970). Because of gains in life expectancy and recent laws protecting the rights of older workers, the chronological age of what might be viewed as an older worker is shifting upward. In a recent study that was a model of sampling appropriate age ranges, Streufert et al. (1990) studied three groups of older adult managers, with the oldest group ranging from age 65 to 75 years. Most studies on work behaviors tend to have upper age limits in the late 50s and early 60s, and tend to have male samples. Because little is known about cognitive declines in young-old compared to old-old, and because there may be a shortage of skilled workers as the baby boomers age, there is an urgent need to include subjects aged 70 years and greater in studies on cognition and work. Also, although there is not a substantial amount of evidence that cognition in women differs from that of men, the psychology of work and aging sheds little light on the behavior of aged women, so women need to be included in samples in appropriate numbers whenever possible.

Another methodological problem that Griew (1970) discussed at length is the challenge for applied psychologists to develop techniques or design jobs to meet the needs and skills of aged individuals. He suggested that there are three techniques one can utilize. The first is a general approach which involves simplifying the component behaviors required. This approach would be exemplified by redesigning components of a job to lighten the cognitive resource demands. Such an approach, as Griew noted would make a job easier for all individuals, not just aged individuals, a point also made by Belbin and Belbin (1969). A second approach is more or less a human factors approach, and involves redesigning tools and tasks in a very specific manner after careful study of the cognitive/motor capabilities of the elderly. The third approach requires that the experimenter generalize from laboratory research, as has been done in the present chapter, to the workplace. He noted that problems with this approach include the potential lack of validity of the laboratory work for the real-world task and difficulties that we have in specifying the components of a work task to make it suitable for laboratory-based interventions. Notable progress, however, has been made in theory development since Griew made his original remarks—both in the psychology of aging and in the psychology of work behavior. I believe that our enhanced understanding of mechanisms underlying cognitive change combined with frameworks for analyzing work behaviors should result in successful joint applications of knowledge in these two important areas.

Although I have focused on the cognitive components of work behaviors in older adults, it is important to recognize that many variables besides cognitive ability impact on work performance (Stagner, 1985). Waldman and Spangler (1989) provided a model of job performance in which cognitive abilities and experience directly affect job knowledge and skills, and thus performance, as Hunter and Hunter (1984) postulated. At the same time, they also included variables such as motives, values, effort, goals, and performance feedback as important determinants of performance. A complete psychology of the aging worker will need to be contextually based, and like the Waldman and Spangler model, include an understanding of individual difference variables beyond age and cognitive ability, as well as variables in the workplace that are external to the worker. Thus, the effects of age-related declines in cognition on work behaviors, in addition to being modulated by experience in the workplace, also will be attenuated by other variables whose age-related trajectories may be positively rather than negatively related to performance.

GENERAL ISSUES AND FUTURE DIRECTIONS

The two substantive topics developed in the present article focused on very different behaviors both in scope and purpose. Medication adherence is a relatively specific behavior of particular importance to older adults due to an increase in multiple chronic conditions with age for which medications are used. In contrast, productivity and work behaviors encompass an almost impossibly broad range of motor and cognitive behaviors and the focus is on vitality, competence, and sustained contributions with age rather than on frailty. Despite the pronounced differences between these two domains, at least a few generalizations can be made about applied cognitive aging research in both areas that presumably apply to other diverse behaviors. First, it seems likely that most of the problems and behaviors on which applied cognitive aging researchers will focus will not be resolved exclusively within a cognitive aging framework. For both medication adherence and work behaviors, the belief systems and motivations of subjects were hypothesized to be important, and in both cases an integrative, contextualist approach was suggested to understand such complex, molar behaviors fully. Related to this point, I believe that for applied cognitive aging work to reach fruition, the work should be guided by complex, but carefully specified, theoretical frameworks, drawn from areas both inside and outside psychology, preferably based on known empirical relationships. It seems likely that causal modeling techniques will become of particular importance in testing such complex frameworks, partially because many of the behaviors of interest will be real-world rather than laboratory-based behaviors. The recent work by Clarkson-Smith and Hartley (1990) on exercise and aging provides an impressive example of sophisticated use of such techniques based on a theoretical framework that integrates many areas of psychology, physiology, and medicine. In addition to comprehensive theoretical frameworks, it will be important to measure both component behaviors underlying real-world behaviors as well as the molar behavior the components comprise (see Streufert et al., 1990, for an interesting example of such a technique), possibly relying on the molecular decomposition, molar-equivalence technique described and utilized by Salthouse (1984). The determination of what the cognitive components of complex real-world behaviors are is a challenging task, and its difficulty should not be underestimated (Griew, 1970). Finally, the two domains reviewed suggest that applied cognitive aging research has great potential to contribute to our understanding of fundamental cognitive processes. For example, it seems certain that the sophisticated methodologies available for measuring adherence behaviors will result in research in this domain contributing to our understanding of basic prospective memory processes in the elderly. Also, research in adherence is a logical area for the development of a more detailed understanding of differences in cognitive processes between the young-old and old-old. Similarly, the study of competence/performance in the workplace surely will result in a substantial elaboration of the literature on expertise and aging. Research on aging and work also has the potential to develop our conceptualizations of plasticity and the potential for cognitive change with age in a manner analogous to the more sophisticated work that exists on measurement of cognitive resources.

In closing, I am convinced that cognitive aging psychology has developed sufficiently to permit conceptual frameworks for real-world problems to be proposed in many areas with substantive research programs developed within them. The present chapter provides only a glimpse of the untapped potential that basic cognitive aging research has for solving real-world problems confronting older adults in society. There is a clear demographic imperative to use basic research findings to improve the quality of life and to sustain productivity of our older citizens. The emerging field of applied cognitive aging represents an exciting, and thus far largely unanswered, challenge to the creativity of both experienced and new investigators in the psychology of cognition and aging. It is time to respond.

ACKNOWLEDGMENTS

Preparation of this chapter was supported partially by grants from the National Institute on Aging (R01 AG060625) and from the AARP Andrus Foundation. I thank Roger Morrell and Lorrina Eastman for help with references and Ray Shaw for thoughtful comments on an early draft.

REFERENCES

Ackerman, P. L. (1987). Individual differences in skill learning: An integration of psychometric and information processing perspectives. *Psychological Bulletin, 102*, 3–27.

Arenberg, D. (1967). Regression analyses of verbal learning on adult age differences at two anticipation intervals. *Journal of Gerontology, 22*, 411–414.

Avolio, B. J., & Waldman, D. A. (1989). Ratings of managerial skill requirements: Comparison of age- and job-related factors. *Psychology and Aging, 4*, 464–470.

Avolio, B. J., Waldman, D. A., & McDaniel, M. A. (1990). Age and work performance in nonmanagerial jobs: The effects of experience and occupational type. *Academy of Management Journal, 33*, 407–422.

Babcock, R. L., & Salthouse, T. A. (1990). Effects of increased processing demands on age differences in working memory. *Psychology and Aging, 5*, 421–428.

Baltes, P. B., Dittmann-Kohli, F., & Dixon, R. A. (1984). New perspectives on the development of intelligence in adulthood: Toward a dual-process conception and a model of selective optimization with compensation. In P. B. Baltes & O. G. Brim, Jr. (Eds.), *Life-span development and behavior* (Vol. 6, pp. 33–76). New York: Academic.

Baltes, P. B., Dittmann-Kohli, F., & Kliegl, R. (1986). Reserve capacity of the elderly in aging-sensitive tests of fluid intelligence: Replication and extension. *Psychology and Aging, 1*, 172–177.

Baltes, P. B., & Schaie, K. W. (1976). On the plasticity of intelligence in adulthood and old age: Where Horn and Donaldson fail. *American Psychologist, 31*, 720–725.

Baltes, P. B., & Willis, S. L. (1982). Plasticity and enhancement of intellectual functioning in old age: Penn State's Adult Development and Enrichment Project (ADEPT). In F. I. M. Craik & S. E. Trehub (Eds.), *Aging and cognitive processes* (pp. 353–389). New York: Plenum.

Belbin, E., & Belbin, R. M. (1969). Selecting and training adults for new work. In A. T. Welford & J. E. Birren (Eds.), *Decision-making and age* (pp. 66–81). Basel, Switzerland: Karger.

Berg, C., Hertzog, C., & Hunt, E. (1982). Age differences in the speed of mental rotation. *Developmental Psychology, 18*, 95–107.

Birren, J. E. (1969). Age and decision strategies. In A. T. Welford & J. E. Birren (Eds.), *Decision-making and age* (pp. 23–36). Basel, Switzerland: Karger.

Birren, J. E., & Fisher, L. M. (1990). The elements of wisdom: Overview and integration. In R. Sternberg (Ed.), *Wisdom: Its nature, origins, and development* (pp. 317–332). Cambridge, England: Cambridge University Press.

Bjork, R. A., & Richardson-Klavehn, A. (1989). On the puzzling relationship between environmental context and human memory. In C. Izawa (Ed.), *Current issues in cognitive psychology: The Tulane Floweree Symposium on Cognition* (pp. 313–344). Hillsdale, NJ: Lawrence Erlbaum Associates.

Blechman, W. (1984). Managing the older arthritic: Can the family help? *Geriatrics, 39*, 131–132.

Blumenthal, J. A., & Madden, D. J. (1988). Effects of aerobic exercise training, age, and physical fitness on memory-search performance. *Psychology and Aging, 3*, 280–285.

Blumenthal, J. A., Williams, R. S., Needles, T. L., & Wallace, A. G. (1982). Psychological changes accompany aerobic exercise in healthy middle-aged adults. *Psychosomatic Medicine, 44*, 529–536.

Cerella, J., Poon, L. W., & Williams, D. (1980). Age and the complexity hypothesis. In L. W. Poon (Ed.), *Aging in the 1980's: Psychological issues*. Washington, DC: American Psychological Association.

Charness, N. (1981a). Search in chess: Age and skill differences. *Journal of Experimental Psychology: Human Perception and Performance, 7*, 467–476.

Charness, N. (1981b). Visual short-term memory and aging in chess players. *Journal of Gerontology, 36*, 615–619.

Charness, N. (1983). Age, skill, and bridge bidding: A chronometric analysis. *Journal of Verbal Learning and Verbal Behavior, 22*, 406–416.

Charness, N., & Bosman, E. A. (1990). Human factors and design for older adults. In J. E. Birren & K. W. Schaie (Eds.), *Handbook of the psychology of aging* (3rd ed., pp. 446–463). New York: Academic.

Clarkson-Smith, L., & Hartley, A. A. (1989). Relationships between physical exercise and cognitive abilities in older adults. *Psychology and Aging, 4,* 183–189.

Clarkson-Smith, L., & Hartley, A. A. (1990). Structural equation models of relationships between exercise and cognitive abilities. *Psychology and Aging, 5,* 437–446.

Cleveland, J. N., & Landy, F. J. (1981). The influence of rater and ratee age on two performance judgments. *Personnel Psychology, 34,* 19–29.

Cohen, G. (1979). Language comprehension in old age. *Cognitive Psychology, 11,* 412–429.

Cohen, G. (1981). Inferential reasoning in old age. *Cognition, 9,* 59–72.

Cohn, N. B., Dustman, R. E., & Bradford, D. C. (1984). Age-related decrements in Stroop color test performance. *Journal of Clinical Psychology, 40,* 1244–1250.

Craik, F. I. M. (1983). On the transfer of information from temporary to permanent memory. *Philosophical Transactions of the Royal Society, London, Series B, 302,* 3341–3359.

Craik, F. I. M. (1986). A functional account of age differences in memory. In F. Klix & H. Hagendorf (Eds.), *Human memory and cognitive capabilities* (pp. 409–422). Amsterdam: Elsevier.

Craik, F. I. M., & Byrd, M. (1982). Aging and cognitive deficits: The role of attentional resources. In F. I. M. Craik & S. Trehub (Eds.), *Aging and cognitive processes* (pp. 191–211). New York: Plenum.

Craik, F. I. M., Byrd, M., & Swanson, J. (1987). Patterns of memory loss in three elderly samples. *Psychology and Aging, 2,* 79–86.

Craik, F. I. M., & McDowd, J. (1987). Age differences in recall and recognition. *Journal of Experimental Psychology: Learning, Memory, and Cognition, 13,* 474–479.

Craik, F. I. M., & Simon, E. (1980). The roles of attention and depth of processing. In L. W. Poon, J. L. Fozard, L. Cermak, D. Arenberg, & L. W. Thompson (Eds.), *New directions in memory and aging: Proceedings of the George Talland memorial conference* (pp. 95–112). Hillsdale, NJ: Lawrence Erlbaum Associates.

Cramer, J. A., Scheyer, R. D., & Mattson, R. H. (1990). Compliance declines between clinic visits. *Archives of Internal Medicine, 150,* 1509–1510.

Davies, D. R., Jones, D. M., & Taylor, A. (1984). Selective and sustained-attention tasks: Individual and group differences. In R. Parasuraman & D. R. Davies (Eds.), *Varieties of attention* (pp. 395–447). Orlando: Academic.

Dustman, R. E., Ruhling, R. O., Russell, E. M., Shearer, D. E., Bonekat, H. W., Shigeoka, J. W., Wood, J. S., & Bradford, D. C. (1984). Aerobic exercise training and improved neuropsychological function of older individuals. *Neurobiology of Aging, 5,* 35–42.

Einstein, G. O., & McDaniel, M. A. (1990). Normal aging and prospective memory. *Journal of Experimental Psychology: Learning, Memory, and Cognition, 16,* 717–726.

Elias, P. K., Elias, M. F., Robbins, M. A., & Gage, P. (1987). Acquisition of word-processing skills by younger, middle-age, and older adults. *Psychology and Aging, 2,* 340–348.

Entwistle, D. B. (1959). Ageing: The effects of previous skill on training. *Occupational Psychology, 33,* 238–243.

Eustace, C., Johnson, C., & Gault, M. (1982). Improvements in drug prescription labels for patients with limited education or vision. *Canadian Medical Association Journal, 15,* 301–302.

Feinberg, J. (1988). The effect of patient–practitioner interaction on compliance: A review of the literature and application in rheumatoid arthritis. *Patient Education and Counseling, 11,* 171–187.

Fernandez, A., & Glenberg, A. M. (1985). Changing environmental context does not reliably affect memory. *Memory & Cognition, 13,* 333–345.

Fisk, A. D., McGee, N. D., & Giambra, L. M. (1988). The influence of age on consistent and varied semantic-category search performance. *Psychology and Aging, 3*, 323–333.

Foos, P. W. (1989). Adult age differences in working memory. *Psychology and Aging, 4*, 269–275.

Fozard, J. L. & Popkin, S. J. (1978). Optimizing adult development: Ends and means of an applied psychology of aging. *American Psychologist, 33*, 975–989.

Fries, J. F., & Crapo, L. M. (1981). *Vitality and aging.* San Francisco: Freeman.

Griew, S. (1970). Methodological problems in industrial aging research. In H. L. Sheppard (Ed.), *Toward an industrial gerontology* (pp. 110–122). Cambridge, MA: Schenkman.

Hasher, L., Stoltzfus, E. R., Zacks, R.T., & Rypma, B. (1991). Age and inhibition. *Journal of Experimental Psychology: Learning, Memory, and Cognition, 17*, 163–169.

Hasher, L., & Zacks, R. T. (1979). Automatic and effortful processes in memory. *Journal of Experimental Psychology: General, 108*, 356–388.

Hasher, L., & Zacks, R. T. (1988). Working memory, comprehension, and aging. A review and a new view. In G. H. Bower (Ed.), *The psychology of learning and motivation* (Vol. 22, pp. 193–225). New York: Academic.

Hess, T. (1984). Effects of semantically-related and unrelated context on recognition memory of different-aged adults. *Journal of Gerontology, 39*, 444–451.

Hilyer, J. C., & Mitchell, W. (1979). Effects of systematic physical fitness training combined with counseling on the self-concept of college students. *Journal of Counseling Psychology, 26*, 427–436.

Horner, K. L., Rushton, J. P., & Vernon, P. A. (1986). Relation between aging and research productivity of academic psychologists. *Psychology and Aging, 1*, 319–324.

Howard, D. V. (1988). Aging and memory activation: The priming of semantic and episodic memories. In L. L. Light & D. M. Burke (Eds.)., *Language, memory, and aging* (pp. 77–99). New York: Cambridge University Press.

Howard, D. V., McAndrews, M. P., & Lasaga, M. I. (1981). Semantic priming of lexical decisions in young and old adults. *Journal of Gerontology, 36*, 707–714.

Hoyer, W. J. (1985). Aging and the development of expert cognition. In T. M. Schlechter & M. P. Toglia (Eds.), *New directions in cognitive science* (pp. 69–87). Norwood, NJ: Ablex.

Hoyer, W. J., Rebok, G. W., & Sved, S. M. (1979). Effects of varying irrelevant information on adult age differences in problem solving. *Journal of Gerontology, 14*, 553–560.

Hultsch, D. F., & Dixon, R. A. (1984). Memory for text materials in adulthood. In P. B. Baltes & O. G. Brim, Jr. (Eds.), *Life-span development and behavior* (Vol. 6, pp. 77–108). New York: Academic.

Hunter, J. E., & Hunter, R. F. (1984). The validity and utility of alternative predictors of job performance. *Psychological Bulletin, 96*, 72–99.

Kahneman, D. (1973). *Attention and effort.* Englewood Cliffs, NJ: Prentice-Hall.

Kausler, D. H. (1982). *Experimental psychology and human aging.* New York: Wiley.

Kausler, D. H., & Kleim, D. M. (1978). Age differences in processing relevant versus irrelevant stimuli in multiple item recognition learning. *Journal of Gerontology, 33*, 87–93.

Kendrick, R., & Bayne, J. (1982). Compliance with prescribed medications by elderly patients. *Journal of the Canadian Medical Association, 127*, 961.

Kiernan, P. J., & Isaacs, J. B. (1981). Use of drugs by the elderly. *Journal of Research in Sociological Medicine, 74*, 196.

Kliegl, R., & Baltes, P. B. (1987). Theory-guided analysis of mechanisms of development and aging through testing-the-limits and research on expertise. In C. Schooler & K. W. Schaie (Eds.), *Cognitive functioning and social structure over the life course* (pp. 95–119). Norwood, NJ: Ablex.

Kline, T. J. B., Ghali, L. M., Kline, D. W., & Brown, S. (1990). Visibility distance of highway signs among young, middle-aged, and older observers: Icons are better than text. *Human Factors, 32*, 609–620.

Lehman, H. C. (1953). *Age and achievement*. Princeton, NJ: Princeton University Press.

Leirer, V., Morrow, D., Pariante, G., & Doksum, T. (1989). Increasing influenza vaccination adherence through voice mail. *Journal of the American Geriatric Society, 37*, 1147–1150.

Leirer, V. O., Morrow, D. G., Pariante, G. M., & Sheikh, J. (1988). Elders' nonadherence, its assessment, and computer assisted instruction for medication recall training. *Journal of the American Geriatric Society, 36*, 877–884.

Leirer, V. O., Morrow, D. G., Tanke, E. D., & Pariante, G. M. (1991). Elders' nonadherence: Its assessment and medication reminding by voice mail. *The Gerontologist, 31*, 514–520.

Leventhal, H., & Cameron, L. (1987). Behavioral theories and the problem of compliance. *Patient Education and Counseling, 10*, 117–138.

Ley, P. (1979). Memory for medical information. *British Journal of Social and Clinical Psychology, 18*, 245–255.

Ley, P., Whitworth, M. A., Skilbeck, C. E., Woodward, R., Pinsent, R. J., Pike, L. A., Clarkson, M. E., & Clark, P. B. (1976). Improving doctor–patient communication in general practice. *Journal of Royal College of General Practitioners, 26*, 720–724.

Light, L. L. (1991). Memory and aging: Four hypotheses in search of data. *Annual Review of Psychology, 42*, 333–376.

Light, L. L., & Albertson, S. A. (1988). Comprehension of pragmatic implications in young and older adults. In L. L. Light & D. M. Burke (Eds.), *Language, memory, and aging* (pp. 133–153). New York: Cambridge University.

Light, L. L., & Singh, A. (1987). Implicit and explicit memory in young and older adults. *Journal of Experimental Psychology: Learning, Memory, and Cognition, 13*, 531–541.

Madden, D. J. (1983). Aging and distraction by highly familiar stimuli during visual search. *Developmental Psychology, 19*, 499–507.

Madden, D. J., Blumenthal, J. A., Allen, P. A., & Emery, C. F. (1989). Improving aerobic capacity in healthy older adults does not necessarily lead to improved cognitive performance. *Psychology and Aging, 4*, 307–320.

Madden, D. J., & Nebes, R. D. (1980). Aging and the development of automaticity in visual search. *Developmental Psychology, 16*, 377–384.

McDaniel, M. A., Schmidt, F. L., & Hunter, J. E. (1988). Job experience correlates of job performance. *Journal of Applied Psychology, 73*, 327–330.

McEvoy, G. M., & Cascio, W. F. (1989). Cumulative evidence of the relationship between employee age and job performance. *Journal of Applied Psychology, 74*, 11–17.

Meisel, S., & Kiely, K. (1981). Graphic prescription labels. *American Journal of Hospital Pharmacy, 38*, 1116.

Mergler, N. L., & Zandi, T. (1983). Adult age differences in speed and accuracy of matching verbal and pictorial signs. *Educational Gerontology, 7*, 73–85.

Meyer, H. H. (1970). The validity of the in-basket test as a measure of managerial performance. *Personnel Psychology, 23*, 297–307.

Morrell, R. W., Park, D. C., & Poon, L. W. (1989). Quality of instructions on prescription drug labels: Effects on memory and comprehension in young and old adults. *The Gerontologist, 29*, 345–354.

Morrell, R. W., Park, D. C., & Poon, L. W. (1990). Effects of labelling techniques on memory and comprehension of prescription information in young and older adults. *Journal of Gerontology, 45*, 166–172.

Morrow, D., Leirer, V., & Sheikh, J. (1988). Adherence and medication instructions: Review and recommendations. *Journal of the American Geriatric Society, 36*, 1147–1160.

Murphy, K. R. (1989). Is the relationship between cognitive ability and job performance stable over time? *Human Performance, 2*, 183–200.

Murrell, K. F. H. (1970). Major problems of industrial gerontology. In H. L. Sheppard (Ed.), *Toward an industrial gerontology* (pp. 71–83). Cambridge, MA: Schenkman.

Navon, D. (1984). Resources—A theoretical soupstone? *Psychological Review, 91*, 216–234.

Over, R. (1989). Age and scholarly impact. *Psychology and Aging, 4*, 222–225.

Page, P., Verstraete, D., Robb, J., & Etzwiler, D. (1981). Patient recall of self-care recommendations in diabetes. *Diabetes Care, 4*, 9698.

Park, D. C., Cherry, K. E., Smith, A. D., & Lafronza, V. N. (1990). Effects of distinctive context on memory for objects and their locations in young and older adults. *Psychology and Aging, 5*, 250–255.

Park, D. C., Morrell, R. W., Blackburn, B., Frieske, D., & Birchmore, D. (1989, August). Medication compliance in rheumatoid arthritis: A new approach. Paper presented at the International Psychogeriatric Association, Tokyo.

Park, D. C., Morrell, R. W., Frieske, D., Blackburn, B., & Birchmore, D. (1991). Cognitive factors and the use of over-the-counter medication organizers by arthritis patients. *Human Factors, 33*, 57–67.

Park, D. C., Morrell, R. W., Frieske, D., & Kincaid, D. (in press). Medication adherence behaviors in older adults: Effects of cognitive interventions. *Psychology and Aging*.

Park, D. C., Puglisi, J. T., & Smith, A. D. (1986). Memory for pictures: Does an age-related decline exist? *Journal of Psychology and Aging, 1*, 11–17.

Park, D. C., Puglisi, J. T., Smith, A. D., & Dudley, W. N. (1987). Cue utilization and encoding specificity in picture recognition by older adults. *Journal of Gerontology, 42*, 423–425.

Park, D. C., Puglisi, J. T., & Sovacool, M. (1984). Picture memory in older adults: Effects of contextual detail at encoding and retrieval. *Journal of Gerontology, 39*, 213–215.

Park, D. C., Royal, D., Dudley, W., & Morrell, R. (1988). Forgetting of pictures over a long retention interval in young and old adults. *Psychology and Aging, 3*, 94–95.

Park, D. C., Smith, A. D., Dudley, W. N., & Lafronza, V. N. (1989). The effects of age and a divided attention task presented at encoding and retrieval on memory. *Journal of Experimental Psychology: Learning, Memory, and Cognition, 15*, 1185–1191.

Park, D. C., Smith, A. D., Morrell, R. W., Puglisi, J. T., & Dudley, W. N. (1990). Effects of contextual integration on recall of pictures in older adults. *Journals of Gerontology: Psychological Sciences, 45*, P52–P57.

Plude, D. J., & Hoyer, W. J. (1985). Attention and performance: Identifying and localizing age deficits. In N. Charness (Ed.), *Aging and human performance* (pp. 47–99). New York: Wiley.

Powell, R. R., & Pohndorf, R. H. (1971). Comparison of adult exercisers and nonexercisers on fluid intelligence and selected physiological variables. *Research Quarterly, 42*, 70–77.

Puglisi, J. T., Park, D. C., Smith, A. D., & Dudley, W. M. (1988). Age differences in encoding specificity. *Journals of Gerontology: Psychological Sciences, 43*, P145–P150.

Rabbitt, P. (1965). An age decrement in the ability to ignore irrelevant information. *Journal of Gerontology, 20*, 233–238.

Rabinowitz, J. C., Craik, F. I. M., & Ackerman, B. P. (1982). A processing resource account of age differences in recall. *Canadian Journal of Psychology, 36*, 325–344.

Rhodes, S. R. (1983). Age-related differences in work attitudes and behavior: A review and conceptual analysis. *Psychological Bulletin, 93*, 328–367.

Rikli, R., & Busch, S. (1986). Motor performance of women as a function of age and physical activity level. *Journal of Gerontology, 41*, 645–649.

Rosen, B., & Jerdee, T. H. (1976). The nature of job related age stereotypes. *Journal of Applied Psychology, 61*, 180–183.

Salthouse, T. A. (1984). Effects of age and skill in typing. *Journal of Experimental Psychology: General, 113*, 345–371.

Salthouse, T. A. (1985a). Speed of behavior and its implications for cognition. In J. E. Birren & K. W. Schaie (Eds.), *Handbook of the psychology of aging* (pp. 400–426). New York: Van Nostrand Reinhold.

Salthouse, T. A. (1985b). *A theory of cognitive aging.* North Holland: Elsevier.

Salthouse, T. A. (1987a). The role of experience in cognitive aging. In K. W. Schaie (Ed.), *Annual review of gerontology and geriatrics* (Vol. 7, pp. 135–157). New York: Springer.

Salthouse, T. A. (1987b). Age, experience, and compensation. In C. Schooler & K. W. Schaie (Eds.), *Cognitive functioning and social structure over the life course* (pp. 142–157). Norwood, NJ: Ablex.

Salthouse, T. A. (1988). The role of processing resources in cognitive aging. In M. L. Howe & C. J. Brainerd (Eds.), *Cognitive development in adulthood* (pp. 185–239). New York: Springer-Verlag.

Salthouse, T. A. (1989). Ageing and skilled performance. In A. M. Colley & J. R. Beech (Eds.), *Acquisition and performance of cognitive skills* (pp. 247–264). New York: Wiley.

Salthouse, T. A. (1990a). Cognitive competence and expertise in aging. In J. E. Birren & K. W. Schaie (Eds.), *Handbook of the psychology of aging* (3rd ed., pp. 311–319). New York: Academic.

Salthouse, T. A. (1990b). Influence of experience on age differences in cognitive functioning. *Human Factors, 32,* 551–570.

Salthouse, T. A., Kausler, D. H., & Saults, J. S. (1988). Investigation of student status, background variables, and the feasibility of standard tasks in cognitive aging research. *Psychology and Aging, 3,* 29–37.

Salthouse, T. A., Mitchell, D. R. D., & Palmon, R. (1989). Memory and age differences in spatial manipulation ability. *Psychology and Aging, 4,* 480–486.

Salthouse, T. A., & Somberg, B. L. (1982). Skilled performance: Effects of adult age and experience on elementary processes. *Journal of Experimental Psychology: General, 111,* 176–207.

Schaie, K. W., & Willis, S. L. (1986). Can decline in adult intellectual functioning be reversed? *Developmental Psychology, 22,* 223–232.

Schmidt, F. L., Hunter, J. E., Outerbridge, A. N., & Goff, S. (1988). Joint relation of experience and ability with job performance: Test of three hypotheses. *Journal of Applied psychology, 73,* 46–57.

Schneider, W., & Shiffrin, R. M. (1977). Controlled and automatic human information processing: 1. Detection, search, and attention. *Psychological Review, 84,* 1–66.

Sharps, M. (1991). Spatial memory in young and elderly adults: The cateory structure of stimulus sets. *Psychology and Aging, 6,* 309–311.

Sharps, M. J. & Gollin, E. S. (1987). Memory for object locations in young and elderly adults. *Journal of Gerontology, 42,* 336–341.

Sharps, M., & Gollin, E. S. (1988). Aging and free recall for objects located in space. *Journal of Gerontology: Psychological Sciences, 43,* P8–P11.

Shaw, R. J., & Craik, F. I. M. (1989). Age differences in predictions and performance on a cued recall task. *Psychology and Aging, 4,* 131–135.

Simonton, D. K. (1989). The swan-song phenomenon: Last-works effects for 172 classical composers. *Psychology and Aging, 4,* 42–47.

Smith, A. D., & Park, D. C. (1990). Adult age differences in memory for pictures and images. In E. A. Lovelace (Ed.), *Aging and cognition: Mental processes, self-awareness, and interventions* (pp. 69–96). North Holland: Elsevier.

Smith, A. D., Park, D. C., Cherry, K. E., & Berkovsky, K. (1990). Age differences in memory for concrete and abstract pictures. *Journal of Gerontology, 45,* 205–209.

Sparrow, P. R., & Davies, D. R. (1988). Effects of age, tenure, training, and job complexity on technical performance. *Psychology and Aging, 3,* 307–314.

Spirduso, W. W. (1980). Physical fitness, aging, and psychomotor speed: A review. *Journal of Gerontology, 35*, 850–865.

Stagner, R. (1985). Aging in industry. In J. E. Birren & K. W. Schaie (Eds.), *Handbook of the psychology of aging* (2nd ed., pp. 789–817). New York: Van Nostrand Reinhold.

Stine, E. A. L., Wingfield, A., & Meyers, S. D. (1990). Age differences in processing information from television news: The effects of bisensory augmentation. *Journals of Gerontology: Psychological Sciences, 45*, P1–P8.

Streufert, S., Pogash, R., Piasecki, M., & Post, G. M. (1990). Age and management team performance. *Psychology and Aging, 5*, 551–559.

Taylor, R. N. (1975). Age and experience as determinants of managerial information processing and decision making performance. *Academy of Management Journal, 18*, 74–81.

Tulving, E., & Thomson, D. M. (1973). Encoding specificity and retrieval processes in episodic memory. *Psychological Review, 80*, 353–373.

Tulving, E., & Schacter, D. L. (1990). Priming and human memory systems. *Science, 247*, 301–306.

Waldman, D. A., & Avolio, B. J. (1986). A meta-analysis of age differences in job performance. *Journal of Applied Psychology, 71*, 33–38.

Waldman, D. A., & Spangler, W. D. (1989). Putting together the pieces: A closer look at the determinants of job performance. *Human Performance, 2*, 29–59.

West, R. L. (1989). Planning practical memory training for the aged. In L. W. Poon, D. C. Rubin, & B. Wilson (Eds.), *Everyday cognition in adulthood and late life* (pp. 573–597). New York: Cambridge University Press.

Willis, S. L. (1989). Improvement with cognitive training: Which old dogs learn what tricks? In L. W. Poon, D. C. Rubin, & B. A. Wilson (Eds.), *Everyday cognition in adulthood and late life* (pp. 545–569). New York: Cambridge University Press.

Willis, S. L., Blieszner, R., & Baltes, P. B. (1981). Intellectual training research in aging: Modification of performance on the fluid ability of figural relations. *Journal of Educational Psychology, 73*, 41–50.

Willis, S. L., & Schaie, K. W. (1986). Training the elderly on the ability factors of spatial orientation and inductive reasoning. *Psychology and Aging, 1*, 239–247.

Winfield, J., & Task Force on Arthritis Patient Education. (1989). Arthritis patient education. *Arthritis and Rheumatism, 32*, 1330–1333.

World Health Organization. (1981). Health care in the elderly: Report of the Technical Group on use of medications by the elderly. *Drugs, 22*, 279–294.

Yesavage, J. A., Lapp, D., & Sheikh, J. I. (1989). Mnemonics as modified for use by the elderly. In L. W. Poon, D. C. Rubin, & B. A. Wilson (Eds.), *Everyday cognition in adulthood and late life* (pp. 598–611). New York: Cambridge University Press.

Yesavage, J. A., Rose, T. L., & Bower, G. H. (1983). Interactive imagery and affective judgments improve face-name learning in the elderly. *Journal of Gerontology, 38*, 197–203.

Zacks, R. T., Hasher, L., Doren, B., Hamm, F., & Attig, M. S. (1987). Encoding and memory of explicit and implicit information. *Journal of Gerontology, 42*, 418–422.

Zandri, E., & Charness, N. (1989). Training older and younger adults to use software. *Educational Gerontology, 15*, 615–631.

CHAPTER TEN

Human Factors
and Age

Neil Charness
University of Waterloo

Elizabeth A. Bosman
University of Toronto

Human factors has been characterized in a number of different ways. Two representative examples are "the discipline that tries to optimize the relationship between technology and the human" (Kantowitz & Sorkin, 1983), and the discipline whose goal is "designing for human use and optimizing working and living conditions" (Sanders & McCormick, 1987). Other terms sometimes used interchangeably with human factors are ergonomics (though ergonomics tends to restrict itself to dealing with the workplace) and engineering psychology, or human engineering. In short, human factors tends to be a discipline with a strong performance orientation, with the central theme being how to design products or processes to enable someone to do a task more efficiently and safely. The question of the appropriateness of the performance goal is left to the user.

As the preceding suggests, human factors is relevant to many aspects of daily living, from the design of household appliances and automobiles to the design of buildings and transportation systems. The following briefly describes a few of the topics that fall within the area of human factors. Anthropometry is concerned with measuring the dimensions and functional capabilities of the human body. More specifically, anthropometry is concerned with measuring variations in the size of various body parts, and the range and strength of movements the body is capable of (Sanders & McCormick, 1987). Human–computer interaction is concerned with how to design computer software and hardware so that the use of computers by people is facilitated (Card, Moran, & Newell, 1983). Transportation engineers are concerned with the issues pertaining to the design of safe and efficient transportation systems (Committee for the Study on Improving Mobility & Safety for Older Persons, 1988), whereas illuminating engineers are concerned with the design of lighting systems for a wide range of indoor and outdoor settings (Kaufman & Haynes, 1981a, 1981b). Individuals focusing upon the man–machine interface attempt to design instrument and control panels so that the control of cars, planes, appliances, and other machines is efficient and relatively errorless (Sanders & McCormick, 1987).

Human factors is a comparatively young discipline: Two of the main journals in this area, *Human Factors* and *Ergonomics*, have just reached their early 30s. The application of human factors to issues in aging is about as old as the societies that spawned these journals. A classic work by Welford (1958), *Ageing and Human Skill*, represents one of the first attempts to link basic laboratory research about aging to practical issues. The long-term interest in this topic in the *Human Factors Society* (see Fozard, 1981) has led to the publication of two special issues on aging in *Human Factors* in the past 10 years (in 1981 and 1990). Nonetheless, there is still a paucity of reliable data on which to base recommendations and design decisions. As Smith (1990) commented in the most recent special issue: "Although the knowledge base for human factors and aging is weak and conceptual thinking is in its infancy, theorizing can play an important role in the emergence of any field of inquiry" (p. 509). As a result, part of our chapter is theoretical and speculative.

There are two primary approaches taken within human factors: (a) studying human capabilities and modifying the tool or the environment to fit the needs of the human user, and (b) modifying the user to work with a difficult-to-change or inherently dangerous tool or environment. The first approach is the more usual one: designing for the user. The second approach more often is subsumed under the issue of training techniques. Both approaches are needed to provide maximal benefit to user populations once the tool or environment assumes even a modest degree of complexity (contrast design and training requirements for a broom vs. an automobile). Given these orientations, differentiating human factors research from applied psychology (see chapter 9) is difficult. Perhaps the easiest way to proceed is to view applied psychology as dealing more with changing the human, and human factors as concerning itself more with changing the environment, usually in a way that improves cost-effectiveness and safety. It should be kept in mind that the nature of the human–environment interaction (see Parmelee & Lawton, 1990) affects both enterprises.

What can the study of human factors offer for older adults? Because aging often is accompanied by negative changes to the human condition, human factors research can play an essential role in improving the quality of life for older people through better design. Older adults now form and will increasingly represent a significant proportion of the population in both the western industrialized nations and the developing nations (Report of the World Assembly on Aging, 1982). "Know the user" is the credo of a good designer. Older users are becoming increasingly commonplace. Further, if environmental conditions interact with age to constrain performance, then the optimal environments for people will change with age.

First, we need to delineate what is mean by the term *older adult*. Traditionally the term has been reserved for those near or past retirement: those 60 years of age and older. In industrial gerontology, the term *older worker* often refers to those in the 40–45 + years range (Smith, 1990). Visual and auditory declines have been documented both cross-sectionally and longitudinally for the decade of the 30s and beyond (Fozard, 1990). Thus, a conservative use of the term older adult should probably be those age 40 years or above, a bit above the halfway point of life expectancy in industrialized nations.

Within the ranks of the older adult there are probably three distinct subgroups: those who are middle-age, those still in the paid labor force (40–64 years); the old, those in the early and middle retirement years (65–74 years); and those who are in late old age (75 + years). Design issues for these three groups will vary. The criteria that design can be measured against fall into three overlapping categories: safety, efficiency, and comfort. A simple extension of traditional human factors approaches can deal with the age 40–64 years group. The primary concerns, we would predict, will center around workplace efficiency and safety. The age 65–74 years group likely will be perceived as targets for improved consumer product design, with safety and comfort (ease of use) being the probable focus. The age 75 + years group will be the target of prosthetic products such as assistive devices that will enhance both basic activities of daily living (e.g., bathing, dressing, toileting and continence, feeding, transferring) and instrumental activities of daily living (e.g., shopping, house and yard work, financial maintenance, and driving), keeping them independent in their homes for as long as possible.

There are three important assumptions that must be met if human factors research is to be a useful complement to the study of aging:

1. It must be the case that optimal safety, efficiency, and comfort conditions for older adults differ from those for younger ones, else designing optimally for the young or the old will suit the entire population. Phrased in statistical jargon, age by condition interactions should be evident for the outcome measure, rather than solely main effects of age. To

be safe, it is almost always better to design for the old when interactions are not disordinal (crossover), because the young may show no changes in performance across conditions, whereas the old do. Older adults may be more sensitive to design flaws, given the perceptual and cognitive changes that usually accompany aging. With disordinal interactions, design decisions are complicated, because different designs are optimal for different age groups. Fortunately, disordinal interactions are relatively rare.

2. It should be the case that variability in performance of older adults is not so great that design guidelines are hopelessly wide and hence too costly to implement. The choice of the term *cost* is intentional. It may be technologically possible to design an automotive vehicle that safeguards the lives of its occupants from a head-on collision at 100 km/hr. But, that vehicle may not be economically viable in the current marketplace. We examine cost–benefit issues later on.

3. To enable population estimates of performance to be meaningful, representative samples of older adults are needed. Such samples very rarely are obtained in laboratory studies, because the usual volunteer samples tend to be quite unrepresentative of their population cohorts (Camp, West, & Poon, 1989; Rosenthal & Rosnow, 1975; Todd, Davis, & Cafferty, 1983). Even survey research encounters difficulties in achieving representative samples, due to nonresponse for questionnaire, phone, and in-person interviews. In the case of laboratory studies, the problems are greater yet, because mobility is a usual requirement for entry into a laboratory setting. In some cases, it may be desirable to bring the lab to the person rather than vice versa. See Kelly and Kroemer (1990) for a good discussion of sampling issues related to anthropometric measurement.

Our chapter is divided up into four main sections. Initially, we summarize age-related changes in perceptual, cognitive, and physical capabilities that have implications for principles of design. We then discuss some specific content areas within human factors and their relevance to older adults. This discussion necessarily is limited by space considerations, and the topics selected were those that have broad relevance for the daily lives of older adults. We begin with a detailed review and analysis of guidelines for optimizing the visual and auditory performance of older adults. Next we focus on a small number of areas of functional human factors: transportation environments, stressing the automobile, and work environments, stressing computer technology. In the third section we examine cost-benefit analysis, a tool that can be used to help make decisions about design implementation. Finally, we outline some guidelines and recommendations for future research.

SOURCES OF PRINCIPLES FOR DESIGN

There are three complementary sources of information about older adult behavior that can provide principles for design: epidemiology, laboratory research, and field studies. Epidemiology of aging deals with population statistics; for instance, determining whether age is a risk factor for the incidence of dementia, disability, and automobile fatalities (see *Second Conference on the Epidemiology of Aging*, 1980). Such research can provide valuable clues about age changes from macroindicators in the population. Nonetheless, descriptive data from epidemiology do not always pinpoint causal factors; rather, such data identify correlates (risk factors). We would classify this approach as problem identification, a top-down approach to design.

Laboratory experiments on aging (more accurately termed quasi-experiments, because age is not a manipulable variable) search for changes in microlevel processes in individuals. The phenomena explored range from the biological and physiological to cognitive and social. Such studies aim at identifying basic mechanisms or molecular processes that can account for age-related changes in performance at a more molar level of description. The expectation is that the identification of such basic processes should be able to provide the framework for causal explanations of any age-related differences in more complex activities, such as driving a vehicle. For instance, by knowing how identification and discrimination thresholds for visual and auditory stimuli change with age, employers should be able to design work environments that meet any special needs of older workers. Laboratory research represents more of a bottom-up approach to design, starting with molecular theories and working toward prediction of molar performance.

Field research involves two facets: observational studies and experimental studies. Observational research provides a careful description of the task environment in which people operate. Studies can be concerned with gross descriptions of typical activity patterns of older adults. The results of one such study by Moss and Lawton (1982), plotted in Fig. 10.1, indicate that television viewing is, after sleep, a very time-consuming activity for old adults. Human factors specialists looking at these patterns might become concerned with ensuring that televisions (and VCRs) function well for older viewers. Another approach might be to discover what barriers have to be removed to permit the activity patterns of dependent older adults to more closely resemble those of younger adults.

At the next level of analysis, field studies may have the goal of cataloging and describing in greater detail all the activities that must be carried out to accomplish a specific task. For instance, Clark, Czaja, and Weber (1990), expanding on Faletti's (1984) pioneering work, provided a sound

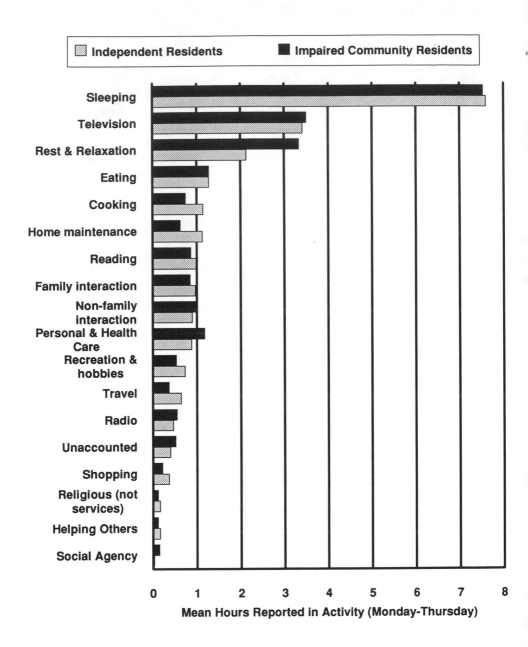

FIG. 10.1.   Mean hours in an activity (adapted from Moss & Lawton, 1982) for independent residents (N = 426, mean age = 75 years) and impaired community residents (N = 164, mean age = 79).

functional analysis of instrumental activities of daily living after careful observation of older adults carrying out tasks such as laundry, cooking, and shopping in their usual settings. By correlating task demands with anthropometric measurements of their population they could identify problem sources (e.g., inappropriate heights for kitchen cabinets) and make suggestions for redesign. Field research involves both top-down and bottom-up approaches to design.

Generalizations About Aging

In general, the results of epidemiological studies, although indicating population trends, are not sufficiently detailed to help in formulating specific design guidelines for older adults. Experimental field studies, although providing valuable information, have not been sufficiently numerous to be useful in formulating general guidelines for design. Our approach has been to use the results of experimental and descriptive studies indicating the nature of age-related changes in perception, cognition, physical size, and motor performance as guidelines for design. Detailed descriptions of these age-related changes are available elsewhere (Charness, 1985; Fozard, 1990; Kelly & Kroemer, 1990; Kline & Schieber, 1985; Koncelik,, 1982; Salthouse, 1985a, 1985b; Stoudt, Damon, McFarland, & Roberts, 1965, 1973; Welford, 1977; Working Group on Speech Understanding & Aging, CHABA, 1988; see also chapters in this volume). We list some of the more salient ones for design in Table 10.1, offering an age epoch approach consistent with the view that there are distinct subgroups of older adults. The rationale for this approach is that design issues can be identified by looking at age-related changes, and predicting their effects on activities. For example, age-related increases in auditory threshold, particularly for high frequencies, have implications for the volume and frequencies of messages and warning signals employed in public places. Decreased physical strength with age has implications for how much strength should be required to open a jar of food or a fire door. Age-related slowing has implications for how much time should be allowed to complete certain activities, such as reading a traffic sign, or crossing a road.

Consistent with this approach, we (Charness & Bosman, 1990b) previously outlined parameters for predicting the performance of older adults, following Card et al. (1983). One of the motivations for collating age-related performance parameters was to try to provide for the possibility of "cookbook" solutions to design.[1] Ideally, designers would like to

---

[1]It must be admitted that extrapolations from theoretical parameters to real-life performance is risky and has had a checkered past, as earlier work on human reliability estimation has shown (Sanders & McCormick, 1987, p. 38). Nonetheless, even poor estimates are better than no estimates at all, given that design decisions must be made daily.

TABLE 10.1
Age Trends Relevant to Human Factors

	Middle Age (45–64 Years)	Old Age (65–74 Years)	Late Old Age (75+ Years)
Perceptual			
Vision	Near focus declining, hence needs reading glasses or bifocals. Increased susceptibility to glare. Less successful dark adaptation. Some decline in static and dynamic visual acuity. Some loss in ability to discriminate colors.	Little focusing ability left, and loss of acuity even with corrective lenses. Less (⅓ compared with young adult) transmission of light through to the retina. Greater susceptibility to glare. Slow dark adaptation. Significant declines in static and dynamic visual acuity, in useful visual field, and in color discrimination ability.	Significant loss of visual acuity (dynamic and static), color discrimination, and extent of the visual field. Significant risk of visual dysfunction from cataracts, glaucoma, and macular degeneration.
Hearing	Some loss at high frequencies.	Significant loss at high frequencies and some loss at middle frequencies. Can be helped by hearing aid. Greater susceptibility to masking by noise.	Significant loss at high and middle frequencies. Likely needs a hearing aid.
Taste, Smell, Cutaneous Sensitivity	Minimal loss.	Minor loss.	Significant loss.
Cognitive			
Response Time	Some slowing in response time.	Significant slowing in response time.	Pronounced slowing in response time.

Working Memory/ Attention	Minor decline in learning ability and ability to divide attention.	Moderate slowing in learning rate and ability to divide attention.	Learning rate is halved from the 20s, and significant declines are observed for dual-task performance.
Knowledge Base	Little change in fluid intelligence, and stability or increases in crystallized intelligence.	Some decline in fluid intelligence and stability or slight decreases in crystallized intelligence.	Significant declines in fluid and crystallized intelligence.
Physical and Motoric			
Size changes	Limited height loss and some weight gain.	Significant height and weight loss coupled with cohort differences that exaggerate these effects.	Cohort is significantly smaller and there is significant loss of height and weight.
Physical Strength	Modest decline in strength and aerobic capacity.	Moderate decline in strength and aerobic capacity. Some bone density loss.	Significant declines in physical strength and aerobic capacity. Significant bone density loss.
Balance and Mobility	Slight declines in balance ability with little mobility loss.	Significant declines in balance ability and some difficulties with mobility.	Balance likely to be impaired and mobility likely to be restricted.
Health	Fairly robust	Greater susceptibility to chronic conditions (e.g., arthritis, diabetes, osteoporosis, hypertension).	The presence of multiple chronic conditions is highly likely.

know facts about their client populations, such as the size of lettering for signs that would be seen by 95% of the population of licensed drivers. Because it is unlikely that a massive effort will be mounted to establish such facts for each possible situation (e.g., for highway sign legibility in daylight, dusk, night, rain, snow, fog), it would be ideal to be able to derive them from laboratory observations. Nonetheless, it is important to stress that such parameters typically are derived from biased samples. If sound recommendations for design are the goal, representative sampling is an important means to that end. For the present, we will have to be satisfied with the first approximations that biased sampling bring us. It is incumbent on human factors research, however, to extrapolate findings based on advantaged volunteers by trying to run studies with less well-off older adults. Candidate populations would be those older adults who are physically or financially dependent, less well-educated, foreign born, rural, ethnic, and female.

DESIGNING FOR SENSORY LOSS

Human factors specialists interested in aging typically have focused upon the design implications of decreased visual and auditory capabilities with age. Such age-related declines are seemingly inevitable, and can have a profound impact upon the lives of older adults. For example, decreased visual activity may hinder the performance of tasks that rely upon vision, such as shopping, cooking, driving, and most occupations. A loss of hearing ability may interfere with the ability to communicate with others, and may lead to social isolation. The age-related changes in visual and auditory capabilities outlined in Table 10.1 have fairly straightforward design implications that can be employed to develop general guidelines for optimizing the visual and auditory environments of older adults (for general discussions, see Boyce, 1981; Regnier & Pynoos, 1987; Sanders & McCormick, 1987; Working Group, 1988). The following presents a review and discussion of these design guidelines beginning first with the visual environment, and then proceeding to a discussion of the auditory environment.

The Visual Environment

Several characteristics of the environment and the task to be performed will affect visual performance. Previously, we (Charness & Bosman, 1990b) identified five categories of environmental and task characteristics that affect visual performance, and for which the optimal value of these characteristics is likely to differ for young and elderly adults. The environmental characteristics were level of illumination and amount of glare. The task characteristics were size of critical visual details, contrast between critical visual details and task background, and the ease of color discrimination. The following discussion expands and elaborates our previous discussion outlining the optimal value of these environmental and task characteristics for older adults. Table 10.2 summarizes guidelines for optimizing the visual environment of older adults.

Level of Illumination

One of the factors that affects visual performance is the level of illumination. In general, increasing the level of illumination results in improved visual performance. However, the benefit of increasing illumination follows the law of diminishing returns; subsequent increases in the level of illumination result in smaller gains in performance level, and at some point further increases in illumination do not result in improved performance. The point at which the function relating performance to level of illumination asymptotes depends on the visual difficulty of the task. For easy visual tasks the asymptote occurs at lower levels of illumination than for difficult visual tasks (Boyce, 1981; Cushman & Crist, 1987).

A consequence of various age-related changes in the eye, senile miosis, yellowing and opacification of the lens, and clouding of the vitreous humor, is that less light reaches the retina of an older adult (Kline & Schieber, 1985). Given that visual performance is in part dependent on the level of illumination, a straightforward implication of these age-related changes is that older adults will require more illumination in order to see well. In general this expectation has been confirmed. Older adults do require more illumination in order to see well, although there is no consensus regarding how much more illumination is required (e.g., Boyce, 1973; Guth, Eastman, & McNelis, 1956; Hughes & McNelis, 1978; Hughes & Neer, 1981; Jaschinski, 1982; Ross, 1978; Simmons, 1975; Smith & Rea, 1978). Results usually differ between studies, and it is difficult to determine the cause of the conflicting results because different studies employ different tasks that vary in visual difficulty, and consequently in the amount of illumination required for optimal performance. In addition, most studies typically have not established the level of illumination at which further improvements in performance are not observed for the oldest subjects (see Smith & Rea, 1978, for an exception). Without this information it is not possible to establish how much more illumination is required to maximize the visual performance of older adults.

In North America, the most extensive guidelines for determining the appropriate level of illumination for a wide range of residential, com-

TABLE 10.2
Guidelines for Optimizing the Older Adult's Visual Environment

---

A. Increase the level of illumination.
   1. Extensive guidelines for specifying the level of illumination for a wide variety of residential, commercial, institutional, industrial and outdoor settings have been developed by the Illuminating Engineering Society IES (Kaufman & Haynes, 1981a).
B. Accommodate for decreased rate and final level of dark adaptation.
   1. Avoid sudden and pronounced shifts in illumination level, particularly at places with changes in floor level, or with other potential hazards such as obstacles, etc. (Regnier & Pynoos, 1987).
   2. Have levels of emergency illumination adequate for older adults:
      (a) The (IES) (Kaufman & Haynes, 1981a) makes the following recommendations regarding emergency illumination for the general population:
         (i) illumination not less than 1% of normal amount, minimum of 5 lux;
         (ii) minimum illumination of 30 lux at all doors and hazards.
C. Control glare:
   1. Location of glare zones:
      (a) Direct Glare Zone: relative to the light source, the zone from 90° to 45°, with 0° being perpendicular to the light source (Cushman & Crist, 1987);
      (b) Indirect Glare Zone: relative to the light source, the reflected glare zone is from 0° to 45° (Cushman & Crist, 1987).
   2. Line of Sight Angle:
      (a) The line of sight refers to the path between the fovea and the object being viewed. Knowledge of where the observer is looking when performing a task makes it possible to position light sources so that they do not cause glare;
      (b) The reference point for determining the line of sight is the horizontal plane defined when the head is upright, and the subject is looking straight ahead. The deviation of the line of sight from the horizontal plane when viewing an object defines the line of sight angle (Kroemer & Hill, 1986);
      (c) Kroemer & Hill (1986) provided the following estimates of line of sight angle for target distances of .5 m to 1 m:
         (i) head and back upright: $-29° \pm 20°$;
         (ii) head and back reclined: $-20° \pm 20°$;
         (iii) head tilted: $-40° \pm 40°$.
   3. Guidelines for controlling direct glare (Boyce, 1981; Cushman & Crist, 1987; Kaufman & Haynes, 1981a; Regnier & Pynoos, 1987):
      (a) position light sources as far away as practical from the operator's line of sight;
      (b) use several small low-intensity light sources rather than one large high-intensity light source;
      (c) use light sources with a minimum of luminous intensity in the direct glare zone;
      (d) increase the luminance of the area around any glare source;
      (e) use task lights with intensity controls and some method for adjusting their position relative to the task;
      (f) reorient the workplace and furniture if necessary;
      (g) shield light sources if necessary.
   4. Guidelines for controlling reflected glare (Boyce, 1981; Cushman & Crist, 1987; Kaufman & Haynes, 1981a); Regnier & Pynoos, 1987):
      (a) position light sources so that no significant amount of reflected light is directed toward the eyes;
      (b) use light sources with diffusing or polarizing lenses;
      (c) use nonreflectant materials on walls, floors, and ceilings;

(Continued)

TABLE 10.2
(Continued)

(d) change the orientation of the workplace, task, and furniture; change the viewing angle, or the viewing direction in order to improve visibility;
(e) keep the illuminance level as slow as feasible;
(f) use indirect lighting;
(g) use a combination of top and side lighting.
5. Architectural modifications that reduce glare (Regnier & Pynoos, 1987):
   (a) overhangs on windows;
   (b) avoid windows at places likely to be the site of falls, such as on stairways and other changes in floor level.
6. Evaluating the potential for glare-related visual difficulties:
   (a) Borderline between comfort and discomfort glare (BCD) index: The BCD indicates the level of illumination at which a light source will produce discomfort glare for individuals of different ages (Bennett, 1988);
      (i) BCD (foot lambers) = 25,000/age(yr.).

D. Increase the size of important visual details.
1. Font size for printed material. The IES (Kaufman & Haynes, 1981a) makes the following recommendations for the general population:
   (a) minimum acceptable font size is 8;
   (b) for prolonged reading font size should be 10 or 12.
2. Letter size for signs. The Government of Canada (1987) recommended the following letter sizes be used on signs to be read by older adults:
   (a) minimum size of 15 mm;
   (b) ratio of letter size to reading distance = 1:100 (i.e., at distances of 100 m, letters should be 1 m; at distances of 100 cm, letters should be 1 cm)
3. Additional means of increasing size of important visual details (Cushman & Crist, 1987):
   (a) decrease the viewing distance;
   (b) use a magnifying glass or microscope.

E. Increase contrast.
1. Increase contrast between visual tasks and background. Some methods for doing this are improving print quality, using white as opposed to gray paper, changing typewriter and printer ribbons frequently, adjusting CRT brightness and contrast controls, using ink pens rather than pencils, and by using contrasting colors for different task objects and the background (Cushman & Crist, 1987).
2. The following luminance ratios for the general population have been drawn from the IES Handbook (Kaufman & Haynes, 1981a) and from Woodson (1981):
   (a) task to immediate darker surroundings: 3:1;
   (b) task to more remote darker surroundings: 10:1;
   (c) reverse the aforementioned luminance ratios if the task is darker than the surrounding area.
3. Use contrast to emphasize changes in floor level and other hazards in the environment (Regnier & Pynoos, 1987).

F. Reduce the difficulty of color discriminations.
1. Regnier & Pynoos (1987) recommended that the following guidelines be used to reduce difficulties in color discrimination:
   (a) avoid discriminations in the blue-green range;
   (b) avoid discriminations among colors of the same hue.
2. A list of colors that are equally discriminable among the general population appears in Woodson (1981), pp. 523–525.
3. For tasks where the difficulty of color discriminations cannot be reduced, or where accuracy of color discrimination is important, provide increased levels of illumination (see Kaufman & Haynes, 1981a; Knoblauch et al., 1987).

mercial, institutional, industrial, and outdoor settings are those of the Illuminating Engineering Society (IES). A detailed discussion of the IES approach to specifying illumination level is beyond the scope of this chapter (see Boyce, 1981; Flynn, 1979; Kaufman & Haynes, 1981a); however, a brief description is provided. The IES approach to specifying illumination assumes a positive linear relationship between task difficulty, as defined by the size of the critical visual details, and level of illumination. In addition, at a given level of task difficulty, other factors that affect task performance, such as the demand for speed and accuracy, reflectance of the area surrounding the visual task to be performed, and the ages of the individuals performing the task, also influence the amount of illumination required to optimize performance. In general, as the demand for speed and accuracy and the age of the individuals performing the task increase, and the reflectance of the task surround decreases, the IES guidelines recommend a higher level of illumination. Whether or not the IES guidelines are adequate for older adults has not been determined.

Given the difficulty in specifying the appropriate amount of illumination, it is sometimes suggested that control of lighting level be given to the individual (Fozard & Popkin, 1978). The assumption underlying such a recommendation is that individuals will select the level of illumination that will maximize visual performance. Although some studies indicate that individuals do prefer the level of illumination that results in optimal performance (e.g., Hughes & McNelis, 1978), others indicate that they do not (Boyce, 1981). The implication is that leaving lighting level under the control of the older adult may not always result in optimal illumination.

Control Glare

Glare refers to any light source that interferes with visual performance by either producing physical discomfort in the observers or reducing the visibility. One way in which glare may be categorized is according to the source of the glare. Direct glare is produced by a light source shining directly into the observer's eyes, for example, the sun or an incandescent light bulb (Boyce, 1981; Cushman & Crist, 1987; Kaufman & Haynes, 1981a). The effect of direct glare upon performance depends on how close the glare source is to the observer's line of sight. Generally, the closer the glare source is to the line of sight, the more likely it is to reduce the visibility of the target, and the lower the level of performance (Cushman & Crist, 1987). Reflected glare is produced by light that is reflected from objects that the observer is viewing, for example, light reflected from VDT screens, pages of books, glass windows. If light is reflected from a uniform surface such as flat paint, the reflected light produces veiling reflections (Boyce, 1981; Cushman & Crist, 1987; Sanders & McCormick, 1987). The effect of veiling reflections is to reduce the contrast between important visual details and the task background, a situation that will result in decreased visual performance (Boyce, 1981; Cushman & Crist, 1987).

Some of the age-related changes in the eye that decrease the amount of light reaching the retina also increase the susceptibility of older adults to glare. Specifically, the yellowing and opacification of the lens and the clouding of the vitreous humor cause light to scatter within the eye which increases the likelihood that a light source will produce glare (Kline & Schieber, 1985). Ironically, increasing the level of illumination also increases the likelihood that a light source will produce glare. Consequently, it has been suggested that in order to control glare, illumination levels should be as low as is compatible with the maintenance of visual performance (Cushman & Crist, 1987).

Table 10.2 presents several guidelines for controlling direct and indirect glare. In general, these guidelines outline practices to be followed when positioning light sources and furniture so that the amount of direct and reflected glare in the environment is minimized. Although these guidelines seem reasonable, their effectiveness and whether or not it is practical to implement them remain to be determined. Several measures exist for evaluating the potential for glare-related visual difficulties (for a discussion, see Boyce, 1981; Kaufman & Haynes, 1981a, 1981b), but only one measure has been found that considers the effects of increased age. The Borderline Between Comfort and Discomfort Glare (BCD) index indicates the level of illumination at which a light source will produce discomfort glare as a function of age (Bennett, 1977). Although the BCD index does indicate that older adults will experience discomfort glare at lower levels of illumination than younger adults, the function presented by Bennett has not been validated in subsequent studies and its predictive validity is unknown.

Size of Critical Visual Details and Contrast

The visual difficulty of a task is affected by the size in degrees of visual angle of the smallest critical visual details to be discriminated, and the contrast between the luminance of the critical visual details and the luminance of the background. Generally, decreasing task difficulty by increasing the size of critical visual details, or increasing the amount of contrast, will result in improved performance (Boyce, 1981; Cushman

& Crist, 1987). Further, it has been found that making the visual component of a task easier by increasing the size of critical details, or increasing contrast, results in greater gains in performance than can be obtained by increasing the level of illumination. The point is that increasing the level of illumination is not a general panacea that will ensure high levels of visual performance. Modifying a task so that its visual component is easier is just as important as providing adequate illumination (Boyce, 1981; Cushman & Crist, 1987).

A number of age-related changes in vision suggest that older adults would benefit from both increased size of important visual details and increased contrast. There is an age-related decrease in visual acuity, even when corrective lenses are worn. This is probably due to among other things cell death on the retina and the scattering of light within the eye, both of which will result in an image that is somewhat degraded (Kline & Schieber, 1985). Although there is evidence to suggest that the visual performance of older adults is better when the size and contrast of important visual details is increased (Blackwell & Blackwell, 1971; Government of Canada, 1987; Ross, 1978), definitive guidelines have yet to be established. For example, the recommended font sizes listed in Table 10.2 may be too small for older adults, and in particular, the minimum acceptable font size of 8 may systematically inconvenience older adults.

The guidelines for improving contrast by using good quality paper and changing typewriter and printer ribbons frequently are again reasonable, but their effectiveness in enhancing performance is unknown. It is also not clear if the luminance ratios listed in Table 10.2 will reduce problems with transient adaptation for older adults. The available evidence suggests that for the general population the luminance ratios in Table 10.2 are overly conservative. Very few real-life environments achieve luminance ratios of less than 20:1, yet problems with transient adaptation are not frequently reported (Sanders & McCormick, 1987). Similarly, studies have indicated that performance on visually difficult tasks is not affected by luminance ratios of 110:1 (Cushman & Crist, 1987). The implication is that for the general population at least, luminance ratios do not have to be as tightly controlled as indicated in Table 10.2. Whether this is also true for older adults is unknown.

Ease of Color Discrimination

The ability to discriminate between colors as indicated by performance on the Farnsworth–Munsell 100 Hue Test decreases with age, particularly for colors in the blue-green range (Fozard, 1990; Kline & Schieber, 1985). Consequently, the difficulty of color discriminations should be minimized, and discriminations among colors in the blue-green range should be avoided. However, several studies have indicated that increasing the level of illumination increases the performance of older adults on the Farnsworth–Munsell, and that the improvement in performance associated with increased illumination is greater for the oldest adults tested (Bowman & Cole, 1980; Boyce & Simons, 1977; Knoblauch et al., 1987). Although the level of illumination that results in optimal color discrimination by older adults has not been established, an implication of these results is that when difficult color discriminations cannot be avoided, the level of illumination should be increased for older adults.

Summary and Conclusions

Although there is consensus regarding what characteristics of the visual task and environment must be controlled in order to maximize the visual performance of older adults, definitive guidelines have yet to be established. Many of the guidelines discussed previously are little more than rough approximations. Research is required to establish the amount of illumination that maximizes the visual performance of older adults for a wide range of tasks and levels of task difficulty. However, it is unlikely that increased illumination alone will be sufficient to overcome the effects of age-related changes in visual capabilities. It seems likely that some combination of increased illumination, increased size of critical visual details, and increased contrast will be necessary to maximize performance. Currently, the optimal size of visual details or optimal amount of contrast for older adults is not known, let alone how these task characteristics interact with level of illumination. Given the increased susceptibility to glare with age, it is important to keep illumination levels as low as is compatible with good visual performance, and manipulate task characteristics in order to improve performance. Further research needs to be done to establish when a glare source is likely to cause discomfort or decreased visual performance in older adults, so that glare-related visual difficulties can be minimized. Finally, human factors research seeking to optimize the visual environment of older adults has focused upon the impact of a limited number of age-related changes in vision, decreased acuity and color discrimination ability, increased susceptibility to glare, and the decreased amount of light entering the eye with age. Research is required to establish the human factors implications of age-related changes in depth perception, visual field size, dynamic visual acuity, and contrast sensitivity (for a related discussion, see Czaja, 1990; Sekuler, Kline, Dismukes, & Adams, 1983).

The Auditory Environment

With regard to the auditory environment, the traditional focus in human factors has been on controlling the level of noise in the environment so that hearing loss is not produced and the ability to perform a task is not negatively affected by excessive amounts of noise (e.g., Kantowitz & Sorkin, 1983; Sanders & McCormick, 1987). An additional concern when dealing with older adults is to facilitate speech understanding and the detection of other important nonspeech sounds (e.g., warning signals), which are compromised by age-related increases in auditory threshold. The hearing ability of older adults is also more adversely affected by noise, reverberation, and echoes, and consequently, it is important to minimize these factors (Fozard, 1990; Regnier & Pynoos, 1987; Working Group, 1988). Table 10.3 elaborates and expands the guidelines we presented previously (Charness & Bosman, 1990b) for optimizing the auditory environment of older adults. As was the case with guidelines for optimizing the visual environment, all of the recommendations in Table 10.3 are reasonable given the nature of age-related changes in hearing. The following evaluates these guidelines, and indicates where additional research is required.

Age differences in auditory threshold provide an initial means for determining the volume of important sounds. In the case of speech, age differences in speech understanding are not well predicted by age-related increases in auditory threshold for pure tones, and consequently, when seeking to maximize speech understanding, it is necessary to consider age differences in speech reception thresholds (Working Group, 1988). However, to accommodate for interindividual variability, in practical applications the volume of warning signals and speech probably will have to be significantly above threshold values. Research is required to determine how loud speech and other important sounds must be in a variety of environments if they are to be heard by the majority of older adults.

Such research also will need to consider the effects of background noise. Although it is clearly necessary to reduce background noise in environments that are likely to be frequented by older adults, in many instances it may be impractical to renovate buildings with sound-absorbing materials and modified acoustics or to eliminate the noise created by heating and cooling systems. A more practical approach would be to determine the levels of background noise that interfere with the hearing ability of older adults and attempt to maintain noise at or below these levels. Another useful approach would be to determine the signal-to-noise ratios required to maximize the hearing ability of older adults (see Working Group, 1988, for a discussion). Such research also should attempt to use noise similar to that commonly found in many everyday environments, rather than employing white noise.

Additional means of facilitating speech understanding, such as avoiding speaking too fast and maximizing the use of visual cues, are dependent primarily on the sensitivity of the speaker to the special needs of older listeners. Consequently, it may be necessary to instruct individuals

TABLE 10.3
Guidelines for Optimizing the Older Adult's Auditory Environment

A. Increase the volume of important sounds.
  1. Pure tones:
    (a) estimates of age- and gender-related differences in auditory threshold for pure tones can be found in Olsho, Harkins, and Lenhardt (1985);
    (b) avoid high frequency (4,000 Hz plus) sounds (Regnier & Pynoos, 1987);
    (c) for warning signals and other important sounds use low-frequency (1,000 Hz to 2,000 Hz) sounds that have reverberation. The rationale for using reverberation in this instance is that the physical sensation of vibration may alert individuals with severe hearing impairment. This may be critical in emergency situations (Regnier & Pynoos, 1987).
  2. Speech:
    (a) estimates of age-related differences in speech reception threshold can be found in Plomp and Mimpen, 1979.
B. Control background noise and reverberation.
  1. Control background noise:
    (a) eliminate where possible constant sources of background noise such as piped in music, air conditioning, etc. (Regnier & Pynoos, 1987);
    (b) use sound-absorbing materials on walls, floors, ceilings, and windows (Regnier & Pynoos, 1987).
  2. Eliminate reverberation and echoes:
    (a) Plomp & Duquesnoy (1980) made recommendations regarding room acoustics for elderly adults;
    (b) when reverberation is present, pausing slightly after grammatically strategic points may facilitate speech understanding (Davidson, Schonfield, & Winkelaar, 1982).
C. Additional methods for facilitating speech understanding.
  1. Facilitate use of visual cues when speaking and listening (Regnier & Pynoos, 1987):
    (a) arrange furniture in a circular or semicircular manner;
    (b) use furniture that can be moved easily;
    (c) restrict the size of conversation groups to between four and six persons.
  2. Avoid speaking too fast:
    (a) normal speaking rate ranges from 140–200 words/min. Speaking faster than this can adversely affect the speech understanding of older adults (Stine & Wingfield, 1987; Stine, Wingfield, & Poon, 1986; Wingfield, Poon, Lombardi, & Lowe, 1985; Working Group, 1988).

working with older adults how to accommodate to the effects of hearing loss. It also seems likely that these guidelines will be most effective when dealing with small groups, and may not be effective in large groups or public places.

TRANSPORTATION

In this section we review human factors issues in transportation, focusing on three different modes of transportation: public transit, walking, and driving. Given the dearth of research into human factors issues concerning older users of public transportation, our discussion concentrates on walking and driving. There are three key aspects to design for any component in the transportation system: efficiency, comfort, and safety. Efficiency usually can be taken to concern the goal of allowing access to a given set of destinations in minimal time and by allocating as little money as possible. Comfort refers to the physical and psychological well-being of users of transportation systems. Safety can be stated crudely as reaching your destination without injury. Comfort and safety sometimes can be viewed as different points on the same continuum. As always, there are tradeoffs between these design specifications. We are interested in the tradeoffs from the perspective of older users.

Given that about 800 people are killed and thousands more are injured every week in automotive accidents in the United States, you have to wonder about the current system's design characteristics. It often happens that the human is the most unreliable component in a system, so design ultimately focuses most intensely on human performance limitations.[2] Mechanical failure of the vehicle is assigned primary responsibility for a very small percentage of accidents, sometimes as little as 1% (Huston & Janke, 1986).

Public Transportation

As Hoag and Adams (1975) pointed out, there is little research into human factors for urban transportation systems. Part of the problem is due to lack of information on anthropometric measurements for the civilian population, and particularly for elderly people (see Charness & Bosman, 1990b; Kelly & Kroemer, 1990, for age-related summary information.) A good example of the problem is discussed by Hoag and Adams (1975) for passenger seating. If a seat is too high, there is excess pressure on the thighs, but if it is too low, excessive effort is needed to rise from the seat. The Hoag and Adams's tables and discussion deal with 99th-percentile women and do not take into account older women who are disproportionately short, a point graphically illustrated in Koncelik (1982, his Figure 8.3). Due in part to age-related height and weight loss and to cohort differences in body size, most older adults of today are smaller and weigh less than more recent adult birth cohorts. Further, depending on the nature of the survey question and sampling technique (Forbes, Hayward, & Agwani, 1991) between 30% and 50% of community-dwelling

---

[2]For the drivers among the readers: How often have your brakes failed to work properly, resulting in your failure to stop at a traffic light or stop sign, compared to your perceptual/cognitive system failing to register (probably under divided-attention conditions) the presence of the traffic light or stop sign?

adults over the age of 65 years report some problems with mobility and likely would have special needs for transportation systems. As has been pointed out (e.g., Ashford, 1981), even when design is for the able-bodied older adult, general frailty may mean a much higher risk of injury (e.g., when buses accelerate or decelerate rapidly and passengers lose their balance). An empirical investigation of age as a risk factor seems worthwhile.

Given that older people tend to be slower and less agile than their younger counterparts, it is probably necessary to ensure that entrance and exit conditions in public transit vehicles meet their needs by widening aisles, providing grab bars, and improving seating. Hoag and Adams (1975) outlined a set of valuable suggestions. Allowing for suitable seating and shelter while passengers wait for transportation to arrive seems necessary. Providing an automated telephone system that enables users to determine when the bus will arrive at a given stop also alleviates waiting problems.[3] Another concern for older adults is fear of crime while using public transit. Hoag and Adams stressed that even though crime is not a frequent event on public transportation,[4] its perceived frequency is what determines acceptability.

Walking

As the most basic form of mobility, walking affords seniors access to their needs both in the home and outside it. In rural communities, when seniors no longer can drive and there is no public transportation available, walking is often the only means to independence. Ashford (1981) cited a study indicating that 87% of local shopping trips by pensioners were done by walking, as were 39% of trips to town centers.

Safety

Older pedestrians are apparently overrepresented in pedestrian fatality statistics (Cross-National Study, 1989). In Germany in 1985, 52% of pedestrian fatalities involved those over 65 years old. In the Dutch city of Groningen, 60% of pedestrian and bicyclist fatalities involved those over age 65 years. Svanborg (1984) indicated that among pedestrians killed in Sweden 48% are 65 years and older. Given that those 65 years and older comprise between 10% and 18% of these populations it is clear that

---

[3]Such a system (Tele-Ride) is in use in several Canadian cities.

[4]Hoag and Adams (1975) cited a 1970 survey of Chicago public transportation users that although less than 0.5% of users either were victims of or witnessed a crime, 70% reported that crime was somewhat likely or very likely.

older pedestrians are highly at risk. (Even assuming that older citizens spend twice as much time in pedestrian-related activity as other segments of the population, they would still be overrepresented.)

It should not be assumed that the driver is always at fault. Evans (1988a) cited data showing that about one third of pedestrians who were fatally injured had blood alcohol levels in excess of .10, above most legal limits. Winter (1984) cited research showing that 18.8% of fatally injured pedestrians aged 65–74 years and 6.7% of those aged 75 + years had been drinking. Mathey (1983) suggested that older pedestrians are particularly prone to unsafe road-crossing practices, such as crossing after a light has turned red, impatient or abrupt crossing, indefinite and indecisive behavior when entering a crossing, miscalculating the speed of approaching vehicles or their stopping distances, and so forth.

How might we improve design to avoid pedestrian accidents? On the changing people side of the human factors equation, Mathey (1983) proposed group training sessions and mass media instruction as potential techniques for influencing unsafe behavior by older pedestrians. However, an evaluation of such interventions by the Organization for Economic Cooperation and Development (Road Transport Research, 1986) suggested that past education and public training techniques have not been very effective in reducing accidents.

The other option is to change the environment in which people walk. Here we have to be speculative because there is virtually no field research to draw on. A frequently voiced complaint by pedestrians is that traffic lights do not permit enough time for crossing. Lengthening traffic lights is one possibility, particularly in view of the slower walking speeds of the elderly and the disabled (see the discussion by Charness & Bosman, 1990b). Whether the benefits outweigh the costs is difficult to determine, as the cost-benefit analysis that we present later indicates. Another suggestion would be to install special bicycle lanes to minimize pedestrian/cyclist accidents. Because older people are at much higher risks for falls generally (Sterns, Barrett, & Alexander, 1985), ensuring that sidewalk and road surfaces are hazard-free, with clear demarcations for changes in depth, makes sense. In countries such as Canada, when winter conditions create ice hazards in most locations, clearing and sanding or salting of walkways is essential.

Comfort

As many have noted, pedestrians are seen as secondary when designing traffic light systems. If there are tradeoffs to be made, the pedestrian is expected to make them. Although there has been a movement to turn parts of city centers into vehicle-free zones (pedestrian malls), it has not made significant inroads in North America, though suburban shopping malls, which afford both safe walking conditions and climate-controlled comfort, have been extremely successful. Also, as most joggers know all too well, the hard paved surfaces of sidewalks and roadways, though ideal for rubber wheels, are not the most comfortable surface medium for walking and jogging and are very unforgiving for falls.

Psychological comfort is important too. Many older adults living in cities will not walk outside at night for fear of being attacked. Fear of crime is much greater than it should be, given the frequency of such attacks.[5] Yet perceptions govern actions. Ensuring that areas are well lit and patrolled by police forces might allay some of the fears of all citizens, not just seniors.

Driving

Within North America, the automobile is the preferred mode of transportation. Even the most cursory examination of traffic on the roads reveals that the vast majority of vehicles are privately owned automobiles usually containing no more than one person. Although walking is an important form of transportation for seniors and the amount and pattern of driving changes with age, driving remains a very important form of transportation for older adults. Loss of the ability to drive because of age-related declines often requires a significant change in lifestyle and is associated with increased dependence.

Safety

Two issues are relevant to evaluating the safety of older adults while driving: likelihood of being involved in an accident as a function of driver age, and likelihood of being killed if involved in an accident as a function of age. As Evans (1988a; 1991) has shown, older drivers are far less likely to be involved in a severe crash (Fig. 10.2) or fatal accident (Fig. 10.3) than 20-year-old drivers, whether statistics are based on fatalities per million licensed drivers or on fatalities per unit distance traveled. The fatality figures are taken from the Fatal Accident Reporting System (FARS). These data are matched to other data bases that record ages of licensed drivers (Federal Highway Administration), as well as to surveys of vehicle use (Nationwide Personal Transportation Study) that estimate mileage of drivers (for a discussion, see Evans, 1988a, 1991). Although integrating such epidemiological data runs a variety of risks (e.g., if there

---

[5]A recent newsletter by the National Advisory Council on Aging in Canada cites studies showing that in 1981, 5% of crimes committed against adults victimized seniors, 39% victimized 39- to 59-year-olds, and 56% victimized 16- to 29-year-olds.

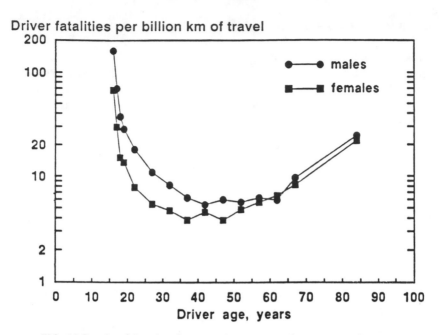

FIG. 10.2. Car-driver involvements in severe crashes per unit distance of travel versus car-driver sex and age. From *Traffic Safety and the Driver* (p. 34) by L. Evans, 1991, New York: Van Nostrand Reinhold. Reprinted by permission.

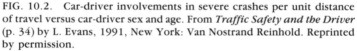

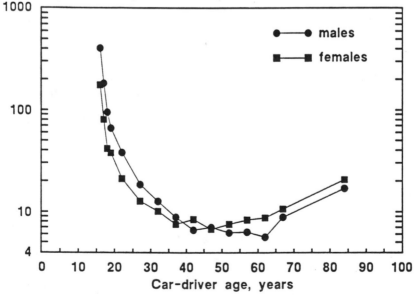

FIG. 10.3. Driver fatalities per billion km of travel versus sex and age. From *Traffic Safety and the Driver* (p. 32) by L. Evans, (1991), New York: Van Nostrand Reinhold. Reprinted by permission.

is age-related under- or overreporting of miles driven, or if older drivers retain their licenses but do not drive), the trends appear to be robust.

However, it should be noted that for both measures a *u*-shaped function is observed, with the peak at age 20 years and declining accident rates until the 40s and 50s, and then a rise which only becomes pronounced above the 70s. Women are less at risk than men over the entire life span for fatalities per million licensed drivers, and become equal to men past the 50s for fatalities per unit distance traveled. The *u*-shaped function suggests that driver inexperience is a critical factor in accident rates in the early years and that declining physical and psychological capabilities are responsible for increases later on, another example of the age/skill tradeoff (Charness & Bosman, 1990a).

Further, older drivers are also less of a risk to pedestrians than younger drivers (Evans, 1988a), whether using a measure such as pedestrian fatalities, or pedestrian fatalities per million licensed drivers, or pedestrian fatalities per unit distance traveled, though with the latter measure there is a noticeable rise for drivers above age 60 years. If a pedestrian is killed by a driver, it is nearly 10 times more likely to be by a 20- to 30-year-old than by a 70- to 80-year-old. In short, though older drivers are more likely to be involved in accidents than middle-age drivers, they are far safer than 20-year-old drivers, no matter which statistic is chosen.

The consequences of being involved in an accident show a different pattern, however. Older drivers and passengers (65 + years) are from three to four times more likely to die from injuries incurred in automobile crashes (Evans, 1988a, 1988b) than younger (20-year-old) drivers. These risk ratios hold whether you examine those wearing seat belts or those not wearing seat belts, as well as for every seating position in the automobile, suggesting that biological factors associated with aging are important (Evans, 1988b). These age-related increases in accident fatalities speak eloquently to the need for a better designed transportation environment, particularly when considering that accidents resulting in nonfatal injuries are about 30 times as frequent as accidents resulting in fatalities. Nonetheless, as Evans (1991) noted, such risk-factor multiples should be kept in perspective. Thirty years ago the fatality rate was three times as high as it is today in the United States, and even today, some countries have fatality rates over three times as high.

Types of Accidents. A number of studies indicate that the type of violation associated with an accident varies with age. Figure 10.4 gives results from Huston and Janke (1986) based on California Highway Patrol data from 1983. Speed is the most frequent violation assessed for nonfatal accidents incurred by young drivers, whereas a right-of-way violation is the most frequent violation associated with older drivers. A very similar

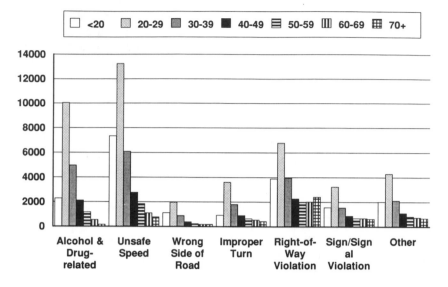

FIG. 10.4. Number of injury accidents categorized by primary type of
violation and age of driver at fault by the California Highway Patrol, 1983,
from Huston and Janke (1986).

picture results from examination of fatal accidents. For younger drivers,
alcohol- and drug-related violations become the overwhelming attributed cause. Right-of-way violations remain the most significant factor for
the oldest adults. These data are remarkably similar to California Highway Patrol data summarized earlier by Harrington and McBride (1970),
indicating that attributed accident causes have remained quite stable over
the years, despite striking changes in the road environment and the automobile.

When you examine the percentage of accident types within age groups
to control for differing frequencies across age groups, the results are even
more dramatic, as seen in Fig. 10.5. It should be noted that there are
problems with the attribution of accident fault. Planek (1972) cited data
showing that 15% of single-car accident fatalities died within 15 min of
their accident from "natural causes," with coronary artery disease the
assumed cause for 94% of these cases. Accidents may follow heart attacks as well as be the precipitating cause. A study by Waller (1967) did
not show a significant relation between cardiovascular disease and 3-year
accident rates or violations (mileage adjusted) for older drivers, though
presence of dementia was a significant risk factor for older drivers for
accidents and the joint presence of cardiovascular disease and dementia
resulted in three times as many accidents as a comparison group of healthy
aged 60 + years drivers.

Age <20

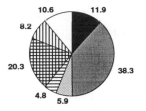

10.6 11.9
8.2
20.3 38.3
4.8 5.9

Age 20-29

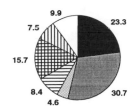

9.9 23.3
7.5
15.7
8.4 30.7
4.6

Age 30-39

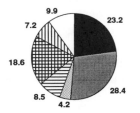

9.9 23.2
7.2
18.6
8.5 28.4
4.2

Age 40-49

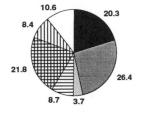

10.6 20.3
8.4
21.8 26.4
8.7 3.7

Age 50-59

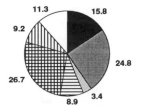

11.3 15.8
9.2
24.8
26.7 3.4
8.9

Age 60-69

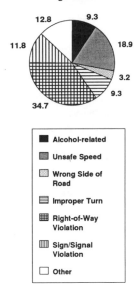

12.8 9.3
11.8 18.9
3.2
9.3
34.7

Age 70+

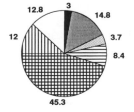

12.8 3 14.8
12 3.7
8.4
45.3

■ Alcohol-related

▨ Unsafe Speed

▦ Wrong Side of Road

≡ Improper Turn

▦ Right-of-Way Violation

▥ Sign/Signal Violation

☐ Other

FIG. 10.5.   Percentage of violation types within age groups for injury accidents, from Huston and Janke (1986).

It is currently not known what is the cause of different types of accidents or why the frequency of accident type varies with age. We would like to suggest that the accident types in Fig. 10.5 denoted by solid shading may be the result of risk taking (driving while impaired or speeding), whereas those indicated by hatching may be the result of breakdowns in perceptual-cognitive processing (failing to see a traffic light, stop sign, or oncoming vehicle). More specifically, a driver is probably aware that driving at excessive speeds or while impaired increases the likelihood of an accident. Thus, accidents involving these factors may be the consequence of risk-taking behavior. Alternatively, accidents involving failure to yield right of way or turning when unsafe seem more likely to result from perceptual or cognitive errors such as inaccurately estimating vehicle velocity, not reacting soon enough to an unexpected hazard, and so forth. Thus, it is possible that for younger adults many accidents are attributable to risk-taking behavior. In contrast, the types of accidents older drivers are involved in could stem from age-related declines in the efficiency of perceptual and cognitive processes (Charness, 1985; Panek, Barrett, Sterns, & Alexander, 1978). General slowing in response time with age (Birren, Woods, & Williams, 1980; Cerella, 1990; Salthouse, 1985a, 1985b) could result in a failure to react quickly enough in emergencies. Age-related changes in visual perception also could predispose older drivers to certain types of accidents. For example, it could be the case that older drivers have a higher percentage of right-of-way accidents because of a decreased ability to judge speeds of oncoming vehicles (Scialfa, Guzy, Leibowitz, Garvey, & Tyrrell, 1991), making them more likely to err in gap detection situations. We first consider changes in visual perception, and then look at the impact of slowing upon the driving performance of older adults.

It might be expected that there would be relationships between accident and violation rates and visual capabilities. Unfortunately, the evidence is not always consistent. Level of visual acuity, either static or dynamic, does not seem to be related in a consistent way to accident records for drivers. In a general review, Planek (1972) cited contradictory studies. The Burg study, using volunteers, found that those with better visual acuity scores had better driving records, though the correlations were generally quite low. The Crancer study compared male drivers between ages 50 years and 70 years who had clean driving records over the previous 6 years and those who had two or more accidents over the previous year, or two accidents and two violations within the previous 24 months. Poor-record drivers had better vision (static and dynamic acuity, glare resistance) than the good-record drivers!

Some have suggested that poor correlations are to be expected given the transient nature of accident-provoking factors. Sivak (1981) pointed out that it is unlikely that safe driving performance exceeds human capabilities "*given* a sober, physically and mentally healthy individual who is not under the influence of fatigue, acute stress, or other undesirable transient states" (p. 62). Unfortunately, people are not always operating vehicles in such ideal conditions. Sivak cited research showing that those in divorce proceedings have twice the accident rate of controls, and that 80% of fatalities in one study had experienced one stressful event in the previous 24 hr. As many have pointed out, old age is often a time of loss and it may be expected that older drivers are disproportionately exposed to stressful conditions.

However, other evidence is consistent with the view that age-related changes in visual perception do affect driving ability. At a very fundamental level, having normal visual fields seems critical to being able to spot events in peripheral vision. It is also known that the size of the visual field shrinks with age (e.g., Cerella, 1985). Johnson and Keltner (1983) screened 10,000 drivers with visual perimetry equipment. They found that there was an age-related increase in visual field abnormalities (about 3% below the age of 60 years, about 13% for those over 65 years of age). Further, for those with binocular visual field loss (1.4% of the sample), accident frequency and convictions over the previous 3-year period were almost double those of age- and sex-matched controls with normal visual fields. Those with monocular loss did not differ significantly from controls in accident and violation frequency, though they were marginally higher.

Being able to read and respond to signs and signals is a critical part of driving. Older adults have much greater difficulty reading and responding to signs in both simulated video tests using sign detection (Evans & Ginsburg, 1985; Woltman, Stanton, & Stearns, 1984) and in simulated road tests using character orientation identification (Sivak, Olson, & Pastalan, 1981). In the latter case, nighttime performance was tested for age groups equated for daytime static visual acuity. In a later study, however, it was found that when older drivers are equated with younger drivers on low luminance acuity, there are no longer any age differences in performance on the orientation identification task (Sivak & Olson, 1982), even in the presence of glare. Older drivers are also slower to make same–different judgments, particularly for symbolic signs (Halpern, 1984), though visibility distance thresholds favor icon over text signs (Kline, Ghali, Kline, & Brown, 1990), particularly in dusklike lighting conditions. Most of these studies have used very small samples (usually 10 or fewer per age group), and those that matched for acuity across age groups may underestimate the true relation because acuity declines with age, particularly static acuity under low illumination (Sturr, Kline, & Taub, 1990).

Similarly, as Mourant and Langolf (1976) noted, much higher intensities and/or larger letter sizes and contrast ratios are required for luminance specifications for automobile instrument panels to accommodate middle-age and older (45 + years) drivers. There is a bit of a balancing act required though, because luminance levels should be kept low enough to maintain dark adaptation (<3.4 candelas/m²) and to avoid disability glare (<17 candelas/m²). Another problem with instrument panels for older adults is that with increased age past the 50s it is difficult to focus at near distances (presbyopia) and also to change accommodative focus between near (instrument panel) and far (road) points. There is some hope that "head-up" displays, already popular in aircraft, will make their way into motor vehicles. Such displays project information onto the windshield at a perceived visual depth that more closely coincides with the resting focus point for older adults (Sojourner & Antin, 1990).

Another significant feature of driving is picking the right stimulus to attend to out of the complex array of objects in the visual field. Individual differences in the ability to identify an object embedded in a field of irrelevant objects represent differences in "field dependence/field indepedence" (Witkin et al., 1954). Field dependence, as measured by the embedded figures test, has been found to be correlated with a measure termed *spare visual capacity*, keeping your eyes closed during straight-road driving for as long as possible (Shinar, McDowell, Rackoff, & Rockwell, 1978). In that study both eyes-open measures and field dependence were higher in a small sample of older (N = 9) than younger (N = 6) drivers. Field dependence measures also have been found to be correlated with accident rates (e.g., Avolio, Kroeck, & Panek, 1985), and particularly for accident rates among older commercial drivers (Mihal & Barrett, 1976). In the latter study, a selective attention measure (dichotic listening task) and a complex reaction-time task (choosing the correct action—braking or turning—from a photograph of a traffic situation) were also significant predictors of accident rates for the preceding 5 years, with the relationships stronger for older (age 45–64 years) than younger (age 25–43 years) drivers. In this study, accident frequency was correlated $r(73)$ = .38 with age.

A more promising approach to examining attention and visual field effects has been to use the useful field of view measure (UFOV; Owsley, Ball, Sloane, Roenker, & Bruni, 1991). Viewers of a video display terminal are asked to make same–different judgments for displays with two central targets (car, truck in two lanes) presented very briefly (12.5 ms to 250 ms) followed by a random noise mask. A secondary task involves radial localization (determining the meridian) for a peripheral object. Pass–fail scoring for UFOV was a significant predictor [$r(51)$ = .36] of prior 5-year accident rates for a group of 57- to 83-year-old Alabama drivers. Cognitive performance on a mental status test was about equally good (r = .34), with the two measures combined accounting for 20% of the variance in accident rates. Prediction was even better when only accidents at intersections were considered. In this instance the proportion of variance accounted for was 29%.

Perhaps the most critical driving performance measure, from an accident avoidance perspective, is following the car ahead of you, and matching your speed and braking to that driver, the "platoon driving" task. A recent field study, albeit with a very small sample (N = 10), showed that the older group (M = 66 years) was no worse than a comparison group (M = 30 years) on brake reaction time, delay, and a correlation coefficient that summarized general following performance, though both groups were much better than brain-damaged younger drivers (Korteling, 1990). Further, little relation was found between laboratory reaction-time tasks and the field measures for either of the older or young control groups. The author attributed the lack of slowing on the realistic task to an effect of driver experience.

Another critical feature of safe driving is the ability to respond quickly to unexpected obstacles, an operation that could be expected to be affected by age-related slowing. Various highway design specifications give 2 s to 2.5 s as the minimal time. Olson and Sivak (1986) arranged for a field experiment of slowing in obstacle avoidance by placing a piece of yellow foam rubber in the driver's lane at a hill crest location where, on average, the obstacle was visible at a distance of about 46 m. Generally, perception-response times of older adults were about the same as the younger ones in the surprise condition (*Median* = 1.1 s, with the 95th percentile response time for both groups about 1.6 s), though the authors did not report significance tests, preferring to plot the percentile response plots for each group. (Perception time, defined as the time to lift the foot from the accelerator pedal, was a bit slower in older than younger adults, but response time, defined as the time to contact the brake pedal from accelerator pedal release, was slightly faster.[6]) Here too, with experienced older drivers, there was little evidence of a problem with slowed response.

The failure to find significant age effects in these field experiments is intriguing given the pervasiveness of age-related decreases in perceptual acuity and slowing. It may be the case that the perceptual, cognitive, and psychomotor changes that occur with increased age are outweighed by the experience that older drivers have accrued, enabling them to compensate for such changes. Still, it would seem to be important to supplement the field study of obstacle avoidance with variables such as divided

---

[6]However, the pattern of slower initiation time and faster movement time has been shown to predict the likelihood of taxi drivers being involved in a "struck-from-behind" accident (Babarik, 1968).

attention (e.g., have the drivers look for street addresses) to simulate a range of typical driving conditions, before concluding that there are no age differences.

Another explanation for the lack of correlation between laboratory and field measures may have to do with the base rate problem. Accidents do not occur very frequently on a per-miles-driven basis. The absolute frequency of accidents should be much greater for commercial drivers,[7] thereby improving the chance to find significant correlations with laboratory variables. Finally, it may be the case that older drivers who suffer accidents share with their accident-prone younger counterparts poor calibration between their confidence in handling risky situations and their competence (Matthews, 1986). That is, young and old drivers may overestimate their ability to handle inherently risky situations compared with their peers; middle-age counterparts rate their abilities as similar to their peers. Such results are consistent with a calibration or metacognition problem.

Redesign to Prevent Older Driver Accidents. How could vehicles and road systems be redesigned to cut down accident frequency? We offer some speculations. Speeding and alcohol and drug abuse are not addressed easily, though these violations assume less importance for older drivers as shown earlier. Better law enforcement may help somewhat (particularly by moving more to issuing warnings than tickets: Van Houten & Nau, 1983), though changing society's attitudes toward these violations is essential to solving the problem. Highway speeding is eliminated easily enough by designing cars that cannot speed (through the use of governors), though this solution has never been acceptable in North American society, which covertly and overtly sells vehicles based on speed and acceleration capabilities. The lowering of the speed limit on U.S. highways to 55 miles/hr during the oil crisis some years ago may well be responsible for some of the recent decline in fatal accidents, because speed at impact is strongly related to severity of injury (MacKay, 1988). Lowering speed limits represents a very inexpensive way to reduce speeding on the highways, assuming that drivers comply. Also, the negative effect of high gasoline prices on travel is a likely cause of fewer deaths. Less travel means fewer accidents.

Right-of-way violations can be minimized with better road design, particularly in highway settings. As Solomon (1985) pointed out, the U.S.

---

[7]We are assuming that commercial drivers are not much more skilled than noncommercial drivers, at least not more skilled by a factor equal to their greater driving distances. The former assumption is consistent with the finding that race car drivers have worse than average accident rates compared to age- and sex-matched controls (Evans, 1991).

Interstate system, which carefully controls access via ramp systems, has mileage-based accident and fatality rates that are one third to one half of those for conventional highways carrying similar traffic loads. Highway construction costs (cited in newspaper articles) are sometimes in the several million dollars/mile range for difficult terrain. Money (1984) cited estimates by the U.S. National Highway Traffic Administration that accidents in the United States annually cost more than $50 billion in lost income, medical costs, insurance costs, and legal expenses. That figure probably can be doubled to arrive at today's costs. It is difficult to justify thousands of miles (billions of dollars) of new highway construction on safety grounds alone unless a very high percentage of accidents could be avoided that way.

Another way to minimize accidents that may be due to failure to notice signs is to improve lighting of signs and possibly to improve headlamp performance, which is critical for night driving (Mortimer, 1988). The older eye transmits light less effectively. But with increased intensity of the light source comes increased opportunity for glare. We concentrate on glare from headlights of motor vehicles. Night driving demands that headlamps provide as much visibility as possible, particularly when the vehicle is traveling at high speeds. Unfortunately, on two-lane roads, increased illumination power for headlamps results in increased visibility for the driver, but also increased glare for the driver on the other side of the road. It is not simply a matter of changing the headlamp beam pattern, because it is necessary for light to be projected into the same plane as the oncoming driver's eyes in order to illuminate road signs (see Olson, 1988). The more light in the plane of the sign, the less expensive the reflective coating on the signs needs to be. So older drivers, who have a greater need for illumination of both the road and road signs, also would suffer the most from the increased glare that any proposed increases in headlamp illumination would bring. Older drivers report much lower frequencies of night driving than younger drivers (Planek & Fowler, 1971), perhaps responding adaptively to the double jeopardy situation that they face.

One high-tech design option for minimizing older driver right-of-way and sign violation accidents is to use radarlike warning devices within automobiles to alert the driver auditorally to possible road hazards or to pedestrians (Yaksich, 1985) and to have lights and signs broadcast a signal that could be translated by a device in the car into different auditory warnings (to supplement the visual one) when drivers approach intersections. Although such devices are technically feasible, it is probably not yet economically feasible to install them in 180 million vehicles and at millions of traffic intersections, though pilot projects are probably warranted. Careful feasibility studies are needed accompanied by cost-benefit analyses. The problem with accidents is that, fortunately, they are still relatively rare events on a per-vehicle-mileage basis, and there is undoubtedly a point of diminishing returns for further investments in safety devices. A totally risk-free transportation system is impossible.

Because it is unrealistic to believe that all accidents can be eliminated through design, minimizing the effects of collision on motorists and pedestrians is a worthwhile goal. It is possible to design vehicles to minimize internal impacts with automobile surfaces (for instance, through installation of air bags), as well as to design external surfaces to minimize injury for pedestrians (MacKay, 1988). Again, cost-benefit analyses are needed to determine whether such modifications are economically viable. Our suspicion is that government regulation probably will be the most fruitful way to prod manufacturers to make the necessary changes, though the current highly competitive marketplace, steeply rising car insurance costs, and an aging population may accelerate the process. Unfortunately, until very recently, safety has not been a selling point for automobiles, probably because people would rather not acknowledge the risk of injury through accidents when contemplating a purchase.

Some have taken the higher risk of accident involvement by older drivers (compared to middle-age drivers) as a sign that stiffer licensing arrangements are needed. As Evans (1991) noted, older drivers are considerably less of a risk to themselves and others than are young drivers. Older drivers reduce their driving distances considerably and drive less during high-risk times such as during rush hour and at night, probably responding adaptively to age-related changes that make driving a less comfortable experience for them. The problem for older drivers is more likely to be one of diminished mobility than diminished driving capability. Nonetheless, high-risk subgroups within the older population, such as of those in the early stages of dementia, should probably be carefully screened.

Another approach to accident avoidance is to redesign the driver, that is, to provide training programs to eliminate unsafe driving practices. Older driver training has become increasingly popular in the United States through programs sponsored by the American Association of Retired Persons (55 Alive/Mature Driving), the American Automobile Association, and the National Safety Council. Formal evaluations of the efficacy of these programs are very infrequent. The few attempts that have been made have not shown any differences in accident rates between volunteer trained groups and waiting group controls. For instance, in one large ($N =$ 10,000) study, because of high dropout rates (only 21% remained in training and provided follow-up accident data) the final samples were no longer random so the lack of differences is not interpretable (McKnight, 1988).

Comfort

As mentioned earlier, seating standards, based on 99th percentile anthropometric data, systematically inconvenience older women, who, ironically, are the fastest growing group of older drivers (Winter, 1984). Seating position is also critical for visibility of the road, and short older women will have a reduced field of vision of the road ahead. One idea for designers would be to adopt an age-weighted driver-related 99th percentile standard. Another would be to provide slightly more expensive seating that has greater adjustment capability.

There is more to comfort in driving than physical comfort. Psychological comfort may well be one of the important factors in the marked reduction in mileage driven by older drivers. Evans (1988a) noted that the average annual distances travelled for male drivers is 31,400 km for those aged 35–39 years and 14,500 km for those aged 65–69 years. (Some of the reduction may well be due to elimination of the need to drive to work following retirement.) Certainly reductions in the amount of driving at night, on highways, and during rush hour by older drivers fits with the idea of psychological discomfort. Because accident risk is directly related to mileage (exposure), such reductions are probably adaptive, though restricting.

There is an interesting ethical dilemma facing designers. Should they succeed in making the driving environment more comfortable for older drivers, whose risk of accident on a per-mileage basis is higher than that of middle-age drivers, more older drivers will be killed and injured as they are encouraged to drive greater distances. Determining how mobility gains balance these accident losses is more than an academic exercise. Unless accident risk (per unit distance traveled) can be reduced at a faster rate than the increase in travel distance we may be spinning our wheels both figuratively and literally with respect to accidents.

In summary, older adults are at much greater risk for personal injury as transportation users, particularly as pedestrians, but also as drivers compared to middle-age adults. Some of the increased risk can be traced to age-related changes in physical, perceptual, and cognitive functioning. Better design can be expected to help mitigate the greater risks, but whether such changes are cost effective is at present unknown. Similarly, older transportation users are probably the least likely segment of the population to be comfortable and secure when using transportation systems. Low-cost design modifications probably could rectify some of this discomfort. Further, in almost every case, modifications aimed at improving the comfort and safety of older users probably would benefit other segments of the population.

THE OFFICE ENVIRONMENT

Human factors will become increasingly concerned with the graying of the labor force. As Fig. 10.6 shows, the work force is aging along with the rest of the population. In the next few decades, those in the 45–64 year age range who have been in balance with new entries in the labor force will practically equal those who have usually been the largest component, 25- to 44-year-old workers.

Human factors research in the office environment has been focused on two main issues: safety and productivity. Safety research usually is concerned with reducing accidents and work-related disabilities (such as back injuries and repetitive strain injuries). A typical concern is the design of safer machine–human interfaces. Productivity concerns focus on the design of better tools, instruments, and displays, as well as on how to structure the sequencing of activities and layout of work space to permit efficient movement within and between activities. Because vision is such an important component, there is a large literature concerning visual characteristics such as lighting, contrast ratios, and display types.

Earlier we outlined the changes in vision and hearing that occur in late middle age. Such changes have profound implications for safety and productivity in a workplace that will depend increasingly on older workers. Perhaps equally important are the cognitive changes that can be expected for older workers, the most salient of which is learning rate. Most memory studies show, for intentional learning situations, that older adults learn less effectively than younger ones (see chapter 2 of this volume). We concentrate on what such age-related changes mean for a workplace that is becoming increasingly volatile and dominated by changes in technology. We focus on the use of microcomputer systems, simply because they represent the most rapidly growing sector of new business equipment. Further, there is some indication that such systems are also finally penetrating the home market.

Computer Use

Probably the prototypical product for human factors research is the computer system.[8] Ten years ago, if you wandered through most offices in North America, you might have seen a few terminals connected to a central mainframe computer. Today, on many desks you will find a micro-computer—some with about the same computing power as that old mainframe and virtually all with better human–computer interfaces. However, be-

---

[8]A survey of Human Factors Society members by Sanders, Bied, and Curran, cited in Sanders and McCormick (1987) showed that 31% worked in the computer and software industry.

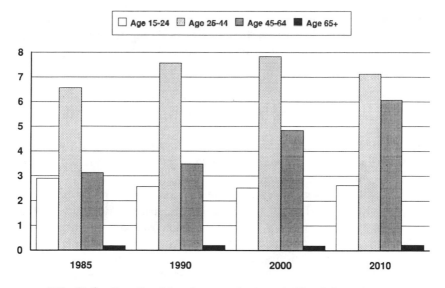

FIG. 10.6. Canadian labor force projections (millions) from Denton, Feaver, and Spencer (1986).

cause of their design, microcomputer systems can stress the visual, manual, and learning capabilities of workers, particularly those of older workers.

Vision

Most microcomputers systems have a screen that transmits light via a cathode ray tube (CRT), much like that in a typical television set. An exception is the laptop or notebook computer, which typically has either a liquid crystal display that is backlit and/or reflects ambient light or a gas plasma display. The challenge with all these device types is positioning, resistance to glare, and presenting high enough contrast ratios for text and graphics so that the viewer easily can perceive what is on the screen. A great deal of research has been done examining screen characteristics affecting legibility, particularly concerning factors such as size, color, and type of text characters. Almost all this research has been carried out using young adults (see for reviews Grandjean & Vigliani, 1980; Helander, 1987).

Positioning can present special problems for presbyopic older adults who use bifocal lens systems. Typically, near vision is in the lower half of the lens and distance vision is in the upper half. If a screen is mounted on top of a computer, an older adult will be forced to tilt his or her head up sharply to use near vision, contravening standard recommendations[9]

---

[9]The Kroemer and Hill (1986) study used subjects of unreported ages, with either uncorrected normal (20/20 Snellen) vision or corrected to normal vision via contact lenses only.

that the screen be about 30° below the line of sight (Kroemer & Hill, 1986; see also Table 10.2). Use of reading glasses designed for near vision only or the addition of a third lens for near distance above the far distance lens may help. As well, monitors often can be placed directly on the desk in front of the keyboard, with the main computer box off to the side. Still, given that older adults tend to have poorer posture (head tilted down), such repositioning may not compensate adequately for all older adults. Laptop computers have the advantage that their screens are positioned quite low in the visual field but the disadvantage that the screens tend to be smaller and that screens (LCD or gas plasma) have lower contrast ratios and are less glare resistant than CRT devices.

As technology has advanced, the density of screen characters has improved on the typical monitor found in a business environment. Only a few years ago, the most popular color screen used a 640 (horizontal) × 200 (vertical) pixel (picture element) matrix with text characters plotted in a 5 × 7 array. The more usual color system today uses a 640 × 480 pixel array with 7 × 9 boxes for text symbols. Early research (e.g., Pastoor, Schwarz, & Beldie, 1983) showed that the denser the array, the better the visual performance through character sizes of 9 × 13, though character size (visual angle) was confounded with density. However, a recent study with a high-resolution monitor showed little difference for a 1-hr reading aloud task with 12 × 14 versus 8 × 9 character matrix sizes (Miyao, Hacisalihzade, Allen, & Stark, 1989). It is unknown whether age is an important factor, but it seems likely that denser, higher contrast displays would be even more beneficial for older viewers. Similarly, instead of using fixed width characters, newer graphical interfaces have attempted to use variable width characters, bringing displays of text more in line with traditional printed text. Such displays may yield a slight reading speed advantage (6%; Beldie, Pastoor, & Schwarz, 1983), but again, it is unknown whether variable width fonts aid older viewers disproportionately. Given the rapid advances in display technology, it seems likely that by the time the relevant research has been conducted, megapixel displays with carefully tuned character fonts will have become commonplace in the office environment. Such displays can eliminate the usual difference in reading speed favoring paper over the CRT, when contrast, antialiasing, polarity, and other factors are optimized, at least for young adults (Gould, Alfaro, Finn, Haupt, & Minuto, 1987).

Input Devices

There is a large human factors literature devoted to control devices (see Sanders & McCormick, 1987, chapter 10), and a growing body on computer input devices (Greenstein & Arnaut, 1988). The keyboard is still the major input device for working with a computer system, though alternatives such as the mouse, touchscreen, trackball, light pen, joystick, and digitizing tablet in combination with menu-driven software are assuming an increasing role. More exotic devices such as the glove and voice-driven, handwriting-driven, or eye movement-driven systems also are being explored. There are also specialized controls for the severely disabled population (e.g., mouth-driven controls).

Much of the research on input devices for computers has focused on the relative merits of such devices, particularly for positioning tasks such as target acquisition. Early work focused on so-called Fitts' Law devices, such as cursor keys, joystick, and mouse (e.g., Card, English, & Burr, 1978), usually showing the marked superiority of the mouse for extended movements across a screen. However, for some applications, a touchscreen yields better performance than the mouse (Karat, McDonald, & Anderson, 1986). We have been unable to locate any published work that examines age effects.

Thus, we can offer only speculative suggestions about input devices. First, the very old are much more likely than young and middle-age adults to suffer from chronic conditions such as arthritis (Verbrugge, Lepowski, & Konkol, 1991) that would make keyboard interaction difficult. Further, older adults are probably less likely to have typing skills than young adults, particularly older men. It can be expected that use of menu-driven software with direct (absolute positioning) addressing devices such as a touchscreen or a light pen would be the best choice for novice older users. Keyboards likely would present the greatest difficulty for nontypists. Devices such as a mouse, trackball, or joystick probably would be intermediate between the two. Menu designs should pay careful attention to target size given expected problems with homing in on small targets. Target acquisition may be exacerbated by hand tremor or arthritis.

Learning

Given the pressures to bring today's complex business software to market quickly, it is more likely that the user must learn to accommodate to the application than it is that the manufacturer or designer will do large-scale studies to test out different interface designs. Efforts must be expended to find effective ways to teach people. In the recent past, it has been claimed that the modal technique for training in small office environments has been to dump the software package in front of the user and ask them to learn it (Czaja, Hammond, Blascovich, & Swede, 1986). Now it is more common for the software designer to include a tutorial, either on line or via a manual, to support training. Some offices also send employees to short seminar courses.

Individual differences only now are being recognized as important mediators of human–computer interaction (e.g., Egan, 1988). A critical, though generally unresolved, issue is whether older adults benefit differentially from some training techniques over others. That is, are there interactions between age and training technique? Some strong claims originated in the early 1960s and 1970s that "discovery learning" techniques were of special benefit to older workers (e.g., Belbin & Belbin, 1972), but the evidence offered in support of this assertion was quite weak. Nonetheless, the idea that people can gain especially from situations where they can actively explore the task environment has resurfaced under other names, for instance, as "exploration training" (Wood & Roth, 1988).

A few studies have contrasted training techniques but have not shown interactions with age for learning software. Gist, Rosen, and Schwoerer (1988) showed that a modeling-plus-tutorial condition was better than a tutorial-only condition, but equally so for young (age < 45 years) and older (age > 45 years) workers learning a spreadsheet. Similarly, no interaction with age was reported by Czaja et al. (1986) in a study of word-processing training. They reported that computer-based training was inferior to instructor-based and manual-based techniques, but equally so for young, middle-age, and older learners. Zandri and Charness (1989) did report an interaction between training technique and age (learning alone or with a peer, with and without preliminary information about computers) for people learning to use a calendar and notepad system on one of three dependent variables. In this case, the old group showed less of a difference in performance on a final test than did the young group as a function of training conditions, though both groups were near perfect. No interactions were evident for time to complete the task or amount of help required. In short, there is little indication that one form of training will be differentially beneficial for older compared to younger computer users.

Generally, though, it can be expected that whatever training regimen is adopted, more time should be permitted for older workers to go through the program and more assistance should be available. Most studies of software training show that older adults acquire new information more slowly than young adults. In word-processing training studies, older adults were either 1.5 times slower (Elias, Elias, Robbins, & Gage, 1987, with trained typists) or 2.5 times slower (Zandri & Charness, 1989, with nontypists) than young adults in proceeding through the self-paced tutorials or test sessions. Gomez, Egan, and Bowers (1986) showed that when a 2-hr time limit was set for completing a text-editing tutorial in their first experiment, age was a significant predictor of those who finished ($M = 41$ years) versus those who did not ($M = 52$ years) in their sample of

33 women aged 26–63 years. Age was also a predictor in Experiment 2 of whether subjects finished the advanced lessons in the second test session. Age was also strongly associated with number of first-try errors and execution time/change (bivariate r values over two experiments averaging about .50), making an independent contribution that was usually greater than other significant predictors such as spatial memory and reading skill. In the two studies that kept track of requests for help from the trainer (Elias et al., 1987; Zandri & Charness, 1989), the oldest group required about three times as much help as the youngest group.

One study, however, reported minimal age differences between young (18–30 years) and old (65–75 years) in knowledge acquired about text editing during a computer-assisted six-session (12-hr) tutorial (Hartley, Hartley, & Johnson, 1984). The study is described only sketchily, but perhaps the extensive training is responsible for the finding of minimal age differences (12 hr vs. 2–3 hr in other studies). Another study (Garfein, Schaie, & Willis, 1988) reported no age differences in acquiring knowledge about spreadsheet software following two 1.5-hr tutorials, though the participants' age range (49–67 years) excluded young adults.

Trying to match the user interface to the user's cognitive representation of the task can pay dividends for young adults, particularly in terms of gains in performance with practice (e.g., Roske-Hofstrand & Paap, 1986; Singley & Anderson, 1989). Nonetheless, mental models are not always successful in producing better performance if they are not well tuned to the given task and individual (see the review by Carroll & Reitman Olson, 1988). Given the expectation that older adults will have less efficient working-memory and problem-solving skills when tackling novel tasks, it seems likely that they would benefit differentially from the "training wheels" approach (Carroll & Carrithers, 1984) of limiting the overall complexity of a software application. What types of gains can be expected with older adults remains to be seen. Rate of change with practice on laboratory tasks is usually equivalent for young and old (see the review by Salthouse, 1990), and occasionally slightly greater for the middle age compared with young adults (e.g., Charness & Campbell, 1988).

Attitudes. As a species, humans are characterized by their remarkable adaptiveness. Usually, when a new tool provides a needed function (e.g., the telephone), it is quickly adopted by the population who need that function, though not always (see Ostberg & Chapman, 1988). However, attitudes can play an important role in determining whether the effort to learn to use a new tool is going to be perceived as being worthwhile and that decision is likely to affect training entry and success (Belbin & Belbin, 1972). Particularly with computer technology, which has a history of being seen as frightening and complex (Lee, 1970), those being urged to learn to use it may not be sufficiently motivated to do so. The critical issue here for human factors is whether attitudinal differences exist between younger and older workers that may hamper training efforts.

There is some evidence to suggest that older adults are less likely to report using new technology such as computers, banking machines, and even calculators. Zoltan and Chapanis (1982) obtained attitude information from a sample ($N = 521$) of professionals (CPAs, lawyers, pharmacists, and physicians) in Washington, DC. They reported that older professionals were much less likely to use computers than younger ones, probably due to training opportunities. They did not report the relation between age and attitudes, though they did find a significantly more positive attitude for users versus nonusers, a variable that is correlated with age in their sample. Arndt, Feltes, and Hanak (1983) found that older individuals were much less likely than younger ones to report use of a word processor in a random sample of secretarial staff at a university. Brickfield (1984) reported a marked decline with age in technology use by a 1981 sample of American Association of Retired Persons members over the age of 45 years. Fig. 10.7 plots the results for their Table 1.

Brickfield (1984) also reported that ". . . older people have less positive views toward a variety of technologies than do younger people" (p. 32), though he did not provide any data. Other investigations generally have not found significant age differences in attitudes toward computers. Krauss and Hoyer (1985) found sex differences (men more favorable) but no age differences in attitudes toward computers. They compared employees and spouses of employees who were retirees at a senior center program on computers to undergraduates at Syracuse University, so selection bias may have played a role. Ansley and Erber's (1988) highly educated older volunteers were virtually equivalent to undergraduate students on 10 subscales measuring attitudes toward computers.

Do attitudes predict performance once someone is involved in a training program? In the Gomez et al. (1986) text-editing study attitudes toward computers tended to be slightly negatively correlated with age ($r = -.3$, $-.2$), though generally uncorrelated with performance, except for a counterintuitive positive relation between attitudes and the time to make an editing change. Czaja et al. (1986) also failed to show significant relationships between computer attitudes and word-processing performance in their study. Zandri and Charness (1989) showed no relation between initial attitudes and final test performance, though initial attitudes were negatively correlated with time to complete tutorial sessions [$r(42) = -.36$] and the amount of help requested [$r(42) = -.34$]. However, attitudes toward computers measured before the final test session were positively

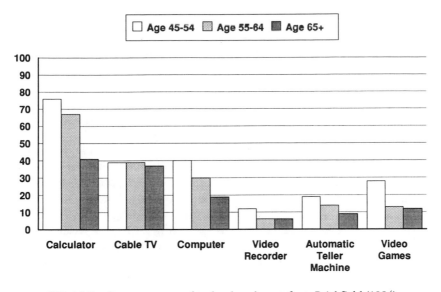

FIG. 10.7. Percentage use of technology by age from Brickfield (1984),
N = 750.

correlated with test performance. All of the experimental studies of software training have used volunteers who may be expected to have more
positive attitudes toward computers than nonvolunteers. Thus, the consistent failure to find a relationship between initial attitudes and performance may not be strongly generalizable. Nonetheless, such negative
results suggest that if extra incentives are offered to older workers to
retrain, their success in the program may not be jeopardized by any negative attitudes that they may hold initially.

Computers probably will continue to play an increasingly important
role in society. The challenge for designers of hardware and software
is to enable easier interaction with these devices, particularly for older
adults. Any age-related disadvantage in familiarity with microcomputers
is likely to be a function of this historical epoch. For future generations
of senior citizens the microcomputer is probably going to be as familiar
(and perhaps as easy to use) as is the telephone for today's generation.[10]
Still, a great deal of basic human factors work needs to be conducted on
age and computer use. Almost every issue that has been addressed with
young populations needs replication with older ones.

---

[10]A slight irony might be perceived when the typical feature-laden office telephone is
visualized. A kind of "Peter Principle" may be at work, where a useful device is complicated to the point where it is just beyond the average user's competence.

COST-BENEFIT ANALYSES

Design, whether concerned with the public or private sector, must deal with the cost-benefit issue. A reasonable characterization is provided by Frost (1975): "Cost benefit analysis is designed to compare two or more solutions to a given problem and to provide a framework in which such comparisons can be usefully discussed" (p. 3). In the minimalist situation, the two solutions can be taken as "doing nothing" and "doing something." Cost-benefit analysis usually involves standardizing outcome variables by determining (and in most cases estimating) their market prices. This quest often leads to fairly speculative exercises, such as determining a monetary value for clean air, travel time, and even a human life. We offer the following example in that spirit.

Consider the case of extending crossing times for pedestrians at signals, discussed earlier. Take the example of a traffic light that allocates more time to east–west traffic than to north–south, with our concern being the pedestrians making the north–south crossing. If we extend the lights for pedestrians by an average of 3 s/light (one project suggested 6 s: Atkinson, 1987) vehicles on the main east–west route are slowed by the same amount.

Assume that in the United States, half of the 2,000 yearly older pedestrian deaths (Sterns et al., 1985) could be avoided this way. This is probably much too generous an estimate, because about half of pedestrian fatalities occur at intersections without signs or traffic lights (Hauer, 1988). Further, drivers who make left turns constitute about one third of the risk to a pedestrian (Yaksich, 1985, Table 3), and they usually have the same green light (except for the case of left-turn signal intersections).

As a first approximation, assume also that the value of a life is $20,000.[11] (See Mooney, 1977, for a detailed discussion of the problem of assigning a monetary value to life.) A saving of about $20 million thus would be realized, before considering health care, police/ambulance costs, and damage to the vehicle that hits the pedestrian, all of which increase the figure. To provide an upper bound on that figure, we might assign a cost of life of $250,000, yielding a savings of $250 million for 1,000 lives. A lower bound might be that only 250 lives are saved by lengthening lights, yielding an interval of $5 million to $250 million saved.

---

[11]This is the limit for accidental death via air travel under the Warsaw convention if travel is not through the United States, and roughly what the annual per capita Gross National Product is for the United States. In the first author's university, one employment benefit is life insurance valued at one times annual salary. Courts often take the position that the value of a life is the expected income that would have been earned if the person would have continued living to their usual life span. This scheme would generate very little value for older adults lives because they are generally retired from paid employment.

The fuel consumption cost of idling an automobile is approximately .8 ml/s (estimated from Chang, Evans, Herman, & Wasiclewski, 1977). Assuming fuel costs of $.25/l ($1/gallon) or $.00025/ml yields .00025 × .8 = $.0002/s of idle time. Being stopped at three of the extended traffic lights per day (about 1,000/year) for, say, 25 million urban vehicles (there are about 180 million registered autos, trucks, and buses in the United States) leads to an estimate of costs ($.0002/s × 3 s delay/ light × 1,000 lights/year × 25,000,000 vehicles) of $15 million. The $15 million fuel cost figure is obviously only approximate, because fuel costs are rising, though engine efficiency is also increasing. Upper bounds on fuel costs are around $65 million, if you assume that fuel costs are $1.20/gallon and 100 million vehicles are idled at three extended traffic lights daily. In short, much of the savings attributed to lengthened light times and diminished fatalities would be reclaimed by increased fuel consumption alone.

More significantly, drivers who are slowed may be losing time from paid employment. Assuming an average industrial wage of $10/hr, the loss of 9 s/day yields a loss of $.025/day. Again, multiplying this by 25 million vehicles yields a cost of about $625,000/day or about $200 million per year. Reasonable upper and lower bounds on cost could come from assuming that there are one to three traffic lights encountered per day, that lost-time costs are valued between $1 (nonpaid time[12]) and $10/hr, and that 10 million to 100 million motorists[13] encounter lengthened lights. The extremes for these assumptions yield a range of lost-time costs from $3 million to $500 million.

We are making the simplifying assumption that only 3 s are lost at each light, whereas a more sophisticated analysis might show that delays cascade in heavy traffic situations (perhaps doubling or tripling the real time loss). Further, the time (and monetary) loss could be even greater if commuters arrive at work feeling highly stressed and take 15 min or so to cool down.

These calculations also fail to consider the off-setting deaths that might be incurred in producing and distributing the additional millions of liters of gasoline consumed during engine-idling time (though these are probably factored into the cost of fuel), deaths attributable to increased pollu-

---

[12]Cost-benefit analyses usually assign value to unpaid time (Frost, 1975). Drivers are willing to pay to use a toll road during leisure travel if they perceive that travel times will be reduced compared to those on a nontoll road, demonstrating that their unpaid time is worth money. Getting there is not always half the fun. Also, any time loss probably should be weighted more highly for older adults, given that it is a nearly exhausted nonrenewable commodity.

[13]We assume that a maximum of 100 million of the 180 million registered vehicles in the United States operate in cities with traffic lights.

tion from burning that fuel, and the "savings" to Social Security of having 1,000 older Americans die prematurely. Further, we have assumed that outcomes for younger pedestrians would be unaffected by crossing time changes.

On the other hand, and undoubtedly more important, the analysis thus far fails to consider potential savings for cases where older pedestrians would ("only") have been seriously injured (or even just frightened when nearly hit) and would have consumed expensive health care, hospital care, and nursing home care. Typically, nonfatal accidents outnumber fatal ones by very high ratios. Hauer (1988) cited figures of about 12,000 pedestrians aged 64 + years injured per year, compared to about 2,000 killed. Elimination of half the injuries, valuing the average cost of such an injury at between $1,000 and $10,000, yields additional benefits of between $6 million and $60 million per year.

Further, this analysis ignores the costs of implementing a scheme to lengthen lights. Aside from personnel and equipment costs (Hauer, 1988, indicated that there are about 300,000 signals installed in the United States), there is also what economists term an *opportunity cost* for such a program. Namely, spending money on this program means that less money is available for other programs that may yield a greater social welfare benefit. As Table 10.4 indicates, from a strictly economic analysis standpoint it sometimes may not "pay" to save lives when all the costs are tallied (with the obvious exception of your own life or the lives of your loved ones). It may prove beneficial in this case to design traffic light systems where a button provides the pedestrian with a longer crossing time, one out of two light changes, or have the system change to longer north–south crossing times after rush-hour periods. Even more important would be a more detailed examination of the 2,000 annual pedestrian fatalities (not to mention nonfatal injuries), followed by field studies, to see to what extent light crossing time is a significant contribut-

TABLE 10.4
Cost-Benefit Analysis of Lengthening Traffic Lights by 3 Sec
to Allow More Crossing Time for Older Pedestrians

Cost	Benefit
Fuel consumption of idled vehicles: $40 million (range: $15 million to $65 million)	Lives saved: 250 to 1,000: $123 million (range: $5 million to $250 million)
Time lost by drivers: $250 million (range: $3 million to $500 million)	Nonfatal injuries prevented: 6,000 $33 million (range: $6 million to $60 million)
Total cost: $290 million	Total benefit: $156 million

ing factor. The difficulty of assigning monetary values to the cost and benefit sides in this very rudimentary analysis indicates why so few cost-benefit analyses are conducted, though they are potentially very informative about hidden costs in decision making. Nonetheless, if human factors specialists are to make claims on societal resources through issuing guidelines for products and processes, they will have to convince the public that changes are worthwhile.

CONCLUSIONS

Earlier, we suggested that if human factors research focusing upon older adults is to produce design guidelines that supplement those obtained from research with younger adults it must be the case that the conditions of optimal safety, efficiency, and comfort for older adults differ from those for younger adults. We have outlined examples of age by condition interactions for visual performance under different illumination levels and auditory performance in the presence of noise. Such interactions are also quite evident for molar tasks such as driving a motor vehicle safely. Although further research is required to identify other environments and tasks for which age by condition interactions are observed, it seems reasonable to conclude that design guidelines should be developed for older adults. Unfortunately, a limitation of human factors research focusing upon older adults is that specific guidelines for design are often lacking, and those that do exist frequently have a weak empirical basis. We would like to suggest some procedures for data collection that may facilitate the development of sound design guidelines. In addition, we outline some additional content areas within human factors that need to be addressed from an aging perspective.

Procedural Recommendations

Our first set of procedural recommendations concerns sampling technique. Specifically, we suggest that research should not employ an extreme groups design, but rather that an attempt be made to incorporate decade samples of older adults, ranging from age 40 years to age 80 years, or beyond, depending on the physical, perceptual, psychomotor, or cognitive functions being investigated. In addition, an attempt should be made to obtain a representative sample. Older adults are a heterogeneous group, and if effective design guidelines are to be developed performance functions that span older adulthood are required. Samples that focus upon a restricted age range and employ volunteer populations who are primarily White, middle-class, healthy community-dwelling adults are likely to underestimate interindividual variability. It is critical to obtain an accurate estimate of performance variability because as was discussed previously, if the performance of older adults is so variable that extremely wide design guidelines are required, it may be too costly to implement many guidelines. Design guidelines that are not economically feasible to implement are of no benefit to older adults.

Although difficult, there are several ways in which a representative sample could be obtained. Research teams may try to link up with ongoing studies that already have identified representative samples. It may be feasible to bring the lab to the participant in order to avoid selective refusal based on mobility constraints. Portable computer equipment can facilitate this process, though it cannot eliminate the need for laboratories, particularly for visual performance studies that require tight control of illumination. At worst, more of an effort can be made to seek out groups that are less likely to volunteer for further validation before any recommendations are made.

Our second procedural recommendation is to extend laboratory research on the physical, psychomotor, perceptual, and cognitive capabilities of older adults and attempt to make it more useful for real-world applications. Predictions from laboratory tasks to real-world tasks (e.g., via the parameter estimates given in Charness & Bosman, 1990b) have not yet been subjected to sufficient empirical testing. There are enough counterintuitive findings in field research to suggest that the road will be a rocky one. It is not enough to show that older adults are slower than younger ones on classic choice reaction-time tasks and then assume that this has implications for braking an automobile. As we have seen, driving experience and the very slow response times of even young drivers to unexpected hazards in the real world put their reaction times out of the range of typical laboratory reaction-time studies. Even in laboratory situations, you can show age-related slowing with choice reaction time in the presence of no age-related differences in performance in a task with high face similarity—typing (Bosman, 1991; Salthouse, 1984). When highway design standards are based on perception-response times of 2 s to 2.5 s, there is an urgent need to look at laboratory situations that sample tasks in this time range.

There are several ways in which the results of traditional experimental studies can be extended to real-world situations. First, better use should be made of epidemiological sources of information about aging. Large-scale population studies are available through governments and industry on health, activity, injury, and disability that can be analyzed by age and other demographic features. Most of these data sets are based on questionnaire response data (which has some weaknesses). Nonetheless, secondary analysis can help to provide new hypotheses that can be explored in future experimental studies. Such data sources are particularly valuable for cost-benefit analyses. In addition, a careful task analysis is a necessary step in the research process. Identifying needs of older adults requires careful observation of performance under lifelike circumstances. The results of epidemiological data and task analysis will aid in the identification of tasks and environments that pose special difficulty for older adults, and thus will better enable experimental studies to focus upon tasks and environments that are relevant to the daily lives of older adults. Finally, more experimental field studies should be conducted. The leap from lab to life sometimes can land you in the abyss of unconsidered variables. It is critical to see whether laboratory effects (of illumination level, noise, etc.) are maintained under typical task conditions found in the home and the workplace.

Content Area Recommendations

We see three content areas where human factors research concerning older adults might expand: anthropometry, safety, and cost-benefit analyses. First, large-scale anthropometric and biomechanical data gathering should be initiated, particularly with respect to dynamic measures such as strength and reach, to provide solid guidelines for the capabilities of older adults. These guidelines probably should be phrased in terms of 95th and 99th percentiles. They also, as much as possible, should be based on the types of challenges faced by adults in their usual environments. For example, age norms should be determined for the type of torque necessary to open a food jar, which is somewhat different from the more commonly used grip-strength measure, though perhaps correlated with it (see Czaja, 1990; Kelley & Kroemer, 1990, for related discussion).

A second important area for human factors research is safety. Older adults are more fragile than are younger ones, and this has serious implications for accident prevention programs, whether dealing with stepstools in the kitchen or automobiles. Detailed analysis of accident data is called for. Centralized recording systems such as the FARS (Fatal Accident Report System, by the National Highway Traffic Safety Administration in the United States) help somewhat, but maintaining information on injury accidents, given their much higher frequency, could be even more useful. Falls during everyday activities now are being studied much more intensively than ever, but the problem here, as with other relatively low-frequency events, is determining the causes so that effective interventions become possible. One option is to make greater use of workers' compensation board injury data, though this will apply only to those still in the labor force. Another possibility is to make greater use of emergency room data bases about product roles in accidents, such as the National Electronic Injury Surveillance System (see, e.g., Czaja, 1990, Table 8).

A third major area for further work is in pinning down the costs and benefits of potential interventions. In our society, for both good and bad reasons, the bottom line is invariably economic. It is unlikely that design guidelines for older adults will be implemented if they are not cost effective. For example, when dealing with a transportation system that constitutes nearly 20% of the Gross National Product, any redesign or intervention may entail a massive investment. Determining the break-even point for such investments is critical in societies with high indebtedness and minimal fiscal flexibility. Including economists and accountants in interdisciplinary teams is one way to proceed.

It is worth returning to the theme that human factors research is likely to set different goals for the different older adult groups. For the middle-aged, it seems likely that redesigning the work environment should satisfy their needs for better visual and acoustic support. Given that the middle-aged do not differ that much from the young on suprathreshold stimuli, it is also likely that younger adults will benefit from such changes. For the old and the very old, however, where the concerns are likely to be focused in the home and transportation environments, it seems more likely that a broader task analysis will be necessary. Functional analysis based on goals of the older person may point the way to better design.

Finally, as we have indicated previously (Charness & Bosman, 1990b), it is necessary to consult with the user as well as with specialists when redesigning. It makes little sense to redesign a food jar for easier opening if it contains high-salt, high-fat, low-vitamin contents. Similarly, there is little need to provide special transportation vans to take immobile older adults to the bank if technology could offer them a better way to manage their finances (and perhaps to socialize while doing so via a video-phone) at home. Human factors research should be conducted in conjunction with, and not just for, older adults.

ACKNOWLEDGMENTS

This work was supported by grants to the authors from the Natural Sciences and Engineering Research Council of Canada (NSERC A0790), Bell Northern-Research, and the National Centres of Excellence Program for the Canadian Aging Research Network (CARNET).

We are grateful to Leonard Evans and Van Nostrand Reinhold for permission to use the two figures on severe crashes and driver fatalities. We thank Pat Telford for help with the literature review, William Forbes for earlier comments on the cost-benefit analysis, Stephen Godwin, Transportation Research Board, for providing us with early drafts of papers on aging and driving, and Don Kline, Kathy Pichora-Fuller, and Bob Dewar for helpful advice. We are indebted to Tim Salthouse and Gus Craik for expert feedback on the first draft.

REFERENCES

Ansley, J., & Erber, J. T. (1988). Computer interaction: Effects on attitudes and performance in older adults. *Educational Gerontology, 14*, 107–119.

Arndt, S., Feltes, J., & Hanak, J. (1983). Secretarial attitudes toward word processors as a function of familiarity and locus of control. *Behavior and Information Technology, 2*, 17–22.

Ashford, N. J. (1981). Transport for the elderly and handicapped. *Applied Ergonomics, 12*, 87–92.

Atkinson, W. G. (1987). *Pedestrian crosswalk signal activation demonstration.* MANOP Services Ltd., 1007 Frederick Rd., North Vancouver, British Columbia.

Avolio, B. J., Kroeck, K. G., & Panek, P. E. (1985). Individual differences in information-processing ability as a predictor of motor vehicle accidents. *Human Factors, 27*, 577–587.

Babarik, P. (1968). Automobile accidents and driver reaction pattern. *Journal of Applied Psychology, 52*, 49–54.

Belbin, E., & Belbin, R. M. (1972). *Problems in adult retraining.* London: Heineman.

Beldie, I. P., Pastoor, S., & Schwarz, E. (1983). Fixed versus variable letter width for televised text. *Human Factors, 25*, 273–277.

Bennett, C. A. (1977). The demographic variables of discomfort glare. *Lighting Design and Application, 7*, 22–24.

Birren, J. E., Woods, A. M., & Williams, M. V. (1980). Behavioral slowing with aging: Causes, organization, and consequences. In L. W. Poon (Ed.), *Aging in the 1980s: Psychological issues* (pp. 293–308). Washington, DC: American Psychological Association.

Blackwell, O. M., & Blackwell, H. R. (1971). Visual performance data for 156 normal observers of various ages. *Journal of the Illuminating Engineering Society, 1*, 3–13.

Bosman, E. A. (1991). *Age-related changes in transcription typing skill.* Unpublished doctoral dissertation, University of Waterloo, Waterloo, Ontario.

Bowman, K. F., & Cole, B. L. (1980). A recommendation for illumination of the Farnsworth–Munsell 100-Hue Test. *American Journal of Optometry and Physiological Optics, 57*, 839–842.

Boyce, P. R. (1973). Age, illuminance, visual performance and preference. *Lighting Research and Technology, 5*(3), 125–144.

Boyce, P. R. (1981). *Human factors in lighting.* Essex, England: Applied Science.

Boyce, P. R., & Simons, R. H. (1977). Hue discrimination and light sources. *Lighting Research and Technology, 9*, 125–140.

Brickfield, C. F. (1984). Attitudes and perceptions of older people toward technology. In P. K. Robinson & J. E. Birren (Eds.), *Aging and technological advances* (pp. 31–38). New York: Plenum.

Camp, C. J., West, R. L., & Poon, L. W. (1989). Recruitment practices for psychological research in gerontology. In M. P. Lawton & A. R. Herzog (Eds.), *Special research methods for gerontology* (pp. 163–189). Amityville, NY: Baywood.

Card, S., English, W., & Burr, B. (1978). Evaluation of mouse, rate-controlled isometric joystick, step keys, and text keys for text selection on a CRT. *Ergonomics, 21*, 601–613.

Card, S. K., Moran, T. P., & Newell, A. (1983). *The psychology of human–computer interaction.* Hillsdale, NJ: Lawrence Erlbaum Associates.

Carroll, J. M., & Carrithers, C. (1984). Blocking learner error states in a training-wheels system. *Human Factors, 26*, 377–389.

Carroll, J. M., & Reitman Olson, J. (1988). Mental models in human–computer interaction. In M. Helander (Ed.), *Handbook of human–computer interaction* (pp. 45–65). Amsterdam: North-Holland.

Cerella, J. (1985). Age-related decline in extrafoveal letter perception. *Journal of Gerontology, 40*, 727–736.

Cerella, J. (1990). Aging and information-processing rate. In J. E. Birren & K. W. Schaie (Eds.), *Handbook of the psychology of aging* (3rd ed., pp. 201–221). San Diego: Academic.

Chang, M., Evans, L., Herman, R., & Wasielewski, P. (1977). Observations of fuel savings due to the introduction of right-turn-on-red. *Traffic Engineering & Control, 18*, 475–477.

Charness, N. (Ed.). (1985). *Aging and human performance*. Chichester, England: Wiley.

Charness, N., & Bosman, E. A. (1990a). Expertise and aging: Life in the lab. In T. H. Hess (Ed.), *Aging and cognition: Knowledge organization and utilization* (pp. 343–385). Amsterdam: Elsevier.

Charness, N., & Bosman, E. A. (1990b). Human factors and design for older adults. In J. E. Birren & K. W. Schaie (Eds.), *Handbook of the psychology of aging* (3rd ed., pp. 446–463). San Diego: Academic.

Charness, N., & Campbell, J. I. D. (1988). Acquiring skill at mental calculation in adulthood: A task decomposition. *Journal of Experimental Psychology: General, 117*, 115–129.

Clark, M. C., Czaja, S. J., & Weber, R. A. (1990). Older adults and daily living task profiles. *Human Factors, 32*, 537–549.

Committee for the Study on Improving Mobility and Safety for Older Persons. (1988). *Transportation in an aging society: Improving mobility and safety for older persons* (Vols. 1–2). Washington, DC: Transportation Research Board, National Research Council.

Cross-National Study: Older people in traffic—How dangerous? (1989). *Ageing International, 26*, 35–38.

Cushman, W. H., & Crist, B. (1987). Illumination. In G. Salvendy (Ed.), *Handbook of human factors* (pp. 670–695). New York: Wiley.

Czaja, S. J. (Ed.). (1990). *Human factors research needs for an aging population*. Washington, DC: National Academy Press. (Available from National Research Council, 2101 Constitution Avenue, NW, Washington, DC, 20418)

Czaja, S. J., Hammond, K., Blascovich, J. L., & Swede, H. (1986). Learning to use a word-processing system as a function of training strategy. *Behavior and Information Technology, 5*, 203–216.

Davidson, H., Schonfield, D., & Winkelaar, R. (1982). Age differences in the effects of reverberation and pause on sentence intelligibility. *Canadian Journal on Aging, 1*, 29–37.

Denton, F. T., Feaver, C. H., & Spencer, B. G. (1986). Prospective aging of the population and its implications for the labour force and government expenditures. *Canadian Journal on Aging, 5*, 75–95.

Egan, D. E. (1988). Individual differences in human–computer interaction. In M. Helander (Ed.), *Handbook of human–computer interaction* (pp. 543–568). Amsterdam: North-Holland.

Elias, P. K., Elias, M. F., Robbins, M. A., & Gage, P. (1987). Acquisition of word-processing skills by younger, middle-age, and older adults. *Psychology and Aging, 2*, 340–348.

Evans, D. W., & Ginsburg, A. P. (1985). Contrast sensitivity predicts age-related differences in highway sign discriminability. *Human Factors, 27*, 637–642.

Evans, L. (1988a). Older driver involvement in fatal and severe traffic crashes. *Journal of Gerontology, 43*, S186–S193.

Evans, L. (1988b). Risk of fatality from physical trauma versus sex and age. *The Journal of Trauma, 28*, 368–378.

Evans, L. (1991). *Traffic safety and the driver.* New York: Van Nostrand Reinhold.

Faletti, M. V. (1984). Human factors research and functional environments for the aged. In I. Altman, M. P. Lawton, & J. F. Wohlwill (Eds.), *Human behavior and environment: Advances in theory and research: Vol. 7. Elderly people and the environment* (pp. 191–237). New York: Plenum.

Flynn, J. E. (1979). The IES approach to recommendations regarding levels of illumination. *Lighting Design & Application, 9*(September), 74–77.

Forbes, W. F., Hayward, L. M., & Agwani, N. (1991). Factors associated with the prevalence of various self-reported impairments among older people residing in the community. *Canadian Journal of Public Health, 82*, 240–244.

Fozard, J. L. (1981). Special issue preface. *Human Factors, 23*, 3–6.

Fozard, J. L. (1990). Vision and hearing in aging. In J. E. Birren & K. W. Schaie (Eds.), *Handbook of the psychology of aging* (3rd ed., pp. 150–170). San Diego: Academic.

Fozard, J. L., & Popkin, S. J. (1978). Optimizing adult development: Ends and means of an applied psychology of aging. *American Psychologist, 33*, 975–989.

Frost, M. J. (1975). *How to use cost benefit analysis in project appraisal.* Epping, England: Gower.

Garfein, A. J., Schaie, K. W., & Willis, S. L. (1988). Microcomputer proficiency in later-middle-aged and older adults: Teaching old dogs new tricks. *Social Behavior, 3*, 11–148.

Gist, M., Rosen, B., & Schwoerer, C. (1988). The influence of training method and trainee age on the acquisition of computer skills. *Personnel Psychology, 41*, 255–265.

Gomez, L. M., Egan, D. E., & Bowers, C. (1986). Learning to use a text-editor: Some learner characteristics that predict success. *Human–Computer Interaction, 2*, 1–23.

Gould, J. D., Alfaro, L., Finn, R., Haupt, B., & Minuto, A. (1987). Reading from CRT displays can be as fast as reading from paper. *Human Factors, 29*, 497–517.

Government of Canada (1987). *Housing an aging population: Guidelines for development and design.* (ISBN: 0-662-15640-4, Catalogue: H-71-3/6-1987E). Canada: National Advisory Council on Aging, Ministry of Supply & Services.

Grandjean, E., & Vigliani, E. (Eds.). (1980). *Ergonomic aspects of visual display terminals.* London: Taylor & Francis.

Greenstein, J. S., & Arnaut, L. Y. (1988). Input devices. In M. Helander (Ed.), *Handbook of human–computer interaction* (pp. 495–519). Amsterdam: North-Holland.

Guth, S. K., Eastman, A. A., & McNelis, J. F. (1956). Lighting requirements for older workers. *Illumination Engineering, 11*, 656–660.

Halpern, D. F. (1984). Age differences in response time to verbal and symbolic traffic signs. *Experimental Aging Research, 19*, 201–204.

Harrington, D. M., & McBride, R. S. (1970). Traffic violations by type, age, sex, and marital status. *Accident Analysis and Prevention, 2*, 67–79.

Hartley, A. A., Hartley, J. T., & Johnson, S. A. (1984). The older adult as computer user. In P. K. Robinson & J. E. Birren (Eds.), *Aging and technological advances* (pp. 347–348). New York: Plenum.

Hauer, E. (1988). The safety of older persons at intersections. In *Transportation in an aging society: Improving mobility and safety for older persons* (Vol. 2) (pp. 194–252). Washington, DC: Transportation Research Board, National Research Council.

Helander, M. G. (1987). Design of visual displays. In G. Salvendy (Ed.), *Handbook of human factors* (pp. 507–548). New York: Wiley.

Hoag, L. L., & Adams, S. K. (1975). Human factors in urban transportation. *Human Factors, 17*, 119–131.

Hughes, P. C., & McNelis, J. F. (1978). Lighting, productivity, and the work environment. *Lighting Research and Design, 8*, 32–40.

Hughes, P. C., & Neer, R. M. (1981). Lighting for the elderly: A psychobiological approach to lighting. *Human Factors, 23*(1), 65–85.

Huston, R. E., & Janke, M. K. (1986). *Senior driver facts* (Report No. CAL-DMV-RSS-86-82, 2nd ed.). Springfield, VA: Technical Information Service.

Jaschinski, W. (1982). Conditions of emergency lighting. *Ergonomics, 25*, 363–372.

Johnson, C. A., & Keltner, J. L. (1983). Incidence of visual field loss in 20,000 eyes and its relationship to driving performance. *Archives of Ophthalmology, 101*, 371–375.

Kantowitz, B. H., & Sorkin, R. D. (1983). *Human factors: Understanding people-system relationships*. New York: Wiley.

Karat, J., McDonald, E., & Anderson, M. (1986). A comparison of menu selection techniques: Touch panel, mouse and keyboard. *International Journal of Man-Machine Studies, 25*, 73–88.

Kaufman, J. E., & Haynes, H. (Eds.). (1981a). *Illumination Engineering Society lighting handbook: Application volume*. New York: Illuminating Engineering Society of North America.

Kaufman, J. E., & Haynes, H. (Eds.). (1981b). *Illumination Engineering Society lighting handbook: Reference volume*. New York: Illuminating Engineering Society of North America.

Kelly, P. L., & Kroemer, K. H. E. (1990). Anthropometry of the elderly: Status and recommendations. *Human Factors, 32*, 571–595.

Kline, D. W., & Schieber, F. (1985). Vision and aging. In J. E. Birren & K. W. Schaie (Eds.), *Handbook of the psychology of aging* (2nd ed., pp. 296–331). New York: Van Nostrand Reinhold.

Kline, T. J. B., Ghali, L. M., Kline, D. W., & Brown, S. (1990). Visibility distance of highway signs among young, middle-aged, and older observers: Icons are better than text. *Human Factors, 32*, 609–619.

Knoblauch, K., Saunders, F., Kusuda, M., Hynes, R., Podgor, M., Higgins, K. E., & de Monasterio, F. M. (1987). Age and illuminance effects of the Farnsworth–Munsell 100-Hue Test. *Applied Optics, 26*, 1441–1448.

Koncelik, J. A. (1982). *Aging and the product environment*. New York: Van Nostrand Reinhold.

Korteling, J. E. (1990). Perception-response speed and driving capabilities of brain-damaged and older drivers. *Human Factors, 32*, 95–108.

Krauss, I. K., & Hoyer, W. J. (1985). Technology and the older person: Age, sex, and experience as moderators of attitudes towards computers. In P. K. Robinson, J. Livingston, & J. E. Birren (Eds.), *Aging and technological advances* (pp. 349–350). New York: Plenum.

Kroemer, K. H. E., & Hill, S. G. (1986). Preferred line of sight angle. *Ergonomics, 29*, 1129–1134.

Lee, R. S. (1970). Social attitudes and the computer revolution. *Public Opinion Quarterly, 34*, 53–59.

MacKay, M. (1988). Crash protection for older persons. In *Transportation in an aging society: Improving mobility and safety for older persons* (Vol. 2) (pp. 158–193). Washington, DC: Transportation Research Board, National Research Council.

Mathey, F. J. (1983). Attitudes and behavior of elderly pedestrians. *International Journal of Aging and Human Development, 17*, 25–28.

Matthews, M. L. (1986). Aging and the perception of driving risk and ability. In *Proceedings of the Human Factors Society—30th Annual Meeting* (pp. 1159–1163). Santa Monica, CA: Human Factors Society.

McKnight, A. J. (1988). Driver and pedestrian training. In *Transportation in an aging society: Improving mobility and safety for older persons* (Vol. 2, pp. 101–133). Washington, DC: Transportation Research Board, National Research Council.

Mihal, W. J., & Barrett, G. V. (1976). Individual differences in perceptual information processing and their relation to automobile accident involvement. *Journal of Applied Psychology, 61*, 229–233.

Miyao, M., Hacisalihzade, S. S., Allen, J. S., & Stark, L. W. (1989). Effects of VDT resolution on visual fatigue and readability: An eye movement approach. *Ergonomics, 32,* 603–614.

Money, L. J. (1984). *Transportation energy and the future.* Englewood Cliffs, NJ: Prentice-Hall.

Mooney, G. H. (1977). *The valuation of human life.* London: Macmillan.

Mortimer, R. G. (1988). Headlamp performance factors affecting the visibility of older drivers in night driving. In *Transportation in an aging society: Improving mobility and safety for older persons* (Vol. 2) (pp. 379–403). Washington, DC: Transportation Research Board, National Research Council.

Moss, M., & Lawton, M. P. (1982). The time budgets of older people: A window on four lifestyles. *Journal of Gerontology, 37,* 115–123.

Mourant, R. R., & Langolf, G. D. (1976). Luminance specifications for automobile instrument panels. *Human Factors, 18,* 71–84.

Olsho, L. W., Harkins, S. W., & Lenhardt, M. L. (1985). Aging and the auditory system. In J. E. Birren & K. W. Schaie (Eds.), *Handbook of the psychology of aging* (2nd ed., pp. 332–377). New York: Van Nostrand Reinhold.

Olson, P. (1988). Motor vehicle headlighting: A classic problem in ergonomics. *University of Michigan Transportation Research Institute Research Review, 18*(6), 1–10.

Olson, P. L., & Sivak, M. (1986). Perception-response time to unexpected roadway hazards. *Human Factors, 28,* 91–96.

Ostberg, O., & Chapman, L. J. (1988). Social aspects of computer use. In M. Helander (Ed.), *Handbook of human–computer interaction* (pp. 1033–1049). Amsterdam: North-Holland.

Owsley, C., Ball, K., Sloane, M. E., Roenker, D. L., & Bruni, J. R. (1991). Visual/cognitive correlates of vehicle accidents in older drivers. *Psychology and Aging, 6,* 403–415.

Panek, P. E., Barrett, G. V., Sterns, H. L., & Alexander, R. A. (1978). Age differences in perceptual style, selective attention, and perceptual-motor reaction time. *Experimental Aging Research, 4,* 377–387.

Parmelee, P. A., & Lawton, M. P. (1990). The design of special environments for the aged. In J. E. Birren & K. W. Schaie (Eds.), *Handbook of the psychology of aging* (3rd ed., pp. 464–488). New York: Academic.

Pastoor, S., Schwarz, E., & Beldie, I. P. (1983). The relative suitability of four dot-matrix sizes for text presentation on color television screens. *Human Factors, 25,* 265–272.

Planek. T. W. (1972). The aging driver in today's traffic: A critical review. In P. F. Waller (Ed.), *Aging and highway safety: The elderly in a mobile society* (pp. 3–38). Chapel Hill, NC: North Carolina Symposium on Highway Safety.

Planek, T. W., & Fowler, R. C. (1971). Traffic accident problems and exposure characteristics of the aging driver. *Journal of Gerontology, 26,* 224–230.

Plomp, R., & Duquesnoy, A. J. (1980). Room acoustics for the aged. *Journal of the Acoustical Society of America, 68,* 1616–1621.

Plomp, R., & Mimpen, A. M. (1979). Speech-reception threshold for sentences as a function of age and noise level. *Journal of the Acoustical Society of America, 66,* 1333–1342.

Regnier, V., & Pynoos, J. (1987). *Housing the aged.* New York: Elsevier.

Report of the World Assembly on Aging. (1982). (Report No. A/CONF.113/31 [Sales No. E.82.I.16]). New York: United Nations.

Road Transport Research. (1986). *Guidelines for improving the safety of elderly road users.* Paris: OECD.

Rosenthal, R., & Rosnow, R. L. (1975). *The volunteer subject.* New York: Wiley.

Roske-Hofstrand, R. J., & Paap, K. R. (1986). Cognitive networks as a guide to menu organization: An application in the automated cockpit. *Ergonomics, 29,* 1301–1311.

Ross, D. K. (1978). Task lighting—Yet another view. *Lighting Design and Application, 8*, 37–43.

Salthouse, T. A. (1984). Effects of age and skill in typing. *Journal of Experimental Psychology: General, 13*, 345–371.

Salthouse, T. A. (1985a). Speed of behavior and its implications for cognition. In J. E. Birren & K. W. Schaie (Eds.), *Handbook of the psychology of aging* (2nd ed., pp. 400–426). New York: Van Nostrand Reinhold.

Salthouse, T. A. (1985b). *A theory of cognitive aging.* Amsterdam: Elsevier.

Salthouse, T. A. (1990). Influence of experience on age differences in cognitive functioning. *Human Factors, 32*, 551–569.

Sanders, M. S., & McCormick, E. J. (1987). *Human factors in engineering design* (6th ed.). New York: McGraw-Hill.

Scialfa, C. T., Guzy, L. T., Leibowitz, H. W., Garvey, P. M., & Tyrrell, R. A. (1991). Age differences in estimating vehicle velocity. *Psychology and Aging, 6*, 60–66.

Second Conference on the Epidemiology of Aging (1980). Proceedings of the Second Conference, March 28–29, 1977, National Institutes of Health, Bethesda, MD. (NIH Publication No. 80-969)

Sekuler, R., Kline, D., Dismukes, K., & Adams, A. J. (1983). Some research needs in aging and visual perception. *Vision Research, 23*, 213–216.

Shinar, D., McDowell, E. D., Rackoff, N. J., & Rockwell, T. H. (1978). Field dependence and driver visual search behavior. *Human Factors, 20*, 553–559.

Simmons, R. C. (1975). Illuminance, diversity and disability glare in emergency lighting. *Lighting Research and Technology, 5*(2), 125–132.

Singley, M. K., & Anderson, J. R. (1989). *The transfer of cognitive skill.* Cambridge, MA.: Harvard University Press.

Sivak, M. (1981). Human factors and highway-accident causation: Some theoretical considerations. *Accident Analysis and Prevention, 13*, 61–64.

Sivak, M., & Olson, P. L. (1982). Nighttime legibility of traffic signs: Conditions eliminating the effects of driver age and disability glare. *Accident Analysis and Prevention, 14*, 87–93.

Sivak, M., Olson, P. L., & Pastalan, L. A. (1981). Effect of driver's age on nighttime legibility of highway signs. *Human Factors, 23*, 59–64.

Smith, D. B. D. (1990). Human factors and aging: An overview of research needs and application opportunities. *Human Factors, 35*, 509–526.

Smith, S. W., & Rea, M. S. (1978). Proofreading under different levels of illumination. *Journal of the Illumination Engineering Society, 8*(October), 46–52.

Sojourner, R. J., & Antin, J. F. (1990). The effects of a simulated head-up display speedometer on perceptual task performance. *Human Factors, 32*, 329–339.

Solomon, D. (1985). The older driver and highway design. In J. L. Malfetti (Ed.), *Drivers 55 + . Needs and problems of older drivers: Survey results and recommendations.* Orlando, FL: Proceedings of the Older Driver Colloquium.

Sterns, H. L., Barrett, G. V., & Alexander, R. A. (1985). Accidents and the aging individual. In J. E. Birren & K. W. Schaie (Eds.), *Handbook of the psychology of aging* (2nd ed., pp. 703–724). New York: Van Nostrand Reinhold.

Stine, E. L., & Wingfield, A. (1987). Process and strategy in memory for speech among younger and older adults. *Psychology and Aging, 2*, 272–379.

Stine, E. L., Wingfield, A., & Poon, L. W. (1986). How much and how fast: Rapid processing of spoken language in later adulthood. *Psychology and Aging, 1*, 303–311.

Stoudt, H. W., Damon, A., McFarland, R. A., & Roberts, J. (1965). *Weight, height, and selected body dimensions of adults—Vital and health statistics* (Series 11, No. 8). Rockville, MD: Public Health Service.

Stoudt, H. W., Damon, A., McFarland, R. A., & Roberts, J. (1973). *Skinfolds, body girths, biacromial diameter and selected anthropometric indices of adults—Vital and health statistics* (Series 11, No. 35). Rockville, MD: Public Health Service.

Sturr, J. F., Kline, G. E., & Taub, H. A. (1990). Performance of young and older drivers on a static acuity test under photopic and mesopic luminance conditions. *Human Factors, 32,* 1–8.

Svanborg, A. (1984). Technology, aging and health in a medical perspective. In P. K. Robinson & J. E. Birren (Eds.), *Aging and technological advances* (pp. 159–168). New York: Plenum.

Todd, M., Davis, K. E., & Cafferty, T. P. (1983). Who volunteers for adult development research?: Research findings and practical steps to reach low volunteering groups. *International Journal of Aging and Human Development, 18,* 177–184.

Van Houten, R., & Nau, P. A. (1983). Feedback interventions and driving speed: A parametric and comparative analysis. *Journal of Applied Behavior Analysis, 16,* 253–281.

Verbrugge, L. M., Lepowski, J. M., & Konkol, L. L. (1991). Levels of disability among U. S. adults with arthritis. *Journal of Gerontology, 46,* 571–583.

Waller, J. A. (1967). Cardiovascular disease, aging, and traffic accidents. *Journal of Chronic Diseases, 20,* 615–620.

Welford, A. T. (1958). *Ageing and human skill.* London: Oxford University Press.

Welford, A. T. (1977). Motor performance. In J. E. Birren & K. W. Schaie (Eds.), *Handbook of the psychology of aging* (pp. 450–496). New York: Van Nostrand Reinhold.

Wingfield, A., Poon, L. W., Lombardi, L., & Lowe, D. (1985). Speed of processing in normal aging: Effects of speech rate, linguistic structure, and processing time. *Journal of Gerontology, 40,* 579–585.

Winter, D. J. (1984). Needs and problems of older drivers and pedestrians: An exploratory study with teaching/learning implications. *Educational Gerontology, 10,* 135–146.

Witkin, H. A., Lewis, H. B., Hertzman, M., Machover, K., Meissner, P. B., & Wapner, S. (1954). *Personality through perception.* New York: Harper.

Woltman, H. L., Stanton, R. H., & Stearns, R. A. (1984). Information sign color evaluation using a video presentation. *Transportation Research Record* (No. 996). Transportation Research Board, National Research Council.

Wood, D. D., & Roth, E. M. (1988). Cognitive systems engineering. In M. Helander (Ed.), *Handbook of human–computer interaction* (pp. 3–43). Amsterdam: North-Holland.

Woodson, W. E. (1981). *Human factors design handbook.* New York: McGraw-Hill.

Working Group on Speech Understanding and Aging, CHABA. (1988). Speech understanding and aging. *Journal of the Acoustical Society of America, 83,* 859–895.

Yaksich, S., Jr. (1985). Interaction of older drivers with pedestrians in traffic. In J. L. Malfetti (Ed.), *Drivers 55 + . Needs and problems of older drivers: Survey results and recommendations.* Orlando, FL: Proceedings of the Older Driver Colloquium.

Zandri, E., & Charness, N. (1989). Training older and younger adults to use software. *Educational Gerontology, 15,* 615–631.

Zoltan, E., & Chapanis, A. (1982). What do professional persons think about computers? *Behavior and Information Technology, 1,* 55–68.

Author Index

553

Subject Index